The FBI Files
Sam Giancana

Tony Dark

"The FBI Files Sam Giancana" by Tony Dark.

Library of Congress number 2004115890

© 2004-2009 Tony Dark.

Published 2004-2009 by HoseHead Productions
2009 Second Edition

Manufactured in the United States of America

ISBN 0-615-12720-7

CONTENTS

Introduction

Someone once said that the FBI does not stand for "Federal Bureau of Investigation" but rather "Forever Bothering Italians." From the viewpoint of the Italian mob nothing is further from the truth. Between the 1920's and the 1950's, this onetime unstoppable organization had (with the exception of bootlegging) forty years of non-interference from the FBI. They ran their empire like a finely-oiled machine. In the eyes of the FBI's founder, J. Edgar Hoover, organized crime was a state issue rather than the Federal government's problem. That all changed in the late 1950's when J. Edgar Hoover unleashed his agents to bring down the leaders of organized crime throughout America.

The Subject

The Patch, a run-down, overcrowded, poor section of Chicago, was in the early 1900's filled with immigrants that would make up the core of America. Southern Italians were the newest group to enter this new-found land, finding themselves as the lowest class among the British, Irish and German citizens of America. They were the new unwanted people and were treated like weeds growing in the grass. Most of the newly arrived Italians would move on from the east coast cities such as New York and Philadelphia and head to Chicago to live the American dream. They would fill many of the houses with 3 to 5 families each as they scrambled to make a new life for themselves.

One young Italian who went by the nickname of "Momo" dreamed of the day that he, an Italian, would become someone who could control police, judges, politicians, hoodlums, chumps and women. He even dreamed of controlling countries. His name was Salvatore Michael Giancana, known to the world as Sam "Mooney" Giancana.

Sam Giancana would fulfill his dreams by becoming the top boss of the Chicago mob and a member of the ruling board of organized crime throughout the world. He controlled top politicians who had ties to presidents of countries and became richer than he could ever imagine. One of the proudest aspects of Giancana's life was that his people, the Italians, came to America with nothing, and within a decade or two were the main controlling power in almost every aspect of one's life.

They controlled the union men who built the roads, the houses, the plumbing, the bricks; the truck drivers who delivered the food for everyone to eat, and the politicians who made the laws and ran the cities. They controlled the shipping docks and the international shipping. They controlled the factories that built America and the banks that held the money.

Sam Giancana's dreams were being fulfilled that is until the United States government decided enough was enough. Organized crime had reached into every aspect of society by the 1950's and J. Edgar Hoover's Federal Bureau of Investigation was pressured to stop the leaders of organized crime and expose everything they had control over. By about 1958, the FBI started investigating the top leaders of the syndicate under the "Top Hoodlum Program" which was designed to put the top bosses away where they could not control their empires. In Chicago, Sam Giancana was the boss and prime target. The plan was to destroy his life, his reputation and contacts, and to strip him of the millions he made on gambling, prostitution, union funds, shake downs, stealing and murder.

Sam Giancana hated publicity, or did he? Many of the people he called "close friends" were movie stars, top entertainers, high profile businessmen, leaders of nations and top political members. Besides his well-known friendships with movie stars Frank Sinatra, Dean Martin, and Sammy Davis Jr., one of his most publicized relationships was that with singer-entertainer Phyllis McGuire. Giancana, the boss of a crime empire who controlled almost every life he came in touch with, and McGuire, a strong woman who controlled her own life and refused to take orders. One craved publicity, one did not, but both got world wide attention as they secretly tried to have a relationship with each other. Their romance later became a cable movie called "Sugartime" in which actor John Turturro played a young Sam Giancana and Mary-Louise Parker played Phyllis McGuire.

The legacy of Sam Giancana lives on through his family. However, it is not what one would think. His oldest daughter, Antoinette Giancana, wrote a book about her life growing up with her powerful father called "Mafia Princess." If that wasn't enough to make Sam Giancana turn over in his grave, she also at one time sold pasta sauce and even posed nude for Playboy Magazine. His nephew, who has the same name as his powerful uncle, releases books about Momo and his uncle's goons.

As of 2008, it was announced that a TV mini-series about Giancana's life was in the works. The rights for the mini-series were acquired from Giancana's youngest daughter Francine. The producer of the mini-series is Nick Celozzi who runs a Chicago acting school for the arts. Nick Celozzi grandmother was Sam Giancana's sister. Celozzi's grandfather is well known in the Chicago land area because he is the owner of Celozzi-Ettleson car dealer ship, a well know business in Chicago who use to have a catchy slogan "*Where you always save more money*" on TV commercials. Nick Celozzi, a Hollywood actor for many years, has had acting parts in many movies and some well known TV shows like "*Walker Texas Ranger,*" "*The A-Team*" and "*Hunter.*" It looks like the Sam Giancana story will continue on.

What You Will Read In This Book

Portrayed in this book are the actual FBI reports that show how the agents went about taking down a mob boss.

The day-to-day reports, the interviews, the development of moles and "rats" inside the mob who were close to Sam Giancana. Where he went, who he met, who he dated, who were his family members and closest friends, his enemies, his cronies and his puppets. Where his money was, how much he had, how much he had made, and how much he had spent.

Shown in these reports is how the FBI agents had a hand in the destruction of Giancana's life and career in organized crime. In the end, Sam Giancana was so miserable from the constant pursuit from the government that he left the mob, his family, friends and the United States, just to find peace. In 1965 Giancana went to jail for refusing to answer questions in a Grand Jury hearing on organized crime in Chicago. He spent one year in Cook County Jail until his release in 1966. Once out, he took his millions and fled the country, traveling all over the world to escape the prying eyes of authorities. It all came to an end in 1975 when Giancana was forced to return to America against his will by Mexican authorities who snatched him from his hill-top mansion and delivered him to the U.S. government to once again testify against his organized crime buddies. Months later while waiting to testify, Sam Giancana was shot in the back of the head while he was cooking food for himself, in his Oak Park home, with a close friend nearby.

About the FBI Files

One thing is for certain, the FBI likes to repeat itself. Among the many different files, the same information is repeated over and over. At the beginning of each new addition to the file, they recap most of the past information they had previously uncovered. The main file for Sam Giancana totaled over 3,000 pages; however, about 1,500 of those pages were the same information typed over and over again. So I have filtered as much of the "repeats" as possible, unless of course the reports included some new information or a correction of a previous fact. As to the completeness of the files, unfortunately some of the pages were missing and only a few of the actual FBI photos were still attached. It is possible that the photos and pages were removed and attached to other files, or simply misplaced. Included in this book is most of the main investigation conducted on Sam Giancana and his activities. Sadly, some of the information the FBI agents gathered was incorrect; names misspelled, information not true and simply wrong. It has to be understood that during an investigation where you have to rely on murderers, thieves, and "bad people," sometime the information is not correct. However, the information in the reports has been mostly left intact, in its original state.

The Mob

Organized crime in America dates back to the 1800's with gangs that had ruled the big cities and small towns throughout the United States. In the early 1900's immigrants belonging to the Italian organizations known as the Mafia and the Camora, came to America to create their own empires of organized crime. The Mafia meaning, "A Sicilian attitude of popular hostility to law and government. A secret society characterized by this attitude in organized crime." The Camora is the name used for the Neapolitan criminal organization from the Naples, Italy area. Once in America, the members of these organizations learned that gangs controlled sections and portions of the cites and towns. In Chicago, it was the "Black Hand" that controlled the streets while Irish and German gangs struggled to maintain territory. While in the 1920's Al Capone and the Capone Gang became the top gang controlling and killing all others which formed into what is know today as the "Chicago Outfit". It was this organization in which Sam Giancana was the top boss from 1957 until 1965.

The FBI Agents

The FBI Agents or "SA's," which they are referred to, stands for "Special Agents." These are the men who put the files together. It is not the work of just one agent, but rather several agents over a 20-year period. The most famous agent investigating was William F. Roemer Jr., who spent many years following Giancana, doing everything in his power to make Giancana's life miserable and to expose his dealings and associates. Roemer wrote about his experiences with Giancana in his book, [Roemer, Man Against the Mob.] However, as you will read, many of the reports not talked about in his book are listed in these files by the other agents who tried their hardest to bring Giancana down.

Reading an FBI file is very easy and self-explanatory. The FBI file contains most of the information learned about the subject who an FBI Agent is investigating. Most of the agents from the 1950's, 1960's and 1970's "hand wrote" what they had learned in a note pad, then turned in the information to their field office in whatever city they represented. That field office in return would send a Teletype or Airtel message of the information to FBI headquarters in Washington, D.C. where top FBI officials would review it and decide what action to take.

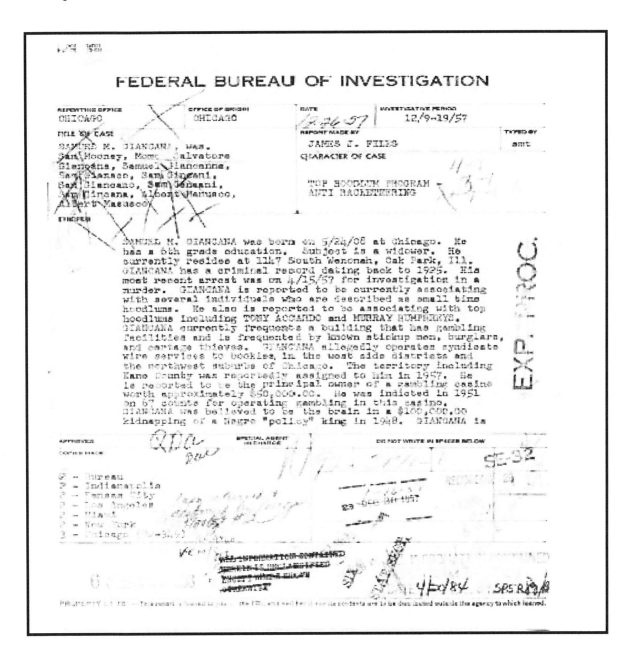

This is an actual FBI page at the beginning of a new report serial. The number in the lower right hand corner of this file, 92-3171-1 is the file number. 92-3171 is the FBI headquarters file number for Sam Giancana and the -1 is the serial number.

DECODED COPY

☐ AIRGRAM   ☐ CABLEGRAM   ☐ RADIO   xx TELETYPE

10:02 PM CDST DEFERRED 6-22-64 DHM
TO DIRECTOR
FROM CHICAGO 222219

SAMUEL M. GIANCANA, AKA. AR.
    CG 6486-C* ADVISED GIANCANA HELD CONVERSATION WITH SEVERAL
ASSOCIATES AT ARMORY LOUNGE SHORTLY AFTER RETURN TO CHICAGO
AREA AND DISCUSSED WEDDING OF SON OF ANTHONY ACCARDO HELD JUNE 10
LAST AND OF NUMEROUS INVESTIGATING AGENCIES WHO HAD PERSONNEL
COVERING AFFAIR. GIANCANA PROCEEDED TO SPEAK AT LENGTH OVER
FBI SURVEILLANCE DURING SUMMER 1963 AND INDICATED THAT HE WAS
UNABLE TO ACCOMPLISH ANYTHING DURING PERIOD OF SURVEILLANCE.
ACCORDING TO GIANCANA "THEY HAD ME TIED UP. I COULDN'T GO
NOWHERE ALONE." GIANCANA CONTINUED THAT HIS COURT PROCEEDINGS
WERE A LAST DITCH EFFORT, WHICH HE DID NOT FEEL AT ITS INCEPTION
WOULD SUCCEED. GIANCANA NOW FEELS THAT EACH AND EVERY CASE
INVOLVING GOVERNMENT OR LOCAL POLICE SHOULD BE BROUGHT TO COURT
IF FOR NO OTHER REASON THAN THE AGENCY IN QUESTION WILL DEFER
FURTHER ACTION UNTIL MATTER DECIDED. GIANCANA BELIEVES THESE
TACTICS SHOULD BE ALSO PURSUED AGAINST LOCAL PRESS THROUGH
LIBEL ACTIONS TO CURTAIL WAVE OF BAD PUBLICITY AFFORDED CHICAGO
HOODLUMS WHICH REDUCES THEIR ACTIVITIES. ✓

RECEIVED: 11:12 PM RDR

ALL INFORMATION CONTAINED
HEREIN IS UNCLASSIFIED
DATE 4-23-84 BY SP5256/CAC

92-3171-1421

12 JUN 23 1964

7 2 JUN 26 1964

If the intelligence contained in the above message is to be disseminated outside the Bureau, it is suggested that it be suitably paraphrased in order to protect the Bureau's cryptographic systems.

The above is an FBI Airgram, "Airtel," an example of what was sent to FBI headquarters every day from field offices in other states with newly gathered information in the investigation of Sam Giancana.

FEDERAL BUREAU OF INVESTIGATION

REPORTING OFFICE	OFFICE OF ORIGIN	DATE	INVESTIGATIVE PERIOD
CHICAGO	CHICAGO	The year	The date it was made

TITLE OF CASE	REPORT MADE BY		TYPED BY
SAMUEL M. GIANCANA, aka	Who made the report		dkc

CHARACTER OF CASE
The number of the file and the agency

In this book, whenever you see this header above it means the beginning of a new file section and represents one of these two pages or similar to them.

The subject Sam Gaincana in a 1950's Chicago Police mug shot photo.

Glossary

Airtel Report — Also known as "Airgram," A special report transported by air between FBI headquarters and an FBI field office in another city.

Associate — Someone working for the mob, but not made a member of the family due to nationality or other reason.

Boss — Leader of the organized crime family. Also could be referred to as Repre sentanda.

Acting Boss — Appointed by the "Boss" to act in the "Boss's" place but not in a permanent capacity.

Under Boss — Appointed by the "Boss" as his immediate subordinate authority, to act in his place. Sometimes called "Zottagob."

Bureau — The Federal Bureau of Investigations "FBI"

Camorra — Criminal organization in Napoli "Naples, Italy." Also covering some of the southern sections of Italy.

Capo — The boss of his crew, a lieutenant appointed by the top mob boss functioning as his immediate authority over the lower order of membership. Short for the Italian phrase capo regime. Other words meaning the same, Caporegima, Caporegine, Copo, Captain.

Commission — Highest known body of authority and policy in the "La Cosa Nostra" com posed of "bosses" of certain "families."

Consiglieri — The adviser of the ruling top mob boss. This position is usually held by a retired mob boss. Title of individual in the "Family" who acts as a neutral advisor within a "Family."

CCC — Chicago Crime Commission. A privately funded organization that special izes in keeping information on organized crime in Chicago.

CG	FBI term for the Chicago Group.
CG-6343-C*	The number given to the hidden microphone installed by the FBI at Celano's Tailor Shop located at 620 North Michigan Avenue in Chicago. This tailor shop was used by top mob bosses to discuss business. It was owned by syndicate figures Jimmy Celano and his brother Louis Celano, the mobs man in Local 134 of the International Brotherhood of Electrical Workers Union in Chicago.
CG-6486-C*	The number given to the hidden microphone installed by the FBI at the Armory Lounge located at 7427 Roosevelt Road, River Forest. The Armory was the headquarters of Sam Giancana. Nicknamed little Mo.
CG-6576-C*	The number given to identify the hidden microphone installed by the FBI in the Democratic offices of the First Ward Organization located at 1 LaSalle Street, in the heart of Chicago, IL.
CPD	Chicago Police Department.
Friend of Ours	Terminology used in referring to an individual or individuals in conversations or introductions connoting their membership. Other phrases, "With Us," "Amici Nostri," and Amico Nostro."
FGJ	Federal Grand Jury.
FNU	First Name Unknown.
La Cosa Nostra	Name of the American Organized Crime family, means "Our Thing" in the Italian language.
Made Man	An official Chicago mobster in the Italian organization. To become a "made" man means you are a ruling mobster and a "member" of the Outfit or the La Cosa Nostra. The term "Made" man is only used for the Chicago mob.

Mafia	Criminal organization in Sicily, Italy.
MM 794-C*	The FBI number given to identify the hidden microphone installed by the FBI at 118th Road, Miami, Florida. This hidden bug was used to uncover the planning stages in the planned killing of Frank Esposito by Jack Cerone, Fifi Buccieri and David Yaras in 1962.
OBS	Obscenity.
PD	Police Department.
RE	Means "About"
Sac	Special Agent in Charge (FBI)
Siji	Sicilians
Soldier	The lowest order of membership, most commonly referred to as Button men, Wise Guy, Good Fella, Soldata.
USDC	United States District Court
West Side Bloc	A group of Chicago politicians under the control of the mob.
Have a Beef	Means one person has a disagreement or is mad at some another person.

Before we get to the file on Sam Giancana, which will explain in detail how he rose to be the boss, an FBI informant, identity not known, was highly trusted because the information he gave was always very accurate. When this informant was interviewed about how Sam Giancana was chosen to be the boss, he gave a different story that is contained in the mail file of Sam Giancana. Here is a portion of that interview:

"The informant advised that at the time that Tony Accardo stepped down from his position of leadership; Samuel "Moe" Giancana and Sam "Teet's" Battaglia were considered to replace Accardo. He advised that most of the members in "The Life" felt that Battaglia was actually stronger at that time and were amazed that Giancana was chosen. While Giancana is boisterous, Battaglia is quiet and ruthless and for this reason, most of the members in "The Life" felt that Battaglia would be chosen.

The informant advised that the Committee set up presently consisted of five members. The committee is headed by Sam Giancana and his associates, Jack Cerone, Fifi Buccieri, Sam Battaglia, and Tony Accardo. He advised that all of the aforementioned individuals are Italian and, of course, in "The Life."

The informant advised that acting in an advisor capacity to the committee is Paul Ricca who never quite regained his position of authority due to his pending deportation.

In addition, acting in an advisory capacity is Murray "The Camel" Humphreys who represents the non-Italian top associates of "The Family." He advised these non-Italian associates of stature are Gus "Slim" Alex, Ralph Pierce, Eddie "Dutch" Vogel, Lenny Patrick, and Jake Guzik.

In addition, acting in an advisor to the committee is Frank "Buster" Wortman who advises on all matters pertaining to criminal activity in East St. Louis, Illinois and Henderson, Kentucky.

The informant advised that Ross Prio is an exceptionally influential individual in "the Family." The informant advised he has heard from various sources that he is also on the committee. However, he has also heard information to contradict Prio's presence on the committee and therefore advised he is not sure of Prio's actual position of leadership in "The Family" other than he is an extremely powerful individual. He advised that the committee at present is heavily weighted with Siciliano members advising that with the exception of Fiore "Fifi" Buccieri and Paul Ricca who are Camorra, the rest are Sicilian.

Informant advised that Samuel "Moe" Giancana was "made" before his being sent to the penitentiary. He advised he was one of Al Capone's associates and by the time, Giancana got out of the "42 Gang" he was "made" or brought into the outfit. He advised further, that Chuckie English and Sam "Teet's" Battaglia, who also were members of the "42 Gang," were "made" years ago, shortly after Giancana was brought into "The Life."

Informant advised that Fiore "Fifi" Buccieri's sponsor was killed right after he brought "Fifi" into "The Life". He advised that Fifi Buccieri ultimately became extremely close to Sam Giancana and actually was a partner in many of Moe's ventures. He advised that Tony "JB" Accardo and Sam "Teet's" Battaglia were both "made" in the days of Al Capone.

The informant estimates that there are approximately 150 Italians in "The Life" in Chicago whereas there are thousands in New York City. He advised that New York City uses "button men" and the soldier system, which includes many more members plus the fact that there is more than one family in New York each with their "button men and individual soldier system." The word Capo régime, the informant explained, is used interchangeably with Don. He advised that this term is seldom used in the Chicago area and if used refers to a head of a section of a town or an overseer. The information advised that the term "button men" is used only in New York City and is not a common term in Chicago. He advised the term "soldiers" is not common to Chicago but if it were it would refer to the individuals who would work directly beneath the Don or Capo who boss a district. He advised the term mustachios refers to old-time Sicilians who were generally kill crazy and handled every problem with a killing. He advised not only is this term dying out but also the individuals to which it applied. He advised today "The Family" members are more suave and have abandoned the old-fashioned ideas."

Anthony "Joe Batters" Accardo and Sam "Mooney" Giancana in a 1950's Chicago Police line up photo.

Chapter 1

Sam "Mooney" Giancana

FEDERAL BUREAU OF INVESTIGATION				
REPORTING OFFICE CHICAGO	OFFICE OF ORIGIN CHICAGO	DATE 1957	INVESTIGATIVE PERIOD Dec. 9 thru Dec. 19, 1957	
TITLE OF CASE SAMUEL M. GIANCANA, aka		REPORT MADE BY James J. Files		TYPED BY dkc
		CHARACTER OF CASE File number 92-3171-1 Chicago File number 92-349-1		

Synopsis:

    Samuel Giancana was born on May 24, 1908 at Chicago. He has a 6th grade education. Subject is a widower. He currently resides at 1147 South Wenonah, Oak Park, Illinois. Giancana has a criminal record dating back to 1925. His most recent arrest was on April 15, 1957 for investigation in the murder of Leon Marcus. Giancana is reported to be currently associating with several individuals who are described as small time hoodlums. He also is reported to be associating with top hoodlums including Tony Accardo and Murray Humphreys. Giancana currently frequents a building that has gambling facilities and is frequented by known stickup men, burglars, and cartage thieves. Giancana allegedly operates syndicate wire services to bookies, in the west side districts and the northwest suburbs of Chicago. The territory including Kane County was reportedly assigned to him in 1957. He is reported to be the principal owner of a gambling casino worth approximately $50,000. He was indicted in 1951 on 67 counts for operating gambling in this casino. Giancana was believed to be the brain in a $100,000 kidnapping of a Negro "policy" king in 1948. Giancana is believed to be the principal owner of enterprises including a motel, a tavern, and an air conditioning business.

    Giancana traveled by plane to an unknown destination from Miami, Florida in 1950 with Tony Accardo and Murray Humphreys. In 1953, he traveled to Los Angeles with Accardo. GIANCANA IS SAID TO CARRY A GUN AT TIMES AND TO HAVE A VICIOUS TEMPERAMENT.

Details:

PERSONAL HISTORY AND BACKGROUND

BIRTH

T-1 informant advised in 1946 that Samuel Giancana claimed that he was born in Chicago, Illinois, on July 16, 1908. Check of records of Bureau of Vital Statistics, Chicago, on 12-16-1957, disclosed no birth record for Samuel Giancana on that date.

T-3 informant, who has furnished reliable information in the past, advised that his records disclose that birth certificate number 5915, filed at the Bureau of Vital Statistics on June 30, 1908, reflects that Gilomo Giancana was born on May 24, 1908, at 223 Ebeten (illegible), and is the second child of Antonio Giancana, age 27, laborer, born at Abruzzi, Italy, and Antonia Desimmona, age 22, born Abruzzi, Italy. This birth was reported by Absentrina Vitale, midwife, 49 Schlot Street, on June 30, 1908. T3 advised that the baptism records of Holy Guardian Angel Church. 717 West Arthington Street, Chicago, reflects the birth of a son to the same parents as above on May 24, 1908. These records reflect the name of this child as Momo Salvatore Giancana.

T-3 advised that Anthony V. Champagne, 5679 West Madison Street, attorney for Giancana, stated on July 9, 1957, that the subject filed delayed series birth certificate number 2965, state file number 201026-1, at the Bureau of Statistics in 1956. This certificate reflects the following: MOMO SALVATORE GIANCANA, Known as SAMUEL M. GIANCANA, born June 15, 1908, at Chicago, son of ANTONIO GIANCANA, born Castelvetrano, province of Tiapani, Italy, and ANTONIA DESIMMONA, also born Castelvetrano. Included is an affidavit from an uncle Andrea Giangano, 7441 Washington Street, Forest Park, Illinois, attesting to the birth of the subject on June 15, 1908. Attached to the certificate is the affidavit of subject that the above statement is true to the best of his knowledge. It was notarized by Anthony V. Champagne on June 29, 1956.

EDUCATION

T-2 informant, who is in a position to furnish reliable information, advised on December 1, 1946, that Giancana's formal education consists of six years of grammar school.

EMPLOYMENT

T-1 informant advised in 1946 that Giancana at that time claimed to be employed at the Central Envelope and Lithograph Company, 426 South Clinton Street, Chicago, where he had worked as a salesman since January 2, 1943, at a salary of $40.00 a week. T-1 advised that M.R. DeTolve, president of Central Envelope and Lithograph Company, had stated in March 1945, that Giancana was employed by that company and had received a salary of $55.00 a week since January 2, 1943. M. R. DeTolve is listed as Giancana's brother-in-law.

Captain Fremont Nestor of the Oak Park Police Department advised SA James Files on December 13, 1957, that he has never known Samuel Giancana to hold regular employment since moving to Oak Park in 1945. Files reflect that subject filed for Selective Service while an inmate of the Federal Penitentiary at Terre Haute, Indiana, on December 14, 1942. At the time of his registration, he did not list any business or employer.

MARITAL STATUS

T-1 informant advised in 1946 that subject claims to have married Angeline De-Tolve on September 23, 1934. A check of records of the Bureau of Vital Statistics on 12-13-1957 disclosed no record of marriage under the date of September 23, 1934. Informant T-3 advised on December 17, 1957, that Sam Giancana was married on September 23, 1933. Subject's wife, Angeline DeTolve Giancana, died on November 24, 1956.

RESIDENCES

Sam Giancana currently resides in a large brick bungalow with his two daughters at 1147 South Wenonah, Oak Park, Illinois. The house sit's on the northwest corner of Wenonah and Filimore in an older residential area of Oak Park. The town is a "dry" suburb and has a reputation as a quiet, law-abiding community. The house purchased in April, 1945, from a real estate firm, when a man using the name Sam Mooney, put down $10,000 in cash as a deposit. Two days later, an attorney using the name "Campagna", (true identity Anthony V. Champagne), called the real estate company and said he would complete the deal for Mr. Mooney. The deal was completed for a total of $22,000 in cash at a loan office at 5200 West North Avenue, Attorney Champagne acting for the subject.

One block to the south of the subject's home is Roosevelt Road, which is the dividing line between Cicero and Berwyn to the south of Roosevelt Road, and Oak Park to the North. Cicero is a suburb with a reputation as the location of various underworld activities. Informant T3 advised in 1957 that subject previous resided at the following addresses:

2822 West Lexington (1945)	1048 South Monitor
2022 West Lexington (1939)	914 South Hermitage (1934)

RELATIVES

On December 13, 1957, Captain Nestor advised that the subject has the following relatives:

Annette Giancana, daughter, born June 23, 1935.
Bonita Lou Giancana, daughter, born April 29, 1938.
Josephine Giancana, sister, residing at 920 South Hermitage, Chicago.
Victoria Giancana, sister, residing 920 South Hermitage, Chicago.
Mary Giancana, sister, residing at 920 South Hermitage, Chicago.

MILITARY INFORMATION

A report of Sam Giancana's physical examination dated February 12, 1944, reveals that he was rejected for military service because of a constitutional psychopathic state and inadequate personality, manifested by strong anti-social trends.

IDENTIFICATION RECORD

The following is the identification record of Sam Giancana as listed in the files of the Identification Division of the Federal Bureau of Investigation under the FBI number 58437. He was arrested May 17, 1926, for investigation by the Evanston, Illinois, Police Department as Sam Giancana and was released. On July 25, 1926, he was arrested by Louisville, Kentucky, Police Department as Sam Giancana for vagrancy and no disposition was listed. He was arrested on September 17, 1926, by the Chicago Police Department on a murder charge and was indicted in the September term of the Grand Jury. Charges were dropped.

On March 12, 1929, Giancana was arrested on a burglary charge at Chicago, Illinois, and on March 26, 1929, was sent to Illinois State Penitentiary, Joliet to serve a sentence of one to five years. On November 13, 1933, Giancana was arrested by the Oak Park Police Department on a charge of "general principles" but no disposition is listed. He was again arrested February 11, 1939, by the Alcohol Tax Unit, Chicago, Illinois, on a charge of conspiracy to violate the Internal Revenue Laws. He was sentenced to four years in Federal Penitentiary and fined $3,700 on October 16, 1939. As a result, thereof he was received at the United States Penitentiary at Terre Haute, Indiana, on October 30, 1940.

The Chicago Police Department arrest records revealed the following identification record for Samuel Giancana; as Sam Gencani he was arrested on September 25, 1925 for larceny of an automobile and was sentenced to thirty days in the Chicago House of Correction. Under the same name, he was again arrested January 18, 1926, and charged with violation of U.S. 22 M.V.L. For this, he was fined $10 and costs. The Chicago Police Department records further reflect that he was arrested June 27, 1927, as Sam Gincana and found not guilty of larceny. He was arrested January 3, 1928, on a charge of disorderly conduct and was fined $50 and costs. Again as Sam Gincana he was arrested March 13, 1928, for disorderly conduct and was fined $200.00 and costs. On February 15, 1929, he was charged with burglary and larceny and his bond on these offenses were forfeited. A charge of robbery on February 20, 1929, was stricken off and an arrest for larceny on March 12, 1929, was nolle prossed on December 24, 1932. The following is a description of Sam Giancana which was obtained from the files of the Alcohol Tax Union:

Name	Samuel Giancana
Date of Birth	July 16, 1908
Height	5'9" and $\frac{3}{4}$"
Weight	160
Hair	Black, slightly wavy receding at temples
Eyes	Brown
Completion	Dark
Build	Medium
Place of Birth	Chicago, Illinois
Occupation	No known legitimate employment
Social Security#	326-18-6902
FBI#	58437
Residence	1147 South Wenonah Avenue, Oak Park, Illinois
Photograph	Available

B. CRIMINAL RECORD

The following is the identification record of
the subject under FBI number 58437, dated July 12, 1946:

Contributor of Fingerprints	Name and Number	Arrested or Received	Charge	Disposition
PD, Evanston, Ill.	Sam Giancana, #14-P	5-17-26	inv.	rel.
PD, Louisville, Ky.	Sam Giancana # 15037	7-25-26	vag.	
PD, Chicago, Ill.	Sam Giancana #C-2757	9-17-26	murder	Indicted Sept. Term G.J.
*	#C-14275 Sam Gincanni, 3-12-29, sent. Joliet Pen. #2807. att. burg. P.G. (On record sheet rec. from PD, Chicago, Ill.)			
SP, Joliet, Ill.	Sam Gincana #2807	3-26-29	att. burg.	1 - 5 yrs.
PD, Oak Park, Ill.	Sam Giancana #2535	11-13-33	G.P.	
Alcohol Tax Unit, Chicago, Ill.	Sam Giancana #5484-M	2-11-39	cons. to viol. Int. Rev. Laws	10-16-39, 4 yrs. Pen. fine: Tot. $2700, penalties Tot. $1000
USM, Chicago, Ill.	Sam Giancana #263	2-11-39	I.R.	sent. to Leaver worth, Kans. 4 yrs. del. to said Inst. 10-28-39
Co. Jail, Chicago, Ill.	Sam Giancana #8229	2-11-39	I.R.	2-15-39 del. to USM.
USM. Lena, Ill.	Sam Giancana # - -	not given (prt. rec. 10-19-39)	liquor vio. - Int. Rev. Laws	4 yrs.
USP, Leavenworth, Kans.	Sam Gincnana #55966	10-28-39	Int. Rev. still. mfg. conc. poss. consp.	4 yrs.
USP, Terre Haute, Ind.	Sam Ginncana #104	10-30-40 (in trans. from USP Leavenworth, Kans.)	Int. Rev. Laws	4 yrs. Disch. 12-14-42 Conditional Release & Prob. from 12-14-42 to 10-15-43 CR.

Contributor of Fingerprints	Name and Number	Arrested or Received	Charge	Disposition
*		Sam Gencani, Chicago, Ill. 9-25-25, larc. of auto; 30 days H. of C.		
*		Sam Gencani, Chicago, Ill. 1-18-26, U.S. 22, M.V.L. $10. and costs.		
*		Following notations received on record sheet from PD, Chicago, Ill:		
*		#C-5755, Sam Gincana, 6-27-27, not guilty larceny.		
*		As Sam Gincana, 1-3-28, $50. and costs. dis. cond.		
*		As Sam Gincana, 3-13-28, $200. and costs dis. cond.		
*		#C-14275, Sam Gincanni, 2-15-29, bonds forf. burg. and larc.		
*		#C-14275, Sam Gincanni, 2-20-29, str. off. robb. (2).		
*		#C-14275, Sam Gincanni, 3-12-29, nolle prossed larc. disch. 12-24-32.		
*		Sam Giancana, #C-62565, PD, Chicago, Ill. G.P.		

The following is the arrest record of the subject under Chicago Police Department number E-27465, checked on December 17, 1957:

Sam Gincana, 9/25/25, 30 days House of Correction, Larc. of auto;

Sam Gincana, 1/18/26, $10.00 and costs, U.S. 22, M.V.L.;

Sam Gincana, 5/17/26, inv., rel.;

Sam Gincana, 6/27/27, not guilty, larceny, 17a, db;

Sam Gincana, 1/3/28, $50.00 and costs, disorderly conduct, 26th District, Judge Gentsel;

Sam Gincana, 3/13/28, $200.00 and costs, disorderly conduct, Judge Finnegan;

Sam Gincanni, 2/15/29, bonds. forf. burglary and larceny, Judge Sullivan;

Sam Gincanni, 2/20/29, str. off. robb. (2), Judge Sullivan;

Sam Gincanni, 3/12/29, Joliet Penitentiary # 2807, attempted burglary, plea of guilty, Judge Sullivan;

Sam Gincanni, 3/12/29, nolle prosse larc., Judge Sullivan, discharged 12/24/32;

Sam Gincanni, 2/11/39, CGV, Chicago, Internal Revenue;

Sam Gincanni, 2/12/45, Inv. DB;

Sam Gincanni, 5/14/46, Inv. 5th District;

Sam Giancana, 11/2/34, GP Off. DB;

Sam Giancana, 3/20/52, SOL (NA) permitting building to be used for handbook.

ASSOCIATES

Association with Subordinates

On December 13, 1957, Captain Nestor advised that Sam Giancana is currently associating with Joey Glimco, hoodlum president of the Teamsters Union Local 777. Another close associate according to Captain Nestor is John Lardino, with alias Edward Nardi, 1201 North Belfort Avenue, Oak Park, Illinois, who has been a suspect in robberies and burglaries. Another associate is Sam "Sambo" Cesario, 1206 North Marion, Oak Park, Illinois, a small time hoodlum who has carried out stickups and operated crap games. Other associates are:

Rocco Potenzo, 900 South Leavitt, Chicago
Tom Potenzo, 3526 West Flournoy, Chicago
James Kenefeck, 19 Bell Avenue, Chicago
J. Kortin, 2511 South 57th Court, Cicero
Netti E. Taglia, 1022 South Menard, Chicago
(FNU) Bucciene, 910 South Paulina, Chicago
R. Mundo, 3245 West Lexington, Chicago
James F. Conroy, 1705 North Bloomingdale, Chicago
Carlo Urbanati, 2929 West Flournoy, Chicago

Captain Nestor stated that he dose not know whether these latter associates have been close to Giancana recently. He stated that they are all individuals whom he would describe as small time hoodlums.

T-4 informant, who has furnished reliable information in the past, advised that on April 10, 1957, that Earnest "Rocky" Infelice is a very close associate of Sam Giancana and that Sam Giancana wields a big club in the determination of what gamblers can operate. Rocky Infelice is Giancana's trigger man. T4 advised on June 4, 1956, that Carmi Fanelli operates the Armory Tap, which is owned by Giancana.

ASSOCIATION WITH OTHER HOODLUMS

1) In May 1954, T-9 informant advised that during May 1954, Giancana went to the Orange Lantern, 1904 West Division Street, where he met John Miroglia and James Capezio. He was greeted warmly by those in the tavern and shared a table with Miroglia and Capezio. The information advised that the subject spent the better part of two hours in the Orange Lantern and when he departed someone was heard to remark that this was the first time in over five years that he had been outside of his own territory in Cicero. The informant advised that of his knowledge, the fact that the subject turned up in the heart of Tony Capezio's territory was very unusual.

2) Lieutenant Joseph Morris, Scotland Yard Detail, Chicago Police Department, advised on an unknown date that at the wake of Giancana's father, Antonio Giancana, at Cermak Funeral Home, Cicero, Illinois, on July 29, 1954, Sam Giancana was visited by the following hoodlums and sat with them in Joe Corngold's Cocktail Lounge near the funeral home, they were:

Tony Accardo	Milwaukee Phil Alderisio
Dominick Brancato	R. S. Roti

Jake Guzik	John Lardino
Pat Manning	Frank LaPorte
Joe Glimco	Dominick DiBello
Tony Mack	Joe Campise
Obbie Frabotta	Anthony DeRosa
Ross Prio	

3) Information was received from Miami Office on January 13, 1956, that Sam Giancana, Murray Humphreys, Tony Accardo, Gus Alex, and Paul DeLucia were attending a conference at the Thunderbird Motel, just north of Miami Beach, Florida.

4) On April 18, 1957, T-6 informant advised that Sal Moretti, who was found murdered on April 12, 1957, was a driver for William "Willie Potatoes" Daddano, (real spelling Daddono) a lieutenant of Giancana's.

5) Captain Nestor advised in 1949 that Sam Giancana was then the right hand man and bodyguard for Tony Accardo.

6) In February of 1950 a report stated that Giancana was listed as one of the biggest hoodlums on the list of the Chicago Crime Commission, being only second to Tony Accardo, who is allegedly head of the alleged crime syndicate in Chicago.

7) During 1946 Giancana was reported (source unknown) to be a close associate of Tony Accardo, Jake Guzik, Hyman Levin, Edward Vogel, and Murray Humphreys, all accredited with being members of the alleged Chicago Crime Syndicate.

8) During 1948, Captain Nestor advised that Louis "Little New York" Campagna, who was incarcerated for extortion in the Brown-Bioff case, visited Sam Giancana at Giancana's home in Oak Park.

9) Informant T-7 advised on August 22, 1957, that he has heard from someone whom he considers a reliable source that Tony Accardo and Paul DeLucia have fallen out of favor with the alleged syndicate because of the publicity they have been receiving. It is rumored that Accardo has been ordered not to roam more than six blocks from his home except to answer court subpoenas. This order was issued by Sam Giancana according to the T7 source.

CRIMINAL ACTIVITIES

GAMBLING

1) T-6 informant advised on June 24, 1957 that Lennie Patrick owns a building on Roosevelt Road which was formerly used as a bath house and as a center for gambling operations. The informant said that this building was remodeled by Patrick about two years ago and is now a Negro rooming house. Upon the demise of this gambling house Patrick and Dave Yaras purchased a bath house on North Avenue in the vicinity of Damen Street and placed Willie Block in charge of this place, which is operated as a bath house open to the public, but which has plush quarters for gambling on the upper floors. T-6 continued that shortly after this place was put in operation a gang led by "Milwaukee Phil" Alderisio broke into the place and smashed the fixtures, furniture, and so forth. T-6 said that it seemed that "Milwaukee Phil" considered this to be his

24

exclusive territory. T-6 stated that the matter was finally arbitrated by Joe Eptstein after Epstein discussed the situation with Sam Giancana and it was decided that Patrick and Yaras could continue to operate but must pay a percentage to "Milwaukee Phil" Alderisio.

2) Captain Nestor advised on December 13, 1957 that Giancana's current headquarters are in an old bank building just east of Austin Avenue on Roosevelt Road in Chicago. Nestor stated that he had learned that Giancana has gambling facilities on the second floor to this building and that Giancana goes there almost nightly. He stated that on one recent evening he surveilled this building and observed 44 individuals known to him to be stickup men, burglars, and cartage thieves entering this building.

3) On April 5, 1957 Captain Nestor advised that his sources have told him that the territory including Kane County was recently assigned to Samuel Giancana and that the assignment was made as of January, 1957.

4) In May 1955, a Federal Grand Jury investigated suspected tax evaders. The particular targets of the probe were gamblers who had neglected to buy wagering stamps and those who falsified their gambling income on income tax returns. Heading the list of those to be subpoenaed was Sam "Mooney" Giancana of Oak Park, who allegedly runs syndicate wire services to bookies in the west side districts and in the northwest suburbs.

5) T-8 informant advised on February 18, 1955, that Giancana recently remolded the building at 4810-12 West 22nd Street in Cicero, Illinois, and converted it into a plush gambling place with roulette wheels, a horse parlor, private rooms for card games, and refreshment facilities.

6) T-9 informant advised in May 1954 that it is general knowledge or at least the belief among the underworld element that the top setup of the "syndicate" insofar as the operation of taverns, handbooks, and minor gangs was concerned, was that Tony Accardo was the top man, then followed by Tony Capezio and Sam Giancana. T-9 stated that of his own knowledge no one operated in the area north of Madison Avenue to just south of Belmont Avenue on the north and from Cicero Avenue on the west to the lake on the east, with the exception of the down town area, without Capezio's okay. The informant stated that the same held true for Cicero and the central west and southwest suburbs, which was the subject's territory. The informant stated that the north and northwest sections of the city and the northwest suburbs are controlled by Rocco Potenzo, who is one the subject's "boys."

7) March 1954 reported that Sam Giancana was a third principal owner of the Wagon Wheel in Norwood Park along with Nick D'Amico and James Davies. The Wagon Wheel is a reputed gambling establishment bring in approximately $50.000. In 1951 then States Attorney, John S. Boyle, had assigned a squad of States Attorney's Police to find Giancana after a capias had been issued and Giancana had failed to appear for arraignment in Criminal Court. He had been indicted on 67 counts for operating gambling in the Wagon Wheel.

8) Information was received in 1948 from an unknown source that Sam "Momo" Giancana was one of the "big shots" in gambling in the vicinity of Roosevelt Road and Halsted Street in Chicago.

9) In October 1955 Giancana was one of six top syndicate gambling bosses to be subpoenaed by a Special County Grand Jury, which was investigation a wave of unsolved bombings.

KIDNAPPING, ROBBERY, LARCENY, BURGLARY, and ALCOHOL TAX VIOLATIONS

In 1926, Giancana and two companions were arrested for the killing of William Girard during the robbery of a south side cigar store. The principal witness in the case was an Alexander Burba. Burba reported to the authorities that he had been offered money and threats of persuade him to change his story. The authorities did nothing to protect Burba and he was shot to death as he opened his front door to his home. The court case fell apart and Giancana was freed. However that same year Giancana served time in Bridewell prison for auto larceny and time in Joliet Prison for burglary. In 1939 Giancana was arrested along with fourteen others for the illegal operation of a 1,000 gallon capacity whiskey still on a farm near Garden Prairie, Illinois. Giancana was sent to Terre Haute Penitentiary on a four-year sentence. It was there he gained the confidence of one Edward Jones, the Negro policy king of the south side. Jones was serving time for income tax violations. Giancana was paroled in December of 1942, and Jones some time later. Both Jones and Giancana remained in touch until May of 1946. Jones was kidnapped by four masked men and held for ransom. Jones was released six days later when the ransom of $100,000 was paid. In July of 1946, it is indicated that Giancana was one of the persons involved in the kidnapping of the policy boss. It appears that the house presently occupied by this subject at 1147 Wenonah Avenue, Oak Park, was vacant at the time when Jones' was snatched and the place could have been used to hide Jones. By the time local authorities learned of the suspected facts the subject was then in residence in the building and there was no opportunity to make a search.

In August of 1952 Theodore Roe, a late Negro policy king was murdered. It was reported that Gus Alex and Sam Giancana had made death threats against Roe in person prior to his death. A similar kidnapping attempt had been made against Roe in which he was able to shoot and kill Leonard Caifano, one of the attackers. At Caifano's wake, police raided the building looking for Leonard's brother Ralph Caifano and Sam Giancana, both believed to be the other two who tried to kidnap or kill Roe. In June 1951, a report stated that two men were with Caifano when he was killed, the two being "Teets" Battaglia and a man known as "Little Caesar." The report also went on to the effect that Roe was to be kidnapped and Giancana was said to have been present at a conference a few days prior to June 18 concerning the kidnapping. The story recited that Giancana was referred to as possibly being the "young bloods" linked with the Capone syndicate. The object of the scheme allegedly was to take over Roe's rich policy interests and the alleged plot, supposed to have been hatched aboard a yacht, had been rented by Caifano.

BRIBERY

Sam Giancana was one of many racketeers involved in the 1951 syndicate horse-meat scandal. This scandal involved the bribing of State Meat Inspectors to pass horse-meat as beef. On March 6, 1952 it was reported that Sam Giancana and Frank Tye were among the racketeers involved in the scandal.

LEGITIMATE ENTERPRISES

ARMORY TAP, Formerly FOREST LOUNGE

A) T-4 informant advised on June 4, 1956, that the Forest Lounge, Niles, Illinois, reputedly the headquarters of Giancana, is now known as the Armory Tap. It is operated by Carmie Fanelli for Giancana. One Carmin Finella, a known associate of Nick George Montos, may be identical with the above individual. Lieutenant Joseph Morris, Scotland Yard Detail, Chicago Police Department advised SA Francis W. Matthys in 1957 that Giancana is believed to have owned the Forest Lounge, 6548 Milwaukee Avenue, Niles, which was operated for him by Rocky Vallo and Leo Zimmerman at one time. The Chicago Crime Commission reported on October 24, 1952, that Sam Giancana and his brother Rocky Giancana owned the Forest Lounge. Rocco Potenzo operated it for them: however, the commission stated that continued checks by its investigation reflected that as of January, 1953, the only gambling they were able to find at this place was a "26" game.

B) Utility Engineering Company, 6201 West Roosevelt Road, Oak Park, Illinois. In October 1955, informant T10 advised that Sam Giancana and Tony Accardo are the actual owners of this air conditioning business although the owner listed on the license is Anthony DePardo, who has an office in Berwyn.

C) Boogie Woogie Night Club, 1709 West Roosevelt Road, Chicago. T-2 informant advised in 1946 that he had learned in 1945 that Giancana owned the Boogie Woogie Night Club. The informant advised that Giancana confirmed in a statement to him that he owned this club. The informant advised that this club was patronized by Negroes exclusively.

D) Windy City Sports Enterprises was reported to be owned by Giancana and republican Illinois state representative James Adduci. It was reported that Adduci scoffed at the idea that Giancana was recognized as the leader of the Mafia in Chicago in 1951.

E) In January 1953, Captain Nestor advised that he had a discussion with four or five individuals regarding the Capone mob's activity in legitimate enterprises and that during the course of this discussion someone in the group, whose identity he was unable to recall, mentioned the fact that the Capone mob was attempting to get a corner on the shrimp industry in the United States. He advised that after being told this rumor he contacted one of his informants whose identity he did not wish to disclose. This informant told Nestor that his information was that Tony Accardo and Sam Giancana were active in the mob's attempts to muscle in on the shrimp industry. This information was furnished as a rumor and has been unable to verify it.

A photo of the Armory Lounge in Forest Park, Illinois in the 1960's

PAST MISCELLANEOUS INFORMATION

Sam Giancana was "made" a member of "The Family" prior to his being sentenced to the penitentiary during the 1930's.

In February 1953, an informant advised that Sam Giancana, a lieutenant of Tony Accardo's, appears at the Rain Box Lounge, 5146 West Cermak Road, Cicero, every Monday night. According to the informant, at the time Giancana holds court in which he settles all disputes amongst members of the hoodlum element, makes his underworld contacts, and is available to any hoodlum who needs money or advice.

Lieutenant Joseph Morris advised that Giancana leases a basement room of the Imperial House, a swanky after theater supper club at 50 East Walton Place as a meeting place. This restaurant is operated by an Italian using the name Ben Scott through whom allegedly Giancana receives his orders.

On June 7, 1955, Lieutenant Morris advised that he had received information that on that date Sam Giancana, Paul DeLucia, Tony Accardo, Sam Hunt, Jack Guzik, Gus Alex, Lester Kruse, and Anthony Ricci, a New York hoodlum, were departing Chicago for Miami via Eastern Airlines. He subsequently advised that through a highly confidential source he had learned that these hoodlums had been tipped off that U.S. Marshall's would be at the airport to serve a grand jury subpoena. As a consequence only DeLucia, Joe Fischetti, and Anthony Ricci made the trip.

Chicago informant advised that in connection with Giancana's position as head of the organized criminal element in the Chicago Area that Giancana was present at the famed Appalachian Meeting held at Appalachian, New York, in November 1957. Giancana was one of three Chicagoans, a second being Anthony Accardo, who were present at this meeting but who managed to escape into the surrounding countryside and escape detection by raiding police officials.

An informant was re-contacted by SA Robert J. Deneen on February 7, 1958. She advised that in using the word "syndicate" when discussing the positions of Tony Accardo, Tony Capezio, and Sam Giancana in May 1954, she could have had in mind no more exact meaning than that which is in general use by the newspapers. This is simply that a smaller group of individuals seem to dominate vice in general in the Chicago area.

The informant stated the use of the word "syndicate" was not meant to indicate that she could positively state that there is any formal organization with a chain of command or definite assignment of responsibility to each member. She stated that underworld characters now seldom use the term "syndicate". When referring to the undefined powers in vice in the Chicago area, they currently speak of "the outfit." A copy of this report is submitted to the Los Angeles Office since a lead is outstanding in that division and Frank Ferraro, who subject reportedly visited in Los Angeles, reportedly now lives in Chicago.

Additional FBI Information

1)   Atlanta report dated 10/4/1927 disclosed that the photograph of Sam Giancana, Chicago number 2767, would be forwarded to the St. Louis Office, in connection with the Mattoon Illinois Interstate Robbery for possible identification by the Cain brothers, Floyd, Roy and Fred, all subjects of Bureau.

2)   John F. McCall, manager of the Hi Speed Motor Express, 2900 West Taylor Street, Chicago, reported on 1-6-1944 that a tractor containing 414 cases of eggs has been stolen. Joseph Iuro, owner of the tavern located at 725 South California, Chicago, on 1-6-1944 named several suspects including Charles English and Sam Marcello, aka "Mooney." On 1-14-1944 English stated that "Mooney" was Moon Giancona "Giancana" instead of Sam Marcello.

3)   In December 1949 a representative of a credit agency in Grand Rapids, Michigan called the Chicago Crime Commission seeking information regarding Sam Giancana, the right hand man of Tony Accardo, head of the Capone gang. It was understood that Giancana was about to take over an AMI juke box distributorship.

4)   On 9-25-1950, William Drury, former Chicago Police Lieutenant was murdered at his home, 1843 Addison Street, Chicago. Later, in an anonymous telephone call to the Chicago FBI office, information was received that "Fat" Leonard, deputy sheriff of Cook County, Illinois, Charles "Chuck" Nicoletti, 2700 block of Lexington, Chicago, Sam Mircelli, 2800 block of Flourney, Chicago, and one "Mooney" (Mooney was believed to be Sam Giancana) were involved in the killing of William Drury.

5)   Thomas F. Kelly Sr., Illinois Sports News, 906 South Wabash, Chicago, advised that the Midwest News Service, 537 South Dearborn Street, Chicago, which was operated by Sam Giancana and others, ceased operations in November 1951.

6)   Dave Sentner advised on 2-20-1952 that some 30 gangsters and underworld characters in Chicago did not have any record in the Chicago Police Department files which raised a question in their minds as to whether or not their files and records had been purged. Sam Giancana record was one of them however, Giancana's was later located.

7)   Virgil W. Peterson, Operating director, Chicago Crime Commission, stated he had learned that Harry Russell, a notorious gambler in the Miami area, flew to Chicago from Miami for a conference with Jake Guzik, Sam Giancana and others which was held on 12-17-1952 in St. Hubert's Grill. The Capone Outfit, according to Peterson, was concerned over an alleged grand jury investigation of income tax violations. Their plans were to pay as much as $5,000 per juror to kill a possible indictment. Tom Kelly, manager of St. Hubert's Grill, regularly furnished rooms for Giancana and the others to hold various conferences.

8)   In 1953 an informant advised that John Drew, Tony Accardo, Mike DePeano and Sam Giancana notorious Chicago hoodlums and racketeers, were attempting to move into control of the Golden Hotel Casino in Reno, Nevada.

9)   Lt, Joseph Morris, Scotland Yard District of Chicago PD advised that "a theory" regarding the adduction of Clem Graver, missing member of the Illinois State Legislature, had been developed. This theory was to the effect that Graver obtained some money from Sam Giancana. This money was to be used to "spring" an unknown individual from jail. Giancana was supposed to have welshed on this deal and three friends of his thereafter "took care" of the victim. These three persons were reported to have been Sam Battaglia, Frank Sortino and Gus Alex. Another informant advised that on 11-1-1953 a meeting was held at the Saxony Hotel, Miami, Florida, which was attended by Sam Giancana and others. The kidnapping of Clem Graver was mentioned and his death was reported to have been ordered by Giancana because Graver had in his possession the proceeds of a robbery and refused to deliver the money to the parents of one of the gang killed in the robbery.

10)   On 6-7-1955 Lt. Joseph Morris advised that Sam Giancana and others had departed that date for Miami. Morris was of the opinion that this might have been a gathering of mob leaders to select a successor to Louis Campagna who had died in Miami on 5-30-1955. Lt. Morris subsequently advised that from a highly confidential source he had learned that Giancana had not left Chicago for Miami on 6-7-1955 as he had been tipped off that the US Marshal would be at the airport to serve a Grand Jury subpoena.

11)   The Criminal Division, Department of Justice, Washington DC, furnished a copy of a letter the Department had received from Edward H. Miller, Atlanta, Georgia dated 12-22-1955 in which he stated in part the following. Alex Greenburg and Willie Bioff were shot on orders of the Syndicate because they refused further shakedowns. Greenburg owed Paul Ricca (Paul DeLucia, Chicago) more than $300,000 and was killed on Ricca's orders. He was shot by one "Trigger" M. Calfam and Sam Giancana.

12)   In 1947 the automobile of James Mirro, former member of the "Red Hawk" gang was seen parked in front of Giancana's home. There was possibly an alliance between Giancana and the "Red Hawk" gang.

13)   In 1948 Lt. Tiny Nester, Oak Park Police, Illinois, had arrested Giancana on a routine pickup several times. After one arrest Nester received a large box of merchandise from Giancana with no name on the package. Nester returned the package with a note that he did not care to receive a gift from such a hoodlum as Giancana.

14)   In 1948 there was a possibility that Tony Accardo would be sent to prison and that Giancana would temporarily fill his top position in the syndicate. On 3-5-1948 Giancana was visited by Louis Campagna concerning

this. Giancana drove a "souped up" 1946 Mercury Sedan. It was also reported that Giancana owned three store buildings west of California Avenue on the north side of Roosevelt Road, Chicago, and spent considerable amount of time there. He was considered one of the most vicious members of the syndicate.

15)   In 1949 Giancana was reported to be the successor to Anthony Accardo as head of the Chicago Syndicate. However, Giancana did no follow instructions to keep the "heat" off his activities and it was indicated that the successor might be Ben Fillichio.

16)   In 1951 the special September, 1951 grand jury, investigating gambling in Cook County, Illinois, had indicted nineteen hoodlums including Giancana. Giancana, a top Capone man, was charged on 67 counts with allowing a building he owned to be used for bookmaking purposes. The building called the Wheel Wagon, 4416 Narragansett, Norwood Park Township. On 11-8-1951 Giancana was a state fugitive when he failed to appear for his arraignment. Neighbors reported that Giancana had not been seen in the neighborhood for weeks.

17)   In 1951 James J. Adduci, Illinois Republican State Representative from Chicago, was described as a former partner of Sam Giancana, an ex-convict in the Windy City Sports Enterprises.

18)   In 1952 Sam Giancana, who was one of the operators of the Midwest News Service, an organization distributing racing news, was reported in February, 1952 as being involved in the multi-million dollar horse meat racket.

1929 Chicago Courts Listing of Sam Giancana

Taxed		
Book		
Page		

Indictment No.
SEP 24 1926

41206

Indictment for Murder

The People of the State of Illinois VERSUS

Diego Ricco
Joseph Pape
Sam Giancana

Bail fixed at $

DISPOSED OF

Date	Entry	Book/Page
OCT - 4 1926	Assign'd to Judge Brothers	AA 56 2
OCT - 4 1926	See order of this date in Journal entire order	AA 56 3
OCT - 4 1926	FLEA OF NOT GUILTY ENTERED Ricco & Giancana	
OCT - 6 1926		
NOV 9 - 1926	No Bill see term — 1926	BB 56 3
" " "	Bail fixed at $2000.00	B 56 5
NOV 16 1926	Ricco & Giancana Sureties in $3000.00 day to day Ricco	
NOV 18 1926	No to set Bail out Cont 24 Nov—17—1926 Pape	B 56 60
" " "	Bail fixed at $2000.00 Giancana &	B 56 67
NOV 26 1926	Seven Sureties in 2000.00 day to day Pape	E 56 85
DEC 16 1926	Assign'd to Judge Brothers	
JAN 10 1927	By Cont Jam —10—1927	AA 56 68
" " "	Demand for trial as to	
JAN 17 1927	No defts Jam — 17—1927 Giancana	B 56 95
JAN 31 1927	" State " — 3 — " Ricco & Pape	
" " "	" deft Merch — term —1927 Eck	B 56 106
MAR - 8 1927	Diego Ricco Surety in $2000.00 Slaughty Giancana	135
APR 28 1927	No deft April—26—1927 Eck	136
	MOTION STATES ATT'Y STRICKEN OFF WITH LEAVE TO REINSTATE	BB 56 141

Taxed		
Book	110	
Page	497	

Indictment No.
SEP 24 1926

41207

Indictment for

The People of the State of Illinois VERSUS

John Rogers
Frank Cornelius
Frank Mille

Bail fixed at $ 3500.00

PLEA OF NOT GUILTY ENTERED

Date	Entry	Book/Page
SEP 28 1926	By Frank Eck —25—1926	Mille AA 56 31
OCT 21 1926	Plea of not guilty Wt E. withdrawn	" 37
OCT 25 1926	Felony & Jury waived Plea of not	
OCT 25 1926	Gty to set finding — Gty to set	

32

NAME _Sam Siverera_

Received _March 26, 1929_
Sentence _1-5_

Term of Court

County _Cook_
Crime _Attempt Burglary_

Color _White_
Hair _Lt. Ch._ Eyes _Hazel_gre_M_
Height _5'8½_ Build _Medium_
Religion _Roman Catholic_
Profanity _No_
Smoke _No_

Age _25_
Nativity _Illinois_
Weight _150_
Education _7th Grade_
Drink _No_
Chew _No_
Associates _#3159_
Father born in _Italy_
Mother born in _Italy_
Children
How long have you lived in the

United States?
Are you a Naturalized Citizen?
Have you taken out 1st Papers?
Are you an Alien?

Parents Living _life_
Left Home What Age _19_
Married _No_
Wife Living

Hereditary Disease
Condition of Heart _endocarditis_
Condition of Lungs _O.K._
Occupation _Chauffeur_
Working when arrested on present charge _66_
How long before if not
Name and address of
Parents or Family, or } Father:- Mr Tony Siverera
Correspondents   920 Bewley Street,
                                      Chicago, Illinois

Previous terms here

3/29/29 Picture #3
Geo. M Couper
25¢ O. Biren

Name of Trial Judge: _John J. Sullivan_
Name of State's Attorney _John A. Swanson_ Term: _March 1929_
Court: _Criminal_
Date of Sentence: _March 14, 1929_

DETAILS OF CRIME

Guilty #50636

Resident or Transient?

General Reputation:

Industrial Habits:

Associates: _Good_
Disposition: _Good_

Was the Crime Attributed to the Use of Liquor? _No_
Previous Criminal Record, so far as known:
10-28-39 Parole WSP Leavenworth Kan 8 slight 4 to Death Mark 1105 4 yrs

Previous terms here

GRADE RECORD

PRISON RECORD HERE PUNISHMENT RECORD

DAYS LOST

REMARKS

Short Time Expires

19

PAROLE RECORD

Application for Parole

Received
From
Residence

Business

Location

Wages Offered

Application Endorsed by

No.

Paroled

Recommended for Discharge

Discharged December 24, 1934

Previous Criminal Record, so far as known

10-28-34 Rec'd W.S.P.

	REPORTS WHILE OUT ON PAROLE		
	DATED	RECEIVED	REMARKS
Jan.			
Feb.			
March			
April			
May			
June			
July			
Aug.			
Sept.			
Oct.			
Nov.			
Dec.			
Jan.			
Feb.			
March			
April			
May			
June			
July			
Aug.			
Sept.			
Oct.			
Nov.			
Dec.			

ACTION TAKEN BY PAROLE BOARD

Before the Board March X 1930 — 1

Passed to: Maximum X — 1

Ordered Paroled December 25, 1932 — 1

DEPARTMENT OF JUSTICE
WASHINGTON

October 1, 1940

To the   Warden, U. S. Penitentiary, Leavenworth, Kansas

WHEREAS, in accordance with the authority contained in title 18, sections 744b and 753f, U. S. Code, the Attorney General by the Director of the Bureau of Prisons has ordered the

transfer of   Sam Giancana, #55966

from the   U. S. Penitentiary, Leavenworth, Kansas

to the   U. S. Penitentiary, Terre Haute, Indiana

NOW THEREFORE, you, the above-named officer, are hereby authorized and directed to execute this order by causing the removal of said prisoner, together with the original writ of commitment and other official papers as above ordered and to incur the necessary expense and include it in your regular accounts.

And you, the warden, superintendent, or official in charge of the institution in which the prisoner is now confined, are hereby authorized to deliver the prisoner in accordance with the above order; and you, the warden, superintendent, or official in charge of the institution to which the transfer has been ordered, are hereby authorized and directed to receive the said prisoner into your custody and him to safely keep until the expiration of his sentence or until he is otherwise discharged according to law.

By direction of the Attorney General,

JAMES V. BENNETT,
Director, Bureau of Prisons.

Pursuant hereunto, I have this _____
day of OCT 3 0 1940_____, 19 , received the above-named prisoner as herein
directed.

REED COZART
Acting *Assistant Director.*

Name _____
Title _____
RECORD CLERK

Facilities available. (Group #2)

COPY.—To be left at institution from which prisoner is transferred

U.S. GOVERNMENT PRINTING OFFICE   16- 12710

6/24/40 Maint
8/5/40 Elec.Shop
9/25/40 Terre Haute

UNITED STATES PENITENTIARY
LEAVENWORTH, KANSAS

RECORD OF ___SAM GINNCANA .___ NO. **55966**

Alias ___None___ Color ___White___

Crime ___Int. Rev. (Still Mfg Conceal Poss Consp Unbond Distille___ Military or Civil ___Civil___

1-4yrs. 2-2yrs. & 5-2yrs. concur.

Sentence ___4___ years ___-___ months ___-___ days.

Fine ___$ 2,700.00 Committed Yes. (5-$500.00 & 2-$100.00 Fines)___ PEN. $1,000.00 Comm #### itted No. (2-$500.00 Pens).

Received at Penitentiary ___Oct. 28th.,1939___ From ___ND-Ill.,Freeport___

Date of Sentence ___Oct. 16th.,1939___ Sentence begins ___Oct. 16th.,1939___

Maximum term ends ___Oct. 15th.,1943___ Minimum term ends ___Nov. 13th.,1942___

Good time allowed ___336___ days, Occupation ___Steam Fitter & Electrical___ Age ___31___ Years

July 16th.,1908

Elgible to parole ___Feb. 15th.,1941___

Action of parole board _____

Trusty Appointment and Grades		
2nd Grade 12-8-39		
1st Grade 1/7/40		

CLO 9/9/40 Med   Criminal History TRANS TERRE HAUTE 10-29-40

8-25-25	Chicago Ill.;larc.of auto.;30 days. H. of C.	
1-18-26	Chicago Ill.;M.V.L.;$ 10.00 and costs.	
5-17-26	Evanston Ill.;inv.;released.	
7-25-26	Louisville Ky.;vag.;dismissed.	
9-17-26	Chicago Ill.;murder.;indicted Sept.G.J.	
6-27-27	Chicago Ill.;larc.;not guilty.	
1-3-28	Chigago Ill.; ? .;$ 50.00 and costs.	
3-13-28	Chicago Ill.; ? .;$ 200.00 and costs.	
2-15-29	Chicago Ill.;burg.and Larc.;bonds forf.	
3-12-29	Chicago Ill.;att'd.burg.;1-5yrs.SP.Joliet Ill.disch. exp. 12-24-32 . .	
11-13-33	Oak Park Ill.;G P.;discharged.	
12-11-39	Chicago Ill.;int.rev.still.;present case.	

* * * *
(OVER)

3/11/40 Disap.Boiler
6/4/40 - " Farm #

DATE	M.A. 13.11 VIOLATIONS	Days Lost
12-7-39	VIOLATION OF INSTITUTIONAL RULES : (104669) While picking up head phones this morning I found this man with a new institution phone cord which had not been issued to him. C. C. SABOR, Junior Officer. DISPOSITION 12-8-39 Reduced to second grade. C. J. SHUTTLEWORTH, Associate Warden.	

* * * * *

Committed Name GIANCANA, Sam   Register Number 55966-L

2. ASSOCIATE WARDEN'S REPORT:

OUTLINE OF OFFENSE: (792)

Unlawfully possessing still; defrauding United States of Tax; Carrying on business as wholesaler; operating distillery without sign; without bond; fermenting mash; concealing goods and commodities; possession unstamped distilled spirits; and conspiracy.

Codefendants: John Greco, Joe Giszi, Richard Cramer, Michael Falco, Angelus Mamdeopulos, Tony Giacalone, Louis Cocenate, Sam May, James Miceli, Elmer Hansen, Ed Simons, Maxwell Wilcox. (dispositions not given).

STATEMENT BY INMATE:

"I'm just a victim of circumstances. I engaged in a telephone conversation with somebody who happened to be in that business. You associate with somebody in that business, you're accused of it. I donated some money to a fellow who wanted to go in business and I wind up with this".

SUMMARY OF IMPRESSIONS:

As is indicated in this statement, subject is a somewhat indignant individual at this time. He is very bitter toward the investigating authorities in this instance. He very reluctantly admitted that he had "donated" funds which were used by other persons in the erection and operation of a distillery. He was inclined to be rather sarcastic in his replies to questions. This is not an unusual attitude in the instance of the hoodlum who has engaged in rather extensive operations. It is rather evident in his own admissions and in the record that subject has been engaged in violations over a rather lengthy period of years. He is essentially a petty criminal and will probably always participate in criminal activity where there is what appears to him to be an opportunity to increase his income. He will prefer those activities which provide a reasonable possibility of some luckless individual, other than himself, assuming the blame for any violation which is discovered. His attitude is poor and he will make little effort toward an adequate institutional adjustment. He will complain and connive and may, as a result, present some disciplinary problem from time to time.

QUARANTINE REPORT indicates that subject has made a satisfactory adjustment during the Quarantine period.

Recommendations:-

TRANSFER: NONE. Benefit by such is not indicated in this instance.
SUPERVISION: MEDIUM. No institutional problem of serious consequence is anticipated; however, some disciplinary problem may arise as a result of his poor attitude.

CJS
wiley

Classification Form 1b
Rev. January, 1939

ADMISSION SUMMARY
(Continued)

Page _____

CINNCANA, Sam (wh-51)

Committed Name

Register Number

5 5 9 6 6 - L

A. FAMILY DATA:

Father	Tony Connenna	56	918 So Hermitage St., Chicago, Ill
Mother	Mary (?) Cinneana	58	Deceased
Bro	Joe	27	918 So Hermitage St., Chicago, Ill
Bro	Charles	20	"
Sis	Mrs Tony (Lena) Campo	35	Address unknown
Sis	Mrs Am (Mary) Cinneana	22	"
Wife	Mrs Sam (Angeline) Cinneana	20	2822 Lexington Street, Chicago, Ill
Dau	Annett Cinneana	5	"
Dau	Bonnie Lu Cinneana	16	months.

PARENTS born in Italy, citizens of Italy, married in the U S., no marital discord, interested in welfare of subject and treated subject well, illiterate, occasional attendants of the Catholic Church, good health during S's childhood

FATHER, arrived in the U. S. at 22, never remarried, a responsible parent, good health now, employed as a fruit peddler, steady worker, moderate drinker.

MOTHER, died of an auto accident at 58 when subject was 16, arrived in the U. S. at 9, at devoted parent, never worked outside the home.

SIBLINGS: Subject is the second of five children, none deceased, relationship with siblings friendly, economic status modest.

Joe   Eighth grade; single, cigar store, never a delinquent
Charles: Seventh grade; "   factory worker "   "
Lena: Eighth grade; married; husband a laborer; husband in USPL 2 years for liquor
MARY: Sixth grade; "   ------------   never a delinquent

MARITAL STATUS: Married (VA2) 9/26/33 at Chicago, Ill No record (VA3) relationship congenial and subject expects to reunite with wife when released, lived together 6 years (VI5)

WIFE: Maiden name: Angeline De Tolve, one year younger than subject, good health, 4 years of hi school, worked as an office worker, prior to marriage, acquainted with subject 5 years, prior to marriage, never previously married (VI5)

ISSUE:
Annette: Good health and with mother (VI5)
Bonnie Lu "   "   "   "
Subject never previously married (VI5)

B. PERSONAL HOME: Born 7/15/08 at Chicago, Ill of Italian extraction

EARLY DEVELOPMENT: Good health during childhood, reared by parents until 25 when he married, no participation in organized boys' activities, delinquency began at the age of 16 when subject was sent to the Ill St Pen for five years for burglary, became permanently separated from parental home at 25 when he married.

EDUCATIONAL HISTORY: Completed the eighth grade (VI5) left school at 14 to work as a salesman and delivery boy.

OCCUPATIONAL HISTORY: Principle occupation: fruit commissioner; last occupation: salesman (VIM) first ~~first occupation: salesman and delivery boy at 14; admits having served~~ salesman (VI3); first job as a salesman and delivery boy at 14; admits having served 5 years in the Ill St Pen for burglary and discharged.

MILITARY SERVICE: None (VI5)

EMPLOYMENT RECORD: Last employer: Central Envelope Co., 415 So Clinton Street, Chicago, Ill @ $60.00 per week (VI4) In fruit business for self at Chicago, Ill from 1935 to 1938.

LEISURE TIME ACTIVITIES: Enjoys normal recreational activites, especially outdoor sports, gambles, non-member of clubs and lodges, occasional attendant of the Catholic Church (VI5) Constructive interests limited, light drinker, non-user of drugs, sexual promiscuity indicated; associated with persons of all types (VI5)

Classification Form 1b
Rev. January, 1939

ADMISSION SUMMARY
(Continued)

Page _____

Committed Name   G I N N C A R A, Sam (wh-31)   Register Number   5 5 9 6 6 - L

B. PERSONAL HOME: —continued from page 1.—
RESIDENCE LAST FIVE YEARS: last residence: Chicago, Ill 2822 Lexington Street from 1935
to 1939. Bona fide residence: Chicago, Ill (VA2-VI5) No migratory habits indicated.

C. ECONOMIC STATUS:
PARENTAL HOME: Subject came from Italian immigrant working-class family living in
moderately comfortable economic circumstances of average social and cultural status.
One brother-in-law has served a term for liquor law violation. Father provided adequately
on a modest economic level; mother never worked outside the home. Home situated in
Chicago, Ill since birth. Parents rented 2-family, 6-room, modern, brick house in good
repair situated in a working-class neighborhood of Chicago, Ill. Furnishings owned by
parents were satisfactory and the home was carpeted. Children were sent to Sunday
School occasionally; home discipline normal; family relations congenial. Father is living
with Joe and Charles in moderately comfortable economic circumstances, self-supporting
and not in need of relief. Mother is deceased.
PERSONAL HOME: Subject left parental home at 25 to marry, never again returning to parental home to live; home ties with father and siblings strong. While single subject
was unstable socially, made a poor industrial adjustment, occasionally engaged in
law violations as a means of support. Lived in marginal economic circumstances, generally
with parents in working-class sections of Chicago, Ill on average standard of living.
While married and living with wife subject was unstable socially, made a fair industrial adjustment, irregular work history, occasionally engaged in law violations
as a means of support. Good health during adult years (VI5) Appreciated family responsibilities and supported family to the best of his ability. Attributes cause of
present trouble to debts and pressure for money. Lived in marginal economic circumstances
on fair standard of living. Owned 2-family, 5-room, modern brick houses (VI5) In
good repair situated in a working-class neighborhood of Chicago, Ill. Owned satisfactory
furniture valued at $300.00 and the home was carpeted. Since marriage wife worked outside
the home as an office worker (VI5) Family has never received relief. Subject at one
time saved $5,000.00; has owned 2 autos but at present subject has no economic resources.
Wife is unemployed and does not need relief (VI5)
SOCIAL AGENCIES INTERESTED: Ginnaro, Toy, Katherin 182865 — 2909 Lexington Street
                            CRA Union 12/17/36 Mts Wash #34135 11/23/34 (VA6)
IMMEDIATE PROBLEMS: None at this time.

D. REFERENCES AND RESOURCES: Father, siblings and wife may be in a position to assist with
readjustment plans. Asserts wife is loyal and that a reunion is planned. Home offered
by father. Has had experience as a fruit commissioner. Has dependents but no economic re-
sources has $2,500.00 group insurance (VI5)
TENTATIVE PAROLE PLANS:
Proposed Parole Advisor: Frank Hart, 5457 So Harman Ave, Chicago, Ill (VI5)
Prospective Employer: Central Envelope and Lithographing Co, 426 S Clinton Street,
Chicago, Ill (VI5)
Probable Destination: Chicago, Ill.

E. ATTITUDES AND CHARACTERISTICS: Subject is the product of Italian immigrant working-
class family living in moderately comfortable economic circumstances of average social
and cultural status; early home life normal; reared by parents until 25 when married.
Reared in moderately comfortable economic circumstances; one brother-in-law delinquent,
having served a penitentiary term for liquor. Subject is unstable socially, irregular
in social habits, extra-legal activities occasional in respect to theft and liquor.
Moral standards questionable, associated with persons of questionable reputation. Residence
stable, industrial habits fair, comprehends slowly, family ties close with father and siblings, interested in personal and parental family, frank, cooperative, moderately alert,
delinquent since 16, complains of hay fever, interested in working as a steam fitter
while here.

FPI Atl. Ga.—6-15-39—1,150,000
—continued on page 3.—

Committed Name ~ CLEVELAND, Sam   Register Number

4.   Medical: November 18, 1939

PHYSICAL EXAMINATION AND CORRELATED HISTORY:

General: A white, male, 31 years, 5'8 and three fourth inches,
                well nourished, well developed, erect and active.
                Blood pressure 118/68.
                Appendectomy in 1928.

Special: None.

Venereal: Gonorrhea   (1928) O.U smear is negative.

                Syphilis denied; Blood tests are negative.

Narcotics: Use denied; no needle scars.

Dental: Calculus, Caries; Gingivitis.
                Rated as B.

Recommendations:

                Treatment: Oral prophylaxis; fillings.

                Work: Regular.

                No limitation as to cell location, dining,
                recreation or disciplinary measures.

                Transfer not indicated.

FPI Atl. Ga.—6-15-39—1,150,000

Classification Form 1b
Rev. January, 1939

ADMISSION SUMMARY
(Continued)

Page _____

Committed Name   GINDRANA, Sam   11/10/39   Register Number   55946-L.

4b. Neuropsychiatric.

PSYCHOLOGICAL: Intelligence. Verbal Test,
Wells' Revised Alpha, Form 5, 11/10/39. Surpasses
9 per cent of the inmate population. Binet Equivalent M.A. 10:7, I.Q. 71.
Non-Verbal Test, Kellogg-Morton Revised Beta, 11/10/39.
Surpasses 47 per cent of the inmate population. Binet
Equivalent M.A. 13:11, I.Q. 93.

Manipulative Skill: Dearborn Form Board #3.
Accuracy surpasses 28 per cent of the inmate population - a poor performance. Speed surpasses 66 per
cent of the inmate population - a good performance.

PSYCHIATRIC: Of dull normal intelligence, this
man has apparently been in business for himself selling
food. Claims he has done well. Asserts his innocence of
the present offense. Says he loaned a man $500 without
knowing the use to which the money was to be devoted,
but later found out that the man ran a still. This fellow,
he says, has not been caught. Bitter about being sent
here. Says he never had anything to do with the illicit
enterprise. Probably is lying. Seems to have a bad anti-
social attitude. Claims that being Italian with a previous
criminal record the cards were stacked against him and
he was sent here for something he did not do. Should do
well here. Interested in learning electrical work, although he does not intend to work at it as a regular
trade, so I believe he should do ordinary labor. No evidence of nervous or mental disease. Prognosis for the
future, I am afraid, is poor.

NEUROLOGICAL: Negative.

DIAGNOSIS: Dull normal intelligence.

RECOMMENDATIONS:

    Treatment - routine.
    Plans - Interested in electrical work and might
            profit by trade training in this. Does
            not intend to work in electrical field
            after he leaves here. Schooling.
    Quarters - regular.
    Work - Would like to work in electrical shop. Says
           not interested in industries. Probably not
           suitable for electrical work.

Classification Form 1b
Re... anuary, 1939

ADMISSION SUMMARY
(Continued)

Page _____

Committed Name QUINCANA, Sam   Register Number   55958

8(a)   WORK HISTORY.

FIRST WORKED FOR PAY AS A SALESMAN AND DELIVERY BOY AT AGE FOURTEEN.
Principal occupation has been operating a fruit sales business.
Has been in the Illinois State Prison.
Has some experience at electrical work.

Test indicates poor manipulative skill. A-59/S-69.

RECOMMEND: ELECTRIC SHOP FOR VOCATIONAL TRAINING.

(b)   EDUCATIONAL HISTORY.

ATTENDED PUBLIC SCHOOL IN A CITY IN ILLINOIS, COMPLETING THE SIXTH
GRADE AT AGE FOURTEEN.
Normal age-grade progress; regular in attendance; satisfactory school
adjustment.

S.A.T. "T"
Rd. A.   11-6   Eng. A.   10-9   Arith. A.   11-11
Gr. R.   8-9   1.   3-7   9/   7-6
R. A.   10-7   2.   6-0   10.   8-1
Mile   10   4.   6-8

Test 8-7. Spread of scores from a low of 3-7 in paragraph meaning
to a high of 7-6 in arithmetic reasoning.
Mental tests indicate ability for subjects of approximately sixth
grade level.

RECOMMEND: CLASS ATTENDANCE OPTIONAL, CELL STUDY COURSES IN
ARITHMETIC REVIEW, VOCABULARY, AND BETTER ENGLISH.
M:8,b

(c)   RELIGIOUS

CATHOLIC
RELIGIOUS OBSERVANCE   PRACTICAL
INTERIOR ATTITUDE   WELL DISPOSED
GENERAL RECOMMENDATION   ATTENDANCE AT SERVICES AND
                                  RECEPTION OF SACRAMENTS.

Committed Name GIANCANA, Sam   Register Number 55966-L

I. CLOSE: Hardened and habitual offender; rather long sentence; previous
sentence for felony; rather poor adjustment at Joliet; considered
custodial risk at this time.

2. MORE: Should be able to adjust here; this institution considered adequate
place of confinement for this type offender.

3. SOCIAL SERVICE: Personal and family background being explored further.
Father and siblings being encouraged to cooperate with readjustment plans.
Marital status being explored further.

4. (a). Oral prophylaxis; fillings.

   (b). Routine.

5. (a). CONSTRUCTION: Construction #4(New Hospital); qualified for such
work; expected to make good adjustment at this type of work;
training should increase subject's industrial competence and aid
in post-release adjustment.

   (b). Class attendance optional. Cell study courses in Arithmetic Review,
Vocabulary and Better English.

   (c). Chaplain's recommendations approved.

6.   P. A. Report to be secured.

Notation: Joliet Penitentiary, Illinois: Subject received 3/26/29 to serve
one to five years attempted burglary; discharged at expiration 12/24/32;
punished four times for violations.

Classification Form 2
Rev. January, 1939

UNITED STATES PENITENTIARY
LEAVENWORTH, KANS.

SPECIAL PROGRESS REPORT

Committed Name **GINNCANA, Sam**   Reg. No. **55966-L**   Date **Sept. 25,1940**

CASE CONSIDERED THIS DATE BY THE CLASSIFICATION COMMITTEE FOR TRANSFER
TO UNITED STATES PENITENTIARY, TERRE HAUTE, INDIANA.

CUSTODY: MEDIUM.

White male, age 31; committed October 28,1939; offense Internal Revenue
Act; four year sentence expires November 13,1942; no detainers; no escape
record; serving first Federal Penitentiary sentence; has previously
served one State Penitentiary sentence; also served one jail sentence,
and arrested numerous times for misdemeanor; served previous sentence for
Attempted Burglary; rather poor adjustment at Joliet State Penitentiary,
Joliet, Illinois; not dangerous offender; married; family ties close
with father, wife, two children, and four siblings; fit for normal manual
labor; residence should stable; bona-fide residence, Chicago, Illinois;
appears suitable for confinement in medium security penitentiary, apparently not custodial risk.

COMMITTEE ACTION: Transfer to UNITED STATES PENITENTIARY, TERRE HAUTE,
                    INDIANA recommended.

NAME Sam Ginncana   NO. 55966   COL. White
Date of sent. Oct.16-1939
DATE REC. Oct.28-1939   FROM ND:Ills.Freeport
                                      (1-4yr.2-3yr.& 5-2yr concur.)
CRIME Int.Rev-Still-Mfg-Conc.Poss-   SENTENCE 4years   AGE 31
Onsp.Unbonded Distiller

ALIASES:

```
U. S. PENITENTIARY
LEAVENWORTH, KANS.
TRANSFERRED
OCT 29 1940
TO: Terre Haute, Ind.
```

F. P. C. ....

FPI INC—FLK—7-25-38—2500—12009-99

Work Assignments

DATE	PLACE	DATE	PLACE	DATE	PLACE
NOV 24 1939	Const. #4 (Hosp)				
FEB 6 - 1940	Labor #2				
___ 1 - 1940	Boiler (Steamfitter) J.J.				
JUN 27 1940	Maint				
AUG 8 - 1940	Eles. Shop				

Cell Assignments

DATE	CELL	DATE	CELL	DATE	CELL
NOV 24 1939	13 - 357				
FEB 17 1940	13 - 363 R				

Work Progress

DATE	PROGRESS	DATE	PROGRESS	DATE	PROGRESS
1939. Nov.	Fair				
Dec.	Good				
1940 Jan.					
Feb					
Mch					
Apr					
May					
June	Fair				
July	Fair				
Aug	Good				

Chapter 2

FEDERAL BUREAU OF INVESTIGATION

REPORTING OFFICE	OFFICE OF ORIGIN	DATE	INVESTIGATIVE PERIOD	
CHICAGO	CHICAGO	1958	February 3, 1958	
TITLE OF CASE		**REPORT MADE BY**		**TYPED BY** dkc
SAMUEL M. GIANCANA, aka		**CHARACTER OF CASE** FBI Air mail Telegram from Louisville Field Office		

Patrolman Howard Cooper, Identification Division, Louisville Police Department, advised SA Edward F. O'Connor on January 29, 1958, that the files of his division reflected an arrest on July 25, 1926, for Sam Giancana, 1422 Taylor Street, Chicago. Louisville Police Department Docket No. 15037 reflects Giancana was arrested on charges of vagrancy on July 23, 1926. Police Docket no. 4903 reflects that on July 24, 1926, case was dismissed, RUC.

FEDERAL BUREAU OF INVESTIGATION

REPORTING OFFICE	OFFICE OF ORIGIN	DATE	INVESTIGATIVE PERIOD	
CHICAGO	CHICAGO	1958	February 14, 1958	
TITLE OF CASE		**REPORT MADE BY** SA James J. Files		**TYPED BY** dkc
SAMUEL M. GIANCANA, aka		**CHARACTER OF CASE** Anti-Racketeering, File 92-3171-8		

Synopsis:

Subject's wife died 11/24/56. In 1942, he listed his brothers as Joe and Charles Giancana and his sister as Mrs. Lena Campo and Mrs. Sam Giancana. Charles Giancana holds liquor license for River Road Inn, which reportedly owned by the subject. A 1957 black Chevrolet registered to James V. Perno has been observed regularly at Giancana's maintains a joint checking account with his daughter, Bonnie, at the Oak Park National Bank. US savings bonds have been purchased in the names of various members of the subject's family in recent years. Records of the Chicago PD reflect Giancana was most recently arrested on April 15, 1957. Records of the US Penitentiary, Leavenworth, Kansas, reflecting subject's file transferred to US Penitentiary, Terre Haute, Indiana. A liquor license for the Forest Lounge reportedly owned by Giancana is held by Rocco Potenzo. On

2/4/58 subject was observed in the company of Michael A. Parise. An automobile registered to Charles Tumminella has been observed parked at the subject's residence. Observation of the Wagon Wheel, gambling establishment, in 1/58 indicated this establishment is currently in operation. Search of real estate records regarding property reportedly owned by the subject disclosed that most of this property is held in trust or an undisclosed beneficiary by various banks. Subject reportedly currently meets with other hoodlums in a private dining room over a restaurant on Chicago's near north side.

RELATIVES

Mr. Wayne Keyser, Parole Officer, United States Probation, and Parole Offices, Chicago advised SA James Files on January 28, 1958 that at the time the subject was committed to the supervision of his office in 1942, he listed the following relatives:

Brothers	Joe Giancana, 918 South Hermitage, Chicago
	Charles Giancana, 918 South Hermitage, Chicago
Sisters	Mrs. Leno Campo
	Mrs. Sam (Mary) Giancana

The subjects furnished the following information regarding these relatives:

Joe has an eight grade education; was employed as a cigar store operator and had never been delinquent.

Charles has a seventh grade education; was a labor and had never been delinquent.

Lena was married to Tony Campo, who served two years imprisonment for liquor violation (no details furnished).

Mary was married to Sam Giancana (no details available).

Records of the Chicago Police Department reviewed on January 22, 1958 by IC Ronald W. Auld reflect the following records for Joseph and Charles Giancana, no police number was located:

Name	Joseph Giancana
Address	2816 West Lexington (as of 2 -7-47)
Sex	Male
Race	White
Age	26 (as of 2-7-47)
Weight	168
Height	5'7"
Complexion	Dark
Build	Medium
Eyes	Brown
Hair	Black
Marital Status	Single
Nationality	American
Occupation	Peddler

ARREST RECORD Joe Giancana

August 16, 1937	Loitering	Discharged 8-26-37
August 24, 1940	Warrant / No peddler's license	Discharged 8-26-40
February 7, 1947	Investigation / Gambling	Discharged 2-10-47

Name	Charles Giancana
Address	920 South Hermitage (as of 9-6-44)
Sex	Male
Race	White
Age	21 (as of 1944)
Weight	160
Height	5'7"
Complexion	Dark
Build	Stout
Eyes	Brown
Hair	Black
Marital Status	Single
Occupation	Peddler

ARREST RECORD

May 20, 1940	Investigation	Discharged 5-21-40
January 13, 1941	Raid	Discharged 1-23-41
August 23, 1943	Reckless driving	DWP 9-8-43
September 6, 1944	Investigation disorderly.	Discharged 9-7-44

A review of the state Liquor License Application for the River Road Inn, 5400 North River Road, Rosemont, Illinois, was made by SA Files on January 15, 1958. This property allegedly owned by subject. These records disclosed that liquor license 12675 had been issued to Charles Giancana on April 27, 1957. The following personal information regarding the license was set out:

| Name | Charles Giancana |
| Residence | 5400 River Road, Rosemont, Illinois (another address had been written here and erased which appeared to be 1304 South _____ok. |

Birth	Chicago
Citizen	Yes
Convicted of a felony?	No

AUTOMOBILES

On January 6, 8, 9, 23, 25 & 31, SA Files observed a 1957 Chevrolet, bearing 1958 Illinois license 1303677, parked in driveway or in front of house at 1147 South Wenonah Avenue, Oak Park, Illinois. This automobile is registered to James V. Perno. The files of the Chicago office contain no information regarding Perno and his connection with subject is not known at this time.

ASSOCIATION WITH SUBORDINATES

On February 4, 1958, Sam Giancana was observed by SA's Vincent L. Inserra, Ralph R. Hill, and James J. Files leaveing his home in company with a white male individual. They entered a 1956 black Chevrolet, bearing 1957 Illinois license 1736 425 and departed. The Chevrolet was driven by the person accompanying the subject. This automobile is registered to Michael A. Parise, 3917 West Drake, Chicago. Chicago files reflect no information concerning this individual.

A white over green 1955 Oldsmobile issued to Charles Tumminella, 7441 West Roosevelt Road, Forest Park, was observed parked at subjects home on January 30, 1958 by SA Lenard A. Wolf. The files of the Chicago Office reflect no information regarding Tumminella.

ASSOCIATION WITH OTHER HOODLUMS

A review of Chicago files reflects the following addresses for hoodlums with whom the subject has reportedly associated:

Names	Addresses
Tony Accardo	915 North Franklin, River Forest
"Milwaukee" Phil Alderisio	4736 West Adams, Chicago
F. S. Roti	211 West 23 Street, Chicago
John Lardino aka "Edward Nardi"	10 North Wells Street, Chicago
Pat Manning	1439 Franklin Ave, River Forest
Frank LaPorte	1816 South Gunderson, Berwyn
Joe Glimco	1213 Blue Island Ave, Chicago
Joe Campise	957 North Harding, Chicago
Al "Obie" Frabotta	3950 Lake Shore Drive, Chicago
Anthony DeRosa	1111 Vernon Park Place, Chicago
Ross Prio	6116 North Forest Glen, Chicago
Jake Guzik (deceased)	

GAMBLING

On January 15, 1958, physical observation of the Wagon Wheel, 6421 West Montrose Avenue, Chicago, a gambling establishment in which Giancana is reported to be a major owner, disclosed that this establishment is currently in operation. An individual in a 1957 Ford appeared to be acting as a look out in a position on Narragansett Avenue, commanding a view of the rear area of the Wagon Wheel. The above auto is registered to J. Pelletiere, 231 North Wisconsin, Villa Park. This individual is described as a white male, approximately 35 years old, 5'9", 165 pounds, black hair, swarthy complexion.

NORTH AVENUE LOUNGE

On December 18, 1957, T-2 informant advised that Ernest "Rocky" Infelice is a muscle man for Sam Giancana. Ernest Infelice, FBI number 308006B, operates the tavern at 8500 West North Avenue, in an unincorporated area of Cook County. The above real estate records reviewed on January 2, 1958, by SA Harold D. Sell reflect that this property was conveyed to Joseph DeTolve (brother-in-law of subject) and wife on May 25, 1951. 1957 taxes for this property were paid by Joseph DeTolve, 3819 Jackson Boulevard, Chicago.

FLAMINGO MOTEL

T-2 informant advised on December 18, 1957, that Giancana is reported to have won the Flamingo Motel, Milwaukee Avenue and River Road, Wheeling, and that prostitute's work out of this motel.

MISOLANIOUS

T-3 informant, who has furnished reliable information in the past, advised in January 1958, that about once or twice a week at about 1:00 p.m. Sam Giancana and Gus Alex together with lesser hoodlums, such as Hy Godfrey and Frank Ferraro, aka "Strongy" meet for lunch in a private dining room located on the second floor of Mike's Fish Restaurant on East Ontario Street in Chicago. T-3 suggested that since all of the above are connected with Chicago gambling activities, these luncheon meetings probably have something to do with gambling. On January 31, 1958, SA Files observed Sam Giancana enter a side door at the above described restaurant at 12:30 p.m.

PERSONAL HABITS AND PECULIARITIES

On January 31, 1958, Father Edmund Skoner, a Catholic priest, advised SA Files that he has no contact with the Giancana family for almost eighteen years. He said he originally became acquainted with the subject when the subject was in the penitentiary in Terre Haute, Indiana. The subject's wife and her mother came to Father Skoner and asked him to assist in seeking the parole of the subject. Father Skoner advised that he went to Terre Haute with the subject's wife and her mother and met Sam Giancana and that later he offered to act as Giancana's parole adviser if he were admitted to parole. Father Skoner advised he has not seen Giancana since that time, but that he gathered from seeing Giancana's name in the newspapers that since then, Giancana had developed into a regular hoodlum, and that he had wondered many times if he had not been "taken in" by the subject's wife. Father Skoner advised that a year or two ago he met a priest who knows the subject, and that this priest mentioned that Giancana remembers him, Father Skoner. This priest, whose name Father Skoner did not wish to disclose, commented that Giancana is always friendly toward the church and has been known to loan slot machines and other coin operated devices for use at church bazaars and the likes.

ADMINISTRATIVE PAGE
The Chicago Division

   1)   Will attempt to establish the current location and identity of subject's brothers and sisters through neighborhood investigation and public sources.

   2)   Will ascertain whether the subject or members of his family are members of Tam O'Shanter Country Club and obtain pertinent information concerning such membership.

   3)   Will conduct investigation to develop further identifying information re garding the following associates of the subject:

Rocco Potenzo, 8857 North Kildare Avenue, Skokie
Michael Parise, 3917 North Drake, Chicago
Charles Tumminella, 7441 West Roosevelt Road, Forest Park
A. Giancana, 175 North Lombard, Oak Park
J. Pelletiere, 231 North Wisconsin, Villa Park

FEDERAL BUREAU OF INVESTIGATION

REPORTING OFFICE	OFFICE OF ORIGIN	DATE	INVESTIGATIVE PERIOD
CHICAGO	CHICAGO	1958	February 28, 1958

TITLE OF CASE	REPORT MADE BY	TYPED BY
SAMUEL M. GIANCANA, aka	Special Agent H.R. McCullough	dkc
	CHARACTER OF CASE	
	Ant-Racketeering, File number 92-3171-9	

Synopsis:

Files of the Los Angeles Office reflect subject Giancana and three other individuals arrived in Los Angeles from Chicago on January 15, 1953 and were met by Anthony R. Pinelli Sr. and Frank Ferraro. Ferraro and his wife operated Tom Tom Caf , Glendale, California from 1952 to 1953. In 1953 Ferraro, according to Los Angeles Police Department, resided in Whittier, California. For the information of the bureau, Chicago and New York, Anthony R. Pinelli, Sr., mentioned in the body of the enclosed report, is the subject of the case entitled, "Anthony R. Ponelli, Sr. was. Anti-Racketeering", Los Angeles (origin) 92-112, Chicago 62-4844. On March 16, 1956, Lt. Phillips advised SA Townsend that Pinelli is an associate of Tony Accardo and Sam Giancana of Chicago.

On October 12, 1955, and October 29, 1955, Lt. Marion B. Phillips, Intelligence Division, Los Angeles Police Department, advised SA Frank H. Townsend that on January 15, 1953, Sam Giancana together with Anthony Accardo, Michael Mancuso, and Dr. Eugene Chesrow arrived at the Los Angeles International Airport from Chicago where they were met by Frank Ferraro and Anthony Pinelli, Sr. All six individuals were immediately questioned by members of the Intelligence Division who threatened to arrest those of the group who had arrived from Chicago if they remained in Los Angeles. Consequently, Giancana, Accardo, Mancuso, and Dr. Chesrow left the same date via air for Las Vegas, Nevada.

According to Lt. Phillips, Frank Ferraro, with aliases Frankie Sortino, "Strongy," at that time resided at 15208 Starbuck Avenue, Whittier, California; he previously resided at 7825 South Paxton, Chicago, Illinois, and in about 1950 he operated the Tom Tom Caf , Glendale, California. However on January 23, 1958, a review of the telephone directories for Los Angeles disclosed no listings for Ferraro or the Tom Tom Caf . On February 19, 1958, Investigative Clerk John Santos obtained a report dated September 5, 1952 from Dun and Bradstreet, Inc. concerning the Tom Tom Caf , a restaurant and bar, located at 806 East Colorado Boulevard, Glendale, California. A review of this report disclosed the following:

The caf , in 1946, was purchased by Frank Sortino, Sam J. Baer, and Harold Baer. Harold Baer withdrew in 1947 and in 1952 Sam Baer sold his interest to Sortino. Thereafter, Sortino was assisted in its management by his wife, Victoria Sortino. The report, which contains no derogatory information, mentions that the Sortino's are generally prompt in their payments. An addendum, dates February 19, 1953, indicated the business was sold to Modern Hotels, Inc. effective February 8, 1953.

The following physical description of Frank Sortino was obtained from a review of the files of the Los Angeles Office:

Name	Frank Ferraro
Sex	Male
Race	White

Age	42 in 1955
Height	5'10" to 11"
Weight	190 Pounds
Build	Medium heavy
Eyes	Hazel
Hair	Black, thick, slightly curly
Complexion	Ruddy

Relatives		
	Wife	Helen Butts
	Father	Joseph Sortino (deceased)
	Mother	Angelina Sortino
	Brothers	Roland Sortino
		John Sortino
	Sisters	Jennie Sortino
		Josephine Musolino
		Frances Sartogrossi
		Mary Napoli
		Helen Giglio

Criminal Record

Sentenced in 1938 in Massachusetts to serve 16 years for armed robbery and forgery.

Update to this file under Sam Giancana, 92-3171- 15 dated 5-6-1958 stated:

On 3-7-58 Detective Sergeant John Broom and Detective William Stenberg, Glendale Police Department, furnished information that Frank Sortino is no longer at the Tom Tom Bar but has a brother, Thomas Sortino, who runs a bike shop on Glendale Avenue just below Monterey in Glendale together with his wife, Marge Sortino. Detective Stenberg stated that he has had frequent contact with Thomas Sortino and Marge Sortino and considers them to be reliable persons who could be trusted to furnish truthful information.

Detective Broom was re-contacted on 3-14-58, at which time he said that he obtained information that Frank Sortino had opened a liquor store in a supermarket somewhere in Arcadia, California.

The following investigation was conducted at Los Angeles by SA William A. Watson:

On 4-11-58, information advised that Frank and Victoria Sortino were continuing to do business at 253 East Gladstone, Azusa, California, under the business name of "The Beverage Shop" which is a liquor store. As of 12-5-57, the Sortino's moved from 1120 East LaFlora Lane, Glendora to 11543 Venice Boulevard, Los Angeles 66, California. It is noted that the last address show above for Sortino is located at an extreme distance from his supposed place of employment, and it is possible that Sortino may have terminated his association with the Beverage Shop or that the management may be in the hands of some other party. This case is being maintained pending for the purpose of further investigation to confirm or eliminate this possibility. The files at Los Angeles contain no additional information concerning Ferraro, aka Sortino, since the date of rerep.

FEDERAL BUREAU OF INVESTIGATION

REPORTING OFFICE	OFFICE OF ORIGIN	DATE	INVESTIGATIVE PERIOD	
CHICAGO	CHICAGO	1958	April 11, 1958	
TITLE OF CASE		REPORT MADE BY		TYPED BY
		SA Frank L. Mellott		dkc
SAMUEL M. GIANCANA, aka		**CHARACTER OF CASE**		
		Chicago Field Office, Title of Case Changed, Now "Samuel M. Giancana, Top Hoodlum Program" File 92-3171-13		

Synopsis:

Neighbor reports Giancana; his three daughters, age 22, 19, 12; his sister and brother-in-law, Marie and James Vincent Perno and their daughter all reside at Giancana's residence, Oak Park. Giancana appears to be frequently away and has no regularity to his arrivals and departures from residents. Physical surveillance at Giancana's residence reflects visits by Dominick Nuccio, hoodlum with extensive criminal record, including suspect in several murder cases; and by William Daddono, aka "Willie Potatoes", described as "Muscle Man" for Giancana. Other known associates of Giancana are Phillip Colucci, one of three brothers described as operating their handbooks and taverns on Chicago's West Side, where they have strong political influence and Anthony V. Champagne, Attorney, who recently refused to testify before Senate Racket Committee regarding allegation he settled a labor dispute with the aid of hoodlums. Giancana described by newspaper articles and informant as close to top of hoodlum hierarchy in Chicago. Effort's to determine subject's financial interest in several properties negative to date.

PERSONAL HISTORY AND BACKGROUND

Nelson A. Locke, 1146 South Wenonah, Oak Park, Illinois, was interviewed on March 25, 1958 at Chicago Midway Airport, where he is employed as a Supervisory Electronics Maintenance Technician for the Civil Aeronautics Administration. Mr. Locke stated he first became acquainted with the subject and his family in November 1955 when he, Locke, moved into the neighborhood, across the street from the Giancana residence. Shortly after this date the subject's wife died, Angeline, died in Florida of a lingering illness, after which the subject's sister and brother-in-law Marie and James Perno, moved into the Giancana home with their daughter Andrea, now about nine, to help take care of the Giancana children. Mr. Locke described the Giancana children as Annette, also known as "Toni" about 22; Bonnie, age 19; and Francine, about 12. Mr. Locke remarked he infrequently sees Sam Giancana in his yard or coming and going, but Giancana has been a rather "mysterious figure", in that he appears to be gone from his home a considerable part of the time, as though he might live elsewhere some of the time, has no regularity to his comings and goings, dose not appear to be gainfully employed yet has an abundance of material wealth, as evidenced by the fine furnishings in his home, his gift of a 1958 Thunderbird car to Bonnie and a 1957 Chevrolet to Annette. Mr. Locke commented that there is a constant movement of people at the Giancana residence due to the arrivals and departures of the members of the Giancana and Perno families as well as by numerous friends, relatives, and associates of both families. Mr. Locke went on to say that when the subject is home he appears to have numerous visitors during the afternoon and evening hours on some days, yet few, if any, visitors on other days. According to Mr. Locke all members of the Giancana and Perno families are close-mouthed regarding Sam Giancana, apparently due to his not revealing to them anything regarding his activities or because he has instructed them not to discuss him or his activities.

Mr. Locke stated that Sam Giancana formerly drove a late model pink Cadillac with gold wheels, but apparently disposed of this car due to the publicity which Giancana and this car received at the time of the murder of Leon Marcus in 1957, at which time Giancana was picked up by the Chicago Police Department for questioning, as it was brought out that Marcus had loaned Giancana approximately $150,000 and held some sort of collateral on the River Road Motel, reportedly owned by Giancana.

Mr. Locke commented as a result of conversations with the Perno's he seemed to recall that Perno works as a foreman or supervisor in a factory and drives a 1956 Chevrolet Bel Air, black in color. The following is a description of James Perno as furnished by Mr. Locke:

Race	White
Sex	Male
Age	35-40 years
Height	5'4"
Weight	130-140 pounds
Hair	Dark
Complexion	Dark
Peculiarities	Is very close mouthed regarding himself and occupations.

Among the frequent visitors at the Giancana home, Mr. Locke remarked, is an elderly Italian woman believed to be named "Tumminello", who has a large family, some of whom also visit the Giancana house.

Records of the Bureau of Records and Communications Chicago Police Department, contained an arrest record pertaining to a James Perno of 919 North Leavitt, Chicago, and records of the FBI Identification Division, under FBI number 1240890 contained information pertaining to a James Perno with alias James Perino. The age reflected in these records is 55 years, and exceeds by approximately 20 years the apparent age of the James Perno residing with the subject, as estimated by Mr. Locke, a neighbor, and as a result of observation by surveilling agents.

ASSOCIATES

Phillip Colucci

It has been observed on various days that a 1958 Chevrolet Bel Air, two door, bearing Illinois license 552255 is parked in the driveway or garage at subject's residence or occasionally at the curb in front of the house. It has been determined that this car is registered to "A. Giancana, 175 North Lombard, Oak Park". Records show that the occupants of 175 North Lombard are Phillip Colucci: wife is shown as Margaret in one instance and Mary in another. Colucci claims residence at 175 North Lombard for the past eight years, previous address not shown. His employment shown as owner, N/W Realty, 2700 Harlem Avenue.

Records of the Chicago Credit Bureau on March 24, 1958 reflected that Mary Colucci is married to Phillip, whose business is the Jockey Club, 8500 West North Avenue, Melrose Park.

Mrs. Clarence Townsend, 179 North Lombard advised SA James Files on February 20, 1958 that the residents on 175 North Lombard are believed to be named Carducci and that he owns or operates a lounge know as the Jockey Club somewhere in the Western Suburbs. Clarence Townsend was contacted by SA Mellott on March 20, 1958, at which time he furnished substantially the same information as that furnished by his wife. Townsend remarked that he and his wife have lived at their present address for about two years and that the previous owner of the house at 179 North Lombard is a James Van Doren, a reputable realtor in Oak Park.

James Van Doren, 419 South Boulevard, Oak Park, advised on March 20, 1958 that he has known Phillip and Mary Colucci as neighbors and socially for the past nine years. Mr. Van Dorn explained that his wife and Mary Colucci have become well acquainted during this time, as a result of which Mary Colucci frequently confides personal information regarding herself, her husband, and her family. Regarding her husband, Mrs. Colucci has stated during recent years that he is a partner in the Jockey Club, a restaurant and lounge, at the Northwest corner of North Avenue and Fifth Avenue in Melrose Park. About 1949 she claimed her husband was engaged in the hotel and restaurant linen supply business; in about 1949-1952 her husband has a Kaizer-Frazer dealership. According to Mrs. Van Doren, Colucci's present employment is believed to be in some way connected with the jukebox business, believed to be the ABC Music Corporation. According to Mr. Van Doren, Colucci is close-mouthed and rarely discussed himself or his activities. During about 1948-1950 Colucci made at least two trips a year to Italy and also made frequent trips to New York but never discussed these trips or his intentions of taking them, but his wife would let the information "slip out." Mr. Van Doren said that Colucci's silence regarding these trips led him to believe that Colucci may have been engaged in the narcotic traffic or as a runner between "Lucky" Luciano and hoodlums in the United States.

Mr. Van Doren said he recalls that when the subject moved into the neighborhood he did not make use of his garage until he had installed powerful flood lights to turn on before he would venture near the garage. Mr. Van Doren said the maiden name of Mary Colucci is Odierno and that her parents operated Jenny's Pizza and Spaghetti House on Route 14, a short distance northwest of Walworth, Wisconsin on the road to Darien, Wisconsin. The Colucci's, according to Mr. Van Doren, have three children, Robert, Phillip and Mary Ann. Mr. Van Doren commented that the Colucci's recently remarked that they are buying a house in River Forest and that he will determine where this house is located.

T1 informant advised in August 1946, that Phillip Colucci is a member of the Colucci Syndicate made up of five Colucci boys, Joseph, Vito, Dominick, James, and Phillip. According to this source, the Colucci's operate sixteen handbooks in the 25th and 27th wards.

Officer Raymond Ray of the Commissioner's Office, Chicago Police Department, advised in 1957 that there are three Colucci brothers, Vito, Joe, and Phillip who are quite active on Chicago's West Side. The Colucci's, according to Ray, are interested in handbooks, taverns and auto agencies. They operate approximately eight books located on West Madison Street, Division Street, and Lawrence Avenue. They operate the Parkise Motors, a Kaizer Frazer Agency, in the 2800 block of West Madison Street; they own and operate a lot of taverns in the 27th Ward and are very strong politically being very close to John Touhy, 27 Ward Democratic Committeeman.

Thomas Bailey, Investigator in Charge, Alcohol Tax Unit, Chicago, made available to the Chicago Office on an unknown date in 1945 the Alcohol Tax Unit case involving Phillip Colucci. According to the file, Phillip Colucci was arrested December 10, 1943 for operation of a "Wild Cat Distillery" at 1315 West Van Buren Street, Colucci's address at that time was shown as 5649 Jackson Boulevard, Chicago. He was described as a white male, born July 24, 1904, 5'5", 170 pounds, stocky build, brown eyes, vertical 1' scar under bridge of nose.

On January 27, 1944, Colucci was held to the Federal Grand Jury under $2,000.00

bond by Alcohol Tax Unit on charges arising from his operation of the illicit distillery. Evidence against Phillip Colucci may not be sufficient to warrant his prosecution, it appears to be more that ample evidence to warrant the prosecution of all other defendants.

T-2 informant advised on April 26, 1945, that in the case of the Alcohol Tax Unit involving Phillip Colucci and four other individuals arrested on December 10, 1943, $2,100 was paid by Colucci to Federal Court bondsman Richard Parker, Jr. and Michael J. Boyle, Assistant United States Attorney to "fix" the case. This informant advised in May 2, 1945 that sometime prior to the first of the year, 1945 he was contacted by Federal Court bondsman Richard Parker, Jr., who wanted to know whether Phillip Colucci could be contacted. The informant said he made contacts through friends of his and talked to Colucci fully and then called Parker back advising him that he could talk to Colucci. He stated that he has talked with the parties concerned and though that a pay-off of $2,100 was made somewhere in the Old Post Office Building.

Arthur Colucci, who was convicted in Federal District Court in 1944 for narcotics violation and deported to Italy in 1948. Chicago Police Department advised on March 11, 1958, that a notation in the files of the Bureau of Identification states that the arrest record pertaining to Phillip Colucci was ordered destroyed on October 30, 1944; reason for destruction and name of the official authorizing the destruction of the record was not shown.

PHILLIP COLUCCI ARREST RECORD

April 6, 1936	Speeding	Fined $5.00
September 16, 1939	Disorderly Investigation	Discharged
May 5, 1941	Accident Investigation	D.W.P.
August 9, 1944	Disorderly Investigation	Discharged
January 3, 1946	Speeding	$6.00 fine
January 24, 1949	Disorderly Investigation	Discharged
February 3, 1949	Traffic Violation	Fined $9.00

DOMINICK NUCCIO
Aka "Lucky", "Joe Delano",
"Ercole Liberatore"

On March 6 and 27, 1958, a 1956 DeSoto, bearing Illinois license 1134605 and registered to Dominick Nuccio, 7436 West Carmen, Chicago, was observed parked at the residence of Sam Giancana. On the latter date this car, driven by a white male in his 60's, was surveilled from the residence of the subject to Foster and Olcott Streets on the Northwest side of Chicago where surveillance was discontinued. This point is located approximately four blocks from 7436 West Carmen, shown on the license registration as the address of Dominick Nuccio.

The files of the Chicago Office reflect the following background information pertaining to Dominick Nuccio with aliases, as compiled June 1, 1950.

PERSONAL HISTORY AND BACKGROUND

Records of the Bureau of Identification, Chicago Police Department, as checked on May 29, 1950, reflected that Dominick Nuccio at that time was 55 years of age and resided with his wife Inez Nuccio at room 602, North Park Hotel, Chicago. These records did not reflect any information as to his education or family and the only legitimate business he has ever been known to be connected with is shown as the Innenudo Tap at 1220

North Park Street, Chicago, which was known as a hoodlum hangout operated by Nuccio.

CRIMINAL ACTIVITIES

Nuccio has been in difficulty with the law enforcement agencies since January 6, 1918, when he was arrested for vagrancy in Chicago and was sentenced to serve sixty days in the House of Correction. Since that time, he has been arrested on 24 occasions, ranging from vagrancy to investigation as a suspect for murder.

The records at the Chicago Crime Commission contain an anonymous letter directed to that Commission under the date of September 8, 1943, which states that Eddie Vogel, who is the alleged leader of the so-called Chicago crime syndicate's slot machine activities in this area, pushed Nuccio out of the Dome Gambling Spot at 7466 Irving Park Road, Chicago.

In August of 1944 it was reported that Dom Nuccio, Dominick Brancato, and Dominick DiBello, gamblers and police characters, were questioned and cleared in the gang killing of Lawrence Mangano.

A list of the murders Nuccio has been questioned in is as follows:

> Dion O'Banion, murdered in 1924.
> Joseph Adducci, murdered September 15, 1934.
> Estelle Carey, murdered February 2, 1943.
> Lawrence Mangano, murdered August 1944.
> Vincent Venvento, murdered September, 1946.
> Doward Falcon, murdered July 10, 1946.
> Tina Jacobs, murdered September 19, 1947.

It was reported in 1948 that Gerald Covelli, a Chicago hoodlum presently believed to be serving a lengthy sentence in the Joliet State Penitentiary for armed robbery. Covelli was listed as a lieutenant of Dominick Nuccio. In December of 1947, Covelli was involved in the hi-jacking of a truck at Chicago, Illinois, and in connection with this hi-jacking was indicted for armed robbery.

In July 1948 a report carried the account of the murder of one Doward Falcon, who on July 10, 1948 was killed in gangland fashion. According to newspaper clippings, Mrs. Inez Nuccio, wife of Dominick Nuccio, charged Falcon with attempting to rape her in Lincoln Park ten day prior to the day Falcon was killed. Falcon was arrested on a complaint of Mrs. Nuccio; however, he denied the charge of rape, but admitted accidentally bumping into her in Lincoln Park. According to the newspaper clippings Mrs. Nuccio was alleged to have told Mrs. Falcon that her husband, Dominick Nuccio, would kill Falcon for this. Falcon was arrested, charged with disorderly conduct, and released on bond. Nuccio was picked up and questioned in connection with this murder and he was released due to insufficiency of evidence to connect him with the same.

T-7 informant advised that as of April 15, 1950, Nuccio, together with Brancato and DiBello, were organizing the 38th Police District for gambling purposes. This informant advised that the above mentioned individuals formerly operated in the 36th Ward, where they are alleged to have the sanction of police authorities in that district.

In March 1950, Captain Thomas A. Kelly of the Town Hall Police District had ordered the arrest of Dominick Niccio, Brancato, and DiBello. These individuals have been arrested many times on gambling and other charges in the Chicago area and are reportedly "three Guzik-Capone gambling syndicate lieutenants". The reason for the order being issued to have these individuals arrested was that it has been learned that they were attempting to organize gambling in the Town Hall Police District and were using violence in efforts to cut themselves in on horse racing profits.

IDENTIFICATION RECORD

The following is the Identification Record of Dominick Nuccio as contained in the files of the Bureau of Identification of the Chicago Police Department.

On January 8, 1918, Nuccio was arrested and charged with Vagrancy. On August 11, 1919, he was arrested and charged with auto larceny and found not guilty. In July 1919, he was arrested and charged with burglary; however, a no bill was returned in his favor. On December 2, 1919, he was sentenced to serve a sentence in the Illinois State Penitentiary at Pontiac, Illinois, on a charge of burglary, and in connection with this burglary charge, charges of assault to commit murder and carrying concealed weapon were stricken off. Apparently Nuccio appealed this conviction for burglary, because on April 28, 1920, the sentence was reversed and his case was remanded to the Trial Court by the Supreme Court of the State of Illinois. There is no further disposition with reference to this burglary arrest and conviction. On April 12, 1921, he was arrested and charged with robbery and turned over to the authorities at Summit, Illinois; however, he was discharged from this arrest. On October 21, 1921, and on January 13, 1922, he was arrested for disorderly conduct and was fined $5.00 and costs for each of these arrest. On May 25, 1922, he was arrested for disposition for this arrest. On October 26, 1922, he was arrested for larceny; however, this charge was not processed by the State of Illinois. On January 24, 1923, he was arrested for attempted burglary and was found not guilty. On May 21, 1931, he was arrested for disorderly conduct and fined $50.00 and costs. On April 1, 1932, he was arrested and charged with investigation and released.

On June 8, 1933, he was arrested for disorderly conducted and fined $25.00 and costs. On August 24, 1934, he was arrested at Milwaukee, Wisconsin, for violation of the United States Internal Revenue Law. However, there is no disposition for this arrest. On October 11, 1934, he was picked up as a murder suspect and released. On November 21, 1944, and on January 31, 1945, he was arrested for investigation and released. On March 11, 1945, he was arrested in a gambling raid and released. On July 15, 1948, and again on August 4, 1949 he was arrested for investigation and released.

DESCRIPTION

The following is the only available description of Dominick Nuccio as reflected in the files of the Bureau of Identification of the Chicago, Illinois, Police Department:

Age	55 (1950)
Height	5' 41/3"
Weight	135 pounds
Hair	Dark
Eyes	Brown
Build	Slender
Occupation	Clerk
Marital Status	Married, wife Inez Nuccio
Present Residence	7436 West Carmen, Chicago
Complexion	Sallow
Teeth	Good
Scars and marks	Three brown moles on right side of face and nose
Chicago police #	D-15232

MICHAEL A. PARISE

As previously reported the subject was observed on February 4, 1958, to leave his home in the company of a white male driving a 1957 black Chevrolet. This car was registered to Michael Parise, 3917 North Drake, Chicago. This car had been observed by SA Mellott on March 17, 19, 27, 1958, parked in the driveway or in front of Sam Giancana's house. Files of the Chicago Office do not contain any references to this individual.

Records of the Bureau of Records and Communications, Chicago Police Department reflected that one Mike Parise, residing at 1025 South Morgan Street, a white male, age 19 in 1932, 5'8", 170 pounds, medium build, brown eyes, black hair, was arrested on December 31, 1932 on disorderly conduct charges and discharged on the same day. These records also reflected that this same Mike Parise was arrested on August 13, 1935 on a man slaughter charge arising from an altercation on August 8, 1935 in the Blacksmith Shop of the city Asphalt Plant, 1533 South Ashland during which a argument occurred and Parsie struck one William Gannon, knocking his down and causing his to suffer a basal skull fracture, from which Gannon died on August 10, 1935. Disposition of this matter is shown as "no bill" on August 17, 1935.

Records reflect that Michael Parise now resides at 3917 North Drake (since August 25, 1956) lived at 1625 North Hermitage on November 10, 1954 and previously lived at 1025 South Morgan, believed to be May 18, 1942 and on Wagoner Road in Glenview, Illinois. Employment on August 26, 1956 is shown as night clerk at the River Road Motel (it is to be noted this property is reportedly owned in whole or in part by Sam Giancana.) The following notations appeared on the Credit Bureau records: U.S. Air Force, 11/10/54: wife Miriam , age 29 in 1943, employment Republic Drill and Tool Company, 223 South Green guard- 4 months.

CHARLES and TONY J. TUMMINELLO

It was observed on February 25 and 28 that a 1955 Oldsmobile was parked in front of the Giancana residence. It has been determined that this car belongs to Charles Tumminello, 7441 West Roosevelt Road, Forest Park. The files of the Chicago Police Department do not contain any reference to Charles Tumminello or to variations in spelling of that name. Bureau will obtain current identify information regarding Tony J. Tumminello, who has been in contact with Sam Giancana. Other persons named Tumminello, possibly known as Tony, have been in frequent contact with the subject at his residence.

ANTHONY V. CHAMPAGNE, Attorney

Captain Fremont Nestor (National Academy) Police Department, Oak Park, Illinois, advised on February 27, 1958 that Anthony V. Champagne, an attorney and associate of Giancana as well as numerous other hoodlums, acts in the capacity of as advisor to keep these hoodlums "out of trouble" by assisting them in hiding their assets and keeping their gambling and other illegal activities under control. In addition, Captain Fremont Nestor stated, Champagne is believed to serve as a "runner" for these hoodlums, assisting them in carrying out their illegal activities with a minimum of trouble, and also enlists the power of the hoodlums for his own ends where necessary.

On March 21, 1958, Anthony V. Champagne invoked the Fifth Amendment repeatedly when the Senate Rackets Committee sought to question him about his connection with the Chicago Restaurant Association. Champagne also refused to tell whether he had received $120,000 for his job as an attorney for the association to settle at a labor dispute, with the aid of hoodlums, for a restaurant chain that the committee refused to identify. Champagne refused to tell whether he knew Tony Accardo, Vincent "The Saint" Inserro, and Sam "Mooney" Giancana.

Champagne refused to tell whether he had been hired to settle a strike for a large restaurant chain or whether he was hired because it was believed that his association with under world figures in Chicago would enable him to settle it. It was at that point that Champagne was asked about Accardo, Inserro, and Giancana. Anthony Champagne succeeded Abraham Teitelbaum, a former Capone family lawyer, as attorney for the Chicago Restaurant Association.

WILLIAM DADDONO,
Aka, "Willie Potatoes"

On February 26 and March 20, 1958, a 19958 Ford Convertible, bearing 1958 Illinois license 936522 was observed arriving and departing from the Giancana residence. This auto is resisted to William Daddono, 8109 West 26th Street, Riverside, Illinois. William Daddono is described as a "muscle man" for Giancana. Records of the Chicago Crime Commission describe Daddono as an ex-convict and hoodlum who has been implicated in crimes arranging from burglary to murder. Additional background information will be obtained regarding him.

OTHER HOODLUMS

The Miami Office advised that on January 9, 1958, Mrs. Arthur Chalk, owner, Chalk's Flying Service, County Causeway, Miami, Florida, advised SA William L. Eddy that her records indicate that on or about May 24, 1950 Sam Giancana departed Miami for Bimini. She advised that her records indicate that also on this flight were Anthony Accardo, Charles Fischetti, and Murray Humphreys.

Duke Camp, Waiter Captain, Chez Paree, a Chicago Nightclub, was interviewed by SA Ralph Hill, Jr. on February 28, 1958. Camp advised that he has been employed by the Chez Paree since approximately 1943 in the capacity of waiter and waiter captain. He said that in this capacity he has become acquainted with the hoodlums that frequent the Chez and by such has been able to determine which of these individuals wield "influence" in the under world circle. Camp related that in the immediate post war years the Chez was regarded by the hoodlum element as a second home but during recent years has been used less frequency. Camp said that every Sunday night the first table at ringside at the Chez is reserved in the name of Jimmy Allegretti, (Allegretti is under investigation by the Chicago Office under the Top Hoodlum Program), for the second show which commences at 12:15 a.m. Camp said that the Sunday night attendance by the hoodlums is regarded as something of a ritual so that Camp and other employees call Sunday night at the Chez "Hoodlum night". Camp advised that the Chez, in his opinion, is Allegretti's command post, Camp said that Allegretti is occasional accompanied by Sam "Mooney" Giancana. Camp said that on these occasions Allegretti is usually subservient to "Mooney".

CRIMINAL ACTIVITIES

T-5 informant advised on April 1, 1958, that she has learned through conversation with criminal elements with whom she associates that Sam Giancana is considered one of the three of four top hoodlums who "run" Chicago, and that he also controls gambling in Cicero.

T-6 informant advised on February 21, 1958 that about February 1948 the Boogie Woogie Liquors, 1709 Roosevelt Road, was sold by Sam Giancana, also known to him as "Mooney", to an individual known to this informant as Rodney Johnson. The bar had previously been used for gambling and was a source of trouble to him as T-6 advised local Italian hoodlums were always fighting in the bar. T-6 said that Frank Barradio was front man for Giancana and had the title to the property. T-6 states that Leon Marcus, slain Chicago banker, had syndicate connections and Marcus put the financial squeeze on

Giancana to repay funds; for this, he was killed by the syndicate.

Walter J. Devereux, Assistant Operating Director, Chicago Crime Commission, made available on April 3, 1958 a memo dated July 15, 1946 prepared by the Crime Commission for its own use. This memo, pertaining to the subject, is set out as follows:

"This subject, under the name Sam Gincana, appears on a list of names of the "42 gang" dated in September, 1929. His address then was 1423 West Taylor, Chicago. On September 24, 1926, Sam Gianeana, Diego Ricco, and Joseph Pape were indicted in Cook County on a charge of murder. This case, before the criminal Court was stricken off with leave to reinstate, when the State indicated they had no evidence. The facts concerning this matter are briefly as follows: William G. Girard, 4157 North California Ave. age 55 years, married, with two children and a barber by trade was shot by Diego Ricco, Joseph Pape, and Sam Gianena, according to a coroner's inquest held September 18, 1926, when the trio held up the deceased in a store at 22nd and State St. on September 12, 1926. A verdict of murder was returned by the inquest jury. Ricco's address was 3863 W. Harrison St., Pape at 1645 W. Taylor and Gianena at 1444 W, Taylor. As indicated above the case against the three men was SOL in court on April 28, 1927. The chief state witness was one Alexander Burba, a taxi driver who was murdered by person or persons unknown on April 8, 1927. Burba's widow informed the police that several attempts has been made to "buy-off" her husband from testifying in the Girard murder case and after he refused, threats were made against him. While Ricco, Pape, and Gianena were sought by the police in connection with the Burba killing, apparently nothing ever came of the investigation.

On December 13, 1926 Sam Giancana, Dominick Caruso, and Joseph Sypher, alias Frank Rollins were indicted by the Grand Jury, Cook County on a charge of burglary. On July 6, 1928, this case was stricken off with leave to reinstate as to Giancana and Sypher and on the same date, Caruso entered a plea of guilty and on May 8, 1929 was sentenced to the penitentiary for 1 year to 10 years. The facts in the case were that a dress shop at 2663 N. Clark Street was burglarized early on morning of July 3, 1926 and 50 dresses valued at $35 each were stolen. The police chased a cab at about 4:40 a.m. July 3, 1926 in which the three defendants were riding and when the cab crashed, Caruso and Sypher were apprehended, Giancana getting away. Fifty dresses were found in the car and Sypher stated the three had stolen the dresses. Giancana was arrested later that morning. Neither Caruso nor Giancana would talk.

On May 10, 1927, Sam Giancana was indicted by the Cook County Grand Jury for larceny of an automobile and on June 27, 1927, the case was dismissed for want of prosecution. It appears that the automobile was owned by Herbert Miller, 1815 Cuyler Avenue, and was stolen on April 26, 1927 and was valued at $1800.00.

On September 27, 1928 it was reported that the bombing for the second time in 11 days of the ice cream plant of A. Giancane, 1510 Taylor Street. Following the first bombing of this place, the police surmised that it was in retaliation for the slaying of Edward Divis, west side gangster. Sam Giancane, son of the ice cream manufacturer, and Dominic Caurso, son of the older Giancane's former business partner had been mentioned in the investigation of the Divis murder, but they had never been found.

On December 5, 1928, Sam Giancana, Thomas Russo, and Tony Orlando were indicted by the Cook County Grand Jury on a charge of larceny. On March 12, 1929, a nolle prosequi was entered by the court as to Giancana and Orlando. On April 19, 1929 the felony was waived and Russo entered a plea of guilty to driving a motor vehicle without the owner's consent and was sentenced to 6 months in the House of Correction and fined $1.00 no costs. The basis of this charge was the stealing of a truck valued at $600 on November 16, 1928.

On December 5, 1928, Tony Orlando, Sam Giancana, and Thomas Russo were indicted by the Cook County Grand Jury on a charge of "Attempting to Commit a Burglary." On March 12, 1929, Orlando and Giancana entered a plea of guilty and Orlando was sentenced that date to serve from 1 to 5 years at Pontiac and Gincana was sentenced that date to serve 1 to 5 years in the penitentiary. On March 12, 1929, the case against Russo was stricken off with leave to reinstate. The facts in this matter were that the trio were found near the scene of a store wherein an attempted had been made to knock a hole through the building wall to gain entry, this being on November 17, 1928. Other facts appear that Joe Cardose saw Orlando get in his truck and drive it away and while Cardose was giving chase in an automobile he was cut off and curbed eight or ten times by Russo and Giancana and as a result he lost track of the truck. The burglary charge and the charge of having burglar tools centered on the fact that the trio attempted to burglaries a store at 3947 West Madison Street at 1:00 or 2:00 a.m. by cutting bricks out of the wall of the building. The police came, found the hole in the wall, and Giancana, Russo and Orlando close by, burglary tools near the hole, and a revolver on the ground close to where Giancana was standing. Four hundred feet away was an automobile which was traced to Giancana. Overalls taken off Giancana were covered with mortar dust.

The files of the Chicago Crime Commission reflect that Sam Giancana was brought into court on September 29, 1928 on a writ of habeas corpus and was discharged. The police had him in custody for two days as a suspect in the bombing of 1510 W, Taylor St., and that he was a known racketeer-that he was a candidate for the leadership of the "42 gang". The police further indicated that they suspected that Giancana had shot one Tony Russell with a shot gun a short while before and that they were desirous of holding the prisoner until they could locate Russell.

The records also reflect the discharge of Sam Giancana on November 21, 1928, in the Municipal Court on a charge of carrying concealed weapons. On February 13, 1945 a story stated that the arrest of Tony Accardo, alias Joe Batters, a Capone hoodlum and Sam Giancana, age 36 of 2822 Lexington Ave. and Daniel Beneduce, 43, of 4285 Glady's Ave., as suspects in the kidnapping of Jack Guzik in April, 1944. Accardo was released and the other two were brought to police court charged with disorderly conduct and released on February 14, 1945.

MISCELLANEOUS

Personal Habits

T-6 informant advised on February 20, 1958 that he believes that Darlene Caifano, wife of Marshall Caifano, a hoodlum under investigation by the Chicago Office, has been "playing around with Sam "Mooney" when Caifano was out of town." About two years ago, according to this informant, "Mooney" gave Darlene Caifano $10,000 to invest in casinos in and around Las Vegas, Nevada. The informant expressed the belief that "Mooney's" real name is Giancana, but that he is commonly known as "Mooney."

Captain Fremont Nestor, Oak Park Police Department, advised that Giancana is known as a former driver for the syndicate and is very adept at driving. When he is being surveilled he then "loses" the surveillance by evasive tactics. Captain Nestor said that experience had shown that it is virtually impossible to physically surveilled the subject due principally to his suspicious nature, which causes his to "inspect" his neighborhood with binoculars and to report the presence in the neighborhood of any cars he feels might be used to surveilled him. On these occasions he or an associate makes the complaint under the name of some neighbor, never his own name. Another obstacle to physical surveillance is that the neighborhood is residential and dose not lend itself to physical surveillance. In addition a local ordinance prohibits the parking of cars on the streets of Oak Park during the night, so that a car that is parked on the street becomes conspicuous.

For these reasons spot surveillances have been adopted as the most practical way to determine the identity of the persons contacting the subject. The details of these surveillances are not being set out in this report except to note the dates on which a particular visitor was observed. Surveillance logs are being maintained in the 1A section of this file.

The main purpose of determining who the subject's visitors are is to consider which one of his associates might lend himself to development as an informant. The need to develop an informant close enough to the subject to know about his activities becomes increasingly obvious, as investigation to date indicates the subject had hidden his assets, both legitimate and illegal, in trusteeships and other devices which enabled him to keep true ownership hidden. In some cases it appears he has placed some of his legitimate and illegal operations, e.g., air conditioning business, gambling places, and motel, in the names of associates who operate them for him and become the owners of record, making the determination of the true owner difficult, if not impossible.

FEDERAL BUREAU OF INVESTIGATION

REPORTING OFFICE	OFFICE OF ORIGIN	DATE	INVESTIGATIVE PERIOD	
CHICAGO	CHICAGO	1958	May 30, 1958	
TITLE OF CASE		REPORT MADE BY		TYPED BY
SAMUEL M. GIANCANA, aka		. Special Agent Robert C. Reed		dkc
		CHARACTER OF CASE		
		FBI Headquarters File number 92-3171-18, Chicago File number 92-349-18 – Anti Racketeering Milwaukee Office		

Synopsis

Subscriber telephone number CE8-1155, Madison, Wisconsin, R. W. Coan, Vice President Coan Manufacturing Company, Madison, which manufactures vending machines. Subscriber telephone number CH8-9888, Lake Geneva, Wisconsin, Angelo and Tony Restaurant and Pizzeria, run by Angelo O'Dierno. Also Jennie's Spaghetti House, one and one-half miles northwest, Walworth, owned by Angelo O'Dierno, SR. O'Dierno family residents Walworth, approximately twenty years, originally from Chicago, Illinois. Milwaukee Division files reflect Angelo O'Dierno considered as possible theft of 47,137 pens, 2320 pencils and 96 desk sets with 66 desk pens from Parker Pen Company, Janesville, Wisconsin, 3/30/49. Available criminal records on O'Dierno's set out.

AT MADISON, WISCONSIN

Information on Richard Coan is in contact with subject. Richard W. Coan of 5614 Raymond Street is listed at vice president at the Coan Manufacturing Company in Madison. The Coan Manufacturing Company manufactures various types of vending machines, including cigarette and food machines. Madison Police Department advised that the department file does not contain any criminal records on Richard Coan.

AT LAKE GENEVA, WISCONSIN

On May 7, 1958 T-2 informant advised telephone number CH8-9888 is listed to Angelo and Tony's Restaurant and Pizzeria, 619 Williams, Lake Geneva, and telephone bills are sent to Angelo O'Dierno, Jr. On May 7, 1958 Albert Stephan, Assistant Chief of

Police, Lake Geneva, advised that Angelo and Tony O'Dierno, who are brothers, don't seem to do a large amount of business at their establishment but both drive Cadillac automobiles. He advised that the brothers have been at the above establishment for approximately two years. The records of the Lake Geneva Police Department reflected no record of Angelo or Tony O'Dierno.

On May 8, 1958 Leo Brancamp, patrolman, Walworth Police Department, advised that to his knowledge the O'Dierno family consists of the following individuals:

Anthony O'Dierno, Sr.
Mrs. Anthony O'Dierno, Sr.
Anthony (Tony) O'Dierno, Jr. son, Howard, Illinois
Frank O'Dierno, son, Zion, Illinois
Angelo O'Dierno, son
Jennie O'Dierno, daughter
James O'Dierno, son, Chicago

Mr. Brancamp advised that Anthony O'Dierno, Sr. has more sons and daughters living in the Chicago area, including a son older than Frank who visits Anthony Sr. approximately every two weeks and that the entire family consists from about fourteen to sixteen children.

Available records in Walworth County Sheriff's office reflect that Norman Lee Williams was involved in a fight with Tony and Angelo O'Dierno on January 2, 1958 at Jennie's Spaghetti House, Walworth. Sergeant Werner Voegeli advised that no criminal charges were made but Mr. William filed an assault suit against the brothers. Sergeant Voegeli advised that he has always been suspicious that the O'Dierno family had an outside source of income other than the restaurants but that he has no information as to what it might be.

FEDERAL BUREAU OF INVESTIGATION

REPORTING OFFICE	OFFICE OF ORIGIN	DATE	INVESTIGATIVE PERIOD	
CHICAGO	CHICAGO	1958	June 17, 1958	
TITLE OF CASE		REPORT MADE BY		TYPED BY
		Special Agent Frank L. Mellott		dkc
SAMUEL M. GIANCANA, aka		CHARACTER OF CASE		
		FBI Headquarters File number 92-3171-21, Top Hoodlum Program – Anti Racketeering		

Synopsis:

Summary Report: Subject presently considered by police, press, Chicago Crime Commission, and informants to occupy one of 3 or 4 top-ranking position in local crime syndicate hierarchy. List of subject's known associates set out, with brief description, where known, of each. Subject claimed that his sole source of income during 1952, 1953, and 1954 resulted from a partnership with Charles "Chuckie" English in gambling at the Chicago racetracks, and in 1955 and 1956 major portion of income received from this partnership. Subject reported to have undergone surgery during recent months for cancer; close relatives confirm subject had been ill but claim nature of illness unknown to them. Subject reportedly having affair with wife of subordinate.

Birth

Father Scola, Pastor, Holy Guardian Angel Church, 717 West Arthington, Chicago, advised SA Mellott on April 28, 1958, that Certificate Number 1191 recorded on Page 56, Volume 6, of the Birth Register maintained by the Church, reflects that Momo Salvatore Giancana was born on June 15, 1908, at Chicago to Antonia Disimone and Antonio Giancana. Father Scola pointed out that both spelling "Giancana" and "Giancano" appear on the certificate and the latter was the name originally recorded, but subsequently changed to the correct spelling of Giancana. Father Scola pointed out that the only data of birth on the certificate is June 15, 1908 and that the name "Gilormo" dose not appear anywhere on the record.

Father Scola added that the name "Momo", as well as the name "Gilormo" and very rare Italian names and that the name "Momo" is generally considered a nickname. Father Scola also explained that the Italian name "Salvatore" is usually translated into the Americanized version of "Sam". Father Scola stated the aforementioned records were originally recorded at the time of Baptism on December 15, 1908, and do not appear to have been amended or altered since that date.

ASSOCIATES

Captain Nestor, Police Department, Oak Park, advised on December 13, 1957, that the subject has been known to associate with the following hoodlums during recent years:

Joseph Paul Glimco

T-4 informant advised on March 17, 1958, that Glimco is associated with various "syndicate" heads in the Chicago area. According to this source, Glimco is President of Local 777, a cab drivers union, who was indicted by a Federal Grand Jury in 1955 for invasion of the Poultry Union in Chicago. In 1956, Glimco was acquitted following a lengthy Federal Court trial. This informant further stated that during prohibition Glimco was a gunman hired to protect beer trucks for the Al Capone syndicate and was later given authority to control the Poultry Handlers Union, but never held an office in that union.

John Lardino

John Lardino, with alias Edward Nardi, 1201 North Belfort Avenue, Oak Park, Illinois, has been a suspect in robberies and burglaries and is presently President or Vice-President of the so-called "Miscellaneous" union, which represents service personnel at night clubs and restaurants.

Rocco Potenzo

Potenzo is reported to be manager of the Forest Lounge, 6548 North Milwaukee Avenue, Chicago, for Sam Giancana. Potenzo attended the annual lawn party on July 5, 1954, at the Anthony J, Accardo residence.

> Tom Potenzo
> 3562 West Flournoy, Chicago

```
        Jay Kortin
        2511 South 57th Court, Cicero

        (FUN) Bucciene
        910 South Paulina, Chicago

        James T. Conroy
        1705 North Bloomingdale, Chicago

        Carlo Urbanati
        2929 West Flournoy, Chicago
```

Captain Nester stated that with the exception of Glimco, and Lardino, he would consider the other persons named above to be "smalltime" hoodlums.

Lieutenant Joseph Morris, Chicago Police Department, advised in the latter part of May 1955, that at the wake of Giancana's father, Antonio Giancana, at Cermak Funeral Home, Cicero, on July 29, 1954, Sam Giancana was visited by the following hoodlums and sat with them at Joe Corngold's cocktail Lounge, near the funeral home:

Anthony J. Accardo

Anthony Accardo is considered by the Chicago Police Department and the Chicago Press to be head of the Chicago crime syndicate, which is highly organized on a local basis and controls gambling activities in Chicago and environs.

Felix Alderisio, with aliases
Phil Alderisio, "Milwaukee Phil"

Alderisio is a Chicago hoodlum who is a close associate of Albert Frabotta, the "enforcer" for the syndicate and Marshall Caifano, with aliases, an organizer for the syndicate. Alderisio is known to have attended the July 5, 1954 and 1955 annual party held at the Accardo residence.

Dominick Brancato

T-4 informant advised that on March 17, 1958, that Brancato is one of the "Three Dom's" (Dom Nuccio and Dom DiBello), who are active in the operation of various Near North Side Chicago night clubs for the syndicate.

Jake Guzik

Deceased Capone mobster.

John Lardino

Described above.

Patrick Mano, with alias
Pat Manning

Patrick Mano was described by T-4 informant on March 17, 1958, as one of the "fronts" for Anthony Accardo and Jake Guzik in the infiltration of the policy racket on the South Side of Chicago. According to this informant Patrick Mano was indicted in 1942 for a policy violation, at which time the policy racket was alleged to be a seven million dollar a year operation in the Chicago area. Mano attended the annual party held by Accardo at his home in 1954, 1955, and 1956.

Frank LaPorte

Frank LaPorte was described by T-4 on as an old time bootlegger whose present activities are concerned with gambling and prostitution in the Calumet City and Chicago Heights area. T-5 informant advised that Frank LaPorte appears to be principal owner and operator of the Owl Club, a big money gambling enterprise in Calumet City, Illinois, and is referred to in that area as an up and coming underworld chief.

Joey Glimco

Referred to above.

Dominick DiBello

Dom DiBello, with aliases Bill DiBello, Sam Lewis, Phil DiBello and Tommy Docino, was described by T-4 as one of the "Three Dom's" who are active in syndicate operations on the Near North Side of Chicago.

Albert Frabotta, with alias "Obie"

Obie Frabotta was described by T-4 as an "enforcer" for the syndicate and an intimate associate of Marshall Caifano, organizer for the syndicate.

Ross Prio

Prio was described by T-4 as an associate of the "Three Dom's" in the operation of various gambling enterprise on the Near North Side of Chicago. Prio is an associate of Marshall Caifano and other hoodlums and in 1955 was alleged to have been partially responsible for the financing and smuggling of the quantizes of narcotics from Canada.

Phillip Colucci

Phillip Colucci is believed to be one of five Colucci boys who operated 16 handbooks in the 25th and 27th Wards.

Dominick Nuccio, with aliases "Luckey", Joe Delano

The lengthy criminal record and description of Dominick Nuccio has been previously reported.

Sam Battaglia, with alias "Teeze"

67

A 1958 Oldsmobile convertible bearing 1958 Illinois license 1119975 has been observed at the Giancana residence on two occasions in March and April 1958. This car is registered to M. Salvatore, 1114 North Ridgeland, Oak Park. It has been determined through investigation that 1114 North Ridgeland is the residence of Sam Battaglia and his wife, Angela.

T-4 informant advised on March 17, 1958, that Battaglia had been intimately acquainted with Paul "The Waiter" Ricca as an "enforcer" for the syndicate. He is a former member of the old "42 Gang" and was a friend of Anthony Papa who was assassinated in gangland fashion while under indictment on a narcotics charge. In 1945, Battaglia was investigated for the murder of Alex Chase, a Hammond, Indiana hoodlum.

Richard Bernas, was
Dick Burna and Rick Burns

A 1954 Oldsmobile bearing 1958, Illinois license 2756726, registered to Richard Burns, with aliases Dick Burna, and Lick Burns, then living at 6634 North Maplewood, Chicago, was a very close friend of Mathew Capone, brother of Al and was at that time employed at the Deerfield Country Club, a plush gambling casino in Lake County, Illinois, with Mathew Capone, cousin of Rocco Fischetti.

Hyman Godfrey

Hyman Godfrey of 1227 East 47th Street, Chicago, has been observed entering and or leaving the subject's residence on several occasions during the period of January and June 1958. Godfrey is described as a long time associate and right hand man of Sam "Golf Bag" Hunt, a prominent Chicago hoodlum.

Charles Fischetti and
Murray L. Humphreys

Charles Fischetti is a brother of Rocco and Joe Fischetti, all of whom have been described by T-4 on March 17, 1958 as former members of the Capone syndicate and are believed to presently operate gambling operations in Chicago for the Crime Syndicate.

Murray Humphreys, "The Camel" described by T-4 on March 17, 1958 as a syndicate hoodlum, who in 1946, with Jake Guzik attempted to "muscle" into a wire service operated by a James Roger (deceased). According to this informant Humphreys is a close associate of Accardo and Ricca and it is alleged that he was partially responsible for the death of Charles "Cherry Nose" Gioe in 1956.

CRIMINAL ACTIVITIES

Current Criminal Activities
Including Definition of
Syndicate

On April 3, 1958, Marshall Caifano, advised SA Ralph R. Hill that he is a member of the syndicate in Chicago and that the syndicate is composed of gamblers. Caifano stated that several members make up a hierarchy of the syndicate and syndicate member are apportioned districts out of which they operate. Caifano stated that the syndicate member in charge of each district receives a percentage of all gambling conducted in his district and controls all gamblers, taking "drastic measures" if they prove untrustworthy. Caifano would not admit that the syndicate controls anything other than gambling nor would he identify the members other than himself who compose this syndicate.

On March 31, 1958, T-6 advised that he is of the opinion that the syndicate in the Chicago area is a highly organized group within this area but unlikely that the organization is extended to a national or international level. He advised however, that the most influential and powerful men in the Chicago organization are widely acquainted throughout the country and that it is only logical to surmise that these men could and do contact their friends in other cities to insure that certain of their wishes are carried out.

T-8 further advised that the syndicate is concerned mainly with organized gambling in all forms and that many other types of crimes attributed to the syndicate are often the result of some personal activity on the part of some individual believed to have syndicate connections. The informant stated that the very nature of the organization structure of the syndicate makes it inevitable for top syndicate figures to turn to criminal activities other than gambling because the opportunity exists and there is revenue to be gained.

According to this informant, Anthony Accardo is the top man in the Chicago area and that the sometimes voiced belief that he has retired is wrong. According to this source, Sam Giancana, alias "Mooney," is final arbitrator of all matters of organizational interest. In addition, Giancana is responsible for the entire Chicago area, the authority to allocate "districts" and to place these districts under control of certain men whom he chooses.

T-8 informant stated that these "district men" are required to pay a certain sum of money each month to Giancana, who in turn, turns over a certain sum to Accardo. The district men are allowed rather wide latitude in the means they exercise to raise this money and any money they make in excess of the amount payable to Giancana may be counted as their profit. The informant pointed out these payments must be made promptly and in cash and failure to meet these obligations are generally deemed to be a fatal mistake.

This informant pointed out that the principal thing that the syndicate has to sell is protection. For example, protection from police action and protection from other hoodlums. The informant noted the fact that gambling is protected from police action and this invariably gives raise to other criminal activity such as prostitution, narcotics, and fencing. The informant pointed out that if the police are compromised in one activity there is a certain reluctance to act in another direction. The informant states that the district man is under considerable compulsion to raise a certain amount of money each month and if gambling revenues are uncertain or inadequate he will turn to any means available.

T-9 advised that through his own experience and information, which has come into his possession, he feels that the four individuals who actually control and guide the syndicate are at the present time Anthony Accardo, Sam "Mooney" Giancana, Paul Ricca, and Ross Prio. This informant states that these persons meet regularly at times at Celano's Tailor Shop on Michigan Avenue, at which time they apparently talk over gambling operations and assign territories and conduct and other business, which should arise.

On April 8, 1957, Captain Nestor advised that his source have told him that the territory including Kane County was recently assigned to Samuel Giancana and that the assignment was made as of about January, 1957.

T-12 informant advised on May 8, 1958, that Sam Giancana controls all syndicate activities on the west side of Chicago and the western suburbs, exclusive of Melrose Park, which is controlled by Rocco DeGrazia.

T-13 informant advised on May 6, 1958, that the west side gambling syndicate head was Sam Giancana whose lieutenant, according to this source is Marshall Caifano. This informant stated the syndicate takes 60 per cent of the take at the book and that 40 per cent is given to the operating. Out of the 60 per cent, the syndicate takes care of all pay offs. Informant was of the opinion that there are approximately 200 handbooks operating in the area confined by the loop west to Cicero and between Madison and Roosevelt Road.

CRIMINAL ACTIVITIES

Gambling

Records of the Chicago Crime Commission reflect that in February of 1950, Sam Giancana was considered one of the principal Chicago are hoodlums and was considered a "general overseer" of the local gambling in Chicago. He is suspected to have spent time in Florida but never at the same time as Tony Accardo as one or the other was always around the local area to make sure that business was conducted as usual.

Other files reflect that in a court observer's report of June 17, 1957 concerning indictment 51-2012, in which Sam Giancana is charged with knowingly permitting a building owned by him for the operation of a handbook, it should be noted that Judge Wilbert F. Crowley heard this case, and that the defense attorney was Michael Brodkin. Giancana entered a plea of not guilty, testimony was heard, and the court found him not guilty.

Another record at the Chicago Crime Commission reflects that in the early part of 1955 alderman J.P. Immel Jr., of the 41st Ward had called upon the Police Commissioner of Chicago and informed him that Sam Giancana was threatening him and pushing him around in an effort to place pin ball machines in the ward.

POLICY

It was reported on June 22, 1951, that Ted Roe claimed that Giancana, in 1946, tried to shake him down. He said that George Jones brought Giancana to him and introduced him under the name of "Mooney". Giancana tried to shake him down for $4,000 and said he and his people could do Roe some good; that they could keep the policy business from getting into the papers. A tussle followed and George Jones told Roe and Giancana not to fight. Roe turned the proposition down. According to the story, Giancana said he wanted to meet with Roe and his lawyer the next day but he did not show up.

A report in 1952 stated that Clifford Davis, who ran the Jones wheels with Ted Roe, capitulated to the syndicate headed by Tony Accardo, and Sam Giancana when Roe was slain August 4, 1952. Davis was to take over as general manager for the mob. The report stated that that Accardo and Giancana control all policy in the city and suburbs, including Evanston and Gary, Indiana. The story stated that the $30,000,000-a-year racket will be run by Davis with a syndicate man actually in control behind the scenes. The syndicate man is said to be George Harrison who had operated three small policy wheels in the Stockyards district.

LEGITIMATE ENTERPRISES

Anthony James DePardo, President, Utility Engineering Company, Oak Park, advised SA Mellott on April 25, 1958 that he has done business with Sam Giancana, known to him as "Mooney" for the past 15 years when Giancana brought in two irons for repair. He became a customer and bought several household appliances during the years. At about the time of the initial purchase Giancana commented he would recommend DePadro to some of his friends. These friends turned out to be some of the other better known "syndicate guys" and apparently they recommended DePadro to other friends, as a result of which many of them became his customers.

Mr. DePardo explained that by the syndicate he meant what everyone else in the Chicago area understands by the term i.e., these members of the criminal organization which controls and directs criminal activities in the Chicago area, and which is referred to in newspaper columns and in everyday speech as the "syndicate." Mr. DePardo named some of the syndicate members as follows, pointing out that each of them have been customers of his at one time or another; Sam Giancana, Tony Accardo, Jake Guzik, Gus Alex, Joey Glimco, Louis Campagna, Paul "The Waiter" Ricca and Ed Vogel. At one time, Giancana owed him approximately $80,000 for furniture, appliances and heating and air conditioning system installed at the River Road Motel, 5400 River Road, Schiller Park. On one occasion, Mr. DePardo related, was he ever paid in any form other than cash. At the time Giancana owed him the approximate $80,000, he came into the office one day and tossed him a bundle of currency wrapped in newspaper and announced it was to be credited to his account. The amount of this bundle was $15,000. DePardo stated he has sold appliances and/or air conditioning systems to many of the members of the "syndicate" but that at no occasion was he ever paid by check.

Mr. DePadro stated that "Toni" Giancana is the subject's daughter who was employed by him at the time he also operated a furniture store next door. He employed her at the request of "Mooney" who stated his daughter was beginning to run wild and he wanted to keep her busy on something. According to DePardo she worked for him about two months in about 1953 as a saleslady but did not show up for work regularly and eventually stopped coming all together. Mr. DePardo offered to make records of his firm available for examination by the FBI and asserted that nothing would be found to show that Giancana, Accardo or other syndicate members own or have any financial interest in the business.

RIVER ROAD MOTEL, formerly
Sunrise Club
5400 North River Road
Schiller Park, Illinois

On April 2, 1957, Leon Marcus, a former Chicago banker, was found shot to death in the city of Chicago. On his person was found a carbon copy of a receipt indicating that the securities company with which Marcus had been connected had loaned Sam Giancana $150,000 and has accepted as security on this loan a mortgage on a west suburban motel. The receipt indicated that $100,000 of the amount had been repaid. The motel was identified as the River Road Motel, which formerly had been the old Sunrise Club, a syndicate house of prostitution which had been closed about two years ago following a newspaper expose. The reputed operator of this motel is Rocco Potenza, who allegedly manages Giancana's gambling house.

On April 5, 1957, it was reported that officials had entered Leon Marcus' safety deposit box in the Southmoor Bank and Trust Company on Chicago's south side where they found four deposit slips showing that Giancana's River Road Motel had been paying $333.33 a month interest on a $100,000 mortgage held by Marcus' Security company; however, Louis Corrington Jr., president of the Southmoor Bank, said that the Giancana loan had been paid off three weeks earlier by an unidentified individual who came in a paid approximately $135,000 in cash.

The trust number 8566 pertains to River Road Motel, 5400 River Road, Schiller Park and is a Land Trust Agreement existing since February 3, 1955 between the Southmoor Bank and the following two beneficiaries of the trust:

Michael Caldarulo
623 South Kildare
Chicago, Illinois

James Perno as trustee
1538 North 24th Avenue
Melrose Park, Illinois

The wording of the agreement describing Perno as "trustee" indicated he is holding his beneficial interest for someone else. In this connection it is to be noted that a James Perno has resided at the subject's residence for the past four years and is married to the subject's niece, Marie Perno, nee Tumminello.

In 1956, a complaint was filed concerning the rape of a woman at the River Road Motel. Named in the complaint as owner-operators of the River Road Motel were Michael Caldarulo, James Perno, Mary Pitarro and Charles Kane.

Mrs. Mary Polinski advised on May 6, 1958 that she is the former Mary Pitarro and that she formerly had a financial interest in the River Road Motel. Mrs. Polinski explained that her husband, Ross Pitarro, who died in 1950, had known Mike Caldarulo since their boyhood. In July or August, 1950, Caldarulo offered Pitarro a portion of some land and buildings he had on River Road as an investment to Potarro, them working as district sales manager for the Permanent Stainless Steel Company. Pitarro considered this a friendly gesture on the part of Caldarulo and saw it as a possible opportunity to make a profit and persuaded his wife it would be a good investment. As a result they brought a half interest in the property, which was put in the names of Mary Pitarro. Mrs. Pitarro went on to say that the property at that time consisted of a tavern, a dining room and kitchen behind the tavern, a five-unit motel. Mrs. Poliwski stated she did not recall the exact amount of cash that her husband put up but she dose recall that he carried a $9,000 mortgage. In November, 1950 her husband died and she retained ownership until the fall of 1951. For about nine weeks shortly after her husband's death she worked at the property, fixing up and cleaning the place.

At the time, she mentioned, many of the customers were real "tough" but she discouraged these persons from frequenting the place by raising prices and as a result building up a good patronage and converted the place into a private key club. A short time later she moved to Detroit, and upon her return some two and one-half months later she went out to the property to see Mike Caldarulo about selling out her interest in the property. She remarked that she read in the paper prior to coming out to the property that the club purchased a federal gambling stamp, and she observed on this visit that a Bingo table was in operation in the cocktail lounge and the place gave the appearance of having been converted into a gambling place. She told Caldarulo that she was interested in selling and accepted his offer of $20,000 for her interest in the property. She pointed out that in 1952 she drove by the property and noticed that all the buildings that existed at the time she had interest in the property had been torn down and replaced by newer, larger and more luxurious buildings. Mrs. Polinski stated that she has had no interest in the place since that time, has not seen Mike Caldarulo since early 1952, and has no knowledge of Charles Kane.

Michael Caldarulo, 623 South Kildare, advised SA Mellott on May 22, 1958, that he would not divulge any information regarding the River Road Motel and that any questions pertaining to it should be directed to his attorney, Anthony V. Champagne. "Charles Kane is the alias of Charles Giancana."

FOREST LOUNGE

The Chicago Crime Commission reported on October 24, 1952, that Sam Giancana and his brother Rocky Giancana owned the Forest Lounge, 6548 Milwaukee Avenue, Niles. Rocco Potenzo operated it for them; however, the commission stated that continued checks by its investigations reflected that as of January, 1953, the only gambling they were able to find at this place was a "26" game. A State Liquor License Application for the Forest Lounge reflects that the license was issued on July 8, 1957 to Rocco Potenzo. Owner of the presises is Russian Et Al, and that his lease expires in 1959. Personal information on Potenzo:

Name   Rocco Potenzo
Age   45
Residence   8857 North Kildare Avenue, Skokie

Property at 4810-12 West Cermak
Cicero, Illinois

T-10 informant advised on February 13, 1955 that Giancana recently remodeled the building at 4810-12 West 22nd (Cermak) Street in Cicero, and converted it into a plush gambling place with roulette wheels, a horse parlor, private rooms for card games and refreshment facilities. According to the deed, this property was listed in ownership of the Pinkert family at one time and the most recent transactions show a mortgage to the Service Savings and Loan as grantee from the Exchange National Bank as grantor under document number 1558454 dated November 9, 1954.

Property at 5941 West Roosevelt Road
Cicero (former bank building)

Anthony James DePardo, president of the Utility Engineering Company advised that it is general information that the old bank building on Roosevelt Road is a gambling joint, and this fact is personally known to him as he installed two, five-ton air conditioning units in the building; for the units and their installation he was paid in cash by Joe Corngold.

Lormar Distributing Company, Chicago, Illinois

Records of the CCC dated July 15, 1957, contain the information that the Lormar Distributing Company was started in January, 1957, by Charles English. It was latter learned that this firm was dealing in counterfeit phonograph records and underselling legitimate market. According to this source, Sam Giancana was supposed to be one of the men "behind the scenes" in this company.

Places of Amusement or Hangouts Frequented

T-11 informant advised prior to March, 1955, that Giancana was a frequenter of Philip's Restaurant and Candy Store at 22nd and Cicero Avenue.

State of Health

T-18 informant advised on May 23, 1958, that the subject has his second operation for cancer about two weeks ago. According to this informant, the matter has been kept in complete confidence and is known by very few persons. The informant expressed the view the condition is malignant and not too much hope for recovery is expected. Mrs. Lucille Brahill, niece of subject, and Mrs. Rose Flood, sister of the subject's late wife, advised on May 27, and May 28, 1958, respectively, that the subject has been hospitalized during recent months and is confined to his home due to illness. Both of these sources have stated that the subject dose not desire to discuss his state of health with family members or friends and the exact nature of his illness is not known to them.

<u>Female Companions</u>

T-18 advised on February 20, 1958, that he believes that Darlene Caifano, wife of Marshall Caifano, had been "playing around with Sam Mooney" when Caifano was out of town. The informant also advised on April 14, 1958, that on the evening of April 11, 1958, he had occasion to observe Darlene Caifano in a night club on the south side of Chicago. During the course of the evening, Darlene Caifano became extremely intoxicated and was overheard to comment regarding certain of her escapades with Sam "Mooney". The informant recalled that Darlene remarked that she frequently had a rendezvous with Sam on Friday evenings.

T-19 informant advised on April 19, 1958, that she is acquainted with Darlene Caifano. She stated that it is common knowledge among the friends and associates of Marshall Caifano that his boss is dating and having sexual relations with Darlene. According to this informant, Darlene was a crude "hillbilly" when Caifano picked her up. He has since, polished and dressed her to the point where she is now a very attractive woman. After this revamping by Caifano, his syndicate boss moved in and started dating her. The informant explained that feeling among the friends and acquaintances of the Caifano's is that Caifano knows of the relationship between his boss and his wife but is afraid to do anything about it. The informant identified Caifano's boss as Sam Giancana. The informant identified pointed out that the irony of this situation is that Giancana has been known to admonish married men in his organization for playing the bright spots and dating too much and then he in turn is dating the wife of his more highly placed men.

FEDERAL BUREAU OF INVESTIGATION

REPORTING OFFICE	OFFICE OF ORIGIN	DATE	INVESTIGATIVE PERIOD
CHICAGO	CHICAGO	1958	August 7, 1958

TITLE OF CASE	REPORT MADE BY	TYPED BY
	Special Agent Frank L. Mellott	dkc
SAMUEL M. GIANCANA, aka	CHARACTER OF CASE	
	FBI Headquarters File number 92-3171-22 Top Hoodlum Program – Anti Racketeering	

Synopsis:

Mary and Phillip Colucci, River Forest, Illinois admit associating with subject's; both deny knowledge that car owned by subjects eldest daughter was registered to their address until car involved in accident. Colucci claims not related to Colucci brothers who operate handbooks and exercise political influence on Chicago's west side. Subject reportedly seen in company of Frank Sinatra in Las Vegas. Examination of legal records gives no indication subject has financial interest in Villa Venice, large restaurant and lounge northwest of Chicago. Subject, using name "Russell Paige", operated on in May, 1958, for rectal disorder and in April, 1956, for colon disorder, but no indication of malignancy. Subject referred to surgeon by, Dr. Carl Champagne, brother of Anthony V. Champagne, notorious hoodlum attorney. Efforts by Deputy United States Marshals during May-July, 1958, to locate subject to serve subpoena for subject's appearance before McClellan Committee unsuccessful to date. Car driven by subject registered to Anthony

DeBendo, Berwyn, but efforts to establish existence of this person unsuccessful.

PHILLIP COLUCCI

Phillip Colucci advised SA Melllot on July 16, 1958 that he knows the subject but dose not associate with him in any way. Colucci remarked that the subject's wife, Angeline, who died about 3-4 years ago, was a fine woman, liked and respected by all who knew her. Colucci said that his wife and Angeline grew up in the same neighborhood and were good friends until Angeline's death. As a result of this friendship, his wife and Angeline visited at each other's homes, and on occasion he would drop his wife off at Giancana's residence but on no occasion has he visited in the Giancana home and, from what he knows of Giancana and his reputation as a hoodlum, he has never desired to associate with him.

Colucci stated the only unlawful activities in which he has engaged was the operation of two handbooks about 20 years ago and bootlegging for a period of about three years about 25 years ago. Colucci emphatically denied being a brother or related in any way to the Colucci brothers, including Joe, Dominick, Vito, and Frank, who are generally known to operate handbook and wield considerable political influence on Chicago's West side.

Mrs. Mary Colucci, wife of Phillip, said that while she and her husband know Sam Giancana, as a result of his marriage to her friend, Angeline, they have never been on friendly terms and, since the death of Angeline, have seen him on only rare occasions. Mrs. Colucci commented that while Giancana's wife was a very warm and loveable person, the subject is extremely "cold" and repels all but a limited few he takes a liking to. Mrs. Colucci said she has read and heard about the subject's gambling activities, but that neither she nor her husband have any knowledge of these activities.

Phillip Colucci admitted being the brother of Arthur Colucci, who was deported to Italy in 1948 following a narcotics conviction, but stated he attempted to help this brother "straighten himself out" and give up his dealings in narcotics but, falling in this, completely severed relationship with his brother and has had no further contacts with him. Colucci said that his other brothers are: Mario Colucci, about 49, who lives in Baragiano, Italy, and Amedeo Colucci, M.D., who lives in Petersburg, Ohio, where he practices medicine with his wife, Maria, also an M.D.

As to his reported interest in the Jockey Club, now the North Avenue Steak House, 8500 North Avenue, Maywood, reportedly owned by Joseph DeTolve, subject's brother-in-law, and operated by Ernest "Rocky" Infelice, a muscleman for the subject, Colucci advised as follows:

He and a partner, Daniel Beneduce, now deceased, leased the Jockey Club in about 1948, or 1949, and operated it as a restaurant and tavern for about four years. Following the death of his partner in about 1953 he decided to go out of business and close the place down. When they first leased the place, one Pasquale Lari, who now operates a motel at about 19th Avenue and North Avenue, in Melrose Park, owned the Jockey Club but during their lease Lari sold all or part of the club to Joseph DeTolve, brother of Angeline DeTolve, the subject's late wife. Since he closed the club in about 1953 or 1954 he has had no further interest in the place, has not frequented it, and has no knowledge as to present ownership or operation of the place.

Colucci stated he has made three trips to Italy since coming to this country at the age of 18, the first of these in 1937, the second in 1939, and the third in 1953. According to Colucci, these trips were made solely for the purpose of visiting his parents residing in Baragiano, Italy, and were in no way related to the narcotic traffic in which his brother Arthur was engaged, or to any other unlawful activities.

Colucci stated his present employment is as a silent partner of Frank Smith in the Garfield Music Corporation, a jukebox rental concern, and as a buyer and seller of real estate. Regarding the first of these employments, Colucci stated his partner is a brother of Fred Thomas Smith, commonly known as "Jukebox Smith" but that this fact was unknown to him when he entered into partnership with Frank Smith. According to Colucci, no pressure of any sort is used by his partner to install the juke boxes in establishments, nor is his firm controlled or influenced by hoodlum elements. Colucci remarked that his nephew, Guido Losasso, collects the coins from the machines and services them, but that the firm is actively operated by Frank Smith. Colucci commented that he desires to get out of this business due to the unsavory reputation the juke box industry has acquired due to the influence of hoodlums who have entered the field.

Colucci added that prior to his operation of the Jockey Club in about 1948, he operated the Rex Bowling Alley, including lunchroom and bar, at 5800 West Chicago Avenue for about 2 to 3 years; the Times Square Grill at the Northwest corner of Lake and Wells Streets in the Chicago Loop, and a restaurant at Taylor and Halsted Streets, then known as the Del Mar Restaurant.

Following is Colucci's description, as obtained from observation and interview:

Name	Phillip Coloucci
Address	13399 Lathrop, River Forest
Race	White
Age	53
Date of Birth	July 24, 1904
Place of Birth	Baragiano, Italy
Height	5'61/2"
Weight	172 pounds
Build	Stocky
Hair	Black, graying
Eyes	Brown
Complexion	Cark
Relatives	Wife, Mary Colucci, nee Odierno, age 39
	Sons Robert, age 15, and Phillip age 9
	Daughter Mary Ann Colucci, age 13

Frank Sinatra

T-1 informant advised in the latter part of June, 1958, that several months ago, Frank Sinatra was appearing at the Sands Hotel show, Sam Mooney was seen in the company of Sinatra at the El Rancho Vegas Hotel in Las Vegas, Nevada. The informant stated that Mooney is a Chicago racketeer whose true name is something other than Mooney but who is commonly known as "Mooney".

Stardust Hotel
Las Vegas, Nevada

T-1 informant advised in the latter part of June, 1958, that one John Drew, formerly of Chicago, who has operated gambling establishments in Reno and Las Vegas, Nevada, is one of the officials of the new Stardust Hotel Casino, Las Vegas. This informant pointed out that Drew has always been the type of person who "fronted" for undisclosed interests in gambling establishment, and it is believed by the informant at the Stardust Hotel, especially for Sam Mooney. The informant described Mooney as a Chicago racketeer whose true name is something other than Mooney but who is commonly known as Mooney.

Villa Venice

An examination of the Land Tract Book stated that on October 24, 1956 the Villia Venice was purchase for $80,000 by Meo's Villa Venice, Incorporated from Albert Bouch. President of Meo's Villa Venice, Incorporated is shown as James Meo and secretary as Stella Meo. In all of the documents, no mention is made of Giancana or individuals other than the Meo are listed above.

Personal Habits and Peculiarities
State of Health

Sam Giancana was admitted to Columbus Hospital, Chicago, on May 10, 1958, under the name of Russell Paige. He was operated on by Dr. Peter Rosi, M.D., for rectal prolapse. DR. Rosi commented that the subject earned the reputation among nuns and nurses at the hospital to be the "coldest" and most anti-social patient they have ever had and, as a result of his surly attitude towards the hospital staff he suggested that the subject leave the hospital on May 20th and complete his recuperation at home or elsewhere. On July 5, he returned for a final examination and was found to be in good health, with no need for further examination.

Current Efforts to Locate the Subject

Deputy United States Marshals Sol Carvelli and James McKeigue, Chicago, advised on various dates during the period May thru July 31, 1958, that efforts by them to locate Giancana for purpose of serving him with a subpoena to appear before the Senate Select Committee on Improper Activities in the Labor or Management Field had been unsuccessful to date. Both Carvelli and McKeigue expressed the view that the publicity given to the matter of serving subpoenas on witnesses to appear before the aforementioned committee caused the subject to go into hiding and that numerous inquiries made by them at places the subject is known to have frequented in the past were unsuccessful in developing any information as to the subject's whereabouts.

On July 14, 1958, Deputy McKeigue advised that he had, on that day, served the subject's daughter, "Toni", with a subpoena directing her to appear before the aforementioned Senate committee. He pointed out that this step was taken in the belief that it would encourage the subject to accept service of the subpoena and appear before the committee rather than subject his daughter to it. Deputy McKeigue advised on July 21, 1958, that this plan did not achieve its expected results, as "Toni" Giancana was excused from testifying before the committee after a letter was produced from her doctor, to the effect that it would be injurious to her mental health to testify. (See Page 100 of this book)

Deputy McKeigue advised on July 18, 1958, that a reliable source known to him reported that the subject was seen at the Turf Club, a gambling place in Cicero, for a brief period of time between midnight and 1:00 a.m. on July 13, 1958.

T-3 informant advised in June and July, 1958, that he has not seen the subject at his home for the past several months. The informant expressed the belief that the subject had probably left the city or was in hiding. This informant also remarked that since the subject's disappearance there has been a considerable decrease in the number of the visitors to the subject's home.

Use of Possible Alias "Anthony DeBendo"

As reported in the past a car registered to Anthony DeBendo, 1828 South Clinton, Berwyn, has been observed parked in front of Giancana's garage on several occasions. Records of the Chicago Police Department do not contain any information pertaining to an Anthony DeBendo. The directory of the West Suburbs, Chicago area, lists a Ruth L. Smith and C.M. Paran as residents at 1828 South Clinton, Berwyn.

Mrs. Ruth Stella, 1828 South Clinton, advised on July 14, 1958, that "Anthony De-Bendo" has not been around for some time, several months, in fact, and when pressed for details as to the identity and whereabouts of DeBendo, and the extent of her knowledge of him, she became confused and evasive, requesting SA Mellott to leave his name and telephone number so that her husband could telephone and give the necessary information regarding DeBendo. Mrs. Stella reluctantly said her maiden name was Ruth Smith but declined to give her husband's first name, occupation or other identifying data. Mrs. Stella admitted she had never seen a person known as Anthony DeBendo, and remarked that the name had "come up" in conversation, but could not recall the parties to the conversation.

Pasquale Stella, advised on July 15, 1958, that he and his wife, Ruth Stella, nee Smith, have lived at their present address since 1952 but that he has no knowledge of an "Anthony DeBendo", dose not know of any car other than his wife's 1953 Cadillac being registered to his address, and dose not have knowledge of Giancana. As to his wife's statement that DeBendo had not been around for several months, Stella remarked his wife had just returned home from the hospital and was probably confused and excited by the interview and gave incorrect information. Stella claimed to be employed for the past five years as a partner with Anthony Rossetti in the Rossetti Construction Company and gave the address of 4300 Milwaukee Avenue, Chicago.

Rumor Regarding Death of Subject

T-5 informant advised on August 1, 1958, that information had recently come to the informant's attention to the effect that the subject, due to be killed by the Syndicate, had been killed and his body dumped in Chicago. However, the captain of the police district in which the body was dumped, not desiring the large-scale investigation which would ensue from the discovery of the body, had some of his more trusted officers removed the body to another police district. This informant explained that the rumor appeared to be ill-found, as it was too unlikely that a police official would have taken such action were the body found in his district, and the fact that the subject's body had not been located gave no credence to the rumor.

FEDERAL BUREAU OF INVESTIGATION

REPORTING OFFICE	OFFICE OF ORIGIN	DATE	INVESTIGATIVE PERIOD
CHICAGO	CHICAGO	1958	October 17, 1958

TITLE OF CASE	REPORT MADE BY	TYPED BY
	Special Agent Frank L. Mellott	dkc
SAMUEL M. GIANCANA, aka	CHARACTER OF CASE	
	FBI Headquarters File number 92-3171-25 Chicago File number 92-349-25 Top Hoodlum Program – Anti Racketeering	

Synopsis:

Information set out regarding following associates of subject: Frank Eulo, Rocco Eulo, Charles Nicoletti, Rocky Prano, Mike Sabatino, and Pasquale Stella. Subject identified as probably identical with gambling boss who told Kane County, Illinois, jukebox operator he and associates were bringing books and slots into county and expressed view to jukebox operator he should "go along" with them. When operator did not acquiesce, he was first pressured by gambling bosses subordinates to get out of business and then treated with fatal or crippling beating with baseball bats. No action taken by local officials. No interstate character. Subject identified in 1954, by being "boss" of corrupt union officials. Information developed that subject owns American Motel, Stone Park, Illinois, and Villa Venice, large restaurant and lounge northwest of Chicago. Subject reportedly was in Cuba during hearings of Senate Select Committee and returned to celebrate conclusion of hearings at Villa Venice with other leaders of crime syndicate. Information advised that subject is currently in Mexico. Numerous efforts made to determine subject's whereabouts non-productive to date.

ASSOCIATES

Frank Eulo, Rocco Eulo
Mike Sabatino, 1104 South
Maple Avenue, Oak Park,

As previously reported, the subject underwent surgery in April 1956, and May 1958, at which time he used the alias Russell Paige and gave as his home address 1104 South Maple Avenue, Oak Park, Illinois. This address is located two and one-half blocks from the subject's home.

Current investigation reflects that the residents at 1104 South Maple Avenue are Frank Eulo, and his wife, Rose, and Mike Sabatino and his wife, Betty. In addition to these individuals, who have been observed entering and leaving this residence, a car registered to Rocco Eulo at 1104 South Maple has been observed parked in the immediate vicinity of this house on two different occasions.

New York letter to Newark dated February 3, 1958, in case captioned "Joseph Profaci, Anti-Racketeering, Top Hoodlum Program", reports that T-2, a New York City investigation agency, has stated that on November 21, 1957, the name of Frank Eulo, 1104 South Maple, Oak Park, was obtained from cards and papers carried by Joseph Profaci, with aliases, who has been described by T-3 as the number one man along Sicilians in New York City and the United States, and as the man to whom leaders of five Sicilian Combinations in the metropolitan area of New York are responsible. Frank J. Ahern, Chief of Police, San Francisco Police Department, has linked Profaci with the Mafia in the United States. Profaci is a top hoodlum of the New York Office.

Bureau of Records and Communications, Chicago Police Department, contained information that on March 6, 1949, Frank Eulo, 1104 South Maple, was arrested at 12th and Albany Streets, Chicago, charged with damaging city property, to which he entered a plea of guilty on March 31, 1949. He was fined $5.00. Eulo did not list his date or place of birth, and gave his occupation as that of clerk.

A car registered to Rocco Eulo, 1104 South Maple, was observed by the Scottland Yard Detail, Chicago PD, at the July 5, 1954, annual party held at the residence of Anthony J. Accardo's, 915 North Franklin Street, River Forest.

Files of the Chicago office reflect that Mike Sabatino had Alien Registration Number 3458962. Information relating to this registration is no longer available in files of the Chicago Office.

George Bond, Sales Manager, Allen Chevrolet Company, 6527 Roosevelt Road, Berwyn, Illinois, advised on August 8, 1958, that he sold a 1958 Chevrolet Impala, white, full power, to Mike Sabatino, 1104 South Maple, on November 30, 1958. According to Mr. Bond, Sabatino is a "collector" for the syndicate. According to Mr. Bond, Sabatino was referred to him by Dom "Butch" Blasi, who handles the purchase of cars for several prominent hoodlums. Further information regarding this is reported under the caption "Automobiles".

Mr. Bond furnished the following information regarding Sabatino:

Name	Michael Sabatino, aka "Mike"
Address	1104 South Maple, Oak Park
Age	41 years, born around 1917
Wife	Betty Sabatino
Relative	Frank Eulo, brother-in-law
Landlord	Rose Eulo
Occupation	"Advertising"
Personal Reference	Tony Russo, 816 N. England Avenue.

CHARLES NICOLETTI, with
Aliases "Chuck", Chuckie"
1700 block on North 19th
Street, Melrose Park, Illinois

T-4 informant advised that he was told by a prominent Chicago gambler, (Joe Epstein, well known and powerful gambler) that Charles "Chuckie" Nicoletti was destined to become a "big man in the outfit". According to this source, Nicoletti has, over the years, proved himself to the "outfit", even to the point of having committed a couple of out-of-town gangster-style murders. This source also advised the information that Nicoletti was recently given one of the best syndicate "districts" in the city. According to this source, Nicoletti is intelligent and capable enough to one day succeed Tony Accardo.

The informant described Nicoletti as a white male, about 35 years old of age, 5'11" tall, 175 pounds, black wavy hair, brown eyes, dark complexion, Italian extraction, and had the following distinguishing characteristics: has gold fillings in upper portion of upper front teeth and slight cast to one eye. The informant stated it was his understanding that Nicoletti has been considered assistant to Sam "Mooney" Giancana.

ROCKY PRANNO, with aliases
Rocky Martel, Rocky Bartel
Aurora, Illinois

Information regarding captioned individual is set out under the caption "Criminal Activities".

PASQUALE STELLA
1828 South Clinton Avenue
Berwyn, Illinois

A 1957 Chevrolet, sport coupe, registered to "Anthony DeBendo," 1828 South Clinton, Berwyn, has been observed park at the subject's garage on numerous occasions during the period of March and June, 1958. A car registered to Anthony DeBendo has also been observed at the annual lawn parties held at the home of Anthony Accardo, leader of the crime syndicate in the Chicago area.

It was subsequently determined that the resident of this address is Pasquale Stella and his wife, Ruth. Both Stella and his wife were evasive and contradicted each other when interviewed concerning "Anthony DeBendo".

Information on file in the Chicago office reflects that on May 4, 1956, T-1 advised that the Dream Bar, 13th and Cicero Avenue, Cicero, which is operated by one Pasquale Stella, is rumored to be actually owned by Sam "Mooney" Giancana, with Stella acting as the front for him. This source advised that Stella is bald with a squint in one eye, and that the bartender at the Dream Bar is one Gus (last name unknown).

The Bureau of Records, Chicago PD, listed that Pasquale Stella, 1234 South 58th Court, Cicero, was arrested on September 22, 1948, with Paul E, Ross, with alias Paul Rossi, thief and jewelry fence; Frank Coduto, 3056 West Jackson Boulevard, and Gus Nordi, 1143 Harrison Street. Charge and disposition not shown, and date information furnished no recorded.

Andrew Aitken, then Chief of Detectives, Chicago Police Department, advised in 1952 that the Paul Ross gang, formerly very active in armed robberies, was again active in local robberies, burglaries, and hijackings. Detective Aitken furnished a list of associates of Paul Ross. Included in this list is the name Pasquale Stella, 1234 South 50th Court Cicero.

CRIMINAL ACTIVITIES

Gambling and Extortion

This section can not be released due to its sensitive information about an informant or victim being taken for a ride to meet Sam Giancana in 1956. It's believed that this man was an operator in a music company and the crime syndicate was attempting to muscle their way into an unknown county. One of the sections follows:

"They drove around various roads including various roads where he heard gangsters had been "taken for a ride". The informant stated that this made him still more uneasy, and he decided to give the appearance of "going along" with any suggestions they would make. He said the "boss" asked him how (Blacked out) he had. And the boss told him and then was told by the boss, "we're going to make you a lot of money with books and slots." He said in order to stall them off he told them he could not give them a definite answer then as he was going to the lakes for three days and for them to see him upon his return next Tuesday to discuss the matter further. He said he was not harmed on the ride and was returned to his automobile.

Upon returning to his automobile he immediately called Sheriff Howard Kellett and told him of the recent ride and asked advice as to how to cope with the situation. Between them it was decided to tell the "musclemen" that he had a silent partner who would not go for their deal and that, therefore, it was all off. At this point the victim was shown several photographs and he picked out the photograph of Sam Giancana as closely resembling the "boss" when he was taken for a ride.

Influence Over Corrupt
Labor Union Bosses

Abraham Teitelbaum, 410 South Michigan, Chicago, advised SAs John B. Tarpey, and Robert C. Holmes on July 23, 1954, that the cost of settling the strike at the Marquis chain of restaurants in the fall of 1953, was $60,000. Mr. Teitelbaum said that Anthony V. Champagne replaced him as Chicago Restaurant Employees International Alliance, AFL. Mr. Teitelbaum remarked that this union's International President is a Mr. Blakely, who is controlled by a "murderer" named John Lardino, alias John Nardico, and that Lardino is controlled by Johnny Moore, alias Claude Maddox, of St. Louis, Missouri. Teietelbaum stated that Maddox's boss is "Mooney" Giancana.

LEGITIMATE ENTERPRISES

American Motel

T-5 informant advised on August 14, 1958 that Sam Giancana, commonly known as "Mooney", is the owner of the American Motel located at 1800 Mannheim Road, Stone Park. Physical surveillance of the American Motel and cars parked in the immediate vicinity during the period of this report shows no indication of the presence of Giancana or any of his associates at this establishment.

Villa Venice

On September 29, 1958, Alfred "Chuck" Meo was interviewed by SAs Frank Mellott and Lester Esarey at Meo's Norwood House, 4750 North Harlem, Norridge, a plush restaurant operated by Chuck Meo. He stated that he and his brother, James Meo, own this restaurant along with the Villa Venice.

He stated that James and his financial interest in restaurants is confined to these two, and that the Franklin House, whose ownership is frequently attributed to them, is owned by two of his nephews, the sons of his brother James.

Meo stated the Norwood House was built with money made available by his wife, Trip, who received a large settlement as a result of being permanently crippled in an airplane crash a few years ago. He stated that the Villa Venice was purchased from Papa Bouche, a friend of the Meo family for many years. Meo stated that his brother, James, was the band leader at the Villa Venice during Bouche's ownership.

Chuck Meo admitted that many of the notorious Chicago hoodlums, including Tony Accardo, Sam Battaglia, and Rocco Fischetti frequent his restaurant, and he is happy to have their business, as they are free-spending customers. He denied they have meetings at his restaurant, and said that they come to his place to enjoy the excellent food that he serves. He remarked that most of these individuals, such as Accardo, Battaglia, and Fischetti, have been known to him for many years as a result of his growing up with them in the Taylor and Halsted sections of Chicago, which is commonly known as the Italian Quarter.

Chuck Meo emphatically denied that any of the hoodlums had a financial interest in either the Norwood House or the Villa Venice, and stated that it is ridiculous to suppose that Sam Giancana has any financial interest in the Villa Venice. Meo added that he has not seen "Mooney" Giancana for at lease 3 or 4 months, and that Giancana rarely frequents either the Norwood House or the Villa Venice.

T-9 informant furnished on September 30, 1958, the following information regarding the Villa Venice, located on Milwaukee Avenue (Route 21) near Wheeling, Illinois:

This well known restaurant and lounge was owned and operated by Albert "Papa" Bouche, until October 1956, at which time Bouche was bought out by the Meo brothers, with the backing of the crime syndicate. Although the ostensible purchasers of the property were the Meo brothers and their wives, Alfred and Trip (Tripolina) and James and Stella, the real operator of the Villa Venice is Sam Giancana, commonly referred to as "Mooney", while Jimmy Meo is the "front". When Giancana appears on the scene, it becomes obvious to all he is the "top dog" in the operation of the place, as all the others, including Jimmy Meo, become subservient to him and jumps at his command. Giancana regards the Villa Venice as his toy and insists on it being run strictly according to his dictates, and he personally rebukes employees when their dress or conduct are not up to his standards.

Although Giancana was frequently at the Villa Venice prior to the recent hearings of the Senate Rackets Committee (McClellan Committee or more properly, the Senate Select Committee on Improper Activities in the Labor or Management Field), he went to Cuba while the hearings were in progress and did not return until the hearings concluded. A day or two after the hearings ended, Giancana and other "wheels" in the syndicate held a private party at the Villa Venice to celebrate the conclusion of the hearings. At this gathering, in one of many private rooms in the Villa, several guards were posted at strategic points on the grounds to challenge anyone not known to them. The Villa has gradually been becoming a headquarters for the crime syndicate, as indicated by closed meetings complete with "lookouts" and by frequenting of the Villa by friends of Giancana, who are paid considerable deference by the Meo brothers.

One of the most current and important projects of the crime syndicate is the preparation of gambling houses scheduled to go into operation when the new sheriff comes into power this fall. Apparently, the syndicate leaders have some assurance that "their men" will get into office of Sheriff of Cook County, which will permit them to open gambling casinos in unincorporated areas outside Chicago and in those suburbs where they now "own" the police. In most cases, these gambling casinos have been and are being converted by Richard Burns from private dwellings located in or near such places as River Grove and Skokie. (According to information on file, Richard Bernas, with alias Richard Burns, is an old-time Capone gang figure, who handles some of the construction jobs for syndicate members.) Some of the upstairs rooms of the Villa it self are being prepared for gambling "after the election". (This informant dose not know the identity of the candidate for sheriff being backed by the syndicate.)

Other information of police tie-ins with organized gambling is the close association with, and apparent subservience of, sheriff's deputies in the area. One of the sheriff's men is one "Pete" (LNU), a detective assigned to Milwaukee Avenue Sheriff's Station, who is at the Villa at least once every week and obviously is a friend and associated of Giancana and the Meo's.

The Maitre d' of the Villa, known to the informant only as "Louie," knows extremely little regarding the duties of a Maitre d', but the word has gone around that he is the son of one of the better known syndicate hoodlums, who requested that Giancana give his son the job, and Giancana obliged. This "Louie" is a white male of Italian descent, approximately 22-24 years of age of slight build.

"Jack" (LNU), a bartender at the Villa, deals in stolen merchandise. This "Jack" is a white male about 38 years of age, approximately 6'1", has dark hair, and wears a mustache. One of the other bartenders is Sylvester Lachiana, who also is a salesman of Hamms Beer for the Terminal Distributing Company.

VILLA VENICE

2855 MILWAUKEE AVENUE at DESPLAINES RIVER
NORTHBROOK, ILLINOIS

LEhigh 7 - 2300 ● SPring 5 - 3535

Armory Lounge
7427 Roosevelt Road
Forest Park, Illinois

Joseph L. Cortino, Chief of Police, Forest Park, Illinois, advised on September 23, 1958, that the Armory Lounge, 7427 Roosevelt Road, is owned and operated by Carmen "Carmi" Fanelli, but that the property on which the restaurant is located is owned by J. Ammarino. Chief Cortino stated that it had been alleged on many occasions that Giancana and Tony Accardo own the place, but that this is not a fact, unless the ownership is hidden. Chief Cortino commented that he knows Fanelli and Ammarino personally and that he eats at the restaurant occasionally; on these occasions, he stated, he has not seen Giancana, although it is possible that Giancana frequents the place when dining out.

PERSONAL HABITS AND PECULIARITIES

Automobiles and Aliases
By Subject

On June 6, 1957, a 1957 Chevrolet Sports Coupe was sold to one Anthony DeBendo. This sale was made by sales manager George Bond. Bond advised on August 11, 1958, that the Chevrolet was sold by him to Dom "Butch" Blasi, who told Bond to make the sale in the name of Anthony DeBendo. In compliance with this request, the records were made out in the name of DeBendo, but DeBendo never made an appearance and the entire transaction was held by Blasi, with down payment and balance being made in cash. Bond stated he could not recall the reason for Blasi to come to him for cars but vaguely recalled that either Blasi or some other hoodlum was referred to Allen Chevrolet by Frank Colucci, one of the West Side Colucci brothers. Bond stated he has since learned that Blasi used to buy cars for crime syndicate members from Bergl Chevrolet Company before coming to him, but that Blasi had a disagreement with Bergl and discontinued doing business with him. In this conversation, Blasi also had a disagreement with him, Bond, over the price offered for Tony Accardo's 1955 Cadillac on a trade-in, and as of that time, about March 1958, Blasi discontinued buying cars at Allen Chevrolet.

In addition to the above described car, which initiated the purchase of cars from Allen Chevrolet Company by Blasi, the following cars were also ordered by Blasi:

A 1958 Chevrolet Impala sold under the name of "Ralph Fisher," 1356 Forest View Road, Skokie, on November 29, 1957. (Ralph Fisher is a known alias of Rocco Fischetti, same address, who has been under investigation as a top hoodlum of the Chicago Office.)

A 1957 Chevrolet convertible, yellow, sold under the name of Clarice Accardo, but ordered and paid for by Blasi. (Clarice Accardo is the wife of Anthony J. Accardo, top hoodlum of the Chicago Office.)

A 1958 Chevrolet Bel Air Sport Coupe sold on October 3, 1957, to James Meo, and a 1958 Chevrolet Impala was sold to Alfred "Chuck" Meo on November 23, 1957. (James and Alfred Meo, brothers, are known associates of Chicago Crime Syndicate members and are under investigation by the Chicago office.)

In addition to the above, one Frank Gentile, 3101 North Marmora, Chicago, a police officer on the Chicago Police Department, was sent in by Blasi and bought a 1958 Chevrolet Bel Air Sports Sedan. Another police officer, John Matassa, believed to head the Chicago Police Department Censor Bureau, ordered a car which was paid for by Blasi and turned over to Matassa. According to Mr. Bond, all cars purchased by Blasi were paid for with $100 bills, never by check. At the time of the purchases, Blasi gave the following phone number where he could be reached: FO6-9709, this number is the phone number of the Armory Lounge in Forest Park.

Current Efforts to Locate the Subject

It was learned that the subject reportedly had or has an apartment above the Pink Clock Tavern, 7635 Roosevelt Road, Forest Park. Spot surveillances in the vicinity of the Pink Clock Tavern during the last two weeks of July and first three weeks of August were non-productive as to any indications the subject or any members of his family were frequenting and part of this building.

On August 21, 1958, the subjects daughter "Toni" Giancana was observed parked at the Pink Clock Tavern. At 11:50 a.m., Toni Giancana was observed to leave the tavern and enter her car accompanied with a white male. They proceeded from the Pink Clock Tavern to the Maywood Sportsman's Club, approximately three-quarters of a mile north of the junction's highway 20 and 64 in DuPage County. Upon arrival at the Sportsman Club, the subject daughter and her male escort were observed to enter what appeared to be a converted barn. Approximately forty minutes later, they left this building re-entering Giancana's car and returned to the Pink Clock Tavern, where the escort was dropped off and "Toni" Giancana then returned to her own residence.

From examination of the membership list of the Maywood Sportsman Club it was determined that Toni Giancana's escort was Carmen J. Manno, 4346 West Van Buren, Chicago, age 27, and employed as a bartender at the Pink Clock Tavern.

Carmen J. Manno, 4346 West Van Buren, Chicago, advised on September 3, 1958 that he has no knowledge of anyone named Giancana. When questioned as to the identity of the young woman in whose company he was on August 21, 1958, he stated that she was known as to only as "Toni" and that he had meet her about three or four weeks previously when she came into the Pink Clock Tavern accompanied by an unknown male escort. Several days later she appeared at the Maywood Sportsman's Club on a Sunday when a registered shoot, open to the public, was being held. On this occasion, she was accompanied by a white male approximately 30 years of age who she identified as her cousin (James Perno). On the occasion of her next visit to the Pink Clock she remarked to him that she was interested in shooting and he offered to take her with to his gun club. She accepted the invitation and, as a result, he has taken her to the gun club on two or three Thursday afternoons and twice on Wednesday evenings. On each of the Wednesday evenings, he picked her up at her house, located on the Northwest corner of Fillmore and approximately Wenonah in Oak Park. On one of these occasions, he met a girl in her 20's names Kay who was introduced to him as "Toni's" cousin (Katherine Tumminello), and a little old gray-haired lady who "Toni" called "Grandma" on one occasion, "aunt" on another. (Mr. Annie Tumminello). On another occasion, he met a girl about 12 or 13 years old named "Fran" who was introduced to him as "Toni's" younger sister.

Manno explained that he is a bachelor and has looked upon his dates with "Toni" as both female companionship and the enjoying of something of mutual interest, i.e. trap and pistol shooting. Manno explained that he has never had an occasion to ask "Toni" whether her last name is and although he vaguely recalls having heard the name "Giancana" he did not attach this name to her. Manno commented that she has observed that on occasions "Toni" dose not appear to be "all there" as she will make some remarks that has no bearing on the topic of the discussion at the moment. Manno said that he dose not believe that "Toni's" father either lives or visits in the building housing the Pink Clock Tavern and dose not recall having seen him in the Tavern itself. Manno stated that he was employed from February 1954 to October 1954 at Janda's, a lounge just west of the Chateau, in Lyons. From October 1954 to April 1955, he was employed at the Magic Lounge, across the street from the Turf Club in Cicero, and from April to June 1955, he was employed at the Turf Club, Cicero. He remarked that he believes his checks were signed by an individual named Joseph Aiuppa, who is known to him and most people as "Joey O'Brien". (Joey Aiuppa is under investigation by the Chicago office as a top hoodlum.)

86

The following description of Manno was obtained by observation and interview:

Name	Carmen Joseph Manno
Sex	Male
Race	White
Age	28
Birth	August 24, 1930, at Chicago
Height	5'9"1/2
Weight	170 lbs
Hair	Dark Brown
Eyes	Hazel
Completion	Medium
Occupation	Bartender, Pink Clock Tavern, (Since 1958)
Military Service	U.S. Naval Reserves- 2 years, 1955 to 1957

T-11 informant advised on various dates in August that efforts by him to locate the subject have been negative, but that the Senate Select Committee is desirous of locating him to appear as a witness before the Committee during the planned fall hearings. Included in the question to be asked the subjects are those relating to subject's efforts to "muscle in" jukebox operations and set up gambling operations in Kane County, Illinois.

T-10 informant advised on August 17, 1958, that Maureen Smith, an alleged prostitute, is Giancana's current girl friend. He advised that she is currently working as a dice girl and prostitute in a tavern on Higgins Road, which was recently raided by State Police on a vice complaint. (Reports reflect that Anthony Romano was arrested as keeper of a house at 9907 Bryn Mawr, Rosemont.) According to this informant, the subject purchased a 1956 white Cadillac convertible for Maureen and she subsequently gave it to her boy friend, one "Doody" (phonetic) who lives in Hyde Park and is out on bond on a burglary charge in which the Chicago Police Department killed his partner "Black Mike." This information advised that Maureen, a brunette, is 20 years of age, is very good looking, and has a nice figure.

On August 20, 1958, this informant advised that Giancana is presently in Mexico. As a result of numerous physical surveillances during the period August 22 - September 5, 1958, and discussions with the following persons, it was determined that no one fitting the description of aforementioned Maureen Smith was observed in the area of the Drift Bar on Higgins Road and 9903 Bryn Mawr Avenue, Rosemont, a house of prostitution; neither was a Cadillac known to have been used by any occupants of those two places:

Lieutenant William Moffat
Officer Mike Erpino
Officer Charles Klusas
Arthur Sholz, Chief of Police, Rosemont
Mrs. Ruth Sprafka
Michael Schessle
Jodie Gray
Toya Barclay, 9903 Bryn Mawr
Sam Volpendesto, 9903 Bryn Mawr

As the information furnished by the aforementioned persons relates to the existence and whereabouts of Maureen Smith and is not otherwise pertinent to this investigation, details of the interviews are not being set out.

FEDERAL BUREAU OF INVESTIGATION

REPORTING OFFICE	OFFICE OF ORIGIN	DATE	INVESTIGATIVE PERIOD
CHICAGO	CHICAGO	1958	December 30, 1958

TITLE OF CASE	REPORT MADE BY	TYPED BY
SAMUEL M. GIANCANA, aka	Special Agent Frank L. Mellott	dkc
	CHARACTER OF CASE	
	FBI Headquarters File number 92-3171-30 Top Hoodlum Program – Anti Racketeering	

Synopsis:

Information regarding associate, Charles Nicoletti, set out. Allegation subject has financial interest in large motel in Stone Park, Illinois, without foundation. Additional information received to effect subject is actual owner of Villa Venice Lounge and Restaurant, northwest of Chicago. Investigation Las Vegas, Nevada, reflects subject not known to have financial interest in Stardust Hotel or other enterprises that city. Chief investigator Chicago Offices, Illinois Secretary of State, has agreed to initial prospective action against subject if and when it can be established he is using fictitious car registration or drivers license. Informants report subject, along with about 10 or 12 other prominent hoodlums, has part of large scale crap game. On 11/2/58 subject denied true identity to Senate Select Committee investigator who approached him to serve subpoena and efforts by Committee and by Chicago Office FBI to locate subject since that date have been unsuccessful.

Charles Nicoletti, also known as
"Chuck", "Chuckie"
1638 North Broadway
Melrose Park, Illinois

Chicago T-1 informant advised on March 17, 1958, that he had obtained information regarding Charles Nicoletti from a responsible official source to the effect that Nicoletti is an associate of Jake Klein, narcotic distributor in the Midwest. According to this source Charles Nicoletti was arrested with Earnest Sansome in connection with narcotics in the 1940's. At the present time Nicoletti owns two or three supermarkets on the near west side of Chicago and is also known to be a "lay-off" man in connection with gambling activities in the Chicago area.

A report dated December 12, 1955, that the Scotland Yard Detail of the Chicago Police Department raided what they called the biggest floating crap game in the city. Lieutenant Joseph Morris, head of this unit, led the raid on the large black garage in the rear of 936 Laflin Street. Among the 71 men taken into custody was Charles Nicoletti, age 42, 2745 Lexington Street, described as a strong arm man for Sam Giancana.

Under Chicago Police Department number 1426506, a Charles Nicoletti was arrested. An entered date May 13, 1943, reflects that Nicoletti was turned over to the United States Marshal, Chicago, on a narcotic violation. He was removed to Miland, Michigan to serve 18 months. He was conditionally released December 24, 1944. This record also reflects that this individual was arrested on May 14, 1942, on "General Principles" and released by the Chicago Police Department and was also arrested on August 16, 1934, for attempted burglary for which he was sentenced one years probation.

The following is a description of Charles "Chuckie" Nicoletti:

Birth	December 13, 1916
Height	5'10"
Weight	180 lbs
Eyes	Brown
Nationality	Italian- American
FBI #	1426506

As of April 24, 1958, Charles Nicoletti was listed as an ex-convict sentenced for narcotics violation and as an old time Capone figure who is now an assistant of Sam Giancana.

LEGITIMATE ENTERPRISE

American Motel
1800 Mannheim Road
Stone Park, Illinois

It is understood that the American Motel in Stone Park is owned and operated by one Louis Klein, who has a reputation in the Chicago land area for honesty and integrity in his role as developer and builder. It is believed that one Charles Pizzo, 2643 North 73rd Court, Elmwood Park, owns the restaurant adjoining the American Motel. Mr. Klein stated that he dose not know Samuel Giancana and has prided himself on being a law abiding citizen who has had absolutely no known relations with criminal elements.

Charles Pizzo, owner of the County Fair Restaurant, which adjoins the Motel at the southwest intersection of Mannheim Road and North Avenue in Stone Park. Mr. Pizzo stated he knows Sam Giancana to be a prominent hoodlum in the Chicago area who has never approached him nor has he been approached by anyone purporting to represent Giancana.

Villa Venice

CG T-2 informant advised on November 5, 1958, that she frequented the Villa Venice. During which time she has came to know many of the personnel employed at the Villa. According to this informant the real boss of the Villa Venice is Sam Giancana, for when he would appear on the scene everyone would "snap to attention." Giancana would inspect the place and would rarely reprimand any of the staff, including the ostensible owners, James and Stella Meo, if the place or they themselves were not clean.

According to this informant the employees referred to Giancana as being "clean crazy" and his desire for cleanliness was almost an obsession with him. This informant stated that there was no prostitution at the Villa or in the gondolas, although it is possible that sexual activities may have taken place on the gondolas; however, the management did not keep any girls for the express purpose of prostitution.

CRIMINAL ACTIVITIES

Possibility of Prosecution of
Subject for Use of Fraudulent
Driver's license and Car Registration

On November 2, 1958, Richard Sinclair, Senate Select Committee Investigator, reported that while surveilling the subject's residence, for attempting to serve Giancana with a subpoena, he observed a man approximating the subject's description leave the house in a 1958 Ford Thunderbird, registered to his niece. This subject proceeded to the Armory Lounge, a hoodlum hangout about one mile from the subject's house. Mr. Sinclair entered the lounge, approached the individual believed to be Giancana and asked this individual if he was Sam. This individual replied "Sam who?" and was told "Sam Giancana" by Mr. Sinclair. This individual denied being Giancana and furnished an Illinois driver's license with the name "Sano" to substantiate his claim.

Mr. Sinclair stated that due to an element of doubt in his mind as to whether this was actually Giancana, who he had not previously seen, he did not attempt to serve the subpoena and left the lounge. A short time later another investigator arrived on the scene with additional photographs of the subject, at which time Mr. Sinclair stated he was able to positively identify the man seen in the lounge as Sam Giancana; however, by this time Giancana had left the restaurant and a short time later his daughter, Bonnie, arrived and drove away in the Thunderbird left there by the subject when he made his departure with an unidentified man. Mr. Sinclair stated that although he did not make his identity known to Giancana, he believes that his identity has probably been correctly guessed by Giancana, in view of his hasty departure from the lounge.

In view of the above the possibility exists that the subject may be using a fraudulent car registration and driver's license. On November 7, 1958, the above matter was discussed with Captain Ed Devorak, Illinois State Police, Harlem and Irving Park Station, for the purpose of determining what prospective action could be taken against the subject and other criminal elements using fictitious registrations. Captain Devorak expressed the view that he could not recall any instance where any of the hoodlums had been arrested for using a fraudulent registration or driver's license. He stated that in those cases where the persons using such became involved in an accident; if it could be shown that they were at fault they would be charged with a substantive traffic violation but not with violation of using fictitious registration or license. Captain Devorak advised on November 14, 1958, that he had discussed the matter with the Attorney General and on the basis of present statutes, it was the opinion of the Attorney General that there is no charge that could be brought against such individuals without running the risk of possible false arrest if the person arrested were to claim that the car had been loaned to him by another party. Captain Devorak expressed the view that these matters are more properly within the province of the Secretary of State's Office.

Daniel H. Conway, Chief Investigator, Chicago Office, Secretary of State's Office, advised that the matter of fictitious and otherwise fraudulent registration and driver's license is a problem which arises frequently and is usually dealt with by recalling the fictitious car registration or demanding the return of the fictitious driver's license. Mr. Conway stated that it is only in rare instances that prospective action is ever undertaken against these violations. Mr. Conway stated that if it could be definitely established that a particular hoodlum, such as the subject, were using fictitious registration, if alone or in conjunction with the use of a fraudulent driver's license, he would be glad to cooperate with a view to taking provocative action against the subject. Mr. Conway pointed out that due to his limited staff it would be necessary to "set up" a situation so that at a particular time and place one or more of his investigators could stop the subject and establish adequate proof that the car registration was actually fictitious and not merely a car borrowed by the subject from one of his associates who would then "cover" for the subject's use of the car. Mr. Conway also pointed out that while criminals are known to occasionally carry "phony" driver's licenses, they usually have a valid driver's license in their own name.

Gambling

CG T-3 informant advised on October 17, 1958, that Tony Accardo, "Mooney" Giancana, Rocco Fischetti, and Joey Aiuppa are four of the better known Chicago area hoodlums who have a part of the "big game," a large scale floating crap game.

CGT-4 informant advised on October 20, 1958, that most of the top hoodlums in the Chicago area are known to him. This informant pointed out that Accardo is a "big guy" but probably in name only. He explained that "Mooney" Giancana has a lot of power and has put a lot of boys in business and if there were ever a showdown and they started counting noses, Giancana's operation and supporters would far out number that of Accardo. This informant went on to say that he has shot craps in the "big game" in the past and remarked that Accardo, Giancana, and Aiuppa are some of the individuals who own part of this game.

PERSONAL HABITS AND PECULIARITIES

Current Efforts to
Locate the Subject

On October 14, 1958, Toni Giancana was observed parked in front of 4346 West Van Buren, the residence of Carmen Manno, who has been courting Toni. Manno, who appeared cooperative on a previous interview, was contacted after the surveillance was discontinued. He stated that Toni Giancana has stopped by on her way home from the dentist. He stated he considered her a nice and likeable girl and that he intended to keep company with her. He remarked that he wants nothing to do with her father, a good part of whose life has been and will be spent in "running from the law," and, for that matter, neither does Toni have much to do with her father.

Manno stated he was introduced to Sam Giancana for the first time about three weeks ago. Since then he has seen the subject on one or two occasions while visiting Toni but that on these occasions Giancana was either leaving or entering the house and "growled out" a greeting as he passed near. Manno stated that on these occasions Giancana appeared to have dropped off or picked up by someone else, as only cars belonging to other family members or relatives were parked in the driveway or at the curb after Giancana had arrived.

Manno was re-contacted on December 4, 1958, at which time he stated he visits the Giancana's almost every other day to visit or pick up Toni, with whom he is now going steady. Manno stated that for the past three weeks at least, possibly four to five weeks, he has not seen the subject at all and believes the subject must be living elsewhere.

During the period of this report, almost daily spot physical surveillances have been made in the vicinity of the subject's residence and possible hangouts of his. Neither the subject nor any cars known to be used by him were observed.

Information given to the U.S. Senate Committee in 1958 on Sam Giancana. He was investigated for his connections with mob layer Anthony V. Champagne.

Anthony V. Champagne has represented a number of the top echelon Capone gangsters. In April 1945, Sam "Mooney" Giancana, one of the leading Capone gangsters in this area, purchased a home at 1147 Wenonah Avenue, Oak Park, Illinois. A deal was consummated for this property for $22,000. Giancana, in company with his attorney, Anthony V. Champagne, paid $22,000 in cash for the house.

For many years one of the most notorious syndicate gambling places had been known as the Wagon Wheel. Income tax returns of Sam Giancana were examined and they reflected that Sam Giancana had reported income of $98,258.10.10 as his share of the proceeds from the Wagon Wheel during the years 1947, 1948 and 1949. In August 1954 the alternate location for the Wagon Wheel gambling operations was at 6416 Gunnisson. On this building was a sign which read, "Building for Sale, Call Estebrook 8-8834." The telephone number was determined to have been listed to Anthony V. Champagne. This is the same building in which the big syndicate crap game was to open in August 1956 and the same sign was still on the building, referring prospective buyers to Anthony Champagne's telephone number.

On March 31, 1957 Leon Marcus, a banker, was the victim of a gang killing in Chicago. Following his slaying there was found on his body a copy of a receipt which Leon Marcus had given to Sam Giancana, reflecting that Giancana had made a $100,000 payment on a loan of $150,000 which had been made to him by Marcus through the Southmoor Securities Company. This loan apparently was made on the River Road Motel in Schiller Park, a suburb of Chicago. On April 11, 1957 the Chicago Daily News carried a story which stated, "Fast talking Nathan H. Glass Thursday told how he arranged two mortgages on the River Road Motel. The plush Schiller Park Motel's topsy-turvy financial history has intrigued investigation since a receipt found on the body of the slain banker; Leon Marcus linked the banker to hoodlum Sam Giancana. Glass, a mortgage broker, revealed that he arranged both mortgages he handled one for $90,000 and the other for $160,000, at the request of Anthony V. Champagne."

Records of the Cook County Building and Zoning Board reflected that the Southmoor Bank and Trust Company, with which Marcus had been affiliated prior to his death, was acting as trustee for unidentified owner of a River Road Motel. The attorney for the unnamed owners of the motel was identified as Anthony V. Champagne.

As an aftermath of the Marcus gang killing, it was developed that Sam "Mooney" Giancana had been wanted for prosecution of an indictment against him on a gambling charge in 1951. When the indictment was returned a copias for the arrest was issued. However, Giancana was never arrested or brought to trial in connection with the indictment. Anthony V. Champagne was quoted in the Chicago News on April 16, 1957 as stating that he recalled having informed an Assistant State's Attorney that Giancana, who was his client when the indictment was returned, was out of town. Champagne claimed that he informed the prosecutor that if Giancana returned he would be advised to surrender. Champagne then claimed he never saw Giancana again. The Chicago Crime Commission, however, received information that on April 10, 1957 attorney Anthony V. Champagne stated that he aided Sam Giancana in obtaining a passport, and gave information regarding delayed birth certificate on file at the Bureau of Vital Statistics. He later stated that a delayed birth certificate was issued under the name Mo Mo Salvatore Giangana and that Sam Giancana's mother was the first of three wives of Anthony Giancana, who died in 1909 or 1910. This would indicate that Champagne had been actually representing Giancana up to the present time.

On the next few pages is a letter sent to Robert F. Kennedy in 1958 from someone who knew the Giancana family and actually had Giancana's daughter over to her house. She wrote Kennedy exposing Giancana.

1146 So. Wenonah
Oak Park, Ill
August 16, 1958

Dear Mr. Kennedy;

In response to your letter I am happy to know that my information may in some way help your investigation.

It has come to my attention that, since the 31st of July Giancana has been arriving at his home, 1147 Wenonah, several afternoons each week between 5 and 6 P.M.

2

He arrives in a different
car each day, driven
by someone else. He
is driven right up
to the garage but
has to cross the patio
in order to enter the
house. By this time
the gardeners have
left and there is
not usually anyone
around the outside
of the house.

Giancana also
spends considerable
time at the following
two places when he
does not wish to be

located.

River Road Motel
5400 River Road
(He owns the motel.)

Armory Lounge
7427 Roosevelt Rd.
Forest Park, Illinois

He is also partial
or complete owner of
Mea's Villa Venice
and I believe he has
some interest in Mea's
Franklin House. Both
are located near the
motel.

He is (4) also associated with Chuck Lorman and Sam English in their record conterfiting business which operates out of Lorman's Record Shop, Roosevelt Road at Austin Ave, Chicago."

I hope that my information may be of some use to you and your committee. I shall be happy to give you further assistance if so requested as long as our correspondence is kept on a purely confidential basis

(OVER)

in the mail the could
tip off Giancana. Fran
and Andrea have been
taught to notice such
things – Thank you for
your consideration,

I shall remain,

Sincerely yours,
Miss Arlene Locke.

P. S.

Due to the fact
that Giancana's
daughter and neice are
frequent visitors at my
home, it would be
appreciated if further
correspondence to me
could be addressed in
envelopes without the
Senate Committee name in
the return address corner.
If they should see a Senate
marked envelope arrive

UNITED STATES SENATE

85TH CONGRESS - 2ND SESSION

BEFORE THE SELECT COMMITTEE ON IMPROPER ACTIVITIES IN THE LABOR MGMT FIELD

ANNETTE GIANCANA,
1147 S. Wenonah
Oak Park, Illinois,

    Petitioner

To: Hon. John J. McClellan, Chairman
Room 101, Senate Office Building
Washington 25, D. C.

MOTION TO QUASH SUBPOENA

Now comes the witness ANNETTE GIANCANNA, through her counsel, and moves this Committee for an order to quash subpoena herein and as grounds for her motion alleges as follows:

1. Your petitioner is presently incapacitated because of ill - health and in no condition to travel from Oak Park, Illinois, and to testify before the committee, forthwith, as directed.

2. The facts pertaining to your petitioner's condition is substantiated by Dr. William F. Parrilli, M. D., 4753 Broadway, Chicago 40, Illinois, whose remarks in connection therewith are contained in a written statement executed under date of July 14, 1958, which will be exhibited herewith.

WHEREFORE, your petitioner, through her counsel, moves the committee to quash its subpoena, executed on July 3, 1958 by the Hon. John J. McClellan, Chairman, and served upon her in Illinois.

ANNETTE GIANCANNA

By her attorney,

Benedict F. FitzGerald, Jr.
983 National Press Bldg., Washington 4, D. C.
Sterling 3 - 1824

SERVICE

This is to certify that I, Benedict F. FitzGerald, Jr., made service in the following manner: I called James Kelley, investigator in the office of Robert F. Kennedy, Counsel for the Committee, on the telephone on July 14, 1958 at 4:45PM and advised him of the petitioner's condition, and forwarded him a copy of same by United States Mail by mailing him a copy addressed to him at his office in the Senate Office Building

Chapter 3

FEDERAL BUREAU OF INVESTIGATION

REPORTING OFFICE	OFFICE OF ORIGIN	DATE	INVESTIGATIVE PERIOD	
CHICAGO	CHICAGO	1959	March 16, 1959	
TITLE OF CASE		REPORT MADE BY Special Agent Ralph Hill Jr.		TYPED BY dkc
SAMUEL M. GIANCANA, aka		CHARACTER OF CASE FBI Headquarters File number 92-3171-31 Top Hoodlum Program – Anti Racketeering		

Synopsis:

Giancana continues to evade service of a subpoena by the Senate Select Committee. Informants report Giancana is normally at home in Oak Park, Illinois, or in the Oak Park vicinity. One informant reports that Giancana recently left the Chicago area for Miami Beach, Florida, in February 1959. Giancana reportedly in Las Vegas, Nevada in January 1959.

RELATIVES

Chicago T-1 informant advised on February 25, 1959 that Sam Giancana's oldest daughter, Annette, is "wacky" and has suffered a nervous breakdown on three occasions in recent years. Annette is scheduled to be married soon to a boy described by the informant as "quiet and stupid".

Associates

Frank Eulo

An investigation revealed that the residents of 1104 South Maple Avenue, Oak Park, are Frank Eulo and his wife, Rose, and Mike and Betty Sabatino. The name Frank Eulo, 1104 South Maple, Oak Park, was obtained from cards and papers carried by Joseph Profaci, who has been described as the number 1 man among the Sicilians in New York City and the United States. Profaci is a top hoodlum in the New York Office.

Chicago T-2 advised on February 19, 1959, that Frank Eulo, in 1932, was sentenced in Chicago to a term of one year to life under the Habitual Criminal Act and in 1933, was indicted for bank robbery. Eulo was acquitted of the charge of bank robbery in Criminal Court of Chicago in 1934. The informant further advised that it was his understanding that Eulo has a position in the International Brotherhood of Teamsters in New York.

John Matassa

Chicago T-2 informant advised on February 19, that John Matassa, formerly a sergeant with the Chicago Police Department, Narcotics Detail, who is presently assigned to the Chicago Police Department, capacity unknown, is engaged as bodyguard and chauffeur from Giancana and has been seen with him recently in the western suburbs of Chicago.

John Schutin

Chicago T-2 informant advised on February 3, 1959, that John Schutin, formerly a patrolman with the 35th District of the Chicago Police Department and who is now an assistant assigned to under Sheriff Tommy Harrison of the Cook County Sheriff's office, has been seen quite often in company with Giancana. Chicago T-2 advised that it is his belief that Schutin is also a personal bodyguard and liaison between the Cook County Sheriff's office and the Chicago Syndicate.

William Daddono, Also Known as "Willie Potatoes"

Chicago T-3 advised on February 23, 1959, that Giancana and one Willie D. (assumed to be William Daddono), has been seen frequently together during the afternoon periods at the Motor World Hotel, 47th and Laramie Streets, Summit, Illinois.

Charles Nicoletti

Charles Nicoletti had been previously reported as an "up and coming" lieutenant of Giancana and who is slated for a high position in the Syndicate.

Nicoletti was interviewed by SA's Vincent L. Inserra and William Roemer on December 16, 1958, at the Cal-Lex Club, California and Lexington Streets, Chicago, Illinois. Nicoletti stated that his main source of income stem from commissions obtained from car dealers, notably Montgomery Automobile Sales and Denemark Cadillac Agency for referrals given to these agencies by him for new car purchases. Nicoletti stated that he get a new Cadillac every year from the Denmark Agency. Nicoletti said that he works part-time as a potato salesman at an alary of $100 a week but declined to name the produce firm or brokerage with which he is connected. He stated he has an interest in tree supermarkets in the Chicago area but declined to name them. Nicoletti admitted that he had been convicted of a narcotics violation in Federal Court in Chicago approximately 15 years ago for which he served a sentence of 18 months.

He was questioned concerning his relationship with various hoodlums in Chicago among them being Samuel Giancana. Nicoletti did not deny knowing these individuals nor did he admit any relationship with them. Nicoletti further declined to answer any questions regarding known hoodlums with whom he was allegedly associated.

La Donna Vivian Collins

Chicago T-2 advised on February 23, 1959, that he had recently received information to the effect that Giancana's latest paramour is an individual named La Donna Vivian Collins. Miss Collins was described as an attractive female in her late twenties or early thirties with little or no connection with other Syndicate girl friends. SA Ralph Hill, attempted to contact Miss Collins at which time she did not desire to discuss any matter with the FBI without being in the presence of her attorney.

Criminal Activities

Margaret Montello advised SA Hill and Robert Buckingham on February 27, 1959, that she has been paramour and mistress of Jeff Manno, one of the notorious Manno brothers, for approximately 13 years. She said that although she is not acquainted with Giancana personally, she has heard through Manno that Giancana was slated to be the number one man in the Chicago Syndicate and was described as a close mouth vicious killer and a person whose influence is unquestioned in the Chicago Midwest area. *(Attached to the file is a Chicago Tribune Newspaper article dated February 22, 1959. Current Efforts to Locate Subject.)*

Physical surveillances have been conducted on January 12, and February 13 at the Armory Lounge and Mike Fish's Restaurant on Ontario Street with negative results.

Chicago T-2 informant advised that he heard from various sources that Mooney Giancana plays poker at Salerno Funeral Parlor, 6300 West North Avenue, Chicago, during the evening hours. He allegedly holds infrequent meetings during daylight hours at the Villa Venice. Giancana allegedly maintains a lavish apartment on the second floor of the building where the Pink Clock Lounge is located and apparently spends a great deal of time in this apartment.

It is to be noted that the Salerno Funeral Parlor is a very large undertaking establishment and wakes are held there nightly and it has been observed that there are usually from 50 to 100 cars parked in the vicinity and in the parking lot.

Physical observation of the Pink Clock Lounge revealed that there is one and possibly two apartments located in this building and that the only name on the mailbox is that of G.S. Miller. Contacts at the Pink Clock Lounge are not considered at this time as being feasible in that the Pink Clock Lounge is owned by one Carmen Tumminello, known associate of Giancana, and the bartender is Giancana's future son-in-law, Carmen Manno, who has been contacted on previous occasions and whose reliability is very questionable.

During the winter months the Villa Venice Restaurant is closed to the public except on Fridays, Saturday, and Sunday evenings. The physical lay-out and location of the Villa Venice is such as to preclude a successful surveillance.

Chicago T-5 informant advised that Giancana is at home on most occasions and conducts his business in the usual manner. He can be seen during the dinner hours at the Armory Lounge, and takes nightly walks around the block at his home.

Chicago T-6 advised that top hoodlums who have been sought by the Senate Rackets Committee have hidden out in the past at a resort known as "The Nest" located near Fox Lake, Illinois. This resort is owned and operated by one Cannatta, a crooked political figure who owns a tavern on West Madison Street in Chicago. Informant was unable to advise whether or not Giancana was one of these persons visiting "The Nets."

Informant T-7 advised on February 6, 1959 that Giancana visits the Galewood Barber Shop located at 6954 West North Avenue on an average of once per week. The informant noted that the shop is operated by a relative of Giancana.

TRAVEL

Chicago T-9 advised on February 13, 1959, that he had learned that Giancana and either Joe Caesar or Joey O'Brien had departed from Florida during the weekend of February 8, 1959. He assumed they would be in Miami Beach, a hangout frequented by many Chicago hoodlums. It should be noted that Joe Caesar is an alias of Joe DiVarco, a Chicago top hoodlum and Joey O'Brien is an alias of Joseph Aiuppa, a Chicago top hoodlum.

FEDERAL BUREAU OF INVESTIGATION

REPORTING OFFICE	OFFICE OF ORIGIN	DATE	INVESTIGATIVE PERIOD	
CHICAGO	CHICAGO	1959	May 14, 1959	
TITLE OF CASE		REPORT MADE BY		TYPED BY
		Special Agent Ralph Hill Jr.		dkc
SAMUEL M. GIANCANA, aka		**CHARACTER OF CASE**		
		FBI Headquarters File number 92-3171-33 Top Hoodlum Program – Anti Racketeering		

Synopsis:

Giancana served with subpoena by Deputy U.S. Marshal, Las Vegas, Nevada, 3/25/59, to appear before Senate Select Committee. Giancana scheduled to appear before this committee during the first week of June, 1959, Giancana gave lavish reception at LaSalle Hotel, Chicago, on 4/4/59 for wedding of daughter, Antoinette, to Carmen Manno. Giancana interviewed at reception by "Chicago Tribune" reporter, spoke views on Syndicate, ex-convicts, and Senate Committee. Giancana allegedly attended gangland meeting held at Miami Beach, Florida, during later part of March, 1959, with Anthony Accardo, and New York, Philadelphia, and Miami hoodlums. Giancana allegedly has taken over Local 110, of the Movie Operator's Union, replacing the now deceased Claude "Screwy" Maddox.

ASSOCIATES

Chicago T-1 advised on April 5, 1959, that the following individuals either attended the wedding reception of Antoinette Giancana, or had been extended invitations to attend. Wedding held at LaSalle Hotel, Chicago. The following named individuals are all well known hoodlums in the Chicago area:

Anthony Accardo	Benny Fillichio
Joseph Aiuppa	Joe Glimco
Felix Alderisio	John Lardino
Gus Alex	Murray Humphreys
Louis Briatta	Rocco Potenzo
Sam Battaglia	Ralph Pierce
Marshall Caifano	Rocco Paternoster
John Cimitle	Charles Nicoletti
William Daddano	Nick Palermo
Joseph DiVarco	Tony Ricci
Frank Ferraro	Joe Fischetti

In addition to the above individuals, the following individuals, who are either on the fringe of Chicago hoodlums or are well known Chicago politicians, were in attendance:

Bernard Glickman
Anthony V. Champagne, Attorney
Richard Gorman, Former Assistant United States Attorney

Pat Marcy, Political
James Adducci, Politician
Michael Brodkin, Attorney

Attached is the Chicago Tribune newspaper interview by Sandy Smith, dated April 4, 1959.

The Miami Office advised by letter dated April 28, 1959, that there was no registration contained at the Thunderbird Motel, Sunny Isles, Florida, under the name of either Anthony Accardo or Sam Giancana, during the months of March or April, 1959.

However, there was a listing of a Miss Marie Accardo (daughter of Anthony Accardo) of 915 Franklin, River Forest, Illinois, was registered as a guest at the hotel from March 9 to March 28, 1959. Miss Accardo was accompanied by one June Elwert, from Chicago.

The Miami Office advised that during the month of March, 1959, the following named hoodlums were residing in the Sunny Isles, Florida, area, at the motels indicated:

Carlo Gambino, Top hoodlum, New York Division, Golden Gate Motel
Anthony Carfano, Top Hoodlum, Cleveland Division, Golden Nugget Motel
Max Weisberg, Top Hoodlum, Philadelphia Division, Golden Nugget Motel
James Plumeri, Top Hoodlum, New York Division, Surfside, Florida resident
Thomas Greco, Top Hoodlum, New York Division, Suez Motel

It is to be noted that the Miami Office advised that Joseph Pischetti and Anthony Ricci are permanent residents in the Miami Beach area, rather than the Thunderbird Motel.

Chicago T-1 was re-contacted regarding the information previously furnished, at which time he stated that a check of his source indicated the possibility that Giancana and Accardo may have stayed at the Dunes Motel in the Miami Beach area, rather than the Thunderbird Motel.

Chicago T-1 advised on May 11, 1959, that the following situation was revealed to him in Springfield, Illinois:

Anthony J. DeTolve, 1038 Sangamon Street, Chicago, an Illinois State Senator, recently introduced a bill into the State Legislature of Illinois providing for the revocation of a State Law which empowers the Secretary of State for Illinois to revoke Illinois Drivers Licenses on the basis of out-of-state convictions for drunken driving. This bill was killed in community by State Senators Thomas McGloon and Bernard S. Neistien, both of Chicago.

Several days thereafter, McGloon, Neistien, and several others were in the dinning room of either the Abe Lincoln or the St. Nicholas Hotel in Springfield and were approached by Senator DeTolve, who was apparently enraged at having his bill quashed. DeTolve told McGloon that, "He (McGloon) would get the word like the others had."

It is noted that DeTolve is a nephew of Michael and James DeTolve, brother-in-law of Sam Giancana. According to the informant, after DeTolve left, Neistien told McGloon that he, Neistien, had received a telephone call several days previous at his hotel, and the voice at the other end said, "This is Sam Mooney. Do you know who I am?" And then said, "Leave my brother-in-law alone and tell all those other guys to leave him alone or else."

LABOR UNION ACTIVITIES

Chicago T-1 advised that he had recently learned that Sam Giancana had taken over Local 110 of the Movie Operators Projectors Union, after the death of Claude

Moore, also known as Claude "Screwey" Maddox. In this connection, it is noted that the following individuals are known to be members of this union:

Sam Aiuppa, Brother of Joseph Aiuppa
John Accardo, Brother of Tony Accardo
Anthony Accardo Jr., Son of Tony Accardo
Charles Giancana, Brother of Sam Giancana

Chicago T-1 said that at this time he had no further details regarding Giancana's association with this union, but expected to gain more information in the near future.

CURRENT FRIENDS

Chicago T-1 advised on April 10, 1959, that he has recently learned that Sam Giancana's paramour is Keeley Smith, wife of Louis Prima, of the well known night-club team of Keeley Smith and Louis Prima. In this connection, it is noted that Chicago T-1 said he had heard from various sources that Prima is "connected" with the Chicago syndicate and for that reason had agreed to play dates at the Chez Paree Night Club in Chicago, for a figure far below that of his average salary, and does so because of the fact that he is partially owned by the syndicate.

FEDERAL BUREAU OF INVESTIGATION

REPORTING OFFICE	OFFICE OF ORIGIN	DATE	INVESTIGATIVE PERIOD
CHICAGO	CHICAGO	1959	June 30, 1959

TITLE OF CASE	REPORT MADE BY	TYPED BY
SAMUEL M. GIANCANA, aka	Special Agent Ralph Hill Jr.	dkc
	CHARACTER OF CASE FBI Headquarters File number 92-3171-36 Top Hoodlum Program – Anti Racketeering	

Synopsis:

Giancana appeared before Senate Select Committee June 9, 1959, and invoked the Fifth Amendment. Senate Committee testimony linked Giancana to Gary, Indiana vice as "absentee commander-in-chief," with John Formosa and Anthony Pinelli. Giancana traveled to Mexico City in 6/11/59, returned to Chicago 6/15/59, and was stopped by U.S. Customs Service in Chicago. Subsequent search of Giancana's personal effects by Customs agents revealed numerous names and telephone numbers. Chicago informant states that Giancana and others presently engaged in attempts to corner bail bond business in Chicago and 5 other large U.S. cities, suggests possibility that purpose of Giancana's visit to Mexico City may have been in furtherance of this plan.

Labor Union Activities

It was previously reported that Sam Giancana had taken over Local 110 of the Movie Projectionists Union after the death of Claude Moore, also known as "Screwy" Maddox.

On June 10, 1959, George Hall, employed as projectionist, wood Theater, Randolph and Dearborn Streets, Chicago, was interviewed by SA's Ralph R. Hill, Jr., and William F. Roemer Jr., concerning the possibility of Sam Giancana's being connected with Local 110. It is noted that T-1 informant had been advised by Hall previously that this local was under the control and influence of Murray Humphreys and / or Sam Giancana. According to T-1, Hall had run for office of business agent of Local 110 against Clarence Jalas, incumbent, unsuccessfully. Hall advised T-1 that his defeat was due to the fact that Humphreys, through Giancana, had managed to swing the vote of the local to Jalas' favor. Hall also advised the information that Jalas had received upwards of $1,500 per year each from certain members of the union in return for favors, such as being allowed to work on choice locations or to work two jobs. Hall advised the informant that the following individuals with hoodlum connections are members of Local 110.

      John Sortino, brother of Frank Ferraro.
      Tony Martin, brother-in-law of Tony Accardo.
      Joe Coscione, former chauffeur for Frank Nitti.
      (FUN) Gioe, brother of Charles "Cherry Nose" Gioe, deceased.
      Morton Weiss, brother of Hymie Weiss.
      John Maritote, brother of Frank Diamond.
      Augie and Tony Circella, brothers of Nick Circella, also known as Nick Dean.
      Frank DeLandi, brother-in-law of Frank Nitti.
      Stanley D'Andrea, brother of Phil D'Andrea.
      The Gigante brothers, brothers-in-law of Paul "The Waiter" Ricca.
      Rocco Eulo, associate of Sam Giancana.
      Alan and Hyman Bioff, brothers of Willy Bioff, deceased.
      William "Red" Campbell, collector of Tony Accardo.
      Sam Aiuppa, brother of Joseph Aiuppa.
      John Accardo, brother of Anthony Accardo.
      Anthony Ross Accardo, son of Tony Accardo.
      Charles Giancana, brother of Sam Giancana.

Hall advised the interviewing agents that he has been a movie projectionist for over 25 years and was at one time close to Eugene Atkinson, former business agent for local 110, now deceased. Hall said that in the 1930's, the hoodlum element in Chicago was interested in moving into the movie projectionist trades, so they set up a school to train operators to replace the operators then in the union. When Atkinson discovered this, he conspired with Hall to blow up the school. Atkinson purchased the dynamite and formulated the plans, but the plot was discovered before it was carried out. Hall advised that he remained silent, was convicted and sentenced to five years in the Illinois State Penitentiary. Hall was discharged in 1939, rejoined the union, which at that time was headed by Atkinson, and became Atkinson's confidant. Atkinson died in 1958, and left an estate valued in the excess of $500,000. In November 1958, Hall and Jalas, who had temporarily replaced Atkinson, were in competition for the election to the office of business agent for Local 110. Hall stated that he had the job virtually sewn up, but Jalas torpedoed him by bringing up the point with the international that he, Hall, was an ex-convict and was, therefore, not qualified for the job. This was brought out at a union meeting held in November, 1958, at which time Hall states that he called Jalas a conniving (Deleted). Joe Montana, hoodlum and close friend of Hall and godfather to Hall's child, was present at this meeting and became so distraught that he subsequently suffered a stroke and at this point is totally disabled. As a result of the meeting, the election was extended until March, 1959, and during the interim, Jalas somehow managed to swing the vote to his, Jalas', favor by convincing the members that he would get them higher wages, better job and better working conditions. Jalas was elected as business agent and is now negotiating a "status quo" contract with the theater owners, which

107

means no wage increase. Hall said that he has no proof of extortion on the part of Jalas in negotiating this contract with the owners, but pointed out that the contract would affect the savings of over $200,000 to them.

Hall said that as far as he knows there is no hoodlum control over Local 110, and said that in fact Jalas wants nothing to do with the hoodlums and dislikes them intensely. It was pointed out to Hall that many hoodlums have close relatives in the local, to whom he replied that these individuals have been with the local for many years and merely indicates that the hoodlums desire their close relatives to be in a legitimate occupation so as to cause them no embarrassment. Hall states that Jalas dose no special favors for them, but merely tolerates them as members of the local.

Hall discounted information that influence was exerted on the local by the late Claude Moore, but said that he had heard that Moore had been the power behind the union but was unable to substantiate this information. Hall said that he had heard some rumors to the effect that Murray Humphreys or Giancana had taken control of the union, but discounted these rumors.

The inconsistency of Hall's remarks were pointed out to T-1, who advised that Hall was obviously lying, and said that he would attempt to gain more substantial information from Hall regarding the information previously furnished.

Travel

Mr. James Bruner, United States Customs Agent advised SA Hill on June 15, that Sam Giancana had arrived at Midway Airport from Mexico City in the early morning. Giancana was searched by Customs personnel at Chicago's Midway Airport upon arrival and no contraband material was found. However, Giancana had in his possession an Illinois driver's license made out to Frank DiSanto, 3436 West Adams, Chicago. Giancana was questioned regarding this driver's license and advised Mr. Bruner that he had "borrowed it," and had no further explanation.

Giancana had a hotel bill in his possession marked paid, from the El Presidente Hotel, Mexico City, registered as Mr. & Mrs. Sam Giancana. Mr. Bruner said that Giancana, who was unaccompanied, stated that he had been there alone. Mr. Bruner said that he did not ascertain how much money Giancana had in his possession, but merely saw a wad of $100 bills and a wad of $50 bills.

Mr. Bruner temporarily confiscated an address book and pieces of paper and notes from Giancana, which are set forth as follows. It is noted that the addresses are being set forth according to various field divisions and not according to their exact sequence in the address book.

Los Angeles Division

Barbara	Cal OL2-1778
Hone	012-5895
Keeley Smith	9488 554 Bar Baraway
Sinatra	Office 5-4977
Home	Crestview 4-7848
Texas	Crestview 4-7848
Shirley Petering	542 San Pablo
Virginia Jumer	OL 4-6394
Hollywood 46	9020 Wonderland Avenue

Business card of Richard L. Mandl, Manager
Thomas Cook and Son, Travel Service
9359 Wilshire Boulevard, Beverly Hills

Miami Division

Lynn Giedrick   Franklin 3-9340
                                 720 Northeast, 26th Street Apartment 205, Miami

Business card of Harry Moss, Jeweler, Eden Roc
Hotel, Miami Beach, Florida, Jefferson 2-2034

Union 6-0287   Tony Goble (believed to be Ricci)

A note stating flight 104 arrived 2:20 Eastern Thursday leaves 11:30 Fisher.
It should be noted that the Fisher as appears in the note may be identical to Joe
Fischetti, who is known to use the alias of Fisher.

New York Division

Beverly   Yonkers, New York
                                 7-2524

Salt Lake City Division

John Drew   2-6122 home

This is believed to be the number, Dunes 2-6122, as John Drew is known to reside
in the Las Vegas area.

Las Vegas

Peter, Ed, Charlie, Janice
This note appeared in Giancana's address under the letter S.

Chicago Division

Easterbrook 9-4412 Home   OR 5-5069 Office BI7-4174-2239
Graceland 7-4459   Barbara
Bittersweet 8-8412   Steve's
Barbara   Austin 7-2917
Connie   Bishop 7-9960
Forest 9-6260   Darline
Hickory 7-7784   Green
Frankie Hart   7-91547
Hump   Esterbrook 8-0301
Jean   Village 8-0301
VA 4-0315   Marie Singer
Nick   Haymarket 1-8680
Morning before noon1   -5459
Eastgate 7-2327   Toddo
Fillmore 5-4128   Violet

The following are business cards and various notes in Giancana's possession:

Note from the Park-Mor Motel, 3800 River Road, contained the following notes:

Hotels in Mexico
EL-Presidente
Acapulco
Pierre-Marcues
La-Perla

Restaurants
Villa-Fontana
Folkolare
Hacaranda
La-Fuente   afro   Astoria

Piece of paper containing the following names and notation and the names they are believed to be:

Gus 2	Gus Alex, Chicago top hoodlum.
Frank 2	Frank Ferraro, lieutenant of Gus Alex.
Paul 2	Paul Ricca, Chicago Top Hoodlum.
Joe 2	Joey Aiuppa or Joe Batters, Chicago top hoodlums.
Rocky 2	Rocky Potenzo, lieutenant of Giancana.
LaPort 2	Frank LaPorte, lieutenant of Tony Accardo and syndicate representative in Calumet City, Indiana.
Curry 2	Francis Curry, coin machine representative for Giancana in the Joliet, Illinois.
Sam Battaglia 2	Syndicate representative for West Side.
English 2	Chuckie English, owner of Lor-Mar Distributing Company and former business partner of Giancana in horse book activities.
Sam Alex 2	Brother of Gus Alex and Chicago hoodlum.
Big AL 2	Big Al Polizzi.
Ross Prio 2	Ross Prio, Chicago top hoodlum and Northwest Side syndicate representative.
Jackie 2	Jackie Cerone, Chicago hoodlum.
John D'Arco 2	Chicago city alderman and representing First Ward
Buddy Jacobson 2	Buddy Jacobson, associate of John D'Arco.
Butch 2	Butch Leydon, associate and chauffeur for Gus Alex and Eddie Vogel.
Potizie 2	
Hyman Furst 1	Owner of Furst and Frust Collection Agency believed to be Collectors for Chicago's bookmakers.
Buddy 2	
Fiffie 2	Fiffie is Joe Corngold, syndicate representative for Cicero and lieutenant of Giancana.
Hump 2	Murray Humphreys, Chicago top hoodlum.
Eddie 2	Eddie Vogel, syndicate representative for the coin machine industry in the Chicago area.
Brodkin 2	Mike Brodkin, syndicate lawyer and partner in the firm of Bieber and Brodkin.
Formosa 2	John Formosa, mentioned earlier in this report as vice over lord in Gary, Indiana.
Nick DiMarco	Unknown
Glickman	
Mar's	Mars is the Mars Oldsmobile Company of Chicago.
Champ	Unknown

Business cards and notes containing the names of the following bondsmen were noted:

The Summit Fidelity and Surety Company,
1135-37 South State Street
Chicago, Illinois
Irwin's Weiner, Branch Manager.
Harrison 7-2848
Victory 2-1250

Eddie Morris
Paddy Cerone
Tony Horton
Drexel Bonding Company.

The following other notes and business cards were in Giancana's possession:

Stuart J. Barnes, Editor
"Mexican American Review"
"The Sales Executive"
Apartado 21975
This card bore the penciled notation of 13-47-22.

Maison Cye, Shirt maker
37 West 57th Street
New York
Plaza 8-0610

David B. Trott   Morris R. DeWoskin
Attorney at Law   Executive House
1 North La Salle Street   71 East Wacker Drivers
Chicago   Chicago

Kathy Steele   Janus Beer Sales
20 East Delaware Place   1901 West Cermak
                                  Broadview, Illinois
                                  Bill Facchini

Miscellaneous

Attempt to Corner Bail Bond Business

On June 17, 1959, Chicago T-2 informant was interviewed at the Criminal Court Building, 2600 South California, by SA's William F. Roemer, Jr. and Paul B. Frankfust.

Chicago T-2 stated he did not know Sam Giancana personally and would not know him if he saw him. He states he dose know him by reputation. He did not know who had given his name to Giancana, but thought an explanation for it might be that at about 10:00 a.m. last Monday, June 15, 1959, he was stopped in the hall of the Criminal Court Building by (Name Deleted). He stated he understood that he was not getting along too well with surety companies he writes bonds with. He said there was a company coming into town which is out of Indianapolis and that "Mooney" was interested in it and Mooney had given him his name. He said (Name Deleted) had mentioned the name of the bonding company he was interested in and said it sounded like United Bonding Company or a name similar to it. The Informant related that he knew who "Mooney" was and who Brodkin represents and further that he, himself, is on a friendly business basis with

111

(blacked out) and (blacked out), who are some of the leading bondsmen in the city and he is aware that they have connections with the outfit. He thought because of his association with these people his name might have been recommended as a person to bring in to represent the colored interests on the south side. Chicago T-2 said he told (blacked out) that he was getting along with him all right with his present companies, but that he was always open to a good proposition.

He said after his initial conversation with (blacked out) he called (blacked out) company, Indianapolis, which company he represents and with whom he is a close friend. He said (blacked out) told him that he heard of the company which (blacked out) had mentioned to him and said that the outfit was behind this company in Indianapolis where a man named (blacked out) was operating it, and that the company was no good. He further state that a hoodlum in Cleveland also had the agency for this company there, but he did not know his name.

Chicago T-2 stated he has given this matter considerable thought and that knowing that the outfit controls certain judges and that there are powerful people behind this operation, he did not fell that he could flatly turn down the invitation to join up with this new company, especially when he knew who was behind it. He said that he had talked to (blacked out) yesterday and had told him that he wanted to stay in business and did not want any "moth" to grow on him in the new company if he thought it was a good thing to do. He felt, therefore, that within the next month or so he very well could be writing bonds for a company that is apparently being backed by the outfit.

Chicago T-2 further remarked that since the bail bond scandal broke a new association of bondsmen has been formed with the purpose of forming certain policies to be followed in the future in a effort to eliminate chicanery on part of bondsmen as well as city officials. Officers in this association are Irv Weiner, President, Ed Morris, Secretary, and Tony Horton as Treasurer.

Chicago T-2 believes that since the outfit is behind this new company they are attempting to freeze out a majority of the other bondsmen and take over the bonding business in other larger cities as well. He said that if Irv Weiner, Pat Cerone, Ed Morris and Tony Horton were to associate themselves with new company, they could sew up ninety percent of the bonding business in Chicago. He further stated that if they had a majority of bonding business in five of the larger cities they would be able to take $15,000 per week out of the business.

Chicago T-2 further inquired as to the present status of Ed and George Jones, former policy wheel operators on the south side, who are now in Mexico City, Mexico. He said he wondered about their present connections with the outfit as he understands when anyone from the syndicate goes to Mexico he finds out that generally they have visited with Ed Johns before they return. He further stated that the son of an Italian hoodlum, whose name he cannot recall, has spent some time with Ed Jones in Mexico. He also advised he had learned that Jones had been to Switzerland on frequent occasions, but dose not know for what reason. He commented that he is also on friendly terms with (blacked out) and knows his wife, and they have been together socially, and he speculated that if Giancana had been to Mexico he possibly could have been in contact with (blacked out) could have given his name to Giancana and possibly have recommended him in this bail bond venture.

Chicago T-3 advised SA's Ralph Hill Jr. and Paul Frankfurt on June 23, 1959, that a new bonding company is being formed in Indianapolis, Indiana, named the United Public Insurance Company, headed by (FNU) Schloss. The General Manager is Jim (O.J.) Helburn or Hilburn. Their address is 108 East Washington Street, Indianapolis. Until recently, this company has engaged almost exclusively in automobile insurance, but about a month or two ago, the company applied to the United States Treasury Department for a Federal Qualification to write bonds in Federal Court. The United Public Company was formed in 1955, with a capital of approximately $500,000. They have suffered heavy losses every year, and during the year 1958 ended with a net loss of $216,000.

After obtaining a state license in Indiana to write bonds in local and state courts, Bob Smith, who had been field representative for Michigan Surety Company for bail bonds, went to Cleveland, and with Dominick Lenardo, formed the Trans American Surety Company, which is to be the general agency for the United Public with exclusive rights nationwide over the bail bond business of this company. Other officers of Trans American are Lou Brady (possibly Louis P. Brady, Cleveland and Miami, Florida hoodlum) and Don Plitzer.

According to the informant, the Trans American Company is completely backed by "the outfit" and has aspirations of cornering the bail bonds business in Chicago, Detroit, Miami, Cleveland, Indianapolis, and East St. Louis. Representatives in those cities are to be Eddie Morris and Irv Weiner, Chicago; Pete Lacovoli, Detroit; "Tuffy" Mitchell, Indianapolis; Moses Massau, Miami; and an unknown Italian hoodlum for East St. Louis.

According to Chicago T-3 informant, the normal procedure for most bail bonds companies is to receive a minimum of ten dollars per one thousand dollars of bonds written. (from the agency), the United Public is making arrangements whereby the Trans American agents had to pay the United States Public only five dollars per thousand. In this matter, the smaller companies will be forced out of business, and the larger agencies, foreseeing a larger profit, will join Trans American. When Trans American has accomplished this end, and thus hopes to control the lions' share of the business.

AIR TEL, AIR MAIL
Date: 7-4-59
To: Director, FBI
From: SAC, Miami
Subject: Sam Giancana, Top Hoodlum Program

Bonita (Bonnie Lou) Giancana, daughter of subject, married Anthony Tisci, 7-4-59, at St. Patrick's Church, Miami Beach, Florida. Tisci is son of Anthony T. Tisci, Secretary to Congressman Roland Libonati from Illinois. Wedding reception held at Fountain bleau Hotel, Miami Beach, Florida. Ralph DiCostanzo, gambler, formerly from Chicago, now resides Miami, Florida, attended reception. No known top hoodlums Miami area observed at wedding reception. Daniel Sullivan, Operating Manager, Crime Commission, Greater Miami, advised he received information Frank Sinatra and Dean Martin, actors, flew in to Miami from west coast for wedding.

FEDERAL BUREAU OF INVESTIGATION

REPORTING OFFICE	OFFICE OF ORIGIN	DATE	INVESTIGATIVE PERIOD	
CHICAGO	CHICAGO	1959	August 18, 1959	
TITLE OF CASE		**REPORT MADE BY**		**TYPED BY**
				dkc
SAMUEL M. GIANCANA, aka		**CHARACTER OF CASE**		
		FBI Headquarters File number 92-3171-38 Top Hoodlum Program – Anti Racketeering		

On 8/3/59 the reception Manager of the Hotel El Presidente, Mexico, Arturo Funes advised that Sam Giancana had occupied Suite 413 at the hotel from 6/11/59 to 6/14/59. Funes stated that he could not recall Giancana and had no information as to the reason for his trip to Mexico City. Giancana's registration card reflected their permanent residence address of 1147 South Wenonah, Oak Park, Illinois.

On 8/13/59 Stuart Barns, the editor of the magazine "Mexican-American Review" and "The Sales Executive," advised that he edits the above-mentioned publications for the American Chamber of commerce in Mexico, with offices at Plaza Santos Degollado 10. Barns advised that by name he dose not recall Sam or Samuel Giancana but related that about the middle of June he had attended a breakfast meeting at a hotel in Mexico with a "gangster-type individual" from Chicago whose sole interest in Mexico appears to be gambling operations of any type.

Barns related that he is associated with a Mexican citizen named Jorge M. Isaac in attempting to establish near Mexico City a Disneyland-type recreation facility which will be known as "City of Shows," and in view of their need for several million dollars in capital for the venture they had been referred in a casual manner to the Chicago investor, who advised them that he would only invest money in an operation if it involved gambling. The explained to him that the only gambling which might occur at the recreation facility would be bingo games in connection with which prizes would be given, and while he indicated some interest in that activity Barns and Isaac, became of his general attitude, held no further conversations with him. Barns subsequently advised that following consultation with his partner, Jorge Isaac, he had ascertained that the Chicago investor had been introduced to them as Bill Scali and that a person in Mexico City who might know more about Scali is one Robert Molliter, who edits a weekly tourist newspaper.

Barns described Scali as follows:

Name	Bill Scali
Age	50-52 born approx: 1907-1909
Height	5'7"
Weight	150 pounds
Build	Slender
Hair	Dark Brown or Black
Eyes	Unknown
Completion	Dark
Characteristics	Wears horn-rim glasses, speaks broken English with what appears to be an Italian accent.

Barnes claimed to be unable to furnish any additional information concerning the activities in Mexico of the individual described above.

FEDERAL BUREAU OF INVESTIGATION

REPORTING OFFICE	OFFICE OF ORIGIN	DATE	INVESTIGATIVE PERIOD	
CHICAGO	CHICAGO	1959	August 25, 1959	
TITLE OF CASE		REPORT MADE BY		TYPED BY
		Special Agent Ralph Hill Jr.		dkc
SAMUEL M. GIANCANA, aka		CHARACTER OF CASE		
		FBI Headquarters File number 92-3171-39 Top Hoodlum Program – Anti Racketeering		

Synopsis:

Chicago informant states that Giancana is on his way out as leader of the Chicago syndicate and is to be replaced by William "Willie Potatoes" Daddono. This information refused by another Chicago informant who states that Giancana presided over a meeting of Chicago syndicate members held on 7/31/59. During this meeting Giancana stated that they had brought a tobacco distributing company and he was going to San Francisco on August 7, 1959, to confer with a person from Honolulu who would "set them up" with cigarette companies. Rocco Potenzo, underling of Giancana, reported on 8/11/59, that Lake County, Illinois gambling is dead. Potenzo has purchased the Corsica Restaurant, the Vegas Motel, and a gambling spot, all in Niles, Illinois. Giancana advised Frank LaPorte, syndicate reprehensive of South Cook, to "get busy" with opening spots in Calumet Park and Calumet City, Illinois. Persons whose names and / or telephone numbers appeared in Giancana's address book were contact with unproductive results. Bonnie Lou Giancana, daughter of subject, was married at Miami Beach, Florida on July 4, 1959, to Anthony Tisci.

Associates

John D'Arco

On July 21, 1959, SA's John Roberts and William Roemer contacted John D'Arco, Alderman, First Ward, City of Chicago, at 100 North LaSalle Street. D'Arco was advised that his name appeared in the possession of Sam Giancana on June 15, 1959. D'Arco merely commented that "a lot of people carry my name around and I can't be responsible for what it means."

He was asked as to whether he was acquainted with Giancana and replied that he had known Giancana in his youth but had not seen him for a long time and dose not associate with Giancana. D'Arco had no further comment to make regarding Giancana.

Louis Stevens

Miss Louis S. Stevens, employed as supervisor, Claims Department, Prudence Life Insurance Company, Chicago, advised SA Ralph Hill Jr. that she had known Sam Giancana for less that one year, having met him "through a friend." She last saw him sometime in May, 1959 and stated that this acquaintanceship was purely on a social basis. And she is not acquainted with Giancana's personal life or means of livelihood. Miss Stevens was very uncooperative and advised SA Hill that she did not desire to discuss the matter any further. It is noted that the telephone number of Miss Stevens appeared in the address book of Giancana, which was found on his person by Customs agents in Chicago on June 15, 1959.

Ralph Becker

Mrs. Ralph Becker advised that she did not know any Giancana and was not acquainted with him. She was unable to explain the appearance of her telephone number in Giancana's address book.

Anita Kollar

Miss Anita Kollar, advised SA Hill that she has dated Giancana on three or four occasions and that her last meeting with him was "several months ago." She said she knew nothing of Giancana's personal life but had heard that he was a "racketeer"; however, she said that Giancana had always behaved like a gentleman in her presence, and she had heard no bad reports concerning his personal life or habits. Miss Kollar was reluctant to discuss anything concerning discussions she and Giancana had, nor would she name any of the places that she went to with Giancana.

Telephone number Filmore 5-4128, which appeared in Giancana's address book with the notation "Violet," is listed to Leo Guardino, 1215 Division, Melrose Park, Illinois. Loe Guardino is a known burglar and a top jewel thief to the Chicago Division. An attempt was made on July 12, 1959, to make contact at the Guardino residence, at which time SA Hill was advised by the occupant of this residence that she did not care to discuss any matter with the FBI.

Listed in the book as "Darline", is Darline Kaliboda, a paramour of Fred DelGeino and Peter Kokenis, 1216 South Austin, Cicero. DelGeino and Kokenis are known jewel thieves and burglars of the Chicago Division. Attempts were made to contact Miss Kaliboda with negative results.

CRIMINAL ACTIVITIES

Chicago T-1 informant advised SA Hill on July 21, 1959, that he had ascertained from an unnamed individual who had "connections with the Chicago crime syndicate" that the following situation exists with the Chicago crime syndicate pertaining to Sam Giancana and others:

The Chicago syndicate hierarchy contains two top positions, the most prominent being that of "The Man." He is comparable to the Chairman of the Board of a large corporation. Directly beneath this position is that of "The Boss." Analogous to this position is that of president of a corporation. "The man" is the overseer and policy maker for the outfit, and the "Boss" carried out his directives. Prior to 1955, the man was Louis "Little New York" Campagna. Upon his death, Paul "The Waiter" Ricca assumed this position. Upon Ricca's semi-retirement, Sam Giancana moved in and took over both positions of "The Man" and "The Boss." From 1952 to 1957 the position was of "The Boss" was held by Anthony "Tough Tony" Capezio, and upon his death by Tony Accardo. Giancana forced Accardo into semi-retirement and assumed the reins of the syndicate. The informant said that as a supposition, one can be "The Man" only if one holds Mafia connections. Accardo was not a member of the Mafia, and therefore was "Boss" and subservient to the directives of "The Man." Accardo it is said stepped down when Giancana moved in, because "when you have a man like Mooney Giancana at your back, you either get out or you die." One reason for Accardo's forced retirement was that he was not anxious to push into new fields of investment for the Chicago syndicate.

Giancana, in his position as overseer, holds court at a place in Cicero during the day, where he gives orders and makes decisions. He is described as a chain cigar smoker, has a volatile personality, breaks out into giggles at unexpected moments, and his orders are curt and to the point. A simple "Yes" or "No" usually suffices. In his position as head of the Chicago syndicate, Giancana controls some five million dollars for investment purposes. According to the informant, among these investments are the All American Motels, the Caravan Motel, and others, unnamed.

According to Chicago T-1, a development had recently occurred which has made Giancana's position untenable. William "Willie Potatoes" Daddono is taking over the syndicate, and Giancana is being forced out. One reason for this, according to the informant, is that Giancana has been embarrassing the syndicate with his off the cuff remarks, his excessive drinking and partying and lavish weddings. Daddono ironically has been Giancana's representative and muscle in the outlying suburbs, such as Kane, Will, and Lakes Counties. Daddono is described as a vicious, unreasoning, and sadistic killer, who enjoys torturing his victims by burning them. According to the Chicago files, Daddono had been described in 1957 as a possible replacement for Sam Giancana in the syndicate. He was a prime suspect in the killing of Salvatore Moretti in 1957. Moretti's body when discovered showed signs of being subjected to cigarette burns.

According to Chicago T-1, when Giancana steps down, he is to assume the position presently occupied by Joey Aiuppa in Cicero. Aiuppa will be allowed to hold certain locations but will not be allowed to expand.

Chicago T-1 further stated that as corroboration for the above information, he, the informant, had a conversation with Joe Bulger in the latter's office at 188 West Randolph Street, Chicago, on July 21, 1959. It is noted that Bulger is described as a syndicate lawyer and was a co-defendant with Paul Ricca in the latter's income tax evasion trial, which resulted in the conviction of Ricca. Bulger advised the informant of the following facts:

The "young turks" are taking over the Chicago syndicate. These men are William Daddono, Marshall Caifano, Phil Alderisio, Jack Cerone, Sam Battaglia, Obbie Frabotta, and Joe Gagliano. According to Bulger, Giancana is unable to control these individuals described as being wild and unreasoning. Giancana, Accardo, and other older members of the syndicate, therefore, are out of the picture. According to Bulger, they have succumbed to pressure both from the Government and from within the organization.

Chicago T-2 advised on July 30, 1959, that Sam Giancana presided over a meeting held in Chicago on that day. Attended by Frank LaPorte, syndicate representative for Southern Cook County; Al Pilotto, lieutenant and body guard of LaPorte; Frank "Strongy" Ferraro, lieutenant of Gus Alex, Chicago top hoodlum; and others, unknown. This meeting was apparently for the purpose of discussing the situation in Southern Cook County with regard to gambling, police payoffs, and possible fields for investment in legitimate enterprises.

LaPorte advised that the Corral Club, a gambling establishment in Calumet Park, had been closed by the raids from the Sheriff's police so that the Corral Club was going to be moved to a place in Calumet City. LaPorte further advised Giancana that they had a word on another gambling place near the Corral Club in Calumet Park, which was located in a garage. The individual who owned the garage was a bit reluctant to lease the space for a gambling operation, but he was "convinced" by Babe Tuffenelli that if he didn't lease the space for an operation, he would be in trouble. LaPorte estimated that it would cost from $6,000 to $8,000 to make this spot ready for an operation but expected no difficulty in starting a large scale gambling operation in that establishment.

"A Chicago Daily news article dated August 8, 1959 is attached to this file at this spot concerning gambling raids."

Chicago T-2 continued with a report on the meeting held May 30, 1959, by stating that Frank LaPorte had contacted the Chief of Police in Calumet City, at which time LaPorte told the Chief that he would be behind the Chief "a trillion percent," that anytime anybody would come "he (LaPorte) would know before him (the Chief)." LaPorte said that he was then going to arrange a meeting between the Chief in Calumet City, Captain McDonagh of the Sheriff's Police, and Captain Jacobs of the State Police so that they would all get acquainted, work together, and "if they have to make a pinch in one of those spots, they can get together so they don't get hurt; otherwise, one man makes a pinch, they might cross one another."

LaPorte further advised that he has a nephew named Allucci who was with Irv Weiner in the bonding business in Calumet City and said that Allucci told him (LaPorte) that he had had an offer from a person named Memerovski to get Weiner and go with him in the bonding business, LaPorte identified Memerovski as the head of the Lake State Insurance Company in Chicago and said that he intended to write bonds with the United Bonding Company in Indianapolis. Giancana told LaPorte to tell his nephew to stay with Weiner.

It is to be noted that report of SA Hill at Chicago dated June 30, 1959, reflects that Giancana was interested in the United Bonding Company of Indianapolis and there was some indication that this company was Outfit connected and would be headed in Chicago by Irv Weiner.

Chicago T-2 then advised that LaPorte knew of an individual who was working for the Sanitary District in Stickney, Illinois, who wanted LaPorte to have Chesrow or someone with the Sanitary Board contacted in order for this individual to get a better job. Giancana advised LaPorte that his (Giancana's) nephew worked for the Sanitary District and that he was never satisfied. Giancana intimated that he and others in the Outfit had obtained jobs for individuals in the Sanitary District and that they were always asking for better jobs. Giancana told LaPorte to tell this person that he would work on it.

Chicago T-1 said that Giancana had been in contact with Moe (LNU) recently. Moe asked Giancana if "we knew anyone named Peazza?" Giancana advised Moe that at that time he did know of a Peazza whom he thought was "working for us" but found out that it is another Peazza from Harvey who was beaten up and robbed of $500. Moe desired to know the identity of the person who held up Peazza so that he could be "interrogated a little bit."

In this connection it is noted that when Giancana was searched by Customs agents on June 15, 1959, he had on his person a written note containing the words "the fellow's name is Peazza from Chicago Heights, regards of Holda."

Chicago T-2 advised on August 11, 1959, that Rocco "Rocky" Potenzo was complaining to Jimmy Celano, Dave Yaras, Hy Godfrey, and others, unidentified, that the authorities in Lake County, Illinois, were closing down all of his gambling establishments. (At this point, it should be noted that Potenzo has been described as Giancana's lieutenant for syndicate activities in northwest Cook County and Lake County, Illinois.) Rocky advised that under sheriff Tommy Harrison of Cook County Police was unable to render any assistance in this regard because of the fact that his (Potenzo's) troubles were emanating in Lake County and in Cook County. Potenzo advised the group that he had a new restaurant called Corsica, the Vegas Motel, and a gambling joint all together at 9000 Milwaukee Avenue, Niles, Illinois.

Potenzo advised Frank (either LaPorte or Ferraro) and Dave Yaras that Lake County was down "real tight," and he was unable to go even in a "sneak spot." Potenzo described a meeting he had with an individual named Ridi who is apparently acquainted with Lake County law enforcement authorities. This individual told Potenzo that he didn't want anything going in Lake County and that included bingo games, bowl games, or anything. Ridi told Potenzo that he was on orders from his boss, and Potenzo replied "well, I'm on orders from my boss, too." Potenzo then told this individual that he has a spot eight miles from his present location, and he never had any complaints. Ridi then told Potenzo that the Chief of Police in Wheeling, Illinois is friendly with Louis (LNU). Potenzo announced to the group "I'm gonna get a joint if I have to open up in a picnic grove, and if they come, I'll go over to the city side." Potenzo said that his new place was in the red, and he needs the money.

LEGITIMATE ENTERPRISES

Chicago T-2 informant stated on July 30, 1959, that Frank LaPorte reported to Giancana that Babe Tuffenelli, through one Manny Smerling, was interested in some 250 cigarette machines located in Elgin, Illinois. The company presently holding these machines is named the Modern Vending Company of Elgin. The owners of the company, who were a man and wife, now divorced, had 500 machines, and the wife desired to sell her share of approximately 250 machines. Tuffenelli, through LaPorte, desired to know if "somebody's trying to get somebody out, and if so, Babe would tell the guy to laid off and leave the thing alone." Giancana evinced some interest in this information and desired to know more particulars pertaining to the operation. Giancana then told Hy Godfrey to inquire through Eddie Vogel (Chicago Top Hoodlum) as to weather or not Eddie had any interest in Elgin. Godfrey advised Giancana that he would ascertain from Vogel, Francis Curry, Black Joe Amato, and William Daddano as to whether or not these individuals maintained any interest in Elgin or DuPage County.

Giancana then advised the group that "we" own tobacco distributing company and have been trying to get direct connections with cigarette companies. Giancana indicated that they had trouble getting the stamp from the State, and after they finally obtained that, they "got on with one company" but indicated that the rest of the companies didn't want to do business with him.

Giancana said that he was going to meet an individual from Hawaii who told Giancana that he would "straighten them up" with all cigarette companies, and Giancana said that he was going to meet this individual in San Francisco on August 7, 1959. Giancana then said that he thought that they could do good business and make some money with this company. He said "maybe we can supply that guy in Elgin."

It is to be noted that Chicago T-2 reported that in a meeting held between Tony Accardo and Gus Alex on August 3, 1959, Tony Accardo advised Alex that he was meeting "a Chinaman" from Honolulu on August 12, 1959, at the Desert Inn, Las Vegas, Nevada. Accardo described this individual as a powerhouse in Honolulu who "does a lot of things with the State."

The Honolulu office advised by radiogram that Kan Jung Luke is president of Loyalty Enterprises, Limited, is an accountant, and has represented Martin Jerome Bromley, top hoodlum of the Honolulu office. Bromley does business as the Coast Cigarette Venders, Los Angeles, California.

The Salt Lake City Office advised that on August 10, 1959, that Kan Jung Luke had reservations at the Desert Inn, Las Vegas, Nevada, for August 12, 1959.

Chicago T-2 stated that Frank Ferraro and Gus Alex held a meeting in Chicago on August 8, 1959, with "Dom (LNU) and (Pete) LNU for the purpose of discussing the formation of the Trans American Surety Company and the possibility of having Irv Weiner brought into it. Ferraro advised them that he would take the matter into discussion but that the final decision would rest with Sam Giancana, who at that time was in Las Vegas.

"Dom" asked Ferraro to have Weiner send him an abstract of the latest Illinois laws governing the bail bond business. "Dom" then indicated that they were opening offices in Philadelphia, Des Moines, Miami, Indianapolis, and Las Vegas.

After "Dom" and "Pete" left, Alex indicated to Ferraro that it would be much better if the Chicago group took over the bonding business rather than allow "that bunch from Cleveland" into it. Ferraro argued that the Trans American Company was already formed and has numerous accounts. At any rate, they (Chicago) were "getting a piece of it" and would ultimately gain total control.

MISCELLANEOUS

It is to be noted that SA Hill maintained a spot surveillance on the residence of Giancana, 1147 South Wenonah, Oak Park, and reported no activity, nor was Giancana presence indicated. As indicated by informants and telephone calls, Giancana appears to be on a constant travel status between the West Coast, Las Vegas, and Miami, Florida, with occasional stopovers in New York City. Neighbors report that they rarely see Giancana and there may be periods of two or three months when he dose not make an appearance in the neighborhood.

Chicago T-3 advised on July 20, 1959, that Giancana, when he is in town, can usually be found during the evening hours at the Armory Lounge at 7441 West Roosevelt Road, Forest Park. The informant stated that there appears to be congregations of hoodlums at the Armory during the evening hours of Tuesday and Friday nights.

Surveillance was maintained on the Armory Lounge by SA's Hill, Roemer, and Roberts on July 21, 1959, from 6:30 P.M. through 10:00 P.M. During that period, individuals identified as Phil Alderisio, Obbie Frabotta, and several unknown individuals were observed entering and departing this restaurant, but Giancana was not observed. It is noted, however, that license number 715962, registered to R. Flood, 5962 West Adams, was seen parked in the lot adjacent to the Armory Lounge.

FEDERAL BUREAU OF INVESTIGATION

REPORTING OFFICE	OFFICE OF ORIGIN	DATE	INVESTIGATIVE PERIOD	
CHICAGO	CHICAGO	1959	October 21, 1959	
TITLE OF CASE		REPORT MADE BY		TYPED BY
		Special Agent Ralph Hill Jr.		dkc
SAMUEL M. GIANCANA, aka		CHARACTER OF CASE		
		FBI Headquarters File number 92-3171-40 Top Hoodlum Program – Anti Racketeering		

Synopsis:

The title of this case is changed to reflect the additional aliases of Sam Flood and John DeSantos. Sam Giancana and Anthony Accardo held a conference in Chicago on 9/8/59 at which time it was disclosed that Giancana is a member of a 12 man "Commission" which appears to be interstate in character and is composed of nationally known hoodlums namely Joe Profaci, Vito Genovese, Thomas Luchese, Joe Zerilli, Joseph Bonnan-

120

no, Steve Magaddino, and John LaRocca. Giancana has spent time recently apparently in furtherance of syndicate activity, on the East Coast, West Coast and Las Vegas. Giancana appeared before the Special Federal Grand Jury, Chicago on 10/5, 6, and 7/59 allegedly concerning hoodlum control of Rush Street night spots in Chicago.

ASSOCIATES

Frank Sinatra

Giancana, upon being searched by Customs Agents at Midway Airport in Chicago on June 15, 1959, had in his possession an address book which contained, among other things, the telephone number Crestview 4-2368 with the name "Sinatra". The Los Angeles Division advised that CG T-1 informant stated that this is the telephone number of Frank Sinatra, 2666 Bmont Drive, Los Angeles which is a non-published number.

CG T-2 advised on September 24, 1959, that at that time Giancana had been in Las Vegas for two to three weeks and had introduced Frank Sinatra to Barbara Grocke at the Sands Hotel. Sinatra was in Las Vegas at that time for a night club appearance.

CG T-3 advised on September 9, 1959, that Giancana had been in Atlantic City, New Jersey apparently during the later part of July or early August, 1959.

The Newark Division advised by Airtel dated September 18, 1959, that investigation at the Claridge Hotel, Atlantic City, New Jersey revealed that the Sinatra party rented the entire first floor of this hotel consisting of ten bedrooms and three parlors from July 25, 1959 to August 2, 1959. The only records of occupants besides Sinatra were his valet; Bob Wagner and Natalie Wood, prominent Hollywood stars, and Sam Kahn, prominent song writer.

The New York Division advised that Joe Fischetti and several other hoodlums were in Frank Sinatra's suite in Atlantic City, New Jersey during Sinatra's engagement at the 500 Club during August, 1959. Information stated that in addition to Fischetti were Jack Entratta from Las Vegas, "Skinny" D'Amato, owner of the 500 Club, and several other individuals who appeared to be hoodlums. CG T-4 advised that it is common knowledge that Fischetti and Sinatra are close friends and that Sinatra has a "hoodlum complex."

CG T-5 advised on September 18, 1959, that Sinatra enjoys surrounding himself with hoodlums and in the informant's opinion; Sinatra would give up his show business prominence to be a hoodlum himself if he had the courage to do so.

Keeley Smith

CG T-2 advised on September 4, 1959, that Giancana is a paramour of Keeley Smith of the noted comedy-song team of Keeley Smith and Louis Prima. The informant advised that Prima is aware of this arrangement, but is helpless to do anything about it. It should be noted that during the search by Customs Agents of Giancana on June 15, 1959, Giancana's address book reflected the name and address of Keeley Smith.

CRIMINAL ACTIVITIES

Chicago T-3 advised on September 8, 1959, that Sam Giancana and Anthony Accardo were in attendance at a conference on that date during which they discussed the crime syndicate picture on a nationwide basis. Giancana said that he had recently been to the East Coast for the purpose of apparently solidifying his position with the East Coast syndicate leaders in an attempt to take command of the syndicate activities properly in the Las Vegas, Nevada and Southwest area. Giancana mentioned that he had made four appointments to see Vito Genovese but that Vito was busy. Giancana then met with Tommy Brown, true name Thomas Luchese, in New York and was somewhat disgusted with these meetings in that Luchese insisted upon bringing up "Jimmy" with him during these meetings. Giancana indicated that most of these conferences were held in Atlantic City, New Jersey. According to Giancana, Genovese had been making trips outside of New York City to Buffalo, Tucson, Arizona, and other places. Genovese made these trips with out the sanction or knowledge at the time of his constituents which contributed toward displeasing both Giancana and Luchese. Accardo told Giancana that a situation like that described by him always exists particularly in the East Coast. Giancana indicated that Joe Bonnanno had gone to Tucson and made his son the boss in the Tucson area so that anyone who goes to the Southwest part of the United States must go to Bonnanno regardless of the reason for being in that area.

It was decided that Bonnanno had no business, claming to be the absolute authority in that section and it was agreed by both Accardo and Giancana that that particular area is "open territory."

Accardo surmised that Bannanno's reason for settling in Tucson lay in the fact that this world put him in a better position to move in on Las Vegas. Accardo told Giancana that he, Giancana, was in a good position because of the fact that the "commission" was increased to 12 individuals as that Giancana needs seven votes for majority and six votes for standoff. Accardo and Giancana said that the following individuals among others are on this "commission":

Thomas Luchese	Steve Magaddino
Joe Bonnanno	Joe Zerrilli (Detroit)
Vito Genovese	Joe Profaci
Raymond (LNU) (Boston)	John LaRocca (Pittsburgh)

Accardo said that at one time the "commission" used to be composed of Profaci, Genovese, Luchese, Joe Ida (Philadelphia), Steve Magaddino, Peter Magaddino, and Accardo.

Giancana said that Joe Ida was in all probability no longer on the "commission" and that there is a vacancy in Philadelphia and discussed the possibility of Dominic (LNU) taking over. Giancana said that in all probability Dominic had backed out because of the fact that this involved too much pressure. The Philadelphia Office advised on September 15, 1959, that Joseph Ida, New Brunswick, New Jersey, rules Italian racketeers in Southern New Jersey and Philadelphia, along with Dominic Olivette, Ida, however, as of March, 1959, had gone to Italy for an extended visit. The Pittsburgh Office advised that Sebastian John LaRocca, Pittsburgh top hoodlum, was in attendance at the Appalachian meeting during November, 1957, and disappeared shortly thereafter. LaRocca returned to Pittsburgh during February, 1959, and presently resides at Ingomar, Pennsylvania.

The New York Office advised on September 23, 1959, that the Jimmy (LNU) referred to as a companion of Luchese is possibly James Napolitano, also known as "Jimmy Nap", former Brooklyn gambler now working in Atlantic City, New Jersey. Jimmy (LNU) could possibly be Vincent Alo, also known as "Jimmy Blue Eyes", New York top hoodlum who is prominent in East Harlem, New York hoodlum activities.

Thomas Luchese and Joseph Profaci are top hoodlums of the New York Office and Vito Genovese, another top hoodlum, is presently out on $150,000 bail concerning a United States Bureau of Narcotics Case.

The Detroit Office advised on October 6, 1959, that Joseph Zerilli is referred to as one of the Judges, peacemakers, or elder statesmen among the Italian gambling syndicate in Detroit. Zerilli is regarded as a final arbiter in disputes among the syndicate members and has been credited with establishing the policy under which the syndicate operates in Detroit. It is noted that Zerilli's son, Anthony Zerilli, is married to Rosalie Profaci, the daughter of Joseph Profaci of Brooklyn, New York, mentioned as one of the members of the "commission."

Chicago T-8 informant advised on August 5, 1959, that Sam Giancana is stated to be the "big boss" and is a member of the top echelon of syndicate crime in Chicago.

GAMBLING

Chicago T-3 informant advised on September 8, 1959 that Giancana was very much perturbed over the Viaduct Lounge in Cicero, Illinois, which has been raided by the States Attorney's Office for Cook County on September 7, 1959. The Viaduct Lounge is regarded as the location of the largest dice game and gambling operation in the Chicago area. The nightly revenue of this establishment runs into the many thousands dollars. During the above described raid States Attorney's Police arrested Rocco Fischetti, Taiquin "Queenie" Simonelli (brother-in-law of Tony Accardo) and Lester "Killer Kane" Kruse as operators of this establishment. Giancana said that he would take drastic measures of retaliation for this raid and mentioned that he would do his best to see that John Stamos, Assistant States Attorney in charges of this raid, is fired.

Political Tie INS with Organized Crime

Chicago T-3 informant advised that Joseph Lohman, former sheriff of Cook County and now state treasurer for Illinois, had been trying to get in touch with Giancana recently for reasons unknown. It was decided that Giancana should attempt to arrange some sort of meeting with Lohman with the possibility in mind of giving Lohman assistance in his quest for forthcoming Democratic Gubernatorial College for the State of Illinois. Accardo and Giancana according to the informant were discussing other possibilities of the next governor for Illinois and mentioned Eddie Barrett, but discounted Otto Kerner because of the fact that Jack Arvey would not want to put him in that position. It was generally agreed, however, that unless the Democratic Party is harmonious the possibility exists that the incumbent Governor William Stratton will be elected for a third term.

Hoodlums "Muscling" of Legitimate Business

Chicago T-3 informant advised that Sam Giancana, Frank "Strongy" Ferraro, and James Celano, among others, held a meeting in Chicago on that date regarding beer distributorship, presently owned by John Fredericks, in which considerable hoodlum money is invested. Among these investors are Celano, Frank LaPorte, and John Drew, a Las Vegas hoodlum formerly from Chicago and now the alleged owner of the Stardust Hotel in Las Vegas. Celano was upset over the financial condition of this distributorship and said that a group of lawyers headed by Angelo Geokaris and John Tomares were interested in buying out Fredericks but that they wanted Fredericks to go into involuntary bankruptcy in federal court. This would involve an investigation and it would disclose that Celano, ET AL, had heavy investments in this enterprise, which would cause considerable embarrassment to all concerned. Celano requested permission from Giancana to approach John Tomares and threaten him with death unless he, Tomares, and Geokaris reconsidered their position; Giancana gave Celano permission to do so and said that he would send William "Willie Potatoes" Daddono over to hear Geokaris.

MISCELLANEOUS

"Attached here is a Chicago Sun Times newspaper article dated October 6, 1959 concerning Sam Giancana's Federal Grand Jury appearance."

FEDERAL BUREAU OF INVESTIGATION

REPORTING OFFICE	OFFICE OF ORIGIN	DATE	INVESTIGATIVE PERIOD	
CHICAGO	CHICAGO	1959	December 28, 1959	
TITLE OF CASE		REPORT MADE BY		TYPED BY
		Special Agent Ralph Hill Jr.		dkc
SAMUEL M. GIANCANA, aka		CHARACTER OF CASE		
		FBI Headquarters File number 92-3171-40 Top Hoodlum Program – Anti Racketeering		

Synopsis:

Sam Giancana in attendance at meeting of Chicago hoodlums held in Chicago in October and December, 1959, and adjudicated on matters of policy. Other members in attendance were Murray Humphreys and Frank Ferraro. Chicago informant states Giancana had acquired an agency known as World Wide Actor's Agency. Giancana fines $100 and coast on 12/6/59, for possession of a fraudulent driver's license, in Chicago.

ASSOCIATES

The information contained in this section should not be construed to indicate all known associates of Giancana. It should be noted that Giancana is known to have associates with most Chicago's known "hoodlums" and the following names of individuals contained in this section are those associates of Giancana who are more or less closely aligned with him and his activities by virtue of their "business" relationships.

Gus Alex
4300 Marine Drive, Chicago

Chicago T-5 advised that Sam Giancana and Gus Alex, together with other lesser "hoodlums", such as Hy Godfrey and Frank Ferraro, meet for lunch in a private dining room located on the second floor of Mike's Fish Restaurant on East Ontario Street, Chicago, about once or twice a week. The informant suggested these meetings were at that time in all probability connected with Chicago gambling activities. Gus Alex is highly placed in the Chicago syndicate and in this connection was placed in charge of the syndicate's activities in the Chicago's Loop section.

Sam Battaglia, also known as "Teetz"
1114 North Ridgeland, Oak Park

The name Sam Battaglia was among those appearing on the list of handwritten names found in Giancana's possession upon his search by Customs agents in June, 1959. Chicago T-3 advised that Sam Battaglia had been intimately acquainted with Paul "The Waiter" Ricca as an enforcer for the syndicate. He was a former member of the old "42 Gang" and in 1945 was investigated for the murder of Alex Chase, a Hammond, Indiana hoodlum.

Chicago T-3 advised that it was his understanding that Sam Battaglia was among those who, with Sam Giancana, were taking over the "Chicago Syndicate" from the people described by the informant as the "older heads" and in this connection, Battaglia was to take command of the western suburb activities.

Richard Bernas, Also known as
Dick Burns
5368 Oakton, Skokie

On January 16, 1958, an Oldsmobile was seen parked in the driveway of the Giancana residence registered at that time to Richard Bernas. Richard Bernas, also known as Dick Burna and Dick Burns, was a very close friend of Matthew Capone, brother of Al Capone, and was at the time employed at the Deerfield Country Club, described as a plush gambling casino in Lake County, Illinois.

Frank Sinatra

Chicago T-1 informant advised on November 24, 1959, that Giancana has taken over the organization known as World Wide Actors Agency which is an agency booking and managing theatrical and night club talent. Among his clientele is allegedly Frank Sinatra. It has been previously reported that Sinatra, a well known star of night clubs, television and movies, is a close associate of Giancana.

Chicago T-1 advised that Sam Giancana new paramour is Marilyn Miller who is on the chorus line at the Chez Paree night club in Chicago. T-1 stated that Giancana has planned to place Miss Miller as the hostess in a night club in Los Angeles, California area; however the name of this establishment at this time is unknown.

Nicholas "Peanuts" Danolfo
Las Vegas, Nevada

Chicago T-23 informant advised that Nick "Peanuts" Danolfo, Pit Boss, Wilbur Clark's Desert Inn Hotel, Las Vegas, met with Sam Flood at the Desert Inn Hotel on August 12, 1959. On October 19, 1959, Danolfo placed a telephone call from the Casino of the Desert Inn Hotel on the behalf of Sam Flood to Beverly Hills, California.

Phyllis McGuire

Chicago T-36 advised that he had reason to become aware of the fact that Phyllis McGuire of the well known singing team of the "McGuire Sisters" had become romantically involved with an individual known to the informant as Sam Flood from Chicago and it was determined later by the informant that the individual known to him as Sam Flood was in actuality Sam Giancana. It was learned that Giancana had rented a home outside Las Vegas and that each night following the McGuire Sisters' appearance Giancana had a car pick up Phyllis McGuire and take her to a house outside of Las Vegas provided by the Ashcraft Realty firm. Also staying in this house in addition to Phyllis McGuire was one or two of Giancana's daughters and possibly another female relative of Giancana's. The informant believed that in the view of this apparent close relationship, the possibility exists that Giancana and Phyllis McGuire may be seriously considering an attempt at marriage. The informant continued that when Giancana made contact with Phyllis McGuire at the Desert Inn Hotel in Las Vegas these contacts were made through the Desert Inn pit boss Nicholas Danolfo; also know as "Peanuts." The informant said that Danolfo is probably one of Giancana's main representatives at the Desert Inn.

Nick Vallo

Chicago T-1 stated that Sonny King, who at that time was appearing as a singer at the Chez Pare night club, was escorted around Chicago by Giancana and all of King's bills including his account at the Drake Hotel were taken care of by Giancana. The informant advised that apparently King is another of Giancana's clientele in World Wide Actors Agency.

Criminal Activities

Chicago T-2 informant advised that on October 15, 1959, a conference was held on that date of Chicago syndicate hoodlums which was attended by, among others, Sam Giancana, Murray Humphreys and Frank Ferraro. Ferraro advised the group that the Cook County States Attorney's Office, through Paul Newey, was making preparations to indict some local officials. Ferraro said that this was probably due to the informants of the FBI and said further that Newey had previously been with the FBI. (Paul Newey, Chief Investigator for the State's Attorney's Office, was formerly an agent for the Federal Bureau of Narcotics). Ferraro contained that he advised Les Trilla that if any official gets indicted, he, Trilla, was going to be responsible. Les Trilla, who owns and operates a cooperage company in Chicago, is the contact man between the Chicago syndicate and the States Attorney's office. Ferraro asked Giancana how he "made out with Tommy Brown" and said "was it all right, same amount." Giancana replied affirmative to this question and then continued by stating that he had told Tony Accardo that Vito (Genovese) has been on the side of the Chicago syndicate.

It has been previously reported that Giancana made a trip to the East Coast at which time he made contact with Tommy Brown, also known as Thomas Luchese, New York top hoodlum and Vito Genovese.

Murray Humphreys then announced that he had recently been East and reported on the case involving Eugene C. James and Louis Saperstein who were under indictment in New Jersey for Labor Extortion. The purpose of this conversation was to ascertain where a certain individual lives on the East Coast and that apparent meaning of this was that there is an individual in that area who has either testified concerning some matter or who is going to testify. Humphreys was desirous of ascertaining this individual's present whereabouts.

Ferraro announced that Les Trilla is having Buddy Jacobson meet at 22nd and Washington with Frank Ferlic and then said that "Jacobson, Trilla, Munizzo and Adamowski, sat down and made a deal. You should get these guys and pinpoint them to find out about all this (obscenity)." Frank Ferlic is First Assistant to State Attorney Benjamin J. Adamowski. Buddy Jacobson is Secretary to Chicago's First Ward Alderman John

D'Arco. Thomas B. Munizzo, a trucking company operator, has been described as a liaison between the Chicago Syndicate and the Mayor's Office.

Ferraro then mentioned obtaining the services of Captain Frank Papa of the Chicago Police Department and placing him as Community Officer of the Central Police District in Chicago. Ferraro stated that D'Arco called Frank Papa about this job and Pape called back and told D'Arco that he did not want it. That afternoon, according to Ferraro, the Mayor got a hold of D'Arco and purposed Frank Papa for this position. The result of this conference was, according to Ferraro, that Frank Papa was installed as new Police Captain of the First or Central Police District in Chicago.

Throughout the above described meeting Giancana appeared to be the final authority involving any matters which may have come up and his answer, whether they were in the negative or the affirmative, were accepted without question.

Chicago T-2 advised that Murray Humphreys and Sam Battaglia held a discussion on that date regarding a recent request from Sonny Capone, son of the late Al Capone, for some $25,000. Humphreys exhibited a letter which he intended to send to Capone which states as follows:

Dear Sonny,

I am in receipt of your letter of October 30, 1959, showing a breakdown of your expenditures of $10,000 plus $5,000 for the doctor and others. This matter has been taken up with the interested parties and rejected. Give my best to your mother.

Yours as ever,
Murray

Humphreys said that the amount requested from Sonny Capone represents that amount that Capone lost in his business in Miami plus doctor fees and others for a woman that Capone "got in trouble with down there." Humphreys said that he had conferred about this situation with, among others, Gus Alex, Frank Ferraro, and Sam Giancana. Giancana voted "absolutely not" on this request.

Chicago T-2 advised that Murray Humphreys and Sam Battaglia held a discussion relating to syndicate meeting places and Humphreys said "The danger in the spot, is putting too much confidence in the operators. Frankie is the one who dose that. I think that you should give the operators more money like $20.00 a month rather then only $5.00 a month because if you want people on your side, you have to give them something. At one time we used the numbers system for meeting spots like 1, 2, 3, and 4, and then we would change back and forth among ourselves, and Sam "Mooney" Giancana would come up to me and say now this month is going to be such and such and so then would change the numbers."

Chicago T-2 advised that a meeting of syndicate hoodlums was held on that date in Chicago and was attended by Frank Ferraro, Sam Giancana, and Rip, (Gus Alex). One of the matters taken up on the agenda was a situation involving a gambling operation in Cicero known as the MGM Lounge which is purportedly operated by Nick Kokinas. Rip advised the group that there was a disagreement in this establishment and the question has come up as to whether or not Koklinas should be put out by a brother of Sam Battaglia. Kokinas was offered only $1,500 to be put out and apparently was unhappy about that satiation. Giancana advised Rip to "tell that Greek to take the $1,500 and get out of there."

"Attached here is a Chicago Sun Times article dated November 6, 1959 concerning Gian-cana."

Miscellaneous

Lloyd Bell, under sheriff, Clark County Sheriff's Office, Las Vegas, Nevada, advised that Sam Giancana is considered as persona non grata in Las Vegas and this if he returns to Las Vegas; he will be thrown in jail on vagrancy charges.

Position of Giancana In
Chicago Underworld Activities

According to Chicago T-4, Anthony Accardo was the top man in the Chicago area and that the sometimes voiced belief that he has retired is wrong. According to this source, Sam Giancana was final arbitrator of all matters of organizational interest. In addition, Giancana was responsible for the entire Chicago area, the authority to allocated "district" and to place these districts under the control of certain men whom he chooses.

Chicago T-4 stated that these "district men" were required to pay a certain sum of money each month to Giancana, who, in turn, turned over a certain sum to Accardo. The district men are allowed rather wide latitude in the means they exercise to raise the money and any money they make in excess of the amount payable to Giancana may be counted as their profit. The informant pointed out these payments must be made promptly and in cash, and failure to meet these obligations are generally deemed to be a fatal mistake. This informant pointed out that the principal thing that the "Syndicate" has to sell is protection. For examples, protection from police action and protection from other hoodlums. The informant noted the fact that gambling is protected from police action and this inevitable gives rise to other criminal activity, such as prostitution, narcotics and fencing. The informant pointed out that if the police are compromised in one activity, there is a certain reluctance to act in another direction. The informant stated that the district man is under considerable compulsion to raise a certain amount of money each month and if gambling revenues are uncertain or inadequate, he will turn to any means available.

Chicago T-5 advised that he felt that the four individuals who actually control and guide the underworld were, at the time, Anthony Accardo, Sam Giancana, Paul Ricca, and Ross Prio. This informant stated that these persons meet regularly at times in Chicago, at which time they apparently talk over gambling operations and assigned territories and conduct any other business which should arise.

Informant advised that officers of unions were close associates of Chicago hoodlums including Sam Giancana, and the unions were controlled by the hoodlum element. James Blakely, a "gunman and long time associate of gangsters" was Chicago International Vice-President of the Hotel and Restaurant Employees and Bartenders Union. Blakely was controlled by John Lardino, a murderer, and if Blakely stepped out of line Lardino had standing orders to murder him from "syndicate" heads through Giancana and others. Giancana was described as an "arch killer" and the boss of the Chicago underworld.

Senate Select Committee on Improper Activities in Labor-Management Relations

Sam Giancana was considered one of the Committee's most important witnesses. He had been directly involved in labor racketeering matters in the Chicago area. Giancana was subpoenaed in Las Vegas after a lengthy attempt by investigators to find him. On 6-9-1959, Giancana invoked the Fifth Amendment to most questions and only laughed when asked how he ranked in the crime hierarchy.

WESTERN UNION TELEGRAM
W. P. MARSHALL, PRESIDENT

DOMESTIC SERVICE	INTERNATIONAL SERVICE
Check the class of service desired; otherwise this message will be sent as a fast telegram TELEGRAM DAY LETTER NIGHT LETTER	Check the class of service desired; otherwise the message will be sent at the full rate FULL RATE LETTER TELEGRAM SHORE-SHIP

1211 (4-55)

NO. WDS.-CL. OF SVC.	PD. OR COLL.	CASH NO.	CHARGE TO THE ACCOUNT OF	TIME FILED
			Senate Select Committee on Improper Activities in the Labor or Management Field	

Send the following message, subject to the terms on back hereof, which are hereby agreed to

25 May 1959

RICHARD E. GORMAN, ESQ.   CONFIRM DELIVERY
1 NORTH LA SALLE STREET
CHICAGO, ILLINOIS

PURSUANT TO SUBPOENA HERETOFORE SERVED UPON HIM,

YOUR CLIENT SAM GIANCANA IS DIRECTED TO APPEAR AT ROOM 101,

SENATE OFFICE BUILDING, WASHINGTON, D. C. AT NINE THIRTY A. M.

WEDNESDAY, JUNE 10, 1959.

                    JOHN L. McCLELLAN, CHAIRMAN
                    Senate Select Committee on Improper
                    Activities in the Labor or Management Field

Giancana, Sam   6-10-59   9 3:0 / AM

Notify: Richard E. Gorman, Atty
         1 North LaSalle St
         Chicago 2, Illinois

Telegram sent 5-25-59   9 AM

                    Tuesday 6/9

Chapter 4

Chicago CG 6343-C advised on January 18, 1960, that on this date Sam Giancana had a conversation as follows with Frank Ferraro:

Giancana: I insulted your friend.

Ferraro: Who?

Giancana: O'Brien (Joey Aiuppa). I said listen, Joey, what the (obscene) do you think, that we're married to you? You get out of work, you send a guy around, what the (obscene) do you think, we don't owe you anything, we're not married to you. We'll help you, sure, but we're not married to you. We're not gonna put anybody out of work to put someone in there. Now, I says, you'll wait until something shows up, and I'll contact you. But this coming around every day, every day, that's a lot of BS. We don't owe them anything. You don't owe them anything, do you?

Ferraro: No.

Giancana: We'll help the guy, that's all right. But we're not gonna fire a guy.

Ferraro: When did you talk to him?

Giancana: Saturday, he came over to the barber shop (Louie Briatta's Barbershop on Polk Street). I said, the minute you guys get out of work, you come over here like we owe you something. We don't owe you anything. We don't owe you fellas anything. I said, you're 50 some years old, you ought to be able to take care of yourself, without going around asking for help here and help there. He said I haven't got a dime, I haven't got this. I said, who's fault is it? It's not our fault that you haven't got anything. What the hell. These guys are making (obscene) nuisances out of themselves.

Ferraro: That's right. I'll tell him the very same thing.

Giancana:	I got mad at him Saturday night. I went to the barber shop, and I said, Louie (Briatta), when I find something, I'll contact you. He said when will that be? I said, I'm working on a deal now, and when I get a spot for you, I'll get you an office. If it don't go through, then you'll have to wait until something shows. I says, and don't come bothering me, I'll get in touch with you. Don't come bothering me, or anybody. We never saw you guys, you never came near us. Them guys are a bunch of (obscene).
Ferraro:	How come Freddy (Fred "Juke Box" Smith) can't manufacture a job for them?
Giancana:	Freddy says he's broke. I says, Joe, a guy insults my intelligence when he tells me he's broke. These guys, Frank, they're like leeches. They think you owe them something.
Ferraro:	That's right. I'm glad you told him off. If he comes here, I'll give him some more.

Joey Aiuppa is a former top hoodlum of the Chicago Office. His base of operations has been Cicero, Illinois, which is in the district controlled for the Chicago Crime Syndicate by Sam Giancana. Information has been developed which indicates that Aiuppa formerly was associated with Fred "Juke Box" Smith.

Later that day on January 18, 1960, Sam Giancana, Murray Humphreys and Frank Ferraro had a conversation concerning Richard Morrison, a well known Chicago burglar who furnished information to the States Attorney, involving a dozen Chicago policemen who were associated with him in burglaries.

At a later date a conversation between Murray Humphrey and Sam Pardy, a bookmaker on the far west side of Chicago took place where Humphreys indicated that Giancana was out of town and since he has been "neglecting things" they don't know what to do. Humphreys also mentioned that Giancana gave a "show girl" a ring, which could refer to songstress Keeley Smith, wife of bandleader Louis Prima. It has been previously reported that Giancana has showered Keeley Smith with affections and allegedly gave her a $5,000 ring. It is apparent that Gus Alex is attempting to buy back this ring, probably for Phyllis McGuire.

FEDERAL BUREAU OF INVESTIGATION

REPORTING OFFICE	OFFICE OF ORIGIN	DATE	INVESTIGATIVE PERIOD
CHICAGO	CHICAGO	1960	February 19, 1960

TITLE OF CASE	REPORT MADE BY	TYPED BY
SAMUEL M. GIANCANA, aka	. Special Agent Ralph Hill Jr.	dkc

	CHARACTER OF CASE
	FBI Headquarters File number 92-3171-46 Top Hoodlum Program – Anti Racketeering

Associates

Marshall Caifano
25 East Delaware Place, Chicago, IL

Chicago informant advised that Murray Humphreys and Frank Ferraro had decided that Marshall Caifano had committed indiscretions with his female companions and nightclubs activities so that it became necessary for Giancana to admonish Caifano concerning these activities and to be more circumspect in his dealings while in public view. It was decided that Giancana should further talk with Caifano to emphasize Caifano's need for the application of discretion while in public. According to this informant, Caifano had attracted a large amount of newspaper publicity during 1959 and 1960 by divorcing his second wife, Darlene Caifano and marrying a Chicago model named Marge Evenson. This marriage dissolved in a divorce action approximately nine months later which in turn received considerable publicity in the Chicago papers. This coupled with the fact that, according to the informant, Caifano was seen on an almost nightly basis nightclubbing on the near north side of Chicago, instigated the actions of Murray Humphreys, et al in Caifano's admonishment. This informant advised that the prime reason for Giancana's intervention was the fact that the informant stated that according to Murray Humphreys, Giancana was probably the closest person among their associates to Caifano.

Vikki Taylor

On February 2, 1960, Mrs. Vikki Taylor, 520 East Drive, North Miami, Florida, advised SA Albert T. Healy that she is the former wife of ex-fighter Jake LaMotta. Upon being showed a photograph of Sam Giancana, Mrs. Taylor stated she recognized him as an individual she had met several times at the Fontainebleau Hotel, Miami Beach, Florida. She said she had met Giancana when she was appearing there on a show which starred Jimmy Durante during the 1957-1958 winter season, and she believes it was in about March, 1958. She denied any knowledge of Giancana's background, associates or activities and claims to have no information concerning him.

Criminal Activities

"Attached is a Chicago Daily Tribune article dated January 8, 1960, containing information on the gang slaying of William Skally."

"Attached is a Chicago American newspaper article dated December 20, 1959 containing information on the gang slaying of mobster Roger Touhy."

Gambling

In February of 1960, it was reported that the Riviera Lounge, 6540 North Milwaukee, Norwood Township, was the site of a gambling raid on November 21, 1959. The club had been found booming with the weekend trade of horse players, dice shooters and poker addicts, some twenty of whom were woman. The operator of the place was identified as Rocco Potenzo, Giancana's partner, who was not caught in the raid. It has been permitted to keep its liquor license. Daniel Ryan, County Board President, ruled that no evidence was presented at a recent hearing on revocation of the license to warrant either revocation or suspension.

Position in the Chicago Syndicate

On December 3, 1959, Peter Herdinger, Detective with the Intelligence Unit, Chicago Police Department, advised SA William Roemer that he believed Sam Giancana is now the number one man in the Chicago syndicate. He said that he believed William Daddono is the number two man and Rocco Potenzo is the number three man.

FEDERAL BUREAU OF INVESTIGATION

REPORTING OFFICE	OFFICE OF ORIGIN	DATE	INVESTIGATIVE PERIOD	
CHICAGO	CHICAGO	1960	July, 14, 1960	
TITLE OF CASE		REPORT MADE BY		TYPED BY
		New York		dkc
SAMUEL M. GIANCANA, aka		CHARACTER OF CASE		
		FBI Headquarters File number 92-3171-50, Samuel M. Giancana, Top Hoodlum Program – Anti Racketeering		

On July 13, 1960, Mr. John Teeter, Administrator of the Damon Runyon Cancer Fund, was interviewed by SA's Frank Gerrity and Thomas Emery. Mr. Teeter explained that his wife, Christine, and her sisters, Dorthy and Phyllis McGuire, comprise the well-known singing trio known as the McGuire Sisters. He related that basically the information he wished to discuss concerned an association which had developed between the subject and Phyllis McGuire during the past year.

By the way of background, Mr. Teeter related that about 5 or 6 years ago he had been contacted in NTC by one Curly Harris, whom he knew as a Frank Costello associate, with a proposition whereby the Damon Runyon Cancer Fund would be the recipient of a substantial sum as a result of the intended liquidation of holding of a group in

Chicago, known as the Italian Welfare League. Teeter was instructed to contact Chicago Attorney Anthony V. Champagne who handled the liquidation proceedings.

After Teeter made contact with Champagne in Chicago, they proceeded together to Oak Park where they stopped at what Teeter described as a rather pretentious home where Champagne introduced him to Tony Accardo. Teeter stated the nature of his trip to Chicago concerning the intended liquidation. After the brief visit with Accardo, Champagne took him to the Italian Welfare League property which was to be disposed of. Though he could not recall the location, Mr. Teeter described the property as an estate originally owned by the Atwater Kent family, which estate had been converted apparently for the purpose of a day camp for underprivileged children or some similar charitable purpose.

Mr. Teeter noted that there had been a meeting called at that time to discuss the proposed liquidation of the property, which meeting was attended by Accardo and a number of other individuals unknown to Teeter. During that time he met a number of individuals, usually by first or last name only, through the Chicago Attorney, Anthony V. Champagne. During the past year, Mr. Teeter has become aware that Phyllis McGuire has become involved romantically with a questionable figure identified initially to Mr. Teeter as one Sam Flood from Chicago. Teeter later determined that Flood is identical with the subject.

Teeter continued that during the past 2 or 3 weeks he had occasion to go to Chicago to visit his wife, Christine, when the McGuire Sisters were appearing at the Club Chez Paree in that city. He related that when he finally got to Chicago on this trip, he arrived at the above mentioned club between the McGuire Sisters' acts and encountered Phyllis in the club with the subject whom she introduced him to Sam Flood. Teeter explained that he recognized Flood as one of the groups he had met in connection with the Italian Welfare League liquidation in previous years, although he did not know the subject's true name at the time.

Mr. Teeter commented that at the time of the above mentioned introduction by Phyllis McGuire the subject replied that he knew Mr. Teeter although they had no further conversation at the time. Teeter could only surmise that the subject must have recalled him from the liquidation proceedings during previous years. Mr. Teeter noted also that the subject was treated with great deference while in the Club Chez Paree in Chicago.

Mr. Teeter stated that he had discussed this problem in general with his wife, Christine, and with Dorothy McGuire, both of whom are very concerned about the subject's attention to Phyllis and her acceptance and apparent approval of these attentions. He remarked that Phyllis McGuire is a headstrong, know-it-all type who is unable to be controlled in situations such as this.

Teeter continued that after the Chicago booking, the McGuire Sisters went to Las Vegas where they had an engagement at the Desert Inn Hotel. Teeter arrived in Las Vegas a day or so after they opened at this hotel and thereafter learned that the subject and his combination driver and cook, one Joe (last name may be Lubino), were in Las Vegas and that Phyllis was continuing in very close contact with the subject. Teeter learned that each night following the McGuire Sisters' appearance, the subject had a car pick up Phyllis and take her to a house outside Las Vegas provided the subject by the Ashcraft Realty Firm.

Teeter stated that while at the Desert Inn, he once had occasion to stop into Phyllis McGuire's dressing room with the McGuire Sisters' manager and as they entered the room, Phyllis was counting a larger stack of bills which was determined to be about $6,500 in hundred dollar bills. By way of explanation, Phyllis told them that she had won the money on the recent fight (probably meaning the Robinson-Fulmer fight). Teeter stated that Phyllis knows nothing of boxing and probably would not know one fighter from another, and he is convinced the money was given to her by the subject.

He added that she also came into possession of an additional $3,500 while at the Desert Inn which she claimed to have won on the gambling tables there. Teeter ex-

134

plained that this was highly unlikely since Phyllis had in debt for about $16,000 at the Desert Inn Casino and thereafter the McGuire Sisters' manager and Teeter had obtained an agreement with some of the Desert Inn owners, including Moe Dalitz and Murray Kleinman, that she was barred from any further gambling, and that the operators had standing instructions not to allow her at this casino. Teeter remarked that Phyllis has also received jewelry from the subject which he ascertains to be worth at least $20,000.

Teeter noted that when the subject contacted Phyllis by telephone at the Desert Inn, he regularly made these telephone contacts through the Desert Inn pit boss, Nicholas Donolfo, who is probably one of the subject's main representatives at the Desert Inn.

Mr. Teeter stated that the McGuire Sisters are currently between engagements, and that Phyllis McGuire is currently in NYC, staying at 525 Park Ave. He related that she has indicated, however, that she plans to travel to either Honolulu, Hawaii, or to the Philippine Islands for an undisclosed reason other than recreation, and that her sisters and Teeter believe that she intends to meet the subject on such a trip.

Teletype
To Director, FBI
From Chicago, File 92-349
Date 7-15-60
Samuel Giancana, aka Sam Flood

One Harry H. Fuller, Manager of the Midwest Ranch of the National Bureau of Casualty Underwriters, Chicago, contacted the Chicago FBI Office upon the suggestion of Dr. Earl McRoberts, a Chicago Sac contact, concerning one Sam Flood. Fuller explained that a way reputable independent oil man and close friend of his, whom he declined to identify, telephonically contacted him in the recent past from Las Vegas, Nevada and inquired about the identity of a Sam Flood. Fuller's source indicated that he had meet Flood in Las Vegas and that Flood is alleged to be an important figure in the Mafia in Chicago. By Mafia, Fuller interpreted this to mean the Chicago Crime Syndicate. Fuller's source claimed that Sam Flood is about fifty years old, of Italian origins and the name did not seem consistent with his appearance. Fuller said that he dose not know the circumstances surrounding the inquiry of his source, who dose not want to be involved in any way. It is pointed out that Sam Flood is an alias of Giancana in Las Vegas and is possibly identical with subject. Flicka McKenna, a former member of the Chez Paree Adorables, a dancing group employed full time at the Chez Paree, Chicago's largest night club, recently advised that Sam Giancana dated Phyllis McGuire while the McGuire Sisters appeared at the Chez Paree approximately six weeks ago in Chicago. Chicago investigation continuing.

FEDERAL BUREAU OF INVESTIGATION

REPORTING OFFICE	OFFICE OF ORIGIN	DATE	INVESTIGATIVE PERIOD
CHICAGO	CHICAGO	1960	September 4, 1960

TITLE OF CASE	REPORT MADE BY		TYPED BY
			dkc
SAMUEL M. GIANCANA, aka	CHARACTER OF CASE		
	FBI Headquarters File number 92-3171- Top Hoodlum Program – Anti Racketeering		

Observed at the Armory Lounge on this date were Anthony J. Accardo, Joseph Glimco, and Carmen Fanelli. Joesph Glimco, President of Local 777, Taxicab Drivers Union, Teamsters Union, was hired as a gunman during prohibition by Al Capone to guard his beer trucks. For this he was given authority to control the Poultry Handlers Union, but never held office in that organization.

John Lardino
1201 North Bellforte
Oak Park, IL

Chicago T-1 informant advised that John Lardino, although officially out as of Local 593 of the Hotel and Apartment Hotel Service Workers and Miscellaneous Restaurant Employees Union where he has been a business agent, was, in actuality receiving approximately $100 a week from the union for an unknown reason. Lardino advised the informant that he was concerned about the fact that Local 593 had been losing its membership and was at that time attempting to exert his influence to increase the membership to the old figures of approximately 12,000 members. Lardino was seeking Murray Humphreys' authorization to follow through in this regard.

Chicago T-5 advised that John Lardino is closely allied with Sam Giancana and is active in the Hotel and Restaurant Workers Miscellaneous Union, although he was recently deposed from this position after appearing before the Senate Rackets committee and taking the Fifth Amendment. Chicago T-15 indicated the "syndicate" has attempted in the recent past to place individuals in this particular organization with the purpose of maintaining control of same and stated that some of these individuals were from Kansas City, Missouri, and Cleveland, Ohio.

FEDERAL BUREAU OF INVESTIGATION

REPORTING OFFICE	OFFICE OF ORIGIN	DATE	INVESTIGATIVE PERIOD	
CHICAGO	CHICAGO	1960	October 14, 1960	

TITLE OF CASE	REPORT MADE BY	TYPED BY
		dkc

SAMUEL M. GIANCANA, aka	**CHARACTER OF CASE** FBI Headquarters File number 92-3171-81 Top Hoodlum Program – Anti Racketeering New York File 92-793

John H. Teeter, (Protected identity), advised that he received the following information from his wife Christine McGuire. Teeter cautioned that neither he nor his wife could vouch for the truth of this information but he is furnishing it as it was received by his wife from Sam Giancana. Subject, Phyllis McGuire and Christine McGuire had dinner at the La Scala Restaurant, New York City, and recently during dinner Fidel Castro and Cuba were discussed. Subject said that Castro was to be done away with very shortly. When the girls registered doubt about this happening then Giancana assured them it was to occur in November and that he has met with the "assassin" on three occasions.

Teeter said that "assassin" was the term used by Giancana. Giancana said he hat met with the "assassin" on a boat docked at the Fontainebleau Hotel, Miami Beach, Florida, and that everything had been perfected for the killing of Castro. Giancana said that the "assassin" has arranged with a girl, not further described, to drop a "pill" in a drink or some food of Castro's.

Giancana also told the sisters that Castro is in advanced stages of syphilis and is not completely rational. Teeter will immediately contact the NYO if he learns anything further on this matter.

New York and Chicago should closely follow this matter and should immediately advise Bureau if any additional data is received regarding alleged plot against Castro. In particular, if information should be received implicated in alleged plot, Bureau and interested offices should be expeditiously advised and recommendations should be furnished concerning close coverage of Giancana with view to identifying any contacts he might make regarding this matter, including physical surveillance.

Miami should immediately furnish its comments regarding possible identity of person who allegedly met with Giancana at Fontainebleau Hotel. However, any inquiries conducted concerning this matter by Miami should be discreet so as not to jeopardize New York source or alert individuals possibly involved to the Bureau's interest.

FEDERAL BUREAU OF INVESTIGATION

REPORTING OFFICE	OFFICE OF ORIGIN	DATE	INVESTIGATIVE PERIOD
CHICAGO	CHICAGO	1960	November 18, 1960

TITLE OF CASE	REPORT MADE BY	TYPED BY
		dkc
SAMUEL M. GIANCANA, aka	**CHARACTER OF CASE** FBI Headquarters File number 92-3171-86 Top Hoodlum Program – Anti Racketeering Weekly Summary Airtel	

It was reported that Murray Humphreys, Gus Alex, Frank Ferraro, Anthony Accardo, and Sam Giancana were to have a meeting at the St. Clair Hotel, Chicago, on 11/18/1960. Hy Godfrey was dispatched to the St. Clair to make the necessary arrangements for a suit.

On 11/18/60, physical surveillance at the St. Clair Hotel disclosed that Hy Godfrey was observed at 10:30 a.m. conversing with Dave Gardner, his contact with the hotel. At 11:35a.m., Sam Giancana, accompanied by Ralph Pierce, entered the hotel and proceeded to the 12th floor.

On 11/16/60 and 11/17/60, Giancana and Rocco Potenzo were, on those dates, at the Armory Lounge, Forest Park.

On 11/17/60, Louis Stevens advised that he had been acquainted with Giancana during 1959, and had met with him on several occasions at the North Avenue Steak House, Maywood, Illinois, which he assumed was owned by Giancana.

On 11/15/60, a physical surveillance at Mike's Fish Restaurant, 161 East Ontario, disclosed the presence of Anthony Accardo, Jack Cerone, Frank Ferraro, Gus Alex, Sam Giancana, and Ralph Pierce.

FEDERAL BUREAU OF INVESTIGATION

REPORTING OFFICE	OFFICE OF ORIGIN	DATE	INVESTIGATIVE PERIOD
CHICAGO	CHICAGO	1960	December 9, 1960

TITLE OF CASE	REPORT MADE BY	TYPED BY
		dkc
SAMUEL M. GIANCANA, aka	**CHARACTER OF CASE** FBI Headquarters File number 92-3171-93 Top Hoodlum Program – Anti Racketeering Weekly Summary Airtel	

On 12/6/60 Sam Giancana was seen at the Armory Lounge at approximately 12:00 midnight. That same date, Carmen Fanelli was interviewed by Bureau Agents in connection with Chicago case captioned "CARMEN FANELLI, PERJURY, Chicago file 74-188." Fanelli was seemingly cooperative to the agents and answered all questions posed to him in connection with his selling of Fox Head 400 Beer in his establishment. Fanelli verified the fact that the meeting between Tony Accardo and heads of the Fox head Brewery for the purpose of placing Accardo in as salesman was held at the Armory Lounge in

1956. During the interview, it was possible for one of the agents to make a physical observation of this establishment on the pretext of having a perfunctory interest in the premises. It was noted that there is a private dining room located in the rear of the restaurant separated from the main building by a door which is approximately 14 x 20 feet in size. It contains an extension telephone, carpeting, and holds two large tables and a small table. This would in all probability be the location of any meetings which would go on in the Armory Lounge between Giancana and other members of his organization.

That interview of Finelli conducted by Agents was reported in detail to Murray Humphreys by Sam (LNU) (not Sam Giancana). The primary concern of Murray Humphreys over this interview was the fact that questions were asked of Finelli as to the actual owner of the Armory Lounge, that is, to whom did Fanelli pay his rent. The owner of the record of this property is Country Investments, Inc., no address. Springfield has been requested to ascertain through the corporation records the identity of this corporation. It would appear that Country Investments, Inc. is in ascertaining the complete identity of this corporation and its officers.

A FBI undercover photo taken in the rear parking lot of the Armory Lounge.

FEDERAL BUREAU OF INVESTIGATION

REPORTING OFFICE	OFFICE OF ORIGIN	DATE	INVESTIGATIVE PERIOD
CHICAGO	CHICAGO	1960	December 16, 1960

TITLE OF CASE	REPORT MADE BY	TYPED BY
		dkc
SAMUEL M. GIANCANA, aka	**CHARACTER OF CASE**	
	FBI Headquarters File number 92-3171-94 Top Hoodlum Program – Anti Racketeering. Weekly Summary Airtel	

The Springfield office advised by airtel mail dated 12/14/60 that the files of the Corporation Division, Secretary of State's Office, Springfield, Illinois, revealed that the Country Investment Corporation, field articles of incorporation on 10/3/56, the incorporators being:

        Carmen Bruno, 1014 North 21st Street, Melrose Park, Illinois
        Peter Gerrine, 920 North 20th Street, Melrose Park, Illinois
        Sam Aiuppa, 910 North 22nd Street, Melrose Park, Illinois

The address of the corporation was listed as 10 North Broadway, Melrose Park, Illinois. It is noted that this corporation owns the property upon which the Armory Lounge is located on.

The annual report of this corporation files 2/29/60 revealed the following officers of the corporation as follows:

        D.J. Bruno, President, 10 Broadway, Melrose Park
        Sam Aiuppa, Secretary, 1546 North 18th Street, Melrose Park
        James Aiuppa, Treasurer, 300 Lawndale Avenue, Melrose Park

It is noted that Sam Aiuppa if the brother of Joseph J. Aiuppa, who is a Chicago top hoodlum and close associate of Sam Giancana's. Aiuppa at one time maintained a high degree of control of gambling interest in Cicero, Illinois.

It was learned that one of Giancana's principal bases for operation as of early 1960 was Gus' Steak House, 4817 West Roosevelt Road, Cicero. The informant stated that Giancana utilized a back room of this establishment for meetings and is usually accompanied by an individual known as Duke (LNU) who always carries a briefcase with him. During these occasions Duke makes telephone calls from Gus' Steak House utilizing the telephone booth and conducts all conversations in Italian. Usually two or three days subsequent to these telephone calls another meeting is called at Gus Steak House which, according to the informant, is attended by hoodlums "from all over the country." Gus Steak House is operated by Gus Kringas.

Information has come to the attention of this office in the past that Gus' Steak House is a well known gambling establishment and these gambling operations are conducted on the second floor. Gus' Streak House is owned by Kyriakos Vavaroutson and Steve Harris, who took over this restaurant from Kringas and one Selemos.

Chicago informant 6343 advised on 12/9/60 that "Mooney" was back in town during the early morning hours. This source further advised that an individual believed to be Giancana was present during a conference between Murray Humphreys, Frank Ferraro, and Gus Alex held on 12/14/ 60. One of the purposes of this conference was a discussion of the possibilities of investments in Las Vegas, primarily the Stardust Hotel.

Although the Carmen Fanelli interview afforded an opportunity to observe close-ly the interior of the Armory Lounge and the location of the probable meeting place for hoodlums gathering, thus adding to the information being gathered on this estab-lishment, it is felt that several other problems must be resolved before the establish-ment of a confidential source can be effected.

FEDERAL BUREAU OF INVESTIGATION

REPORTING OFFICE	OFFICE OF ORIGIN	DATE	INVESTIGATIVE PERIOD
CHICAGO	CHICAGO	1960	December 30, 1960

TITLE OF CASE	REPORT MADE BY	TYPED B'
		dkc
SAMUEL M. GIANCANA, aka	CHARACTER OF CASE	
	FBI Headquarters File number 92-3171-96 Top Hoodlum Program – Anti Racketeering. Weekly Summary Airtel	

On 12/8/60, an informant advised SA John J. Matthews that Rinaldo Spaderm, whose true name is Robert Jacobs, has been a personal friend of Richard Fanning for many years, and that he was quite upset at the recent assassination of Richard Fanning. Spaderm stated that he had been attempting to learn the reason for Fanning's murder from Marty Fanning, Richard's brother. On 12/21/60, Spadern stated the opinion of most of Fanning's associates in that Mooney Giancana was responsible for his death. Accord-ing to Spaderm, Fanning and Lester Belgrad work together on a shake-down racket. They preyed on business men at local hotels, placing these individuals in compromising posi-tions. Fanning would engineer the matter and Belgrad would represent himself as a law enforcement officer.

On several occasions the victims were individuals close to the Syndicate. Fanning and Belgrad were warned to desist and when they ignored the warning, both were killed.

Chicago informant 6343 advised that Hy Godfrey, a messenger boy for top hood-lums, had a conversation with an unidentified person, during the course of which he mentioned that that Sam Giancana was out of town. According to this informant, it would appear that Giancana had been out of town since before Christmas.

Officer Hugh Phillips of the Chicago Police Department gave information that Anthony Phillips, William "Potatoes" Daddono, and (FNU) Carramone are presently at-tempting to muscle into the garbage disposal business.

12-30-1961, Salt Lake City File 139-17. Arthur James Balletti was charged by the State of Nevada with three counts, invasion of privacy, a felony. The other two charges are misdemeanors for alleged "recording of telephone conversations" of Dan Rowan and Phyllis McGuire. All items seized at the time of arrest of Balletti except two cameras will be retained by Clark County Sheriff's Office until conclusion of trial of Balletti. Balletti on interview denies monitoring telephone conversations and claims individual who traveled to Las Vegas with him used name Harrison and actual identity unknown to Balletti.

Additional FBI information

1) Frank Sheehan, Chicago PD officer advised that Charles Leonardi was listed on an application for a Retail Liquor Dealer's License as the president of the Black Onyx Night Club Inc., Chicago. Sheehan stated that he heard that Leonardi was a nephew of Sam Giancana. On 4-15-1960 Leonardi admitted he was a stepbrother of Giancana in that his mother married Giancana's father. He denied associating with Giancana and said he had not seen him for five or six months.

2) Report on Gambling Conditions in the Chicago area stated that Sam Giancana and Charles English had a partnership wagering at race tracks. English did the betting and received 20% of the winnings while Giancana, "the money man in the venture," received 80% of the winnings. Individuals who failed to obey the dictates of the underworld leaders have been beaten and in some instances, although never factually substantiated, killed.

3) CG-6343-C advised in October, 1960 that James Stavros ran as Democratic committeeman of Wheeling Township, Chicago, and after the election, Stavros started "shaking down" the bar owners and everyone else in Wheeling Township. He said that Sam Giancana and others decided that John F. Scanlan would talk to Stavros to straighten him out.

4) Frank Ferraro and Sam Giancana, according to CG 6343-C held a conference on April 4, 1960 which was as follows:

Giancana: I want to talk to you just a minute.

Ferraro: Ok.

Giancana: I went to Las Vegas and made all those arrangements
                with Johnny (John Drew). He said he didn't want to
                be disturbed so I got hot and said to Willie "Potatoes"
                let's go back they won't allow no hoods there.

Ferraro: No hoods?

Giancana: None at all. No, no hoods.

Ferraro: I ain't a known hood.

Giancana: Someone will put the finger on you through from Chi-
                cago.

Ferraro: (Obscene) them. I didn't lose anything there anyway.

    This short conversation apparently means that Giancana and Willie Daddono, who is Giancana's lieutenant, had been to Las Vegas where they had been in contact with Johnny Drew, the floor manager of the Stardust Hotel. Apparently, Giancana received no satisfaction there, and coupled with the fact that Las Vegas has recently had a drive on hoodlums in that area, Giancana and party returned to Chicago.

Chapter 5

FEDERAL BUREAU OF INVESTIGATION

REPORTING OFFICE	OFFICE OF ORIGIN	DATE	INVESTIGATIVE PERIOD
CHICAGO	CHICAGO	1961	January 6, 1961

TITLE OF CASE	REPORT MADE BY	TYPED BY
		dkc
SAMUEL M. GIANCANA, aka	**CHARACTER OF CASE** FBI Headquarters File number 92-3171-97 Top Hoodlum Program – Anti Racketeering. Weekly Summary Airtel	

Information was received from CG 6343-C on 11/14/60, wherein an individual believed to be Sam Giancana discussed this Standard Garbage Disposal Company and the difficulties this company has been encountering with the Garbage Disposal Association. Apparently the association had been utilizing pressure in order to stop the Standard Disposal Company from expanding their business. It was Murray Humphreys contention that an Antitrust suit should be filed against the Disposal Association and go through legitimate channels to exert pressure against the association rather than using muscling tactics.

GC informant advised on 1/4/61, that the Standard Disposal and Metal Company is a hoodlum controlled operation. The informant stated that Lenny Patrick (Chicago top hoodlum) and Dave Yaras (known to the Miami Office) are working together arranging and lining up stops and customers for this disposal company. Informant said that he knew for a fact that Patrick had approached the owner of Marty's Food Market, Inc., to line up this individual as a customer for Standard Disposal Company. It was the same person who was the victim of Lennie Patrick's muscling tactics in a shake-down of super markets in 1958.

On 1/5/61, SA's Ralph Hill and Vincent L. Inserra interviewed Dave Kaye who identified himself as the sales director and vise president of the Standard Disposal and Metal Company at 1216 South Sangamon. Kaye was interviewed in his office at that address. Kaye was visibly disturbed over the presence of agents and commented immediately to the agents that he is a parolee from the state of Florida and had been convicted of attempted murder in Miami in 1954, however, would not go into lengthy detail as to circumstances surrounding his conviction other then to state that he was sent to Miami from Chicago in 1951 by Eugene "Jimmy" James, the then vice president of International Laundry Workers Union and head of Local 46 in Chicago. Kaye was sent to Miami as deputy receiver and organizer in an attempt to organize the Laundry Workers in south Florida area. Kaye advised that he was paroled from Florida Penitentiary on March 24, 1959, and his parole was sponsored by Eugene James. Kyle stated he received a 20 year sentence and his parole expires in 1975.

Kaye said that the Standard Disposal and Metal Company was organized about a year ago and now has 175 to 180 stops, both residential and industrial, picking up garbage and scrap. He said that they have been in difficulty with the Salvage Association which has, according to Kaye, "formed a monopoly for restraint of trade" and that the association is attempting to put them out of business by closing them out of dumping grounds, pressuring trucking companies to keep them from purchasing trucks and using economic pressure on their potential customers. Kaye insisted that the business had been obtained by underselling competition, that this is strictly legitimate and that no muscling tactics are utilized, he said that he knows Dave Yaras "slightly" but denied knowing Lenny Patrick. He stated that neither Yaras nor Patrick are at this time working for this company and to the best of his knowledge have never been utilized as salesmen for the Standard Disposal. He said the operations of the Standard Disposal Company are financed by the Guaranteed Trust and Savings. It is noted that the Guaranteed Trust was formerly the Southmoor Bank and Trust, whose president was Leon Marcus, slain in gangland style in 1956, after which much speculation was made to the effect that the killing was carried out under orders of Giancana.

On 1/2/61, Giancana was observed at the Armory Lounge in the evening hours in company with Nick D'Amico, John Jarelli and Joe Marks. Giancana was observed being dropped at the Armory Lounge from a car occupied by Giancana and two other individuals. This automobile after dropping Giancana proceeded to 915 Franklin Street in River Forest where it was observed that Anthony Accardo departed from his vehicle and proceeded into his residence at that address.

CG informant advised that that Gus' Steak House in Cicero, mentioned previously, utilized gambling on the second floor and that the whole layout is operated by Frank Sharkey, an ex-convict. Sharkey is probably Frank "Sharkey" Eulo, 1104 South Maple, Oak Park, a close associate of Giancana's.

FEDERAL BUREAU OF INVESTIGATION

REPORTING OFFICE	OFFICE OF ORIGIN	DATE	INVESTIGATIVE PERIOD
CHICAGO	CHICAGO	1961	January 13, 1961

TITLE OF CASE	REPORT MADE BY	TYPED BY
		dkc
SAMUEL M. GIANCANA, aka	**CHARACTER OF CASE** FBI Headquarters File number 92-3171-98 Top Hoodlum Program – Anti Racketeering. Weekly Summary Airtel	

Thunderbolt Motel
(formerly River Road Motel)
5400 River Road, Rosemont, Illinois

According to an informant whose identity is to be protected, furnished information from his files pertaining to the trust agreement for the River Road Motel. On 7/26/54, trust agreement was transferred from the Pioneer Trust Savings Bank to the Southmoor Bank and Trust. The original mortgage was held by Guarantee Reserve Life Insurance Company of Hammond, Indiana, Ben Jaffe officer. Amount of the mortgage was then $90,000 and sole beneficiaries of the trust were Michael Caldarulo and Nathan Ladon.

On 1/17/55, Ladon's and Caldarulo's interest was transferred to Anthony V. Champagne. On 2/3/55, Anthony Champagne's interest was transferred to Michael Caldarulo (35 per cent) and James Perno (65 per cent). On 3/24/55, the Southmoor Securities deposited $150,000 to the Southmoor Bank and Trust and took over $100,000 of the mortgage on the River Road Motel with the Southmoor Bank and Trust holding $50,000. On 11/3/55, Caldarulo's and Perno's interest was conveyed to Anthony Champagne and on the same date Champagne's interest was transferred again to Caldarulo and Perno. On 2/5/57, the Southmoor Bank and Trust assigned all interests in the River Road Motel to the Guarantee Reserve Life Insurance Company of Hammond, Indiana, based upon installment note held by the Guarantee Reserve Life Insurance Company of $160,000 signed by James Perno and Michael Caldarulo as trustees.

The informant said that in relation to the last transaction mentioned above, shortly after the mortgage of Southmoor Securities and Southmoor Bank and Trust was satisfied, Mr. Leon Marcus was slain in gangland fashion and on his person was discovered a receipt reflecting that the River Road Motel paid $150,000 to the Southmoor Bank and Trust signed by H.L. Marcus. The $50,000 mortgage of the Southmoor Bank and Trust was paid and placed with the bank. The remaining $100,000 still remains on deposit at the Guarantee Bank and Trust and has never been claimed. The informant explained that the $100,000 could be claimed at any time by the executor of the state of Leon Marcus, however, almost 4 years has elapsed since that time and the $100,000 still remains on the books at the Guarantee Bank. It is the informant's belief that this money in actuality belongs to Sam Giancana who is not disposed at this time to lay claim to it and the estate of Leon Marcus probably, on orders from Giancana will not lay claim to the $100,000.

Regarding Michael Caldarulo mentioned as a beneficiary of the trust, he is a nephew by marriage of Giancana. Nathan is Nathan "Butch" Ladon, well known to the Chicago office as runner and messenger boy for Syndicate hoodlums, the most prominent being Gus Alex, Eddie Vogel, Frank Ferraro, and Murray Humphreys. James Perno is also a nephew by marriage of Giancana's. Ben Jaffe has been prominently mentioned in the past as a "financial wizard" and expert in investment of the Chicago Syndicate money into legitimate channels particularly in hotels, motels and night clubs in Las Vegas and Miami areas.
"Attached here is a Chicago Daily News article dated 5/22/57 about Ben Jaffe."

West Suburban Disposal Company
3945 West 5th Avenue
<u>Chicago</u>

On 1/10/61, SA's Ralph Hill and Vincent Inserra interviewed John Ponson, president of the company, Isadore "Izzy" Scarmuzzo, general foreman and Rudolph "Rudy" Fratto, who identified himself as a "salesman" for the company. Ponson complained bitterly of the fact that his company is being "muscled" by the Chicago Scavenger Association which has, according to Ponson, successfully strangled all competition attempted by anyone who is desirous of entering the scavenger industry. He said that his trucks have been followed and the drivers harassed and threatened, his trucks have not allowed on dumping grounds and potential customers have been pressured by member companies of the scavenger association not to do business with West Suburban Company. He denied any hoodlum affiliation with his company and said that all business has been conducted strictly on a legitimate basis with no muscling or pressuring tactics utilized. He admitted that William Daddono Jr., was a charter member of the corporation, however, he also admitted that he neglected to add the Jr. after the name Daddono. He said, however, that Daddono has absolutely no connection with the corporation financially or otherwise. When asked for his reasoning for placing Daddono's name on the corporate charter he explained that Daddono's name has significance in certain areas and was of great help to him on a "name dropping" basis in obtaining new customers.

Ponson furnished a list of his customers consisting of about 200 names, a majority of these customers are night clubs and taverns known in the past or alleged to have been in the past as hoodlum or syndicate affiliated. Rudy Fratto claimed that he obtained most of the customers for the service; however, Ponson when interviewed separately claimed that he had obtained most of the customers. Fratto was immutable to questioning; however, he admitted that his daughter is married to William Daddono Jr., son of William "Willie Potatoes" Daddono, a top lieutenant for Giancana. Fratto is the brother of Frankie "One Ear" Fratto and Luigi Fratto (true name), aka., Lou Farrell, a top hoodlum of the Omaha Division, who similarly attempted to open a scavenger business in Des Moines, Iowa. When these individuals were questioned as to whether they had criminal records, Ponson admitted that he had been arrested for assault and battery on approximately 25 occasions; Isadore Scarmuzzo admitted that he had served time in Leavenworth Penitentiary. However, would not disclose the nature of this sentence and Rudolph Fratto admitted that he "has a small sheet for some ridiculous alcohol charge."

"Attached here is a Chicago Sun-Times article captioned "Kup's Column" dated 1/13/61, concerning the Disposal Company."

Officer Lee Gerhke, Chicago Police Department, advised on 1/9/61, that on 1/5/61 Sam Giancana was observed at the Armory Lounge. Officer Gerhke stated that he attempted to place Giancana under surveillance leaving the Armory Lounge; however, Giancana and his driver proceeded at a high rate of speed with the lights off and after a few blocks managed to elude the surveillance. Officer Gerhke stated that during the late evening hours, Giancana was again observed and was placed under surveillance, this time driving a 1959 Ford Convertible registered to Hazel Sweazy. Giancana was accompanied by a female, whose identity was unknown to officer Gerhke. When Giancana made this surveillance he again proceeded at a rate of speed exceeding 85 miles on a heavily traveled boulevard in Oak Park, with his lights off. While the Intelligence unit was attempting to keep Giancana under surveillance at that rate of speed Officer Gerhke's automobile and Giancana's automobile were surrounded by squad cars of the Oak Park Police Department. After officer Gerhke identified him self he advised Oak Park Officers of the identity of Giancana at which time one of the officers mentioned that this was an opportunity to have Giancana placed under arrest and charged with wreckless driving, driving without lights, etc. The officer then made a telephone call and after a few moments came out and released Giancana giving no explanation. Giancana then roared off at a high rate of speed and the surveillance was of course discontinued by the officers.

On 1/10/61, CG 6343-C advised that Giancana had departed the Chicago area sometime during the day of 1/8/61, and was believed to be in the Miami, Florida area. This same informant reported that Murray Humphreys departed for Miami on 1/12/61, and that Frank Ferraro left for Miami on 1/13/61.

Associates

Phyllis McGuire

John Teeter advised agents on September 20, 1960, that he had received information from Christen McGuire that Frank Sinatra, the notes singer, is a messenger for the underworld and had delivered money to Charles "Luckey" Luciano in Atlanta. With regards to underworld messengers, Teeter advised that Phyllis McGuire told Christen McGuire that she would act as a messenger for Giancana. Teeter further advised that Giancana reportedly offered Phyllis McGuire a half million dollars in cash, a home, car, and a chauffer, to marry him, but she turned him down. Phyllis has reportedly told her sister that she dose not love Giancana and has no intention of marrying him.

Jimmy Dino

A New York City informant advised in October 1960, that Marilyn Miller, a former chorus girl from the Chea Paree Night Club in Chicago, was the favored mistress of

147

Giancana's, who was currently having an affair with Phyllis McGuire. According to the informant, Marilyn Miller advised that Giancana was at that time in New York, staying at the Hampkin House, using an alias other that those he normally uses for the purpose of his courtship of Miss McGuire.

Giancana was accompanied by one "Obie" and was in contact with Charles Tourino, and Jimmy Dino. It was further ascertained by the informant that Dino had business meetings in his room at the Savoy Hilton Hotel in New York City. NY informant advised that Jimmy Dino was in possession of $100.000.00 in cash which might possibly be turned over to Frank Reed, Carmine Lombardozzi or John Franzese, aka. "Sonny."

Charles Nicoletti

It is to be noted that a meeting of west side hoodlums are meeting practically every night from about 6 to 8 p.m. in the Garden Lounge in the Bismarck Hotel. They are Charles "Chuckie" Nicoletti, Ju Ju Grieco, Tony Spilotro and William "Potatoes" Daddono. An informant has been developed, and these men appear to trust him 100%. While they have not told him specifically what type of "pick-ups" he is to make for them, he assumed that for the most part, it will be money owed to the "syndicate" on the west side. He feels that they believe that he is better qualified to handle some of their contacts than the men listed above. He pointed out for example, that Tony Spilotro is a young "punk" who is trigger happy, impulsive, and therefore, not suited for certain types of operations in which these men are involved.

The informant advised that during a conversation he was having with syndicate men on election night, November 8, 1960, these men were checking every ten or fifteen minutes, by phone, with the election headquarters, to determine how Daniel Ward was fairing in the contest. It seems Ward, who was running for States Attorney for Cook County, is the man who the organized crime in Chicago very much wants in that post, and as the evening wore on and it was apparent that Ward would win, these men were quite elated, which indicated to the informant that organized crime in Chicago felt Ward could be controlled by them after he assumed office in the near future.

Rocco Pranno

Chicago informant advised on September 28, 1960, that for approximately the last four week, Rocky Pranno and his associates have stayed away from Kane County entirely. He stayed that business is slow in the county and Pranno is doing nothing to push business in any way. The informant stated that Pranno, along with a person who goes under the name of Mike Marino, has opened the "Key Club" located on the Southwest corner of North Avenue and Mannheim Road, Stone Park, Illinois. He stayed that the club is supposed to actually be owned by Pranno and Marino, about whom he knows nothing. He added the club is small, only holding about 40 people and when in the club, a short while ago could see no evidence of gambling.

It was further related that it appears that William Daddono, who formerly had exclusive rights to McHenry, Kane, and DuPage County, Illinois, has apparently lost out in his fight with Sam Giancana for the territory and Giancana now has exclusive rights to the area. He states that both Pranno and Tony Pirotti, who served in the same capacity as Pranno in DuPage County, were Daddono's men and from what he has learned, Pirotti is out entirely in DuPage County and at the present time he and Daddono are opening a jukebox route out of Freeport, Illinois. He stated that Pirotti, who resides in DuPage County, is only supposed to spend his weekends in DuPage County and during the week resides at Freeport. He stated that due to the shifting in power in the three counties, it is entirely possible that this is the reason that Pranno is staying out of Kane

County. The informant stated that Julius Cohen, who did the collecting in the county on the machines under Daddono, is still serving in the same capacity, however, Cohen only spends two days a week in Kane County, and at that time he leaves as rapidly as possible after his work is complete.

It is the informant's opinion that either Pranno or the others have done something wrong in the country or they are going to attempt to start something new. He stated that business is so poor due to all the law enforcement authorities in the county clamping down on Pranno. As to DuPage County, the informant states that the top man for organized crime in DuPage County is a man known as Joe and "Jencke"; however, he knows nothing of this man. He states that the next line appears to be a man who goes under the name of Joe Pray and Joe Tee. He states that he knows nothing about this individual. The informant related that from what he understands, there is little operation in DuPage County with the exception of a few small handbooks.

Marilyn Miller

Reference is made herein to information contained under the Associates Section, wherein Marilyn Miller is described by an informant as a mistress of Giancana. Marilyn Miller's address in Chicago was 900 North Rush Street, and she was described as about 23 years old, 5'4", brown hair, green eyes, very attractive. Marilyn Miller advised the informant that Giancana had allegedly spent $100,000 on her during the past years and named Giancana as Chicago's number two man, who was to take over when the number one man (apparently Anthony J. Accardo) is sent away on income tax violations.

The informant advised that Marilyn Miller had been attempting to telephonically contact Giancana at Townhall, which the informant believes is in Chicago. The informant said that Miss Miller had written a letter to Giancana addressed to Miss Violet Delregino, Amber Light Club, 5534 West Cermak Avenue, Cicero, Illinois. According to the informant, Miller stated that this club is owned by Giancana and she has reached him there in the past. Miss Miller stated to the informant that Violet Delregino is a switchboard or telephone operator connected with this establishment. This lounge has long been known as a gambling establishment operated by Joseph "Fifkie" Corngold, an associate of Giancana. Corngold is an old time Capone mobster.

The informant further advised that she learned that Phyllis McGuire, as of October, 1960, was leaving on a tour for seven weeks and would hit "all of his places," which Miller implied meant places in which Giancana has an interest. According to the informant, Miller advised that Phyllis McGuire has to be nice to Giancana because of his connections and friends in the entertainment field, despite reported rumors among theatrical people that McGuire is attempting to "shake" Giancana so that she can marry someone else.

Chicago T-7 advised on January 5, 1961, Miss Miller had been telephoned by one Joey Pignatello from Miami, Florida. Informant stated that Miller indicated that Giancana was with Pignatello as he utilized this person as a body guard.

Plot to Kill Fidel Castro

Informant advised that everything has been perfected for the killing of Castro. Giancana said that the "assassin" had arranged with a girl, not further described, to drop a pill in a drink or some food of Castro's. Giancana also said that Castro was at that time in the advanced stages of syphilis and was not completely rational.

FEDERAL BUREAU OF INVESTIGATION

REPORTING OFFICE	OFFICE OF ORIGIN	DATE	INVESTIGATIVE PERIOD
CHICAGO	CHICAGO	1961	January 20, 1961

TITLE OF CASE	REPORT MADE BY	TYPED BY
		dkc

	CHARACTER OF CASE
SAMUEL M. GIANCANA, aka	FBI Headquarters File number 92-3171-102 Top Hoodlum Program – Anti Racketeering. Weekly Summary Airtel

Chicago informants reported they have not seen Giancana in the Chicago area during the past week. Records of the Playboy Club, a swank key club at 116 E. Walton Street, Chicago, reflect that Sam Flood is a customer. If anything arise, contact Vic Lownes, Lownes is one third owner of the Playboy Club. Flood was recommended by Don Medlevine, former owner of the Chez Paree. Flood is a used alias of Giancana.

FEDERAL BUREAU OF INVESTIGATION

REPORTING OFFICE	OFFICE OF ORIGIN	DATE	INVESTIGATIVE PERIOD
CHICAGO	CHICAGO	1961	February 3, 1961

TITLE OF CASE	REPORT MADE BY	TYPED BY
		dkc

	CHARACTER OF CASE
SAMUEL M. GIANCANA, aka	FBI Headquarters File number 92-3171-103 Top Hoodlum Program – Anti Racketeering. Weekly Summary Airtel

It was reported that Giancana was back in the Miami, Florida staying at the Fontainebleau Hotel. Records of the Playboy Club were checked on 1/27/61, and it was ascertained that Sam Flood has a key to this establishment giving a residence address of 2801 North Sheridan Road, Chicago. A pretext inquiry was made at 2801 North Sheridan Road, which is a multi story luxury type apartment building and it was ascertained that there is no Sam Flood listed as a tenant therein. It was noted; however that Donald Medlevine is a tenant in apartment 1520. According to records of the Playboy Club, Medlevine was given as the sponsor for Giancana's membership. There was annotation on Giancana's card made in large capital letters and heavily underlined to the effect that no correspondence or communications were to be sent to this member and all inquiries should be directed to Vic Lownes, partner of the Playboy Club.

It is noted that the Playboy Club has received much newspaper publicity in the recent past and it has been rumored in the newspaper articles that the Chicago hoodlums element was attempting to take over the club. Mr. Arnold Morton, one of the partners in the Playboy Club advised on 1/27/61, that several hoodlums, whom he did not care to name, had made overtures of attempting to get an interest in this establishment. They were told that if they carry through any threats or continued to express an interest in the operation of the Playboy Club that they would be exposed in the next issue of Playboy magazine. At that point the hoodlums backed off and made no further overtures.

Detective Lee Gerhke, Chicago Police Department Intelligence Unit, advised SA Ralph Hill that he had ascertained from a confidential source that Giancana had a financial interest in the following enterprises

R & S Liquors
Forest Lounge
Lormar Distributors
Shrimp boats operating out of Cuba

This Division has been aware of the alleged interest of Giancana in both the Forest Lounge and the Lormar Distributors. The Forest Lounge, which is now closed, was operated by Rocco Potenza, a lieutenant of Giancana's and Lormar Distributors at 5954 West Roosevelt Road is operated as a record distributing center by Chuckie English, a lieutenant of Giancana's. Officer Gerhke also advised that he had ascertained recently that Giancana utilized as one of his hang outs that Galewood barber shop, 6964 West North Avenue, Chicago. He stated that they observed William Aloisio, aka. "Willie Smokes" and Felix "Milwaukee Phil" Alderisio at this barber shop on 1/29/61.

FEDERAL BUREAU OF INVESTIGATION

REPORTING OFFICE	OFFICE OF ORIGIN	DATE	INVESTIGATIVE PERIOD
CHICAGO	CHICAGO	1961	February 10, 1961

TITLE OF CASE	REPORT MADE BY	TYPED BY
		dkc

SAMUEL M. GIANCANA, aka	**CHARACTER OF CASE** FBI Headquarters File number 92-3171-111 Top Hoodlum Program – Anti Racketeering. Weekly Summary Airtel

Sergeant Frank Nash, Intelligence Unit, advised on 2/8/61 that the IU had recently set up a dummy juke box corporation in Chicago for the purpose of investigating the Commercial Survey Company at 110 Franklin Street, Chicago. Although these are separate firms, they are, in actuality, one in the same, and the purpose of these companies is a shake-down of juke box operations in the Chicago area, which nets these companies in excess of $100,000 per machine by these companies on a "subscription" basis. If any questions are given, the purpose of the company is to "investigate stolen and broken juke boxes."

The Commercial Survey Company is headed by Michael Dale and Joseph Gagliano, and the Recorded Music Service Association is headed by Earl Keyes, who is also General Manager of the Apex Amusement Company which is Eddie Vogel's organization. The Commercial Survey Company is, in fact, controlled by Chuckie English, a partner of Giancana. English has also the Lor-Mar Distributing Company, which has been investigated in the past as has the Commercial Survey Company in connection with muscling in the recording and Juke Box field.

Sergeant Nash stated that some of the muscle artists employed by the Recorded Music Service Association and the Commercial Survey Company are Ernest "Rocky" Infelice, James "Cowboy" Mirro, William Messino, and Americo DiPietto. All of these individuals are well known to the Chicago Division as musclemen for Syndicate hoodlums and well known burglars in the Chicago area. Infelice and DiPietto, in addition, own the North Avenue Steak House, which just recently burned to the ground from a fire of undetermined origin.

Sergeant Nash continued that shortly after the dummy corporation was set up by himself he was contacted by one Harry McCulloch, a former Chicago Police Sergeant now in the employ of the Commercial Survey Company as "investigator," to subscribe to the services of both the Commercial Company and the Recorded Music Company, at a cost of $1.15 per month per machine in operation. Sergeant Nash said he politely declined the subscription and on a daily basis received threatening telephone calls from McCulloch and other individuals. The last contact Sergeant Nash has was by an individual who telephonically advised Nash that if he did not subscribe to the service of the Commercial Survey Company he would be submitted to a "private and personal meeting." Nash said that this threat was not carried out; however, the dummy corporation was disbanded shortly thereafter for the purpose of investigating the newly formed scavenger companies in Chicago.

West Suburban Scavenger Service

Sergeant Nash advised that he is on a special assignment as this time regarding both West Suburban Scavenger Service and the Standard Disposal Company. Nash said that the IU has a "confidential source" in the West Suburban offices, and it was determined from this confidential source that William Daddono on several occasions passed on instructions to the West Suburban Co. as to new customers to be contacted for business. Nash said that on 2/4/61 a meeting was held at the MGM Lounge in Cicero. Among the automobiles noted in the lot were those of William Daddono, Rudy Fratto, and others whose identities have not yet been determined. It has been determined that Standard Disposal Co. is controlled by Sam Giancana and Gus Alex.

It has been learned that Standard Disposal Co. is actually a Syndicate operation whereby the West Suburban Co. is apparently an independent operation run by William Daddono. Daddono has been instructed by Gus Alex, through an intermediary, to give back some of the customers that he had obtained in the West Suburban Co. to the Standard Disposal Co.

Mrs. Hazel Sweazy advised SA Ralph Hill that she has been a social acquaintance of Giancana's for a few months and has dated him on occasion. Mrs. Sweazy stated that in her opinion Sam Giancana is a "perfect gentleman" and is being unduly harassed by the various law enforcement agencies. She said Giancana has told her he is a "retired gambler" and that she is inclined to believe his statement. She said she dose not believe Giancana is a mobster as disclosed by the newspapers articles and that if she did believe this she would no longer associate with him.

Chicago informant 6343-C advised on 2/7/61 that Anthony Accardo and Gus Alex held a conference on that date during which Accardo brought up the fact that it was foolish for Giancana to hold meetings at the Armory Lounge in view of the fact the police have been known to conduct surveillances on a regular basis's.

FEDERAL BUREAU OF INVESTIGATION

REPORTING OFFICE	OFFICE OF ORIGIN	DATE	INVESTIGATIVE PERIOD	
CHICAGO	CHICAGO	1961	February 13, 1961	
TITLE OF CASE		REPORT MADE BY		TYPED BY
				dkc
SAMUEL M. GIANCANA, aka		CHARACTER OF CASE		
		FBI Headquarters File number 92-3171-112 Top Hoodlum Program – Anti Racketeering. Airtel teletype		

Arrangements complete for as plant from which to observe Armory Lounge. Fisur will be instituted from fixed location, the Naval Ordnance Plant, Forest Park, IL. Commencing twelve midnight February 14, 1961. Chicago informant reports seeing Giancana's car at Armory Lounge on 2/10, but did not observe Giancana. Plans being formulated for pretext interview with Anthony V. Champagne, Giancana's attorney and suspected channel for legitimate transactions of Giancana. Purpose is to observe physical setup of his offices for possible future penetration and or confidential source. Chicago PD advised that Giancana may have been at the wedding of Ross Prio's daughter, 2/11, although no positive identification was effected. Miami reports Giancana was observed in the Miami area, primarily at the Fontainebleau Hotel. Miami Beach. Giancana interviewed by Dale County investigators at the hotel at which time Giancana advised he was a "retired bookmaker" and was in Miami for the purpose of relaxation and rest. Giancana offered county agents a $100 bill which was declined. Giancana is considered ARMED AND DANGEROUS.

FEDERAL BUREAU OF INVESTIGATION

REPORTING OFFICE	OFFICE OF ORIGIN	DATE	INVESTIGATIVE PERIOD	
CHICAGO	CHICAGO	1961	February 15, 1961	
TITLE OF CASE		REPORT MADE BY		TYPED BY
		Ralph Hill Jr		dkc
SAMUEL M. GIANCANA, aka		CHARACTER OF CASE		
		FBI Headquarters File number 92-3171-114 Top Hoodlum Program – Anti Racketeering		

Synopsis:

Revised FBI Identification Record of Giancana, under FBI NO. 58437 set forth. Giancana allegedly has new messenger and "advise man" Joseph Borsellino. Information regarding dealings of Ben Jaffe, financial manipulator and head of Guarantee Reserve Life Insurance Company, Hammond, Indiana, set forth.

Associates

Sam Battaglia

Officer Lee Gerhke furnished SA Ralph Hill pertaining to an investigation recently conducted by the Intelligence Unit of the Chicago Police Department regarding Sam "Teets" Battaglia. On August 25, 1960, Officers of the intelligence Unit ascertained that Sam Battaglia has a race horse farm located in Poplar Grove, Illinois, which is about 13 miles west of Elgin. The name of the farm is Free Meadows Stock, Horse Breeders; listed to the caretaker whose name is Emil H. Meyer. The officers made a pretext call to this farm and ascertained that Sam Battaglia on August 25, 1960, was in Pennsylvania, but would return to the farm on August 27, 1960. It was mentioned that Rocco Salvatore was the chauffeur for Battaglia and was at the farm on August 24, 1960. Battaglia at that time was allegedly in Pennsylvania for the purpose of attending a Little League Baseball game in which his son was participating.

The pretext call also ascertained that Rocco Salvatore drives Battaglia to this farm almost every day in the early morning hours and they both return to the Casa Madrid in Melrose Park, IL, where they remain for about 2 hours during which time Battaglia checks up the daily receipts of gambling at the establishment and then proceeds to his home at 114 North Ridgeland Avenue, Oak Park. Officer Gerhke said that he learned on November 28, 1960, from a confidential source that Sam Battaglia had informed Rocco DeGrazia that he, Battaglia, was the new partner at the Casa Madrid and that DeGrazia was relegated to the status of receiving $250 per week.

Joseph Borsellino

Officer Lee Gerhke, mentioned above, advised SA Hill on January 10, 1961, that he had learned recently that Joseph Borsellino whose residence address was given as 2327 South Austin Boulevard, Cicero, was an "advance agent" for Sam Giancana and in this capacity made frequent trips to New York, Miami, and Las Vegas for the purpose of making arrangements for Giancana to meet with hoodlums personages in those areas. It was learned that the possibility exists that Borsellino may possibly be an employee of Giancana as a muscle man to handle disputes with any revolting factions in Giancana's organization.

Chicago T-1 informant advised that Joseph Borsellino, age 31, surrendered to the New York Police Department on May 10, 1959, and admitted that he slugged one David Burke in a sidewalk brawl over a woman outside of the Beau Brummel, an East Side supper club. Burke was dead when the police arrived at the scene of the incident which occurred at approximately 3:00a.m. Borsellino admitted that he struck Burke and knocked him to the sidewalk after an argument which started over Borsellino's companion, a 24 year old model, one Eve Cafferty. The charges to Borsellino were subsequently dismissed in New York City. The informant said that in his opinion, Borsellino was a man who is capable of performing any crime including murder for the persona in organized crime in the Chicago area.

Joseph Corngold

Chicago T-3 advised that Joseph "Fifke" Corngold had occasion to complain to Frank "Skid" Caruso, who is associated with Jimmy "The Bomber" Catuara, about the fact that one of Caruso's men had become drunk and disorderly at the bar operated by Corngold in Cicero and had threatened one of Corngold's lieutenants. Corngold's men, in turn, later roughed up one of Caruso's men and the situation for a time was one which might have resulted in possible repercussions. The informant stated, however, this situation was amicably resolved.

John Lardino

Detective Lee Gerhke advised that he had recently come into possession of information pertaining to the J. L. Cartage Company, 8330 Center Street, River Grove, Il, owned by J. L. Lardino, residence address 1201 Bellforte, Oak Park. According to his information, Pandin Records Company and Frank V. Pantaleo and Company were also listed as occupants of the address listed above. According to detectives, Frank Pantaleo is a close associate of hoodlums and has done numerous building and repair jobs for them. Pantaleo was reportedly remodeling the home of Charles English, 1131 North Lathrop, River Forest. Walter Blick, representative for the Panteleo Construction Co. advised Detective Gerhke that the J. L. Cartage Co. rents space at 8330 Center Street and is owned by John Lardino.

Rocco Potenzo

On January 19, 1961, Potenzo was observed at the Sunshines Restaurant, Milwaukee and Harlem Avenues, Niles, by SA's Ralph Hill and Vincent Inserra. Chicago T-8 advised that Rocky Potenzo recently related that he has "taken over" as a Chief Lieutenant for Sam Giancana, a large territory in the northwestern portion of Chicago and in the northwestern suburbs. According to this informant, Potenzo has been known to frequent the H & H Restaurant on North LaSalle Street in Chicago and some years ago drove a cab for the Diamond Cab Company and then went to Cuba where he operated a gambling casino in Havana hotel. Potenzo, from time to time, spends part of the winter tourist season in Miami, Florida.

Rocco Pranno

Chicago T-9 advised SA Hill that Rocco Pranno runs the Village of Stone Park, IL, with an iron fist. Stone Park is a small suburb located approximately five miles west of Chicago and immediately west of Melrose Park, IL. The informant said that he has occasion to learn from a Village Trustee in Stone Park that Rocco Pranno, through the Chief of Police, one Signorella, and others, had been opposing a political group in Stone Park which has been fighting Pranno and company. This political group is contemplating running some candidates on a ticket in April, 1961, which is opposed to Pranno and his influence. One of the village trustees has been threatened by Pranno with dire consequences if he runs on the opposing ticket for village trustee or for any position in Stone Park. These threats have been made by Rocco Pranno in person and telephonically. This village trustee was instructed in Rocco Pranno's auto to get out of politics in Stone Park and to "keep his mouth shut." According to the informant, the individuals involved along with Pranno, in running Stone Park, are Ciro Gulino, Village President; Albert Pranno, brother of Rocco Pranno; Andrew P. Signorella, Chief of Police of Stone Park.

The following is the identification record of Rocco Pranno under FBI No. 785212:

Contributor of Fingerprints	Name and Number	Arrested or Received	Charge
Paw Paw, Mich	Rocco Pranno	5/2/34	Not Given
Wheaton	Rocco Pranno	5/2/34	Robb. with a gun
Chicago PD	Rocco Pranno	5/2/34	D.C.
Chicago	Rocco Pranno	11/19/34	Robbery
Berwyn	Rocco Pranno	5/28/35	Susp.
Maywood	Rocco Pranno	6/6/35	Susp.
River Forest PD	Rocco Pranno	9/19/35	Armed robb.
Chicago	Rocco Pranno	11/7/35	Robbery
Chicago	Rocco Pranno	10/17/45	Burglary
U.S. Army	Rocco Pranno	3/9/46	
Chicago	Rocco Pranno	1/15/46	Burg.

     In 1935, Lieutenant Charles Egan, then of the States Attorney's office of Cook County, advised that a holdup gang was then in existence in Melrose Park, IL, who were perpetrating armed robberies of golf clubs in the area. These bandits were identified as Mike Derrico, Rocco Pranno, and George Bougadis.

     On August 21, 1935, the State's Attorney's Office of Cook County apprehended Rocco Pranno, at which time these individuals confessed to various holdings in a confession was obtained from Pranno to the effect that in a barn in the rear of his sister's home at 158 North 20th Street, Melrose Park, IL, were hidden a considerable number of weapons. Based upon this confession, the States Attorney's Office searched the barn and found a cache of weapons including the following:

        Three .38 caliber revolvers;
        One 7.65 automatic pistol;
        One sawed off 12 gauge shotgun;
        One 12 gauge Winchester pump gun;

     Included with the arsenal were oxygen tanks, acetylene tanks and an acetylene torch and other tools utilized in burglaries. Pranno, in an interview with an FBI agent in 1935, admitted that the equipment found in the barn was to be used in a bank burglary which was to take place on Labor Day of that year.

     Lieutenant Charles Calleindo advised SA John O'Leary in 1946 that on one occasion he arrested Rocco Pranno in the act of burglarizing a store in Melrose Park, Illinois. At that point, Pranno drew a gun and fired but the revolver misfired. Pranno was taken to the States Attorney's office by Calleindo and charged with burglary and assault. This charge was reduced to malicious mischief and Pranno was sentenced to 30 days.

In 1955 Officers Stan Lang and Herb Mertes of the DuPage County Sheriff's Office, alleged that DuPage activities including coin machines and pinball machines, were controlled by Anthony Perotti. Assisting Perotti in the control of DuPage County was Rocco Pranno. Information has been reported previously to the effect that Pranno, in 1958, took over juke boxes and coin machine operations in Kane County, IL. The principal business in Kane County was Aurora-Kane County Amusement Company located at 1029 St. Charles Road, Elgin. As of June, 1958, the Aurora-Kane County Amusement Company had 60 pinball machines and 40 bowling alley type machines operating in Kane County.

Chicago T-11 reported that Robert "Rocco" Pranno is an ex-convict and front man for Sam Giancana. A front man for Pranno was Ralph Francis Kelly, former owner Kane County Amusement Company, who is being held as "captive" in his own business. Pranno and Kelly are still paper partners in the company but were only operating ten pinball machines and about 50 bowling machines. It was the informant's opinion that Pranno had been ordered not to "push" coin machines in that area in view of Senate Crime Communion investigations which had been held in 1959 pertaining to that situation. This informant also stated that allegations had been received that Sam Giancana and William Daddono were fighting one another for the control of the "syndicate." The conjecture was that in the event that Daddono gained control, Pranno would be out in Kane County.

Referenced report reveals that Giancana was observed by SA Ralph Hill at Rocco Pranno's and Mike Moreno's Key Club in Stone park on November 5, 1960, having proceeded from O'Hare Field where he arrived on a flight from San Francisco.

Frank Szafran

Reference is made above to Sam Giancana being observed at the Key Club in Stone Park. The automobile which was utilized by Giancana was registered to Frank Szafran. Chicago Police Department files indicate that Frank Szafran his last know address as 5847 North Oconte Avenue, Chicago. He was born on 11/25/1920, at Lowell, Mass, is 5'8" tall and weighs 170 lbs. He was arrested on 9/23/1958, for disorderly conduct; the complainant was Ruth Wiederhold. He was arrested on 9/30/1958, for disorderly conduct. The complainant was Mary Szafran, his wife. Frank Szafran last known employment listed as a bartender at the Forest Lounge for Rocco Potenzo.

Rudolph Fratto

Mr. Fratto said that he is a "Store Salesman" for the West Suburban Company and that prior to his entering in this field was an organizer for the local Upholsters Union. Fratto said that he is the brother of Lew Farrell, true name Luige Fratto. He also said he has another brother named Frank Fratto, whom Rudolph said is commonly called "Frankie One Ear."

Chicago T-1 stated that Rudolph Fratto, also known as "Rudy", "Guy" and "John Farrell," is well known as one of the notorious Fratto brothers of Luigi, Frankie, and Rudy and in this connection is closely associated with many of Chicago's organized hoodlums.

Chicago T-1 advised on January 27, 1961, that he was in possession of a letter which he received anonymously on that date. He advised that he is not aware as to whom the sender may have been, however, this letter states as follows:

"Why dose this guy stay out of the papers Rudy Fratto, this guy is Barney Baker's partner, he and Barney are known GOONS for the Teamsters. Rudy stays out of the news. Rudy and Barbey are bodyguards for Jimmy Hoffa when Hoffa is in town. You must pass them at the door to see Hoffa when at the Shoreland Hotel. Rudy is the brother of Iowa gang boss Lew (Farrell) Fratto. Also, Rudy's daughter is married to the son of Willie "Potatoes" Daddono. This puts Rudy in a strange spot with Hoffa. Hoffa is obligated to the Mafia. Two weeks ago at the Shoreland, Lew Farrell met with Hoffa for two days, the reason, should Joey Glimco fall. Willie and Lew want Rudy to move in Glimco's spot. Last year Rudy and Barney gave a severe beating to John Mahoney, organizer for the produce drivers union. John was talking too much. Rudy can be seen at the home of Daddano two or three times a week for orders. He drives a blue Olds. He lives at 1518 Harlem, River Forest. Last week after Lew left Hoffa, he had a big meeting at his mother's home. Present were Paul Dorfman, Barney Baker, Rudy, Willie and others."

Las Vegas, Nevada, Enterprises

Investments and Hotel Casino's
Las Vegas, Nevada

The information contained herein pertains largely to three hotels in the Las Vegas, Nevada area, namely the following:

>   Stardust Hotel
>   Riviera Hotel
>   Desert Inn Hotel

Chicago T-46 advised on January 28, 1960, that Charles "Babe" Baron had advised Murray Humphreys, previously described, at that time a floor manager of the Riviera Hotel in Las Vegas, that he had met with "Mooney" pertaining to the situation in Las Vegas whereby John Roselli had been getting into difficulty with the hotel and casino operators in the Las Vegas area. Giancana, according to Chicago T-46, advised Baron that he was to consider himself as his, (Giancana's) representative in Las Vegas.

Murray Humphreys advised T-1 informant that it had to become necessary for him to recently severely admonish John Roselli for his attitude and demeanor in Las Vegas. Humphreys further advised the informant that Charles Baron was given instructions to consider himself as not only Giancana's, but as Humphreys' representative in Las Vegas.

Chicago T-3 advised in December, 1960, and January, 1961, that Sam Giancana, Anthony Accardo, John Drew, Morris "Moe" Dalitz, Murray Humphreys, and two unidentified individuals from Cleveland, Ohio, one of whom was probably Morris Kleinman, had recently negotiated a "contract" whereby Giancana and the Chicago group acquired an undisclosed number of points or shares in a three-way deal which was not clear to the informant but which apparently involved the Riviera, Desert Inn, and Stardust Hotel Casinos in Las Vegas, Nevada.

The informant stated that the ground work for these negotiations was laid a number of years ago by Anthony Accardo and Paul DeLucia, also known as Paul "The Waiter" Ricca. Ricca is currently completing a three-year sentence at the Federal Penitentiary in Terre Haute, Indiana, for income tax evasion. Negotiations were further facilitated by the efforts of Eugene C. James, who made several trips to Las Vegas, Nevada, to negotiate with individuals in that area, according to the informant. James, for his part in the negotiations, will receive approximately $1,000 per month from Giancana while James is in the penitentiary. This $1,000 a month will actually be contributed by John Drew from a latter's interest which is $6,000 a month. According to the informant, the kingpin in the negotiations in Las Vegas was Giancana, ably assisted by Anthony Accardo and Murray Humphreys.

According to the informant, the negotiations are not quite complete at this time.

However, for all practical purposes, the contract is sealed and the only part remaining will be the "picking up pf loose ends." The informant clarified the latter by stating that it will be necessary now to obtain clearance from the Nevada Gaming Commission and other State of Nevada officials for individuals that Giancana plans to place as officials continued that the contribution given by this group amounts to approximately $36,000 per month. The return of this investment is unknown to the informant.

Chicago informant continued that Murray Humphreys, Gus Alex, and Frank Ferraro were also included in these negotiations although they did not take an active part in the final stages.

It was also learned that Murray Humphreys had recently instructed Sidney Korshak, described as a prominent Chicago attorney, that Korshak was not to become involved in certain transactions in Las Vegas, which also involved the Chicago group of Humphreys, Giancana, and Frank Ferraro. Humphreys himself was interested in the Stardust Hotel and, therefore, Korshak was not to have any interest therein.

It was advised that Gus Alex and Murray Humphreys told the informant that Sam Giancana had issued orders to the effect that he did not want any interests outside of Chicago to divert any funds emanating from the Las Vegas gambling casinos to interests other than the group represented by Chicago. It was noted by the informant that one Nick, possibly Nick Civella of Kansas City, Missouri, had arranged through Eugene James to obtain points in certain gambling casinos in Vegas. It was the understanding that Nick would receive a certain amount of money on a regular basis for his part in these negotiations as would Eugene James; however, Nick was to receive a regular amount and from the amount he received, was to pay Eugene James for his, part. The informant stated it was apparent to him that Nick was to receive $6,000 a month for his part in the negotiations.

Criminal Activities

Gambling

Gus' Steak House
4819 Roosevelt Road
Cicero, Illinois

Chicago informant advised on December 16, 1960, that Gus' Steak House, which is a restaurant opened by the "gambling syndicate." The informant stated that quite often Sam Giancana was known to the informant as "Mooney", comes into the restaurant and is always accompanied by a man known as "Dutch", who carries a brief case. Giancana sits at the bar while Dutch places long distance telephone calls and that's when he gets the party, he speaks to them in Italian. Usually a day or so later, men come in from all over the country and are usually accompanied by a man with a brief case, they then proceed to the back room and Giancana then issues instructions that they are not to be disturbed.

The informant said that the upstairs of Gus' Steak House is completely devoted to gambling, they have a horse book, dice tables, card tables, and black jack tables. The whole layout is operated by an individual known to the informant as Frank Sharkey. Sharkey according to the informant is an ex-convict. This informant is identical to Frank "Sharkey" Eulo, a close friend of Giancana and an individual who is reported to be his brother-in-law.

Chicago informant T-16 advised on January 26, 1961, that Gus Kringles, operator of Gus Steak House, is the contact man for "syndicate" activities in the near western suburbs of Chicago. His contacts are with Giancana, Sam Battaglia, and other unidentified Cicero gamblers.

Airliner Lounge
Higgins and River Roads
Rosemont, Illinois

CG T-18 advised SA Robert Baker that the Airliner Lounge, 9465 Higgins Road, was operating as a horse book parlor in the lounge as well as his apartments located on the second floor of the building. Informant states that operation therein is run by Rocco Potenzo, but it was the understanding of the informant that Sam Giancana is the actual operator. The Lounge ostensibly had a direct line to a "sports center" in downtown Chicago and race results are relayed through a loud speaker set up in the lounge, in sufficient detail to apprise the better of the first three positions in the race at the time the race is actually being run.

According to the informant, the Mayor of Rosemont is an individual 34 years of age and fairly well off financially. Informant states that he knows of no instance whereby the Mayor accepted a payoff from Giancana or Potenzo but he is concerned over the bookmaking operation in the Airline Lounge, however, dose not know how to cope with it. A man, who did not identify himself, approached the Mayor of Rosemont, stating that he was authorized to extend an invitation for the Mayor and any other person that the Mayor might choose to fly to Las Vegas for a two week trip with all expenses paid. This individual told the Mayor, "I am sure you will enjoy the gambling since you won't lose." Informant noted regarding the sports center mentioned above that it has a direct wire to a similar sports center in New York City and this is operated without the knowledge of the Bell Telephone Company.

CG T-18 advised that one of the persons connected with the Airliner Lounge and the SOS Lounge located directly across the street from the Airliner in one Mel Vaci. The license of the Airline Lounge is listed to Henry Hodl.

Labor Union Activity

CG T-3 advised in January, 1961, that Eugene C. James former president of Local 46 of the International Laundry Workers Union had been recently replaced by Gus Zapas. Although Zapas in not president of this local, he is business agent and for all practical purposes exerts the same amount of control over the local's activities as did James. James is presently undergoing one-two year sentence in the state of New Jersey for labor extortion. Zapas, according to the informant, was sponsored by Sam Giancana who apparently thinks of him. This was contrary to the thinking of Gus Alex who, according to the informant, is not in favor of Gus Zapas being associated with this local inasmuch as Alex dose not trust him. It would seem, however, according to the informant, that Giancana's word in this regard is final.

Armory Lounge
7427 West Roosevelt
Forest Park

CG T-21 advised on January 21, 1961, that Giancana was observed at Armory Lounge on that date at 3:00p.m. The informant also observed two automobiles drive up and go inside the lounge. The cars were registered to Guido DeChiaro, 128 North 24 Street, Melrose Park and D. Sibilano 5541 West Belmont, Chicago.

Detective Lee Gerhke advised SA Hill that Guido DeChiaro is the father-in-law of Michael Urgo, who was shot and killed in front of his, Urgo's home in Elmwood Park, while protecting DeChiaro from a robbery or kidnapping attempt. DeChiaro is the owner of B & M Appliances, also known as M & D Music Company, operators of juke boxes and pinball machines. According to Gerhke, his information is that DeChiaro was invading the territory of Joe "Baggy Pants" Perrino, Joe "Long Pants" Perroti, George Bellison and Joe "Black Joe" "Nigger Joe" Amato.

An inquiry into the death of Michael Urgo was held and a verdict of murder by persons unknown was returned. It is noted that Guido DeChiaro resides at 1725 Thatcher Avenue, Elmwood Park, immediately next door to Joseph "Gags" Gagliano, who according to Detective Gerhke, is a close associate of Giancana and Tony Accardo.

A FBI undercover photo from the Agents car of the Armory Lounge

FEDERAL BUREAU OF INVESTIGATION

REPORTING OFFICE	OFFICE OF ORIGIN	DATE	INVESTIGATIVE PERIOD	
CHICAGO	CHICAGO	1961	February 18, 1961	
TITLE OF CASE		REPORT MADE BY		TYPED BY
				dkc
SAMUEL M. GIANCANA, aka		CHARACTER OF CASE		
		FBI Headquarters File number 92-3171 Top Hoodlum Program – Anti Racketeering. Airtel teletype		

Daily summary, Maher, Chicago PD Intelligence unit has been investigating situation involving purchase of six hundred thousand dollars worth of electronic equipment from RCA with military specs. Bulk of equipment is some five thousand radios suitable for installation in Military jeeps. Info came to the attention of Maher Jan when he arrested Marshall Caifano, Chicago top hood, Charles Delmonico, son of Charles Tourino, and Harold McClintock, Official of Disabled American Veterans. Arrest made as apart of investigation in three gangland murders which occurred in Chicago in December 1960. Caifano was suspect, and was accompanied by two listed above at time of arrest. McClintock had in possession invoice from RCA Cannonsburg, PA. Maher indicated that this equipment can be utilized only I military units, and he was told by one source that this equipment will probably go to Cuba. Charles Delmonico gave residence as Detroit, but true address is Miami Beach. Caifano made a call from California to Delmonico's residence in Miami. Caifano according to investigation conducted, this office reflected Caifano negotiating for casino's in Cuba.

Investigation in Miami and New York reflects Sam Giancana to have been in recent contact with Charles Tourine. Giancana has made numerous visits to Miami area in recent past, purpose of visits unknown. New York informant has reported that Giancana has made tentative plans for doing away with Fidel Castro. Discreetly ascertain through established sources details about purchased of above equipment at RCA, keeping in mind possibilities of neutrally act violation to be protected from premature disclosure. New York furnished known background of McClintock. Chicago is aware of the fact that CIA has in past made purchases of military equipment for anti-Castro forces through covert channels, however, nature of instant purchase is unknown by Chicago. Bureau requested to consider ascertaining through appropriate liaison with CIA any covert anti Castro activity in this regard. Investigation conducted at Guys and Dolls Bar, Niles, February 16, 1961, reveals Frank Szafran, chauffeur and associate of Giancana's, employed there as bartender. During investigation, several hoodlums appearing individuals approached Szafran and asked for "Moe and Rocky." Moe is possibly Giancana and Rocky is Rocco Potenzo, Giancana's lieutenant.

FEDERAL BUREAU OF INVESTIGATION

REPORTING OFFICE	OFFICE OF ORIGIN	DATE	INVESTIGATIVE PERIOD	
CHICAGO	CHICAGO	1961	February 23, 1961	
TITLE OF CASE		**REPORT MADE BY**		**TYPED BY** dkc
SAMUEL M. GIANCANA, aka		**CHARACTER OF CASE** FBI Headquarters File number 92-3171 Top Hoodlum Program – Anti Racketeering. Daily Summary Airtel		

Gustay Allgauer, owner, Allgauer's restaurant, old Heidelberg and Allgauer's Villa Moderne, interviewed 2/21/61. Emphatically denied any connection with Giancana. Allgauer extremely hostile at outset of interview stated "not a dime have I ever given to hoodlums." Allgauer said he has never had personal contact with Giancana, and saw Giancana when subject was observed by Allgauer registering for room at Villa Moderne with an unknown blond about three weeks ago. Allgauer suggested that Leo Olson, former manager at his fireside restaurant, may be tie in with Giancana for following reason. Olson acquired a thirty thousand dollar home shortly after the fire at fireside. Then "purchased" the Villa Venice Club shortly after that. Allgauer stated "Olson didn't have fifty cents for any purchase." Stated unequivocally that Villa Venice is owned by Giancana. Above information corroborated by Chicago informants who have stated that Olson is definitely a front for Giancana at the Villa Venice.

Later restaurant has been alleged for some time to be owned by Chicago hoodlums, and has been utilized for weddings of syndicate hoodlums and there relatives. Last used as site of reception for wedding of daughter of Ross Prio, 2/11/61. Investigation continuing on this situation. Allgauer advised in addition to above that Murray Humphreys, Gus Alex, Frank Ferraro and Hy Godfrey have been utilizing old Heidelberg Restaurant for luncheon engagements for last several weeks. Alex, Ferraro and Godfrey last observed in this restaurant 2/20/61. John Matassa observed at Armory Lounge on a nightly basis. Matassa is a retired Chicago Police man formerly on narcotics detail and is known as bodyguard and chauffeur for Giancana. Chicago informant reports that in addition to this, Matassa has been assigned by Giancana to examine loot taken from lucrative burglaries of furs and jewelry, and take choice items for Giancana. This informant stated that Giancana utilizes Stop Lite Lounge, Cicero, as place where Giancana maintains two large safes containing money, jewelry, ect. This place is short distance from Gus's Steak House, large scale gambling operation of Giancana. Stop Lite is known hangout of thieves, and is also alleged to be gambling operation.

FEDERAL BUREAU OF INVESTIGATION

REPORTING OFFICE	OFFICE OF ORIGIN	DATE	INVESTIGATIVE PERIOD	
CHICAGO	CHICAGO	1961	February 24, 1961	
TITLE OF CASE		REPORT MADE BY		TYPED BY
				dkc
SAMUEL M. GIANCANA, aka		CHARACTER OF CASE		
		FBI Headquarters File Number 92-3171 Top Hoodlum Program – Anti Racketeering. Daily Summary Airtel		

Giancana observed at Armory Lounge during evening of 2/23/61. Chicago informant states Joe Pignatello, driver and chauffeur for Giancana and other hoodlums, had purchased a night club in Chicago and is possible replacing Marshall Caifano in influence in Chicago near north side clubs. He drives a 1960 Cadillac, observed at Armory Lounge during surveillance. License registered to U.S. Auto Leasing Co. Chicago, and leased to Joseph Pignatello. Lease expires March 18, 1961, and Pignatello had advised he dose not desire to utilize services of this company during the coming year. Above car formerly leased to Deluxe Cigarette Service, Chicago, which is operated by Eddie Vogel, Chicago hoodlum.

Chicago informant advised this date that Giancana, William Daddono and George Dix have recently taken over gambling activities in Robbins, IL, a Chicago suburb populated mainly by Negroes. Informant states his opportunity to be employed in the big game in Robbins.

FEDERAL BUREAU OF INVESTIGATION

REPORTING OFFICE	OFFICE OF ORIGIN	DATE	INVESTIGATIVE PERIOD	
CHICAGO	CHICAGO	1961	March 2, 1961	
TITLE OF CASE		REPORT MADE BY		TYPED BY
				dkc
SAMUEL M. GIANCANA, aka		CHARACTER OF CASE		
		FBI Headquarters File number 92-3171 Top Hoodlum Program – Anti Racketeering. Daily Summary Airtel		

Miami advised that Martin Dardis, enforcement officer, stated that Giancana possibly in Las Vegas. Las Vegas advised that Joe Pignatello rented an apartment at the Diplomat House, Las Vegas, for one month, for one occupant. Noted that Pignatello has been alleged to be an advance agent for Giancana, and in this capacity, preceded Giancana to those areas where Giancana intends to visit. Pignatello, in summer of 1960, rented a home near Las Vegas wherein Giancana, family, and Phyllis McGuire resided for one month. Joe Borsellino, described as bodyguard for Giancana, and Sidney Korshak, also in Las Vegas. Las Vegas conducting extensive investigation to ascertain if Giancana is present in that area.

B. K. Bruno, president of Country Investmants, Melrose Park, owner of property on which Armory Lounge located advised this corp. founded by himself, Sam and James Aiuppa, brothers of Joseph Aiuppa, Chicago hoodlum. Purpose of corp. is investing in small parcels of real estate. Armory Lounge building and property purchased by Corp. in 1956 from Joseph Annarino. Denied that Joey Aiuppa or Giancana except by reputation. Investment in Armory Lounge strictly business, no known hoodlum connections. Alderman Thomas Rosenberg, Chicago, re-contacted this date about info previously furnished to effect that he was in New York City in October, 1960, to attend the world series, accompanied by Sam Kaplan, Milt Stern, Bernard Cohn, and unidentified steel man from Pittsburg. Rosenberg stated on reflection that Alderman John D'Arco, Chicago, was also in attendance in New York, and stayed in room reserved by Rosenberg. Noted that D'Arco is known associate of Chicago hoods, and is acquainted with Giancana, also stated he forgot about D'Arco until after original contact by agent. Rosenberg stated he thinks he, Rosenberg, is under consideration for U.S.D.C. Judgeship and wants to keep the record clean.

FEDERAL BUREAU OF INVESTIGATION				
REPORTING OFFICE	**OFFICE OF ORIGIN**	**DATE**	**INVESTIGATIVE PERIOD**	
CHICAGO	CHICAGO	1961	March 7, 1961	
TITLE OF CASE		**REPORT MADE BY**		**TYPED BY**
		Ralph Hill Jr.		dkc
SAMUEL M. GIANCANA, aka		**CHARACTER OF CASE** FBI Headquarters File number 92-3171-135 Top Hoodlum Program – Anti Racketeering		

Synopsis:

Charles Giancana, Anthony V. Champagne, interviewed and declined to furnish pertinent information regarding activities of Sam Giancana. John Matassa, alleged chauffeur of Giancana, interviewed and denied being employed by Giancana. Chicago informant states main wire service for gambling in northwest suburb of Niles, IL, is out of Riviera Lounge, run for Giancana and Rocco Potenzo. Potenzo offered Village President of Rosemont, IL, $1,000 per month to operate wire service in that village. Identities of licenses of some of Giancana's alleged operations set forth. Chicago informant stated Giancana in partnership with Gustey Allgauer at latter's restaurant in the Villa Modern Motel, Highland Park, IL. Allgauer interviewed and denies above, states Giancana in owner of Villa Venice, Wheeling, IL.

Relatives

Charles Giancana, also known
As Charles Kane

Charles Giancana was interviewed by SA Ralph Hill Jr. and Thomas Parrish on February 28, 1961, at the Thunderbolt Motel, 5400 River Road, Rosemont, IL. Giancana stated that he is the youngest brother of Sam Giancana and operates the Thunderbolt Motel, formerly known as the River Forest Motel. He said the property and buildings are owned in trust and said that if the Agents desired to obtain further information regarding this trust they should contact the attorney for the trust, Anthony V. Champagne. Giancana took the interviewing Agents on a tour of the premises, which revealed that this property has undergone extensive remodeling and rebuilding, and now includes, in addition to the motel units, a first class restaurant named "Mr. Anthony's," two cocktail lounges, a night club, and a swimming pool. Giancana evaded questioning pertaining to Sam Giancana's business and said that his contacts with his brother are very infrequent and that he sees him on an average of three or four times per year. He described Sam Giancana as "a kid considerate family man, who never hurt anyone in his life."

Giancana stated that the family consists of four sisters and two brothers, in addition to him self. The other brother is Joseph "Pepe" Giancana with whom Charles Giancana states he has very little contact and is not acquainted with the facts pertaining to Joseph Giancana's livelihood. He said that the parents, both of whom are deceased, are of Sicilian origin and were both born in Sicily.

Anthony V. Champagne

Champagne has been described in the past as attorney for Sam Giancana and was described by Charles Giancana above as the attorney for trust relating to the Thunderbolt Motel.

Champagne was interviewed on February 15, 1961, by SA Ralph Hill Jr. and Vincent Inserra at his office at 1 North LaSalle Street, Chicago, IL. Champagne exhibited a friendly attitude towards the interviewing Agents and declined all questions pertaining to Giancana for the reason which he stated "Mooney is my client on two or three dealings and I therefore exercise my privilege concerning information pertaining to him." Champagne stated that he finds it extremely difficult to locate Giancana when and if he needs him for consultation and other than this had nothing more to say relating to his client.

John Matassa

Matassa has been described by Joseph Morris, Deputy Superintendent, Chicago Police Department, as a "hoodlum cop" and one who is alleged to be a chauffeur and bodyguard for Giancana. Matassa is presently on Disability Retirement from the Chicago Police Department.

John Matassa was interviewed on March 1, 1961, at his residence 1655 North Nashville, Chicago, by SA Hill and John Russell Jr. Matassa was advised that information had been received to the effect that he was a close associate of Giancana and had been utilized by Giancana on occasion as chauffeur. Matassa was visibly upset at the onset of the interview and became more so as the interview progressed. He said, "you received this information from that (obscene) Morris and I'll tell you right now that I have never chauffeured Giancana, but that, if he asked me to chauffeur him, I would gladly do so." Matassa at that point became vitriolic and said that the reason he was chosen by Morris as being an associate of "hoodlums" is because he is of Italian abstract and because of the fact that he was born and raised in the Taylor-Halsted section of Chicago, which is the locale of many of these individuals, including Giancana. He said that for that reason he "became acquainted with Giancana and grew up with him." It was pointed out to Matassa that he, Matassa, was considerably younger than Giancana, in addition to which Giancana was not raised in the Taylor-Halsted section but in the Grand Avenue section, which is quite a distance removed from the former section. Matassa then stated he has been acquainted with Giancana through the years through family connections and said that his wife's mother and Giancana's father both died on the same date and that, for that reason, he attended both wakes.

Matassa then said that he became acquainted with "hoodlums" due to the fact that he was a detective on the Narcotics Detail of the Chicago Police Department for seven years and in this capacity knew many persons of unsavory character, because of the fact that, "you could hardly expect me to do my work in the basement of a church." He was then asked if that statement indicated that persons such as Giancana, were involved in the sale of narcotics and stated unequivocally that this is not so and that no information had ever come to him to the effect that the "so-called hoodlum element" had ever dealt in narcotics or in prostitution. In his opinion, the scope of the "syndicate operations was limited to primarily gambling." In that connection, he said that on occasions he would allow a bookmaker "to take me to Fagman's (men's clothing store in the Sherman Hotel, Chicago) and buy me a new hat.

Matassa said that he frequents many places which are also frequented by Giancana; namely the North Avenue Steak House in Maywood, the Armory Lounge in Forest Park, and other establishments located in Cicero. He said that he visits the Armory Lounge on two or three nights a week where he occasionally plays Gin Rummy and converses with his good friend Carmen Fanelli.

He said that during these occasions in which he dines in these establishments he occasionally sees Giancana and other persons but has no conversation with them due to the fact that they feel that to converse with him would, in effect, place him, Matassa, in jeopardy in his job. He stated that he is a very close friend of Frank Sinatra and whenever Sinatra comes to Chicago he acts as personal bodyguard and chauffeur for him in return for which Sinatra gives him paid vacations to Las Vegas and Miami.

Matassa exhibited a letter of recommendation to Governor Otto Kerner of IL, which was written by William Randolph Hearst Jr. of Hearst Publications. This letter recommended Matassa for the job of personal chauffeur of Kerner. Matassa said that he did not obtain this position because of the fact that Superintendent Morris interfered and cause him to be turned down for the appointment.

Donald J. Medlevine

According to the records of the Playboy Club in Chicago, Giancana is carried as a member and all correspondence pertaining to Giancana is to be directed to Donald Medlevine.

Medlevine was interviewed by SA Hill on February 15, 1961, and stated that he is the former co-owner of the Chez Paree night club of Chicago, which is now closed. He said that he is slightly acquainted with Sam Giancana but knows him only as a former patron of the Chez Paree. He said that he has had no dealings with Giancana other than that above.

Thomas Rosenberg

It has been previously reported that Giancana was residing at the Hampshire House, New York City, from October 6-10, 1960, where he was allegedly registered under the name of Thomas Rosenberg, 1 North LaSalle Street, Chicago.

Alderman Thomas Rosenberg, 1 North LaSalle Street, was interviewed on February 20, 1961, By SA Hill and John Roberts and advised that he is the Alderman for Chicago's 44th Ward. He advised that from October 6 thru the 10, 1960, he was registered at the Hampshire House, New York City, for the purpose of attending the World Series, then in progress in New York. He said that he was accompanied by Sam Kaplan, Milt Stern, Bernard Z. Cohn, and an unidentified steel man from Pittsburgh. He said he did not know Sam Giancana, except by reputation, and states that Giancana was definitely not, as far as he knew, in contact with any of his associates at the Hampshire House.

Alderman Rosenberg re-contacted SA Hill on March 2, 1961, at which time he stated that he recalled after the original contact by SA Hill that Alderman John D'Arco of the First Ward of Chicago, had asked him to obtain a room at the Hampshire House for him to attend the World Series. Alderman Rosenberg said he complied with Alderman D'Arco request and obtained a room for him. He said he went out with Alderman D'Arco on several occasions during this visit in New York, but reiterated that he did not observe Sam Giancana. It is noted that Chicago T-3 stated on several occasions during the latter part of 1960 that Alderman John D'Arco of the First Ward was in contact with many Chicago "hoodlums" such as Murray Humphreys, Gus Alex, and Frank Ferraro.

FEDERAL BUREAU OF INVESTIGATION

REPORTING OFFICE	OFFICE OF ORIGIN	DATE	INVESTIGATIVE PERIOD
CHICAGO	CHICAGO	1961	March 13, 1961

TITLE OF CASE	REPORT MADE BY	TYPED BY
		dkc

SAMUEL M. GIANCANA, aka	**CHARACTER OF CASE**
	FBI Headquarters File number 92-3171-151 Top Hoodlum Program – Anti Racketeering. Daily Summary

Leo Scott, assistant manager of the Villa Modern Motel, advised Villa Modern leased by international Motel, Inc. Subsidiary of Jupiter Oil Co., limited. Informant advised Gus Allgater is presently attempting to get rid of the Old Heidleberg Restaurant. Spot check at Armory Lounge, and Giancana's hangouts and residences did not reveal his presence. Chicago informants state Giancana is aware of investigation and as a result has not been frequenting known hangouts.

FEDERAL BUREAU OF INVESTIGATION

REPORTING OFFICE	OFFICE OF ORIGIN	DATE	INVESTIGATIVE PERIOD	
CHICAGO	CHICAGO	1961	March 17, 1961	
TITLE OF CASE		REPORT MADE BY		TYPED BY
				dkc
SAMUEL M. GIANCANA, aka		CHARACTER OF CASE		
		FBI Headquarters File Number 92-3171 Top Hoodlum Program – Anti Racketeering. Daily Summary		

Anthony Giroliami, Alderman, Chicago contacted this date at his request regarding Evanston and Red Top Cab Companies. Noted that CG informant reported previously of Giancana's interest in these firms. Giroliami, former law partner and associate of deceased alderman, Pasty Petrone, advised closely associated with Fred Bartoli and Sam Levine, current operators of both cab firms listed. When asked if Joey Glimco had an interest in the Flash Cab Co., Giroliami replied no.

FEDERAL BUREAU OF INVESTIGATION

REPORTING OFFICE	OFFICE OF ORIGIN	DATE	INVESTIGATIVE PERIOD	
CHICAGO	CHICAGO	1961	March 20, 1961	
TITLE OF CASE		REPORT MADE BY		TYPED BY
				dkc
SAMUEL M. GIANCANA, aka		CHARACTER OF CASE		
		FBI Headquarters File number 92-3171-162 Top Hoodlum Program – Anti Racketeering. Memorandum		

Synopsis:

Current inquiry disclosed Giancana attempting to employ two Chicago jewel thieves as muscle men and paid killers. Giancana pressured his way into partnership at gambling club Wagon Wheel which now has gambling take averaging $1,000 per day.

Giancana Attempts to Hire Muscle Men and Killers

A Chicago informant has advised that Giancana offered Chicago jewel thieves Steve Tomares and James D'Antonio employment in his organization. They were to be paid $150 per week and were to be placed on a "stand-by basis." Their duties would be to take care of any job requiring strong-arm tactics or killing in connection with activities of the Giancana group. The informant advised Tomares and D'Antonio turned the proposition down because "they might have to kill their friends."

Giancana Muscled Into Gambling at the Wagon Wheel

The informant advised that the Wagon Wheel was run as a gambling operation for many years by Nick D'Amico. D'Amico yielded to pressure by Giancana and took him in as a "partner" at the Wagon Wheel. The Wagon Wheel is now operating as a horse book and racing wire service, affording poker and dice games at the same location. The average take for the horse racing operations runs to approximately $1,000 per day.

The Riviera Lounge is run by Salvatore Mercurio. This club has a horse book operation and is the scene of operations for strip girls and prostitutes. Each evening the money from operations at the Wagon Wheel is collected and turned over to a Giancana associate, Rocco Potenzo, at the Rivera.

Oil Company Leases Property in Which Giancana May have Interest

Recent investigation has indicated that Giancana had an interest in the Villa Modern Motel, Northbrook, IL. Mark Friedman, vice president of the Jupiter Midwest Oil Company, advised on 3/14/61, that the company in January 1961 leased the property occupied by the Villa Modern Motel. Friedman was questioned concerning the possible interest of Giancana in the Villa Modern and he denied any such connection. When questioned further concerning the history of the leasing transaction in connection with Villa Modern, Friedman terminated the interview and asked the agents to meet him in the office of his lawyer if any further information was desired.

FEDERAL BUREAU OF INVESTIGATION

REPORTING OFFICE	OFFICE OF ORIGIN	DATE	INVESTIGATIVE PERIOD
CHICAGO	CHICAGO	1961	March 20 , 1961

TITLE OF CASE	REPORT MADE BY	TYPED BY
		dkc
SAMUEL M. GIANCANA, aka	**CHARACTER OF CASE** FBI Headquarters File Number 92-3171 Top Hoodlum Program – Anti Racketeering. Daily Summary	

Chicago PD Intelligence unit observed Giancana 3/17/61, at the Monclare Funeral Home in Chicago, attending the wake of Joseph "Crackers" Mendino, Chicago hoodlum who died of heart attack on March 16, 1961. Accompanying Giancana was Anthony Accardo, Sam Battaglia, Marshall Caifano, Sam and Chuck English, and numerous other persons stated by PD to be known hoodlums. Los Angeles advised there are numerous firms carried that area as B&K. Inquired with several of these firms negative of knowledge of RCA radio phone equipment. Noted that Chicago advised four thousand radio phones obtained from RCA as gift to Dave were sent to B&K Wholesalers, LA. Mrs. Koolish contacted at LA, stated Abraham Koolish now located in Chicago. Mrs. Koolish disclaims knowledge or receipt of radio phones.

FEDERAL BUREAU OF INVESTIGATION

REPORTING OFFICE	OFFICE OF ORIGIN	DATE	INVESTIGATIVE PERIOD
CHICAGO	CHICAGO	1961	March 20, 1961

TITLE OF CASE	REPORT MADE BY	TYPED BY
		dkc
SAMUEL M. GIANCANA, aka	**CHARACTER OF CASE** FBI Headquarters File number 92-3171-163 Top Hoodlum Program – Anti Racketeering. Memorandum	

Synopsis:

Giancana's brother is building additional motel units at cost of approximately $200,000. Possibility of subject investing in this venture being explored. Anthony Giroliami, Chicago Alderman, denies that Giancana had interest in two Evanston, IL, cab companies. Giancana group building plush restaurant and lounge at Stone Park, IL.

Giancana's Brother Adding Motel Units

Charles Giancana, brother of the subject, was contacted on 3/16/61 and confirmed that he contemplates adding 48 motel units to the Thunderbolt Motel which he operates. He indicated the cost would be around $200,000. Charles was questioned about the possible investment of money by Sam Giancana and he denied that the subject has any affiliation with the motel. He was also asked about hoodlum investments in the legitimate business and the reason why these interests as rule are handled on an undercover basis and kept secret. Charles stated that the primary reason for this concealment is that if hoodlum affiliations were revealed the resulting publicity would cause the general public to believe that muscle was involved in these establishments.

Chicago Alderman Claims Giancana
Has No Interest in Two Cab Companies

Information had been developed that Giancana possible had an interest in the Red Top Cab Company and the Evanston Cab Company, both Evanston, IL. Anthony Giroliami, Chicago Alderman, advised on 3/17/61 that he is close associate of Fred Bartoli and Sam Levine, the current operators of the Red Top and Evanston Cab Companies. Giroliami stated that Giancana has absolutely no interest in either one of these companies. The alderman stated that Bartoli was formerly a vice president of the Flash Cab Company. This organization and the Evanston Cab Company have had a running feud continuing for the past several years. According to Alderman Giroliami the Flash Cab Company had utilized a Chicago Police Officer to monitor telephone calls made to Evanston Cab Company and to use this information in an effort to divert business from the Evanston Cab Company.

A Chicago informant had advised that Bartoli and Levine have expressed a half million dollars for new equipment. The informant said he had heard the Evanston Cab Co. had taken in five new partners who were allegedly hoodlums but whose identities were unknown to the informant.

Giancana Group Building Plush Restaurant and Lounge

An informant has reported that a Giancana group consisting of Rocky Infelice, James Mirro, and Americo DiPietto, who were former operators of the North Avenue Steak House, are involved in a new venture. They are building a plush restaurant and lounge with facilities for meeting and gambling. This establishment will be known as the Lido Motel and is located at Stone Park, IL. It is now in the process of refurnishing and is expected to open within a few months.

FEDERAL BUREAU OF INVESTIGATION

REPORTING OFFICE	OFFICE OF ORIGIN	DATE	INVESTIGATIVE PERIOD	
CHICAGO	CHICAGO	1961	March 23, 1961	
TITLE OF CASE		REPORT MADE BY		TYPED BY
				dkc
SAMUEL M. GIANCANA, aka		**CHARACTER OF CASE**		
		FBI Headquarters File Number 92-3171-173 Top Hoodlum Program – Anti Racketeering. Daily Summary		

Re, Joseph Pignatello. Las Vegas advised instant that Pignatello arrested on 3/22/61, by Clark County Sheriffs Office for working without a permit. At time of arrest he was driving car belonging to Nicholas Peter Danalfo, Las Vegas hoodlum. Pignatello had in his possession $7,500, stated intention to purchase fifty percent of Anjoe's Restaurant.

FEDERAL BUREAU OF INVESTIGATION

REPORTING OFFICE	OFFICE OF ORIGIN	DATE	INVESTIGATIVE PERIOD
CHICAGO	CHICAGO	1961	March 23, 1961

TITLE OF CASE	REPORT MADE BY	TYPED BY
SAMUEL M. GIANCANA, aka		dkc
	CHARACTER OF CASE	
	Treasury Department Bureau of Customs Department, Chicago. Chicago File Number 6-328	

Our file relative to the above subject shows that he arrived at Midway Airport from Mexico on the morning of June 15, 1959; an agent was dispatched to the airport and assisted in the search of Mr. Giancana. While no contraband was found as result of the search, Mr. Giancana had in his possession in excess of $2,500 in U.S. currency. He also had in his possession Illinois driver's license No. D253-2600-9291 issued in the name of Frank DeSanto, 3463 West Addams Street, Chicago, Illinois. The driver's license was detained at the time of then search and was turned over to a representative if the office of the Secretary of State, Chicago, and receipt obtained therefore.

Mr. Giancana was in possession of birth certificate executed in the name of Salvatore Giancano wherein date of birth was shown as June 15, 1908; however, a driver's license in his name showed he was born on July 16, 1908.

FEDERAL BUREAU OF INVESTIGATION

REPORTING OFFICE	OFFICE OF ORIGIN	DATE	INVESTIGATIVE PERIOD
CHICAGO	CHICAGO	1961	March 27, 1961

TITLE OF CASE	REPORT MADE BY	TYPED BY
SAMUEL M. GIANCANA, aka		dkc
	CHARACTER OF CASE	
	FBI Headquarters File Number 92-3171 Top Hoodlum Program – Anti Racketeering. Daily Summary Airtel	

Las Vegas advised that individual who resembles Giancana observed deplaning on March 24, 1961. Efforts being made to verify Giancana's presence. Rose Flood, sister-in-law of Giancana, contacted by Agents, she is not aware of any of his business, described him as a fine gentleman. Spot check at the Thunderbolt Motel revealed Charles Giancana to be in conference with village president of Rosemont, D. Stephens.

During spot check of Key Lounge, Stone Park, known hangout of Giancana run by henchman Rocco Pranno, individual resembling Pranno was noted making a phone call while agent was taking down vehicle license numbers, shortly thereafter, agent was approached by Stone Park Police Chief Signorella, who desired to know agent's identity and business. Signorella was told routine inquiries were being made. Signorella offered assistance, which was declined, and left. Noted that Signorella is alleged to be a cousin of the Pranno brothers.

Spot check made at Crest Lounge, Franklin Park, reveals presence therein of Rocky Infelice, and Americo DiPietto, same group who previously owned North Avenue Steak House, alleged Giancana operations. Attempts made this date to interview Dr. William Nestos, known abortionist and hoodlum doctor, with negative results.

FEDERAL BUREAU OF INVESTIGATION

REPORTING OFFICE	OFFICE OF ORIGIN	DATE	INVESTIGATIVE PERIOD
CHICAGO	CHICAGO	1961	March 28, 1961

TITLE OF CASE	REPORT MADE BY	TYPED BY
		dkc

TITLE OF CASE	CHARACTER OF CASE
SAMUEL M. GIANCANA, aka	FBI Headquarters File Number 92-3171 Top Hoodlum Program – Anti Racketeering. Daily Summary Airtel

Gerard Murray was contacted on March 27, 1961. Murray described as bookmaker in 45th Ward of Chicago, controlled bookmaking activities for deceased alderman Charles Weber. Murray beaten with baseball bats by unknown assailants during week of March 20, in front of his home in Chicago. During contact Murray confirmed fact that he has been chief bookmaker for Weber since the late 1920's. Murray knows Tony Accardo, Murray Humphreys, Ralph Pierce, Ross Prio and other old time hoodlums intimately. During Weber's control, Murray ran gambling on independent basis, no problem with syndicate hoodlums. Shortly after Weber's demise, two hoodlums, Dennis O'Keffe and Eddy Howard, passed word around to Murray's customers that bets were to be made to them, on instructions of Mr. Giancana and Mr. Alderisio.

Contact was made with Murray by Albert "Obbie" Frabotta and Alderisio in December, 1960, at which time Murray was told to "retire." He was contacted again by a hoodlum, whose identity Murray would not disclose, and urged to get out of the business, Murray disappeared from Chicago several months, returned to Chicago March 17, 1961, noted strange cars in neighborhood one or two nights, and on night of March 21, was attacked by three men whom he could not identify. Murray received severe bruises in the abdominal region, legs, and head. Murray is 62 years of age. Murray furnished information regarding syndicate control districts in Chicago from personal knowledge that hoodlum influence is broken down by hoodlums the same as the Chicago police breaks down their districts, which is as follows; Town Hall, Albert Frabotta and Phil Alderisio, Chicago Avenue and Hudson Avenue; Ross Prio and Joseph DiVarco, Sheffield Avenue; Joseph Mendino, died March; Shakespeare, Andy Lucius, William Aloisio and Frank Cerone, Summerdale and Rodgers Park, Lennie Patrick, Damen Avenue, Bob Fiore, aka, Callaham. States Marshall Caifano in partnership with Sam Battaglia, controls west side Chicago. Advised has additional detailing of syndicate gambling but due to physical condition from beating would have to recuperate further before relating same. Murray said he intends to contact Ralph Pierce, William Aloisio, Ross Prio and Rocco DeGrazia to ascertain reason for beating. Said one possibility, in addition to bookmaking, is fact that he and Weber at one time had beer concession at Riverview Park, Chicago, linquished this to syndicate, fronted by Bob Schmidt. Told Schmidt recently he wanted his piece back, was advised not possible. Murray told Schmidt he would take it anyway. Murray states problem of independent gamblers, Chicago, became apparent when new group, headed by Giancana, came into power shortly after war, and replaced old timers such as Accardo.

Arrangements made to re-contact Murray at infrequent intervals at place away from residence or known hangouts. Investigation continuing.

FEDERAL BUREAU OF INVESTIGATION

REPORTING OFFICE	OFFICE OF ORIGIN	DATE	INVESTIGATIVE PERIOD	
CHICAGO	CHICAGO	1961	April 4, 1961	
TITLE OF CASE		REPORT MADE BY		TYPED BY
		Agent Ralph Hill Jr.		dkc
SAMUEL M. GIANCANA, aka		CHARACTER OF CASE		
		FBI Headquarters File number 92-3171-185 Top Hoodlum Program – Anti Racketeering		

Maywood Park Harness Association
Maywood, Illinois

Director William Duffy, Chicago Police Department, IU, advised on March 22, 1961 that "West side hoodlums" have been congregating at the Maywood Park trotting course and said that these individuals were taking bets at the track in competition with the pari-mutuel system. This system was tolerated by the track inasmuch as these persons operated openly with complete disregard for track authorities. The reason for these individuals placing bets at the track instead of going to the pari-mutuel window were primarily as a convenience and also to maintain the odds of a particular horse in a satisfactory manner, in that patrons of these tracks generally feel that to bet at the windows tend to lower the odds. These book makers then upon receiving a large number of bets on a given horse will then protect their bets by shoveling a large amount of money into the pari-mutuel window, thus lowering the odds and assuring a "cushion" on the bets that they had taken.

A physical surveillance was instituted by Sa Ralph Hill and Harold Sell at Maywood Park Harness Association on March 23, 1961, at which time the above situation was observed; however, the only individuals known to the agents were Rocky Infelice, James "Cowboy" Mirro, and Americo DiPietto. These individuals are close associates of Sam Giancana.

Wagon Wheel
Norwood Park, IL

Roswell T. Spencer, Chief Investigator, States Attorney's Office, Cook County, advised SA Hill on April 9, 1961, that investigators from his office raided a gambling establishment on April 7, known as the Wagon Wheel, located at Montrose and Narragansett in Norwood Park. This establishment is actually located behind a dairy products establishment and is the location of a lucrative gambling operation allegedly operated for Sam Giancana by Nick D'Amico. The officers arrested the following individuals and charged them as being keepers of the gambling house, Benny D'Amico, Anthony Vertucci, Thomas Russo, Tony Tiglio, and Michael Romanelli.

In addition to those individuals, several patrons not yet identified were arrested and held for an indefinite period. In addition to the books and records of this establishment, the officers confiscated some $2000 in cash from the safe within.

CG T-9 advised that Nicholas D'Amico operated the Wagon Wheel as his own independent book making and gambling enterprise for about 20 years and was not bothered by any of the so-called "syndicate" representatives. This situation changed, however, upon the appearance of Sam Giancana and company upon the scene shortly after World War II. Giancana then declared himself as partner in the Wagon Wheel and as a result, D'Amico has now been relegated to the status of employee and receives less then 10 per cent of the total winnings.

Miscellaneous

CG T-2 advised on March 31, 1961, that on many occasions, the Armory Lounge has closed on a temporary basis and during these periods, is utilized by Sam Giancana and his associates. The informant cited an instance in approximately 1959 whereby the Armory Lounge was closed; however, a performance was given to a close group of individuals, among whom was Giancana, and this performance was given by Frank Sinatra and Dean Martin. Informant states that these two individuals, well known entertainers, are close associates of Giancana.

This informant also advised of the situation whereby Giancana became enamored with a female located in a western suburb of Chicago during the summer of 1958, having met this person while the latter was employed as a waitress at the Pedicone Restaurant in Lyons, IL. This female was at the time the paramour of one Angelo Fasel and had two children born out of wedlock by this individual. She has been going with him since approximately 1955. The informant stated that Giancana, upon meeting this person, apparently became immediately infatuated with her and proceeded to shower her with gifts, an automobile, and a mink coat. He was apparently extremely jealous of any relationship she may have had with any other individual and evidently discovered the fact that she was still the girlfriend of Angelo Fasel. This person was admonished on several occasions by Giancana at the Armory Lounge and at other locations pertaining to this relationship and was told that it must cease immediately and during one of these occasions, the woman was advised that if Fasel did not cease his relationship with her, Giancana would see to it that "his legs were broken." Apparently these admonitions were not taken in a serious vein, so that in July, 1960, Angelo Fasel, who at the time was residing at 1018 South Second Avenue, Maywood, disappeared and has not been seen or heard from since. His apartment was vacated and all of his belongings remained behind with the exception of his automobile. His automobile similarly has not been seen since. This female made some inquiries regarding the possibility of locating Fasel and was told that she had best forget about the whole matter and forget that she ever heard the name. The informant stated that the person then made inquiry of Giancana regarding Fasel's disappearance, to which Giancana replied, "Who is Fasel?"

Angelo Fasel is the subject of a case captioned, "Dominic Frank Christiano, ET AL, River Forest State Bank, River Forest, Illinois, 3/17/55 Bank Robbery." Chicago File 91-1500, and Bureau File 91-8342. Fasel was named as the participant in this bank robbery and also as the person who drove the get-away car. Dominic Christiano was shot and killed on September 27, 1955, near Willow Springs, IL, and his body was dumped from a moving car. Fasel was described as a close associate of Ernest "Rocky" Infelice and James "Turk" Torello. This bank robbery was perpetrated by four individuals and an amount in excess of $54,000 was obtained. These individuals, all wearing hooded masks, utilized Thompson machine guns in a well planned robbery which took a total of one and a half minutes to complete. Fasel was convicted in 1957 to four months in the State Penitentiary at Vandalia, IL, for a burglary committed in Zion, Illinois.

FEDERAL BUREAU OF INVESTIGATION

REPORTING OFFICE	OFFICE OF ORIGIN	DATE	INVESTIGATIVE PERIOD
CHICAGO	CHICAGO	1961	April 4, 1961

TITLE OF CASE	REPORT MADE BY	TYPED BY
SAMUEL M. GIANCANA, aka		dkc
	CHARACTER OF CASE	
	FBI Headquarters File number 92-3171 Top Hoodlum Program – Anti Racketeering. Daily Summary	

Records of the Illinois State Liquor Commission, Chicago, reflected Nardulli as secretary of the Mist Club Corp., Chicago. Noted that the Mist Club has been alleged in past to be under Giancana's control and is place frequented by Giancana. Name of Frank Nardulli carried as licensee of Amber Light Lounge, Cicero. Amber Light mentioned previously as meeting place of Giancana's. Frank Nardulli Jr., Stone Park, interviewed this date and admitted that he is so called secretary of Mist Club, but stated that he knows nothing of operation, did not contribute any money toward it, and does not know name of other officers. He says he is not acquainted with Giancana, does not know name of operator of the Mist Club, and has only been there on one or two occasions. He stated that he has never heard of the Amber Light Lounge, and denied knowledge of being carried as licensee.

Chicago informant advised that Giancana counts among his closest associates, Frank Sinatra, Dean Martin, and Peter Lawford.

Giancana, at Armory Lounge, placed a phone call to Frank Chesrow, president of the board of sanitary district trustees, Cook County and proceeded to admonish Chesrow severely for something, slammed phone down at end of conversation and stated to informant "That will fix that so and so end." Informant stated that Giancana was acquainted primarily with Giancana's three known assistants, John Matassa, Joseph Pignatello, and Dom Blasi.

FEDERAL BUREAU OF INVESTIGATION

REPORTING OFFICE	OFFICE OF ORIGIN	DATE	INVESTIGATIVE PERIOD
CHICAGO	CHICAGO	1961	April 13, 1961

TITLE OF CASE	REPORT MADE BY	TYPED BY
SAMUEL M. GIANCANA, aka		dkc
	CHARACTER OF CASE	
	FBI Headquarters File number 92-3171-184 Top Hoodlum Program – Anti Racketeering. Daily Summary	

Miami advised investigation that office to date regarding possible Giancana property in Florida. Informant stated that approximately one year ago Giancana had Lake Worth residence completely redecorated and refurnished. Furniture then in the home was given away. Furniture dealings were made by one Sibilano, a furniture dealer located on

West Belmont Street, Chicago.

Leslie Kruse is believed to be Lester "Killer" Kane, member of the Chicago Crime syndicate and partner of Rocco Fischetti and others in the "Big Game" now located in Will County, IL. Kruse is close associate of Ralph Pierce and fled with Pierce to Mexico in fall of 1960 to avoid possible service of subpoena to appear in Tony Accardo's tax trial. He is the owner of the Nu Way Beer Coil Service Company and the Nu Way Plumbing Company, which has recently been mentioned in Chicago newspapers as having lucrative city pluming contracts. It is noted that Jerrold Wexler advised that Nu Way Pluming did the pluming work at the Villa Moderne Motel, Northbrook, an alleged Giancana Interest. Richard Bernas, aka, Richard Burns, resides at 5268 Oakton Street, Skokie, approximately two houses away from Lester Kruse. He has been characterized in the past as a close associate of Kruse, Rocco Fischetti, and Giancana and other Chicago hoodlums. He was described as a "guiding light" of the old Capone organization, and is alleged to be a cousin of the Capone's and Fischetti's. Chicago informants indicate that Burns is the individual who handles most contracts and construction work for so called syndicate gambling spots, restaurants, motels, etc. Burns did remodeling work for the Villa Venice Restaurant, Wheeling, which has been utilized by Giancana and others recently for wedding receptions, private parties and luncheons. In spring of 1958, Sam "Butch" English made a telephone call to John McDonald at Lake Worth, Florida. McDonald interviewed by Agents in July, 1958, and stated he received no call from English and said only other person residing with him at the time was Dick Burns, self employed in the construction business, it is noted that name of Burns utilized by Giancana while residing in Lake Worth. John McDonald, deceased, was a coin machine operator in the Chicago area and close associate of Chicago syndicate members. Eugene Bernstein, mentioned as notary for Lake Worth property, is well known tax accountant for such individuals as Anthony Accardo, Murray Humphreys, Gus Alex, Etal.

FEDERAL BUREAU OF INVESTIGATION

REPORTING OFFICE	OFFICE OF ORIGIN	DATE	INVESTIGATIVE PERIOD	
CHICAGO	CHICAGO	1961	May 11, 1961	
TITLE OF CASE		REPORT MADE BY		TYPED BY
				dkc
SAMUEL M. GIANCANA, aka		CHARACTER OF CASE		
		FBI Headquarters File number 92-3171 Top Hoodlum Program – Anti Racketeering. Teletype to Chicago		

The Bureau desired a special survey be made of the Sam Giancana-Charles English horse betting partnership in view of the lucrative new profit realized by this venture in 1959 and 1960 racing season at the Sportsman and Hawthorne Race Tracks, Chicago. Survey should include but not be confined to examination of all Giancana's and English's winnings and losing pair mutual tickets including manner in which winnings tickets are maintained and submitted to their attorney since normally these tickets would be turned in when cashed.

FEDERAL BUREAU OF INVESTIGATION

REPORTING OFFICE	OFFICE OF ORIGIN	DATE	INVESTIGATIVE PERIOD	
CHICAGO	CHICAGO	1961	May 12, 1961	

TITLE OF CASE	REPORT MADE BY	TYPED BY
SAMUEL M. GIANCANA, aka		dkc
	CHARACTER OF CASE	
	FBI Headquarters File number 92-3171 Top Hoodlum Program – Anti Racketeering. Daily Summary	

James Perno, nephew of Giancana, and resident in Giancana's home, interviewed at the Central Envelope and Lithograph Co., May 11, 1961, about his association with Giancana. He advised that he is employed as maintenance supervisor at the Central Envelope Co., is married to Giancana's niece, Marie Perno, nee Tumminello, and resides with his family. The Central Envelope Co. is controlled by Michael DeTolve, brother-in-law of Giancana. Perno advised that he is and has been a trustee of the Thunderbolt Motel, Rosemont, IL, since its inception. He admitted that Giancana and Michael Caldarulo were the original owners of this property and co-beneficiaries of the trust, but does not know if Caldarulo still maintains an interest therein. He said that he agreed to be trustee for this motel after being requested to do so by Anthony V. Champagne, attorney. He advised that he has not received any compensation in capacity as trustee and knows no part relating to the affairs of the Thunderbolt Motel.

Concerning Giancana, he advised that he comes and goes during the day when Perno is working so does not know when he is home. He has no personal knowledge of any affairs or investments of Giancana, business or otherwise, and states last saw Giancana at the residence two weeks ago. Said Giancana is out of town, declined to say where. He stated he and his wife care for Giancana's youngest daughter, Francine. Declined to furnish any further info, except brief background on Giancana's other two daughters.

CG T-64 advised that Butch Ladon told Gus Alex of Joseph Pignatello's problems in Las Vegas and complained that Pignatello still did not have a work permit and had called him, Ladon, from Las Vegas. Alex stated that he had called Pignatello about this situation also.

FEDERAL BUREAU OF INVESTIGATION

REPORTING OFFICE	OFFICE OF ORIGIN	DATE	INVESTIGATIVE PERIOD
CHICAGO	CHICAGO	1961	May 12, 1961

TITLE OF CASE	REPORT MADE BY	TYPED BY
SAMUEL M. GIANCANA, aka	William F. Roemer Jr. & Ralph Hill Jr.	dkc
	CHARACTER OF CASE	
	FBI Headquarters File number 92-3171 Top Hoodlum Program – Anti Racketeering	

Associates

Alex Dimilio

CG T-1 advised on April 11, 1961, that Alex Dobilio who owns the railway lounge and Railway Restaurant located at Clark and Polk Streets, Chicago, and who owned Staley's Restaurant located on Clark Street between Van Buren and Jackson, Chicago, is an individual generally regarded as a "bomber" and arsonist for Sam Giancana. Informant stated that Dobilio owns the building which is occupied by Blackie's Restaurant located at Polk and Clark Street, Chicago.

CG T-1 said that Dobilio is a very close personal friend and trusted lieutenant of Sam Giancana and advised that Nobilio learned the trade and the techniques of bombing and arson from one James Belacastro, now deceased. Dobilio ran at one time a hard card service distribution concerning horse racing for the entire area of Cook County. Informant described hard cards as sheets containing information relating to current odds on horses running in the various tracks throughout the country.

Alex Dimilio of 144 West Mason, Chicago, advised that he at one time was the owner of the restaurant located on the northwest corner on Clark and Polk Street, Chicago, but had recently sold that establishment. He advised that he had also had an interest in Blackie's Restaurant located on the second floor of the above describing building and is now employed by his brother Tony Dimilio in Dimilio's Bar located on the northwest corner of Clark and Polk Street, directly across the street from the Railway Lounge.

Dimilio was shown a photograph of Sam Giancana taken in 1956 and he immediately identified the photograph as that of Giancana stating that he had "grown up" with Giancana in Chicago in the days of his youth. He stated he has not seen Giancana for over 25 years and described Giancana as "the big man." When asked as to his explanation for the term "the big man" Dimilio shrugged his shoulders and said "that is the way everybody describes him as." Dimilio was asked if he ever had been associated with Giancana other than as that of boyhood companion and stated emphatically that he had never had any dealings of any nature with Giancana.

Dimilio was asked if he had ever been arrested for any reason and stated that he had been arrested on numerous occasions as his occupation at one time was that of "bootlegger" and "beer runner" in that prohibition days. He said he has been arrested many times since for various charges, however, declined to describe the charges for which he was arrested. He said he was last arrested about ten years ago and explained the fact that "it took me a long time to grow up" and said he has not been in trouble since his last arrest.

Dimilio was again asked if he had ever had any dealings with Giancana and was asked if he had ever been employed by Giancana in capacity of "bomber" or arsonist.

Dimilio denied the allegations and again stated that he had had no dealings whatever with Sam Giancana, on a business or professional basis at any time.

Charles Nicoletti

Charles "Chuckie" Nicoletti was interviewed on May 4, 1961, concerning Blackie's Restaurant which has been closed for the past six months, Nicoletti said that he also has an interest in this restaurant; however, due to poor business he was forced to close it down. Further Nicoletti admitted attending the wedding reception of Anthony Accardo's daughter held at the Villa Venice on April 27, 1961. He also indicated that Sam Giancana was present at their reception; however, declined to go into detail concerning Giancana's activities or his associations with Giancana.

Charles "Chuck" English

Chuckie English, business associate of Sam Giancana in racing partnership, was interviewed for approximately 12:20 PM until 1:45 PM. The interview took place on the sidewalk out side of English's place of business, Lormar Distributing Company, 5945 West Roosevelt, Chicago.

At the outset of the interview, English remarked, "there is an anti-Italian campaign being conducted throughout the United States by newspapers and the Government." English stated that these were no federal judges in the Northern District of Illinois of Italian extraction, no senators, only one Congressman, very few police officers, and no member of Mayor Daley's Cabinet of that extraction. He advised that he could not understand why the Federal Government constantly investigated Sam Giancana as "Sam is a sick man and should be left alone. His stomach is being removed piece by piece and the investigation by the Government is contributing to all this sickness." English stated that he, himself, is being treated for a heart condition. He stated that he has a high cholesterol count and displayed a container of yellow capsules which he stated he is forced to take because of this condition. English denied the existence of any "syndicate" in the United States and stated "It is merely sensationalism on the part of newspaper and figments of their imagination." English mentioned Sandy Smith, Chicago Tribune crime reporter as a prime example of this. He stated that when he appeared before the Senate Rackets Committee in 1959, the council for the committee "Took all the material for his questions directly from newspaper articles."

English advised that he was banned from Hawthorne Race Track for a period of ten days in 1960, but it now permanently banned from Washington Park because of newspaper publicity. English stated his name appeared on the front page of the individuals under attack by a special new task force of the Justice Department. English inquired, "Why put me on the front page? I have never been convicted of any crime. I did a year on the installment plan (i.e. total detention time for a variety of arrest amounted to that time), but no more."

English was asked that if there is no syndicate in Chicago, how come there are no independent bookmakers. He stated that he did not know whether or not there are any independent bookmakers in Chicago at this time, but that ten years ago, when he was a bookie, no one bothered him. English stated, "I do not have nickels to rub together now because of all this investigation and bad publicity." He stated that the Lormar Distributing Company was formerly a very profitable venture, but business steadily declined since the arrest of him and his former employee, George Hilger, by the States Attorney's Police in April, 1958, for allegedly counterfeiting phonograph records. He stated that business contacts such as Sears, Roebuck and Company, Montgomery Wards, Woolworth's, ect., contacted him after this incident and advised that they would not purchase additional records.

English denied any connection with Commercial Phonograph Company in which Willie Messina, allegedly a body guard of Tony Accardo, reportedly may have an interest. English claimed that when he was big in the phonograph business, he did not use strong arm tactics although he was "wrongly accused of doing so."

He advised that he recently moved to a new home at 1131 North Lathrop Avenue, River Forest, where he rides with his wife, daughter and son-in-law. He admitted an eight grade education and that he was in difficulty as a youth for shoplifting, etc, remarking, "Everybody up in my old neighborhood did the same thing."

English stated that in 1943, he was drafted into the United States Army but served only three days at which time he was discharged due to the fact that his wife was seriously ill.

English constantly referred to newspaper and investigations during the interview remarking, "Tony Accardo never would have been convicted of income tax evasion if he had not been so called hoodlum and although Jimmy Hoffa was found not guilty by the Government, they continue to investigate him."

English denied that Americo DiPietto or Ernest "Rocky" Infelice were working at the race track making "book" for him. Concerning Giancana, English further advised that Sam is un-married and can date woman and feels that "it is improper for the Government to interview who he dates to find out about his activities."

When asked why Giancana refused to talk to FBI Agents, English remarked, "Sam would have nothing to gain as he is an uneducated man and you Agents are college graduated, lawyers, skilled interviewers and could talk him into saying something detrimental to his interests." When asked if he was a silent partner in any business ventures, English remarked, "It would be ridiculous. Why put up 50 G's to get a percent of a business giving me 10 G's a year or $1.00 for every $5.00 invested. The other partner would have to pay taxes on the profit, and I would take the chance of getting in trouble with the IRS for failure to report the income.

English was then asked what if the silent partner had 90 per cent of the business instead of merely ten percent? He declined to answer the question. It was noted that English was attired in an expensive looking blue silk suit. English displayed the label of this suit which indicated that it was a Hickey Freeman Suit from a Maurice Rothchild Store. English stated that he acquired this suit for $65.00 from a booster or shoplifter.

Concerning his alleged race track partnership with Sam Giancana, he stated that it is on his income tax records and it is confidential. He would not comment further in this regard.

Frank "Sharkey" Eulo

Frank Eulo was interviewed at Gus' Steak House after Eulo reluctantly admitted to his identity and advised as follows:

He has long been a gambler by occupation and has operated various poker and dice games in the Cicero area. Concerning the gambling operations at Gus' Steak House, he claimed that he is presently the sole operator of this enterprise. This includes only the operation of the dice and poker games. At first Eulo denied that there was any race wire service operating at Gus' Steak House; however, later admitted that there was such an operation. This race wire service is operated by one Mike Bakes, who is from the Chicago South Side and who has a gambling stamp for this type of operation.

Concerning Sam Giancana, Eulo claims to have known Giancana since 1920, having known him since boyhood days. According to Eulo, Giancana is not connected in any way with his gambling operation at Gus' Steak House and claims to know nothing about Giancana's activities. About 5 years ago Eulo had a partner ship in his gambling operation with a man named "Queenie" Simonelli, a brother-in-law of Anthony Accardo. Eulo again stated that he alone has the gambling operation at this establishment and that Gus Kringas is the owner of the premises of Gus' Steak House.

In connection with his current gambling activities, records are maintained for Eulo by the D & B Booking Service in Chicago, which moved to another location just down the street from its last. One Tony DiBiase operates this bookkeeping service and claimed that these records are available for review if necessary.

By the way of background information, Eulo stated that he was born February 17, 1907 at Chicago. He resides at 1838 North 77th Court, Elmwood Park, IL, with his wife Rose Eulo nee Nicastro and one son. In 1933, Eulo served 9 years on a 1 to life sentence in Chicago for armed robbery.

Gus Kringas

Gus Kringas, bartender, Gus' Steak House, Cicero, advised that the owner of this establishment was not available and that he is not an employee. He said that he is presently employed as a laborer for the Bureau of Sanitation, City of Chicago, having been so employed for the past 7 years. He is employed at 819 South Kolmar, which is the located in the 29th Ward and his supervisor is one Julius Otto. He said that he is merely helping out at Gus' Steak House for his brother, George Kringas, who is part owner of this restaurant with one Peter Rantis of Berwyn, IL. He added that his brother George can be contacted daily at Margo's Restaurant, 4859 West Roosevelt. He explained that the restaurant at Gus' Steak House has been closed for the past six months and that the lounge section is still in operation. He also stated that he resides at 4037 West Van Buren, Chicago.

Kringas denied knowing one Frank "Sharkey" Eulo who has been reported to operate the gambling game at this establishment. He also denied knowing Sam Giancana and claimed to know nothing about a gambling operation at this location. During the interview, Frank Eulo was observed entering Gus' Steak House and greeted Gus Kringas by his first name at which time the interview of Kringas was terminated.

Shy locking

On April 17, 1961, Duane Seavey telephonically contacted the Chicago Office and asked SA Frank Matthys be given the message that Sam Giancana had called Seavey and told him to come to Giancana's home. He was then on his way to meet Giancana. Agent Matthys called Seavey at his home. He had advised that he had, in past years, run up a gambling debt of about $3,000.00 at Rocco DeGrazia's place in Melrose Park. The syndicate put him in touch with a juice man and he found himself so in debt that he could not get out. After being given the mob's customary ultimation, he filed voluntary bankruptcy proceeding in the United States District. He scheduled this gambling debt and was finally discharged.

Duane Seavey advised he had incurred some $2,450 in gambling debts, which he was unable to pay. He identified these gambling debts as followed:

Norman Becker, also known as "Minnie", Casa Madrid Restaurant, Melrose Park, IL, poker game, $2,150.00.

Gus Liebe, doing business as Viaduct Lounge, Cicero, IL, $200.

Joe Aiuppa, doing business as Towne Hotel, Cicero, IL, $200.

At his meeting with Giancana on April 17, 1961, Giancana told him that repayment was expected. He ordered him to repay the dept at the rate of $300.00 every quarter starting July 15, 1961, for three years. Giancana told him that if payments were made regularly, he would not force Seavey to borrow from a juice man. Present at this time was one whom Seavey identified as probably Jack Cerone. Seavey did not agree to repay this debt.

Giancana replied to Seavey, "You know that doesn't mean anything to us. You still owe the money." Mr. Seavey said he left the matter unanswered and about one month later he received a visit at his home from one Joe Shiminutes. Mr. Shiminutes advised that he was sent to collect the money and that he, Shiminutes, was one of "Skarkey Eulo's boys." He advised Seavey that "Them people want that money right away." Seavey replied that he was unable to pay at that time, whereby Shiminutes said "them are bad people." A week later Seavey went to Gus' Steak House and gave Mr. Shiminutes two checks for $100 each. When both of the checks were returned for wrong signature, Mr. Seavey said he suffered a mild heart attack and spent several days in the hospital.

He said while Seavey was in the hospital, Shiminutes came to his residence a few times looking for Seavey. Once discharged from the hospital, Seavey was visited by Shiminutes at his residence where Shiminutes demanded repayment of the two previous checks which had returned. Seavey gave Shiminutes $200 in cash and was then told by Shiminutes that "they" wanted $300 more, upon receipt of which they would cancel the remainder of the obligations. Shiminutes then advised Seavey "If Mooney "Giancana" had known that you had suffered a heart attack, he would not have sent me out to see you."

Sam Lewis

Chicago T-1 advised as followed on May 11, 1961, in Chicago. Concerning Sam Lewis, owner of the Paar Loan Company, Chicago, he advised that Sam Lewis and Bill "Action" Jackson appeared at his home Sunday night, May 7, 1961, and advised that it was mandatory that he meet with them the following Monday to discuss the loan of approximately $10,000.00 which he owed to the Paar Loan Company.

He advised that at 10:00 pm, May 8, he meet Sam Lewis on the street in the vicinity of Eddie Foy's strip joint and the end result of the meeting was that he was to pay at least $1,000 within the next two weeks to the Paar Loan Company. Lewis advised that he has received instructions from Lester Kruse to the effect that under no circumstances was he to harm him but could insist upon payment of the debt.

He advised that Jackson admitted that he had been recently arrested by the FBI for receiving stolen property in connection with a truck theft. Jackson said that he was not directly involved in the theft, however, he had gone to the drop to pick up some merchandise and that he was arrested at the stolen truck and trailer by agents of the FBI.

Sam Lewis in conversation May 8, 1961, also advised that he had paid $2,000 to some Chicago Police official in order that his son, Robert "Bobby" Lewis, was made a Sergeant on the Chicago police force. Lewis also advised that he paid $2,500 in order to get his other son, Eddie Lewis, into the Intelligence Unit of the Chicago Police Department. Lewis's other son, Sam Lewis Jr., is presently a detective working out of the Detective Division, Burglary Unit, Chicago Police Department.

He advised further with reference to Sam Lewis and his associates, that he has recently been in touch with an individual known to him only as Zaza, who is described as white, male, Italian extraction, 5'7", 190 pounds, badly marked face, husky build, an individual who runs the Diversey Districts for Sam Lewis. Zaza collects from the various books and picks up pay-off money which has been brought to Sam Lewis. Formerly, Sam Lewis and Joe "Crackers" Mendino, recently deceased, ran the Diversey District for the "Outfit." He advised that since "Crackers" Mendino's death, Leonard "Needles" Gianola had taken Mendino's place and is now working with Lewis.

It is interesting to note that "Milwaukee Phil" Alderisio very rarely goes into the district any more because there are bad feelings between Alderisio and Leonard Gianola. He advised that he does not know specifically what brought about these bad feelings. An individual by the name of Bill Gold assists Zaza in collecting in the Diversey District. Bill Gold runs horse rooms and large poker games in the district. Gold is also a "power house" in the Hudson Avenue Chicago Police Station and can get practically and every thing fixed for the "Outfit." He said that Zaza also told him with regard to race wires that there is a "big switchboard" in Melrose Park, IL, where there are 35 to 40 telephones. This operation is supervised by Rocco DeGrazia and the overall authority lies with Jackie Cerone. Zaza explained that information from all over the country comes into this switchboard and then it is passed on to the Chicago districts horse parlors and other gambling establishments by the switchboard. Zaza stated that this switchboard is located in a home and has been operating for some time. Most of the race wire information comes from "out east." Recently, there has been much criticism by members of the "Outfit" and gamblers in general that the service provided "out east" is extremely slow and inefficient.

Most of the hoodlums, including Zaza, Bill Gold, Leonard Gianola and Sam Lewis, can be found at night at the Rae Minks Delicatessen in the Diversey District. With specific reference to the Paar Loan Company, he advised that the office is run and supervised by Jackie Lewis, a daughter-in-law of Sam Lewis. She supervised the operation of the office and the legitimate end of the loan business. He advised that it is very possible that Sam Giancana is a silent partner in this operation inasmuch as he hears Lewis speak of Giancana on many occasions; however, Lewis had never specifically said that Giancana is a partner in the business. However, one Don Parrillo, who lives in Oak Park, is an actual partner of the Paar Loan Company and should appear on the books.

With reference to the Frontier Loan Company located on West Madison Street, Chicago, another "6 for 5" loan operation, this is owned by and run by Fifi Buccieri. He also advised that "Piggy" Joyce operates a large crap game and "6 for 5" loan business off Chicago Avenue. "Piggy" Joyce is a very close associate of Joe "Gags" Gagliano and also hangs out at Rae Minks Delicatessen located at the corner of Pine Grove and Diversey Avenue.

He advised that "Milwaukee" Phil Alderisio has been going to Rae Minks Delicatessen on a more or less regular basis for lunch and can generally be found there between 1:30 pm and 2:30 pm. He advised that Alderisio occasionally makes meets at this place as there is a nice dining room in the back.

He advised that he recently learned that the Mist located in the vicinity of 6400 Montrose is a joint operated by Sam Giancana and that many of the known hoodlums congregate there at various times.

FEDERAL BUREAU OF INVESTIGATION

REPORTING OFFICE	OFFICE OF ORIGIN	DATE	INVESTIGATIVE PERIOD	
CHICAGO	CHICAGO	1961	May 23, 1961	
TITLE OF CASE		REPORT MADE BY		TYPED BY
				dkc
SAMUEL M. GIANCANA, aka		CHARACTER OF CASE		
		FBI Headquarters File number 92-3171-231 Top Hoodlum Program – Anti Racketeering. Daily Summary		

Reference is made to daily summaries pertaining to interviews with Charles English and Dominick "Butch" Blasi. CG informant advised that she was contacted by Blasi and by prearrangement with this office, advised Blasi, she had been contacted by the FBI regarding her relationship with Giancana, and was uncooperative. Blasi then asked informant to appear at the Armory Lounge for a "conference." Informant stated there were several people at the Lounge at the time she appeared, all conferring individually with Blasi. Informant unable to identify any persons there, but assumed they had all been either interviewed or contacted by the FBI, since that seemed to be the main topic of discussion. Blasi asked informant exact nature of contact by FBI, was told that her name had come up as one of Giancana's girl friends. Blasi at the time was drinking heavily, which according to the informant, was unusual. Giancana was not present, and indications were that he had left the area.

Blasi advised the informant that he, Blasi, had been contacted by the FBI and he told the agents to "get lost." Blasi said he figures the FBI is "trying to get close to me since I am the closet person to Sam." Informant then accompanied Blasi to a new establishment, a private club located on Central Avenue in Cicero, IL, where Blasi continued drinking. Blasi advised informant that Giancana had informant on his mind constantly and assured informant that he would get in touch with her as soon as he came back in town, advising the informant that Giancana considered her as "his girl." While still in the Armory, the informant overheard Blasi make phone call to unknown person and advised that person to, "get rid of all these apartment buildings we've got." Informant unable to clarify the above statement.

FEDERAL BUREAU OF INVESTIGATION

REPORTING OFFICE	OFFICE OF ORIGIN	DATE	INVESTIGATIVE PERIOD	
CHICAGO	CHICAGO	1961	June 2, 1961	
TITLE OF CASE		REPORT MADE BY		TYPED BY
				dkc
SAMUEL M. GIANCANA, aka		CHARACTER OF CASE		
		FBI Headquarters File number 92-3171-241 Top Hoodlum Program – Anti Racketeering. Daily Summary		

Department Attorney Robert Rosthal, Attorney General Special Group handing organized crime, advised this date that he contemplates subpoena of Phyllis McGuire and subpoena of books and records of the Red Top Cab Company in near future. Subpoenas and appearances will be in connection with regular Grand Jury proceeding in Chicago, on sterling Harris Ford situation. Purpose of subpoenas will be to explore possible Giancana interest in Evanston cab co. and disclosure of personal transactions and expenditures of Giancana through his relationship with Phyllis McGuire.

FEDERAL BUREAU OF INVESTIGATION

REPORTING OFFICE	OFFICE OF ORIGIN	DATE	INVESTIGATIVE PERIOD	
CHICAGO	CHICAGO	1961	June 13, 1961	
TITLE OF CASE		REPORT MADE BY		TYPED BY
				dkc
SAMUEL M. GIANCANA, aka		CHARACTER OF CASE		
		FBI Headquarters File number 92-3171-264 Top Hoodlum Program – Anti Racketeering. Daily Summary		

One Sam Giancana rented a house in Las Vegas, Nevada, for Phyllis McGuire during the engagement of the McGuire Sisters at the Sands Hotel, commencing June 12, last for one month. Giancana is alleged to have staffed the house, and included one of his own associates, one "Chop Chop." Latter person unknown to this office.

Giancana is believed to spend most of his time with Phyllis McGuire, remaining out of the public eye. Exact location of this house is not presently known. Las Vegas being requested to ascertain full details be this situation and follow closely, Chicago PD intelligence unit advised that they are doing some investigation about insurance claims of the North Avenue Steak House, which was destroyed by fire several months ago. The amount of the claim is in the neighborhood of one hundred thousand dollars. Investigation has disclosed that among the claimants are Americo DiPietto, Ernest Infelice, and one Joe Marks. Name Joe Marks and Infelice show in chattel mortgage from Melrose Park, IL, bank, although not shown on the insurance records. It appears that the claim is at least double that amount which should be claimed, and as a result, the insurance companies do not intend to reimburse any of the claimants. Noted that the property on which the North Avenue Steak House was located is owned by James DeTolve, brother-in-law of Sam Giancana. CG informant advised he observed some papers in an auto driven by Frank Bruno, known to the informant as a "juice man" and an associate of Giancana. These papers contained several addresses in the vicinity of Harlem and North Avenue, Chicago, with notations about tax due, among of income from each address, ect. Informant was unable to obtain any figures or amounts. Address supplied by informant are all in receivership, from the bankrupt assets of Esposito and Company, builders, whose activities were alleged in the past to be closely aliened with Anthony Accardo. Esposito and Company went into receivership some months ago. Investigation continuing.

FEDERAL BUREAU OF INVESTIGATION

REPORTING OFFICE	OFFICE OF ORIGIN	DATE	INVESTIGATIVE PERIOD	
CHICAGO	CHICAGO	1961	June 15, 1961	
TITLE OF CASE		REPORT MADE BY		TYPED BY
		Special Agent Ralph Hill Jr.		dkc
SAMUEL M. GIANCANA, aka		CHARACTER OF CASE		
		FBI Headquarters File number 92-3171-304 Top Hoodlum Program – Anti Racketeering		

Charles Giancana

Sam Giancana's brother Charles Giancana, manager of the Thunderbolt Motel, advised that he had not seen his brother in several weeks and stated definitely that he had not observed his brother in Mr. Anthony's Restaurant located in the motel several months ago. He stated he did not know at the present time where is his brother was. He was asked if Sam Giancana was the sole proprietor of the motel and he stated, "I don't know, I only work here."

Chicago informant T-20 advised that for several weeks prior to June 20, 1961, Giancana, accompanied by, among others Joseph "Pepe" Giancana, another brother, have been meeting at Mr. Anthony's Restaurant at least two to three times per week. The informant was unable to identify the other persons accompanying Giancana except on one occasion during the week on June 1961, when Giancana was accompanied by Anthony Accardo.

Charles Tumminello

Charles Tumminello, nephew of Sam Giancana, was interviewed at his residence, 1301 South Maple Street, Berwyn, on May 26, 1961. At the outset of the interview the Agents identified themselves, but Tumminello declined to invite the Agents into his home and examined credentials in great detail for approximately five minutes. He demanded to know if the visit was social or business and inquired as to how it fitted specifically into the investigative authority of a Bureau Agent.

Tumminello appeared highly incensed, hostile, and displayed a vitriolic temper during the interview. Tumminello rambled in a non-specific manner stating he was angry at the obvious campaign currently in effect in the United States aimed at downgrading the Italian race. He stated persons of Italian descent are persecuted and subjected to intense ridicule by "dirty" newspapers and television programs such as the "Untouchables" which attack Italian people. He stated he has suffered from a persection complex all of his life and has been prevented from securing a good job because he is a "Chicago Italian" and worst of all a Catholic. Tumminello suggested that the FBI direct their investigation activities "at poor executive leadership in the United States Government and senators and congressmen in Washington who play poker and run around with woman.

During the interview it was noted that Tumminello became highly emotional, chain smoked, and at times bordered on being incoherent. During one point in the interview the name of Sam Giancana was mentioned and at this time Tumminello stated that if Giancana's name was mentioned again, the interview would be terminated and the Agents would be asked to leave. He stated however, that Giancana did not provide any money toward the purchase of the apartment house which is now his residence. He stated he and James Perno purchased the apartment house from Charles Giancana at a price of $55,000.

Tumminello stated that Sam Giancana dose not help out with family affairs as many people might be lead to believe and stated as an example one of Giancana's sisters is employed at the Central Envelope Co. as a laboring type position. It should be noted that during the interview Tumminello refused to answer many questions, spoke in generalities, and tried to provoke a discussion on a number of controversial subjects with the interviewing agents.

Peter Epsteen

Mrs. Jane Epsteen advised that she was divorced from Peter Epsteen, an associate of Giancana. She stated her former husband's closest friends are Irving Gordon, political power house in the Chicago's First Ward, Lester Kruse, Pat Marcy, Rocco and Joe Fischetti. In recent years he has become more intrigued with the so-called hoodlum element because of their introducing him with various entertainment celebrities, including Frank Sinatra, Peter Lawford, Sammy Davis Jr. and Mae Britt. She recalled that after his first meeting with Sinatra, Epsteen had attempted to obtain his services in making a commercial for his Pontiac agency. Numerous attempts at this were unsuccessful. Later, he brought this to the attention of Joe and Rocco Fischetti and soon thereafter, Sinatra agreed to the commercial as a favor without charge. However, Epsteen did give him two Pontiacs which he accepted. She believed that they first met Sinatra at the home of John Formossa, which is located south of Chicago in Indiana. She understands that Formossa is in charge of gambling in the Northern Indiana area and that he probably operates houses of prostitution.

Approximately three years ago, she and her ex-husband were vacationing in Las Vegas, Nevada, at the same time as Formossa, Peter Lawford, and Sam Giancana. At that time Formossa complained that Sinatra did not talk to him because he was interested in helping Senator Kennedy obtain the presidential nomination. She stated she was of the opinion that Sinatra would not be able to divorce himself completely from his former hoodlum associations because she had heard from an unrecalled source that the hoodlums were responsible financially for his comeback as an entertainer. She stated she also gained the impression that the hoodlums in Chicago did not want Senator Kennedy to get the nomination and that they were disturbed when Sinatra took an active interest in Senator Kennedy's campaign.

She stated that she originally met Peter Epsteen while she was attending high school in 1947 and they were married in 1949. Shortly after their marriage, he was employed as a salesman for Esserman Motors in Chicago and later as Sales Manager where he became reacquainted with Henry Susk, a former schoolmate, and presently a Pontiac dealer in Chicago. Over the years this friendship has grown and Susk has introduced Epsteen to many hoodlums.

In 1952 after a near nervous breakdown and a severe ulcer, he borrowed money from Susk and with approximately $30,000 which he had inherited in from relatives; he opened a Dodge auto dealership in Chicago and later the Peter Epsteen Pontiac Agency. Part of the reason that she had sought a divorce was because of his association with known hoodlums, which caused a normal interruption in his home life. On numerous occasions she has asked him about hoodlum ownership of his business and he has repeatedly denied to her that the hoodlums have control of any of his business affairs and that his relationship with them is purely social. This friendship has made it possible for him to sell the "hoodlum and their friends" many cars in recent years.

Mrs. Epsteen has met many hoodlums at various cocktail parties in private homes and public places. She was exhibited photographs of numerous Chicago hoodlums and she identified the following:

Gus Alex	Ross Prio
Murray Humphreys	Sam Giancana
Lester Kruse	Butch Lason
Marshall Caifano	Jimmy Allegretti
Rocco Potenzo	Eddie Vogel
Joe Fischetti	Rocco Fischetti

She added that although she had heard Anthony Accardo and Frank Ferraro, she dose not recall having ever met them socially. She added that she has met many other hoodlums and near racketeers from all parts of the United States, but dose not recall them by name at the present.

Of the many times that she met with the various hoodlums, their wife's, and girl friends, they never discussed business as they have little or no respect for any woman. Much of the information that she has learned concerning her former husband's associates came from overhearing conversations when various hoodlums visited with her husband at home. She recalled that one evening Irving Gordon and her husband were discussing the fact that in their opinion the organized hoodlums in Chicago had Arthur Adler murdered and they stated they would like to ask about the death of Adler but were afraid to discuss it with Rocco and Joe Fischetti. In February 1959, she and husband were vacationing in Miami Beach, Florida, and after their arrival they began observing several hoodlums whom she had previously met. She was unable to recall the name but does recall that two or three of them were from New York City and one was an individual who owned a large night club is Salt Lake City. There were also numerous Chicago hoodlums including Gus Alex, Jimmy Allegretti, Murray Humphreys, Marshall Caifano and Sam Giancana. They also saw Rocco Fischetti who advised them to stay away from him and the other named individuals as long as Sam Giancana was in town. She observed none of the wives or girl friends and therefore assumed that it was a big business meeting of the hoodlums which they held in various cities throughout the United States, according to her understanding.

She advised that she has meet Gus Alex and his wife, Marianne, on numerous occasions and knows that they particularly enjoy dining out at the Pavilion Restaurant in Deerfield, IL, and the Imperial House in Chicago. She is also of the opinion that Alex uses this restaurant as meeting places to discuss his gambling business with his hoodlum subordinates. She has also been at several night clubs in the party of Sam Giancana and considers him as "partly crazy." He is an extreme practical joker and she has seen him set fire to the pants of people in his party and observed him cut the microphone wires on Joey Bishop, a comedian, when he was performing at the Fontainebleau Hotel in Miami Beach. Whenever he "pulls this type of trick" neither the people he is with or the management of the club object to his action and she assumes from this that he is "boss of the whole bunch."

Mrs. Epsteen advised that there are many places in Chicago that this group likes to frequent and the only one that she could recall at present was the Armory Lounge. She and her husband use to go their for Italian food, but in recent years her husband told her that he was not suppose to go there because Sam Giancana held meetings there and further that he did not like to be around Giancana. Mrs. Epsteen stated that she would gladly cooperate with the FBI and that she would be available for re-contact within the next few days and further that she would attempt to locate any records of writings which may be in her home that would be of pertinence to the Government.

Ernest Infelice
8500 West North Avenue
Maywood, IL

Ernest Infelice, associate of Sam Giancana, known to the informant as "Rocky" and "Mike" from Chicago who had previously visited the New York area to dispose of stolen property and who were described by the informant as "syndicate men." Investigation determined that individuals who apparently accompanied Infelice were Pete DiPietto and Frank Gallo.

Information was advised that the group that Rocky was associated with now hangs out at the Guest House, Franklin Park, which is the new headquarters of the North Avenue Steak House gang. The incorporators of the Guest House are:

Constantino DiStasio
1306 North 15th Avenue
Melrose Park, IL

Andrew Massa
2322 West Huron
Chicago, IL

James Capezio
1635 North Latrobe
Chicago, IL

Lester Kruse, also known as
Leslie E. Kruse
5206 Oakton Street
Skokie, IL

Chicago informant advised Lester Kruse, an associate of Gus Alex, presently owns a large amount of American Telephone and Telegraph stock which may have been purchased in the name of Dick Bernas, it being noted that Bernas is a close associate of Lester Kruse and lives in a close proximity of Kruse's home. Kruse advised the informant that John Drew of Las Vegas, who operates the Stardust Hotel in that city, was in bad shape financially as he owes Jake "The Barber" Factor between $25,000 and $50,000. Kruse advised the informant that Drew also owes Sam Giancana a large amount of money and had been told that this money must be repaid within 30 days. The money owed by Drew to Giancana is being demanded to be repaid by Gus Alex who, according to the informant, is Drew's partner in the Stardust Casino. Alex is pressuring Drew to repay this amount inasmuch as Alex's equal and partner in the Stardust is Giancana. The informant said that Alex realizes that he must stay on a friendly basis with Giancana so that Giancana will not become displeased with drew.

Informant continued that in connection with the profits from the Stardust Casino, Las Vegas, Lester Kruse, John Drew, Ralph Pierce, Gus Alex, and Sam Giancana have a "piece" of the profits of the casino. Informant stated that Drew is Alex's representative at the Stardust and Tommy McDonald is Giancana's representative at the Stardust. Informant identified Tommy McDonald as a former partner in the Singapore Restaurant in Chicago.

Attempts were made to interview Lester Kruse at his residence at which time SA Ralph Hill was advised by an individual who refused to identify herself at this residence that, "I don't know where Mr. Kruse is. I will have him get in touch with you."

Mannie Skar
Skar Construction Company
Chicago, IL

Chicago informant T-1 advised that the Sahara Motel on South Cicero Avenue in Chicago's Midway Airport is partially owned by one Mannie Skar who formerly operated the Skar Construction Co. with Leon Marcus (deceased) of the Southmoor Bank and Trust Securities, who was murdered in gangland style in 1957. The informant stated that Skar is closely associated with Anthony Accardo, Sam Giancana, and Lester Kruse.

The informant related an instance whereby recently Accardo cut short a fishing trip in the Keys off of the state of Florida to attend the 13th birthday party of Skar's son. He advised that Giancana also attended this party and gave a $1,000 bill to Skar's son in an envelope as a present.

Miscellaneous

A Chicago informant that in connecting with the Evanston Cab Company in which "Milwaukee " Phil Alderisio, Obbie Frabotta, Fred Bartoli, Butch Loverdi and others have a financial interest, represents an investment of better that one million dollars by the criminals involved in its operation. He stated that the radio equipment alone that was placed in the cabs was valued at better that $250,000.

He advised that he first leaned of the Evanston Cab Company nine or ten months ago when Phil Alderisio and Butch Loverdi had a conversation with him. On this occasion Alderisio asked him if he knew of any cab drivers needing a job who were interested in working in a suburb. He stated that he might be able to help Alderisio in this connection and inquired where the cab company was located. Alderisio advised that he and Loverdi "had" the Evanston Cab Co. He further advised that one Sam Levine, also engaged in the operation on the cab company, was in the United States Army and in the same outfit with Butch Loverdi. He further advised that Bartoli operates the company as acting manager with Sam Levine. He also stated that the Evanston Cab Co. through the efforts of Lester Kruse, associate of Gus Alex, who has much influence in Skokie, where he resides, had obtained a franchise whereby the Evanston Cab Co. may now cross into Skokie from Evanston and carry on business in Skokie.

On May 31, 1961, SA Hill telephonically contacted Sam Levine at which time SA Hill was advised by Mr. Levine that he would consent to an interview with SA Hill only in the presence of his attorney, Mr. Charles Bellows.

Chicago T-1 advised on June 13, 1961, that he learned that James "Cowboy" Mirro, former associate of Nick George Montos who, at one time, was a top ten fugitive of the Federal Bureau of Investigation, is a partner in the partnership of the Thunderbolt Motel with Sam Giancana. Informant stated that this motel was formerly known as the River Road Motel.

Angelo Volpe advised that he has done booking making on a small-scale in the past and was the proprietor of the Veterans Cab Co. which consisted of one taxicab which he operated out of his home until approximately 1958. Volpe advised that during the time he drove his cab, he was in the habit of dropping in at the Mist Club which is located at 6412 West Montrose Street and as a result, became acquainted with Eugene Rinaldi, who was the proprietor of the club. Volpe stated that Rinaldi suggested to him during 1959 that he come into the business and set up a corporation if he desired. Volpe said that Rinaldi told him that business was bad, but that if business picked up, he would accept $5,000 as soon as Volpe was "on his feet." Volpe stated that during February, 1959, he contacted Sam Gimini and Frank Nardulli and suggested that they set up a corporation and take over management of the Mist Club. Volpe advised that Gimini, who is the treasurer of the corporation, lives at 2030 Madison Street, Bellwood. Vople advised that he set up the corporation through the D & B Booking Agency. The Mist Club, under the name "Must Club" was incorporated with Volpe listed as president, Nardulli as Secretary, and Gimini as Treasure. At the time he obtained a liquor license, Volpe advised that it was his idea to change the name for Mist to Must in order to make the creditors believe that the old Mist Club was out of business and was now a new establishment. Volpe added that this did not work out and the Mist Club was consequently hounded by creditors. Volpe stated that during the latter part of 1959, Eugene Rinaldi had difficulties with a girl friend and committed suicide. Volpe stated that although he was aware that the Mist Club possessed a notorious reputation for being a place frequented by known hoodlum's ten or fifteen years ago, he hardly ever noted any known hoodlum at the club during the time he had an interest in it. He stated that on several occasions, one or two known hoodlums were pointed out to him at the club, but he soon forgot their identity.

Volpe advised that he dose not know Sam Giancana, has had no dealings with him whatsoever, and emphatically advised that Giancana had no financial interest in the Mist Club. He advised that he is aware that an individual named Nickie Vallo frequented the Mist Club in the company of various beautiful women and was always neatly dressed. He stated, however, that he knows of no other interest that Vallo might have in the Mist Club and stated that he is certain that he has no financial interest in the club. He said he does not know Vallo's whereabouts or have any idea as to where he might be located.

Volpe advised that during May, 1961, he came to the definite conclusion that the Mist Club was not making any money and so decided to delete himself from the corporation which he had originally set with Nardulli and Gimini. He stated he advised them that he was quitting and told them to delete his name when they applied for a liquor license in the name of the club during May, 1961. Volpe advised that he no longer has any interest in the Mist Club and stated that Nardulli and Gimini are the sole corporate members and that to the best of his knowledge; no one else had been named as President and General Manager in Volpe's place. Volpe advised that he is the brother of Dominic Volpe and advised that he had purchased beer from his brother for the Mist Club during the time he was president. He stated he also worked for his brother, Dominic during 1949, when his brother was in partnership with Jack West at Arlington and Washington Streets. Volpe advised that he is a veteran of World War II and is the father of five children.

Giancana was observed meeting two individuals on June 29, 1961, at the Green Gables Ranch, one possibly identical with Paul Emilio D'Amato, Newark top hoodlum.

Gambling

Gus' Steak House
Cicero, Illinois

Chicago T-65 was re-contacted on June 18, 1961, and advised that an individual he had previously referred to as "Dutch" who accompanied Giancana was in actuality named "Butch." It is noted that this description fits that of Dominic "Butch" Blasi.

Police Tie

Ralph Cantonese
Chicago Police Department

Chicago T-19 advised that in 1958 Dean Martin and Frank Sinatra came through Chicago preparatory to going on location to film the movie "Some Came Running" in Indiana. At the time they arrived in Chicago, they were met at the airport in an automobile driven by Captain Cantonese who was accompanied by Joseph Pischetti. According to the informant, the party then proceeded to the residence of Anthony Accardo, where Dean Martin and Frank Sinatra "performed" for Accardo.

The informant also advised that Captain Ralph Cantonese was now a Captain at New City Precinct is a very close friend of Tony Accardo and Sam Giancana. He stated that Cantonese has been associated with "outfit" individuals for many years. By the way of interest, he stated that Cantonese used to attend the 4th of July parties given by Tony Accardo at his residence and said that Cantonese used to wear a false mustache and dark glasses and travel to the party by taxicab so that his identity would not be revealed.

Anthony Champagne

Mr. Anthony V. Champagne advised SA Hill on May 16, 1961, that his client, Giancana, had contacted his and advised him to relay a message to SA Hill to the effect that he, Giancana, did not desire to be interviewed on any matter. Mr. Champagne said that inasmuch as he was merely relaying the desired of his client, he did not feel that it was within his purview to attempt to persuade Mr. Giancana to make him self available for an interview.

FEDERAL BUREAU OF INVESTIGATION

REPORTING OFFICE	OFFICE OF ORIGIN	DATE	INVESTIGATIVE PERIOD	
CHICAGO	CHICAGO	1961	June 23, 1961	
TITLE OF CASE		REPORT MADE BY		TYPED BY
				dkc
SAMUEL M. GIANCANA, aka		CHARACTER OF CASE		
		FBI Headquarters File number 92-3171-282 Top Hoodlum Program – Anti Racketeering		

On June 21, 1961, Giancana possibly in conference that date with Gus Alex, Frank Ferraro, Ralph Pierce, Sam Battaglia. Unknown, not identified, but possibly Battaglia or Giancana, asked general question of above group "have you been interviewed by Roemer and Hill." Referring to FBI agents, it was learned that Lester Kruse mentioned that he, John Drew, Ralph Pierce, Gus Alex, and Giancana have "a piece" of the profits of the Stardust Hotel and gambling casino in Las Vegas. Giancana's representative at the Stardust is Tommy McDonald. The informant relates Drew owes considerable amount of money to Giancana and is being pressured by Gus Alex to repay this amount since Drew is Alex's representative at the Stardust and in order to remain on a friendly basis with Giancana, the debt must be repaid.

Joseph Pignatello is on film location with Frank Sinatra, in Utah, and will be interviewed soon.

FEDERAL BUREAU OF INVESTIGATION

REPORTING OFFICE	OFFICE OF ORIGIN	DATE	INVESTIGATIVE PERIOD	
CHICAGO	CHICAGO	1961	June 28, 1961	
TITLE OF CASE		REPORT MADE BY		TYPED BY
				dkc
SAMUEL M. GIANCANA, aka		CHARACTER OF CASE		
		FBI Headquarters File number 92-3171 Top Hoodlum Program – Anti Racketeering. Daily Summary		

Chicago files reflect one Nick Cecola as an associate of Chicago hoodlum Tony Capezio (deceased), and Mario John Lupo (deceased), in the 1940's. He was interviewed in July 1959 by Agents in connection with perjury case, as a possible witness. He was listed as being employed at his brother Frank Cecola's bar, at the Noble Inn Lounge, in Chicago. Chicago has no objecting to any local action taken against Giancana relative to any local arrest for failure to register as an ex-convict or any other local action that would embarrass Giancana, it be noted that Chicago hoodlum Marshall Caifano was in disfavor with local Chicago hoodlums following his difficulties with the Las Vegas authorities last year.

Motion pictures should be taken of Giancana and Phyllis McGuire particularly with the purpose in mind of utilizing such film before the Grand Jury at Chicago and to induce fullest cooperation on the part of Phyllis McGuire after suitable motion pictures are taken and the possibility of complete coverage explored.

FEDERAL BUREAU OF INVESTIGATION

REPORTING OFFICE	OFFICE OF ORIGIN	DATE	INVESTIGATIVE PERIOD	
CHICAGO	CHICAGO	1961	June 29, 1961	
TITLE OF CASE		REPORT MADE BY		TYPED BY
				dkc
SAMUEL M. GIANCANA, aka		CHARACTER OF CASE		
		FBI Headquarters File number 92-3171-287 Top Hoodlum Program – Anti Racketeering. Daily Summary		

Informant advised that on June 29, 1961, he assisted one Connie Pitt of Pitt Realty Agency, Chicago, attempt to collect a debt owed to Pitt, whose true name is Cornelius Pitt, by two individuals connected with Chicago art galleries. These two ndividuals gave a check in the amount of five thousand dollars, claiming that he could not come up with any more at that time. When pressured by the informant as to the reason, both individuals claimed that they had recently been given fifty thousand dollars by Sam DeStefano on a "juice" loan at an interest rate of five percent per each week or month. According to informant, money given to these persons by DeStefano was actually Sam Giancana's money, and DeStefano is acting as Giancana's personal representative in the "juice" field. Noted that DeStefano was re-interviewed by Agents on June 28, 1961, about his association with known Chicago hoodlums, and explained that he is in the "loan business", stated that his policy is to loan basis of taking a percentage of the business in return for the loan. Denied that this was juice, but stated he also makes individual loans to persons for seven per cent interest. He said he had a loan company, but declined to identify it. DeStefano is known to this office as a vicious loan shark who has been alleged to have committed numerous murders as a part of the enforcement of his collections. Noted also that correspondence has been alleged to have committed numerous murders as a part of the enforcement of his collections. Noted also that correspondence has been directed to Giancana from the Chicago art galleries. It is known that the Chicago art galleries have been utilized as a meeting place for Chicago hoodlum Edward Vogel.

A wire tape placed on the telephone of Dan Rowan of the comedy team of Rowan and Martin by Arthur James Balletti and one J.W. Harrison, not further identified. Balletti is employed by Edward DuBois, a former Bureau Agent who runs a private investigating agency in Miami, Florida. Balletti admits to having been assigned to survey Rowan in Las Vegas, Nevada, and was accompanied by J. W. Harrison, not further known to him who was supplied by Robert Maheu, another former Bureau Agent.

FEDERAL BUREAU OF INVESTIGATION

REPORTING OFFICE	OFFICE OF ORIGIN	DATE	INVESTIGATIVE PERIOD	
CHICAGO	CHICAGO	1961	July 19, 1961	
TITLE OF CASE		REPORT MADE BY		TYPED BY
				dkc
SAMUEL M. GIANCANA, aka		CHARACTER OF CASE		
		FBI Headquarters File number 92-3171-340 Top Hoodlum Program – Anti Racketeering		

CG T-6 advised that Lester Kruse's status with the Giancana organization is such that he is definitely over Ralph Pierce and Rocco Potenzo. In this capacity, is overlord of lucrative gambling operations at J & J Picnic Grove, Will County, IL. Operation is run primarily for Giancana and Gus Alex, and has 7 investors who keep bank at this operation at the quarter of a million dollar level at all times. Operation is now run on sneak basis in view of local heat, however, continues to be a lucrative source of income.

FEDERAL BUREAU OF INVESTIGATION

REPORTING OFFICE	OFFICE OF ORIGIN	DATE	INVESTIGATIVE PERIOD	
CHICAGO	CHICAGO	1961	July 27, 1961	
TITLE OF CASE		REPORT MADE BY		TYPED BY
				dkc
SAMUEL M. GIANCANA, aka		CHARACTER OF CASE		
		FBI Headquarters File number 92-3171-330 Top Hoodlum Program – Anti Racketeering. Daily Summary		

Dominic "Butch" Blasi observed entering Armory Lounge carrying a large briefcase. Blasi was unaccompanied, indicating Giancana is not in town. It was learned that Giancana hoodlums, composed of lesser hoodlums as William Daddono, meet at the Lilac Lounge, located at Wolf and Cermak Roads, near Chicago, on Wednesdays and or Thursday afternoons. Also observed meeting at the lounge was Joseph Glimco. Armed and Dangerous.

FEDERAL BUREAU OF INVESTIGATION

REPORTING OFFICE	OFFICE OF ORIGIN	DATE	INVESTIGATIVE PERIOD	
CHICAGO	CHICAGO	1961	August 1, 1961	
TITLE OF CASE		REPORT MADE BY		TYPED BY
				dkc
SAMUEL M. GIANCANA, aka		CHARACTER OF CASE		
		FBI Headquarters File number 92-3171-371 Top Hoodlum Program – Anti Racketeering. Daily Summary		

Synopsis:

Title changed to reflect additional aliases of Giancana, aka, R. J. Landolt, and Goldfield as reflected by investigation. Giancana interviewed by Bureau agents at O'Hare Airport on 7/12/61; was arrogant, belligerent, uncooperative, blasphemous, and refused to furnish any information relating to his activities. Phyllis McGuire interviewed same date and furnished same information relating to her association with Giancana. Investigation reveals that Giancana spent much of the past month in company with Phyllis McGuire at Las Vegas, Newark, and New York City. Interviews with other associates of Giancana set forth. Informants report that Giancana spent some of his time in Las Vegas for the purpose of solidifying his interest in that area.

Sam Giancana

Samuel M. Giancana was interviewed at the O'Hare International Airport after arriving from Phoenix, Arizona. Giancana was a passenger on this flight under the name of Mooney Cecola. Giancana was approached by Agents as he departed from the plane. He brushed off the attempts of the agents to identify them selves and stated that he was well aware of the fact that the Agents were representatives of the FBI. He stated that he had absolutely nothing to say to the agents. From the very outset and throughout the interview, Giancana was alternately obscene, abusive, and sarcastic. At no time did he exhibit a friendly or cooperative attitude. He asked relative to the reason for the interview and at this point was questioned concerning his knowledge of the wire tapping of the hotel room of Dan Rowan in Las Vegas. Giancana replied that he had absolutely no comment and had absolutely nothing to say. He refused to admit that he is acquainted with the identity of Rowan and repeated effused say any comment concerning that situation. When asked whether he was acquainted with Robert Maheu, Giancana very belligerently refused to make any comment or to indicate in any manner that he was aware of the identity of Maheu.

Giancana became very abusive and obscene and very heatedly advised that he was well aware of the FBI's investigations of him. He stated that he is aware of the identity of SA Ralph Hill Jr., and aware of the fact that SA Hill has talked to numerous girlfriends, relatives, and other associates of his.

At this point, Giancana requested the agents to move away from him and leave him alone. It was pointed out to him that he was in a public waiting room of American Airlines and that the Agents had every right to be situated where they were. It was pointed out to Giancana that he was not under arrest and that the FBI had no interest in detaining him. It was made clear to him that he had every opportunity to leave his present location and that the FBI had absolutely no objections to his re-boarding

198

his airplane en-route to New York. It was pointed out to him that as far as the Agents were concerned there was absolutely no reason for his presence in Chicago and there was no objection to his leaving without plans to return.

At this point in the conversation, Giancana created a disturbance by accusing passengers who had disembarked from American Airlines Flight 66 of being FBI Agents. At this point, Giancana requested the identity of SA William F. Roemer, Jr. and when told, advised he was well aware of SA Roemer's identity. When it was pointed out to him that this seemed to be unusual since SA Roemer has been in no way concerned with any investigation of Giancana, Giancana replied that he was aware of this and was also aware of the individuals whom SA Roemer has been investigating. He also advised that he is aware of the fact that SA Roemer is a "member of the bar."

At this point, Giancana asked the agents if they had ascertained how many men he had killed. Giancana was asked if he could furnish the Agents information in that regard and said that he could not remember; however, he though he might have to be responsible for a killing shortly, looking at the Agents while making the remark. He was asked if that remark was a threat to the Agent and denied making any threats and said that it was not a threat. Giancana referred again to investigations being conducted regarding his activities and made a remark, "my sister-in-law told me all about you, Hill, about the treats which you made if she refused to furnish information. She also told me that you told her that I had killed 13 men." The agent emphatically denied the above remark by Giancana and asked him if he was referring to an interview conducted of Mrs. Rose Flood, a sister-in-law of Giancana's. Giancana shrugged his shoulders and merely replied, "Don't worry, I have it all down in writing."

At this point, Giancana then, represented his ticket, and announced in a loud voice in the presence of everyone in the waiting room that he was, "going to get the hell out of here and go to Cuba." Giancana thereupon re-boarded his plan en route to New York City.

After approximately five minutes, when it apparently became obvious to Giancana that Miss McGuire was not aboard the airline and apparently did not intend to board, Giancana again disembarked from the airline. He approached the Agents, again in the waiting room of American Airlines and in a loud voice again became very abusive and obscene concerning his inconveniences and the fact that Miss McGuire has separated herself from him. He stated that the U.S. Government had lost all its fineness and that "American citizens might as well be in Russia" due to the treatment which he was receiving. It was again pointed out to Giancana that the Agents had no desire that he remain in Chicago and would be very happy if he remained of Flight 66 en route to New York City.

Giancana again remarked, "This country is getting just like Russia where a man is not free to escort a young lady where he pleases. Why don't you investigate these dope fiends?" He was asked if that remark implied that he had information relating to narcotics and his reply to that question was, "Why aren't you investigating the Communists?" Giancana was asked if he was dissatisfied with this country and replied, "I love this country and I would sacrifice my life for it." He said, "I proved this not long ago." He was asked to clarify that last remark and he refused to comment.

Giancana then sarcastically asked the Agents if they had found out that he owned 25 per cent of Marshall Fields, 20 per cent of Carson's, and 20 per cent of Goldblatts Department stores to which the Agent asked if this were a statement on his part and he replied, "Yes, I own all of these places" again in a sarcastic manner. He was asked if he had any interest in Las Vegas, Nevada, and he stated that, "I own 99 percent of Las Vegas." Giancana then asked what the Agents desired to know and invited a question about his activities. The question then put to him was if he would confirm the allegations that he was the head of organized criminal activities in Chicago. He replied, "I'm not the head of anything and I don't know what you are talking about." After making this remark, Giancana uttered a few more obscenities.

Giancana then stated, "If you want to talk to me give me a subpoena and I will appear before the Grand Jury and answer and every question put to me." He was asked if he meant by this that he would answer every question truthfully or if this meant that he would stand on his Constitutional guarantee of the 5th Amendment. He replied, "That all depends on the question."

Giancana advised the Agents that he was aware of the fact that the FBI would make every attempt to "frame" him into the penitentiary, at which point Agents advised Giancana the FBI conducts its investigations on an impersonal unbiased manner and that the history of this organization is not that of "framing" anyone and this is certainly not the intention of the purpose of this investigation. Giancana then referred to his prison sentence, stating, "If I go to the penitentiary this time, I'll go like a man just like I did the other time and you know what I'm talking about." The Agents stated that they did not know what he was talking about and he replied, "I went like a man then even though I was a victim of circumstances." He was asked how he was a victim of circumstance in the instances were he had been given jail terms and he refused to comment further about how he was victimized.

Giancana was asked if he was acquainted with John D'Arco, an Alderman of the First Ward of Chicago. At this point, Giancana said, "Whose D'Arco?" It was pointed out to Giancana that Mr. D'Arco had commented at one time recently that he was acquainted with Mr. Giancana and knew him well. At this point, Giancana directed an obscene remark to Mr. D'Arco and requested that Agents to pass on the obscenity to Mr. D'Arco. He was asked if he knew Murray Humphreys and he stated he did not know Murray Humphreys. He was asked if he knew Gus Alex and he replied, "No, I don't know Gus Alex. Do you think I know everyone in the world?"

Giancana then indicated that he was aware that the Agents intended to report the results of this interview of him to their "boss," who in turn would report the results to their "super boss," who would thereupon reported to his "super boss," and "super super boss," and he said, "You know what I mean, I mean the Kennedy's." He then said, "I know all about the Kennedy's and Phyllis (McGuire) knows a lot more about the Kennedy's and one of these days we are going to tell all." When asked for clarification of his comments in this regard. Giancana uttered an obscenity and refused further comment.

Giancana then made a reference to Aldi Stevenson and vaguely criticized his conduct in office and the manner in which he has involved the United States in the Cuban situation. When asked for clarification in this regard, Giancana stated that he has knowledge that Stevenson directed, "That mess in Cuba" and stated that Stevenson is a "bookworm" who had no common sense.

Giancana then advised that the United States Government is not as smart as it would like to think it is. He stated that he knows that the United States Government made a deal with Fidel Castro during the Batista Regime to furnish support to Castro and assist him in assent to power in Cuba on the condition that when Castro came into power he would eliminate gambling in Cuba. Giancana stated, "Now that deal has boomeranged on you, hasn't it?" When it was mentioned to Giancana that at least one good affect of the above situation might have taken place in that his interests in Cuba were destroyed, Giancana then became very emotional and abusive and commented that he had never been in Cuba and had no interest in Cuba. When asked whether the individuals who ran gambling in Cuba during the Batista Regime were subordinates, Giancana refused to comment. He also refused to identify Charlie Baron as an associate of his.

At this point, Giancana advised that it is his firm belief that he is being "persecuted" due to the fact that he is a member of the Italian nationality. When it was pointed out to him that the investigation by the FBI of Murray Humphreys and Gus Alex have been pursued just as vigorously as the investigation of him and that Humphreys and Alex are not Italians, Giancana then uttered a string of obscenities and indicated that by far the majority of the individuals investigated b the U.S. Government were of Italian descent. He pointed out that it was his opinion that the FBI, "Not only prosecuted but persecuted Italians." When asked for specifics concerning what he intended to indicate by this comment, Giancana again referred to the fact that he was not being allowed to associate with his girlfriend in a normal fashion. It was pointed out to Giancana again that Miss McGuire accompanied other Agents for a purpose of interview entirely under her on volition.

On more than one occasion during the interview, Giancana advised that he did not intend to, "Take this thing sitting down." He very heatedly stated, "I'm going to light a fire under you guys and don't forget that." When asked for clarification of his comments, Giancana refused and further comment. When asked how he enjoyed his recent visit to Florida, Giancana very sarcastically said, "Yes, I have been in Florida and I own the Fontainebleau, The American, and the Diplomat." When asked whether it was true that he owned the Eden Roc, Giancana sarcastically affirmed the Eden Roc also.

When requested whether he would desire that the Agents telephonically contact Butch Blasi in order to provide him transportation form the airport, Giancana replied "Yes, call Butch and tell him to bring two shotguns with him." When asked whether he intended that remark as a threat to the Agents, Giancana replied that he did not.

Giancana facetiously referred to the fact that in Russia if you commit a crime they merely shoot you rather that sent you to prison. His next comment was that "I think I will kill myself. Why don't you give me a pistol so I can do this?" Giancana made remarks throughout the interview to the effect that he was going to kill himself. Regarding his general health, Giancana remarked that he "had a cancer"; however, he did not elaborate on this and stated, "If you want to find out any more about my health, see my doctor." When asked as to the identity of the doctor, he refused to disclose his identity.

On frequent intervals during the conversation with Giancana, it was pointed out to him that he was not under arrest and that the FBI had no intention of detaining him. Giancana frequently during the conversation proclaimed in a loud voice scattered with obscenities, "Get away from me you (obscene) and quit bothering me. I don't want to talk to you." At each such instance, it was pointed out to Giancana that he was free to leave at any time, that he was in a public place and that he was not by any means being detained.

The conversation was terminated upon the appearance of Miss McGuire whom Giancana had previously referred to during the conversation as "the Mrs." He was asked if he was married to her and he said sarcastically "I married her a long time ago." Upon Miss McGuire's appearance, Giancana stated to her in a loud and clear voice "Why don't you tell them to go to hell like I did?" Giancana accompanied by Miss McGuire, them left the interviewing area.

SAM M. GIANCANA
August, 1961

201

Dominic "Butch" Blasi

The records of the Sheriff's office, Muston, Wisconsin, reflect the following information pertaining to Dom Blasi:

On the evening of March 15, 1949, Dominic Blasi, Anthony James Sperna, and Mike Martorano were arrested by the Sheriff's office, Muston, Wisconsin, at which time a search of the automobiles in which these individuals were driving reflected that in the locked trunk of this car was a black Gladstone suitcase containing five loaded pistols and one machine gun.

The official records show that Dominic Joseph Blasi of 1138 Taylor Street was arrested by the Sheriff's Office at 11:00PM in possession of 1948 black Ford which was apparently the property of Anthony Sperna. The weapons in their possession were a .38 caliber Smith and Wesson revolver, a Mauser 7.5 automatic pistol, a .38 caliber Colt automatic, a .22 caliber H and R Sportsman's revolver, and one MP 40 machine gun with pistol grip as well as ammunition for all guns. Blasi at that time stated he was employed as a street paver for the city of Chicago, placed in the job by one Frank Esposito. Blasi was also part owner of the Harrison-Kedzie Realty Company, 3204 Harrison Street, Chicago.

On March 23, 1955, Dominic Blasi was interviewed by SA's Joe Wheeler and Francis Stefanak at which time Blasi furnished the following information:

He stated that he was currently the co-owner of a tavern, "Jim's Corner," 2859 West Roosevelt Road, Chicago. Blasi said he could usually be reached at the tavern address. Blasi advised that he and his partner, whom he declined to name, had paid $4,000 for the tavern in May or June, 1954, and expected to sell it in the near future for $6,5000. He stated they had each taken approximately $100 per week as salary and had placed the balance of profits in a bank. Blasi said the tavern was a profitable business but has all colored trade, and he is anxious to sell.

Blasi said he intended to book horses at the various Chicago race tracks during the 1955 racing season. He claimed to be able to make between $7,000 and $8,000 booking horses during the season and would in addition receive a bonus and other unnamed considerations at the completion of the season.

Blasi advised that he currently resides in Oak Park, IL, with his wife and three children. He declined to furnish his home address or phone number. He added that he was not at this time engaged in any criminal activities and would be available at any time for "show up."

It is noted that the above statement was made by Blasi in connection with line of questioning used during this interview which concerned a recent holdup of a Milwaukee grocery store which resulted in the apprehension of Mike Messina, an associate of Blasi.

Blasi stated that there is a barber shop located at 1074 West Polk Street, which is operated by Louis Briatta and which is used as a hangout for politicians, including John D'Arco, First Ward Alderman and hoodlum. Blasi advised that on occasion many years ago, he perpetrated an armed robbery out of Chicago. When he returned from this job, he was called on the carpet since the individual he had robbed had "Chicago" connections with the "syndicate." He said in his case he was permitted to keep the money he had obtained, however, he had heard of other similar cases where the money had been returned to the victim. Blasi then added, "I have other bosses over me and I'm not referring to my wife."

George Bond, General Manager, Allen Chevrolet Company advised that a 1957 Chevrolet convertible was sold to a Clarice Accardo which was purchased in cash. Bond stated that at no time during his arrangements for the sale of this car did he see any member of the Accardo family, but that all business was transacted by a person known to him as "Butch" Blasi.

Leslie Kruse

Chicago T-1 stated that Leslie Kruse is extremely nervous over the current investigation by the Justice Department into organized crime activities, and has advised of his intention to leave the Chicago area for an extended period, but his destination is unknown to the informant. Kruse's position in the Giancana organization by stating that Kruse passes orders directly on to Rocco Potenzo.

Chicago informant T-1 advised on August 3, 1961, that Leslie Kruse had been complaining of the fact that Jake "The Barber" Factor was having a great deal of trouble due to a split of profits from the Stardust gambling casino in Las Vegas. According to the informant Factor leases the area used by the Stardust and an agreement was made to pay Factor "off the top" of the profits from gambling in the casino. Factor has not been receiving his share of the profits and is in the process of arguing with the Chicago group of this situation.

He also advised that he recently learned that Louis Silver, who is one of the top owners of the Croydon, Eastgate, and St. Clair hotels and who intends to take over the Ambassador hotel chains in Chicago, has a son-in-law named Robert Lifton, who is one of the seven top men operating the Trans-Continental Investment Company, which has offices at Los Angeles and New York. He described this investment company as a "billionaire outfit" in which Leslie Kruse has invested as well as Rocco Fischetti, Gus Alex, and Sam Giancana.

Phyllis McGuire

Chicago T-26 advised on June 27, 1961, that an individual who appeared to be Sam Giancana was observed at the ranch rented by Phyllis McGuire in Nevada. McGuire at the time was sunbathing while the individual who resembled Giancana was spraying her with a garden hose. During that time a car registered to one Nickolas Cecola was observed at the ranch. Nickolas Cecola was fingerprinted on December 27, 1957, when he applied for a position as "boss man" at the Silver Slipper Casino in Las Vegas. He was formerly employed at the Owl Club, Calumet City, IL.

Chicago T-15 advised that Phyllis McGuire had been receiving psychiatric treatment in New York for the past several months and said that Miss McGuire may be carrying a gun in her possession at all times, which possibly was given to her by Giancana. It is the opinion of the informant that Phyllis McGuire has been given a tremendous amount of jewelry by Giancana during the past several months. Informant stated that the McGuire sisters are scheduled to be in London, England for an engagement during the months of October and November, 1961, and there are indications that Giancana is making plans to be in England at the time of the engagement of the McGuire Sisters. The informant also advised that Giancana and McGuire were at the New Latin Casino, Haddonfield, New Jersey. During this period of time, Giancana was seen accompanied by Paul D'Amato. In of June of 1961, Giancana has reportedly presented a 35 carat diamond ring to Miss McGuire, which she has worn on only a very few occasions due to the fact that she dose not want to appear ostentatious. The informant estimates that Miss McGuire has been given jewelry, the market value of which would total over $300,000.00. These gifts have been given to Miss McGuire during the past several months. He also added that the possibility existed that Miss McGuire may as of this date be pregnant, and was attempting to induce Giancana to marry her.

On July 12, 1961, Phyllis McGuire departed alone from a plane at O'Hare Airport, Chicago, at which time she was met by SA Vincent Inserra and John Bassett, and requested an interview. Miss McGuire inquired as to the nature of the interview, at which time she was advised that it concerned he association with Sam Giancana.

At the outset, Miss McGuire became hostile, and stated that she had become highly upset in the recent past because of apparent attention afforded her by the FBI while in the company of Giancana, and also of various attempts to interview her in this connection.

At this point, Miss McGuire became high excited, raised her voice, and berated and belittled apparent methods used by the FBI in the past to determine her association with Giancana. She complained of constant surveillances throughout the country while in the presence of Giancana by the FBI. When queried as to how she knew that the persons in question were FBI agents, she replied, "I just know they are, and I'm getting tired of this harassment". Miss McGuire emphatically stated that she was going to bring this matter immediately to the attention of the FBI in Washington. She went on to elaborate that her brother-in-law, John Teeter, is a close friend of J. Eagar Hoover Director of the FBI, and she would see to it personally that this entire matter would be brought to Mr. Hoover's attention through Teeter. Miss McGuire at one point got out of her chair, and in a high pitched voice, and while demonstrating with her hands, rambled in generalities about FBI harassment and tactics alleged by her in various parts of the United States wherever she had been appearing with her sisters and when accompanied by Giancana. She pointed out that she has been interviewed by the FBI at her Park Avenue apartment in New York City after repeated attempts to contact her, which displeased her greatly. She related another occasion concerning an FBI interview of Dan Rowan of the Rowan-Martin comedy team, which took place at Rowan's apartment in Hollywood, California. She explained that she at one time dated Rowan frequently and, as a result of this association, Rowan apparently had been contacted for information concerning her and Giancana, which had been made known to her by Rowan. At this point Miss McGuire again became highly excited, at which time she was advised that if she were unable to control her emotions, the interview would have to be terminated. It was explained that the interviewing Agents were attempting to solicit her full cooperation concerning the activities of Giancana. It was pointed out that in view of her present attitude and apparent lack of cooperation that a Federal Grand Jury was to convene in Chicago, on July 30, 1961, and she might possibly choose to appear before this Grand Jury in this connection, and that there was a subpoena outstanding for her appearance.

McGiure advised that she had no objections to appearing before the Grand Jury; however; claimed that she was not being uncooperative and that as an entertainer it was her nature to speak loudly and demonstrate with her hands. She went on to point out in detail that the veins in her neck always protruded while forcefully expressing her self.

Miss McGuire apologetically explained to the Agents that she was sorry if she had displayed hostility during the interview up to this point that she would answer any questions and desired that the interview continue. She explained that she first met Sam Giancana approximately two years ago at the Desert Inn Hotel in Las Vegas, where the McGuire Sisters Trio were appearing. She went on to explain that between performances she would occasionally fill in as a card dealer at the "Blackjack" table as a novelty. On one evening while at this table, she was introduced to Giancana by a person whose name she could not recall, and subsequent to this meeting Giancana remained at the table where he joked and heckled her in a playful manner. On this same evening, she departed Las Vegas with the Trio for another singing engagement and did not see Giancana again for about three months when he contacted her at her New York Apartment. Thereafter, she continued to see Giancana in various parts of the United States wherever the McGuire Sisters Trio was appearing. According to McGuire, this included Miami, Chicago, New York, and Las Vegas, and other cities in this country. She recalled that while in Miami she resided in the Deauville Hotel on Collins Avenue, and he visited her at her room at this hotel. She was of the opinion that Giancana took an apartment in the Carleton Hotel during his visit. In regards to Giancana's visits to Miami, McGuire said that she knew of no residences owned or occupied by Giancana in the Miami, Florida, area.

Miss McGuire said that during her meetings with Giancana in various parts of the country, she noted that he was greeted and respected by hotel managers, businessmen, and top personalities in the entertainment field, and apparently most of these individuals were well acquainted with Giancana. When questioned in this regard, she was unable to specifically furnish names of these individuals, with the exception of Jimmy Durante and Joe E. Lewis.

According to Miss McGuire, Giancana advised her that he was a retired Chicago bookmaker and he knew nothing further concerning Giancana's source of income. She stated she has noted that newspapers have referred to Giancana as a "Chicago Syndicate" figure and learned from newspapers that Giancana had been in prison on two occasions. She also said that she could not understand why Giancana was not in jail if he was a criminal as the papers allege. She stated that during the period she had known him; Giancana appears to be a gentleman and displays a great fatherly interest in his children. According to Miss McGuire, she has very frequently dated Giancana since first meeting him and is fond of him. She advised she in not married to Giancana but declined to advise whether or not she contemplated marriage to Giancana in the future.

When questioned in regards to expenditures made by Giancana during the two-year period she has known him, McGuire replied that she had never observed Giancana making large gambling wagers at any of the Las Vegas casinos in her presence, or for that matter, elsewhere in the country. It was pointed out to McGuire that in view oh her close association with Giancana it should be safe to assume that he had given her gifts on occasion, as a token of their friendship. She advised that Giancana had presented her with approximately five gifts during their association, but in view of a disagreement they had experienced recently, she had returned all of the gifts. McGuire at first declined to describe the gifts or their approximate value, stating that she could not understand of what possible value this would serve the FBI, especially in view of the fact that all gifts had been returned. When attention was again directed to the five gifts she had mentioned, McGuire stated that she distinctly recalled that she distinctly recalled that she mentioned "several" gifts, and did not specify a figure of "five". She contained by stating that she had received a total amount of three gifts from Giancana during the time she has known him, and that these gifts consisted of an evening bag and two items of jewelry. Miss McGuire was asked to describe the jewelry and also to advise what, in her opinion, was the total value of each gift. She declined to furnish this information, stating that she could not accurately recall the description and approximate value of each item, and would not want to be in error of any estimate which she might furnish to the Agents, in the event this information might possibly cause Giancana trouble.

McGuire advised the after giving the matter serious thought, she estimated that the combined value of the three gifts given to her by Giancana amounted to less than $5,000. She hastened to add that she had received much more expensive gifts in the past from other suitors. She added that in the event she were required to appear before a Federal Grand Jury at a future date, she would be unable to furnish any more complete information regarding the identity and value of gifts presented to her by Giancana, that she just furnished to the Agents.

McGuire was asked if it was not true that she had recently received a 1961 Cadillac as a gift from Giancana. She said she did not purchase a Cadillac, but it was purchased for her with he own funds from her personal bank account. She advised the purchase came about as a result of a conversation she had with Giancana in Las Vegas. She said that Giancana told her that he would arrange for the purchase of a Cadillac through a close friend, who was in the Cadillac business. The car was delivered to her in Las Vegas from the Denemark Cadillac Agency in Chicago on June 14, 1961.

Prior to leaving the interview room, Miss McGuire again apologized for her behavior at the outset of the interview. She stated that she greatly appreciated the attitude of the interview agents in tolerating her poor conduct, which had been caused by being "high strung" and nervous from overwork. McGuire inquired as to whether or not continued associating with Giancana might jeopardize her career in the entertainment field and possibly expose her to unfavorable publicity. She was advised that any continued association with Sam Giancana would have to be of her own choice and that the FBI could not advise her in this regard.

She stated that she is currently reading an edition of a book entitled "Mafia" and stated that based on her association with Giancana she did not believe it was possible that a man as "gentle" as Giancana could be involved in any similar type activity. She advised that if this could be true she would like to learn more about the man, inasmuch as she has worked hard during her life to become a success in the entertainment field and would not want to lose her present status. It is noted that McGuire wept briefly as preparations were being made to leave the interview room. She requested the names of the interviewing Agents, and was furnished same written on a piece paper. She advised that she would look forward to several days of rest in New York prior to going to New Jersey and suggested that she might possibly desire to be afforded another interview with Agents John Bassett and Vincent Inserra in the near future, inasmuch as she had developed a feeling of trust during the interview.

The interviewing Agents escorted Miss McGuire to the departure area of American Airlines, where she was reunited with Giancana at which time he was obviously irritated and made unfavorable comments to the Agents in a loud voice. As Agents left Miss McGuire with Giancana in the lobby, Giancana exclaimed in a loud voice, "Take a good look". McGuire was observed to break away from Giancana and again approached the agents stated "I wish to apologize for Mr. Giancana's conduct and hope that you will disregard it. He told me that I should not have talked to you, but I told him that I could not be like him because I'm nice."

Activities of Sam Giancana in Las Vegas

Chicago T-2 advised on July 7, 1961 that Giancana was in conference with John Drew and Joe Pignatello. According to this informant John Drew is one of the officials of the Stardust Casino and the Stardust Hotel, Las Vegas. During this conference, the possibility of Joe Pignatello and John Drew of attaining the restaurant known as the Coach and Four located in Las Vegas, for approximately $135,000 was brought up. The possibility of John Drew or others acquiring some interests in or near Searchlight, Nevada, was also brought up during this conference. Searchlight, Nevada, is located on United States Highway number 93 approximately 60 miles southwest of Las Vegas. Most of the businesses in Searchlight are owned by one Willy Martello who, according to this informant, is attempting to expedite more traffic in the town of Searchlight so that his business may profit accordingly. According to the informant the possibility exists that John Drew possibly through Sam Giancana will attempt to buy out Willy Martello or build a new establishment in the town of Searchlight.

Chicago T-35 advised that Giancana, Pignatello, and others, one of whom was possibly John Roselli, mentioned earlier, were in conference in Las Vegas, during which time slot machines and locations in Las Vegas were discussed, however, informant was not familiar with those places discussed by Giancana and the others in this group.

Five Chicago informants all advised that during the latter part of June and early July, 1961, which indicated that Giancana's purpose in being in Las Vegas and to further his romantic relationship with Phyllis McGuire. All of the above informants stated that the relationship between Giancana and McGuire is the aggressor in this affair and has been urging Giancana to marry her whereas Giancana apparently is putting off any such union.

FEDERAL BUREAU OF INVESTIGATION

REPORTING OFFICE	OFFICE OF ORIGIN	DATE	INVESTIGATIVE PERIOD
CHICAGO	CHICAGO	1961	August 7, 1961

TITLE OF CASE	REPORT MADE BY	TYPED BY
SAMUEL M. GIANCANA, aka		dkc

CHARACTER OF CASE

FBI Headquarters File number 92-3171
Top Hoodlum Program – Anti Racketeering.
Daily Summary

Americo "Pete" DiPietto, previously described as part of the North Avenue Steak House gang with Ernest Infelice, James "Cowboy" Mirro, we're interviewed at the Guest House Restaurant. DiPietto was outwardly friendly; however had nothing to say regarding his activities, other than stating he is a legitimate business man. He would not comment on Giancana, stating he had nothing to say in that regard. Interview was of short duration.

FEDERAL BUREAU OF INVESTIGATION

REPORTING OFFICE	OFFICE OF ORIGIN	DATE	INVESTIGATIVE PERIOD
CHICAGO	CHICAGO	1961	August 10, 1961

TITLE OF CASE	REPORT MADE BY	TYPED BY
SAMUEL M. GIANCANA, aka		dkc

CHARACTER OF CASE

FBI Headquarters File number 92-3171
Top Hoodlum Program – Anti Racketeering.
Daily Summary

Symbol number assigned to Armory Lounge microphone surveillance is CG 6486-C. Technical problems about completion of this microphone surveillance now in process of possible solution. Problems involve outside connection and completion so that may be monitored at office. Alternative plan is hook up to apartment in vicinity and established monitoring plant there. Physical surveillance conducted on Dominic Blasi this date to establish whether or not Giancana is in Chicago area. Blasi performed violent evasive tactics to negate surveillance. At time physical surveillance instituted, Blasi was with Dominic Sisilano, furniture dealer for Giancana group. Physical surveillance discontinued after Blasi was observed nearing Armory Lounge. Records of Walston and Company, Stockbrokers, Chicago, checked, and ascertained that Dominic Blasi is prominent customer of this company, as are Bonita, Antoinette, and Francine Giancana, daughters of subject.

FEDERAL BUREAU OF INVESTIGATION

REPORTING OFFICE	OFFICE OF ORIGIN	DATE	INVESTIGATIVE PERIOD
CHICAGO	CHICAGO	1961	August 14, 1961

TITLE OF CASE	REPORT MADE BY	TYPED BY
		dkc
SAMUEL M. GIANCANA, aka	**CHARACTER OF CASE**	
	FBI Headquarters File number 92-3171-367 Top Hoodlum Program – Anti Racketeering. Daily Summary	

Records of the IRS Chicago fail to reflect filing of tax return by John Matassa from years 1955 through 1959. States possible but not probable that Matassa filed under different name and address. Matassa described as retired Chicago Police man. "hoodlum cop", close associate and bodyguard for subject, reportedly enjoys high living standard although only means of support is disability pay from PD. Chicago source who resides adjacent to Armory Lounge, Chicago meeting place of subject. Sam Giancana observed at Armory Lounge conversing with female identified as Bergit Clark, Elmhurst, out side of lounge. In view of unusual increase of activity at the Armory Lounge, installation of hidden microphone will be delayed.

FEDERAL BUREAU OF INVESTIGATION

REPORTING OFFICE	OFFICE OF ORIGIN	DATE	INVESTIGATIVE PERIOD
CHICAGO	CHICAGO	1961	August 18, 1961

TITLE OF CASE	REPORT MADE BY	TYPED BY
		dkc
SAMUEL M. GIANCANA, aka	**CHARACTER OF CASE**	
	FBI Headquarters File number 92-3171-379 Top Hoodlum Program – Anti Racketeering. Daily Summary	

Letter received Chicago Office August 15, 1961, from anonymous source attributes recent gangland style death of William "Action" Jackson, former PCI of Chicago office, and known collector for hoodlum "Juice" men, to Giancana, and associates Sam Battaglia, "Milwaukee Phil" Alderisio, Willie "Potatoes" Daddono and John Matassa. Letter furnished name and address of Renee Conway, described as girl friend of Nicky Vallo, Chicago hoodlum, who would "talk" if interviewed and under impression she was in a "tight spot". Conway described as living life in luxury under sponsorship of Vallo, and having no other visible means of support. Letter states that if John Matassa and Nick Vallo interviewed and forces to talk they could furnish the answers involving the death of "Action" Jackson. Chicago will interview Conway and Matassa in view of above info.

FEDERAL BUREAU OF INVESTIGATION

REPORTING OFFICE	OFFICE OF ORIGIN	DATE	INVESTIGATIVE PERIOD	
CHICAGO	CHICAGO	1961	August 22, 1961	
TITLE OF CASE		REPORT MADE BY		TYPED BY
				dkc
SAMUEL M. GIANCANA, aka		CHARACTER OF CASE		
		FBI Headquarters File number 92-3171-391 Top Hoodlum Program – Anti Racketeering. Daily Summary		

Giancana observed in conference with unknown person, probably one of the Meo Brothers. CG 6486-C advised on August 18, that Mrs. Anthony Accardo and daughter Marie, Mr. and Mrs. Frank Ferraro, Hy Godfrey, and Mrs. Marie Capezio, widow of the late Tony Capezio, attended a dinner party at the Armory Lounge on that date. Not definitely known if Giancana in attendance.

FEDERAL BUREAU OF INVESTIGATION

REPORTING OFFICE	OFFICE OF ORIGIN	DATE	INVESTIGATIVE PERIOD	
CHICAGO	CHICAGO	1961	August 25, 1961	
TITLE OF CASE		REPORT MADE BY		TYPED BY
				dkc
SAMUEL M. GIANCANA, aka		CHARACTER OF CASE		
		FBI Headquarters File number 92-3171-386 Top Hoodlum Program – Anti Racketeering. Daily Summary		

Recently provided information to the effect that the late William "Action" Jackson, who was found killed in gangland style August 11, 1961, had been associated with Sam Lewis in the operation of the Parr Loan Company, Oak Park, who in turn, according to the informant, is a partner of Sam Giancana. Informant advised in addition that the building in which this loan company is located is owned by Chicago PD Captain Louis Capparelli, who has been described in part as an associate of Chicago hoodlums. Anonymous source and other informants, speculating on Jackson's demise, have stated that Jackson was in trouble in the juice racket and was killed by Sam DeStefano, also, that he ran a poker game in Cicero for the outfit and was killed in retaliation of refusing to shut down. Noted that Cicero has been a target of chief investigator of the States Attorney, Roswell Spencer, and as result, certain operations in Cicero have been ordered to shut down until heat cools.

Renee Conway interviewed at Chicago and admitted being Nicky Vallos and acquainted with Giancana. Vallos previously described as associate of subject and possibly involved in the death of William "Action" Jackson, a former collector and juice man who was killed. Will re-interview in near future.

FEDERAL BUREAU OF INVESTIGATION

REPORTING OFFICE	OFFICE OF ORIGIN	DATE	INVESTIGATIVE PERIOD	
CHICAGO	CHICAGO	1961	August 31, 1961	
TITLE OF CASE		REPORT MADE BY		TYPED BY
				dkc
SAMUEL M. GIANCANA, aka		CHARACTER OF CASE		
		FBI Headquarters File number 92-3171 Top Hoodlum Program – Anti Racketeering. Daily Summary		

Donald Parrillo, advised Agents he is president of the Parr Finance Company which is family business located in Oak Park. It is noted informant described Parr Finance Company as a hoodlum operated juice business run by Parrillo who is front man for subject and Sam Lewis who actually owns the business. Parrillo admitted William "Action" Jackson was employed as eighty five dollars a week as a collector for Parr Finance Co.

FEDERAL BUREAU OF INVESTIGATION

REPORTING OFFICE	OFFICE OF ORIGIN	DATE	INVESTIGATIVE PERIOD	
CHICAGO	CHICAGO	1961	September 5, 1961	
TITLE OF CASE		REPORT MADE BY		TYPED BY
				dkc
SAMUEL M. GIANCANA, aka		CHARACTER OF CASE		
		FBI Headquarters File number 92-3171 Top Hoodlum Program – Anti Racketeering. Daily Summary		

Chicago informant has related that Giancana's brother Joseph "Pepe" Giancana is working for Giancana through Frank Eulo in operation of gambling establishment in Cicero known as the Royal Caf .

FEDERAL BUREAU OF INVESTIGATION

REPORTING OFFICE	OFFICE OF ORIGIN	DATE	INVESTIGATIVE PERIOD
CHICAGO	CHICAGO	1961	September 7, 1961

TITLE OF CASE	REPORT MADE BY	TYPED BY
SAMUEL M. GIANCANA, aka		dkc

CHARACTER OF CASE

FBI Headquarters File number 92-3171
Top Hoodlum Program – Anti Racketeering.
Daily Summary

An individual who resembled Giancana seen entering Armory Lounge yesterday in afternoon. Physical surveillance at Armory lounge late 9/6/61, observed automobiles registered to Dom Blasi, and Tony Accardo's brother-in-law Tarquin Simonelli.

FEDERAL BUREAU OF INVESTIGATION

REPORTING OFFICE	OFFICE OF ORIGIN	DATE	INVESTIGATIVE PERIOD
CHICAGO	CHICAGO	1961	September 12, 1961

TITLE OF CASE	REPORT MADE BY	TYPED BY
SAMUEL M. GIANCANA, aka		dkc

CHARACTER OF CASE

FBI Headquarters File number 92-3171
Top Hoodlum Program – Anti Racketeering.
Daily Summary

According to CG 6486-C, Giancana in conference with individual named Bob (LNU). This person has been tentatively identified as Robert Petrone, brother of Patrick Petrone, deceased former alderman of the 28th Ward, Chicago. Petrone is one of the owners of the Oasis Dispensing Company. Information was received some time ago to the effect that this company was under the control of Joseph Glimco, in view of fact that it had exclusive vending rights in all yellow cab garages in Chicago. Petrone would be a logical candidate to fill vacancy of Alderman in 28th ward caused by promotion of Anthony Girolami, incumbent. Contact was had with Girolami in an effort to ascertain the nature of the meeting with Giancana; however, no information was obtained.

FEDERAL BUREAU OF INVESTIGATION

REPORTING OFFICE	OFFICE OF ORIGIN	DATE	INVESTIGATIVE PERIOD	
CHICAGO	CHICAGO	1961	September 16, 1961	
TITLE OF CASE		REPORT MADE BY		TYPED BY
				dkc
SAMUEL M. GIANCANA, aka		CHARACTER OF CASE		
		FBI Headquarters File number 92-3171-417 Top Hoodlum Program – Anti Racketeering. Daily Summary		

Chicago 6486-C , advised that Dominic Blasi previously had Amber Lounge in Cicero, from which he carried on bookmaking activities. He moved this operation to the Mitchell Tavern, Cicero, where it was run for him by Willie Williams with the handling stamp being issued under the name of Helen Michelle, William's girl friend. This operation was raided by the Cook County State's Attorney's Investigators last week.

FEDERAL BUREAU OF INVESTIGATION

REPORTING OFFICE	OFFICE OF ORIGIN	DATE	INVESTIGATIVE PERIOD	
CHICAGO	CHICAGO	1961	September 18, 1961	
TITLE OF CASE		REPORT MADE BY		TYPED BY
		Special Agent John Bassett		dkc
SAMUEL M. GIANCANA, aka		CHARACTER OF CASE		
		FBI Headquarters File number 92-3171-409 Top Hoodlum Program – Anti Racketeering		

Associates

Nicholas Cecola
135 West Cleveland Street
Las Vegas, Nevada

CG T-35 advised in July, 1961, that Sam Giancana advised John Drew of the Stardust Hotel Casino, Las Vegas. Cocola is to be considered as a close associate of Giancana and one who can be helpful concerning the situation in Las Vegas. It is noted that Nick Cecola was issued a work permit card in Las Vegas, on June 28, 1958, at which time he listed his employment as Box Man at the Stardust Hotel.

Nicholas Cecola was interviewed on August 9, 1961. He stated he was born August

16, 1900, in Louisiana but spent most of his life in Chicago. There he had been engaged in the gambling business for the past 40 years, mostly in the Chicago area. In 1957, he came to Las Vegas and obtained employment at the Silver Slipper Casino.

Cecola was asked if he knew the following individuals: Gus Alex, Murray Humphreys, and Frank Ferraro. He said he had heard the names, and in years past he may have seen them, but does not know them personally. Then he was asked if he was acquainted with Sam Giancana and he said he had known Giancana for 20 years, although he had never worked for him. Cecola was asked if he ever talked to Giancana within the last month, but declined to name a specific date or place and declined to furnish topic of conversation except that it was merely casual conversation.

Cecola was asked if he were working at the Stardust to watch out for interest of Giancana or anyone else who might have a hidden interest and he said no, that he was a casino employee, just like all the other employees. He said he had no knowledge of anyone having a hidden interest at the Stardust Hotel or any hotel and he had no information that anyone was "skimming off the top" at the hotel. He said he had never helped make a count of the money at the hotel, and never participated in any policy decisions. Cecola was asked who gave him the message to contact Giancana recently in Las Vegas and Cecola declined to identify this individual.

He said he knew Joseph Pignatello, having first known him in Chicago and more recently had seen him in Las Vegas a few times. He had heard the name Johnny Roselli, but was not acquainted with Roselli. Cecola said he had known Anthony Accardo for a number of years, but had never worked for Accardo. He said that Milton Jaffe and Yale Cohen are the big bosses in the casino at the Stardust and his immediate boss is John Dickson, shift boss at the Stardust. Cecola said that he knows many people through out the United States in all walks of life, hence he feels the fact he knows Sam Giancana and Tony Accardo does not mean anything since he has been in the gambling business for so many years.

John D'Arco

Chicago T-1 advised that John D'Arco, Alderman of the First Ward, recently discussed with him the contact FBI Agents made with him approximately two years ago. D'Arco stated that the FBI informed him of the fact that his name was on a list of Chicago hoodlums found on Giancana's person when Giancana returned to this country from Mexico. Informant advised that he D'Arco what significance of the list was and why his name was on it. D'Arco advised the informant that the list was a compilation of names which Giancana had made of persons he wanted his daughter to invite to her wedding which took place shortly after his interview with FBI Agents. D'Arco said that these were the persons whom Giancana wanted at the wedding in view of his friendship with them. Informant advised that he asked D'Arco why he did not admit to the reason for the list whereby D'Arco replied that he did not know whether the FBI was aware of the impending wedding and he did not want to admit that he was so close to Giancana that he would be invited to the wedding as a special invitee of Sam Giancana himself.

David Halper

Davis Halper, former owner of the Chez Paree restaurant in Chicago. He stated the Chez Paree had to close because it was not making any money After it closed, Ben Goffstein, President of the Riviera Hotel, Las Vegas, gave him a job as a publicity representative an official greeter to guests for the hotel. He added that he wrote letters to former patrons of the Chez Paree and to other persons that he knew in Chicago giving them the "pitch" on coming to Las Vegas and staying at the Riviera Hotel. He stated that he had been doing quite well and that Goffstein seemed very well pleased with his work.

Halper stated he knew Sam Giancana very well, and that Giancana came to his restaurant on many occasions. He added that if he had had more customers like Giancana; his place of business would not have gone broke, as Giancana was a good spender and came to eat at his place many times. Halper added he knew Charles "Baba" Baron, and has known him for many years. He added he and Baron used to "run a book" together in Chicago in the late 1930's.

Halper added that he knew Murray Humphreys, Gus Alex, and Frank Ferraro by name only. He stated he may have met then at his restaurant as customers, but dose not know them personally. He stated he knew John Drew, John Roselli, and Moe Dalitz by name and sight only, and that he had no business connection with any of them in any way.

FEDERAL BUREAU OF INVESTIGATION

REPORTING OFFICE	OFFICE OF ORIGIN	DATE	INVESTIGATIVE PERIOD
CHICAGO	CHICAGO	1961	September 21, 1961

TITLE OF CASE	REPORT MADE BY	TYPED BY
SAMUEL M. GIANCANA, aka		dkc
	CHARACTER OF CASE	
	FBI Headquarters File number 92-3171 Top Hoodlum Program – Anti Racketeering	

The last subject called meeting for today in Chicago, of which Chuck (probably Chuck English) and some of the boys, Joey Glimco, and others were to be in attendance. Meeting to be held at 800 Milwaukee Avenue, Tammy's Snack Shop. Discreet physical surveillance will be conducted.

FEDERAL BUREAU OF INVESTIGATION

REPORTING OFFICE	OFFICE OF ORIGIN	DATE	INVESTIGATIVE PERIOD
CHICAGO	CHICAGO	1961	September 29, 1961

TITLE OF CASE	REPORT MADE BY	TYPED BY
SAMUEL M. GIANCANA, aka		dkc
	CHARACTER OF CASE	
	FBI Headquarters File number 92-3171-430 Top Hoodlum Program – Anti Racketeering	

Casa Madrid Lounge, notorious gambling den, Melrose Park, was raided by the States Attorney Police September 22, 1961. Based on information furnished by this office, twelve persons in the raid were arrested and $22,000 confiscated from safe. Open gambling operation found in progress. Among those arrested were Rocco DeGrazio, Joseph

Battaglia, brother of Sam Battaglia, Chicago and Giancana's reprehensive in western suburbs. One Bart Bartell, subject of ITSP case, Chicago, arrested by Bu Agents, Chicago, and Chicago PD, subsequently turned over to Melrose Park PD with no federal violation established. Bartell furnished information to Chicago informant today to the effect that Melrose Park PD desires $500 to fix case, and are attempting to ascertain identity of informant who furnished original information regarding ITSP. George Guerine, Melrose Park lawyer assigned to defend Bartell, advised Bartell that Charles "Chuckie" Nicoletti is now, "in command" of Melrose Park. Notes that Nicoletti is another Giancana lieutenant, and a Chicago TH, and maintains pretentious residence in Melrose Park.

FEDERAL BUREAU OF INVESTIGATION

REPORTING OFFICE	OFFICE OF ORIGIN	DATE	INVESTIGATIVE PERIOD	
CHICAGO	CHICAGO	1961	October 7, 1961	
TITLE OF CASE		REPORT MADE BY		TYPED BY
				dkc
SAMUEL M. GIANCANA, aka		CHARACTER OF CASE		
		FBI Headquarters File number 92-3171-434 Top Hoodlum Program – Anti Racketeering		

Chicago 6486-C advised that the original information pertaining to the identity of the "stool Pigeons" working for Ross Spencer in the States Attorneys Office came from the Chicago Police Department. This is James Hoy, who has been with Stated Attorney's Police for three years, formerly worked on vice detail, Chicago PD. Spencer was previously apprised of fact that Hoy has been shaking down prostitutes when working for Chicago PD, however, stated at time he could not remove Hoy since he, Hoy, had been in States Attorneys Office so that his hands were tied politically.

Chicago 6486-C also advised that Dominic Blasi and Sam Giancana went over the figures concerning the collection from an undetermined period from operations in western suburbs of Melrose Park, Elmwood Park, Franklin Park, and others. Gross figure was $47,432, less expenses of $13,117. Of expenses, named, 660 went to States Attorneys Office, 300 to Joseph Aiuppa, and 300 to William Daddono. Blasi advised he "used to give Julius a little money." Julius not identified any further; however, it is noted that Ed Julius, IRS Agent, was mentioned previously by this informant as furnishing information relating to the investigations of the hoodlum element to the hoodlums. Blasi advised that he carried out Giancana's orders by moving by moving operations into Elmwood Park, Forest Park, and other areas. An unknown individual advised Giancana that the government had issued a summons to the Central National Bank for the papers regarding a trust agreement for "the hotel". This was probably the Towne Hotel, Cicero, long believed to be Giancana's. Informant advised; however, that Giancana's name does not appear on trust, there fore the summons presents no particular problem insofar as Giancana is concerned. The unknown could possible have been Robert Ansoni, in that he mentioned name of Ortenzi as being on trust. Only other person connected with Towne Hotel is Joey Aiuppa, in addition to Ortenzi and Ansoni. Ross Prio held a conference with Giancana concerning the numbers operation in Chicago, particularly The Buffalo and Lucky Strike Wheels. Prio was up set over fact that the Big Wheel had lost five Sunday's in succession, sometimes as much as 60 to 70 thousand on each Sunday. He then decided to close this operation on Sundays so that the weekly of day to day profits would be greater. Prio advised that as an example, the wheel wins on an average of $10,000 per day to the operation. Noted that information had been previously received to the effect that the daily take from the numbers and policy went from the "bank" to the Rush Street Currency Exchange, operated on the record by Ross Prio Junior, from where it got into the hands of the syndicate. Above information bears this out.

FEDERAL BUREAU OF INVESTIGATION

REPORTING OFFICE	OFFICE OF ORIGIN	DATE	INVESTIGATIVE PERIOD
CHICAGO	CHICAGO	1961	October 9, 1961

TITLE OF CASE	REPORT MADE BY	TYPED BY
		dkc

SAMUEL M. GIANCANA, aka	CHARACTER OF CASE
	FBI Headquarters File number 92-3171-436 Top Hoodlum Program – Anti Racketeering

Chicago 6486-C advised that Giancana held a conference with an unknown politician, possibly James Adducci, Illinois State Representative and leader of the so called "West Side Bloc" regarding political matters within Chicago. The unknown proposed an individual named Willie Greco to fill Alderman or Ward Committeeman position in the 26th ward. Unknown asked Giancana what position he "wanted" filled in 26th ward, Giancana indicated he wanted that of committeeman. Unknown chastised Giancana for not letting him, Giancana's, family know of Giancana's whereabouts, even when in Chicago area, indicating that Giancana does not live at resident address and does not have any contact with his family.

FEDERAL BUREAU OF INVESTIGATION

REPORTING OFFICE	OFFICE OF ORIGIN	DATE	INVESTIGATIVE PERIOD
CHICAGO	CHICAGO	1961	October 10, 1961

TITLE OF CASE	REPORT MADE BY	TYPED BY
		dkc

SAMUEL M. GIANCANA, aka	CHARACTER OF CASE
	FBI Headquarters File number 92-3171-452 Top Hoodlum Program – Anti Racketeering. Attached File 92-636, Detroit

Chicago Teletype case entitled "James Riddle Hoffa, Miscellanies". Chicago 6486-C advised that Felix Alderisio advised Dominic Blasi that Jimmy Hoffa called and wants Sam Giancana to call him that evening. Alderisio indicated very important that call be made and that meeting is to be held apparently this evening in either New York or Detroit. It is noted that James Hoffa is at present time in Portland, Oregon, however, returning to Detroit this date. Informant advised that Sam Giancana informed Phil Alderisio that they should contact Paul "Red" Dorfman to obtain a loan from James Riddle Hoffa because "Dorfman belongs to Hoffa". Allen and Rose Dorfman were owners of record of the insurance companies which handled all insurance for the Teamsters Union. Paul "Red" Dorfman actually owned and operated these companies and assisted Hoffa in obtaining the Presidency of the Teamsters Union.

FEDERAL BUREAU OF INVESTIGATION

REPORTING OFFICE	OFFICE OF ORIGIN	DATE	INVESTIGATIVE PERIOD
CHICAGO	CHICAGO	1961	October 11, 1961

TITLE OF CASE	REPORT MADE BY	TYPED BY
		dkc
SAMUEL M. GIANCANA, aka	**CHARACTER OF CASE** FBI Headquarters File number 92-3171-451 Top Hoodlum Program – Anti Racketeering	

Informant advised that on October 6, 1961, he was in the vicinity of Giancana briefly, at which time John Matassa advised Giancana that "they" are finding out too much about the activities of their group, and as a result "they" know everything, Giancana advised Dominic Blasi to see if Anthony Girolami and Frank Chesrow "have a beef," nature of which was not described by Giancana. Girolami is Alderman of the 28th Ward in Chicago, and clerk of probate court, Cook County. Frank Chesrow, known to be close associate of Giancana and Anthony Accardo, is president of the board of the sanitary district, Cook County. John Matassa advised Giancana that he heard from a newspaper source that someone, not identified by Matassa, is getting an important job in a governmental position, and that the information came straight from Washington. Indicated this job was important, implied that the recipient of the job is part of their group.

FEDERAL BUREAU OF INVESTIGATION

REPORTING OFFICE	OFFICE OF ORIGIN	DATE	INVESTIGATIVE PERIOD
CHICAGO	CHICAGO	1961	October 14, 1961

TITLE OF CASE	REPORT MADE BY	TYPED BY
	Special Agent Ralph Hill Jr.	dkc
SAMUEL M. GIANCANA, aka	**CHARACTER OF CASE** FBI Headquarters File number 92-3171-447 Top Hoodlum Program – Anti Racketeering	

Chicago 6486-C advised that an unknown individual was in a lengthy conference with Giancana during the late evening hours of this date. It is believed possible this person was Louis Brady, well known Miami and Cleveland hoodlum and first cousin of

Pete Milano, head of the organized criminal activity, Cleveland area. Chicago 6343-C advised on January 18, 1961 that Lou Brady had made some negotiations regarding the sale or purchase of Paul DeLucia's Florida home, and in addition he fleeced Giancana out of $90,000, after which he disappeared and was believed to be in Texas. The individual in conference with Giancana mentioned bail bond business, "Paul" I Florida, and was explaining, almost beseechingly, to Giancana about what happened regarding allegations concerning him. He blamed his nephew, one Pete, as the individual who had a business in Cleveland, borrowed some money, and that his nephew mishandled the company. Apparently Pete had cone to Giancana about that time and placed the blame on this individual. Mentioned being in the Fontainebleau Hotel, Miami, apparently some time ago with Giancana, Paul, possible DeLucia, and John Formusa. This person told Giancana that shortly after the difficulty involving Pete and after he learned that Giancana was displeased, he left his home and hid out in Texas. He said, "I left that night, never talked to anybody, went to Texas like a hermit, in the middle of Siberia, where you have to send away for a pound of macaroni. Finally, the next thing I know the US Marshal woke me up at 1:45 in the morning, and I wound up in New York to answer the indictment." He then went into a lengthy discussion of a new corporation he had formed, called spectronics, offered Giancana a group floor proposition, described this as a tremendous operation, named some of the members of the board of directors as the governor of Indiana, a general now with Hallicrafters TV, the president of the General Telephone Company and the president of the Sylvania Television Company. Giancana appeared very much interested. This individual mentioned going to Miami Friday, October 13 and wanted Giancana to give him a note to give to Joe Fischetti or another person in Miami allowing this person to operate in that area. Request was refused by Giancana, who said he would go there personally next month and take care of it. Giancana apparently bought the story of Brady, and they appeared to depart amiably.

FEDERAL BUREAU OF INVESTIGATION

REPORTING OFFICE	OFFICE OF ORIGIN	DATE	INVESTIGATIVE PERIOD
CHICAGO	CHICAGO	1961	October 17, 1961

TITLE OF CASE	REPORT MADE BY	TYPED BY
		dkc

SAMUEL M. GIANCANA, aka	**CHARACTER OF CASE** FBI Headquarters File number 92-3171-448 Top Hoodlum Program – Anti Racketeering

Chicago 6343-C advised that Anthony Accardo, Frank Ferraro, and Jack Cerone were in vicinity of the informant that date when Accardo advised of plans for his son's new travel agency. Accardo desired to place his son in the Riviera Hotel, Las Vegas, to attract business for this agency, but in order to do so he needed authority from Giancana. Ferraro advised that "Moe" was out of town, whereupon Accardo asked Ferraro if it would be satisfactory to ask Murray Humphreys for this authority. They decided to discuss it at lunch at Pete's Fish's Restaurant.

FEDERAL BUREAU OF INVESTIGATION

REPORTING OFFICE	OFFICE OF ORIGIN	DATE	INVESTIGATIVE PERIOD	
CHICAGO	CHICAGO	1961	October 26, 1961	
TITLE OF CASE		REPORT MADE BY		TYPED BY
		Special Agent John Bassett		dkc
SAMUEL M. GIANCANA, aka		CHARACTER OF CASE		
		FBI Headquarters File number 92-3171-472 Top Hoodlum Program – Anti Racketeering		

Villa Venice
Wheeling IL.

Attention is directed to information previously reported relating to the fact that the Villa Venice Restaurant which was formerly owned by the Meo brothers had been sold by the Meo's to one Leo Olsen, however, in actuality it has been alleged that Olsen was merely fronting in this enterprise for the Giancana interest.

Chicago T-42 advised on September, 1961, that Albert Meo had complained to Sam Giancana that Richard Bernas and others had not fulfilled their promise to pay some $40,000 representing the indebtedness of the Villa Venice. According to the informant apparently no money in terms of cash had changed hands with this restaurant and arrangements had been made with the Oak Park National Bank, Oak Park, Illinois, whereby a loan was negotiated of some $40,000 to be "paid" to Albert Meo by the new owners of the Villa Venice. According to T-42 the promise was made to Meo to the effect that this money would be paid.

Robert Petrone

In June 20, 1961, Mr. Robert R. Petrone, President, Oasis Dispensing Company, 3259 West Chicago Avenue, and owner of Robert R. Petrone Real Estate Agency advised he has been acquainted with Joseph Paul Glimco since approximately 1958 when he was introduced to him by an unknown person at a "political party", subsequently met Glimco at a wake about a year ago, and talked to him in his union office. This was the extent of their relationship. He related that his last meeting with Glimco was precipitated by a telephone call from Glimco asking Petrone if he could get him some bath soap. Glimco stated that Petrone's uncle, Bob Petrone, a former 26th Ward Republican Committeeman, used to purchase this soap fro Glimco that this "soap contract" was unknown to him, but that he would attempt to locate it and get some boxes of bath soap for Glimco.

Petrone further advised that he eventually located this soap contact, purchased some boxes for Glimco, took them to the union office, was paid, and has not seen or heard from him since that time. He stated Glimco has absolutely no interest in Oasis Dispensing Company, was never an employee or a share holder, and never received any gratuities, commissions, or compensations of any kind. Petrone advised that he has approximately 25 vending machines in Yellow and Checker Cab locations in Chicago as well as Evanston Cab Co. and the Blue Cab Co. Oak Park. These consisted of eight Checker locations, twelve Yellow locations, three Evanston locations, and two Blue Cab locations on Lake Street, in Oak Park, IL. He stated that he personally obtained these accounts approximately four years ago by "open soliciting the presidents of Checker and Yellow Cab." He also advised he has known Freddie Bartoli of Evanston Cab Company for about ten years and this friendship enabled him to get his machines into this cab company.

Petrone further advised that at the time he obtained his cab vending machine locations, he did not know Glimco; therefore, Glimco had nothing to do with securing these locations. He further stated that his company has," over 150 stops with over 500 vending machines", and the machines at cab locations contained candy, milk, orange juice and lemonade. Petrone advised that when he first met Glimco he told him that he had a number of these machines in taxicab locations but nothing further was discussed about the machines. He further advised that none of the cab companies received any commission payments for the privilege of storing these machines, although industrial locations normally receive a ten per cent commission of all monthly sales. When asked why the cab companies do not receive commissions, Petrone remarked; "the matter of commissions was never brought up. When should I bring it up if they are not aware of it? They believe that they were doing their own employees a favor by installing these machines and they never even considered the fact that they were also doing me a favor.

Petrone advised that no commissions are paid to Freddie Bartoli at Evanston Cab Co. "because Freddie and I are friends and the installation of these machines was just a matter of friendship." When asked if he ever loaned Glimco money or if Glimco ever asked for money, Petrone remarked, "what would he need money from me for? He is the president of a union and should not need anything."

Petrone advised he has never met any member of the Glimco family, does not know how many are in the family, and has never been in the Glimco home. He further stated he has received no phone calls from Glimco, exchanged no correspondence with him, and knows nothing further about him.

FEDERAL BUREAU OF INVESTIGATION

REPORTING OFFICE	OFFICE OF ORIGIN	DATE	INVESTIGATIVE PERIOD
CHICAGO	CHICAGO	1961	November 3, 1961

TITLE OF CASE	REPORT MADE BY	TYPED BY
		dkc
SAMUEL M. GIANCANA, aka	**CHARACTER OF CASE**	
	FBI Headquarters File number 92-3171-475 Top Hoodlum Program – Anti Racketeering.	

Charles Giancana interviewed at Thunderbolt Motel regarding his brother. Giancana was more reticent that in the past to discuss his brother's activities. He stated he has not seen his brother. He suggested his brother may be over seas.

Joey Aiuppa, close associate of Giancana, is in operation of Cicero gambling establishment, was in contact with Frank Ferraro and James Celano in the vicinity of Chicago 6343-C yesterday and advised group that regarding his operations in Cicero, he has been holding "down" for six weeks, did not indicate any hope of reopening in near future.

FEDERAL BUREAU OF INVESTIGATION

REPORTING OFFICE	OFFICE OF ORIGIN	DATE	INVESTIGATIVE PERIOD
CHICAGO	CHICAGO	1961	November 8, 1961

TITLE OF CASE	REPORT MADE BY	TYPED BY
SAMUEL M. GIANCANA, aka		dkc

	CHARACTER OF CASE
	FBI Headquarters File number 92-3171-480 Top Hoodlum Program – Anti Racketeering.

Contact was made with George Graziadei on this date. Graziadei introduces interviewing agents to Joseph Bulger, who announced that he had been retained by Graziadei, and Graziadei must decline to answer all questions. Noted Bulger was codefendant of Paul DeLucia in the income tax case in which DeLucia was convicted in 1958. Bulger has also been described as former head of the Italian American Union and alleged in past to be head of the "Mafia" in the Chicago area. Questing was directed along the lines of the transaction involving the attempted purchase of an interest in the New Frontier Hotel, Las Vegas. Bulger stated that the whole deal was a hoax, and Graziadei was made the patsy. Involved were Charles Leggett, aka Robinson, a convicted swindler, Warren Baylay, former owner of the New Frontier, and Frank Wester, businessman. Bulger said that the New Frontier is a losing proposition, and it would have been impossible for Graziadei to make any money on it. He was asked if Sam Giancana had anything to do with the New Frontier. Bulger said that he did not; however, when asked if Giancana had other interest in Las Vegas, Bulger replied that he understands that Giancana does have other interest in Vegas but declined to name them. During the entire conversation, Graziadei said not one word.

FEDERAL BUREAU OF INVESTIGATION

REPORTING OFFICE	OFFICE OF ORIGIN	DATE	INVESTIGATIVE PERIOD
CHICAGO	CHICAGO	1961	November 9, 1961

TITLE OF CASE	REPORT MADE BY	TYPED BY
SAMUEL M. GIANCANA, aka		dkc

	CHARACTER OF CASE
	FBI Headquarters File number 92-3171-505 Top Hoodlum Program – Anti Racketeering.

Chicago informant advised yesterday that Sam Giancana has delegated Charles "Chuck" Nicoletti as his personal emissary of Cicero, IL, and in that capacity controls all gambling activity in that area. Directly under Nicoletti are Frank "Sharkey" Eulo and Joseph "Pepe" Giancana. Informant advised that Cicero is closed as to "big action"; however, there are four or five places in Cicero that are operating, among them being the MGM Lounge, operated by Nick Kokenes. Joseph "Fifke" Corngold is now living in

Phoenix, Arizona, and has a direct line from his Arizona residence to Cicero so he can get immediately the results of the betting line and results of sporting events.

FEDERAL BUREAU OF INVESTIGATION

REPORTING OFFICE	OFFICE OF ORIGIN	DATE	INVESTIGATIVE PERIOD	
CHICAGO	CHICAGO	1961	November 13, 1961	
TITLE OF CASE		REPORT MADE BY		TYPED BY
				dkc
SAMUEL M. GIANCANA, aka		CHARACTER OF CASE		
		FBI Headquarters File number 92-3171-484 Top Hoodlum Program – Anti Racketeering.		

Informant reports that Giancana group of lieutenants have new meeting place in Cicero, in the penthouse of the Shamrock Motel, Cicero. This group, including Rocco Fischetti, William Daddono, Chuck English, and occasionally Giancana, met at lease twice a week there. The "big game" gambling operation, formerly at J & J Pickic Grove, now located in Niles, IL, at the operational headquarters of Rocco Potenzo.

Information today states that Sam DeStefano, a independent hoodlum characterized as a money lender and local court fixer, was arrested by the Chicago Police following DeStefano's assaulting and threatening of Chicago Tribune reporter William Doherty.

FEDERAL BUREAU OF INVESTIGATION

REPORTING OFFICE	OFFICE OF ORIGIN	DATE	INVESTIGATIVE PERIOD	
CHICAGO	CHICAGO	1961	November 17, 1961	
TITLE OF CASE		REPORT MADE BY		TYPED BY
				dkc
SAMUEL M. GIANCANA, aka		CHARACTER OF CASE		
		FBI Headquarters File number 92-3171-489 Top Hoodlum Program – Anti Racketeering.		

Chicago 6343-C advised that Anthony Accardo, Gus Alex and Frank Ferraro held a conference on that date during which various matters were discussed, among them being the fact that the young Tony (Anthony Ross Accardo) had a dinner date with other men at the Armory Lounge for wild duck dinner. Also discussed was the fact that the Tribune newspaper had written about "The Twelfth Street Guys" however nobody got "pinched". Information was reported that the Tribune wrote about Giancana associates Frank Eulo, Gus Kringas, and his brother Joe "Pepe" Giancana and their gambling operations in Cicero. Ferraro then bemoaned the fact that "them guys out there won't answer to us, only

222

to Moe". Then stated that he couldn't go over Moe's head. Accardo told Ferraro that in Moe's absence "they" should come to him since Moe "wasn't there". This may be referring to the fact that there has been considerable activity in the western suburbs, particularly Cicero, involving Cicero and other western suburb operations. One significant point is the fact that several of the recent gangland slayings in this area relate to Cicero Police. Apparently there is rift or at least a separation of organization between the suburbs and the group meeting in the vicinity of the informant.

FEDERAL BUREAU OF INVESTIGATION

REPORTING OFFICE	OFFICE OF ORIGIN	DATE	INVESTIGATIVE PERIOD
CHICAGO	CHICAGO	1961	November 18, 1961

TITLE OF CASE	REPORT MADE BY	TYPED BY
		dkc
SAMUEL M. GIANCANA, aka	**CHARACTER OF CASE** FBI Headquarters File number 92-3171-492 Top Hoodlum Program – Anti Racketeering.	

Chicago 6486-C observed two unknown individuals held a conference last night, a large porting was unintelligible due to back ground noise and whispers. However, certain significant portions were ascertained to pertain to Sam DeStefano. The conversation stated "he should be here any day, anything important, go to Moe, (referring to the fact that Giancana is expected back shortly) he's (DeStefano) crazy. He's a danger to Giancana, fighting the Tribune. In the event I run into him, get him in the car and finish him myself, knock him off, in the car." The name DeStefano was mentioned in conversation along with enough events to identify subject of conversation as DeStefano. This conversation reflects that the Giancana group is concerned about DeStefano's erratic nature enough to seriously consider killing him, and they are apparently discussing the correct method to perform this killing, however, the final word awaits the return of Giancana from Europe.

FEDERAL BUREAU OF INVESTIGATION

REPORTING OFFICE	OFFICE OF ORIGIN	DATE	INVESTIGATIVE PERIOD
CHICAGO	CHICAGO	1961	November 23, 1961

TITLE OF CASE	REPORT MADE BY	TYPED BY
		dkc
SAMUEL M. GIANCANA, aka	**CHARACTER OF CASE** FBI Headquarters File number 92-3171-502 Top Hoodlum Program – Anti Racketeering.	

Chicago 6486-C advised that John Matassa, Dominic Blasi, and Carmen Fanelli spent several hours reminiscing over past associations between themselves, Frank Sinatra and Tony Bennett, well know entertainers. From conversation, when ever Bennett and Sinatra are in Chicago, Giancana, accompanied by Matassa and Blasi, act as unofficial greeters. Among places frequented by group were the Chez Paree, now closed, the Mist Club, The Amber Light, and Armory Lounge, all known hangouts and possible enterprises of Giancana. Apparently on these occasions, Sinatra and Giancana held contest as to who could spend the most money buying drinks and trinkets for everyone. No mention made to as to the whereabouts or expected return of Giancana to this area.

FEDERAL BUREAU OF INVESTIGATION

REPORTING OFFICE	OFFICE OF ORIGIN	DATE	INVESTIGATIVE PERIOD
CHICAGO	CHICAGO	1961	November 30, 1961

TITLE OF CASE	REPORT MADE BY	TYPED BY
		dkc
SAMUEL M. GIANCANA, aka	**CHARACTER OF CASE** FBI Headquarters File number 92-3171-506 Top Hoodlum Program – Anti Racketeering.	

Carlo Bosica, self admitted Cicero gambler and bookmaker, interviewed regarding his activities. He advised he has been making book in Cicero since 1937 at several locations. He was asked if he knew Giancana and denied knowing him, later admitted being acquainted with him, but denied that Giancana or anyone shared his income from gambling. He stated that all of the so called information of syndicate control of gambling in Cicero was a myth, and not based upon fact. It should be noted that Boscia has been known for year as being an influential bookmaker in Cicero and is an acquaintance, if not an associate, of Giancana. Information received that Sam Giancana has arrived in Puerto Rico with Phyllis McGuire.

FEDERAL BUREAU OF INVESTIGATION

REPORTING OFFICE	OFFICE OF ORIGIN	DATE	INVESTIGATIVE PERIOD	
CHICAGO	CHICAGO	1961	December 6, 1961	
TITLE OF CASE		REPORT MADE BY		TYPED BY
				dkc
SAMUEL M. GIANCANA, aka		CHARACTER OF CASE		
		FBI Headquarters File number 92-3171-520 Top Hoodlum Program – Anti Racketeering.		

According to Chicago 6486-C, Giancana met with Lenny Patrick at the Towne Hotel, Cicero, 12/2/61 regarding the dispute between Patrick, an individual believed to be Alderisio, and Louis Ciriano, bookmaker. Ross Prio accompanied Giancana at this meeting. The meeting was called for the purpose of avoiding an open clash between the Jewish Group, headed by Patrick, and the Italian group, regarding certain gambling operations in Chicago's Loop and in the Rogers Park, or North Side diction of Chicago. Prior to going to the meeting, Ross Prio discussed the lucrative gambling opportunities in Puerto Rico, and told Giancana that he, Prio, has had a gambling operation going there for some time without the benefit of a license, and has the backing of the government there. Informant advised further that Giancana ordered Edward Vogel to place orders for his coin operated machines from Joel Steen, of Worldwide Distributing Company. It has been alleged in the past that Giancana is the man behind the scene in the operation of Worldwide. The meeting between Giancana and Vogel pointed out the fact that Giancana is the main recipient of the funds received from Vogel's operations, and receives the lions share. The money brought into Giancana from individuals represented all operations in Cicero, Forest Park, Puerto Rican lottery, African American policy, and Vogel's coin machine business. Several guards remained in the vicinity of the informant all night of December 2 and 3. Apparently to insure that nothing happened to the money. The individual believed to be Leslie Kruse advised Giancana that a person in Jack Cerone's organization was discovered surreptitiously showing certain books and records during off office hours to an outsider. It was decided that this person should be confronted with these facts after which disciplinary action would follow. From the context of all the conversations, it would appear that gambling in the Chicago area is definitely at a minimum, to the point where there individuals are hunting our sources of income. From the fact that considerable money was brought in, however, there is still gambling going on controlled by the Giancana group. The situation involving Sam DeStefano was mentioned by the two individuals meeting with Giancana, however, no indication was given as to the contemplated action, if any, against DeStefano.

FEDERAL BUREAU OF INVESTIGATION

REPORTING OFFICE	OFFICE OF ORIGIN	DATE	INVESTIGATIVE PERIOD
CHICAGO	CHICAGO	1961	December 7, 1961

TITLE OF CASE	REPORT MADE BY	TYPED BY
		dkc

	CHARACTER OF CASE
SAMUEL M. GIANCANA, aka	FBI Headquarters File number 92-3171-525 Top Hoodlum Program – Anti Racketeering.

On December 4, Charles English was appeared in the vicinity of the informant and held a lengthy conference concerning several topics. One topic of conversation concerned fact that English had been thrown out of Chicago racetracks where he had been wagering in order to further the partnership relationship between himself and Giancana. English also bemoaned the fact the a certain building contract which he had been negotiating with Frank Chesrow, Sanitary District of Cook County, failed and Chesrow had not given him any of these contract awards. English mentioned that Frank Sinatra and the Reprise Record Company either owed a friend of his or the reverse, to which Giancana instructed English to have the friend institute legal proceeding for the recovery of some $14,000 due. English mentioned that he had been picked up recently by the Chicago PD for questioning in recent gang land slayings and was told by the homicide chief to "tell your boss to quit throwing those bodies in the city and throw them in the county." English advised Giancana that he felt like telling the PD "the next one will be dumped in the City Hall." Giancana in company with Phyllis McGuire at Kit Kat Club, Chicago.

FEDERAL BUREAU OF INVESTIGATION

REPORTING OFFICE	OFFICE OF ORIGIN	DATE	INVESTIGATIVE PERIOD
CHICAGO	CHICAGO	1961	December 13, 1961

TITLE OF CASE	REPORT MADE BY	TYPED BY
		dkc

	CHARACTER OF CASE
SAMUEL M. GIANCANA, aka	FBI Headquarters File number 92-3171-547 Top Hoodlum Program – Anti Racketeering.

Giancana in conference with John D'Arco, Alderman, First Ward, Chicago. D'Arco presented Giancana with $33,710 from undetermined source. Noted that D'Arco, known in the past to be an associate of Gus Alex, Murray Humphreys and Giancana. D'Arco is in control of the Chicago's Loop area, and is close to Mayor Daley. Context of conversation indicates that D'Arco is more that a mere associate of these hoodlums, rather, he is part of the operation. He discussed with Giancana sums of money owed by various individuals, and a "treasury" was discussed but not identified. Also discussed was the subject of the next sheriff of Cook County. Giancana indicated he had given the ok for Peter McGuire to run for office on the Republican ticket.

FEDERAL BUREAU OF INVESTIGATION

REPORTING OFFICE	OFFICE OF ORIGIN	DATE	INVESTIGATIVE PERIOD
CHICAGO	CHICAGO	1961	December 15, 1961

TITLE OF CASE	REPORT MADE BY	TYPED BY
		dkc

	CHARACTER OF CASE
SAMUEL M. GIANCANA, aka	FBI Headquarters File number 92-3171-543 Top Hoodlum Program – Anti Racketeering.

Regarding conversation between John D'Arco and Sam Giancana on December 12, Giancana advised D'Arco that he expects to be out of town for a few days, but will be back for Christmas. D'Arco and Giancana discussed placing an individual in a civil service job in Washington, however, did not name him. From the conversation, it appears that this person is young or Italian extraction, and is highly thought of by the conversant, who discussed possibility of making him a judge in five years. It should be noted that a Chicago informant close to D'Arco discussed placing a man, through Representative Roland Libonati, into the Department of Immigration, informant would not divulge name of this person.

CG 6486-C advised late yesterday and last night that Giancana was in conference with several individuals, one known as "Nose." Nose was paid $11,000 by Giancana to take care of four persons untilized by nose for some recent jobs. Three persons unidentified, one identified as "Johnny the Bug." Conversation indicates that Nose has untilized the four men in jobs of importance, possibly recent gangland killings. Mentioned had to get one person in an alley, another in a home. Stated caliber of jobs not too good and that they were lucky, because if they were caught, it would be "katy bar the door." These men are being paid $3,000 a piece, and $1,000 from "Johnny the Bug." Noted the informant reported several months ago discussion wherein Giancana and unknown individual discussed a pending hit. Following this conversation Giancana ordered some furniture for a Chicago area girl friend though a person believed to be Dominic Sibilano, furniture dealer. Giancana indicated to him that he may go to Miami.

FEDERAL BUREAU OF INVESTIGATION

REPORTING OFFICE	OFFICE OF ORIGIN	DATE	INVESTIGATIVE PERIOD
CHICAGO	CHICAGO	1961	December 19, 1961

TITLE OF CASE	REPORT MADE BY	TYPED BY
		dkc
SAMUEL M. GIANCANA, aka	**CHARACTER OF CASE** FBI Headquarters File number 92-3171-545 Top Hoodlum Program – Anti Racketeering.	

Butel request identities of victims of gangland slayings on Chicago during recent past. Among these are the following: John Hennigan, former Chicago informant 6090-C, killed November 13, 1961 in front of his home; Al Testa, burglar and gambler, killed October 8, 1961; William "Action" Jackson, killed August 12, 1961; Al Brown, burglar, killed October 1961; John Gentile, bartender, killed in front of his home, October 9, 1961. All of above slayings remain unsolved as of this date. Motives for most are unknown, although believed to be involved in loan sharking racket and connected with gambling activities. At least one slaying, that of Hennigan, was as result of belief by Giancana organization that he was an informant for the States Attorney's Office, Cook County. John Matassa and Dominic Blasi in vicinity of informant, but advised that most Chicago hoodlums expect to be in the Miami area over the holidays and all important decisions relating to Chicago activities to be held after beginning of new year.

FEDERAL BUREAU OF INVESTIGATION

REPORTING OFFICE	OFFICE OF ORIGIN	DATE	INVESTIGATIVE PERIOD
CHICAGO	CHICAGO	1961	December 21, 1961

TITLE OF CASE	REPORT MADE BY	TYPED BY
		dkc
SAMUEL M. GIANCANA, aka	**CHARACTER OF CASE** FBI Headquarters File number 92-350-Sub E Top Hoodlum Program – Anti Racketeering. Daily Summery	

Sam Giancana and Bernard Glickman discussed the forthcoming heavyweight fight title match between Floyd Patterson and Sonny Libton. Glickman complained bitterly of the treatment given him by Frank Carvo and Frank Palermo and stated that he had been double-crossed in his operations. Glickman feels that there will be up to 15 million dollars involved if the title match comes off and assured Giancana that Liston would do anything that he, Glickman, asked. Giancana told Glickman to follow through on that situation and that he, Giancana, would see to it that the proper persons were notified.

FEDERAL BUREAU OF INVESTIGATION

REPORTING OFFICE	OFFICE OF ORIGIN	DATE	INVESTIGATIVE PERIOD
CHICAGO	CHICAGO	1961	December 22, 1961

TITLE OF CASE	REPORT MADE BY	TYPED BY
		dkc

TITLE OF CASE

SAMUEL M. GIANCANA, aka

CHARACTER OF CASE

FBI Headquarters File number 92-3171-552
Top Hoodlum Program – Anti Racketeering.

Giancana had a conversation with an unknown person connected with Jimmy Hoffa's associate Paul Dorfman in the insurance business in Chicago. Unknown complained of fact that Dorfman has been holding out on them, meaning Giancana, on proceeds of business, and has reneged on several transactions.

Ross Prio stated to Dominic Blasi that he, Prio, had control over refrigeration warehouses in Wisconsin in the cheese industry and was responsible for the passage of a bill relating to the pasteurization of milk used for cheese.

FEDERAL BUREAU OF INVESTIGATION

REPORTING OFFICE	OFFICE OF ORIGIN	DATE	INVESTIGATIVE PERIOD
CHICAGO	CHICAGO	1961	December 27, 1961

TITLE OF CASE	REPORT MADE BY	TYPED BY
		dkc

TITLE OF CASE

SAMUEL M. GIANCANA, aka

CHARACTER OF CASE

FBI Headquarters File number 92-3171-558
Top Hoodlum Program – Anti Racketeering.

Giancana not seen or heard from, although his associates, Butch Blasi and John Matassa were present, and they spent most of the day distributing Christmas gifts to associates. Theodore Kay was interviewed by Agents. Kay claimed to be $40,000 in debt to juice operators in Chicago, namely Willie Messina, George Bravos, Rocky Joyce, and Fiore Buccieri. Loans obtained as result of gambling losses over the years at games controlled by Giancana organization. Kay states his interest payments on these loans amounts to $300 per week, as opposed to his weekly salary of $160. States he was steered to juice men by John "Johnny the Bug" Varelli.

FEDERAL BUREAU OF INVESTIGATION

REPORTING OFFICE	OFFICE OF ORIGIN	DATE	INVESTIGATIVE PERIOD
CHICAGO	CHICAGO	1961	December 28, 1961

TITLE OF CASE	REPORT MADE BY	TYPED BY
		dkc
SAMUEL M. GIANCANA, aka	CHARACTER OF CASE	
	FBI Headquarters File number 92-3171-563 Top Hoodlum Program – Anti Racketeering.	

Chicago 6486-C advised that Sam Giancana held a conference with John D'Arco, Alderman of Chicago's First Ward, close associate of numerous other top Chicago hoodlums, and apparently a member of the Giancana organization. Informant related that during conference, D'Arco again discussed forthcoming election for office of sheriff of Cook County. Qualities of various potential candidates which would favor hoodlum element were pointed out to Giancana by D'Arco. It was suggested by D'Arco that Jack Johnson, warden, Cook County jail be contacted to which Giancana agreeable. Giancana re-contacted by Bernard Glickman, Chicago fight manager, who pleaded with subject to contact Carbo and Palermo group and thereby with Chicago backing, insure Glickman of getting piece of Sonny Liston, current heavyweight title challenger. Giancana has agreed to aid Glickman, claiming motive is as a favor and desires no part of promotion of title fight.

FEDERAL BUREAU OF INVESTIGATION

REPORTING OFFICE	OFFICE OF ORIGIN	DATE	INVESTIGATIVE PERIOD
CHICAGO	CHICAGO	1961	December 29, 1961

TITLE OF CASE	REPORT MADE BY	TYPED BY
		dkc
SAMUEL M. GIANCANA, aka	CHARACTER OF CASE	
	FBI Headquarters File number 92-3171-556 Top Hoodlum Program – Anti Racketeering.	

Chicago informed a conference was held between Giancana, and possibly Vince Garrity and Pete Granata. Garrity is former local disc jockey now trustee for Chicago Sanitary Department. Reportedly backed by James Stavros, who is a Democratic committeeman, wheeling Township, and is a $1,000 month investment for Chicago Sanitary District. Granata rose in politics as Republican Ward committeeman after Joe Porcaro, former committeeman jailed in 1957 for bribery. Granata, strong in rackets in Maxwell, Halsted area, maintains offices at Taylor and Blue Island. Discussion in conference indicates Giancana doubts if republican can be successful candidate for sheriff. Garrity and Granata are contacting various potential candidates who receive Giancana ok to persuade them to run for political offices. Giancana appears to place credence in suggestions made by Granata.

Additional FBI Information

1) It was reported that in 1961 the death of Jack Henningan was ordered by Giancana because he had furnished information to the Cook County States Attorney's Office which resulted in raids on gambling establishments.

2) On 2-15-1961 Captain Hansel H. Tower, US Naval Air Station, Pensacola, Florida, furnished a copy of letter received by Admiral Robert Goldthwaite, Commanding Officer of the Pensacola Station which was signed "Cook USA." According to a penciled notation on the margin, ONI furnished on 2-20-1961 a Photostat of a second letter received by Admiral Goldthwaite and signed "Cook USA."

This unknown subject, Cook USA wrote concerning a plague the CP was planning to spread, called Operation saw and said Admiral Goldthwaite was one of the officers chosen to spread the plague. He stated they had an electronics truck which would project chemicals plus plague infested insects and flees that would cause a terrible lot of deaths in the armed forces and among civilians also. The writer of these letters stated that approval of men to man these operations went all the way back to Chicago to Sam Giancana and others. He said the Party paid heavily to Giancana and the others but that the great Giancana would personal supervise the right Muggs to carry out the operation. Some people in Los Angeles, including children, were to be the first victims and Giancana was to handle this operation in Los Angeles.

3) The Las Vegas Office advised on 3-17-1961, that Ray Addaticchio, Jr., Chairman, Nevada Gaming Control Board, described the Board's "Black Book" as a list of individuals whom they considered undesirable and unwelcome in the state of Nevada. This book had been disseminated to 39 leading casinos in the state of Nevada. The list, which was set out, contained the name of Sam Giancana, FBI NO. 58437, who was at that time residing in Chicago.

4) LV-49-C advised in July 1961 that Sam Giancana had recently been in Las Vegas and purchased an interest in the Coach and Four Restaurant, and set John Drew up as a "dummy owner." John Drew was possibly the "front man" for the Chicago criminal element at the Stardust Hotel, Las Vegas.

5) It was reported in January 1961 that Sam Giancana, Anthony Accardo, John Drew, Morris "Moe" Dalitz, Murray Humphreys and two unidentified individuals from Cleveland, Ohio, had negotiated a "contract" whereby Giancana and the Chicago group acquired an undisclosed number

of points or shares in a three-way deal which apparently involved the Riviera, Desert Inn and Stardust Hotel Casino in Las Vegas. Individuals believed to be fronts or representatives for Giancana in his hidden interests were Charles "Babe" Baron, John Roselli, Tommy McDonald, Ike Epstein and John Drew.

6) Information concerning the confidential assignment of Robert Maheu (former Bureau Agent) for CIA and Maheu's contacts with Sam Giancana. In connection with CIA's operation against Castro, Maheu was o be used as a "cutout" in contacts with Giancana. Since the underworld controlled gambling activities in Cuba under the Batista Government, it was assumed that this element would continue to have source and contacts in Cuba which perhaps could be utilized successfully in connection with CIA's clandestine efforts against the Castro Government. Maheu obtained Giancana's assistance in this regard and he gave every indication of cooperating with Maheu. As of May, 1961 none of Giancana's efforts had materialized but several of the plans were still working. Mahue said he had received valuable assistance from Giancana, which, in turn, was furnished to the CIA

7) Edwin Walter Julius was the IRS agent in Chicago who, according to a highly confidential informant, had allegedly furnished information to Sam Giancana concerning the investigation of Giancana by the IRS. To further establish Julius' suspected cooperation with the hoodlum elements, Chicago recommended that false information be furnished to Julius concerning an investigation by Giancana. If Julius leaked this information to the associate of Giancana he might, in turn, possibly advice Giancana in the presence of the Bureau's highly confidential source which would definitely connect Julius with the hoodlum element.

8) CG-6486-C reported on 12-7-1962 that Sam Giancana conferred with Felix (Milwaukee Phil) Alderisio concerning the interest of Chicago area hoodlums in Jamaica gambling activities. Alderisio informed Giancana that Marvin Billett, who was director of the largest hotel in Jamaica, would probably front for the Chicago hoodlums at this hotel, as it was believed gambling would be legalized in Jamaica. Alderisio also discussed with Giancana the fact that Miami top hoodlum Charlie White had apparently offered Billett $100,000 to front for White and the Miami hoodlums. Giancana instructed Alderisio to send word to White that Billett "belongs to us, leave him alone and if you don't we're gonna have to knock him in the head. Tell him we're trying to get in business with the guy without any money."
It was suggest that Joseph Glimco might possibly obtain a loan through Jimmy Hoffa for the purchase of this hotel but Giancana stated that emphatically that Glimco and Hoffa were no longer close associates and Glimco would not be able to obtain anything from Hoffa. Giancana

then stated that perhaps Allen Dorfman, who operated the Union Insurance Agency at Chicago, was a close associate of Hoffa and might be able to assist in obtaining a loan.

9) CG-6486-C stated on 12-6-1961, John Roselli held a conference with Sam Giancana to discuss a tightening of control of Chicago hoodlum interest in various Las Vegas hotel and gambling casinos. Rosselli referred on several occasions to Louis Lederer and indicated he could be the "front" man for several of their operations. It appeared to informant that they discussed operating through Lederer and Sidney Korshak, well known Chicago and Palm Springs, California attorney. On 12-19-1961 Giancana held a conference with Lederer to discuss local politics, including potential candidates for the office of Sheriff of Cook County. Giancana was highly displeased because he believed that the candidates for sheriff could not be bought and would not play ball with the organization.

Chapter 6

FEDERAL BUREAU OF INVESTIGATION

REPORTING OFFICE	OFFICE OF ORIGIN	DATE	INVESTIGATIVE PERIOD
CHICAGO	CHICAGO	1962	January 3, 1962

TITLE OF CASE	REPORT MADE BY		TYPED BY
	Special Agent Ralph Hill Jr.		dkc
SAMUEL M. GIANCANA, aka	**CHARACTER OF CASE**		
	Headquarters File number 92-3171-573 Top Hoodlum Program Anti Racketeering		

Synopsis:

Sam Giancana, accompanied by Phyllis McGuire toured Europe via London, Rome, Madrid from 10/ 12 to 11/ 28/ 61, and re-entered the U.S. on 11/30/61 by way of San Juan, Puerto Rico. Giancana observed in Chicago in company with McGuire on 12/2/61. Information developed linking Giancana with the Worldwide Distributing Company and the Apex Amusement Co., Chicago, and with certain Nevada gambling casinos and hotels. Among these being the Cal Nava Lodge, Lake Tahoe, Nevada. Informants report that the Giancana organization is at present at a low ebb in gambling income in the Chicago area due to federal, state and local investigation, and has made tentative plans to look into gambling possibilities in Puerto Rico, Jamaica, and West Indies. Investigation reflects a serious rift between Giancana and associate Frank Sinatra.

Associates

Joseph Aiuppa

Joseph Aiuppa has been described as a long-time associate of Giancana, who controls certain phases of gambling activity and also who controls several striptease establishments and bars in Cicero, IL.

Chicago T-41 advised during December of 1961, that Joseph Aiuppa was in contact with Sam Giancana shortly after the latter's returned from his European tour. Aiuppa had been sought by the U.S. Marshal's Office, Chicago, for the service of a subpoena to appear before the Senate Rackets Committee investigating taverns and burlesque house and particularly the American Guild of Varietl Artists and infiltration of persons such as Joseph Aiuppa therein.

Lenny Patrick

Lenny Patrick was in conference with Sam Giancana on 1/3/62. Patrick advised Giancana he was to receive $10,000 from a new source of income but claims to be shorted approximately $20,000. Patrick apparently concerned over figures relating to actual income taken in, and income reflected for tax purposes.

John D'Arco

John D'Arco advised the informant that he was concerned that certain money owed to Giancana by Rocco DeStephano who owes $40,000 to DeStephano's company, went out of business recently. D'Arco told this informant that he also discussed with Giancana the fact that he, D'Arco, was interested in obtaining a Civil Service position in Washington for a certain friend of his in the hope that this individual would soon obtain the necessary experience to be a valuable assistant to the Giancana organization.

Apex Amusement Company
Chicago, IL

Reference is made to information above pertaining to Edward Vogel and instructions given him by Giancana to purchase machines for Apex from the Worldwide Amusement Company.

Chicago T-51, stated that Vogel had presented the books of his coin operated business to Giancana for inspection recently and that at that time gave Giancana some $36,000 representing Giancana's interest in the operation of that particular business for a two month period. The total amount was in excess of $43,000; however, Vogel reclaimed close to $8,000 at his end of the business. In addition to the above sum, Vogel then presented the books and records pertaining to the Apex Amusement Company and gave Giancana $213,000 representing the amount from the Apex Amusement Company for an unspecified period of time. Of this amount Giancana kept $106,750 and returned the remainder to Vogel.

Jamaica
British West Indies

Chicago T-47 advised during the late fall of 1961, that Felix "Milwaukee Phil" Alderisio was in contact with Sam Giancana relating to the possibilities of opening a gambling casino in Jamaica if and when the proposed legalized gambling in that island takes place. Alderisio advised the informant that through Frank Balistrieri of Milwaukee, Wisconsin, contact had been made with an individual who had numerous connections in the hotel industry in Jamaica. This individual whose name is Gleason is willing to "front" for Giancana, in Jamaica if this group so desires. Alderisio advised the informant, however, a slight problem has arisen whereby Charles Tourino of Miami, as associate of Giancana, has also cast avarice looks toward Jamaica and has made contact with the same individual as Alderisio. He has also offered this individual an additional $100,000 to front for him. Alderisio told the informant, however, that problem will be straightened out shortly after he has "a talk" with Tourine.

San Juan, Puerto

CG T-24 advised during the fall of 1961, that Ross Prio mentioned to the informant that he recently been in contact with Samuel Giancana relating to the possibilities of looking into large scale investments in gambling casinos in Puerto Rico which is legitimate and controlled by the Commonwealth Government. Prio advised the informant that the possibilities are manifested in Puerto Rico in that there are few large scale operations there at the present time with the largest one as being in the informant. Prio felt that in view of the fact that gambling has been curiously curtailed in the Chicago area, Puerto Rico would be the logical spot in which to continue to receive profitable returns of their investments.

Prio also indicated to the informant that some time ago he started with the okay of the Commonwealth Government a gambling enterprise in Puerto Rico more or less on the trail basis and at the present time is continuing. Prio told the informant that Giancana was only luke warm to the suggestion of Puerto Rico gambling in that there was tight Governmental control and the hours are restricted from 8:00 to 2:00.

Stone Park, Illinois

Peggy Helm Iagulli advised that her husband is currently confined in prison having been found guilty of counterfeiting. She advised she is currently engaged in divorce proceedings against her husband. She stated that she former-ly worked for Rocco Pranno in the Diamond Lounge. This establishment is located next door to what used to be the Key Lounge and is now known as D'ors Lounge. Peggy Iagulli advised she was a part-time bartender at the Diamond Lounge and worked in the back room of the lounge where she obtained coffee and drinks for the individuals engaged in card games which took place in the rear of the es-tablishment. She stated that during the day-time hours the back room was used as a horse betting parlor.

She further advised that Don Hanke, who resides in Addison, is a close associate of Pranno and is his constant companion. She also advised that Frank Zito is also associated with Pranno and is in charge of all dealers in the card games. She stated that the dice table is run by Tommie Young.

She advised that there is a buzzer attached in the back room whereby the bartender or someone in the front portion of the building is able to press a buzzer, thus warning individuals in the back room if anyone enters the tavern who appears to be a policeman.

She advised that Al Pranno, Rocco Pranno's brother, actually provided the money which enabled Rocco to purchase the Key Lounge. She stated that Mike "The Brew" Marino built the Key Lounge and subsequently Mike sold out to Rocco Pranno. She stated that the money for this purchase was produced by Al Pranno and certain people whose identities she was not aware of but who were from St. Louis and Kansas City. She advised that the Key Lounge was not a money-making operation due to the fact that Rocco Pranno operated it as a "clip joint." She stated it required $50 to obtain a key to the Gold Room and that individuals who frequented the Gold Room simply ran up a tab and were billed at the end of the month. She stated these bills were invariably much higher than the actual amount of the tab these individuals had run up.

She stated she has seen Marshall Caifano, Willie "Potatoes" Daddono, and Sam Giancana at the poker games in the rear room of the Diamond Lounge. She stated that Rocco Pranno's backers at the Key Lounge were upset over the fact that it was not a money-making operation and exerted pressure on him to open up the establishment to the public.

FEDERAL BUREAU OF INVESTIGATION

REPORTING OFFICE	OFFICE OF ORIGIN	DATE	INVESTIGATIVE PERIOD
CHICAGO	CHICAGO	1962	January 5, 1962

TITLE OF CASE	REPORT MADE BY	TYPED BY
		dkc
SAMUEL M. GIANCANA, aka	CHARACTER OF CASE	
	FBI Headquarters File number 92-3171-572 Top Hoodlum Program – Anti Racketeering. Daily Summary	

During the late hours of January 2, Joseph Costello of Chicago Heights, a known hoodlum associate and political powerhouse of the area, conversed with Giancana at length regarding the fact that Costello, who owns a liquor distributing business with heavy commitments to the Schenley Distillery, is being given undue and unfair competition by Joe Fusco, a Schenley Distributor for the Chicago area known and also a known associate of hoodlums. Fusco owns the Gold Seal Liquor Company, a highly lucrative enterprise. Costello is also concerned over the fact that Frank LaPorte, a Chicago top hoodlum, allowed Walgreen's Drug Store to obtain a liquor license for the Chicago Heights and Calumet City areas. Costello feels that all liquor business and other business should be conducted only by Costello and or LaPorte and their interests. Costello stated he was coming to Giancana with this situation in view of the fact that he, Giancana, is the avoidant. Giancana instructed Costello to meet with Joe Fusco and straighten him out and use Giancana's name if necessary. Fusco is to be instructed to cease this "unfair" competition with Costello. Costello was also instructed to get together with Frank LaPorte when the latter returns from California and meet with Giancana and Costello in the vicinity of the informant so that they can discuss their mutual interests and avoid any serious difficulty in the Chicago Heights area.

FEDERAL BUREAU OF INVESTIGATION

REPORTING OFFICE	OFFICE OF ORIGIN	DATE	INVESTIGATIVE PERIOD
CHICAGO	CHICAGO	1962	January 6, 1962

TITLE OF CASE	REPORT MADE BY	TYPED BY
		dkc

	CHARACTER OF CASE
SAMUEL M. GIANCANA, aka	FBI Headquarters File number 92-3171-581 Top Hoodlum Program – Anti Racketeering. Daily Summary

CG 6486-C advised that Giancana had a lengthy discussion with John D'Arco. The topic conversation was the proposed slating of Rosewll Spencer, former FBI agent, now Chief Investigator for the States Attorney's Office, Cook County, for the office of Sheriff, Cook County. D'Arco had been attempting to negotiate with Mayor Richard J. Daley of Chicago in an effort to dissuade Mayor Daley from allowing Spencer's candidacy. Apparently thus far D'Arco has been unable to swing enough influence to attain this goal and bemoaned the fact that Daley is now the most powerful man politically Chicago has ever had, so much that the prominent Chicago Wards politicians and no longer able to swing individual influence with the mayor. D'Arco mentions that when he discussed Spencer with the mayor, the mayor compared Spencer with O. W. Wilson, Superintendent of the Chicago Police Department, at which time D'Arco stated he thought Wilson would be better that Spencer. Then he screamed to Giancana "O.W. Wilson we can work around but this guy (Spencer) is too (obscene) smart to work around. This (obscene) has got us (obscene), absolutely (obscene)." D'Arco referred to Spencer as "FBI stool pigeon (obscene)." D'Arco stated in reference to Dan Ward, the States Attorney of Cook County, that, "I told Slim (Gus Alex) when Ward didn't take the money, I told Slim we're in trouble," which established definitely that Ward was offered organization money to ease off on the organization and turned down the offer. D'Arco made reference to the Kennedy administration and said, "That (obscene) Kennedy is laughing and boasting all over the country." D'Arco then discussed the possibility of Richard Ogilvie wanting the election for sheriff and stated that, "Although Ogilvie may get the Republican endorsement he could not beat a democrat. Our thing is to not have Spencer get on." It was mentioned that if the race for Sheriff was between Ogilvie and Spencer that, "Then we're between an (obscene) and a sweat." D'Arco stated, "This is the worst situation we have ever been in. It used to be there wasn't nobody that we weren't able to reach."

FEDERAL BUREAU OF INVESTIGATION

REPORTING OFFICE	OFFICE OF ORIGIN	DATE	INVESTIGATIVE PERIOD
CHICAGO	CHICAGO	1962	January , 1962

TITLE OF CASE	REPORT MADE BY	TYPED BY
		dkc

TITLE OF CASE: SAMUEL M. GIANCANA, aka

CHARACTER OF CASE

FBI Headquarters File number 92-3171-603
Top Hoodlum Program – Anti Racketeering.
Daily Summary

Information was received pertaining to possible gangland killing disclosed. Gus Vivirito was shot on the street near his house by unknown assailants. He was hit four times by bullets fired form unknown caliber weapons. There were allegedly two assailants involved. According to the Chicago PD Vivirito is 44 years of age, is employed as a photography salesman and notes found on his person indicate that he is heavily in debt to the gambling element. They also stated that Vivirito was on the day before at 5941 West Roosevelt Road, Cicero, a sometime gambling operation controlled by Giancana. The Chicago PD further advised that the telephone number of the States Attorney's Office was found on his person which indicates that Vivirito may have been an informant for that office, advised that Vivirito had been approached on several occasions to furnish information to them which would lead to successful gambling raids; however, if Vivirito declined, it is not known. As of instant date Vivirito is in critical condition but steadily improving. A bullet, however, entered his neck and apparently severed his vocal chords so he is unable to speak. It is believed that he was shot by Miles O'Donnell, who runs a gambling operation on Roosevelt Road.

FEDERAL BUREAU OF INVESTIGATION

REPORTING OFFICE	OFFICE OF ORIGIN	DATE	INVESTIGATIVE PERIOD
CHICAGO	CHICAGO	1962	January 10, 1962

TITLE OF CASE	REPORT MADE BY	TYPED BY
		dkc

TITLE OF CASE: SAMUEL M. GIANCANA, aka

CHARACTER OF CASE

FBI Headquarters File number 92-3171-580
Top Hoodlum Program – Anti Racketeering.
Daily Summary

On January 4, Sam Giancana was in conference with an unknown individual who appears to be an upper echelon hoodlum probably from the Midwest. From the context of this conversation the possibility exists that the unknown could be Nicholas Civella, a Kansas City Top Hoodlum or Frank Wortman, a St. Louis Top Hoodlum. The Riviera Hotel in Las Vegas was mentioned as was Frank Sinatra, Dean Martin, and Sammy Davis, Jr. Giancana advised that Frank Sinatra lied to him when he inferred to Giancana that in the event John Kennedy was elected Sinatra would be able to control the investigation through the Kennedy's on Giancana. Giancana stated that he had sent Johnny Roselli out to Sinatra. The unknown stated that he was recently convicted for state income tax violations and received a six month sentence and a $500 fine which conviction was an out growth of apparently a Federal Grand Jury proceeding. Referring again to Nevada, Giancana was advised by the unknown that Frank Sinatra, Moe Dalitz, Ross Miller, and others are "your people." Giancana indicated that the organization has been in Nevada for ten years and placed many people on the payroll in that area. The unknown asked Giancana what he intended to do about this situation and Giancana replied, "as soon as all these (obscene) is over with, we go to work" indicates that the Jewish element or those responsible for his troubles in Las Vegas can expect reprisals from Giancana. Giancana also complained that Red Skelton, the well known comedian, had been taken over by Jack Entratter, who in turn thus far refused to share the profits from Red Skelton with the organization.

FEDERAL BUREAU OF INVESTIGATION

REPORTING OFFICE	OFFICE OF ORIGIN	DATE	INVESTIGATIVE PERIOD	
CHICAGO	CHICAGO	1962	January 12, 1962	
TITLE OF CASE		REPORT MADE BY		TYPED BY
				dkc
SAMUEL M. GIANCANA, aka		**CHARACTER OF CASE**		
		FBI Headquarters File number 92-3171-577 Top Hoodlum Program – Anti Racketeering. Daily Summary		

CG 6486-C reported that during Giancana's last contact, he conferred with Rocco Potenzo, operator of the Rivera gambling establishment. Potenzo brought in $1400 from gambling for an unspecified period, and appeared to be very unhappy over prevailing unprofitable conditions. He complained that one Bunkie, or Donkey, phonetic, owes his operation $3100, whereby Giancana issued instructions for Sam Battaglia to handle the collection of this amount. The only individuals in the vicinity of the informant during the past few days have been John Matassa and Dominic Blasi, indicating that Giancana is still probably out of town.

FEDERAL BUREAU OF INVESTIGATION

REPORTING OFFICE	OFFICE OF ORIGIN	DATE	INVESTIGATIVE PERIOD	
CHICAGO	CHICAGO	1962	January 17, 1962	
TITLE OF CASE		REPORT MADE BY		TYPED BY
				dkc
SAMUEL M. GIANCANA, aka		CHARACTER OF CASE		
		FBI Headquarters File number 92-3171-589 Top Hoodlum Program – Anti Racketeering. Daily Summary		

CG 6486-C advised that Giancana, in conversation with unknown politician, came to the conclusion that for the present, there are no persons who could meet the specifications required by Giancana to fill the aldermanic position he desires. Giancana places the part of the blame of his present day woes and trials on "dollar hunger" politicians, such as John D'Arco. D'Arco, according to Giancana, does not meet present day standards of conduct required of politicians in Chicago, and is unable to come to the front and make speeches enabling other politicians and Government to recognize the needs of "our people," referring to the Italians. Unknown mentioned that the only person placed on the Democratic slate of candidates for the forthcoming elections, satisfactory to him and to Giancana, is Anthony G. Girolami, candidate for Clerk of the Probate Court of Cook County. Giancana went on further in his denunciation of D'Arco, describing him as a, "nice fellow, but he was always conniving around, making contacts, unable to get up and defend his people." Unknown suggested that D'Arco be instructed to make more speeches, recommended that Giancana reconsider his opinion of D'Arco, which was rejected by Giancana. Unknown suggested that the next alderman in D'Arco's position concentrate on obtaining the goodwill of his constituents and ward residents, rather than attempt to sell them insurance, as they have done in the past. Mentioned that it is wrong for public officials to put the fix in for everyone, but save the instrument of influence peddling on the fix for emergency matters. Mentioned that as far as "Our People" are concerned, money is secondary to recognition and prestige.

FEDERAL BUREAU OF INVESTIGATION

REPORTING OFFICE	OFFICE OF ORIGIN	DATE	INVESTIGATIVE PERIOD	
CHICAGO	CHICAGO	1962	January 18, 1962	
TITLE OF CASE		REPORT MADE BY		TYPED BY
				dkc
SAMUEL M. GIANCANA, aka		CHARACTER OF CASE		
		FBI Headquarters File number 92-3171-594 Top Hoodlum Program – Anti Racketeering		

As the bureau is aware, considerable information has been received of late from CG 6486-C which reflects a serious rift between Sam Giancana and Frank Sinatra, which stems primarily from Sinatra's inability or lack of desire to intercede with Attorney General Robert Kennedy on behalf of Giancana. According to this source, Sinatra and Giancana have severed their relationship.

It would appear that an approach to Sinatra at this time for an interview regarding his real association with Giancana would be propitious, particularly if Giancana's feeling that Sinatra has "gone to the other side" is correct.

It is also pointed out that, as of this date, the exact identity of the individual in contact with Giancana on 12/2/61 is unknown. It was believed to be possibly John Drew, however, Las Vegas had advised that from the dates indicated, this was not possible. For the information of Los Angeles, John (LNU), when conferring with Giancana on the above dates, stated he had visited for several days at the home of Frank Sinatra where he and Sinatra had discussed Giancana and the fact that Sinatra indicated to John that he had attempted to intercede with the Attorney General on behalf of Giancana.

Authorization is requested for an interview with Frank Sinatra in an attempt to determine what Giancana's interest in Cal-Neva Lodge, Lake Tahoe, Nevada are. Note that CG 6436-C indicates Giancana had extensive holdings therein. Also find out the degree of Giancana's hold prime entertainment personalities to wit; Tony Bennett, Louis Prima, Red Skelton, Dean Martin and Keely Smith.

FEDERAL BUREAU OF INVESTIGATION

REPORTING OFFICE	OFFICE OF ORIGIN	DATE	INVESTIGATIVE PERIOD	
CHICAGO	CHICAGO	1962	January 19, 1962	
TITLE OF CASE		REPORT MADE BY		TYPED BY
				dkc
SAMUEL M. GIANCANA, aka		CHARACTER OF CASE		
		FBI Headquarters File number 92-3171-592 Top Hoodlum Program – Anti Racketeering. Daily Summary		

Chicago informant advised that one Jimmie Contursi who is a new associate of Giancana. Contursi described as tough gunman who has part of bookmaking operations on South Side of Chicago. He reportedly has been associated with bookmaking all his adult life and in past acted as fence for "hot" diamonds. He was suspected several years ago in burglary of Cacciatore Currency Exchange.

FEDERAL BUREAU OF INVESTIGATION

REPORTING OFFICE	OFFICE OF ORIGIN	DATE	INVESTIGATIVE PERIOD
CHICAGO	CHICAGO	1962	January 23, 1962

TITLE OF CASE	REPORT MADE BY	TYPED BY
		dkc
SAMUEL M. GIANCANA, aka	CHARACTER OF CASE	
	FBI Headquarters File number 92-3171-594 Top Hoodlum Program – Anti Racketeering. Daily Summary	

Interview with Frank Sinatra for information concerning his relation ship with Sam Giancana not being authorized at this time. You should, however, remain alert to the possibility that further evidence will suggest a stronger probability than is presently indicated that Sinatra has broken with his hoodlum connections completely enough to establish that he will furnish information concerning them. In the event of further developments along this line, a further recommendation for interview will be considered.

(Attached a note from the Las Vegas Field office) Frank Sinatra has been uncooperative when interviewed several times in the past in connection with out Criminal Intelligence Program. He has consistently failed or refused to furnish any information concerning his hoodlum associates. Giancana has made one or two disparaging remarks recently concerning Sinatra but there is no evidence to indicate that they have fallen out or that Sinatra is at odds with any of his other hoodlum acquaintances to the extent that he would furnish information on these people to the FBI. In view of the extremely slight chance that anything of value could be developed through interview with Sinatra plus the always present possibility that our highly confidential source might unavoidably be compromised, authority for such interview is being held in abeyance pending further information indicating that Sinatra has broken with his underworld connections and might be in a mood to cooperate with the FBI.

FEDERAL BUREAU OF INVESTIGATION

REPORTING OFFICE	OFFICE OF ORIGIN	DATE	INVESTIGATIVE PERIOD
CHICAGO	CHICAGO	1962	January 24, 1962

TITLE OF CASE	REPORT MADE BY	TYPED BY
		dkc
SAMUEL M. GIANCANA, aka	CHARACTER OF CASE	
	FBI Headquarters File number 92-3171-600 Top Hoodlum Program – Anti Racketeering. Daily Summary	

Bureau has requested identity be ascertained of individual in conference with Giancana on January 13, 1961. This person has been tentatively identified as Rocco Armando, personal bailiff of Chicago Judge Daniel Covelli. Chicago informant advised some time ago that Armando is "a man to watch," as he is close to Chicago hoodlums and to

First Ward Alderman John D'Arco. In this capacity, he is alleged to act as intermediary between the hoodlums and the court. John Drew was in conference with Giancana mostly about Las Vegas enterprises.

FEDERAL BUREAU OF INVESTIGATION

REPORTING OFFICE	OFFICE OF ORIGIN	DATE	INVESTIGATIVE PERIOD	
CHICAGO	CHICAGO	1962	January 25, 1962	
TITLE OF CASE		REPORT MADE BY		TYPED BY
				dkc
SAMUEL M. GIANCANA, aka		CHARACTER OF CASE		
		FBI Headquarters File number 92-3171-599 Top Hoodlum Program – Anti Racketeering. Daily Summary		

You will recall CG 6486-C asterisk discussing with Giancana and possibly Rocco Armando on January 13, the political situation in Chicago with particular reference to the First Ward Alderman position. The name of Frank Annunzio was mentioned as a possibility to replace John D'Arco as alderman, but was rejected by Giancana as a person not to be trusted. Annunzio is a partner with D'Arco in the Anco Insurance Company, which is one of D'Arco's enterprises. Giancana's present distrust of Annunzio stems from the fact that Giancana was instrumental in the rise in prominence of Annunzio, who then showed his disloyalty to Giancana by inviting Attorney General Robert Kennedy to Chicago for Columbus proceedings which was sponsored by the Italian American People of Chicago. Giancana stated he personally likes Annunzio, but cannot trust him.

Annunzio was interviewed on January 13, 1962, at his office, the Lake Personnel Service. Annunzio displayed a, "cooperative attitude and gave a lengthy dissertation on the present outlook and position of the legitimate Italian American citizenry in Chicago." He deplored the fact that the Italian American's of Chicago is represented politically by personages such as John D'Arco, Anthony Girolami, Peter Granata, Vito Marzullo and the like, stated the respectable Italian has moved to the suburbs and therefore exerts no control in the old wards where they were born and raised. He admitted knowing Giancana, however, was evasive to direct questioning as to Giancana's influence in political affairs. Annunzio was head of the Illinois Department of Labor under then Governor Adlai Stevenson. He is chairman of Lodge 19, Sons of Italy, chairmen of the Italian welfare league, and is prominent in the affairs of Italian Americans.

CG 6486-C advised on January 20, that a party was held at the Armory Lounge, attended by John Matassa, Butch Blasi, Eddie (LNU) and others unnamed.

CG 6502-C advised that Gus Alex and Butch Ladon discussed a party to be held that night "at Carmies place," attended by them and Eddie Vogel. This would be the Armory Lounge, owned by Carmen Fanelli. That party was a mixed affair with males and females present. Giancana was definitely not present.

FEDERAL BUREAU OF INVESTIGATION

REPORTING OFFICE	OFFICE OF ORIGIN	DATE	INVESTIGATIVE PERIOD
CHICAGO	CHICAGO	1962	February 1, 1962

TITLE OF CASE	REPORT MADE BY	TYPED BY
SAMUEL M. GIANCANA, aka		dkc

	CHARACTER OF CASE
	FBI Headquarters File number 92-3171-607 Top Hoodlum Program – Anti Racketeering. Daily Summary

Refer to information previously submitted pertaining to an interview with (blacked out) that he stated his interview be held in confidence. According to Chicago informant went directly to John D'Arco and reported the fact that he had been interviewed by the FBI regarding Giancana and Murray Humphreys. Noted has (blacked out) as a possibility of development under the Top Echelon Criminal Informant Program. In view of his apparent closeness and loyalty to John D'Arco and therefore D'Arco's associates, it is felt that his potential in now greater for future development. Further interviews are contemplated in the near future. Noted that Joseph Glimco was interviewed regarding his association with Giancana and others, and although he admitted being acquainted with Giancana, stated the he has never asked Giancana for anything, but if Giancana asked a favor of him, he, Glimco, would do everything in his power to oblige.

FEDERAL BUREAU OF INVESTIGATION

REPORTING OFFICE	OFFICE OF ORIGIN	DATE	INVESTIGATIVE PERIOD
CHICAGO	CHICAGO	1962	February 2, 1962

TITLE OF CASE	REPORT MADE BY	TYPED BY
SAMUEL M. GIANCANA, aka		dkc

	CHARACTER OF CASE
	FBI Headquarters File number 92-3171-620 Top Hoodlum Program – Anti Racketeering. Daily Summary

CG 6486-C advised last night that Sam Giancana held a series of conferences with Gus Alex, Eddie Vogel, and John D'Arco. Conference with Vogel and Alex mostly drowned out by juke box music, however, pertinent portions of conversation obtained were Giancana advising Alex and Vogel to "tell everyone, including Willie "Potatoes" Daddono, that everything is off, this is it because of the G." Continued by stating, "tell them that what I did was for their benefit, and I did what was right. We ain't spending another nickel."

CG 6502-C advised on 1/25, by way of corroboration of the above, that Gus Alex advised an unknown bookmaker to tell everyone that, "we are cutting the cord." Giancana conference with John D'Arco advised D'Arco that, "everyone is on their own, they got to make it anyway they can." Most of conversation between D'Arco and Giancana related to the intensive investigation conducted on Giancana. As an example, D'Arco advised Giancana of the fact that Frank Annunzio was interviewed by "Hill and Roemer," D'Arco stated that Annunzio advised agents that President Kennedy can thank the Italian ward politician for delivering the Illinois vote to Kennedy during the past election, and the thanks they get is investigation of Italians. Actually, Annunzio stated the Italian ward politicians such as D'Arco, stole the vote in Chicago, and gave it to Kennedy, thus in effect winning the presidential election for Kennedy. D'Arco ranted and raved about the intensive investigation being conducted and that they (Hill and Roemer) are knocking their brains out, talking to everyone. D'Arco moaned throughout conference that, "We are through, there's no place to go." Giancana agreed, stated, "This is it. Don't worry about it, we'll make a living somehow, history repeats itself. They think the (obscene) had been flying, but watch it fly now. I told everyone they're on their own, go ahead and make a living, but you're on your own." Inference here is that the working bookmaker, muscleman, juice operator, ECT, will now revert to his former occupation of stickups and crimes of violence to make a living. Giancana stated, "Now that we're out of the city and out of the county, we'll just move to Indiana and set up headquarters in Hammond, with houses (of prostitution) and everything." D'Arco stated that intensive investigation by FBI is aimed at getting at Giancana and his source of income by attacking his underlings and the organization, to which Giancana agreed. D'Arco complained bitterly about Mayor Richard J. Daley and his organization, and the fact that Daley has thrown off D'Arco and his associates, now that he has reached national prominence. He compared Daley with Giancana by stating, "Moe (Giancana), Daley is as powerful with his group as you are with us. You give us orders we follow them without asking why. We just do it." D'Arco complained of the fact that Daley had allowed Spencer (Roswell T. Spencer) to be placed on the ticket for sheriff, which fact was discovered by Spencer who complained to certain unnamed persons who in turn reported D'Arco's animosity toward Spencer to Mayor Daley. D'Arco reminded Giancana that he, Giancana, ordered D'Arco to campaign against Spencer and inferred that Giancana had thus placed D'Arco in the middle. Giancana indicated to D'Arco that for the present, he is not going south, after which D'Arco requested and received permission to leave town.

FEDERAL BUREAU OF INVESTIGATION

REPORTING OFFICE	OFFICE OF ORIGIN	DATE	INVESTIGATIVE PERIOD	
CHICAGO	CHICAGO	1962	February 3, 1962	
TITLE OF CASE		REPORT MADE BY		TYPED BY
				dkc
SAMUEL M. GIANCANA, aka		CHARACTER OF CASE		
		FBI Headquarters File number 92-3171-609 Top Hoodlum Program – Anti Racketeering. Daily Summary		

Advised early February 1, that Giancana held court over dinner in the vicinity of the informant and announced that he had just returned from Florida. He related that a person probably identical with Joseph Glimco told Giancana about the details of his interview with the FBI. Giancana told the group about his interview be SA's Roemer and Hill in July, 1961, whereby he used abusive and profane language. He was also told about the interview of Peter Granata. Giancana attempted to act unconcerned about the interviews of his associates and other investigation, but was obviously upset about this situation. He stated, "They don't know nothing about me, they don't know where I go or where I been, so (obscene) them." During early mornings of date Giancana conferred with Rocco Potenzo. Potenzo advised Giancana that he is through with bookmaking, and has not even purchased a Federal Stamp for horse booking.

FEDERAL BUREAU OF INVESTIGATION

REPORTING OFFICE	OFFICE OF ORIGIN	DATE	INVESTIGATIVE PERIOD	
CHICAGO	CHICAGO	1962	February 6, 1962	
TITLE OF CASE		REPORT MADE BY		TYPED BY
				dkc
SAMUEL M. GIANCANA, aka		CHARACTER OF CASE		
		FBI Headquarters File number 92-3171-608 Top Hoodlum Program – Anti Racketeering. Daily Summary		

Giancana in conference with Anthony V. Champagne, his attorney, pertaining to his income tax return for 1961. Champagne was upset over the fact that Giancana, through all his traveling around the country and in Europe, had spent funds beyond that amount he shows on his return. Giancana assured Champagne that he only stayed in cheap hotels, spent little money on his European tour, and as par as his travel in this country is concerned, the government can not prove anything.

Giancana stated, "They find the broad (Phyllis McGuire), then they see me with her, but they don't know how I got there. They never see me buy any plane tickets." It was decided that Giancana would claim on his return largely capital gain income from sale of his Roosevelt Road property, not described.

FEDERAL BUREAU OF INVESTIGATION

REPORTING OFFICE	OFFICE OF ORIGIN	DATE	INVESTIGATIVE PERIOD	
CHICAGO	CHICAGO	1962	February 6, 1962	
TITLE OF CASE		REPORT MADE BY		TYPED BY
				dkc
SAMUEL M. GIANCANA, aka		CHARACTER OF CASE		
		FBI Headquarters File number 92-3171-617 Top Hoodlum Program – Anti Racketeering. Daily Summary		

Advised last night that Jack Cerone, Chicago top hoodlum, held a discussion with Sam Giancana, where by Cerone advised that "the G" has recently been making inquiries in Miami Beach hotels and motels regarding Chicago hoodlums such as Frank Ferraro and Giancana. Cerone advised Giancana that he has a house rented in Miami off of Biscatne Boulevard near 95th street causeway from February 9 through May 10, 1962; Cerone offered use of home to Giancana stating that he, Cerone, is going down Friday or Monday to stay alone for a while and if Giancana desired to use the home, he will call Butch Blasi for confirmation. Cerone is having his car driven to Miami on February 8, by some unknown individual. Noted that this source advised that Giancana stated to Cerone, "There is a call out in the last couple of days that back in the east. They might decide that we will get together down there." Above indicated Giancana has been in telephonic contact with East Coast top hoodlums and implies the possibility of a conclave to be held in Miami February 9, and Ross Prio and Murray Humphreys are currently in Miami.

FEDERAL BUREAU OF INVESTIGATION

REPORTING OFFICE	OFFICE OF ORIGIN	DATE	INVESTIGATIVE PERIOD
CHICAGO	CHICAGO	1962	February 7, 1962

TITLE OF CASE	REPORT MADE BY	TYPED BY
SAMUEL M. GIANCANA, aka		dkc

	CHARACTER OF CASE
	FBI Headquarters File number 92-3171 Top Hoodlum Program – Anti Racketeering. Daily Summary

It is recommended that two agents from Chicago Division be sent to Miami to assist in identifying hoodlums from there area who, it is believed, are possibly contemplating a meeting in the Miami area in the immediate future. It is recommended that SA's Ralph Hill and John Roberts travel to Miami relative to the proposed meeting.

Intensive investigation is being continued to determine the movements of Chicago area hoodlums in this regard and all feasible stops have been placed. Miami will be immediately advised of any information coming to our attention as to the departure of any of the top Chicago hoodlums traveling to that area. Jackie Cerone's car is a 1960 dark blue Cadillac convertible with light blue top.

FEDERAL BUREAU OF INVESTIGATION

REPORTING OFFICE	OFFICE OF ORIGIN	DATE	INVESTIGATIVE PERIOD
CHICAGO	CHICAGO	1962	February 8, 1962

TITLE OF CASE	REPORT MADE BY	TYPED BY
SAMUEL M. GIANCANA, aka		dkc

	CHARACTER OF CASE
	FBI Headquarters File number 92-3171-613 Top Hoodlum Program – Anti Racketeering. Daily Summary

CG 6486-C advised during the early hours of 2/6, that Giancana continued his discussion with Jack Cerone pertaining to visitors, if any, which Cerone may have had in his home recently, particularly political personages. Cerone assured Giancana that since his arrival back in Chicago on 2/3, he had no visitors. Giancana reminded Cerone that he was visited by Tony Accardo, to which Cerone replied in the affirmative. He stated, however, he has never allowed politicians in his home. Giancana cautioned Cerone most strongly that he is never to contact any politicians on the telephone, nor is he to visit them in their homes. Any meets must be made away from residences. He reminded Cerone that their existence, in effect depends on their political allies, and, "they can't be dirtied." Giancana was highly concerned over recent contacts by agents of this office with political personages, such as John D'Arco, Peter Granata, ET AL, regarding their association with Giancana and others. He is apparently more concerned over this situation than any other. Giancana made observation that gambling in Miami is wide open just like at Hot Springs. CG 6486-C advised that on 2/6, there was a constant loud playing of the juke box. There were meeting and discussions carried on, however, not possible to hear any conversation, except that the conversant, with Giancana, was Bernard Glickman, former fight manager, mentioned by source. Glickman is apparently, with Giancana's approval and backing, attempting to set up corporation.

Miami reports the following New York hoodlums reportable in the Miami area; Vincent Alo, Salvatore Granello, John Biele, Alex DeBrizzi, Anthony Solerno, Carmine Lombardozzi, Carlo Gambino, Joseph Biondo, Thomas Greco, Joseph and Salvatore Profaci, James Napoli, Salvatore Peritore, Morris Levy, and Salvatore Serrago.

FEDERAL BUREAU OF INVESTIGATION

REPORTING OFFICE	OFFICE OF ORIGIN	DATE	INVESTIGATIVE PERIOD	
CHICAGO	CHICAGO	1962	February 9, 1962	
TITLE OF CASE		REPORT MADE BY		TYPED BY
				dkc
SAMUEL M. GIANCANA, aka		CHARACTER OF CASE		
		FBI Headquarters File number 92-3171-614 Top Hoodlum Program – Anti Racketeering. Daily Summary		

The following Chicago hoodlums are known to be in Miami area: Ross Prio, Murray Humphreys, whose whereabouts are known; Rocco Fischetti, Dominic DiBello, Charles and Sam English, and Joseph Aiuppa. Edward Vogel is "out of town," believed to be in Miami, where he is to meet Gus Alex, according to CG 6502-C. As of late 2/7, Giancana and Alex still in Chicago. CG 6486-C advised yesterday Giancana held conference with individual believed to be identical with Charles Nicoletti regarding installation of pin balls and other coin devices, and purchase of liquor store, bar and restaurant in Melrose Park, IL. No discussion held regarding traveling plans on part of Giancana.

FEDERAL BUREAU OF INVESTIGATION

REPORTING OFFICE	OFFICE OF ORIGIN	DATE	INVESTIGATIVE PERIOD	
CHICAGO	CHICAGO	1962	February 10, 1962	
TITLE OF CASE		REPORT MADE BY		TYPED BY
				dkc
SAMUEL M. GIANCANA, aka		CHARACTER OF CASE		
		FBI Headquarters File number 92-3171-623 Top Hoodlum Program – Anti Racketeering. Daily Summary		

Chicago informant advised that Leslie Kruse had made an emergency trip to Miami and Palm Beach this date to, "Sell his home in Lake Worth, Florida."

Based on very limited info furnished by Chicago source relative to possible residence to be used by Jack Cerone and Sam Giancana. This info fits an unlimited number of houses in this area. House believed to be one to be utilized by these top hoodlums has been located and investigation reflects owner and occupant highly unreliable. Despite this handicap, through detailed planning, ingenuity and imaginative efforts by Bureau personnel, two independent highly confidential sources have been established in house and are in operating condition, effective this date. Source designated as MM 794-C source advises new occupants, identities not yet established, at residence today. Investigation reflects this residence under lease by Rocco Fischetti, Chicago hoodlum, for next 2 ½ months for $3,500.

FEDERAL BUREAU OF INVESTIGATION

REPORTING OFFICE	OFFICE OF ORIGIN	DATE	INVESTIGATIVE PERIOD	
CHICAGO	CHICAGO	1962	February 13, 1962	
TITLE OF CASE		REPORT MADE BY		TYPED BY
				dkc
SAMUEL M. GIANCANA, aka		CHARACTER OF CASE		
		FBI Headquarters File number 92-3171-621 Top Hoodlum Program – Anti Racketeering. Daily Summary		

Chicago informant advised Giancana and Willie "Potatoes" Daddono are reported to be partners in a motel, location not known. Informant states Al Wainer, Chicago liquor store operator, is a close friend of Daddono and may be partner with Daddono in hotel or apartment building. Wainer described as a close friend of Tony Accardo and Chicago juice men. Informant observed Dominic Blasi and John Matassa in conference, nothing of pertinence discussed.

Investigation conducted by Chicago PD Intelligence unit during May, 1961, on Louis Briatta telephonically contacted John D'Arco and Frank Esposito at their Hollywood, Florida, homes. In view of known close association between D'Arco and Esposito as well as Esposito's North of Miami address indicates strong possibility Esposito could be the "Frank" (LNU) discussed in hit proposed for Miami area.

FEDERAL BUREAU OF INVESTIGATION

REPORTING OFFICE	OFFICE OF ORIGIN	DATE	INVESTIGATIVE PERIOD
CHICAGO	CHICAGO	1962	February 14, 1962

TITLE OF CASE	REPORT MADE BY	TYPED BY
		dkc
SAMUEL M. GIANCANA, aka	**CHARACTER OF CASE** FBI Headquarters File number 92-3171-622 Top Hoodlum Program – Anti Racketeering. Daily Summary	

Referenced info furnished by confidential source concerning possible "Hit" victim recently referred to as "Frank," for which Giancana's approval was obtained. Possibility exists that one of the following individuals named Frank could be victim in question. Frank Annunzio, partner of John D'Arco, Chicago Alderman, in Anco Insurance Company, Chicago, and former head of the Illinois Department of Labor in 1952. Frank Caruso, controls gambling on Chicago's South Side subservient to Chicago top hoodlums Frank Ferraro and Gus Alex. Frank Eulo, a lieutenant of Giancana and gambler in Cicero. Frank Ferraro, a Chicago top hoodlum connected with criminal activities in the First Ward in Chicago under D'Arco. Frank Fratto, an ex-convict in the storm window business and brother of Omaha top hoodlum Lou Farrell. Frank Buccieri, brother of Fiore Buccieri, who is a lieutenant of Giancana. Frank Gentile, a Chicago Police officer in First District who is a bag man for various hoodlums and on the payroll of the English brothers. Frank LaPorte, boss of illegal activities in Southeast Cook County, IL. Frank LoVerde, partner in Phil Alderisio at Club 19 in the Rush Street area. Frank Teutonica, Chicago west side juice man who was questioned in gangland slaying of William "Action" Jackson. Frank A. Esposito, a Chicago labor official with strong hoodlum ties and close associate of John D'Arco. Esposito has residence at 5401 North Surf, Hollywood, Florida, telephone WA 20370. Noted D'Arco had residence at 5405 North Surf. Esposito considered most logical victim, base on info furnished by Miami.

FEDERAL BUREAU OF INVESTIGATION

REPORTING OFFICE	OFFICE OF ORIGIN	DATE	INVESTIGATIVE PERIOD
CHICAGO	CHICAGO	1962	February 15, 1962

TITLE OF CASE	REPORT MADE BY	TYPED BY
		dkc
SAMUEL M. GIANCANA, aka	**CHARACTER OF CASE** FBI Headquarters File number 92-3171 Top Hoodlum Program – Anti Racketeering. Daily Summary	

Funeral held recently at Kringas and Marzullo's Mortuary for Danny Allegretti who died February 1, was attended by many of Chicago's prominent criminals. Allegretti reportedly not engaged in criminal activities, but delivered jukeboxes for his brother-in-law, William Daddano. Deceased was father of John and Anthony Allegretti, Chicago police officers. John presently stationed at Shakespeare area, formerly worked narcotics squad as partner of John Matassa. According to information, deceased not related to Chicago hoodlum Jimmy "Monk" Allegretti.

FEDERAL BUREAU OF INVESTIGATION

REPORTING OFFICE	OFFICE OF ORIGIN	DATE	INVESTIGATIVE PERIOD
CHICAGO	CHICAGO	1962	February 16, 1962

TITLE OF CASE	REPORT MADE BY	TYPED BY
		dkc
SAMUEL M. GIANCANA, aka	CHARACTER OF CASE	
	FBI Headquarters File number 92-3171-624 Top Hoodlum Program – Anti Racketeering. Daily Summary	

Conference held between Sam Giancana and Chicago gambler Morris Pearl regarding Dunes Hotel transaction involving point share offer by Pearl. Pearl stated he was in contact with Sid Wyman at the Dunes in Las Vegas who advised Pearl that he, Wyman, owns 50% of the Dunes. He then offered some points to Pearl, in turn offered to cut Giancana on the deal if he was interested. Giancana evinced an interest, whereupon Pearl stated he would look into this further. Conversation touched above current Justice Department investigation now being conducted on organized crime. Pearl stated, "I remember you telling me before Kennedy came in that there was gonna be fireworks, but I never expected nothing like this." Giancana stated, "I just got back the other day, and we got everybody tagged out. They (government) are investigating only certain individuals, in certain cities in certain areas." Pearl asked, "You mean outfit?" to which Giancana replied in affirmative. Interpretation of above would conceivably be that Giancana feels the government investigation is concentrated on individuals such as himself, Gus Alex, and others, hoping to get Giancana through his underlings. This could be reason why Giancana, upon returning to this area, ordered people under his control that from now on, "they're on their own." Pearl, aka "Pottsie" currently owns and operates a 1961 Lincoln with Illinois license plates. This vehicle was observed at the wedding of Jack P. Cerone Jr., in 1961. Groom was son of Jack Cerone, prominent west side gambler and constant companion of Tony Accardo. Pearl observed at "Spranze" Swanson wedding. Mike Spranze, father of the bride, is west side gambler and Capone associate. Pearls vehicle also observed at lawn party given by Tony Accardo at his River Forest home. Chicago source advised that Pearl enjoys frequent Gin games with Morris Maishie Baer true name Morris Saletko.

FEDERAL BUREAU OF INVESTIGATION

REPORTING OFFICE	OFFICE OF ORIGIN	DATE	INVESTIGATIVE PERIOD	
CHICAGO	CHICAGO	1962	February 20, 1962	
TITLE OF CASE		REPORT MADE BY		TYPED BY: dkc
SAMUEL M. GIANCANA, aka		CHARACTER OF CASE		
		FBI Headquarters File number 92-3171-632 Top Hoodlum Program – Anti Racketeering. Daily Summary		

Re: Proposed meeting of hoodlums. Illinois Secretary of State Records reflect 1962 Illinois registration issued to Mario Partipilo for Oak Park, IL. No photos on file at the Chicago PD for Joseph Matarrese, Richard Pausteri, Mike Donofrio or Partipilo.

FEDERAL BUREAU OF INVESTIGATION

REPORTING OFFICE	OFFICE OF ORIGIN	DATE	INVESTIGATIVE PERIOD	
CHICAGO	CHICAGO	1962	February 21, 1962	
TITLE OF CASE		REPORT MADE BY		TYPED BY: dkc
SAMUEL M. GIANCANA, aka		CHARACTER OF CASE		
		FBI Headquarters File number 92-3171-637 Top Hoodlum Program – Anti Racketeering. Daily Summary		

The following information contained in Chicago files about Esposito as follows: Frank A. Esposito, aka Frankie X, age 62, is president of District Council of Construction and General Laborers. He bosses 35,000 men in 18 locals of the International Hod Carriers, Building and Common Carriers Union. Anonymous letter received Chicago office August 1961, contained information which subsequent investigation proved reliable, in part, stated John Matassa, former Chicago Policeman and current bodyguard and chauffeur of Sam Giancana, was on the payroll of Frank Esposito. In addition to Phil Alderisio, Joey O'Brien, and William Daddono, all prominent Chicago hoodlums and lieutenants of Giancana. Investigation of Louis Briatta, May 1961, reflected that Briatta made a long distance call to Esposito March 19, 1961, at Hollywood, Florida. Briatta is a lieutenant of Chicago top hoodlum Gus Alex, and reportedly makes all handbooks collections for Alex in the First Ward (Loop Area).

The Chicago Tribune newspaper reported September 1960, Esposito scheduled for "Heart-to-Heart Talk" with his lieutenant, Al Pilotto, because Pilotto named by South Suburban Beer Distributor in Accardo tax trial as assistant to Tony Accardo selling beer in Calumet City and Chicago Heights, IL. Pilotto described as head of Local 5, Chicago, for Esposito and former bodyguard for south suburban syndicate chief, Frank LaPorte. Gerald J. Covelli, while under indictment for ITSMV violation, Houston, August 1959, claimed Esposito allied with Chicago "outfit." One requested Covelli to arrange property purchase in Chicago for which tremendous profit planned by Esposito after Federal Loan obtained to put up building. Profit would depend on inflated material, prices and kickbacks. However, plan failed to materialize. Information in December 1947, revealed Esposito in telephonic contact with Paul DeLucia, a prominent Chicago hoodlum now under deportation proceedings at Chicago. Although above interest apparent reason for proposed gangland slaying not evident to Chicago Office. Investigation in this regard continued by Chicago office and bureau and Miami will be advised. Chicago PD, observed Giancana in front of the Armory Lounge this afternoon, walking in easterly direction to Pink Clock, another hoodlum hangout.

FEDERAL BUREAU OF INVESTIGATION

REPORTING OFFICE	OFFICE OF ORIGIN	DATE	INVESTIGATIVE PERIOD
CHICAGO	CHICAGO	1962	February 24, 1962

TITLE OF CASE	REPORT MADE BY	TYPED BY
		dkc
SAMUEL M. GIANCANA, aka	**CHARACTER OF CASE** FBI File number 92-3171-634 Top Hoodlum Program – Anti Racketeering. Daily Summary	

Chicago PD observed Giancana at the Armory Lounge late evening of February 22 and 23. Giancana in conference with person possibly identical with Lou Brady. Conversation related to proposed nine and one half million dollar hotel deal which is scheduled for completion in 1963. Brady to take plans, drawings and specification to Miami over weekend and confer with member of Taylor Construction Co., who has agreed to handle the job. Exact site of proposed hotel not yet known, possibly Reno, Nevada area. Giancana advised he will be leaving Monday for a few days, he did not indicate destination.

Informant advised that one Carl Milano, Cleveland hoodlum, arrived in Chicago from Cleveland two weeks ago specifically for a conference with Giancana. Lou Brady and Milano known to be close friends.

Pretext inquiry to locate Frank Esposito at Chicago negative. Miami advised by separate communication.

FEDERAL BUREAU OF INVESTIGATION

REPORTING OFFICE	OFFICE OF ORIGIN	DATE	INVESTIGATIVE PERIOD	
CHICAGO	CHICAGO	1962	February 25, 1962	
TITLE OF CASE		REPORT MADE BY		TYPED BY
				dkc
SAMUEL M. GIANCANA, aka		CHARACTER OF CASE		
		FBI Headquarters File number 92-3171 Top Hoodlum Program – Anti Racketeering. Daily Summary		

Physical surveillance instant vicinity of Jack Cerone's Miami residence reveals that guest of Cerone's is definitely no Sam Giancana. This individual strongly resembles Joe Gagliano, partner of Cerone.

FEDERAL BUREAU OF INVESTIGATION

REPORTING OFFICE	OFFICE OF ORIGIN	DATE	INVESTIGATIVE PERIOD	
CHICAGO	CHICAGO	1962	February 27, 1962	
TITLE OF CASE		REPORT MADE BY		TYPED BY
				dkc
SAMUEL M. GIANCANA, aka		CHARACTER OF CASE		
		FBI Headquarters File number 92-3171-638 Top Hoodlum Program – Anti Racketeering. Daily Summary		

Former paramour of Giancana advised SA John Bassett, that inasmuch as she had reached the conclusion that Giancana ordered execution of Angelo Fasel whom suddenly disappeared July 15, 1960. She desires to reestablish contact with Giancana. States her objective will be to determine through Giancana and associates if he was directly responsible for Angelo Fasel's execution. Informant feels no problem faced in reestablishing contact inasmuch Giancana of opinion that her child is his. She states she was intimate with Giancana during period her child was conceived, however, claims Giancana unaware child actually fathered by Fasel. Child christened 1960 at which time Dominic "Butch" Blasi and wife, Constance, (Blacked out by government) at Giancana's request. Informant claims Giancana attempted to contact her several times during past year through Blasi, but she refused to talk. Informant feels she is held in higher esteem than Phyllis McGuire by Giancana, this strengthened by fact that he is of opinion he is father of her child. Informant plans to solicit funds to finance medical treatment for her child. Informant advise that if Giancana desires to continue relationship, she will discreetly furnish info concerning all activities and contacts.

FEDERAL BUREAU OF INVESTIGATION

REPORTING OFFICE	OFFICE OF ORIGIN	DATE	INVESTIGATIVE PERIOD	
CHICAGO	CHICAGO	1962	March 1, 1962	
TITLE OF CASE		REPORT MADE BY		TYPED BY
				dkc
SAMUEL M. GIANCANA, aka		CHARACTER OF CASE		
		FBI Headquarters File number 92-3171-639 Top Hoodlum Program – Anti Racketeering. Daily Summary		

CG 6486-C advised that Dominic "Butch" Blasi and Joe Porcaro, member of the "West Side Bloc" and candidate for Republican township committeeman of Norwood Park Township, also known as one of group of politicians controlled by Chicago hoodlums, held a conference. Conversation indicated that in recent past, Giancana ordered Peter Granata, Illinois State Representative and First Ward Republican committeeman to contact Cook County Sheriff Frank Sain concerning placement of two of Porcaro's workers on payroll of the Metropolitan Sanitary District. Conversation revolved around possible future political maneuvers on part of Porcaro involving Republican Ward Committeeman Hannenburg and John D'Arco. Text reveals large control by Giancana over "West Side Bloc."

FEDERAL BUREAU OF INVESTIGATION

REPORTING OFFICE	OFFICE OF ORIGIN	DATE	INVESTIGATIVE PERIOD	
CHICAGO	CHICAGO	1962	March 3, 1962	
TITLE OF CASE		REPORT MADE BY		TYPED BY
				dkc
SAMUEL M. GIANCANA, aka		CHARACTER OF CASE		
		FBI Headquarters File number 92-3171-643 Top Hoodlum Program – Anti Racketeering. Daily Summary		

CG 6486-C reports Dominic Blasi and person identified as Fiore "Fifi" Buccieri in brief conference today. Text of conversation appears to revolve around contemplated killing probably set for today at Chicago. Identity of victim unknown. Buccieri will be "leaving the joint at 11 o'clock sharp." Blasi will pick up "Philly", Felix "Milwaukee Phil" Alderisio and Jackie (possibly Jack Cerone) to take unknown destination and "get out." Although victim not known, inasmuch as Buccieri, Alderisio and Jackie Cerone mentioned, all of which mentioned in connection with slaying scheduled for Miami recently. Victim possibly Frank Esposito. Info disseminated today to Chief Investigator R.T. Spencer who advised he had informed the Chicago PD Labor Detail that he had reliable info emanating in Miami relative to this matter.

FEDERAL BUREAU OF INVESTIGATION

REPORTING OFFICE	OFFICE OF ORIGIN	DATE	INVESTIGATIVE PERIOD
CHICAGO	CHICAGO	1962	March 8, 1962

TITLE OF CASE	REPORT MADE BY	TYPED BY
		dkc
SAMUEL M. GIANCANA, aka	**CHARACTER OF CASE** FBI Headquarters File number 92-3171-644 Top Hoodlum Program – Anti Racketeering. Daily Summary	

CG 6486-C reports Giancana in conference evening 2/20 with person probably identified as John Formusua, Indiana top hoodlum and frequenter of Las Vegas or Johnny Roselli, front man for Giancana in Las Vegas gambling enterprises. Unknown person apparently acting as middle man between unknown banker and Giancana concerning 9 ½ million dollar hotel or motel deal, which could be completed June, 1963. The site for property probably Las Vegas. "John" probably John Drew also front man for Giancana in Las Vegas established referred to as person who would place "key men in key spots." Apparently Sid Korshak, prominent Chicago attorney, designed to handle legal end. Subsequent to contacts made by unknown middle man and "Butch" Blasi.

CG 6486-C advised Hy Godfrey and Dominic Blasi discussed insurance business at length at the Armory Lounge. Godfrey operates insurance agency at 1660 East 55th Street, Hyde Park, IL. He stated he recently signed Lennie Patrick up for a $40,000 life policy. Claims Patrick was "on payroll." He also added he "just wrote one half million dollar accident and death policy on Hump and his old lady." Murray "Hump" is Chicago top hoodlum Murray Humphreys. Godfrey suggested Giancana obtain one quarter million dollar life insurance in view of frequent airline trips. He stated that Nicky Kokenes finally paid up insurance first time in eight years. Kokenes is manager of MGM Lounge and allegedly makes payoffs to Frank Papa at Chicago race tracks. Papa is Chicago Police captain on leave in charge of security at Arlington and Washington Race Track, Chicago area. Godfrey indicate well acquainted with Elmer "Dutch" Dowling, lieutenant of St. Louis top hoodlum Frank "Buster" Wortman who was a victim of gangland slaying together with Wortman strong arm man Mel Beckman at Bellview, IL. Godfrey and Blasi indicated they are not aware of reason for killing but stated "Buster will find out." Both disused the advanced state of Shingles "Nervous Disorder" suffered by Murray Humphreys and suggested it had progressed too far for treatment. Godfrey of opinion disease will attack vital organs and finish Humphreys.

FEDERAL BUREAU OF INVESTIGATION

REPORTING OFFICE	OFFICE OF ORIGIN	DATE	INVESTIGATIVE PERIOD	
CHICAGO	CHICAGO	1962	March 9, 1962	

TITLE OF CASE	REPORT MADE BY	TYPED BY
		dkc
SAMUEL M. GIANCANA, aka	**CHARACTER OF CASE** FBI Headquarters File number 92-3171-646 Top Hoodlum Program – Anti Racketeering. Daily Summary	

CG 6486-C reported that Giancana and an unknown female in Armory Lounge briefly today. Information regarding William "Smokes" Aloisio in connection with Willie Messina. Messina is Chicago ex-convict alleged strong arm and "hit man" for syndicate. He is a close associate of Joe "Gags" Gagliano and the Bravos brothers in a large Chicago juice operation. Messina described by informant as "Little Shrimp," formerly utilized by Tony Accardo as a house bodyguard.

FEDERAL BUREAU OF INVESTIGATION

REPORTING OFFICE	OFFICE OF ORIGIN	DATE	INVESTIGATIVE PERIOD	
CHICAGO	CHICAGO	1962	March 10, 1962	

TITLE OF CASE	REPORT MADE BY	TYPED BY
		dkc
SAMUEL M. GIANCANA, aka	**CHARACTER OF CASE** FBI Headquarters File number 92-3171-648 Top Hoodlum Program – Anti Racketeering. Daily Summary	

Chicago informant advised that she had left message with Carmen Fanelli requesting Giancana to make contact with informant. Informant also advised that Sam DeStefano had hair dyed black, wears crew cut and frequents Guest Lounge on a nightly basis. States Willie "Potatoes" Daddono, Tony DeRosa, and Buck Ortenzi were also in conference at Guest Lounge during week.

FEDERAL BUREAU OF INVESTIGATION

REPORTING OFFICE	OFFICE OF ORIGIN	DATE	INVESTIGATIVE PERIOD
CHICAGO	CHICAGO	1962	March 12, 1962

TITLE OF CASE	REPORT MADE BY		TYPED BY
			dkc
SAMUEL M. GIANCANA, aka	**CHARACTER OF CASE** FBI Headquarters File number 92-3171-649 Top Hoodlum Program – Anti Racketeering. Daily Summary		

Lester "Killer Kane" Kruse, close associate of Giancana, confided that Rocco Potenzo is presently operating a large profitable "New York crap game" on Milwaukee Avenue in Niles, IL. Kruse related Potenzo operating game for Giancana as he has other Giancana interests in past.

FEDERAL BUREAU OF INVESTIGATION

REPORTING OFFICE	OFFICE OF ORIGIN	DATE	INVESTIGATIVE PERIOD
CHICAGO	CHICAGO	1962	March 15, 1962

TITLE OF CASE	REPORT MADE BY		TYPED BY
			dkc
SAMUEL M. GIANCANA, aka	**CHARACTER OF CASE** FBI Headquarters File number 92-3171-652 Top Hoodlum Program – Anti Racketeering. Daily Summary		

Chicago informant advised he was frequenting the Cicero area and in this connection talked to Joey Aiuppa and Aiuppa's brother Sam. In the conversation that followed the informant asked Aiuppa why he was getting the cold shoulder in the Cicero area inasmuch as others in a like position he had been in the past are now allowed free run of Cicero games. He specifically noted Chuck Nicoletti and Frank Teutonica. The informant advised the Teutonica is on bad paper with the outfit in Cicero and has been run out of town. Informant was unable to obtain further information about this situation.

FEDERAL BUREAU OF INVESTIGATION

REPORTING OFFICE	OFFICE OF ORIGIN	DATE	INVESTIGATIVE PERIOD
CHICAGO	CHICAGO	1962	March 16, 1962

TITLE OF CASE	REPORT MADE BY	TYPED BY
		dkc
SAMUEL M. GIANCANA, aka	CHARACTER OF CASE	
	FBI Headquarters File number 92-3171-654 Top Hoodlum Program – Anti Racketeering. Daily Summary	

CG informant advised Dave Yaras is presently checked into Tides Motel, North Sheridan Road, for indefinite period. Noted Yaras is a Chicago hoodlum who discussed Chicago "hit job" recently with Jack Cerone while in vicinity of Miami.

FEDERAL BUREAU OF INVESTIGATION

REPORTING OFFICE	OFFICE OF ORIGIN	DATE	INVESTIGATIVE PERIOD
CHICAGO	CHICAGO	1962	March 16, 1962

TITLE OF CASE	REPORT MADE BY	TYPED BY
		dkc
SAMUEL M. GIANCANA, aka	CHARACTER OF CASE	
	FBI Headquarters File number 92-3171-661 Top Hoodlum Program – Anti Racketeering. Daily Summary	

Chicago informant advised he has recently become acquainted with brother of Fiore "Fifi" Buccieri. Chicago investigation had developed info with strong indication Buccieri is hired "hit man" for Giancana. Informant advised "Fifi's" brother while under influence of liquor confided that the only person he fears is his own brother inasmuch as he claims "Fifi" would kill a relative as quick as anyone else. Information to maintain contact and attempt report activities of Buccieri.

Informant learned that Dave Yaras presently living at the Tides Motel, Chicago claims Yaras has substantial financial interest in the Mid West Triumph Company, which also supplies other Chicago hoodlums with sports cars.

FEDERAL BUREAU OF INVESTIGATION

REPORTING OFFICE	OFFICE OF ORIGIN	DATE	INVESTIGATIVE PERIOD
CHICAGO	CHICAGO	1962	March 20, 1962

TITLE OF CASE	REPORT MADE BY	TYPED BY
SAMUEL M. GIANCANA, aka		dkc

CHARACTER OF CASE

FBI Headquarters File number 92-3171-655
Top Hoodlum Program – Anti Racketeering.
Daily Summary

CG 6486-C advised no pertinent activity over weekend, noted that Giancana was in the Fontainebleau Hotel, Miami Beach, Florida as of March 15, last. McGuire Sisters singing team scheduled for engagement at Fontainebleau for night of March 17, last.

Miami requested to maintain contact with Sid Levenson, night manager, about Giancana's expected departure.

About situation with Frank Esposito, Chicago union official, proposed victim of gangland slaying as reported by MM 794-C, bureau authority is requested for interview with Esposito regarding his association with the Chicago criminal organization, in order that this situation may be fully exploited. Strong possibility may exist that Esposito may be persuaded to furnish information to bureau regarding his dealing with this organization. It is felt that this interview should be conducted at earliest possible time in the event the proposed killing is still being contemplated.

FEDERAL BUREAU OF INVESTIGATION

REPORTING OFFICE	OFFICE OF ORIGIN	DATE	INVESTIGATIVE PERIOD
CHICAGO	CHICAGO	1962	March 21, 1962

TITLE OF CASE	REPORT MADE BY	TYPED BY
SAMUEL M. GIANCANA, aka		dkc

CHARACTER OF CASE

FBI File number 92-3171-656
Top Hoodlum Program – Anti Racketeering. Daily Summary

Phyllis McGuire is staying with her sister, Christine, in Fort Lauderdale until end of March. Giancana not known to be there. McGuire Sisters scheduled for two week performance at Basin Street East, NYC, commencing April 2, 1962.

FEDERAL BUREAU OF INVESTIGATION

REPORTING OFFICE	OFFICE OF ORIGIN	DATE	INVESTIGATIVE PERIOD	
CHICAGO	CHICAGO	1962	March 23, 1962	

TITLE OF CASE	REPORT MADE BY	TYPED BY
		dkc

TITLE OF CASE	CHARACTER OF CASE
SAMUEL M. GIANCANA, aka	FBI Headquarters File number 92-3171-657 Top Hoodlum Program – Anti Racketeering. Daily Summary

John Drew, Las Vegas TH, currently in Chicago at the Drake Hotel. Drew is an associate of Giancana and has been described as one of Giancana's fronts in that area. Attempts being made for microphone surveillance coverage of Drew at the Drake.

David Yaras, Miami hoodlum, who figured in proposed Frank Esposito killing, checked out of the Ties Motel, Chicago, today and is believed to be en route back to Miami.

FEDERAL BUREAU OF INVESTIGATION

REPORTING OFFICE	OFFICE OF ORIGIN	DATE	INVESTIGATIVE PERIOD	
CHICAGO	CHICAGO	1962	March 24, 1962	

TITLE OF CASE	REPORT MADE BY	TYPED BY
		dkc

TITLE OF CASE	CHARACTER OF CASE
SAMUEL M. GIANCANA, aka	FBI Headquarters File number 92-3171-659 Top Hoodlum Program – Anti Racketeering. Daily Summary

MM 794-C advised that Jack Cerone was to meet Sam (LNU) at Puccini's Restaurant, Miami, on March 22. Miami ascertained that Cerone, accompanied by Rocco Fischetti, CG TH, were in Puccini's, where Cerone met Santos Trafficante, Cerone, Fischetti and Trafficante them met several other unidentified persons in the restaurant. Giancana not observed. John Teeter, NY source, advised yesterday that Giancana plans to spend the weekend with Phyllis McGuire at Fort Lauderdale, Florida.

FEDERAL BUREAU OF INVESTIGATION

REPORTING OFFICE	OFFICE OF ORIGIN	DATE	INVESTIGATIVE PERIOD
CHICAGO	CHICAGO	1962	March 26, 1962

TITLE OF CASE	REPORT MADE BY	TYPED BY
SAMUEL M. GIANCANA, aka	Agent Ralph Hill Jr.	dkc

CHARACTER OF CASE
FBI Headquarters File number 92-3171-668 Top Hoodlum Program – Anti Racketeering

Chicago T-1 advised in February 21, 1961, that Frank Buccieri, brother of Fiore, works closely with Joe Spotivecchio in a loan shark operation located at 5th Avenue and California Streets in Chicago. This building is known as Parker's restaurant. According to the informant there was at that time a considerable amount of horse betting in the restaurant.

"Attached her is a Chicago American Newspaper article dated April 12, 1961, concerning Frank Buccieri."

Jack Cerone
2000 West 77th Street
Elmwood Park, Illinois

CG T-42 advised that Jack Cerone was in contact with Sam Giancana for the purpose of making arrangements for a trip to Miami. On March 7, 1962, Jack Cerone was observed by SA's Hill, George Stadtmiller, and Warren Donavan at the Eden Roc Hotel, Miami Beach, in company with Rocco Fischetti, Joseph Fischetti, William Aloisio, Lou Rosanova and their wives. Cerone was seen conversing briefly with James Hoffa in the lobby of the Eden Roc. It is noted that Hoffa was in Miami at that time for purpose of attending a Teamsters council meeting.

On March 3, 1962, Cerone, Aloisio and the Fischetti brothers, together with Dave Yaras and their wife's, were observed dining at Puccini's Restaurant on 79th Street, Miami, Florida, by SA's. On the same date the above group was observed in the Casanova Room of the Deauville Hotel, Miami, where they apparently were in attendance to observe the McGuire Sisiters singing team which was playing an engagement at that time at the Deauville Hotel.

CG T-60 advised that Jack Cerone while in Florida was in contact with Sam Giancana. It will be shown elsewhere in this report of Giancana's activities while in the Miami area during March, 1962.

Illegal Activity

Gambling

CG T-58 advised that he had recently been at the Show of Shows located at 1312 South Cicero Avenue, Cicero, IL, which was formerly known as the June

Bug. This show also contains a bar called the Dream Bar. He stated that during the day there is a crap game and card game going at this location as well as a horse book. He said that the results from the races are broadcasted over a public address system and that between races; music can be heard from these speakers. He said that this operation is run by Frank "Sharkey" Eulo for Sam Giancana. He said that this establishment as far as gambling moves then to the Royal Cafa located at 4817 West Roosevelt on the second floor, where cards are played. He advised that the split of the profits from this gambling establishment is 50% for Giancana and 50% for Eulo and his associates. In addition there is a handbook operation in a barber shop at 4850 West Madison Street, Chicago.

He advised that he is acquainted with an individual named Turk, whose last name may be Torello, and who frequents the Stop Light Lounge located at Roosevelt Road and Cicero Avenue. He described Turk as male, white, early 40's, 5'9", 175-180 pounds, husky build. He stated that Turk is engaged in "juice" and gambling activates and works in close association with Joe Aiuppa, Fifi Buccieri and Mario DeStefano.

CG T-48 advised in January, 1962, that Fiore Buccieri was in contact with Giancana during January, at which time he turned in the collection from Forest Park and Cicero, IL, and from the Puerto Rican Lottery. The amount was undetermined by the informant. Buccieri also furnished money from the Pangini game which is a Greek card game.

FEDERAL BUREAU OF INVESTIGATION

REPORTING OFFICE	OFFICE OF ORIGIN	DATE	INVESTIGATIVE PERIOD	
CHICAGO	CHICAGO	1962	March 27, 1962	
TITLE OF CASE		REPORT MADE BY		TYPED BY
				dkc
SAMUEL M. GIANCANA, aka		**CHARACTER OF CASE**		
		FBI Headquarters File number 92-3171-662 Top Hoodlum Program – Anti Racketeering.		
		Daily Summary		

Based upon bureau authority, attempt made to contact Frank Esposito instant date, Chicago, for interview. Ascertained that Esposito is "out of town." Miami ascertain if Esposito currently in Hollywood, Florida, residence and discreetly attempt to determine his expected date of return to Chicago. In the event Esposito is not contemplating an early return to Chicago, Miami is requested to exhaustively interview Esposito for his connection with the hoodlum element.

FEDERAL BUREAU OF INVESTIGATION

REPORTING OFFICE	OFFICE OF ORIGIN	DATE	INVESTIGATIVE PERIOD
CHICAGO	CHICAGO	1962	March 28, 1962

TITLE OF CASE	REPORT MADE BY	TYPED BY
SAMUEL M. GIANCANA, aka		dkc

CHARACTER OF CASE

FBI Headquarters File number 92-3171-665
Top Hoodlum Program – Anti Racketeering.
Daily Summary

Chicago informant advised no success to date making contact with Giancana. She observed Marshall Caifano, Felix Alderisio, James "Cowboy" Mirro and James "Turk" Torello at Guest House Lounge, Franklin Park, on March 25. She now stated that she understands that Giancana is so securely involved with Phyllis McGuire, she doubts whether he will consider another female involvement at this time.

FEDERAL BUREAU OF INVESTIGATION

REPORTING OFFICE	OFFICE OF ORIGIN	DATE	INVESTIGATIVE PERIOD
CHICAGO	CHICAGO	1962	March 31, 1962

TITLE OF CASE	REPORT MADE BY	TYPED BY
SAMUEL M. GIANCANA, aka		dkc

CHARACTER OF CASE

FBI Headquarters File number 92-3171-681
Top Hoodlum Program – Anti Racketeering.
Daily Summary

Chicago informant advised that Sam Giancana is the real authority behind the World Wide Distributors, Inc., Chicago, distributors of juke box and coin operated machines. The slot machines and other gambling machines are crated and stamped as juke boxes, then shipped to England and Puerto Rico. Informant also stated that Giancana is the actual power behind Eddie Vogel in the control of coin machine and juke boxes in the Chicago area. Giancana had ordered Vogel to make is juke box purchases from Joel Stern at World Wide.

FEDERAL BUREAU OF INVESTIGATION

REPORTING OFFICE	OFFICE OF ORIGIN	DATE	INVESTIGATIVE PERIOD	
CHICAGO	CHICAGO	1962	April 4, 1962	
TITLE OF CASE		REPORT MADE BY		TYPED BY
				dkc
SAMUEL M. GIANCANA, aka		CHARACTER OF CASE		
		FBI Headquarters File number 92-3171-681 Top Hoodlum Program – Anti Racketeering. Daily Summary		

Re: interview with Frank Esposito. SA Ralph Hill, through Esposito's Chicago union office, made telephonic contact with Esposito at Hollywood, Florida, instant, told Esposito that it was a matter of urgency and to his benefit that he be interviewed immediately. Esposito agreed to such an interview, advised that he expects to fly to Chicago within the next few days, would contact SA Hill upon arrival. Stated he is under a doctor's care in Florida. Esposito not given any idea for the need for this interview. Miami was advised to alert local authorities that Esposito is in Hollywood at the present time. Giancana known to be in Chicago today.

FEDERAL BUREAU OF INVESTIGATION

REPORTING OFFICE	OFFICE OF ORIGIN	DATE	INVESTIGATIVE PERIOD	
CHICAGO	CHICAGO	1962	April 5, 1962	
TITLE OF CASE		REPORT MADE BY		TYPED BY
				dkc
SAMUEL M. GIANCANA, aka		CHARACTER OF CASE		
		FBI Headquarters File number 92-3171-682 Top Hoodlum Program – Anti Racketeering. Daily Summary		

CG 6486-C advised yesterday that Giancana held brief conferences with Rocco Potenzo and Fiore Buccieri. Potenzo complained bitterly over the fact that Lester Kruse had been giving him "unfair competition in the operation of gambling establishments in that section." Noted that Kruse recently opened a large scale poker, dice and roulette operation near Half Day, IL, in competition with Potenzo's similar type operation in Niles. Potenzo stated, "I'm gonna have to whack that guy, that's the only language he knows." Giancana calmed Potenzo down by stating, "Don't worry, the first time he gets busted, he'll never open again." Buccieri brought in the monthly proceeds from gambling in Cicero and Forest Park, IL. Also proceeds from the juice operation.

FEDERAL BUREAU OF INVESTIGATION

REPORTING OFFICE	OFFICE OF ORIGIN	DATE	INVESTIGATIVE PERIOD
CHICAGO	CHICAGO	1962	April 13, 1962

TITLE OF CASE	REPORT MADE BY	TYPED BY
		dkc
SAMUEL M. GIANCANA, aka	CHARACTER OF CASE	
	FBI Headquarters File number 92-3171-688 Top Hoodlum Program – Anti Racketeering. Daily Summary	

CG 6486-C disclosed Dominic Blasi and Tarquin "Queenie" Simonelli, brother-in-law of Tony Accardo, in lengthy discussion while conducting some type of manual labor at Armory Lounge. Blasi and Simonelli discussed acquisition of new telephone for lounge and Blasi told of warning Giancana for using telephone except to arrange meeting dates. Blasi mentioned the he will deliver quantity of "leads" to John Kringas. Kringas is owner of Gus' Steak House, notorious Cicero gambling establishment.

FEDERAL BUREAU OF INVESTIGATION

REPORTING OFFICE	OFFICE OF ORIGIN	DATE	INVESTIGATIVE PERIOD
CHICAGO	CHICAGO	1962	April 14, 1962

TITLE OF CASE	REPORT MADE BY	TYPED BY
		dkc
SAMUEL M. GIANCANA, aka	CHARACTER OF CASE	
	FBI Headquarters File number 92-3171-689 Top Hoodlum Program – Anti Racketeering. Daily Summary	

Noted Armory Lounge closed until April 24, due to illness of Carmen Fanelli, owner who entered hospital for an operation. However, looks like Giancana will continue to utilize lounge for meetings during period lounge is closed.

FEDERAL BUREAU OF INVESTIGATION

REPORTING OFFICE	OFFICE OF ORIGIN	DATE	INVESTIGATIVE PERIOD	
CHICAGO	CHICAGO	1962	April 17, 1962	
TITLE OF CASE		REPORT MADE BY		TYPED BY
				dkc
SAMUEL M. GIANCANA, aka		CHARACTER OF CASE		
		FBI Headquarters File number 92-3171-690 Top Hoodlum Program – Anti Racketeering. Daily Summary		

Re Interview of Frank Esposito, proposed victim of gangland slaying. Ascertained that he has returned to Chicago area and is now confined to hospital for undetermined reason. Office secretary refused to disclose whereabouts and messages to contact office thus far unanswered. Efforts being continued to locate for interview.

FEDERAL BUREAU OF INVESTIGATION

REPORTING OFFICE	OFFICE OF ORIGIN	DATE	INVESTIGATIVE PERIOD	
CHICAGO	CHICAGO	1962	April 17, 1962	
TITLE OF CASE		REPORT MADE BY		TYPED BY
				dkc
SAMUEL M. GIANCANA, aka		CHARACTER OF CASE		
		FBI Headquarters File number 92-3171-691 Top Hoodlum Program – Anti Racketeering. Daily Summary		

CG 6486-C advised that during early hours of April 13, Giancana held court again in outer room with several hoodlums, among them being John Matassa, Les Kruse, Dominic Blasi and others. Mentioned being followed around in Florida by "nine FBI guys."

FEDERAL BUREAU OF INVESTIGATION

REPORTING OFFICE	OFFICE OF ORIGIN	DATE	INVESTIGATIVE PERIOD	
CHICAGO	CHICAGO	1962	April 19, 1962	
TITLE OF CASE		REPORT MADE BY		TYPED BY
				dkc
SAMUEL M. GIANCANA, aka		CHARACTER OF CASE		
		FBI Headquarters File number 92-3171 Top Hoodlum Program – Anti Racketeering. Daily Summary		

CG 6486-C reported yesterday that Giancana and unknown person in conversation relating to renovation of rear interior of Armory Lounge. Giancana pointed out contour of joints and supports and discussed knocking out wall in rear of Lounge to gain additional six feet of foot space. Measurements were taken and unknown suggested using services of Giancana's son-in-law (probably Carmen Manno) in connection with redecoration. The lounge is closed until April 26, it would appear work would begin prior to opening date.

In view of risk of disclosure of CG 6486-C during altercations, it was deemed advisable by Chicago to temporarily discontinue this source until completion of contemplated construction. At 3:00AM today, removal of CG6486-C was successfully completed with out incident.

FEDERAL BUREAU OF INVESTIGATION

REPORTING OFFICE	OFFICE OF ORIGIN	DATE	INVESTIGATIVE PERIOD	
CHICAGO	CHICAGO	1962	April 21, 1962	
TITLE OF CASE		REPORT MADE BY		TYPED BY
				dkc
SAMUEL M. GIANCANA, aka		CHARACTER OF CASE		
		FBI Headquarters File number 92-3171-696 Top Hoodlum Program – Anti Racketeering. Daily Summary		

Chicago informant who has interest in several race horses and is a close contact with gamblers and bookmakers in Chicago, states Fiore "Fifi" Buccieri is overseer of large organization in Chicago area where number type gambling devices and bookmaking are operated on large scale. Regarding these operations, informant claims Buccieri reports directly to Giancana. Included in activities of Buccieri organization is large scale "juice" operation with collectors and musclemen who report directly to Buccieri.

Noted CG 6486-C recently reported Buccieri, aka "nose" is a hit man who fulfills contracts upon direct order of Giancana relayed to him by Dominic "Butch" Blasi.

FEDERAL BUREAU OF INVESTIGATION

REPORTING OFFICE	OFFICE OF ORIGIN	DATE	INVESTIGATIVE PERIOD
CHICAGO	CHICAGO	1962	April 25, 1962

TITLE OF CASE	REPORT MADE BY	TYPED BY
SAMUEL M. GIANCANA, aka		dkc

CHARACTER OF CASE

FBI Headquarters File number 92-3171-698
Top Hoodlum Program – Anti Racketeering.
Daily Summary

The Following information developed on Eden Land and Building Company, "ELBC", which Dominic Blasi holds the title of vice president in. Alleged owner of company Edward Lachen, former Livery Service chauffeur for Flash Cab Co. and possessor of Chicago PD arrest record. Jump from Livery chauffeur to head of ELBC highly questionable. Original organizer is Frank V. Pantaleo, subject of inquiry by the Senate Investigation committee and associate and building contractor for John Lardino, Charles English, Jack Cerone and Joey Glimco. All under investigation in connection with hoodlum matters. Frank Cerone, hoodlum and convicted criminal is connected with construction of ELBC homes. IRS investigation determined large sums of hoodlum money being invested in ELBC, Schiller Park, IL. Big money behind this company is reportedly Jack and Frank Cerone and Frank V. Pantaleo, all well known Chicago hoods. In view of Pantaleo's association with Cerone, Lardino, and Glimco, IRS of opinion his interest in ELBC far more than concrete construction.

FEDERAL BUREAU OF INVESTIGATION

REPORTING OFFICE	OFFICE OF ORIGIN	DATE	INVESTIGATIVE PERIOD
CHICAGO	CHICAGO	1962	April 27, 1962

TITLE OF CASE	REPORT MADE BY	TYPED BY
SAMUEL M. GIANCANA, aka		dkc

CHARACTER OF CASE

FBI Headquarters File number 92-3171-702
Top Hoodlum Program – Anti Racketeering.
Daily Summary

Frank Esposito, proposed victim of gangland slaying by Jack Cerone, interviewed instant on preliminary basis. Esposito advised that he was recently released from Columbus Hospital, where he was confined for gall bladder trouble. He was told that the interview was for his benefit and personal safety that agents desired to talk with him regarding his personal situation. He desired to know specifically his problem, and he was advised that he was being considered by "certain persons" to be "Hit." Esposito was non committal, however, was obviously shaken over the information. He stated he would get in touch with the formal interview this date, claimed sickness as the primary cause. Roswell Spencer, former SA, Chief Investigator, States Attorney's Office, advised of Esposito's returning to the Chicago area. Spencer was previously furnished the information relative to the fact that Esposito was believed to be the subject of a proposed hit. This information was furnished in such a way to completely protect the source and yet given sufficient credence to this situation.

FEDERAL BUREAU OF INVESTIGATION

REPORTING OFFICE	OFFICE OF ORIGIN	DATE	INVESTIGATIVE PERIOD	
CHICAGO	CHICAGO	1962	May 9, 1962	
TITLE OF CASE		REPORT MADE BY		TYPED BY
				dkc
SAMUEL M. GIANCANA, aka		CHARACTER OF CASE		
		FBI Headquarters File Number 92-3171-713 Top Hoodlum Program – Anti Racketeering. Daily Summary		

The MGM Lounge is a known gambling establishment of Giancana's operated By Nick Kokenes, who, according to CG 6343-C, was forced to turn over his place to Sam Battaglia. The Turf Lounge is operated by Joey Aiuppa and specializes in Burlesque.

FEDERAL BUREAU OF INVESTIGATION

REPORTING OFFICE	OFFICE OF ORIGIN	DATE	INVESTIGATIVE PERIOD	
CHICAGO	CHICAGO	1962	May 16, 1962	
TITLE OF CASE		REPORT MADE BY		TYPED BY
				dkc
SAMUEL M. GIANCANA, aka		CHARACTER OF CASE		
		FBI Headquarters File number 92-3171-720 Top Hoodlum Program – Anti Racketeering. Daily Summary		

CG 6343-C advised yesterday that Louis Celano conversed with his brother, James Celano about the fact a "non union job" was being performed at 7427 West Roosevelt, location of the Armory Lounge. Noted that Louis Celano is business agent of Local 134, IBEW. Investigator for the local was sent out to investigate and was "thrown off." Celano states he then went out to location and talked with Tarquin "Queenie" Simonelli on the job. Giancana then came out dressed in work cloths, supervising construction. Giancana suggested to Celano that he move his car since "the FBI is all over the place." Remodeling being done at Armory Lounge. Giancana's suspicious set out above are obviously erroneous inasmuch as no surveillances have been conducted at this location for some time.

Charles "Chuck" Nicoletti was interviewed at his residence in Melrose Park. Nicoletti cordial but extremely evasive while discussing hoodlum activities in Chicago area. Noted Nicoletti and "Milwaukee Phil" Alderisio were arrested by Chicago PD on May 2, 1962, while both were lying on the floor of a car with fictitious registration in the Rush Street Area. Circumstances indicate both lying in wait for unknown intended victim prior to arrest. Both offered one thousand dollar bribe to arresting officers, neither have attempted to retrieve car from PD pound. Nicoletti denied bribe and presence in car with Alderisio to Agents. He stated, "We wasn't in that car. We was only near it." Politely denied any contact with Giancana and evaded questions concerning his activities within the Giancana organization. When asked if it was true he controlled Melrose Park and Cicero for Giancana to which he had no comment. He stated, "I'm getting old and slowing down, I like you guys and would like to talk to you, but don't want my head handed to me some night." When asked for an explanation of that comment he stated, "Well they might think I'm a stool pigeon."

Nicoletti concluded by stating he might possibly contact agents telephonically at Chicago offices if his attitude changes.

FEDERAL BUREAU OF INVESTIGATION

REPORTING OFFICE	OFFICE OF ORIGIN	DATE	INVESTIGATIVE PERIOD	
CHICAGO	CHICAGO	1962	May 19, 1962	
TITLE OF CASE		REPORT MADE BY		TYPED BY
				dkc
SAMUEL M. GIANCANA, aka		CHARACTER OF CASE		
		FBI Headquarters File number 92-3171-726 Top Hoodlum Program – Anti Racketeering. Daily Summary		

Norman Blubock, Chicago America reporter, advised in confidence yesterday that a contact of his was very close to Joseph Bulger, criminal lawyer and head of the Italo American Union in Chicago, stated to Blubock yesterday that in conversation with Bulger recently, Bulger disclosed that a meeting of top national syndicate figures was held in Florida three months ago as a result of which Giancana is to be retired very shortly. Having had advanced knowledge of this, Giancana had been investing his money in every enterprise he is able to. Among these enterprises which Giancana owns or is heavily invested in are the following: Sahara Motel North, Thunderbolt Motel, American Motel, Concord Motel and Lido Motel, all in Chicago area: Bellwood Savings and Loan, Almira Savings and Loan, Oak Park Savings and Loan, and Bellwood shopping center.

It should be noted that Bulger, aka Joseph Imburgio, is the former mayor of Melrose Park, IL, and was a codefendant in the tax income trial of Paul DeLucia. Bulger had been described in the past by informants whose reliability is unknown, as one time head of the "Mafia." Bulger, however, has been known in the past to make precipitous statements concerning Giancana. He stated several years ago that Giancana was to be replaced shortly by William Daddono.

It should be noted that Giancana, along with Carlo Gambino and others, were in Miami Beach, Florida, during last month and issued unusual orders that "everyone in on his own."

272

FEDERAL BUREAU OF INVESTIGATION

REPORTING OFFICE	OFFICE OF ORIGIN	DATE	INVESTIGATIVE PERIOD
CHICAGO	CHICAGO	1962	May 21, 1962

TITLE OF CASE	REPORT MADE BY	TYPED BY
SAMUEL M. GIANCANA, aka	Agent Ralph Hill Jr.,	dkc

CHARACTER OF CASE
FBI Headquarters File Number 92-3171-725 Top Hoodlum Program – Anti Racketeering

Synopsis:

Chicago informants indicate Giancana to be heavily invested in the World Wide Distributing Company of Chicago. World Wide allegerdly is in the process of shipping gambling type devices throughout the country and into foreign commerce. Informants allege that Giancana has interest in the construction of the Sahara North Motel, an elaborate structure located near O'Hare Field. Giancana is allegedly married to Phyllis McGuire of the McGuire Sisters singing team. McGuire Sisters are scheduled to appear at Las Vegas, Nevada, for a four week engagement commencing 5/15/62. Informant relating to gambling operations of the Giancana organization, particularly on-track horse bookmaking, set forth.

Associates

Louis Celano, Business Agent,
Local 134, International
Brotherhood of Electrical
Workers, Chicago, Illinois

CG T-2 advised that Louis Celano was in contact with Giancana concerning the fact that a non-union job was being performed during the re-modeling of the Armory Lounge. It would appear that any investigation on the part of Celano, according to the informant, was negated by the appearance of Giancana.

Frank Esposito
1701 North Natoma
Chicago, Illinois

It is noted that Frank Esposito, also known as "Frankie X", is the president of the Cook County Municipal Workers and Street Laborers Union, Local 1001, and is on the board of directors of the AFL-CIO Construction and General Laborers District at Chicago. In this position he has control of some 18,000 members of this union. Esposito was born on January 3, 1900 in Italy and maintains a winter residence located at 5401 North Surf Street, Hollywood, Florida.

CG T-3 advised during the fall of 1961 and during the winter of 1962, that Esposito is very close to John D'Arco, First Ward Alderman for the city of Chicago. Through this association of D'Arco and by virtue of his earlier Chicago experiences, Esposito is considered by the informant to have been a close associate of Sam Giancana. The informant speculated that Esposito was responsible for obtaining of employment for individuals and relatives of individuals who are or who have been associated with Giancana in the past. This is accomplished through Esposito's control over many municipal laborers jobs in the Chicago area.

During the early winter of 1962, CG T-4 advised that for an unknown reason Giancana ordered the execution in gangland style of Esposito, said execution to be carried out off the beaches of South Florida during the month of February, 1962. According to the informant, the "contract" for this proposed killing was given to Jack Cerone, a member of the Giancana organization for many years and considered by the informant to be among the top personnel in the Giancana organization.

According to CG T-4, Cerone had gathered a crew of individuals and went to Florida for the primary purpose of carrying out the execution ordered by Giancana of Esposito. Among the individuals selected to fulfill the execution were the following: Frank "Skippy" Cerone of Melrose Park, alleged cousin of Jack Cerone; Fiore "Fifi" Buccieri of Chicago, who according to this informant and CG T-3 maintains a top level position in the Giancana organization and is the enforcer and collector for all the Giancana organizational activities on Chicago's west side extending into the western suburbs including Cicero and Forest Park, IL; Dave Yaras, currently of Miami, Florida, and one time resident of Chicago, for many years a member of Chicago's organized criminal element and considered to be a partner of Leonard Patrick of Chicago's north side. Yaras maintains a residence in Miami and is gainfully employed as a representative of the Susco Automobile Rental Agency of that city. He was considered as a primary suspect in the killing of William Ragen of the Continental Press and Wire Service, Chicago, in 1946; James "Turk" Torello of Chicago, who according to CG T-4 has been utilized in the past in gangland killings and has past history in the Chicago area as a thief, burglar and "muscle man" for the various illegal enterprises, of the organized criminal element in Chicago. He has been described as a member of the "North Avenue Steak House gang", which name is derived from a restaurant by that name, since burned down, operated by Torello and other underworld associates; Vincent "The Saint" Inserro is a long time theft, hoodlum and bookmaker in the Cicero, Illinois area; and Lou Rosanova, long time associate of Jack Cerone and considered as a sometime stolen merchandise fence, gainfully employed as a tailor in Chicago.

Although the contract for the purposed killing was given to Cerone, the informant advised that Buccieri would be primarily responsible for the carrying out of the contract and for the organization of those individuals several of which are mentioned above who were to perform the final act. The informant advised that Cerone was not making progress in the execution and that because of the fact that Esposito rarely, if ever, left the premises of his Hollywood, Florida residence, and according to the orders of the contract it was necessary that Esposito must be abducted and without the knowledge of any of his relatives or associates and without the benefit of witnesses observing such an abduction. The immediate plan was to steer Esposito to an isolated spot preferably near the water from where he would be taken to a boat and then he was to be dismembered and his parts were to be scattered into the Atlantic Ocean. According to the source, it was necessary to make the killing of Esposito appear to be nothing more than a disappearance. One plan was Dave Yaras was to invite Esposito to dinner or for Yaras to place a phone call to Esposito to meet one of the group. Another possibility was to "accidentally" meet Esposito on the beach and invite him for a little ride in the boat. Frank "Skippy" Cerone had made arrangements for the rental of a power boat and Dave Yaras had made proper arrangements for the use of an automobile, possibly stolen, containing license registration which would be untraceable.

Upon receipt of the above information from CG T-4 Sheriff Allen Michell of Broward County, Florida on February 14, 1962, was advised of the fact that there were plans in the making to do bodily harm and possibly kill Esposito. The above information was also furnished to Chief Investigator Roswell T. Spencer of the States Attorney's Office, Cook County, Illinois, and to Joseph C. Morris, Deputy Superintendent of police for the city of Chicago.

Frank Esposito returned to Chicago in April, 1962 and on April 27, 1962, he was interviewed by SA Ralph Hill telephonically. Esposito, who refused to be interviewed in person, advised that he had recently been released from Columbus Hospital, Chicago, where he was confined for a gall bladder condition. He was advised of the fact that he was being considered as a possible victim for a proposed gangland slaying, however, he refused to be committed to a formal interview claiming sickness as a primary purpose for such a refusal.

FBI's surveillance photo of John D'Arco (left) and Frank "Frankie X" Esposito (Right) in Hollywood, Florida, February 1962.

Phyllis McGuire
525 Park Avenue
New York City

It has been reported that Giancana and Miss McGuire have been enamored of each other and have been observed in each other's company on frequent occasions since the summer of 1960. CG T-9 advised on May 9, that he has learned from several sources in and around Chicago that Giancana is positively married to Phyllis McGiure of the McGuire Sisters singing team. The date and the place of this marriage is unknown to the informant but it would appear that the marriage was some months ago.

Illegal Activities

Gambling

CG T-13 advised that in the Chicago organized criminal element, particularly with reference to the gambling operation, the number one individual is Samuel Giancana. One of Giancana's chief subordinates in his gambling empire is Fiore Buccieri, who has been pertinently utilized as an executioner for the organization.

He also added that he had learned recently that on Salvatore DeRosa, also known as "Salam" is connected with an attempted interest of the organization into Puerto Ricanganes. DeRosa's close associate is "Turk" Torello, and at one time operated the North Avenue Steak House in Melrose Park. This steak house has been described as a one time hangout for many of the Giancana organization.

On Track Bookmaking

CG T-14 advised that through his association with Buccieri, who is also a large scale bookmaker, it has been explained to him that Don Angel, operating through a blind company, Camera Construction Company, is actually the biggest bookmaking operation for both horses and sports events in the entire Chicago area. He advised that Don Angel's true name is Don Angelini. About a year and a half ago Angel associated himself with William Kaplan in the Angel-Kaplan Sports Service and is the individual most directly associated with the large bookmaking activities. He advised that this bookmaking operation of Don Angel will never accept a bet less that $100 and will accept lay-off money from small bookies throughout the city and suburbs. He advised that Camera Construction Company generally had two telephone numbers assigned and that the numbers are generally changed every two weeks. He advised that the numbers presently in use which were given to him on March 27, 1962. He advised that one calls either of the numbers to place large bets and the party answering will say Camera Construction Company and then the better is identified and known bets will be accepted and odds given. He advised that Fifi Buccieri is extremely close to this organization and is in fact a part of it; however, he has been unable to learn Buccieri's exact position in the operation.

He advised that one of Buccieri's associates is an individual known to him as "Spotty", an individual not identical with "Spa" Spotteveccio. He advised that through observation and information received from sources close to Buccieri and "Spotty" that Joe "Spa" is a "nobody" or flunky for Buccieri and his associates.

He advised that when Sportsman's Race Track is operating, "Spotty" can generally be seen at the trotters almost every night. He further advised that "Spotty" handles the more important payoffs and collections for the Camera Construction Company operation and is an individual closely associated with Buccieri. He advised with specific reference to betting on hockey games that the Camera Construction Company operates on a %10 margin at all times. He advised that the odds are bet on hockey games by half-puck or puck margin. In other words, a bettor would place a bet with the Camera Construction Co., for example, taking the Chicago Black Hawks with a one puck advantage and one placing a $100 bet would pay an additional $10 for the use of Camera Construction Co. services. In other words, if the bettor lost his bet to the Camera Construction Co. his payment would be $110. This 10% is, according to Buccieri, never decaled in connection with income tax or tax wagering stamps. He advised that most all the heavy betting and lay-offs on hockey games in the Chicago area would be handled through the Camera Construction Co. He advised 10% margin applies only to sporting events exclusive of horse racing.

He explained that the 10% allowance on bets won by the booking organization allows them to disregard handicapping as it applies to sporting events. With regard to the publications put out by Angel and Kaplan, he advised that he learned through Buccieri that there is an individual in St. Louis, Missouri, who actually does the handicapping for the Angel-Kaplan organization. This individual, who is unknown to him and according to Buccieri information, sees that the handicapping information is walked across the Missouri-Illinois Line and then transmitted from East St. Louis to Chicago where the publications are made up. He advised that this is done specifically to circumvent the new federal laws.

He advised that he is in a position to supply the new telephone numbers of Camera Construction Co. each time the numbers are changed. He further advised that he sees "Spotty" from the time to time at the track and will obtain his license number the next time he sees this individual.

He advised with specific reference to the track operations in the Chicago area, particularly pertaining to harness racing, he advised that on-track betting by bookies is a tremendously big money maker for the operators of the track and the Outfit. He advised with specific reference to Maywood in the current racing season that there are 40 bookies operating at the track and that their gross bets are actually larger than the bets placed with the track at the pari-mutuel windows. He said that each of these bookies pays $125 per week for the privilege of accepting bets at the track. He advised again with specific reference to the Maywood operation that there are two Pinkerton employees and one Chicago Police Lieutenant, recently promoted from Sergeant, on leave, assigned to the track. He advised that these three individuals make all the pickups from the bookies on the track. He said that these three individuals check off the bookmakers and pick up the $125 on Monday night. This payment would cover the following week. He advised that Sportsman's Race track operates the same except on a larger scale. In both instances the bookie are supervised by Chuck and Sam English. Chuck and Sam English are always present at Sportsman's and supervise the operation of the bookie and represent the "Outfit" in the large bookmaking operation at both tracks. He advised that Chuck and Sam English can always be seen at Maywood, however, due to the smaller amounts of wagered at Maywood they are not at the track every night. With reference to Maywood, he advised that he has heard from individuals connected with the bookies and also the individuals operating the track that Nathan Ellenm, President of Maywood, and Sam Wiedrick, another high official at Maywood, receive a large percentage of the amount collected from bookmakers each week. He further advised that at least 20% of the money goes directly to (FNU) Dygert, another individual high in the operation of the Maywood Track. He advised that the take for the track operators at Sportsman's is at least three times greater than that at Maywood and that most of the money taken from the bookies is channeled into (FNU) Johnson, who operates Sportsman's, an individual who has appeared before the Senate Subcommittee and a person who was a close personal friend of Al Capone in the Capone era. He further advised in connection with the operation at Sportsman's that Johnson's son-in-law has the entire photo concession at Sportsman's Park and photographs, develops and processes the photographs of all photo finishes. If large amounts of "Outfit" money are ridding on a particular horse the photographs can be altered assuming the horse is a front runner. He advised that sometimes it takes twenty minutes for the photo to be developed in connection with a specific race.

He said ordinarily it only takes a few minutes to develop a photograph and released the results to the public. The way, he stated it is, "who is to say which way you draw the wire." In some instances a dead heat is judged where this type of a finish would benefit the bookies.

He advised that if on-the-track bookies were not allowed to operate at the track the purses available for the horse owners operating at the track would be greatly increased. However, if the horse owners should complain about the on-the-track bookies they are advised that they will not be allowed to race their horses at this particular track if they make a complaint.

He went on to say that through his association with Fifi Buccieri, "Cowboy" Mirro and some of their associates he became acquainted with one Joe "The Jap." He advised that Joe "The Jap" is a powerful man in policy and Puerto Rican gambling games in both Gary, Indiana, and Chicago, IL. He advised that Joe "The Jap" has become quite wealthy through this gambling operation and now owns large real estate holdings in the northwest section of Chicago. He further advised that one of Joe "The Jap's" closest associates is one "Salam." He advised that "Salam" works about three hours per night and will drive every night to Gary, Indiana, where he selects numbers for the following day and makes drawings for the following day's gambling activities. He further transports money from Gary to the Chicago area. He advised that he knows "Salam" and has played cards with him at Parkers Restaurant, a noted gambling spot for cards players on the northwest side of Chicago. He advised that "Salam" would always start his trip each night from Parkers, however, he never returned to Parkers with the money. He advised that "Salam" is also a close associate of Fifi Buccieri and he assumed that rather than bringing the money and the selections to Parkers it would be brought to Hacking Brothers Finance Company with whom Buccieri is closely associated and where the money could easily be stored. He advised that about six months ago most of these individuals left the Parkers Restaurant and are now hanging out at the Stop Light Lounge in the southeast corner of Cicero Avenue at Roosevelt Road in Cicero, IL.

On May 8, 1962, SA Ralph Hill and Vincent Inserra conducted a physical surveillance at Sportsman's Park Race Track, Cicero, IL, between the first and fifth races at the track. The following individuals were observed in activity which appeared to be taking bets and receiving money from individuals at the track. It could not be said as a certainty that bookmaking was taking place from these observations; however, the activities did not appear to be the type which were conducive to the efficient operation of the pari-mutuel system:

Charles English	Sam English
Sam DeRosa	George Bravos
Nick DeGrazio	Donald Angellini

He advised that he has recently been in contact with Rocky Infelice, who formerly owned the North Avenue Steak House, which Infelice burned for insurance purposes last year. He advised that Infelice now attends the Maywood Race Track trotting events almost every night and advised that Infelice has two sons, both red-headed, who are now bookmakers for bookmakers at Maywood Race Track. He advised that Rocky Infelice apparently controls these two boys, however, they accept the bets. He further advised that he has recently been in contact with Jeff Manno, one-time prominent policy individual in the city of Chicago. He advised that Jeff Manno also attends Maywood and I generally in the company of James "Cowboy" Mirro, who is a partner of Rocky Infelice. He advised that Jeff Manno is driving a re Pontiac latte-model and has a job with the "Green Sheet" in downtown Chicago. He advised that Manno is taken care of by "Outfit" members inasmuch as he took the rap for seven or eight policy men years ago and spent considerable time in prison. He advised that today Manno has no power at all and is simply an errand boy and runner for other hoodlums. He advised that Manno is attached to the Fifi Buccieri organization and provides some service to individuals connected with the Fifi Buccieri bookmaking operation.

With reference to the "Salam" who he mentioned previously, he positively identified a photograph of Salvatore "Salam" DeRosa as being identical with the "Salam" who he made reference to previously. He advised, however, that he has not been in contact with "Salam" for a period of nine months. He advised he was closely associated with "Salam" and played ziginette with "Salam", Buccieri, and others at Frank Parker's Restaurant, a noted hangout for the Buccieri organization. He advised that "Salam" talked freely and advised that he was closely associated with Joseph Eto, also known as "Joe the Jap", also known as "Joe Montana." DeRosa advised that he was a runner for the "Joe the Jap" bolito operation in Gary, Indiana. On a number of occasions DeRosa complained to him that the "Mexicans" in Gary would puncture his tires when he made his late night tips. He advised that DeRosa is also closely associated with Joe Fullouci of Hacking Brothers and acts as a collector for the Hacking Brothers operation. He theorized that due to the close association of Fifi Buccieri, Salvatore DeRosa and others individuals in the Buccieri operation with Hacking Brothers that Hacking Brothers would be a depository for funds collected by DeRosa. He advised that if the money did not go directly to Hacking Brothers it would certainly be delivered to Joe Eto.

With reference to Joe Eto, he advised that his individual is closely associated with on George Colucci, who operates a large tobacco company in the City of Chicago. He advised that Colucci and "Joe the Jap" also operated a front organization which supplied cigarette vending machines to various customers in the City of Chicago. Colucci supplied the cigarettes from his warehouse for the machines and also provided a service for repair of the machines. He advised that as Colucci established locations "Joe the Jap" would follow with installations of number-type gambling devices and games such as jar games, punchboards, ect. He advised here again both of these individuals were closely associated with Buccieri and Buccieri would act as "overseer" of this operation as well as the gambling operation.

In conversation with Buccieri he advised that the name of Sam Giancana was held in deep reverence by Buccieri and his associates indicating that Buccieri had a certain area which he advised to the best of his knowledge was from 22nd Street and Madison Street and from Cicero Avenue to some line east and close to the downtown area of Chicago. He advised he did not know how far east this would go. He advised that Buccieri was in charge of operations in this area and that he would report to Sam Giancana. With reference to Joe Eto, he advised that Eto has shown him several two-story building which Eto now either owns or controls. Eto explained how he came in possession of these buildings as follows:

He advised that one Carlo Morrelli, the brother of "Blackie" Morrelli, borrowed about $3,000 of "juice" money from Hacking Brothers arranged by Buccieri and Joe Eto; the building construction loans were also made to Morrelli at high rates of interest. Carlo Morrelli was also a gambler and became deeply in debt to the Buccieri operation. In order to secure these debts, the three building involved were turned over to Joe Eto. Whether or not they were turned over on paper or not he did not know, however, Eto has told Jim that the building are his. He advised that Carlo Morrelli still lives in one of the buildings and advised that they are located on the northeast corner of Chicago and Central Park Avenue. He advised that they are about two doors east of Central Park on Chicago Avenue and are adjoining building which are white brick. He further advised that "Blackie" Morrelli presently runs a gambling joint primarily designed for card playing for the Buccieri outfit located next to the Stoplight Lounge on the corner of Cicero Avenue and Roosevelt Road.

Another individual closely associates with Fifi Buccieri's organization is an individual known as a white, male, 35 years old. He advised Gizzi's brother is a big gambler and bookmaker, particularly in baseball and basketball and other sports events.

He advised Gizzi's brother is a "big man" in bookmaking circles in Chicago and has wide hoodlum connections. He advised that Joe Gizzi by virtue of the job he has with the freight company must represent some hoodlum interest in the freight company itself. He advised that Gizzi himself is a big bettor betting thousands on sporting events and has influence at the Maywood Race Track and is widely known to bookmakers and "Outfit" people at this race track. Gizzi hangs out at Russell's, which is a restaurant located in the vicinity of Thatcher Avenue and North Avenue.

He advised that the bondsman Eddie Morris is also closely associated with Fifi Buccieri. Morris has an individual working for him nicknamed "Schibble Nose Pocky," who is another associate of Jeff Manno, and an individual closely associated with Fifi Buccieri. He advised that "Schibble Nose Rocky" is also a bookmaker at Maywood Race Track and has made considerable sums of money in this activity since Maywood has opened this season.

He advised that a hanger-on, an individual who undoubtedly supplies information to the Buccieri organization, is one Frank Gentile, a Chicago Policeman, who has been associated with hoodlums for years. He advised that Buccieri told himself that Gentile years ago provided good service in connection with the police department's investigation of gangland slayings and for his leaking information received large sums of money from the Outfit. He gambles frequently with Buccieri, however, has lost considerable sums of money and Buccieri and his associates now treat Gentile as a "bum." On one instance that he recalls "Spotty" took Gentile's gun away from him and fired a bullet into the floor at Frank Parker's Restaurant between Gentile's feet just to show him who was boss.

He advised that another individual associated with the Buccieri organization is one Joe "Spa" Spadavecchio. He advised that Spadavecchio is by far the weakest member of the Buccieri group and is an individual who is both nervous and afraid of being deeply involved in hoodlum operations.

He advised another hangout of the Buccieri group is the Pink Clock and the card playing establishment east of the Stop Light Lounge. He advised that with respect to the large bookmaking operation that is overseen by Don Angeline, Danny Leonardi and Carlo (LNU) are individuals who actually make book and run the place. They are immediately supervised by "Big John," who is an enforcer for the Buccieri group and gives Danny Leonardi and Carlo their orders. He advised that "Spotty" Mann is simply a runner for this group, collecting bets and making payoffs, however, he is a flunky and not an important member of the organization.

He advised that with respect to the Fifi Buccieri organization from what he has gathered from conversations with Buccieri and others in the group, it is set up in the following manner:

Buccieri, of course, reports directly to Sam Giancana. Directly beneath Buccieri is an individual named "Big Frank" (LNU), an Italian individual. He advised that this is a very powerful man and exerts influence for Buccieri with particular respect to the loan companies. "Big Frank" also has a nephew, Johnny DeBello, who hangs out at Milano's Restaurant as a juice collector. Johnny DeBello is not important particularly, however, "Big Frank" has tremendous influence in the organization. He advised that the two enforcers, who are collectors and muscle men reporting directly to Fifi Buccieri and "Big Frank", are Tony "Pineapples" Eldorado and Joe DeGaul. DeGaul (possibly Joe Ferriola) is the most trusted muscle man in the group and he has seen him inflict physical pain on other individuals and in his opinion this individual is a sadist killer, apparently enjoying the sight of individual's pain. He advised that directly beneath the tow enforcers are the workers who run the various gambling operations. These individuals are not bosses but more like sergeants and workers in the group. People that would fall into this category would be; Donald Angelini, Joe Spotaveccio, "Big John", "Spotty" Mann, Danny Leonardi and Carl (LNU). Directly beneath these individuals are the runners and individuals. Falling in this category would be individuals such as Salvatore DeRosa, Jeffo Manno, and James "Cowboy" Mirro.

280

FEDERAL BUREAU OF INVESTIGATION

REPORTING OFFICE	OFFICE OF ORIGIN	DATE	INVESTIGATIVE PERIOD
CHICAGO	CHICAGO	1962	May 25, 1962

TITLE OF CASE	REPORT MADE BY	TYPED BY
SAMUEL M. GIANCANA, aka		dkc

CHARACTER OF CASE
FBI Headquarters File number 92-3171-748 Top Hoodlum Program – Anti Racketeering. Daily Summary

You were advised during February last that MM 794 stated that Jack Cerone was discussing gangland slayings, mentioned "plants" in automobiles they utilized for these killings. Recently the Chicago PD arrested two Giancana lieutenants, Felix Alderisio and Charles Nicoletti in an automobile registered to a fictitious name and address. During search of automobile by detectives several days later, elaborately concealed compartments were discovered in the auto, controlled by switches under the dash. One compartment, located behind the front seat, was large enough for a rifle or shotgun. Another compartment was located hidden under the radio speaker. It is noted that ten gangland slaying have occurred in Chicago immediately prior to and after the arrest of the above two, who appeared in municipal court, Chicago, yesterday, and were discharged by reason of "insufficient evidence." They were charges with disorderly conduct and driving a car with fictitious license and registration.

FEDERAL BUREAU OF INVESTIGATION

REPORTING OFFICE	OFFICE OF ORIGIN	DATE	INVESTIGATIVE PERIOD
CHICAGO	CHICAGO	1961	May 29, 1962

TITLE OF CASE	REPORT MADE BY	TYPED BY
SAMUEL M. GIANCANA, aka		dkc

CHARACTER OF CASE
FBI Headquarters File number 92-3171-738 Top Hoodlum Program – Anti Racketeering. Daily Summary

Chicago informant advised that Carmen Fanelli, owner of the Armory Lounge, died on May 22, 1962 of lung cancer, and was buried at Queen of Heaven Cemetery in Hillside on May 26, 1962. Informant states that among those at the wake preceding the funeral were Anthony Accardo and Jack Cerone, however, did not observe Giancana. Informant states that practically every gangland figure from Chicago's west side was in attendance at wake. Giancana advised at Armory Lounge on May 22, overseeing remodeling work being done.

FEDERAL BUREAU OF INVESTIGATION

REPORTING OFFICE	OFFICE OF ORIGIN	DATE	INVESTIGATIVE PERIOD
CHICAGO	CHICAGO	1962	June 12, 1962

TITLE OF CASE	REPORT MADE BY	TYPED BY
		dkc
SAMUEL M. GIANCANA, aka	CHARACTER OF CASE	
	FBI Headquarters File number 92-3171 Top Hoodlum Program – Anti Racketeering. Daily Summary	

Giancana observed in Forest Park, IL, three blocks from the Armory Lounge, driving a 1962 Pontiac Tempest. He wandered up and down the street a few times until he drove by a 1962 Pontiac which was obviously in the process of meeting with Giancana. Giancana apparently didn't like circumstances of the meeting, and gave the wave off to the individual awaiting him, who in turn spead off at a high rate of speed. It was ascertained that it was Jack Cerone driving the other automobile.

FEDERAL BUREAU OF INVESTIGATION

REPORTING OFFICE	OFFICE OF ORIGIN	DATE	INVESTIGATIVE PERIOD
CHICAGO	CHICAGO	1962	June 16, 1962

TITLE OF CASE	REPORT MADE BY	TYPED BY
		dkc
SAMUEL M. GIANCANA, aka	CHARACTER OF CASE	
	FBI Headquarters File number 92-3171-769 Top Hoodlum Program – Anti Racketeering. Daily Summary	

Giancana observed at Armory Lounge, shortly thereafter, Joseph Cortino, Chief of Police, Forest Park, appeared and went inside. According to informant, only two persons there were Giancana and Cortino. Informant advised he spoke with Dominic Blasi who advised that the new license for the Armory Lounge is in the name of Carmen Fanelli's widow.

FEDERAL BUREAU OF INVESTIGATION

REPORTING OFFICE	OFFICE OF ORIGIN	DATE	INVESTIGATIVE PERIOD
CHICAGO	CHICAGO	1962	July 3, 1962

TITLE OF CASE	REPORT MADE BY	TYPED BY
SAMUEL M. GIANCANA, aka		dkc

	CHARACTER OF CASE
	FBI Headquarters File Number 92-3171-789 Top Hoodlum Program – Anti Racketeering. Daily Summary

Confidential source, Chicago, advised recently that Eernest "Rocky" Infelice, together with Americo DiPietro and James Torello had recently purchased Pedicone's Restaurant, Lyons, IL., and utilized the basement office there for meetings. Access available there in through this source, noting that Pericone's is undergoing remodeling.

FEDERAL BUREAU OF INVESTIGATION

REPORTING OFFICE	OFFICE OF ORIGIN	DATE	INVESTIGATIVE PERIOD
CHICAGO	CHICAGO	1962	July 12, 1962

TITLE OF CASE	REPORT MADE BY	TYPED BY
SAMUEL M. GIANCANA, aka		dkc

	CHARACTER OF CASE
	FBI Headquarters File Number 92-3171-811 Top Hoodlum Program – Anti Racketeering. Daily Summary

Re Armory Lounge and re installation of CG 6486-C. Entry made instant, one unit installed, not yet operative due to mechanical problems not present at time of original installation. Remodeling process as site changed telephone wiring system. Original meeting room now a storage room containing linens, meat locker, deep freeze, ect. Survey indicates Giancana probably will meet in rear of dining room where large booth is set up with telephone extensions. Bug coverage suitable for this spot and rear storage room.

FEDERAL BUREAU OF INVESTIGATION

REPORTING OFFICE	OFFICE OF ORIGIN	DATE	INVESTIGATIVE PERIOD	
CHICAGO	CHICAGO	1962	July 25, 1962	
TITLE OF CASE		REPORT MADE BY		TYPED BY
				dkc
SAMUEL M. GIANCANA, aka		CHARACTER OF CASE FBI Headquarters File Number 92-3171 Top Hoodlum Program – Anti Racketeering. Daily Summary		

Examination of physical premises reflects that during major repairs to premises three new telephones drops were brought from the pole to the side of the building. These drops do not enter the building through the old system. New equipment is placed on exterior wall on the outside of the premises and bypasses old main frame. In view of the known weakness in the Oak Park branch of the telephone company, early reentry is scheduled whereby the installation can be brought to the external wires from within.

FEDERAL BUREAU OF INVESTIGATION

REPORTING OFFICE	OFFICE OF ORIGIN	DATE	INVESTIGATIVE PERIOD	
CHICAGO	CHICAGO	1962	July 13, 1962.	
TITLE OF CASE		REPORT MADE BY		TYPED BY
		Ralph Hill Jr.		dkc
SAMUEL M. GIANCANA, aka		CHARACTER OF CASE FBI Headquarters File number 92-3171-799 Top Hoodlum Program – Anti Racketeering.		

Miscellaneous

CG T-51 advised that through the last several years has had many female associates. He appears to prefer as girl friends those individuals who are in the entertainment field. Among them are the following known by the informant to have been associated with Giancana:

Janice Harper, Los Angeles, California.
Honetmelon, A singer for Chicago whose true name is not known.
Keeley Smith, Former wife of Louis Prima, singing star.
Phyllis McGiure, Member of the McGuire Sisters singing team.
Hazel Sweazy, Of Forest Park.
Vickie LaMotta, Ex-wife of former middleweight champion Jake LaMotta.

Among Giancana's closest male associates, according to CG -51 are the following:

John Matassa
Dominic Blasi
John Formusa
Paul "Skinny" D'Amato

Chicago T-1 advised on May 20, 1962, that he had interviewed Manny Skar recently about the operation of the Sahara Motel North, at which time Skar advised that he was the sole owner and operator of the motel. He denied the information that he had accepted a cent of hoodlum money for the motel, but declined to furnish his source of financing, which he stated came to a total cost of 10.4 million dollars. He denied to the informant that he had ever met Sam Giancana and that he would take a lie detector test on that fact. He admitted being acquainted with Marshall Caifano; however, stated that this was strictly a social acquaintanceship.

It is noted that Manny Skar appeared on a pre-taped television interview on Channel 7, WBKB, Chicago, on the occasion of the opening of the Sahara Inn North, June 6, 1962. During this appearance, Skar read a prepared statement in which he admitted past mistakes and denied being associate with the hoodlum element, stating that the Sahara Inn was his operation and his alone.

John Magill, Yacht Broker, advised that Manny Skar owns a 55 foot 1962 Chris Craft motor cruiser in Buraham Harbor. He advised that the boat is named "Sahara" and is tied up in a slip around number 50. Magill advised that the boat is worth at least $80,000.

Chicago T-3 advised that he had learned that Sam Giancana, William Daddono, Sam Battaglia, Gus Alex, known to the informant as "Slim," were heavily invested in the Sahara Inn North.

FEDERAL BUREAU OF INVESTIGATION

REPORTING OFFICE	OFFICE OF ORIGIN	DATE	INVESTIGATIVE PERIOD
CHICAGO	CHICAGO	1962	July 31, 1962

TITLE OF CASE	REPORT MADE BY	TYPED BY
		dkc
SAMUEL M. GIANCANA, aka	**CHARACTER OF CASE** FBI Headquarters File Number 92-3171 Top Hoodlum Program – Anti Racketeering. Daily Summary	

About Armory Lounge and reactivation of CG 6486-C. Re-entry made at location July 27, last, in further attempt to establish location of terminal leads. Tentatively established that terminal wires located under ceiling. Further investigation and re-entry necessary to establish positively the location of these wires in order that source may be reactivated.

FEDERAL BUREAU OF INVESTIGATION

REPORTING OFFICE	OFFICE OF ORIGIN	DATE	INVESTIGATIVE PERIOD
CHICAGO	CHICAGO	1962	August 10, 1962

TITLE OF CASE	REPORT MADE BY	TYPED BY
		dkc
SAMUEL M. GIANCANA, aka	**CHARACTER OF CASE**	
	FBI Headquarters File Number 92-3171-835 Top Hoodlum Program – Anti Racketeering. Daily Summary	

CG informant advised that a party was held at the Sahara Inn North, Manny Skar's establishment, in honor of Keely Smith, one time paramour of Giancana's, who was appearing at Sahara Night clubs. Among those in attendance were John Matassa, Felix Alderisio, Marshall Caifano, Frank "Skippy" Cerone, Skar, Frank Buccieri and others.

According to informant, Giancana was scheduled to appear either at the party or later at Pepe's club located near the Sahara. In connection with the Sahara, informant advised that Skippy Cerone, who resides in Schiller Park, location of Sahara, has much to say as to operation of this establishment, and is liaison with Schiller Park authorities. Bureau will noted that Cerone is cousin of Jack Cerone and was observed in Miami Beach last winter with other Chicago hit men.

FEDERAL BUREAU OF INVESTIGATION

REPORTING OFFICE	OFFICE OF ORIGIN	DATE	INVESTIGATIVE PERIOD
CHICAGO	CHICAGO	1962	August 15, 1962

TITLE OF CASE	REPORT MADE BY	TYPED BY
		dkc
SAMUEL M. GIANCANA, aka	**CHARACTER OF CASE**	
	FBI Headquarters File Number 92-3171-856 Top Hoodlum Program – Anti Racketeering. Daily Summary	

Giancana with numerous individuals at Armory Lounge yesterday. Informant (protected identity) advised that he met with Giancana during evening of August 12, last, stated strictly social meeting, however, admitted being acquainted with Giancana. According to source, fighter Sonny Liston met with Giancana on two occasions last winter regarding Giancana intervening to have the Liston-Patterson fight take place.

FEDERAL BUREAU OF INVESTIGATION

REPORTING OFFICE	OFFICE OF ORIGIN	DATE	INVESTIGATIVE PERIOD
CHICAGO	CHICAGO	1962	August 21, 1962

TITLE OF CASE	REPORT MADE BY	TYPED BY
		dkc
SAMUEL M. GIANCANA, aka	**CHARACTER OF CASE** FBI Headquarters File Number 92-3171 Top Hoodlum Program – Anti Racketeering. Daily Summary	

Informant reports that Pat Marcy, Alderman John D'Arco's secretary for the First Ward of Chicago, had ordered practically all burlesque places in the First Ward closed in order that the convention traffic which normally haunts these places will be diverted to the new glitter gulch section of Chicago, which includes the Sahara Inn and an establishment named "Pepe's", near the Sahara. In support of this, it is noted that "Pepe's" features top flight entertainment and is managed by Gus Alex's associate, Steve DeCosta. It is owned by one Frank Panteleo, associate of Giancana and William Daddano. Informants report that Frank Sinatra has plans for the construction of a new supper club directly across the street from the Sahara, and expects to have gambling therein. Noted that all these establishments are in Schiller Park, IL, an area which contains a village administration friendly to the interest of Chicago hoodlums.

FEDERAL BUREAU OF INVESTIGATION

REPORTING OFFICE	OFFICE OF ORIGIN	DATE	INVESTIGATIVE PERIOD
CHICAGO	CHICAGO	1962	September 5, 1962

TITLE OF CASE	REPORT MADE BY	TYPED BY
		dkc
SAMUEL M. GIANCANA, aka	**CHARACTER OF CASE** FBI Headquarters File Number 92-3171-860 Top Hoodlum Program – Anti Racketeering. Daily Summary	

CG 6486-C advised over Labor Day weekend of the presence of several of Chicago's better known hoodlums, including Giancana, Jack Cerone, Dominic Blasi, John Matassa, Felix Alderisio, and others not identified. One of the unknowns, who appeared during the early evening of September 1, is a politician who was ordered at the time, out of politics for an unknown reason. Giancana held a general bull session with these individuals, however, nothing of significance was noted, except that Giancana was highly irritated over some situation, appeared to be generally dissatisfied.

FEDERAL BUREAU OF INVESTIGATION

REPORTING OFFICE	OFFICE OF ORIGIN	DATE	INVESTIGATIVE PERIOD
CHICAGO	CHICAGO	1962	September 14, 1962

TITLE OF CASE	REPORT MADE BY	TYPED BY
		dkc
SAMUEL M. GIANCANA, aka	**CHARACTER OF CASE** FBI Headquarters File Number 92-3171-868 Top Hoodlum Program – Anti Racketeering. Daily Summary	

CG 6486-C advised that Leslie Kruse briefly discussed matters with Dominic Blasi, the nature unknown; however, Les was instructed to have Frank Buccieri "get a hold of the little guy out west." Later Fifi Buccieri entered into discussion with an unknown, mentioned "he'll take the Puerto Ricans; I'll take the rest, give everything else to Ross." Giancana reported to be back in town from seeing Phyllis McGuire in Las Vegas.

FEDERAL BUREAU OF INVESTIGATION

REPORTING OFFICE	OFFICE OF ORIGIN	DATE	INVESTIGATIVE PERIOD
CHICAGO	CHICAGO	1962	September 19, 1962

TITLE OF CASE	REPORT MADE BY	TYPED BY
		dkc
SAMUEL M. GIANCANA, aka	**CHARACTER OF CASE** FBI Headquarters File Number 92-3171-873 Top Hoodlum Program – Anti Racketeering. Daily Summary	

Chicago informant advised that Giancana observed entering Armory Lounge with Charles English and Sam English. Later that day Giancana held one conference with James Celano, the tailor and occupant of premises under control of CG 6343-C, conferred with Giancana concerning a favor he desired from Giancana. During conversation, Celano described his interview by FBI agents and said that he threw the agents out of his office. Giancana was not impressed.

FEDERAL BUREAU OF INVESTIGATION

REPORTING OFFICE	OFFICE OF ORIGIN	DATE	INVESTIGATIVE PERIOD	
CHICAGO	CHICAGO	1962	September 21, 1962	

TITLE OF CASE	REPORT MADE BY	TYPED BY
		dkc
SAMUEL M. GIANCANA, aka	**CHARACTER OF CASE** FBI Headquarters File Number 92-3171-882 Top Hoodlum Program – Anti Racketeering. Daily Summary	

Norman Glubock advised he received an anonymous tip that a large party of hoodlums would be at the Sahara Inn Motel during the night of September 21, 1962. Noted that Frank Sinatra and Dean Martin are due in town over weekend, and scheduled to stay at Sahara Inn, purpose to see heavyweight fight. CG informant advised that Manny Skar, owner of the Sahara, is having anniversary celebration that evening.

CG 6286-C revealed that preparations being made for some sort of affair on 9/22. No details known. Source also revealed presence of Fifi Buccieri and possibly Miami hoodlum Dave Yaras, discussing some matter involving checks.

FEDERAL BUREAU OF INVESTIGATION

REPORTING OFFICE	OFFICE OF ORIGIN	DATE	INVESTIGATIVE PERIOD	
CHICAGO	CHICAGO	1962	October 18, 1962	

TITLE OF CASE	REPORT MADE BY	TYPED BY
		dkc
SAMUEL M. GIANCANA, aka	**CHARACTER OF CASE** FBI Headquarters File Number 92-3171-908 Top Hoodlum Program – Anti Racketeering. Daily Summary	

CG informant advised he accompanied Sam English to the Sahara Inn Motel on 10/16. When English and informant called upon Manny Skar, some kind of deal was struck.

FEDERAL BUREAU OF INVESTIGATION

REPORTING OFFICE	OFFICE OF ORIGIN	DATE	INVESTIGATIVE PERIOD	
CHICAGO	CHICAGO	1962	October 27, 1962	
TITLE OF CASE		REPORT MADE BY		TYPED BY
				dkc
SAMUEL M. GIANCANA, aka		CHARACTER OF CASE		
		FBI Headquarters File Number 92-3171-916 Top Hoodlum Program – Anti Racketeering. Daily Summary		

CG 6486-C advised that John D'Arco was scheduled to met with Sam Giancana on October 25, 1962. CG 6576-C advised on October 25 last that D'Arco, Chicago First Ward Alderman, reported briefly on results of his meeting with Giancana, to Pat Marcy, secretary to First Ward Alderman. D'Arco confirmed his suspicions that Giancana has secretly passed word on to his organization to quietly go out for Richard Ogilvie in the forth coming election for Cook County Sheriff, in opposition to Roswell Spencer. D'Arco appeared to be upset over this situation. Marcy stated he had been advised by Tony Mack (Anthony DeMonte, Chicago hoodlum) that he, Mack, is pushing for the election of Ogilvie.

FEDERAL BUREAU OF INVESTIGATION

REPORTING OFFICE	OFFICE OF ORIGIN	DATE	INVESTIGATIVE PERIOD	
CHICAGO	CHICAGO	1962	November 9, 1962	
TITLE OF CASE		REPORT MADE BY		TYPED BY
				dkc
SAMUEL M. GIANCANA, aka		CHARACTER OF CASE		
		FBI Headquarters File Number 92-3171-918 Top Hoodlum Program – Anti Racketeering. Daily Summary		

CG 6486-C has reported on the presence of Giancana in the vicinity of the source daily since 11/2, last. Accompanying Giancana has been a group known to be Charles English, John Matassa, Dominic Blasi, Roy (LNU) and Tarquin Simonelli. Giancana appears to be subtly engaged in making final arrangements for opening of Villa Venice club instant. Only break in this pattern was election eve, when group concentrated on recent national election. This source advised that John D'Arco had promised 8,500 votes to be delivered from First Ward for Elmer Conti, Republican candidate for County Treasured. Noted that John D'Arco, according to 6576-C advised that he had orders to deliver votes on behalf of Conti. Also noted that First Ward only delivered 5,100 votes on behalf of Conti.

New York informant advised this date that in conversation with Lenny Gaines, a writer for singer Eddie Fisher, Gaines advised him that Gaines, Frank Sinatra, Fisher and Sam Giancana recently flew from Los Angeles to Reno en route to Lake Tahoe, Nevada, in Sinatra's private plane. Giancana was presented to Gaines as Sam Mooney and Gaines was further advised that Mooney was "The Doctor." During the flight Sinatra and Giancana sat together and conversed privately, excluding the rest of the group.

Fisher was to appear at the Desert Inn commencing November 5, 1962 for an engagement paying $100,000 a week. Approximately two weeks ago, Frank Sinatra telephonically contacted Fisher and advised him that he had "Done Fisher a big favor," in that Sinatra had cancelled his Desert Inn appearance and arranged for him to appear in a Chicago nightclub, commencing November 8, 1962 at $15,000 a week. Gaines indicated that this arrangement was made at the request of Giancana and that Fisher is extremely upset, but is fulfilling engagement.

FEDERAL BUREAU OF INVESTIGATION

REPORTING OFFICE	OFFICE OF ORIGIN	DATE	INVESTIGATIVE PERIOD
CHICAGO	CHICAGO	1962	November 23, 1962

TITLE OF CASE	REPORT MADE BY	TYPED BY
		dkc
SAMUEL M. GIANCANA, aka	CHARACTER OF CASE	
	FBI Headquarters File Number 92-3171-928 Top Hoodlum Program – Anti Racketeering. Daily Summary	

CG 6576-C advised November 21 last that John D'Arco is about to be deposed from his position on orders from Anthony Accardo, backed up by Giancana. Pat Marcy assured D'Arco that Gus Alex will be able to change Giancana's order about D'Arco, and that Gus Alex personally assured Marcy that he is working on this situation 24 hours per day. This fact explains presence of Alex, Frank Ferraro and Hy Godfrey in vicinity of CG 6486-C on November 20, last. They were undoubtedly attempting to locate Giancana for a conference about D'Arco. Alex advised Marcy that he has been unsuccessful to date in locating Giancana, who is expected back in Chicago. D'Arco complained that he cannot rest until Giancana comes back.

FEDERAL BUREAU OF INVESTIGATION

REPORTING OFFICE	OFFICE OF ORIGIN	DATE	INVESTIGATIVE PERIOD	
CHICAGO	CHICAGO	1962	November 28, 1962	
TITLE OF CASE		REPORT MADE BY		TYPED BY
				dkc
SAMUEL M. GIANCANA, aka		CHARACTER OF CASE		
		FBI Headquarters File Number 92-3171-929 Top Hoodlum Program – Anti Racketeering. Daily Summary		

CG 6576-C advised that recently that Giancana, unhappy over recent developments, is purging some of his controlled wards, namely, the First and 25 Ward under Vito Marzullo and John D'Arco. Negotiation now going on between Giancana and Gus Alex to countermand this order, with reference to D'Arco. D'Arco suggested to Pat Marcy that he is going to run for reelection regardless, Marcy told him if he does that, he will "get hit", and the same will happen to Marzullo. Giancana returned to Chicago area November 21, last, made contact at Armory Lounge, appeared at Villa Venice 11/6 last at Frank Sinatra opening of Villa Venice. Most of Giancana organization was also present there.

FEDERAL BUREAU OF INVESTIGATION

REPORTING OFFICE	OFFICE OF ORIGIN	DATE	INVESTIGATIVE PERIOD	
CHICAGO	CHICAGO	1962	December 1, 1962	
TITLE OF CASE		REPORT MADE BY		TYPED BY
				dkc
SAMUEL M. GIANCANA, aka		CHARACTER OF CASE		
		FBI Headquarters File Number 92-3171-944 Top Hoodlum Program – Anti Racketeering. Daily Summery		

CG 6576-C advised November 29 last that John D'Arco and Buddy Jacobson were scheduled to meet with unknown. In view of past information from sources that Giancana has been meeting at Czech Lodge in North Riverside, physical surveillance instituted there for purpose of, if Giancana located, providing sufficient harassment to direct him to places where coverage can be afforded. Giancana's auto observed in parking lot at Czech Lodge. Agents proceeded inside, and after considerable searching of private rooms for dinners, located Giancana in heavy conference with D'Arco. Jacobson was standing guard out side. From previous information furnished by source, D'Arco was there to plead his case to Giancana to remain as Alderman of the First Ward.

Agent brushed past Jacobson and approached Giancana and D'Arco. Greeted Giancana with "Hi Moe" and extended handshake to D'Arco with greeting, "Hello John." Noted that both Giancana and D'Arco known personally to agent. Agent then left immediate room. Giancana left approximately 20 minutes later while agents discussion with Jacobson. After departure of Giancana, agents attempted to talk to D'Arco. D'Arco abusive and obscene and appeared to be greatly upset.

D'Arco refused to admit that he knew agent who has interviewed him several times. It became apparent that D'Arco had lied to Giancana and denied knowing agent possibly for reason that he had not advised Giancana of previous contacts with agent. From info obtained from other source that date, discovery of Giancana and D'Arco by FBI is of great concern.

Giancana, Accardo and Ricca held conference today at Armory Lounge at which time Giancana advised he instructed D'Arco to meet with agents to determine extent of their knowledge of situation. He is extremely upset that not only did D'Arco disobey but was instead abusive of agents. Accardo likewise upset under theory that agents will now take every avenue available to undermine D'Arco. Apparently until yesterday's discovery, D'Arco still considered to be kept as Alderman by Giancana. Due to discovery 11/29 last, Chicago group is at tremendous disadvantage, so, according to Accardo, the Government knows of meet between D'Arco and Giancana, but "we don't know how much they know." Latest plan is to fake a heart attack for D'Arco, put him in the hospital and leak word that due to illness, he is unable to continue. His successor will be one or two handpicked men, either Fred Roti or Anthony DeTolve. Main concern is Mayor Daley's response to picked candidate. Accardo complained they cannot handle Daley like they could handle former Mayor Kelly and Frank Nash. They are afraid that Daley may put in his own man.

FEDERAL BUREAU OF INVESTIGATION

REPORTING OFFICE	OFFICE OF ORIGIN	DATE	INVESTIGATIVE PERIOD
CHICAGO	CHICAGO	1962	December 3, 1962

TITLE OF CASE	REPORT MADE BY	TYPED BY
		dkc
SAMUEL M. GIANCANA, aka	**CHARACTER OF CASE**	
	FBI Headquarters File Number 62-9-9-1128 Activities of Top Hoodlum Program Airtel Summery	

CG 6486-C who reported on 11-30-1962, of a conference between Anthony Accardo, Paul DeLucia and Sam Giancana, stated the main topic of conversation for this conference concerned the First Ward of Chicago, now headed by John D'Arco, reported in the past by this source and others as a close associate of the Chicago syndicate. The conference was as follows:

Accardo: You can still make up your mind, but if you give in there, Moe.

Giancana: Sure.

Accardo: Now, if you let that business that happened out there (referring to disclosure by FBI Agents at Czech Lodge, 11-29-62), interfere and change your plans, you're leaving yourself wide open for criticism. They'll say, the (obscenity) "G" caused this and you were talking to so and so and were seen, and what the hell. You can't do this Moe.

DeLucia: (adds comment, but speaks in broken English).

Accardo:	And that (obscenity) Gussie (Gus Alex). What is he so interested in all of a sudden? What's his play in this?
Giancana:	I don't know, all of a sudden, he puts the bug in my ear.
Accardo:	(obscenity).
DeLucia:	Don't let nobody tell you what to do.
Giancana:	I'm not.
Accardo:	And you can't be giving these guys (FBI) abuse. You got to talk to them. That (obscenity) Louie, he won't even shake hands with the guys, not that I give a (obscenity). That's your story, Moe..you can ask him if you want to, if he wants to be a senator. I'm almost sure that with the Senator ship he gets that pension. How many years did he put in the Senate? Two? Two terms. The Senator ship you can give him. What he loses in one place he can pick up in another place. There's a pension there too. It didn't make any difference. There's got to be so many days before a special election, of course, they got to have time to make a petition. For the Senator ship. The primary is in February.
Giancana:	No, it's all over, last month.
Accardo:	I'm speaking of the Special. The primary is in February for the Mayor and Alderman. Election is in April. Now if there's anything that you want to do, if you want to change your plans, give us a little notice, and we'll give it a going over. Listen, they know how we feel. You can use us for the hatchet men.

CG 6576-C has been reporting for several days that John D'Arco is being deposed from his position as alderman by Giancana, et al and D'Arco and his associates in the First Ward are extremely upset by this situation and have been attempting to have the decision reversed. One of the prime movers behind D'Arco in this move is Gus Alex. Based upon information FBI Agents conducted surveillance at the Czech Lodge, North Riverside, and uncovered a meeting between D'Arco and Giancana in a private alcove of the restaurant.

Accardo begins the conference by insisting that Giancana maintain his position in removing D'Arco from the First Ward in spite of the surveillance referred to. It is suggested that D'Arco be given a State Senator's job which was the position he held prior to becoming Alderman.

The conversation continues as follows:

DeLucia:	How did the "G" find out?
Accardo:	It had to be somebody down there, in that Ward. They tailed him to meet, you understand? They know he's in trouble. Who told them he's in trouble? Who told them that he's in trouble? How can they help? He'd have to tell something on us, so they pinch us, and get us out of the way, and then they got a free play. Moe, here's another thing. When you were checking these people, did you?
Giancana:	Oh, yeah.

DeLucia: (can't decipher)

Giancana: Well, they told Buddy (Jacobson), they're checking on me.

Accardo: They know, they got to know.

Giancana: Well, they ain't got no love for me.

Accardo: Well, you wouldn't have any love either, if you want to know. Anyplace he
            can ram it into us, he's gona ram it. (*Don't know whether they are refer-
            ring to FBI or D'Arco. As far as Chicago Agents are concerned, he's right*).

Giancana: Well, they said, he's in trouble, they want to help, and this and that.

Accardo: Well, when that (obscenity) told the FBI that they had no business there
            and everything else, and if anybody did it, it was Rodi. (Whispers)
            well the other guy, what they been doing, they can smooth
            over. Listen, Moe, we're not here to try to steer you wrong. Follow
            through with your plan. Tell your story tomorrow. Listen, (obsceni-
            ty) the G. We're going through with our plan. Don't back up Moe, don't back
            up. What ever them guys has got to come out, that's why they're begging
            for time. So whatever they got hid, they can cover it up, that's my opinion.

Giancana: No, no.

Accardo: Well, listen, I may not be right. I'm, just speculating out loud.

DeLucia: Take for example, the juice.

Accardo: Just that alone is enough. That's a hell of an operation.

DeLucia: Remember once before, when we first started?..... They went to Esposito and
            said, you're in trouble, we'll help you. (Whispers). (*Referring to Frank Es-
            posito, slated to be executed in February of 1962 in Florida. Esposito
            is another First Ward standby and has offices in the same building as
            D'Arco*).

Accardo: What do you think of this plan?

Giancana: That's all right.

Accardo: He won't go to nobody, Moe, listen, if you want to put the kid in position,
            that's all right, but ..it would be a disturbance, you understand? I'll find
            out about the senator ship. This next election. The one guy ain't gonna
            help. Ask him that question. Give the guy a senator ship, he's like
            a (obscenity) bump on a log there, anyway. Its Republican dominated.
            When Kelly and them guys were there the Senate was always
            Republican, but they had it locked up. We'll make room for him.
            I think the other kid has more seniority rights than
            that Flando (ph) kid, not that I want to knock him out of the box..
            he can't be nothing on any committee, he can only be a member. The
            chairman is what counts. I think, personally, you're starting the kid off
            too high. This is a pretty big jump. Then that Roti,
            if there was anybody entitled to seniority rights, it would

be him. He was a senator, then we took him out. We took him
out with Libonati, when they redistricted. There was two senators, and we
had to lose one, so we knocker him out of the box, and put
Libonati there. I think watch-a-min-call-it is a good man.

DeLucia: Remember when we.. Kelly?.......them was the days.

Accardo: You're going back a ways. Listen, you're put in the same position as we
were when we put in for Committeeman, First Ward, you remember, Kelly
sent word that he did not want Freddy Morelli. Jake (Guzik) sent back word
he said, you tell that big Irish (obscenity) that we are
gonna put Freddy Morelli is and we are gonna elect him and if he
don't like it, tell him to get somebody else to run against him and
we'll beat the (obscenity) out of him. That's when they sent Duffy
into the First Ward, remember? Started hosing us.
But then we got to Duffy. But then we didn't have no Nash. If
we had a Nash, he'd listen to us. We can't go to the Mayor.

DeLucia: Somebody is a stool pigeon.

Accardo: If you make your move, you start, and ..we shouldn't have twenty.

Giancana: Now wait a minute (whispers)..

Accardo: This guy starts talking about the guy. Listen, if we back up now, we back
up for the Government. And we never back up to the Government.

Giancana: (obscenity) (obscenity) (obscenity)

DeLucia: Should we follow through?

Accardo: Follow through with what?

DeLucia: With, uh-about this.

Accardo: But you don't, he's not gonna say, he's gonna follow through on the original program, of course, you want two see what they got to say.

DeLucia: Well, what you gonna say ..he's a (obscenity) stool pigeon.

Accardo: Well, you can't say that. You don't know. The question is, how do they know
about this? The telephone call didn't tell them anything about this troble.

DeLucia: Here's what we do. We leak something out, and see what they do.

Accardo: That's a good way to do it.

DeLucia: I know it'll get out.

Accardo: Then if we get harpooned again, they'll say, well, you said you had (obscenity) for the guy.

DeLucia: How did they find out? He goes out, he goes here and there, he talks to
this guy and that guy, and who knows who says what? So plant something.

Accardo:	That's good. Find out about this election .. He asked last night if I wanted to come downtown. He called me this morning. He wanted to tell me the story.
Giancana:	When did he do this?
Accardo:	After you got through with them.
Giancana:	Last Night?
Accardo:	He said, I got to see you. The G has got a pot of gold on them, but the question is where? Where? Where? Let's take the whole circle. You got Louie (Briatta), you got Frank (Esposito), you got Joe Laino, you got Pat (Marcy), Granata, you got ..
DeLucia:	It's one of them, no question about it.
Accardo:	You don't know where it's leaking from. The original place where you can assume where it's leaking is but where was it carried on from there? The conversation. After it was picked up by them people, so much to our misfortune, the meet was made to order for them.
Giancana:	That (obscenity) John (D'Arco), the guy walks in to our room and looks. That Roemer. He spots us. He says, hello Moe, hi John and he walks away. John then says, who was he? I said, don't you know? That's Roemer. He says, oh my god, no, no, I didn't know. Then we move out of there, into the other room and who the (obscenity) walks in but that (obscenity) Hill. John and I sit at the round table. So we sit there for a while and before I leave, I say, talk to them. So I leave.
Accardo:	We don't pay attention ..that's what I told you.
Giancana:	Well, he gives them this and that, and uh.
Accardo:	Before this happened, we could say, (obscenity), the G. Let them conjure. We're talking here and talking there, you understand? But now .. now you got to try to pacify them when they talk to you. Don't call them dirty words or anything. Don't pay attention. Just walk away from them. Let's pay attention. Just walk away from them. Let them talk. You guys, hollering go (obscenity) and this and that. Them poor (obscenity) they're just like us, they got a job to do. We know what to do and we do it.
Giancana:	I know.
Accardo:	Now the worst story to me was Frank's story. Being out with a whore, that redhead broad, in the (obscenity) room all day, and on the boat, so ..so when his wife got that paper, it was agonizing that much more. You wonder who was wrong in the fight between the two. The husband and the wife. Know what I mean? ..(talking low)....he was telling me hasn't got a dime. So who's fault is it he hasn't got a dime? (back to D'Arco) at the same time, then you hurt yourself if you back up. It's worst of all if you back up. If there's anything you want us to add, if you think of anything, we'll be playing gin tonight. All right Moe?
Giancana:	Yeah.

297

Accardo: There's something there, in that Ward, that they want to cover up that they don't have time to do right now. That's in my mind. I'm just thinking out loud. That's more important. Well, this is too bad. That thing yester- day completely (obscenity) the whole deal. Now, that other (obscen ity), that Louie Briatta, he's got plans now for a big house, in Lincoln Towers, in Lincolnwood or Skokie, for what he wants, it has to be over a hundred thousand.
And he's spending money, where is his (obscenity) money coming from? He's not making that much. (pause) ... listen, Moe, we aren't here to try to twist your mind. We're just giving you what is practical. Practi- cal advice, that's all. We're not here to try to distort you.
Just remember, you can't back up. Even by backing up, you make us look bad on top of it. Cause if anybody was to get the benefits of it, we should have got those benefits. But with what they know, and with what we know, the G was there and nobody else. Now you're getting frightened. Don't back up.
You understand what I'm trying to convey? That other (obscenity) yesterday morning. I can get more out of him by just listening. He'll come over and sit down, and have coffee, and I'll say, what's new, ..what's new downtown. But the point is, he's now calling him a (obscenity). Before, he wasn't. Well, Moe, if you accidentally change your mind, please give us a warning, will you?

Giancana: Yeah, I will.

Accardo: So we get caught flat footed. You tell them, how do you fellas sum up the situation? See what they say. It's more important to see that they got to say, not what we got to say. We already said what we got to say they may say, keep him. They may say that. Then you got to tell them the story. I think the first guy that opens his mouth is gonna he Hump. He'll say, (obscenity) the G.

Giancana: Oh yeah.

Accardo: Listen, anything that happens in the First Ward is gonna be you know. The reason they only give us a little blast is, it's a controlled ward, and they can't do nothing, but if you try to get outside of that (obscenity) ward, then you'll see some action. Tomorrow, try to follow through. Tell Gus, and tell John is going to the (obscenity) hospital, then when he gets back from the hospital, he can't go on. Give the credit to him. Give him the cardiogram and everything, show the heart trouble, then put it in Kup's column. So the Jew is now in there as Avougat. That (obscenity) re- ally reaches out, doesn't he? (Referring probably to Meyer Lansky, Miami, Florida).

Giancana: Sure does.

Accardo: Well, let's go home and go eat. Got to stick to my daily routine ..that (obscenity) Gussie, he was gonna make a hero out of him. He was gonna go up and punch him in the nose. Making a martyr out of him. I say, Hump is gonna say (obscenity) the G and Gussie is gonna say, let's keep him. Right? That's the way I got it figured ..we shouldn't chastise the guy. He should make his move after, that's the way I look at it. What, are you guys all getting afraid of the (obscenity) Government now? What are we gonna do, go back or go forward? If we make a move like this, we might as well let the (obscenity) Government take it all Gussie asked me, what are we meeting for? I said, I don't know what the (obscenity) it's all about. Ask him.

DeLucia: (Whispers)........

Giancana: Yeah, yeah, ...I get you.

Accardo: We'll make arrangements to get him (John D'Arco) in the hospital and set the thing up. So there won't be no embarrassment, on anybody's part. Believe me, I think, through there's more than pride involved here. More than pride. They're hiding something.

The main concern here of Accardo is the possibility of an informant being utilized among the first ward representatives of the syndicate. One of their primary aims now is to attempt to undercover this informant whom they believe is a live informant and not some type of confidential coverage.

Accardo is also convinced that John D'Arco and his associates in the First Ward are fighting this decision primarily because they are hiding something and need time to cover up whatever they are hiding.

The "pot of gold" referred to by Accardo as being in the possession of the "G" is apparently a reference to the informant. They are taking under consideration the possibility that this informant may be Louie Briatta, Frank Esposito, Joe Laino, Pat Marcy or Pete Granata.

It is interesting to note that Accardo during this conversation chastises Giancana and the other active members of the syndicate for provoking much of the intensified investigation by the FBI by the use of abusive language, arrogance and so forth toward the Bureau agents. It is Accardo's feeling that if the hoodlums merely walk away and say nothing to the agents, such provocations will not exist.

In order to save John D'Arco's "pride" in this situation, Accardo suggests that they fake a heart condition for D'Arco, put him in the hospital and leak word to Chicago newspaper columnists.

Arrangements were made during this conference for a meeting among these three plus for 12/1/62, at an unknown location. This conference was for the purpose of finalizing the disposition of the case against John D'Arco. Giancana was strongly urged by Accardo and DeLucia to maintain the stand taken by these three and not give in to the others who are apparently in favor of maintaining D'Arco in his present position as First Ward Alderman.

FEDERAL BUREAU OF INVESTIGATION

REPORTING OFFICE	OFFICE OF ORIGIN	DATE	INVESTIGATIVE PERIOD
CHICAGO	CHICAGO	1962	December 4, 1962

TITLE OF CASE	REPORT MADE BY		TYPED BY
SAMUEL M. GIANCANA, aka	Ralph Hill Jr.		dkc
	CHARACTER OF CASE FBI Headquarters File Number 92-3171-937 Top Hoodlum Program – Anti Racketeering		

CG 6486-C advised November 30 last that Accardo, in discussion with Giancana and Paul DeLucia, stated "I see they made the Jew an avagaud and he's really reaching out." CG informant advised recently that he had learned that Meyer Lansky has risen strongly in hoodlum circles, noted this informant is close to Accardo. Possibility exists that "Jew" referred to by Accardo is Lansky.

CG 6486-C advised further that one Andy Flando, former Chicago politician and until recently with the Sanitary District, was in contact at source with Charles English, pleading his case. He had been accused of playing around with Mayor Daley. English advised Flando that as far as Giancana is concerned, he, Flando, is all right and not in trouble.

FEDERAL BUREAU OF INVESTIGATION

REPORTING OFFICE	OFFICE OF ORIGIN	DATE	INVESTIGATIVE PERIOD
CHICAGO	CHICAGO	1962	December 5, 1962

TITLE OF CASE	REPORT MADE BY		TYPED BY
SAMUEL M. GIANCANA, aka			dkc
	CHARACTER OF CASE FBI Headquarters File Number 92-3171-936 Top Hoodlum Program – Anti Racketeering. Daily Summary		

CG 6576-C advised December 3, last that Pat Marcy indicated to an unknown that John D'Arco was taken ill suddenly and is now in a hospital, location not identified. This follows with Accardo's suggestion to have D'Arco fake a heart attack to save face with his being deposed as First Ward Alderman. Source advised that they are now in the process of obtaining petitions for the candidacy of Anthony DeTolve, Giancana's nephew, as First Ward Alderman.

FEDERAL BUREAU OF INVESTIGATION

REPORTING OFFICE	OFFICE OF ORIGIN	DATE	INVESTIGATIVE PERIOD	
CHICAGO	CHICAGO	1962	December 6, 1962	

TITLE OF CASE	REPORT MADE BY	TYPED BY
		dkc
SAMUEL M. GIANCANA, aka	**CHARACTER OF CASE** FBI Headquarters File Number 92-3171-939 Top Hoodlum Program – Anti Racketeering. Daily Summary	

Daily Summery December 5, concerning possible gangland killing, East St. Louis, of Virgil "Doc" Summers. CG 6343-C advised 12/5, that a conference between Gus Alex, Anthony Accardo, and Paul DeLucia. Alex informed Accardo that "contract given him was consummated Sunday last" referring possible to killing of Virgil Summers Sunday, 12/2 last, East St. Louis. Alex advised of intense efforts to locate "the little guy" and expected to locate the little guy Thursday, 12/6, when he was expected home. Alex told Accardo that he may expect a call Thursday in the event he is successful. This conversation immediately followed that concerning contract consummated Sunday. Possibility exists this may be Neal "Little Monk" Summers, ex-bank robber and brother of Virgil Summers who was last known to reside in Mt. Vernon, IL. In far down state section, identical with Springfield file 91-420. Summers brothers were reputed to have robbed syndicate gambling spot in Chicago years ago. This killing could be retaliation for killing of Elmer Dowling and Beckman, St. Louis several months back. Latter two were henchmen of Frank Wortman, who was in Chicago 11/28 last looking for Giancana and Murray Humphreys for some unknown reason.

The following was obtained 11/28, last from CG 6486-C. Not considered significant at time, however in view of recent gangland killing of Doc Summers over the weekend, Springfield consider as possibility. Following was whispered and covert between Fifi Buccieri and James "Turk" Torello, known henchman of Buccieri and Giancana and known executioner. "A good spot let me hit him we'll have to bring it to the cigar (Giancana) sight the scope in for 20 yards." Buccieri advised Torello he has point 270 rifle with hollow point cartridges which "explodes inside after it hits you."

FEDERAL BUREAU OF INVESTIGATION

REPORTING OFFICE	OFFICE OF ORIGIN	DATE	INVESTIGATIVE PERIOD	
CHICAGO	CHICAGO	1962	December 13, 1962	

TITLE OF CASE	REPORT MADE BY		TYPED BY
			dkc
SAMUEL M. GIANCANA, aka	**CHARACTER OF CASE**		
	FBI Headquarters File Number 92-3171-938 Top Hoodlum Program – Anti Racketeering. Daily Summery		

Efforts have been made during the past several days by Agents to contact Anthony DeTolve, Giancana's nephew and new candidate for First Ward Alderman to replace John D'Arco. DeTolve according to CG 6576-C, apprised Pay Marcy of Agents attempts to contact him and was advised by Marcy to advise agents that he has nothing to discuss with them. Efforts to contact DeTolve are continuing.

CG 6486-C reported December 11 last that Frank Wortman was with Jack Cerone, that date, and revealed that Wortman was ordered to Chicago by Giancana and Anthony Accardo for unknown reason, relating to his recent trial of income tax. Wortman in highly intoxicated condition was advised by Cerone not to worry about this situation.

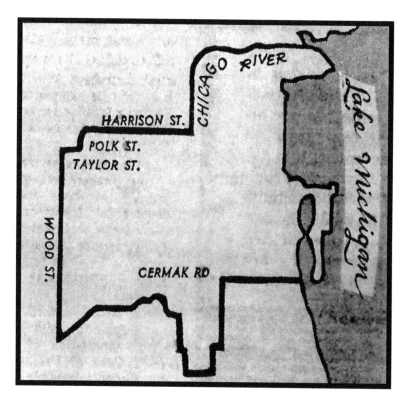

A map of the old First Ward as it appeared in the 1960's while Giancana was boss.

FEDERAL BUREAU OF INVESTIGATION

REPORTING OFFICE	OFFICE OF ORIGIN	DATE	INVESTIGATIVE PERIOD
CHICAGO	CHICAGO	1962	December 14, 1962

TITLE OF CASE	REPORT MADE BY	TYPED BY
SAMUEL M. GIANCANA, aka		dkc

CHARACTER OF CASE

FBI Headquarters File Number 92-3171-941
Top Hoodlum Program – Anti Racketeering.
Daily Summary

CG 6576-C advised yesterday that Pat Marcy complained Giancana is not in town so that Marcy's hands are tied in getting ward set up for new Alderman, Anthony DeTolve, and mentioned that if DeTolve had held a press conference as planned, "the whole organization would have gone down the drain." Marcy advised that Anthony Tisci, Attorney and son-in-law of Giancana, will be the person who will control DeTolve for the organization. Consensus is that DeTolve is completely helpless to conduct ward business without being led by the hand by Marcy.

FEDERAL BUREAU OF INVESTIGATION

REPORTING OFFICE	OFFICE OF ORIGIN	DATE	INVESTIGATIVE PERIOD
CHICAGO	CHICAGO	1962	December 19, 1962

TITLE OF CASE	REPORT MADE BY	TYPED BY
SAMUEL M. GIANCANA, aka		dkc

CHARACTER OF CASE

FBI Headquarters File Number 92-3171-945
Top Hoodlum Program – Anti Racketeering.
Daily Summary

CG 6576-C advised that Pat Marcy described meeting he held with Giancana recently, probably over past weekend. Whereby Giancana promised Marcy that John D'Arco would be retained as First Ward Committeeman. Giancana gave Marcy complete responsibility for handing of First Ward, told him to continue in his work as he had in the past. All decisions will be passed to Marcy from Giancana through Anthony Tisci. DeTolve is going to be told nothing except bare essentials. Marcy is to tutor DeTolve in fine points of graft in First Ward, and after four years, decision will be made as to whether or not DeTolve is to be retained.

FEDERAL BUREAU OF INVESTIGATION

REPORTING OFFICE	OFFICE OF ORIGIN	DATE	INVESTIGATIVE PERIOD	
CHICAGO	CHICAGO	1962	December 20, 1962	
TITLE OF CASE		REPORT MADE BY		TYPED BY
SAMUEL M. GIANCANA, aka		Ralph Hill Jr.		dkc
		CHARACTER OF CASE		
		FBI Headquarters File Number 92-3171-947 Top Hoodlum Program – Anti Racketeering		

Villa Venice Supper Club
Milwaukee Avenue

It has been reported that the Villa Venice Supper Club has been an enterprise of Giancana's since approximately 1960. From April 1960 through spring 1962, the Villa Venice was unutilized primarily for private parties, weddings, etc., and was not considered as a money-making proposition. During the summer months and early fall the Villa Venice underwent a remodeling and reopened on November 9, 1962. The featured entertainer for the opening was Eddie Fisher. He was followed by Sammy Davis Jr., and then by Frank Sinatra and Dean Martin. During the week of the engagement of Martin and Sinatra, the act was joined by Sammy Davis Jr. Following the appearance of Martin and Sinatra, Sammy Davis Jr., remained at the Villa Venice through December 4, 1962. Following December 4, 1962, the Villa Venice was closed and plans are not known at this time as to their reopening.

Leonard Olsen was interviewed at the Villa Venice. Olsen stated that he is presently the sole owner of the Villa Venice since about 1961. He explained that he originally came to the Villa Venice in 1960 when he worked for the Meo Brothers from whom he later purchased the Villa Venice. He said this establishment is incorporated under the name of the New Villa Venice, incorporated and that he owns all of the stock of this corporation. He said after extensive remodeling, the Villa should have seating for about 800 to 900 people. Olsen went on to say that the Villa Venice is scheduled to open on November 9, 1962, and the maitre d' of this club will be Nick Sankovich, former manager of the Chez Paree Night club in Chicago.

Olsen further advised that he has known many hoodlums over the years due to his work in the restaurant. He said Ross Prio was a frequent of his old establishment. He went of to say that Ross Prio's wedding was reception was held at the Villa Venice during February, 1961. Many hoodlums were in attendance at this social event, however, he feels that he is not in a position to turn down this business because of the reputation of these individuals. He added that the cost of the Prio wedding was $4,092.40, which he believes was paid for by Prio.

Current Position of Giancana in Organized Crime

Sam Giancana is generally considered as the number one gang leader in the country today, is ruthless, without human feelings. Giancana, if given a blanket authority by the "national board" of syndicate leaders, would be responsible for an untold number of gangland killings in this area. As it stands now, he must be at least a bit discriminating as to whom he picks as the next victim. The Giancana organization is now more cohesive group then ever, due largely to the fact that the intensive investigation being conducted on their affairs by law enforcement had curtailed their activities, there fore their income. It is now necessary for them to band together in a "sink or swim" effort. During the fat years prior to Appalachian, there was considerable disharmony in the organization, attributed to greed among the members.

Giancana is out of the Chicago area on an average of three weeks out of every four weeks, on business known only to himself. He confides in no one as to his itinerary, and calls in on a periodic basis when out of town to handle any problems which may have arisen during his absence. Not even Dominic Blasi, Giancana's number on lackey, is aware of Giancana's whereabouts. When Giancana calls in, he generally calls the Armory Lounge. When Giancana is in town, he can generally be seen at the Armory Lounge in a nightly basis. He meets his contacts at the Armory, and when secrecy is a necessity, Giancana will meet the party in the vicinity of the Armory, in an automobile. Giancana carries his secrets to the extent that some of the members of his group are unknown to there members, so that it is possible that at least part of the Giancana organization is unknown to investigative agencies. He identified two of Giancana's top lieutenants as Fiore Buccieri and Charles English.

Physical Surveillance by Agents

The Flamingo Motel contains a combination restaurant and lounge and in the restaurant section, Thomas Potenzo, brother of Rocco Potenzo and Sam "Slicker Sam" Rosa with two other unidentified individuals were observed drinking coffee and shortly there after were seen steering a customer from the Flamingo Motel to the Quonset Hut wherein the gambling was located. Then Giancana and Rosa departed heading for the Villa Venice where they were observed conferring with several unidentified individuals at the bar section of the Villa. Rosa was seen being joined shortly thereafter by William Daddono and Thomas Potenzo. Rosa separated and headed back to the Flamingo Motel.

CG T-19 advised that a large gambling operation is presently being conducted in the vicinity of the Flamingo Motel at River Road and Milwaukee Avenue. This operation is under the control of Rocco Potenzo. Operating this game for Potenzo is an individual known as Sam Slick, whose true name is believed to be Sam Rosa, a well known Cicero gambler. This gambling operation includes dice, all forms of cards and roulette, and is presently operating in a large Quonset Hut immediately north of the Flamingo Motel and in back of a gas station located on River Road. The Quonset Hut has a false front and displays a sigh of a phony oil company that occupies approximately 20 feet behind which is a large well-constructed an furnished room which is used for gambling purposes.

Potenzo and his underlings have been contacting their customers and offering them free reservations at the Villa Venice for the feature attraction of Eddy Fisher, Sammy Davis Jr., Frank Sinatra, Dean Martin, etc. Gambling patrons are also offered free shuttle service from the Villa Venice to the gambling establishment, which is less than a mile away from the Villa Venice. The service station attendant on whose property the Quonset Hut is located serves as a lookout for this operation and is believed to have walkie-talkie communications with individuals in the motel and Quonset Hut.

Associates

Phyllis McGuire

CG T-20 advised that Sam Giancana had been able to persuade Frank Sinatra to give a part to Phyllis McGiure in the film "Come Blow Your Horn."

FEDERAL BUREAU OF INVESTIGATION

REPORTING OFFICE	OFFICE OF ORIGIN	DATE	INVESTIGATIVE PERIOD	
CHICAGO	CHICAGO	1962	December 27, 1962	

TITLE OF CASE	REPORT MADE BY	TYPED BY
		dkc
SAMUEL M. GIANCANA, aka	**CHARACTER OF CASE**	
	FBI Headquarters File number 92-3171-651, Top Hoodlum Program – Anti Racketeering. Daily Summary	

Proposed meeting of hoodlums Miami Beach. CG informant, who is in a position of trust with the Chicago hoodlum element, advised Fiore "Fifi" Buccieri, is a killer for the Chicago syndicate. In addition to alias "Fifi", Buccieri addressed as "nose" by intimates. Informant obtained this info from Joey "D" Delmonico. Also considered possible executioner for the mob. Milwaukee informant reported July, 1960 that Buccieri maintains firearms range in Lake Geneva summer home where Buccieri and associates test weapons. Inasmuch as CG 6486-C recently reported person identified as "Nose" used as an executioner for Giancana, photo of Buccieri being sent to Miami under separate cover to assist in identification as involved in contemplated Frank Esposito case.

Additional FBI information

1) Bureau memo dated 2-13-1962 concerning "Jamaica Gambling Activities" set out the following: As a result of information developed by highly confidential sources in Las Vegas it was determined that Nevada gambling personality, John Frank Drew, had traveled to Jamaica. The sources indicated that Drew, who owned 5% of the hoodlum controlled Stardust Hotel in Las Vegas and was reportedly a front man in Las Vegas for Sam Giancana and the Chicago underworld organization, was traveling to Jamaica to develop gambling casinos in that area.

2) Activities and close association between Frank Eulo and Sam Giancana exist. Eulo stated that he had known Giancana since boyhood days dating back to the 1920's, and was described as an errand boy for Giancana in the north section of Cicero, Illinois. It was reported on 2-23-1962 that Eulo operated a crap and card game in Cicero for Giancana and he split of the profits was 50-50. Eulo was reputed to be brother-in-law of Giancana. Eulo's wife, Rose Eulo, was probably related to Giancana. On 8-23-1962 Eulo had returned his gambling operations from the area of 49th Avenue and Roosevelt Road to the Dixie Lounge, 1410 S. Cicero Avenue, Cicero.

3) NK-2251-C reported on 4-16-1962 that Ray De Carlo, Anthony Russo and

Joe Polverino had a conversation that Ray heard Mooney "Giancana" was going to live at Palm Beach, Florida. Ray also told Russo, who had been refused permission to go to Palm Beach, that he should have gone to Mooney and ask him, "I might be able to get something in Palm Beach, it would it all right with you?"

4)   Las Angeles informant advised that he was approached by Irving Dworett who advised him that certain people could expand his business of vending machines in Chicago for a ten percent cut of the ownership. Shortly after this there was a meeting in the vending machine office with about thirty hoodlums present, which included Sam Giancana, Louis Tom Dragna or Los Angels, and Felix Alderisio. Source stated that while he was there, the hoodlums voted as to whether he would be allowed to operate his vending machine business and they all voted to "take him." After the vote source said Alderisio punched him around and that he received several subsequent beatings from this group. Above informant said he also attended a meeting held at Giancana's residence in Melrose Park, Illinois, when about sixteen Italians and Sicilians were present including Giancana. Informant was beat up at this meeting. Dragna mentioned that Mickey Cohen was involved with Coast Vending and Giancana said that Dragna should walk right over Cohen. LA informant also advised that in 1962 Morris Litberg was offered a proposition whereby for ten per cent of his company his vending machine business could be greatly expanded. Shortly after this he attended a meeting in his vending machine office with several Chicago hoodlums including Giancana, Alderisio, and Lou Farrell from Omaha. At the conclusion of this meeting, Litberg was punched around by Alderisio. He was also of the opinion that Alderisio wanted very much to be the big boss and take over from Giancana.

5)   Chicago informant advised that on 8-8-1962, a party was held in honor of Keeley Smith, night club singer, in her room at the Sahara Inn Motel, Chicago. Smith was the feature attraction at the Gigi Room of the Sahara Inn North. Participating in this party were Giancana, several other hoodlums, and numerous prostitutes. About 2:00 p.m. every day John Matassa picked up Smith in a car and drove her to an unknown destination. Smith was a one time paramour of Giancana.

6)   Norman Glubock, Chicago informant and reporter for the Chicago American newspaper, disclosed that Paul Perkins, who operated the O'Hare Taxi Corporation at Mannheim and Higgins Roads at O'Hare Airport, had recently organized a new cab company called the White top Cab Company. According to source, Perkins was observed conferring near his office with Romeo Torsiello and Sam Giancana. Torsiello was the night manager of the Thunder Bolt Motel located at 5400 River Road, Chicago, which was operated by Charles Giancana, brother of Sam. Informant said that the bank rolling for the White Top enterprise came from Sam Giancana. Donald Stephens, Village President, Rosemont, Illinois, stated that Torsiello was the owner of the White Top Cab Company and a brother-in-law of Charles Giancana. He also stated that Jeep Daddono, related to Willy "Potatoes" Daddono, was supervisor of the taxicab drivers.

7)   Mrs. Edward Reilly furnished information in November 1962 regarding activities at a tavern by the name of "Pal Joey's" located at 5120 N. Sheridan Road, Chicago. Reilly identified Sam Giancana from a photograph as being fre-

quent patron of this tavern. She also identified a photograph of Joseph Bor-sellino as the apparent owner and operator of the tavern. Borsellino makes trips for Giancana to New York, Miami, and Las Vegas for the purpose of making arrangements for Giancana to meet with hoodlum personages in those areas.

8) CG-6486-C advised that Alfred Meo had contacted Sam Giancana regard-ing $40,000 indebtedness of the Villa Venice restaurant which had not been paid to him by Richard Bernas and others involved in a deal when the club was sold. Source said later that Giancana had made available $25,000 to Bernas for his use when he needed it. On 12-27-1962 it was reported that entertainers Eddie Fisher, Sammy Davis Jr., Frank Sinatra and Dean Martin had recently appeared at the "New Villa Venice" at Chicago. They drew large crowds at the Villa Ven-ice which cut down considerably on the attendance at the Sahara Inn, owned by Manny Skar. Source said Skar made no mention of the reported connections of Sam Giancana with the Villa Venice.

9) On 9-28-1962, LV-69-C advised that Eddie Fisher had been obtained for the entertainment to open for several well-known entertainers. Giancana sent a message to thank Morris Barney Dalitz, one of the top stockholders at Las Ve-gas, for obtaining Fisher for the opening of the club.

10) Chicago informant furnished information that the Aloha Club at 2443 West Madison was owned by Johnnie Marola, who had a connection with Sam Giancana. Butch Loverdi ran the Club 19 which was a notorious "strip joint" in the Rush Street area of Chicago. Butch was known to be a front man for Milwaukee Phil Alderisio and Sam Giancana. The Talk of the Town night club on North Clark Street in Chicago was operated by Hunk Galiano. Galiano was directly connected to Sam Giancana.

11) On 10-4-1962, CG-6486-C advised the following discussion took place between Sam Giancana, John Matassa, an unknown male and two unknown females:

Giancana:	No no, she still wants to keep her career. She told me, she wants to marry me, but under one condition. I want to sing, she says.
Unknown Female:	You mean Phyllis? (McGuire)
Giancana:	Yeah.
Unknown:	I don't know, the night I was there she was hollering pretty good.
Matassa:	That was on of her off nights. You don't know what happened before that.
Unknown Female:	I never saw her except that one time.
Matassa:	There's a lot more to it.
Giancana:	What do you think happened? We went to this restaurant, and who's picture do you think is sitting right above us?

Unknown female:	Keely Smith?
Giancana:	No. Wilma.
Unknown Female:	Does she know her?
Giancana:	Yeah. I told them to take that picture down. Please, I says, give me one more chance.
Unknown Female:	Who's Wilma? Is she in show business?
Giancana:	No, she was a girl I knew. Someone told her when she was in Vegas, Someone pointed her out. Then she sat down and talked to the girl. Someone sent her (McGuire) one of the Wichell's columns, about a month ago. The article said, love is fading away, Keely Smith was in Atlantic City with Frank Sinatra, and I (Giancana) was there and was all over her. He's given up McGuire and is going back to Keely. So someone from New York sent her the clipping. So I called, and she was just going on, so I said, I'll call you later, so she called at four in the morning and said, you dirty (Obs). I says, what happen? She said, don't you know what happened? Did you see Keely Smith, she said? I said no, I knew she was around, but I didn't see her. She said, well, I got the article right here. I said, well, you don't believe everything you read, do you? And she said, well, I believe this one. My God in Heaven.
Unknown Female:	When you gonna marry her?
Giancana:	Well, she gave me an ultimatum. She says, I got to have an answer. I got to know by Christmas, or it's all off.
Unknown Female:	Well, what the hell. You have your own life to lead. How old is she?
Giancana:	Thirty.
Unknown Female:	Ever been married?
Giancana:	Oh yeah. She was married.
Unknown Female:	You got the ultimatum, huh?
Giancana:	Yeah. Or else, she says. (Laughs) By Christmas.
Unknown Female:	Well, then it's time to back off. I don't believe in that.
Unknown Female 2;	Well, I do. Why should she waste her time.
Giancana:	She cries all the time. She keeps coming back. She packs up and leaves, then she comes back. I've lasted about tow or three years with her. It was a lot of fun.
Matassa:	Oh, yeah, you had a ball.
Giancana:	Yeah, a lot of fun.

309

Matassa:	She was good for you at the time.
Giancana:	Yeah. Those girls do a good job. But she carries the whole act. She'd like to sing alone. Now she gets to expect a little kibbitz between songs. Like that (obs) Hill, she sees him all the time. In the audience. (Goes into dissertation about FBI) She can smell those guys. (Talks about FBI interview, July 1961)..those two guys about a year ago talked to her. They said, come on now, what about him? She says, I have my own money. I know he's a very nice fella, and I like his company, period.
Unknown Female:	That's exactly what they said to me.
Giancana:	I think I'll go call her. I'll be right back.
Unknown Female:	It's not definite.
Matassa:	He's got an ultimatum. By Christmas, or else. It's pretty well set. I don't see it, though. Funny things happen. Right now, I lay three to one nothing happens.
Unknown Female:	Well, the nerve of her, giving him an ultimatum.
Matassa;	I can't see him getting married.
Unknown Female:	No man wants to get married when he gets an ultimatum.
Matassa:	I'll make that five to one. I can't see it. He likes her, though. It's a very close association. I seen it time and again. She's a girl of good character. He respects her. She's quick tempered, and doesn't let a thing go by her.

Chapter 7

FEDERAL BUREAU OF INVESTIGATION

REPORTING OFFICE	OFFICE OF ORIGIN	DATE	INVESTIGATIVE PERIOD
CHICAGO	CHICAGO	1963	January 10, 1963

TITLE OF CASE	REPORT MADE BY	TYPED BY
SAMUEL M. GIANCANA, aka		dkc

CHARACTER OF CASE
FBI Headquarters File Number 92-3171-954
Top Hoodlum Program – Anti Racketeering.
Daily Summary

CG 6576-C advised on 1/8 last that Pat Marcy and Ben Filicio, discussed Cook County Sheriff's office. Ben was desirous in learning if Richard Cain, Chief Investigator, Cook County Sheriff's office, is on payroll of Chicago syndicate inasmuch as Ben has a problem with Cain involving Ben's stores. Marcy assured Ben in confidence, "I've got Cain and I've had him for seven years. Cain does everything I tell him to do. We have no problems with Ogilvie as long as I have Cain."

Ben was then advised by Marcy that Giancana has issued specific instructions regarding Cain that utilization of Cain's services are to be handled strictly by Marcy and or Buddy Jacobson. If Cain's services are desired on specific occasions, Giancana is to be advised and upon making his decision he will advised Marcy to give the proper instructions to Cain.

FEDERAL BUREAU OF INVESTIGATION

REPORTING OFFICE	OFFICE OF ORIGIN	DATE	INVESTIGATIVE PERIOD
CHICAGO	CHICAGO	1963	January 14, 1963

TITLE OF CASE	REPORT MADE BY	TYPED BY
SAMUEL M. GIANCANA, aka		dkc

CHARACTER OF CASE
FBI Headquarters File Number 92-3171-955
Top Hoodlum Program – Anti Racketeering.
Daily Summary

CG 6486-C advised that Charles English discussed situation with Dominic Blasi whereby English's ward, Chicago's 29th, is undergoing political change similar to the First Ward, the difference being that the incumbent alderman, Tom Bourke, is suffering from cancer, thereby necessitating a replacement. John Kringas, brother of Cicero gambler Gus Kringas, was original choice; however, attendant publicity precluded this, therefore, compromise candidate Marvin Browning was chosen. Browning is known associate of English and accompanied him to Phoenix, Arizona, in November, 1962.

FEDERAL BUREAU OF INVESTIGATION

REPORTING OFFICE	OFFICE OF ORIGIN	DATE	INVESTIGATIVE PERIOD
CHICAGO	CHICAGO	1963	January 16, 1963

TITLE OF CASE	REPORT MADE BY	TYPED BY
		dkc
SAMUEL M. GIANCANA, aka	**CHARACTER OF CASE** FBI Headquarters File Number 92-3171-956 Top Hoodlum Program – Anti Racketeering. Daily Summary	

CG 6476-C advised that Giancana and Charles English in vicinity of informant discussing various matters. English bemoaning fact that federal government is closing in on the organization and there apparently is nothing that can be done about it. English made various and sundry inflammatory remarks about the Kennedy administration, pointed out that the Attorney General's raising of ransom moneys from Cuban invaders was muscle which would make Chicago syndicate look like amateurs.

Note Chicago sources have indicated that Giancana accompanied by Phyllis McGiure, the Accardo's and the Cerone's, were recently in Acapulco, Mexico.

FEDERAL BUREAU OF INVESTIGATION

REPORTING OFFICE	OFFICE OF ORIGIN	DATE	INVESTIGATIVE PERIOD
CHICAGO	CHICAGO	1963	January 21, 1963

TITLE OF CASE	REPORT MADE BY	TYPED BY
		dkc
SAMUEL M. GIANCANA, aka	**CHARACTER OF CASE** FBI Headquarters File Number 92-3171-959 Top Hoodlum Program – Anti Racketeering. Daily Summary	

It should be noted that First Ward politician Peter Granata is on the appropriation committee of the Illinois legislature and therefore will be able to influence pending legislation for Giancana.

FEDERAL BUREAU OF INVESTIGATION

REPORTING OFFICE	OFFICE OF ORIGIN	DATE	INVESTIGATIVE PERIOD	
CHICAGO	CHICAGO	1963	January 25, 1963	
TITLE OF CASE		REPORT MADE BY		TYPED BY
				dkc
SAMUEL M. GIANCANA, aka		**CHARACTER OF CASE**		
		FBI Headquarters File Number 92-3171-963 Top Hoodlum Program – Anti Racketeering. Daily Summary		

CG 6576-C advised today that Pat Marcy conferred with Buddy Jacobson and told Jacobson he met with Giancana early instant about several matters, including fact that Anthony Accardo wants Marcy to place Accardo's son-in-law, Palmer Pyle, with Anco Insurance Company at $400 per week. Marcy is concerned since he cannot afford to pay this amount and designated Jacobson to meet with Accardo to explain that he can only pay Pyle $200 per week. Marcy and Jacobson both agreed that Accardo, "still has a lot to say," even though Giancana is boss. Marcy advised that Giancana is placing Andy Flando, Jr., in the 17th District as a state representative to replacing Euzzino. Giancana also offered to place Fred Roti as senator to fill vacancy of Anthony DeTolve. Marcy is most concerned over fact that Giancana is making these decisions involving First Ward without conferring with Marcy. Marcy has to date meet with Giancana afternoon instant.

FEDERAL BUREAU OF INVESTIGATION

REPORTING OFFICE	OFFICE OF ORIGIN	DATE	INVESTIGATIVE PERIOD	
CHICAGO	CHICAGO	1963	January 29, 1963	
TITLE OF CASE		REPORT MADE BY		TYPED BY
				dkc
SAMUEL M. GIANCANA, aka		**CHARACTER OF CASE**		
		FBI Headquarters File Number 92-3171-962 Top Hoodlum Program – Anti Racketeering. Daily Summary		

CG 6486-C advised that Charles English was in discussion that date with Dominic Blasi and Fiore Buccieri. English advised his brother, Sam English, is in Arizona for the purpose of attempting to sell unknown movie Production Company on utilizing his ranch property in Arizona for

313

movie location site. He is also attempting to obtain contracts from Air Force for training films.

The following information regarding the recent wave of fires of questionable origin in Chicago area restaurant, the most recent being the Prime Steak House, Stickney, IL, 1/23, last, owned by Nate Passaro, associate and sometimes partner of Dominic Blasi. According to source, Blasi, on day after fire, made arrangements to meet with Passaro and James Torello, in vicinity of Armory Lounge, to discuss recent fire. Blasi mentioned to Torello that fire was probably caused by overheated boiler. On 1/25 last, Fiore Buccieri advised Blasi and Charles English that he had just come from the scene of the fire, which was still smoldering and described it as "beautiful with beautiful insurance." Noted steak house insured for a quarter of a million dollars, was total loss.

FEDERAL BUREAU OF INVESTIGATION

REPORTING OFFICE	OFFICE OF ORIGIN	DATE	INVESTIGATIVE PERIOD
CHICAGO	CHICAGO	1963	February 1, 1963

TITLE OF CASE	REPORT MADE BY	TYPED BY
		dkc
SAMUEL M. GIANCANA, aka	**CHARACTER OF CASE** FBI Headquarters File Number 92-3171 Top Hoodlum Program – Anti Racketeering. Daily Summary	

Donald Stephens, Mayor, Village of Rosemont, IL, advised yesterday that he and P.J. Greco, building contractor purchased the Thunderbolt Motel, Rosemont for total price of $520,000. Stephens advised he will not use services of Charles Giancana in management of motel. He advised, however, restaurant and cocktail lounge being leased to one Frank Sarno, and head bartender will be Thomas Potenzo, brother of Rocco Potenzo. Stephens admits Giancana continues to utilize private office of Thunderbolt, on occasion, as private meeting place. Stephens states in addition that he, Stephens, met with Paul DeLucia and Anthony Accardo at the Flamingo Motel, at which time Accardo stated he desire to purchase a bowling alley and lounge under construction across the street from the Thunderbolt, for $500,000 cash, for his son-in-law, Palmer Pyle, wants Stephens to guarantee liquor license.

FEDERAL BUREAU OF INVESTIGATION

REPORTING OFFICE	OFFICE OF ORIGIN	DATE	INVESTIGATIVE PERIOD
CHICAGO	CHICAGO	1963	February 7, 1963

TITLE OF CASE	REPORT MADE BY	TYPED BY
		dkc

	CHARACTER OF CASE
SAMUEL M. GIANCANA, aka	FBI Headquarters File Number 92-3171-969 Top Hoodlum Program – Anti Racketeering. Daily Summary

CG 6486-C advised over past weekend that Giancana held dinner party in vicinity of informant with members of his group and females. Source advised that Dominic Blasi was making arrangements with unknown to sell Eden Land and Development Company for about $300,000.

FEDERAL BUREAU OF INVESTIGATION

REPORTING OFFICE	OFFICE OF ORIGIN	DATE	INVESTIGATIVE PERIOD
CHICAGO	CHICAGO	1963	February 15, 1963

TITLE OF CASE	REPORT MADE BY	TYPED BY
		dkc

	CHARACTER OF CASE
SAMUEL M. GIANCANA, aka	FBI Headquarters File Number 92-3171 Top Hoodlum Program – Anti Racketeering. Daily Summary

CG 6576-C advised John D'Arco returned from Florida and discussed current situation with Pat Marcy. Marcy filled in D'Arco with fact that Giancana in not happy with Anthony DeTolve, whereby D'Arco stated desire to talk to Giancana for possible reinstatement. D'Arco told that Giancana is out of town, due back instant or 2/15 next. Marcy advised that Giancana is perturbed concerning recent gambling raids in south Cook County and in Lake County, IL, and fact that although the organization had under sheriff Rich Cain in their pocket, they cannot get next to Ross Spencer, Chief Investigator. It appears that one of persons closest to Giancana at present time is Anthony Tisci.

FEDERAL BUREAU OF INVESTIGATION

REPORTING OFFICE	OFFICE OF ORIGIN	DATE	INVESTIGATIVE PERIOD
CHICAGO	CHICAGO	1963	February 21, 1963

TITLE OF CASE	REPORT MADE BY	TYPED BY
		dkc
SAMUEL M. GIANCANA, aka	**CHARACTER OF CASE**	
	FBI Headquarters File Number 92-3171-975 Top Hoodlum Program – Anti Racketeering. Daily Summary	

CG 6486-C advised that Giancana was in conference with Rocco Potenzo, hoodlum and controller for Giancana of Northwest suburbs, concerning gambling operations in Northwest. Potenza stated the Big Game, formerly at River Road and Higgins Road, Rosemont, Illinois, closed and had moved to factory leased by Potenzo and legit business, to be used for two weeks on trial basis as area's largest crap, roulette and poker operation.

Giancana ordered Potenzo and his cronies to stay away from Tunderbolt Motel, recently sold by Giancana to (Blacked out by government), now known as Caravelle. Restaurant and lounge is under control of Potenzo. Potenzo argued he had a right to be there, however, Giancana was insistent.

CG 6576-C advised John D'Arco and Pat Marcy discussed Giancana, fact that he arrived in Chicago 2/17/63, is going to Florida in very near future. Giancana observed at a large party at Armory Lounge 2/19/63. John D'Arco is making arrangements for Giancana through Lou Koren. Giancana was offered apartment there, declined. Miami note Lou Koren is connected with King Cole Hotel, Miami.

Miami be alert for presence of Giancana and others from Chicago, including Dominic Cortina, Donald Angelini, and James Mirro who are staying at the Golden Nugget Motel.

FEDERAL BUREAU OF INVESTIGATION

REPORTING OFFICE	OFFICE OF ORIGIN	DATE	INVESTIGATIVE PERIOD
CHICAGO	CHICAGO	1963	February 25, 1963

TITLE OF CASE	REPORT MADE BY	TYPED BY
		dkc
SAMUEL M. GIANCANA, aka	**CHARACTER OF CASE**	
	FBI Headquarters File Number 92-3171-978 Top Hoodlum Program – Anti Racketeering. Daily Summary	

CG 6576 advised 2/22/63 that Giancana arrived at Chicago and is scheduled to meet with John D'Arco and Pat Marcy about First Ward Aldermanic election.

FEDERAL BUREAU OF INVESTIGATION

REPORTING OFFICE	OFFICE OF ORIGIN	DATE	INVESTIGATIVE PERIOD	
CHICAGO	CHICAGO	1963	February 25, 1963	
TITLE OF CASE		REPORT MADE BY		TYPED BY
		SA Ralph Hill Jr.		dkc
SAMUEL M. GIANCANA, aka		CHARACTER OF CASE		
		FBI Headquarters File Number 92-3171-976 Top Hoodlum Program – Anti Racketeering		

Influence of Sam Giancana
In the Political Activities
First Ward, Chicago

Anthony DeTolve

Reference is made to report of SA Ralph Hill at Chicago dated 12/20/62, relating to the activates of Giancana in the First Ward and which reflects that John D'Arco is to be replaced by Anthony DeTolve, Illinois State Senator and nephew by marriage of Giancana.

"Attached here is a Chicago American newspaper article dated 12/26/62 pertaining to Anthony "Busy Busy" DeTolve."

Chicago T-1 advised that the attendant newspaper publicity given the First Ward situation reflecting disclosures of Giancana being tied in with the First Ward organization as well as the obvious incompetence of Anthony DeTolve has necessitated a decision by Giancana to possibly replace DeTolve as First Ward Alderman with an individual with more intelligence and political know-how. According to this informant, DeTolve is not aware of the fact that he is under consideration to be replaced and is making plans at full speed for taking over the First Ward upon the election, 2/26/63.

CG T-2 advised that Giancana has issued specific instructions to Anthony Tisci to the effect that Tisci will be direct liaison between Giancana and the First Ward. Giancana's instruction are to be relayed from Tisci to Pat Marcy. CG T-2 is an individual who is consideration as possible alderman for the First Ward is Michael A. FioRito, an attorney with offices as 30 North LaSalle Street, who maintains a permit residence in Wilmette, IL.

CG T-2 advised in February, 1963, that Anthony Tisci was in contact with Giancana regarding the First Ward situation. Of prime concern to Giancana, according to this informant, is the government investigation concerning his, Giancana's, activities. As a result Giancana is being extremely cautious in his contacts particularly with politicians and individuals of prominence.

Giancana's Activities
Outside of First Ward Area

CG T-3 advised that Giancana will in all probability replace the incumbent State Representative from the 17th District of Illinois, Andrew Euzzino, with one Andy Flando, Jr. Flando is a former official with the Chicago Sanitary District.

This informant stated that Giancana is also considering the placement of Fred Roti as an Illinois State Senator from 17th District to replace the incumbent Anthony DeTolve. This information stated Giancana conferred with Pat Marcy concerning this particular situation on January 25, 1963.

CG T-4 advised that First Ward Alderman John D'Arco returned to Chicago during the middle of February, 1963, from his winter residence in Hollywood, Florida. Informant stated that one reason for D'Arco's vacationing in Florida was to validate the story circulated to the effect that he had recently suffered a heart attack which necessitated long recuperation and also is creating a vacancy in the aldermanic position in the First Ward.

"Attached here is Chicago Daily News" article dated 1/17/63, concerning D'Arco's health."

CG T-1 advised that Giancana traveled to Acapulco, Mexico in company of Phyllis McGuire during middle of January, 1963. Also reported in Acapulco at same time were Anthony Accardo, Jack Cerone and Charles English all accompanied by their wives.

CG T-7 advised Giancana in Miami, Florida in February 1963. At that time Giancana was in contact with William "Potatoes" Daddono. Giancana had been spending an average of one out of three weeks in the Chicago area since Christmas, 1962.

FEDERAL BUREAU OF INVESTIGATION

REPORTING OFFICE	OFFICE OF ORIGIN	DATE	INVESTIGATIVE PERIOD
CHICAGO	CHICAGO	1963	February 28, 1963

TITLE OF CASE	REPORT MADE BY	TYPED BY
		dkc

SAMUEL M. GIANCANA, aka	**CHARACTER OF CASE** FBI Headquarters File Number 92-3171 Top Hoodlum Program – Anti Racketeering. Daily Summary

CG 6486-C advised 2/27/63 that Giancana spent most of afternoon in vicinity of source, conversing with Charles English and other associates, gloating over results of Municipal election 2/16/63. He stated, "That will teach that like (obscene) Kennedy who runs Chicago." Comment on excellent appearance of Mike FioRito, newly elected Alderman, First Ward. Made appointment to meet unknowns during late evening 2/27/63.

CG 6576-C advised yesterday Marcy waited in for a call from Butch Blasi as to where and when he was to meet with Giancana that date. Marcy held conference wit FioRito, instructed him as to deportment while being alderman, said being conducted on First Ward by Sheriff's Office, that even if this case got to grand jury, it would be handled by Dan Ward, Democratic States Attorney, and there will be "no problem."

FEDERAL BUREAU OF INVESTIGATION

REPORTING OFFICE	OFFICE OF ORIGIN	DATE	INVESTIGATIVE PERIOD	
CHICAGO	CHICAGO	1963	April 4, 1963	
TITLE OF CASE		REPORT MADE BY		TYPED BY
				dkc
SAMUEL M. GIANCANA, aka		CHARACTER OF CASE		
		FBI Headquarters File Number 92-3171-991 Top Hoodlum Program – Anti Racketeering. Daily Summary		

CG 6486-C reported Giancana returned to Chicago from unknown point on 4/2/63. In brief conference with John Matassa. Matassa, now a business agent for a Teamsters local in Chicago, told Giancana of Jimmy Hoffa's recent tirade against Robert Kennedy, said Kennedy conducting personal vendetta against hoodlums at Government expense. John Matassa, Eddie Vogel and others observed at St. Clair Hotel, Chicago, during late evening of 4/2/63.

FEDERAL BUREAU OF INVESTIGATION

REPORTING OFFICE	OFFICE OF ORIGIN	DATE	INVESTIGATIVE PERIOD	
CHICAGO	CHICAGO	1963	April 11, 1963	
TITLE OF CASE		REPORT MADE BY		TYPED BY
				dkc
SAMUEL M. GIANCANA, aka		CHARACTER OF CASE		
		FBI Headquarters File Number 92-3171-993 Top Hoodlum Program – Anti Racketeering. Daily Summary		

CG 6576-C advised that Pat Marcy met with Giancana on April 4 last, at midnight in Giancana's automobile in the vicinity of Roosevelt and Austin Avenues. Has not yet disuse results of meeting, although noted that during meet with Marcy 4/1/63, Giancana and Marcy discussed reorganization of West Side political bloc.

CG 6486-C advised that Giancana, Anthony Accardo and Paul DeLucia met in the vicinity of source 4/5/63. Most of conference out of hearing of source, however, topic of conversation generally referred to Vito Marzullo, 25th Ward Alderman being deposed by Giancana. Accardo announced that his youngest son, Joseph Accardo, is graduating from Calley Forge Military Academy this year and through congressman Roland Libonati is arranging for Joseph to attend a U.S. Military Academy commencing with academic year 1964.

FEDERAL BUREAU OF INVESTIGATION

REPORTING OFFICE	OFFICE OF ORIGIN	DATE	INVESTIGATIVE PERIOD
CHICAGO	CHICAGO	1963	April 17, 1963

TITLE OF CASE	REPORT MADE BY	TYPED BY
		dkc

	CHARACTER OF CASE
SAMUEL M. GIANCANA, aka	FBI Headquarters File Number 92-3171-994 Top Hoodlum Program – Anti Racketeering. Daily Summary

Chicago informant advised of the following situation regarding Giancana's handling of the political situation in Chicago's wards. Giancana has been displeased with the informant for some time now, since the informant was unwilling to do certain favors for Giancana in the past elections. Giancana also feels that the informant does not owe complete allegiance to the Giancana organization, and for those reasons is giving strong consideration toward ordering the informant to immediately relinquish his position in the ward. If Giancana so orders, the informant will then go to Mayor Daley and turn in his resignation.

It is certain that Al Tomaso, newly elected Alderman of the 28th Ward, is completely in the pocket of Giancana and is co-operating one hundred percent with the organization. The informant stated that he is considering meeting with Giancana in the near future to attempt to make peace with him and remain on his good side.

FEDERAL BUREAU OF INVESTIGATION

REPORTING OFFICE	OFFICE OF ORIGIN	DATE	INVESTIGATIVE PERIOD
CHICAGO	CHICAGO	1963	April 24, 1963

TITLE OF CASE	REPORT MADE BY	TYPED BY
		dkc

	CHARACTER OF CASE
SAMUEL M. GIANCANA, aka	FBI File Number 92-3171-996 Top Hoodlum Program – Anti Racketeering. Daily Summary

Anthony Tisci, son-in-law of Giancana and reported by CG 6576-C to be an important cog in the First Ward operation, was interviewed by SA Ralph Hill on 4/22/63, telephonically, inasmuch as he refused to be interviewed personally. He stated that the relationship between him and Giancana is that of son-in-law and father-in-law; he knows nothing of his business and cares less. He stated he is tired of continuous interrogation by law enforcement, particularly the FBI. Apparently IRS and other agencies have interviewed him and left him with the impression this was the FBI.

Immediately after concluding the interview, Tisci reported to Pat Marcy of the contact and exactly what was said, after proper embellishment.

FEDERAL BUREAU OF INVESTIGATION

REPORTING OFFICE	OFFICE OF ORIGIN	DATE	INVESTIGATIVE PERIOD	
CHICAGO	CHICAGO	1963	April 26, 1963	

TITLE OF CASE	REPORT MADE BY	TYPED BY
		dkc
SAMUEL M. GIANCANA, aka	**CHARACTER OF CASE** FBI Headquarters File Number 92-3171-995 Top Hoodlum Program – Anti Racketeering. Daily Summary	

CG 6486-C advised 2/25/63 that a general discussion was held that date with participants being Charles English, Tarquin Simonelli, Dominic Blasi and Sam Giancana.

It was established definitely during this discussion that the Giancana organization does not have a financial interest in the Sahara Inn North Motel, recently foreclosed upon by the Marshall Savings and Loan Association. English went into some detail concerning the fact that the loan granted to Manny Skar, operator of the Sahara Inn, was fraudulent; however, he does not believe it can be proved. English said that money was paid under the table to officials of the Savings and Loan institution for the granting of the loan. Giancana stated that the reason Skar went under was that he spent money lavishly and could not keep pace with prosperity.

The group discussed gambling briefly and decided that what this country needs to pull itself out of the hole is to legalize gambling needs in certain locations throughout the nation.

FEDERAL BUREAU OF INVESTIGATION

REPORTING OFFICE	OFFICE OF ORIGIN	DATE	INVESTIGATIVE PERIOD	
CHICAGO	CHICAGO	1963	April 30, 1963	

TITLE OF CASE	REPORT MADE BY	TYPED BY
	. SA Ralph Hill Jr.	dkc
SAMUEL M. GIANCANA, aka	**CHARACTER OF CASE** FBI Headquarters File Number 92-3171-998 Top Hoodlum Program – Anti Racketeering	

Synopsis;

Michael FioRito, handpicked candidate of Giancana for First Ward of Chicago, elected as First Ward Alderman in February, 1963. Informant reported Giancana not satisfied with activities of his "West Side Block" politicians and is planning major reshuffling. Anthony Tisci, son-in-law of Giancana interviewed and denied association with Giancana other than father-in-law to son-in-law. Giancana continues to spend considerable time outside of the confines of Chicago.

Political Connections

Anthony Tisci
1 North LaSalle Street
Chicago, Illinois

It had been previously reported that Tisci, son-in-law of Giancana by virtue of his marriage to Bonnie Giancana, is a prime factor in Giancana's political maneuvering in Chicago's First Ward. Tisci is slated for high political offices in the future. In spite of their relationship however, Giancana is giving strong consideration toward sponsoring Tisci in the not too distance future as a member of the United States House of Representatives now held by Roland V. Libonati.

The following represents an interview with Tisci by SA Ralph Hill Jr. on April 22, 1963. It is noted that Tisci refused to be contacted in person so that this interview was conducted telephonically.

Anthony Tisci, identified himself as an attorney with offices at 1 North La Salle Street, Chicago, and a son-in-law of Samuel M. Giancana of 1147 South Wenonah Street, Oak Park, Illinois. Mr. Tisci said that he is married to Bonnie Giancana, a daughter of Sam Giancana.

Tisci advised that his relationship with Sam Giancana is the same as any normal relationship between son-in-law and father-in-law. He advised that Giancana is the grandfather of his children, that he enjoys a close personal relationship with Giancana however, this relationship does not extend to Giancana's business dealings. Mr. Tisci advised that he does not feel that he is at liberty to discuss any personal matters relating to Giancana and said he is "sick and tired of continuous interrogation by law enforcement agencies." He further stated that he does not desire to be contacted in the future regarding any matter in connection with Sam Giancana.

Political Maneuvers in First Ward, Chicago

Reference reported reflects that Anthony DeTolve was ear-marked by the Giancana organization to replace the incumbent alderman of the First Ward John D'Arco. Due to newspaper publicity concerning DeTolve's selection as First Ward Alderman candidate for the municipal election caused a reconsideration of his selection.

Pat Marcy, according to this informant, was told to choose a candidate for the First Ward whose background would be such so as not to create the type of publicity afforded Anthony DeTolve. The selection decided upon was Michael FioRito who at that time was a registered voter and resident in the 33rd Precinct of Winnetka. After considerable maneuvering FioRito was listed as a resident of the Conrad Hilton Hotel for a period of thirty days prior to the election of February 26, 1963. Any indication of prior registration in Winnetka was erased.

Although Anthony DeTolve was carried as the regular candidate for alderman of the First Ward of Chicago, FioRito was carried as a "write in" candidate and the result was a landslide vote in favor of FioRito in the elections in February.

Giancana remained in the Chicago area during the period immediately prior to and during the municipal elections to lend his personal supervision to events surrounding this election.

Political Maneuvers by Giancana
Organization in "West Side Bloc"

It has been reported in the part, of the fact that the Giancana organization over the years has absolute control over certain West Side Chicago Ward organizations. Notable among these in addition to the First Ward of Chicago, are the 25th and 28th Wards. The 25th Ward is headed by Alderman Vito Marzullo. The 28th Ward has a newly Alderman Al Tomaso. The Ward Committeeman for the 28th Ward is Anthony Girolami, who was the former First Ward Alderman and is now the newly elected Clerk of Probate Court of Cook County. Included among the members of the West Side Bloc is Congressman Roland V. Libonati, previously described as a long-time associate of Giancana and other prominent members of the organization and who now represents the 7th Congressional District of Illinois in the United States House of Representatives.

Chicago T-3 advised in April, 1963, that Giancana has held a series of meetings with certain of his close confidents and as a result has tentatively decided to replace these individuals mentioned in the following manner:

Congressman Libonati will be replaced by Alderman Marzullo and after short period of time Marzullo will be replaced as Congressman of the 7th United States Congressional District by Giancana's son-in-law Anthony Tisci.

Chicago T-9 advised that Giancana has lost all confidence in Anthony Girolami, mentioned above, and is considering removing Girolami from the position of 28th Ward Committeeman and give all power in that ward to Al Tomaso. The problem Giancana had with Girolami is the fact that Girolami refused to accede to request of Giancana in the latter's attempt to make Joe Porcaro as Alderman of the 28th Ward. As indication of Giancana's power, according to Chicago T-9, Girolami will accept a directive of Giancana to remove himself from the political scene without further ado.

Gambling

Chicago T-11 advised on various dates from March thru April, 1963, that a full scale gambling operation was in progress daily in the basement of the tavern located at 1442 South Cicero Avenue, Cicero, Illinois. This game was operated by Joseph "Pep" Giancana, brother of Sam, and Frank "Sharky" Eulo, a known gambler and associate of Giancana's.

Travel

On February 10, 1963, Sam Giancana was observed at Jilly's Restaurant in New York City in company with Frank Sinatra, "Fat" Frank Shor, Jack Benanty, and Skinny D'Amato. This group later proceeded to Frank Sinatra's apartment in the Waldorf Tower Hotel. At this time Giancana enjoyed an illicit relationship with an unknown female.

ASSOCIATES

Phyllis McGuire

Chicago T-13 advised that Giancana visited Miss McGiure at the Breakwater Towers Apartments at Ft. Lauderdale, Florida. He further advised that is seems apparent that Giancana is not married to Miss McGiure which fact is upsetting to Miss McGiure who apparently is the aggressor in an attempt to effect a marital relationship. Reports that Sam Giancana trying to break up the McGuire Sisters singing trio. Giancana trying to convince Phyllis she should go solo. Giancana is trying to convince Phyllis that he can make her a big movie star if she will leave the trio.

CG T-3 advised that Giancana has given Phyllis McGuire over half a million dollars worth of jewelry since he began "going with her."

Al Koslow

CG T-3 had advised that Sam Giancana has been in the company of Al Koslow on occashion when Giancana has been in New York City area. Informant advised that Koslow is the son of Nat Koslow, the founders of Nat Koslow Jewelers at 724 5th Avenue, New York City. During the time Koslow met with Giancana he and his brother, Marvin, were in possession of some watches and a 27 carat uncut diamond. During an interview with Marvin Koslow he stated the 27 carat diamond belonged to Sam Giancana and he, Marvin, had been trying to sell it for him. Koslow did indicate that this stone was not stolen, but did not indicate either as to where Giancana had obtained it from. Koslow stated that Giancana had advised him in the past that if he is ever questioned by any authorities, he is to give them a story which Giancana had concocted to the effect that he, Marvin, had formerly gone with Phyllis McGuire and through this relationship had become acquainted with Giancana.

Some time ago Chicago informant advised that Giancana had told him he could get a 27 carat uncut diamond for $100,000 and it was worth $200,000 to $300,000.

FEDERAL BUREAU OF INVESTIGATION

REPORTING OFFICE	OFFICE OF ORIGIN	DATE	INVESTIGATIVE PERIOD	
CHICAGO	CHICAGO	1963	May 3, 1963	
TITLE OF CASE		REPORT MADE BY		TYPED BY
				dkc
SAMUEL M. GIANCANA, aka		CHARACTER OF CASE		
		FBI Headquarters File Number 92-3171-999 Top Hoodlum Program – Anti Racketeering. Daily Summary		

CG 6576-C advised that Anthony Tisci and Buddy Jacobson, following recent meetings with Giancana, have learned that Giancana has decided to place Pat Marcy in control of all syndicate associatated politicians including ward committeemen and aldermen. Giancana has indicated complete dependence upon Marcy's decision in all matters and will issue orders that all matters of policy will henceforth be discussed with Marcy prior to being enacted. The forgoing obviously will place Marcy as one of the most powerful persons in Chicago politics.

Indications have been received that Marcy plans to utilize the locations of CG 6610-C for meetings with these individuals. Giancana has also reiterated that John D'Arco is not to be retained as ward committeeman and is to be deposed off with in the next few months.

324

FEDERAL BUREAU OF INVESTIGATION

REPORTING OFFICE	OFFICE OF ORIGIN	DATE	INVESTIGATIVE PERIOD	
CHICAGO	CHICAGO	1963	May 14, 1963	
TITLE OF CASE		REPORT MADE BY		TYPED BY
				dkc
SAMUEL M. GIANCANA, aka		**CHARACTER OF CASE** FBI Headquarters File Number 92-3171-1001 Top Hoodlum Program – Anti Racketeering. Daily Summary		

CG 6576-C advised on 5/13/63 that Giancana recently held conference with one Hy Godfrey. It was learned that Giancana and Hy discussed the present situation concerning an election of a future alderman for the First Ward.

FEDERAL BUREAU OF INVESTIGATION

REPORTING OFFICE	OFFICE OF ORIGIN	DATE	INVESTIGATIVE PERIOD	
CHICAGO	CHICAGO	1963	June 14, 1963	
TITLE OF CASE		REPORT MADE BY		TYPED BY
				dkc
SAMUEL M. GIANCANA, aka		**CHARACTER OF CASE** FBI Headquarters File Number 92-3171-1028 Top Hoodlum Program – Anti Racketeering. Daily Summary		

Physical surveillance of Giancana on 6/11/63 reflects subject remained at residence during entire stay with exception of two short trips of about 30 minutes each to Armory Lounge. Giancana in presents of Dominic Blasi and Anthony Tisci. On 6/12/62 Giancana observed at O'Hare Airport to board a flight to Honolulu.

Honolulu advised Giancana observed in company with middle ages woman and two young girls who are believed to be Marie Perno and Giancana's two daughters arriving in Honolulu, at which time they traveled to the Sheraton Surfrider Hotel, Waikiki, where Giancana is registered under the name of Jack Perno.

It was determined that reservations for this group were booked by Frank Sinatra during Sinatra's stay at this hotel.

Sam Giancana

Miss Perno

James Perno

Mrs. Perno

FEDERAL BUREAU OF INVESTIGATION

REPORTING OFFICE	OFFICE OF ORIGIN	DATE	INVESTIGATIVE PERIOD
CHICAGO	CHICAGO	1963	June 15, 1963

TITLE OF CASE	REPORT MADE BY	TYPED BY
		dkc

TITLE OF CASE	CHARACTER OF CASE
SAMUEL M. GIANCANA, aka	Headquarters File Number 92-3171-1028 Top Hoodlum Program – Anti Racketeering. Daily Summary

It was learned to day from Chief of Police, Warner Brothers Studio, Los Angeles that Frank Sinatra did not report for work today advising studio he was going to Cal-Neva Lodge for a few days. For information Las Vegas, it was discreetly ascertained that Sinatra was suppose to join Giancana at Surfrider Hotel, Honolulu, today. Las Vegas through discreetly determine if Sinatra as Cal-Neva and advise.

FEDERAL BUREAU OF INVESTIGATION

REPORTING OFFICE	OFFICE OF ORIGIN	DATE	INVESTIGATIVE PERIOD
CHICAGO	CHICAGO	1963	June 22, 1963

TITLE OF CASE	REPORT MADE BY	TYPED BY
		dkc

TITLE OF CASE	CHARACTER OF CASE
SAMUEL M. GIANCANA, aka	FBI Headquarters File Number 92-3171-1055 Top Hoodlum Program – Anti Racketeering. Daily Summary

Continued investigation into attempts by Chicago hoodlums to open gambling in Dominican Republic reflects Chicago hoodlum Les Kruse has made two trips to Dominican Republic, first of which made 5/29/63, in company of Giancana. Information received Chicago reflects Kruse plans to make continued trips on bi-weekly basis to Santo Domingo, Dominican Republic to continue negotiation about installation of a casino in that city.

Information reflects Kruse has obtained financial backing in this matter from several ranking Chicago hoodlums most prominent of which are Ralph Pierce, Rocco and Joseph Fischetti. In view of above, it is strongly felt that the purpose of Giancana's impending ventures in Dominican Republic. It is further assumed by Chicago Division that purpose of Anthony Accardo's trip to Paris is to meet with Giancana and help in negotiations for above noted gambling ventures. Giancana is presently in Hawaii.

FEDERAL BUREAU OF INVESTIGATION

REPORTING OFFICE	OFFICE OF ORIGIN	DATE	INVESTIGATIVE PERIOD
CHICAGO	CHICAGO	1963	June 25, 1963

TITLE OF CASE	REPORT MADE BY	TYPED BY
		dkc
SAMUEL M. GIANCANA, aka	**CHARACTER OF CASE** FBI Headquarters File Number 92-3171-1075 Top Hoodlum Program – Anti Racketeering. Daily Summary	

Extensive and intensified investigations for the past three years of Giancana, midwest representative of National Commission and recognized hear of organized crime, Chicago, has developed no prosecutable violation but has substantiated that no pertinent organized crime decisions in Chicago area, including gangland slayings, are made with out Giancana's authority.

FEDERAL BUREAU OF INVESTIGATION

REPORTING OFFICE	OFFICE OF ORIGIN	DATE	INVESTIGATIVE PERIOD
CHICAGO	CHICAGO	1963	June 27, 1963

TITLE OF CASE	REPORT MADE BY	TYPED BY
		dkc
SAMUEL M. GIANCANA, aka	**CHARACTER OF CASE** FBI Headquarters File Number 92-3171-1059 Top Hoodlum Program – Anti Racketeering. Daily Summary	

As set forth previous communications 24-hour surveillance coverage of Giancana was instituted at 11:40 p.m. on 6/23/63 upon Giancana's return to the Chicago area from Hawaii. During the initial hours of this surveillance Giancana was chauffeured by Tarquin Simonelli to his residence and following the leaving of Giancana at his home, Simonelli departed to the Armory Lounge. It was noted that Simonelli attempted on several occasions within the next three hours to return to Giancana's residence apparently of strange vehicles in the area continued on past the residence and did not attempt to make contact with Giancana. At approximately 2:30 a.m. Giancana departed his residence on foot and proceeded to the Armory Lounge.

It was learned from CG 6486-C that Giancana had several meeting planned for that evening but because of a suspected surveillance of his activities had issued instructions to Simonelli to advised persons supposedly meeting with him to cancel the proposed meetings.

During the morning hours, Giancana journeyed to the Fresh Meadows Golf Course where he met and played 27 holes of golf with John "Haircut" Campanalli, a former large bookie operating in Cicero, Illinois, who is the holder of a federal wagering stamp. Campanalli's partner William Indelli both controlled bookmaking at 4702 West Cermak Road; Sam Pardee, associate of Murray Humphreys, Anthony Accardo in the Erie-Buffalo policy wheel operation, and other Chicago hoodlums. Pardee is a particular favorite of Giancana and that as of approximately two years ago has been given several spots in the western suburbs where gambling operations were taking place as pick ups. By this, certain individuals are entrusted to pick up receipts from various gambling throughout the Chicago area, of which they retain 50% of the monies collected and turned in 50% to Giancana. According to informant, Pardee was given two spots which were formerly handled by Marshall Caifano; Lou Suriano, a Chicago bookmaker who lives down the street from Jack Cerone in Elmwood Park and which Cerone uses Suriano's home to hold meeting with other Chicago hoodlums; and Anthony Tisci. Upon the completion of Giancana's golf match he attempted to lose surveilling Agents by driving on heavily traveled thoroughfares and in an extremely reckless manner and on at least one occasion was noted to almost cause a serious accident due to his reckless driving. Upon Giancana's return to his residence, due apparently to a loss of self control, Giancana was noted to drive his personal vehicle into the side of the garage. In departing from his car to survey the damage caused, Giancana in his haste neglected to place the brakes on the vehicle and at such time as he departed the vehicle, the vehicle began to roll away from him into the street causing him further loss of self control which was extremely obvious to surveilling Agents.

At approximately 7:30 p.m. on 6/24/63, an individual approached surveilling units and identified himself as George Leighton, a Chicago attorney. Following the departure of Leighton, Giancana was observed attempting to take photographs of Agents and in fact of all foreign cars noted in the neighborhood. Giancana did not depart from his residence for the rest of the night.

On 6/25/63, Giancana was joined by Anthony V. Champagne in the early morning hours. Champagne departed after conferring with Giancana for about 30 minutes' duration. It is noted that James Perno departed the residence of Giancana for a period of about one hour and upon his return he was observed to carry several movie cameras, some with telescopic attachments. At this time Giancana again began to further his hobby of taking home movies and began to take photos of everything and everyone in sight.

FEDERAL BUREAU OF INVESTIGATION

REPORTING OFFICE	OFFICE OF ORIGIN	DATE	INVESTIGATIVE PERIOD
CHICAGO	CHICAGO	1963	June 30, 1963

TITLE OF CASE	REPORT MADE BY	TYPED BY
		dkc
SAMUEL M. GIANCANA, aka	**CHARACTER OF CASE** FBI Headquarters File Number 92-3171-1083 Top Hoodlum Program – Anti Racketeering. Daily Summary	

Chicago surveillance continuing with every possible effort being made to avoid any contact with Giancana or to give him any justifiable reason to complain in court concerning out activity. Although we are most discreet in out surveillance activity Giancana continuing his efforts to closely approach agents and photograph them when possible. When agents suspect such activity agents promptly drop surveillance in effort to avoid such incidents.

A car belonging to Illinois State Senator Jerry Dolezal was parked adjacent to Armory Lounge. Four well dressed elderly males entered lounge at time when Giancana arrived. Shortly after arrival of Dolezal, Giancana departed Armory and processed alone in personal vehicle in ten block area in vicinity of Armory Lounge apparently in an attempt to lose surveillance vehicles. When unsuccessful in this regard Giancana returned to Lounge. At approximately seven thirty PM Giancana departed lounge in company of Charles English, Anthony Tisci and his wife. Shortly after their departure Dolezal vehicle observed departing Armory Lounge.

During the late evening hours Charles English approached surveillance agents and requested to talk to them. He was interviewed for two hours by SA's Marshall Rutland and William Roemer Jr. During interview they were joined by Anthony Tisci. During course of conversation Tisci admitted Giancana's reasons for commencing court action were "desperation measure and were caused by his extreme agitation over FBI surveillance." Tisci continued that, "We are putting all our eggs in one basket."

During course of interview English, slightly intoxicated, admitted to be highly upset over FBI investigation into Lormar Distributing Company which company is headed by English and he requested agents to arrange an interview between him and agent assigned to Lomar investigation.

It was apparent from interview all members of Giancana's organization extremely apprehensive over FBI's latest maneuver to closely survey all of Giancana's movements and fell some action imminent on agents advised English they are available for interview and English advised Giancana had declined his suggestion that Giancana meet with FBI.

Giancana on 6/29/63 has gone out of his way to obtain photos of agents, and has noted to travel al least two blocks to approach agents for this purpose. Agents are being extremely discreet remaining a considerable distance from Giancana and any contact with Giancana and his associates are caused by him proceeding considerable distance to contact agents. Every effort being made on part of agents to prevent incident.

FEDERAL BUREAU OF INVESTIGATION

REPORTING OFFICE	OFFICE OF ORIGIN	DATE	INVESTIGATIVE PERIOD
CHICAGO	CHICAGO	1963	July 2, 1963

TITLE OF CASE	REPORT MADE BY	TYPED BY
SAMUEL M. GIANCANA, aka		dkc
	CHARACTER OF CASE FBI Headquarters File Number 92-3171-1082 Top Hoodlum Program – Anti Racketeering. Daily Summary	

CG 6486-C advised on 7/1/63 that Pat Marcy in a conversation with John D'Arco and Mac (LNU) discussing the current FBI surveillance of Giancana at which time Marcy pointed out that he was certain that the FBI had a definite purpose for their actions which would become apparent in due time. Later in the day Marcy was visited by Anthony Tisci who indicated to Marcy that he was preparing to file an amendment to the original complaint which would serve in fact to have the FBI furnish information as to the purpose of their investigation. This source indicates that Tisci feels Judge Austin, the presiding justice in this matter was more than favorable to Giancana's complaint and while they did not feel that they will be able to gain an injunction against the surveillance, they hope to possibly determine what the FBI's reasons are for same.

FEDERAL BUREAU OF INVESTIGATION

REPORTING OFFICE	OFFICE OF ORIGIN	DATE	INVESTIGATIVE PERIOD
CHICAGO	CHICAGO	1963	July 14, 1963

TITLE OF CASE	REPORT MADE BY	TYPED BY
SAMUEL M. GIANCANA, aka		dkc
	CHARACTER OF CASE FBI Headquarters File Number 92-3171-1127 Top Hoodlum Program – Anti Racketeering. Daily Summary	

The Chicago division is in receipt of several letters from local individuals who strongly support the FBI's position in the Giancana case. Jack Brickhouse, noted Chicago sportscaster and official of WGN radio and television station, contacted the Chicago office on this date and advised that in regard to the Giancana matter, persons of responsibility in the Chicago area with whom he has discussed the situation have indicated they are behind the FBI in their stand on the matter and all have indicated some question as to the reasons behind Judge Austin's stand in this matter.

Brickhouse continued that the general feeling is that judge Austin was wrong in his upholding of Giancana's motion regarding this matter.

FEDERAL BUREAU OF INVESTIGATION

REPORTING OFFICE	OFFICE OF ORIGIN	DATE	INVESTIGATIVE PERIOD	
CHICAGO	CHICAGO	1963	July 16, 1963	
TITLE OF CASE		**REPORT MADE BY**		**TYPED BY** dkc
SAMUEL M. GIANCANA, aka		**CHARACTER OF CASE** FBI Headquarters File Number 92-3171 Top Hoodlum Program – Anti Racketeering. Daily Summary		

Proceedings in Giancana matter commenced today before Judge Richard Austin. As Bureau will recall, two motions are presently pending before Austin. One motion presented by plaintiff Giancana requesting injunction against FBI surveillance of Giancana. The other motion is Government's motion to dismiss Giancana's motion based on government's contention that court lacks jurisdiction in this matter. Government represented primarily by U.S. Assistant Attorney John Peter Lulinski, assisted by Frank McDonald and Thomas James. Lengthy argument referring to confidential nature of FBI records under departmental order. Lulinski requested subpoena be quashed immediately with no testimony from sac.

Austin agreed to quash all portions of subpoena except that portion which demanded the number of agents assigned to surveillance. Lulinski advised Judge that Sac under departmental order could not testify as to number of agents without prior consultation with attorney general. Judge gave government until 2:00 PM today to contact attorney general regarding matter.

Lulinski then made excellent presentation prior to Giancana witnesses being heard. Austin declined to rule on motion and instructed Giancana's attorney George N. Leighton to present witness. After consulting with department, USA's office declined to cross examine any witness as they felt that to do so would weaken governments contention that one; court lacked jurisdiction and two; that to properly cross examine government would be weakening position that information in our files must be confidential recognizing that to properly cross examine government would have to indicate knowledge and results of investigation. Government did, however, object to testimony of each witness as irrelevant and immaterial and objected to numerous questions asked by plaintiff's attorney.

First witness was Shirley Cross, Leighton's secretary who testified she visited Giancana's residence in Oak Park and observed automobiles in the vicinity of residence. Also testified that she observed that when Giancana departed residence, vehicles were behind him.

Next witness was Rose Flood, Giancana's sister-in-law. She testified basically same as Cross, however, indicated she had been at Giancana's residence on almost daily basis.

Next witness was Carmen Skembare, professional photographer. He testified as to accompanying Giancana and observing vehicles which appeared to be behind Giancana at residence and golf course.

John Madigan, official of CBS, Chicago, testified that CBS took pictures at Giancana's residence and at Fresh Meadows Golf Course which were not shown.

However, when shown on TV no FBI agents or equipment identifiable.

Howard Erickson, manager of Fresh Meadows Golf Course, testified that Giancana had played golf there on several occasions and that individuals whom he described as Federal Agents had been at the golf course at the same time. He was unable to identify Federal Agents as being FBI.

Charles "Chuck" English testified that he had played golf at Fresh Meadows with Giancana and had observed men on golf course whom he believed to be FBI agents. He stated he could identify Bill Roemer based on a conversation Roemer had with him. He testified later that he had an interview with SA Roemer and another agent whom he only knew as Marshall at the Armory Lounge. He testified conversation related to gambling and general matters, none of which was uncomplimentary to agents or Bureau.

James Perno, nephew of Giancana, testified that he lives with Giancana, and observed vehicles in area and had photographed same.

Ricker, private investigator, for John T. Lynch Investigation Agency, testified he had been hired by Giancana to travel with him on one day, July 14, 1963. He testified as to vehicles which appeared to follow Giancana but was unable to make any identification. Sam Giancana took witness stand obviously for purpose of getting films admitted which he had jointly taken with Perno, He testified that an agent whom he knew as Roemer and one other agent attempted to interview him one night in the vicinity of the Armory Lounge. He claims agents suggested he leave the country and that he "never said a word to them." The testimony of English, Perno and Giancana were replete with inaccuracies and false statements. Their testimony will be carefully reviewed for possible perjury. Sac was called to stand on two separate occasions and except for identification matters claimed privilege under departmental order 260-62 on instructions of attorney general received by wire today latter portion of which stated, "Johnson is instructed not to produce any of the documents called for and not to give any testimony in this matter."

Questions involved identity of individuals and vehicle in films as well as questions intended to solicit admission of surveillance by FBI. On several occasions Austin instructed Sac to answer, however, Sac, continued to claim privilege under 260-62. Austin dismissed Sac, courteously from stand on both occasions with no mention made of contempt of court. All of the films shown reflected numerous unidentified cars in vicinity of golf course, church, Giancana residence and cemetery. No witness was able to positively identify vehicles or occupants as FBI property or personnel.

Leighton indicated to Austin that he might have one witness to be heard at 10:00 am tomorrow namely Giancana's maid Alveria Foster who is presently vacationing in New York. He indicated except for her plaintiff has completed his case.

Lulinski and McDonald strongly of opinion Leighton has not established harassment or misconduct and they are unable to arrive at a factual basis on which Austin could grant injunction against FBI. During entire hearing, Austin appeared extremely hostile to government and solicitous to Leighton. Austin not as hostile at close of session as earlier in day.

Surveillance discontinued earlier today when Giancana appeared headed for Chicago Loop area. Discreet efforts being made to pick up surveillance of Giancana with every effort being made to preclude incident which can be used by Giancana. USA's office strongly concurs that surveillance should continue.

FEDERAL BUREAU OF INVESTIGATION

REPORTING OFFICE	OFFICE OF ORIGIN	DATE	INVESTIGATIVE PERIOD	
CHICAGO	CHICAGO	1963	July 31, 1963	
TITLE OF CASE		REPORT MADE BY		TYPED BY
				dkc
SAMUEL M. GIANCANA, aka		**CHARACTER OF CASE**		
		FBI Headquarters File Number 92-3171-1141 Top Hoodlum Program – Anti Racketeering. Daily Summary		

Bureau authority requested to recontact CG 6486-C for the purpose of making relocation based on results of investigation by this division which indicates that present position of above source completely inadequate to monitor conversations and meetings of Giancana and subordinates. As previously pointed out investigation indicates Giancana now holds "court" in front area of Armory Lounge.

It is felt that reinstallation should be accomplished at earliest possible date as it is felt that Giancana is holding discussions about top level hoodlum matters. Full security can be assured at this time. Pending authority by Bureau, Chicago contemplates re-entry early morning hours August 6, next.

Source advised that on July 20, last Giancana golfing at Fresh Meadow Golf Course with Johnny "Haircut" Campanalli and two other unknown males, nothing Giancana reportedly at Lake Tahoe, July 27, last.

FEDERAL BUREAU OF INVESTIGATION

REPORTING OFFICE	OFFICE OF ORIGIN	DATE	INVESTIGATIVE PERIOD	
CHICAGO	CHICAGO	1963	August 5, 1963	
TITLE OF CASE		REPORT MADE BY		TYPED BY
		SA Marshall Rutland		dkc
SAMUEL M. GIANCANA, aka		**CHARACTER OF CASE**		
		FBI Headquarters File Number 92-3171-1163 Top Hoodlum Program – Anti Racketeering		

Synopsis;

On June 28, 1963, Sam Giancana instituted a suit in United States District Court, be for Judge Richard Austin in which he sought to enjoin the FBI from surveilling him in his daily movements. Government attorneys argued case on basis that Judge Austin had no jurisdiction in the matter, and based on that reasoning did not argue merits of case nor did they cross-examine any witnesses, two of whom were Giancana and Charles English. Judge Austin refused the government request to take case to Court of Appeals for decision as to jurisdiction before arguing case on merits. Austin denied government motion to defer cross-examination. On July 16, 1963, Austin issued temporary injunction restricting FBI surveillance and cited SA Marlin Johnson for contempt, for failing to answer certain questions regarding surveillances. Unites States Attorney's Office presenting request to 7th District Court of Appeals, on July 25, 1963. Giancana known to have traveled to California, Canada, Hawaii, Pennsylvania, New York, Dominican Republic, Florida and Chicago since April, 1963. Information received Giancana considering operating gambling interest in Dominican Republic. During stay in Hawaii in May, 1963, Giancana left with, and in daily company of Frank Sinatra. Twenty-four hour surveillance of Giancana indicated Giancana to be in constant association with several Chicago hoodlums and bookmakers.

Information Concerning Proper
Gambling Interest in Dominican Republic

CG T-4 advised that on May 23, 1963, Leslie Kruse, David Russell and Palmer Johnes traveled to Santo Domingo, Dominican Republic. This informant advised that he had learned that Russell was interested in acquiring a hotel and gambling casino and gambling casino in Santo Domingo and had invited Kruse and Jones to accompany his on this trip so that they might advise him in matters pertaining to the gambling business and hotel business. This informant stated that Russell was a former Chicagoan presently living in Bay Harbor Highlands, Florida, and has known Kruse, from the Chicago days, to be familiar with gambling matters and operations in that city. Jones, presently a resident of Palm Beach County, Florida, was reportedly engaged in the hotel business in Chicago, Illinois. He advised that while in the Dominican Republic this group met with Sam Giancana who was introduced to the group by Kruse as Sam Russo.

Miscellaneous

During the course of an investigation being conducted upon activates of Sam Giancana, SA Marshall Rutland while driving a Bureau car was stopped at red light at the intersection of Des Plaines Avenue and 22nd Street. While awaiting the single to change a car chauffeured by Charles English pulled abreast of the Bureau car. While both vehicles were stopped at the intersection English opened a conversation with the agent pertaining to his recent dinner at the Czech Lodge and during the conversation extended an invitation to the agent to "join us at out next stop." Agent Rutland assumed the reference to "us" referred to Sam Giancana, Anthony Tisci and a female believed to be the wife of Tisci who accompanied English in his vehicle.

SA Ruthland contacted SA William Roemer who was the occupant of a second surveillance unit and advised him of the invitation extended by English. SA Roemer proceeded to the parking lot of the Armory Lounge located on Roosevelt Road in Forest Park. Within the period of several moments English's car arrived at the lot and the four occupants were observed to depart from the vehicle, with all except English proceeding into the lounge. English hailed SA Roemer and waved him over to join him, which SA Roemer proceeded to do. While awaiting the arrival of SA Ruthland who was parking his vehicle, English initiated the conversation by stating, "I want you and me and him to go over to the Pump Room for the rest of the night." SA Roemer advised English that the agents were not interested in night clubbing with Giancana and English but were interested in talking to them in regard to certain of their activities in which the FBI had an investigative interest. At this point SA Ruthland joined English and Roemer.

After questioning the agents as to why they were so interested at this time of Giancana's movements but before awaiting an answer English suggested that they accompany him inside the Armory Lounge for the purpose of continuing their conversations. Upon entering the Lounge the agents proceeded to take position next to English at the bar located in the front portion of the building. The conversation at this point turned to generalities concerning general topics. During one point of the conversation English stated that one of the things that has exited Giancana to a great extent is the fact that he has been unable to get together with any of the girls during this period. English further commented that this was one of the things that has so irritated Giancana at the time of an FBI interview held approximately one year ago, which occasion of Giancana's arrival in Chicago with Phyllis McGiure. English contended that Giancana was attempting at that time to make an impression upon McGiure and because of the presence of the FBI he was greatly embarrassed and humiliated. It was pointed out to English that the FBI had not initiated any action that would have caused Giancana to become embarrassed. Their purpose for being at the airport was merely to interview Miss McGiure and that it was Giancana's own actions which brought him into contact with the FBI. At this point English was advised to offer Giancana the opportunity of talking to the agents. English was observed to proceed to a table at which Giancana was seated and was noted to converse with Giancana for two or three minute period. Upon English's returned to the agents he advised then that he had passed on their request to Giancana who he stated told him that he was not interested in a conversation at this time.

English then went into a conversation regarding his life long friendship with Giancana and stated that he owed a great deal to Giancana for the opportunities which Giancana has afforded English throughout his lifetime. English stated that he and Giancana have been friends for 35 years and, "I won't leave him now that he's in trouble." During this conversation English advised he has made his money through gambling and stated that as of several years ago he was perhaps one of the biggest gamblers in the United States. At this point English attempted to engage the agents in a discussion as to the laws both local and federal regarding gambling and what exactly constituted a gambling violation. The agents pointed out to English that for a legal opinion as to what constituted a violation or gambling laws he should consult with Anthony Tisci, who was observed to be seated at a table with Butch Blasi in another portion of the room. At this point English turned and hailed Tisci and requested that he joins the group, which he did.

Tisci's initial remarks concerning the recent surveillance of Giancana and with out prompting he began a conversation pointing out to the agents that he felt that through their use of binoculars the agents were in actuality spying into the household of Sam Giancana. Tisci continued that he felt this improper because within the household were several young woman whose privacy was being invaded. The agents were quick to advise Tisci that at no time were agents peering into the window of Giancana's home with their binoculars and that Tisci, if he were realistic in his opinions would admit that this was certainly a far fetched statement to make. At this point the agents told Tisci that the conversation to that point with English had been in a very friendly level to which English agreed and Tisci advised that if he desired to continue making such wild accusations that his company was not desired.

After several minutes conversation Tisci warmed to the agents and at one point admitted the reason of trying to do away with FBI investigation into Giancana's activities. According to Tisci, "We are putting all our eggs in one bucket."

After agents had left the Armory Lounge English approached SA Roemer who was driving away in an automobile and told him that he had been instructed by Giancana to tell the agents that if "Kennedy" desired to talk to him it would be all right with Giancana and that "Kennedy" should go through the guy he knows about. English implied that this individual was Frank Sinatra, but did not actually say so. English advised that this message should be given to "Kennedy." "Off the record or on the record, whatever you want to do." This concluded the contact of English.

CG T-6 advised that leaders of the outfit, upon learning of English's interview with the FBI, were extremely upset, and advised that one of these persons, Frank Ferraro, planned to see Anthony Accardo and Paul DeLucia for the purpose of having them talk with Giancana regarding his recent activities and more specifically of his association with English. It was learned that Ferraro indicated that word had gone out some time ago that all hoodlums, upon being contacted with FBI agents were to refuse to talk to the contacting agents. It was learned by this source that one particular point was their belief that English in his discussion with the FBI, had admitted the association between Frank Sinatra and Giancana. The full details as to the reason for their concern were not given, however, there appeared to be the underlying reason that Sinatra was more closely associated with Giancana and the hoodlum element than had been publicly known.

CG T-17 advised that Giancana has shouted a steady tirade of verbal abuse on each occasion that he observes Sheriff's Police following him and further that Giancana's attorney, George Leighton, has indicated further legal proceedings will be taken to enjoin the Sheriff's Police from the surveillance of Giancana.

CG T-9 advised that Peter Granata, Representative to the Illinois State Legislature, had become extremely apprehensive as to his movements, an had indicated to associates in Chicago that he was of the opinion that he was being constantly watched by the FBI for the reason that they felt that he was Sam Giancana's man in Springfield.

Associates

Porfirio Rubirosa

Porfirio Rubirosa, the former ambassador to the United States from the Dominican Republic, was talked of by Giancana whom he was planning to contact in France during June of 1963, concerning gambling in the Dominican Republic.

Frank Sinatra

Investigation reflected that Giancana spent time with Frank Sinatra in Hawaii during May of 1963. During this time. Giancana while living under the alias of J.J. Brackett, resided in the same suit at the Surfrider Hotel in Hawaii. It was noted that following the conclusion of their stay that Sinatra paid the entire bill for all persons at the hotel.

During June of 1963, CG T-3 advised that Frank Sinatra, Ava Garner, Phyllis McGiure, and Sam Giancana met in the New York area, and proceeded to Sinatra's home in New Jersey where they spent the evening.

According to CG T-3, Frank Sinatra at the request of Giancana, obtained a part in his latest picture "Come Blow Your Horn" for Phyllis McGuire.

Legal Proceedings Instituted By Giancana

On June 28, 1963, George Leighton, Attorney, appeared before Judge Austin in the U.S. District Court, representing Sam Giancana in a civil action whereby Giancana appeared as the plaintiff in a suit against J. Edgar Hoover, Director of the FBI and Marlin Johnson, Agent in charge of the Chicago Division of the FBI, whereby Giancana pressed for "equitable relief." Since this time Leighton presented a motion on behalf of Giancana for a temporary restraining order and for temporary injunction as to surveillance conducted by FBI. At this time Giancana also presented a complaint in which he duly swore all allegations set forth therein were true in substance and in fact.

FEDERAL BUREAU OF INVESTIGATION

REPORTING OFFICE	OFFICE OF ORIGIN	DATE	INVESTIGATIVE PERIOD
CHICAGO	CHICAGO	1963	August 8, 1963

TITLE OF CASE	REPORT MADE BY	TYPED BY
		dkc

TITLE OF CASE: SAMUEL M. GIANCANA, aka

CHARACTER OF CASE
FBI Headquarters File Number 92-3171-1169
Top Hoodlum Program – Anti Racketeering.
Daily Summary

A Chicago hoodlum presently under indictment who has been furnishing information to this office advised that a move is underway by Chicago hoodlums to oust Giancana as head of organized crime group in Chicago. According to informant, the person who would be placed in charge if movement if successful is Jack Cerone, long time lieutenant of Anthony Accardo. Informant pointed out that Cerone has Accardo's blessing in this movement. This source advised that Cerone has the backing of many of Chicago's younger hoodlums mainly Fifi Buccieri, Joe Gagliano and Willie Messino. The source continued that this move is similar to that attempted by William Daddono in the past, however, main difference is Cerone has backing of Accardo because of lack of publicity upon activities of Cerone. This situation being followed closely.

FEDERAL BUREAU OF INVESTIGATION

REPORTING OFFICE	OFFICE OF ORIGIN	DATE	INVESTIGATIVE PERIOD
CHICAGO	CHICAGO	1963	August 14, 1963

TITLE OF CASE	REPORT MADE BY	TYPED BY
		dkc

TITLE OF CASE: SAMUEL M. GIANCANA, aka

CHARACTER OF CASE
FBI Headquarters File Number 92-3171
Top Hoodlum Program – Anti Racketeering.
Daily Summary

CG informant advised that this date that in recent contacts with persons close to Sam Giancana he has learned that a general feeling of apprehensiveness pervades the Giancana organization. Few remarks are being made by any of these person's as to their opinions regarding what Giancana plans to do in the future in regard to the running of the Chicago criminal organization. This informant advises that Giancana is giving no directions to his underlings and as a result the general situation is in a state of chaos. It is pointed out that adding to this general state of confusion Giancana has absented himself from the Chicago area for the past two weeks and apparently has given no indication as to when he will return. In regard to the reasons for Giancana's leaving the

Chicago area, it was learned by the informant who is close to many of Chicago's hoodlums, that Giancana's departure was caused by a fear that the FBI would reinstitute the
surveillance upon his daily activities and would again leave him in a position where
he would be unable to go about his daily activities in an unhampered manner. According
to the informant Giancana, in conversation with other hoodlums, had indicated that he
is considering leaving the country with a possible destination being Brazil. The Chicago division feels that this information has some merit based on the comments of Murray Humphreys made in the past that Giancana should attempt to do everything in his
power to get away from the FBI surveillance and to remain in some location where such
surveillance could not be reinstituted. It is felt that a strong possibility exists that
a recent meeting held at Staley's Restaurant by nine of Chicago's leading hoodlums was
probably for the purpose of deciding how Giancana should govern himself based on current happenings. It is further felt highly likely that a decision was made in which it
was recommended to Giancana that he leave Chicago. The informant continued that because
of recent publicity attendant upon the hoodlum situation in Chicago Marshall Caifano is
also making plans to leave the country. He advised that aside from the general consternation caused by the Giancana situation it has been learned by the hoodlums that internal revenue is reportedly going to indict three Chicago hoodlums sometimes prior to the
end of this year. The names of these hoodlums are unknown thereby causing a great deal
of anxiety among at least a half a dozen of the leading hoodlums. CG 6588 informant is
a close associate of Phil Alderisio, advised that Alderisio stated to him that, "If my
name gets in the papers on this thing anymore, I'm going to get out of here for at least
3 months and turn everything over to you."

This source further advised that Alderisio stated that recent newspaper publicity
has visibly shaken Alderisio who is convinced that federal activity in Chicago area and
resulted publicity is prelude to numerous federal indictments. Hoodlums believe purpose of publicity to sway public opinion and favor future federal prosecutions. The same
source advised Jimmy Allegretti told source that all branches of federal government
are working together against syndicate and pointed out recent fast action of Supreme
Court in Giancana matter was a "world's record." Allegretti told source, "The feds really mean business now and this increased pressure and publicity is hurting the Outfit."

The informant who is in daily contact with Lester Kruse and one William
McGuire, a lieutenant in Kruse's gambling enterprises, advised that according to Kruse
the FBI's action against gambling in Northern Illinois has wrecked the Kruse operation to the extent that overhead on buildings formerly used for gambling purposes, now
standing idle, is costing Kruse and his associates a "small fortune." Gambling employees out of work for the past several months are now broke and clamoring for jobs from
the Kruse organization. The organization to date had refused to pay these people even
though they have been employees for over twenty years, and have been unable to find
jobs for them in Las Vegas or elsewhere. Kruse advised informant that as his Illinois
gambling revenue is partially non existent revenue from other Kruse enterprises must
be increased. Informant advised that William McGuire representing Kruse's interest had
a meeting with Carl (LNU) who represents Taylor and Company and Hunt and Company,
manufactures of dice and gambling equipment and both formerly owned by Joey Aiuppa.
McGiure place a large order with Carl for what the informant terms "ace, duce, flats",
a type of dice which, although not loaded, have a shaved side which increases the percentage of craps and hence increases the house tax. Kruse indicates that by increasing
revenue from other establishments revenues lost in Illinois can be made up.

FEDERAL BUREAU OF INVESTIGATION

REPORTING OFFICE	OFFICE OF ORIGIN	DATE	INVESTIGATIVE PERIOD
CHICAGO	CHICAGO	1963	August 20, 1963

TITLE OF CASE	REPORT MADE BY	TYPED BY
		dkc
SAMUEL M. GIANCANA, aka	**CHARACTER OF CASE** FBI Headquarters File Number 92-3171-1183 Top Hoodlum Program – Anti Racketeering. Daily Summary	

Advised this date that Chicago hoodlums presently attempting to organize gambling operations in Mexico. Informant advised that Anthony Accardo visited Nick Circella aka Nick Dean, deported Chicago hoodlum presently residing in Mexico City approximately three months ago to further negotiations. He continued that Augie Circella, brother of Nick Dean and operator of Chicago burlesque house, has met with Accardo at least six times in the past three months and recently received one hundred and fifty thousand dollars from Accardo, presumably "Outfit" money and not Accardo's which was carried to Dean in Mexico by female whose identity unknown to informant at this time. Informant continued that Paul DeLucia "Ricca" is also actively engaged in furthering this Mexican operation with Accardo. Informant further advised that within past 30 to 90 days Ricca has steadily been assuming more responsibility in hoodlum activities and that as of this date in one of five persons actually running the "Chicago Picture." The informant stated that Sam Giancana, Gus Alex, Tony Accardo, and Paul DeLucia are four the top five however, is unaware at this time of the fifth person.

FEDERAL BUREAU OF INVESTIGATION

REPORTING OFFICE	OFFICE OF ORIGIN	DATE	INVESTIGATIVE PERIOD
CHICAGO	CHICAGO	1963	August 22, 1963

TITLE OF CASE	REPORT MADE BY	TYPED BY
		dkc
SAMUEL M. GIANCANA, aka	**CHARACTER OF CASE** FBI Headquarters File Number 92-3171-1184 Top Hoodlum Program – Anti Racketeering. Daily Summary	

CG 6486-C advised that Giancana's chauffer, Butch Blasi, in answer to question about contact with subject stated that he has been in contact with Giancana only once in the last two weeks. Blasi stated that Giancana indicated at the time that he was trying to stay out of public light and was not going to contact anyone other than his son-in-law Anthony Tisci. Blasi indicated that Giancana did not want to use any phones to relay messages.

CG 6576-C advised on same day that Anthony Tisci confided to Pat Marcy that Giancana had telephonically contacted Tisci on that date from Florida and indicated that he would be returning to Chicago area in two or three days.

FEDERAL BUREAU OF INVESTIGATION

REPORTING OFFICE	OFFICE OF ORIGIN	DATE	INVESTIGATIVE PERIOD
CHICAGO	CHICAGO	1963	August 28, 1963

TITLE OF CASE	REPORT MADE BY	TYPED BY
SAMUEL M. GIANCANA, aka		dkc

CHARACTER OF CASE

FBI Headquarters File 92-3171-1189
Top Hoodlum Program – Anti Racketeering.
Daily Summary

CG 6486-C advised subject in Chicago and together with associates indicated concern over IRS raid on bookies at Sportsman's Park Race Track, Cicero. Chuck English extremely upset over this raid on his on-track book makes. Giancana stated, "Now the G will try to find out who is getting that money. Well, maybe that will keep them busy."

Source revealed subject and group in possession of electronic equipment, radio receivers and recorders, some battery operated and good for a distance of 18 yards, other utilized in personal cards.

Giancana, reading from an early edition of the August 27, 1963, Chicago Tribune newspaper and stated, "Look at this. Here's this movie, Johnnie Cook, listen, the inside of the La Cosa Nostra, this flicker was shot long before the disclosures of Joe Valachi. Boy, they're cashing in all right."

FEDERAL BUREAU OF INVESTIGATION

REPORTING OFFICE	OFFICE OF ORIGIN	DATE	INVESTIGATIVE PERIOD
CHICAGO	CHICAGO	1963	August 31, 1963

TITLE OF CASE	REPORT MADE BY	TYPED BY
SAMUEL M. GIANCANA, aka		dkc

CHARACTER OF CASE

FBI Headquarters File Number 92-3171-1191
Top Hoodlum Program – Anti Racketeering.
Daily Summary

CG 6486-C in locality usually visited by Giancana when in Chicago, indicated on August 26, last, subject in close proximity. Giancana responded to inquiry by Chuck English as to why he plays golf with unknown male when he comes to Chicago. "Well when you come back who can you get to play with that you won't beat up. Do you know?"

FEDERAL BUREAU OF INVESTIGATION

REPORTING OFFICE	OFFICE OF ORIGIN	DATE	INVESTIGATIVE PERIOD	
CHICAGO	CHICAGO	1963	September 4, 1963	
TITLE OF CASE		REPORT MADE BY		TYPED BY
				dkc
SAMUEL M. GIANCANA, aka		CHARACTER OF CASE		
		FBI Headquarters File Number 92-3171-1196 Top Hoodlum Program – Anti Racketeering. Daily Summary		

CG 6576-C advised that Lt. Mark Conlin, First District Policeman met on 9/3/63, with Pat Marcy and was given sum of $3,220 for payoffs to policemen in First District as monthly payoff. Marcy advised during conversation that sum was collected from eight joints.

The only individual amount mentioned during conversation was the sum of $150 which is Conlin's allotment. The name of several individuals, possibly captains holding the position of watch commanders were given, however, the amounts each received were not mentioned. Of particular note were Marcy's specific instructions to Conlin to remember and pay off Mandel (First District vice detective who had been causing so much trouble through his enforcement to local laws in Loop strip joints.) Conlin was emphatic in his reply that Mandel was being taken care of.

Of further note was Conlin's consternation over the fact that he had just recently been called in by IRS and questioned as to his connections with the First Ward. Marcy advised that no leak had come from his, Marcy's office and told Conlin not to be worried. However, he cautioned Conlin to be very careful of his actions and not to spend any of the money at this time. He also cautioned Conlin to make sure that his expenditures were not such that he could be caught on spending more than his salary would allow.

IRS questioning of Conlin apparently stemmed from letterhead memo submitted March last advising that Agency of fact that Conlin was bagman for First District. From tone of Marcy's conversation there is no indication that he felt at time of conversation that tie-in came from his office.

FEDERAL BUREAU OF INVESTIGATION

REPORTING OFFICE	OFFICE OF ORIGIN	DATE	INVESTIGATIVE PERIOD
CHICAGO	CHICAGO	1963	September 6, 1963

TITLE OF CASE	REPORT MADE BY	TYPED BY
		dkc

SAMUEL M. GIANCANA, aka	**CHARACTER OF CASE** FBI Headquarters File Number 92-3171-1195 Top Hoodlum Program – Anti Racketeering. Daily Summary

CG 6576-C advised that Pat Marcy did not attend the wedding of a member of Jack Cerone's family because of orders given to him by Moe (Giancana) after he was noted in attendance by police officials at the wake of Mike Spranze, a former Chicago hoodlum. Marcy stated that, "Moe ate my (obscene) good for going to that and gave me orders that I was not to go to any more wakes or weddings. "

This informant further advised that Marcy is presently utilizing an additional room in his present office building, however, exact location not known at this time. Possibility exists this is space formerly covered by CG 6610-C and efforts being made at this time to determine that possibility.

FEDERAL BUREAU OF INVESTIGATION

REPORTING OFFICE	OFFICE OF ORIGIN	DATE	INVESTIGATIVE PERIOD
CHICAGO	CHICAGO	1963	September 12, 1963

TITLE OF CASE	REPORT MADE BY	TYPED BY
		dkc

SAMUEL M. GIANCANA, aka	**CHARACTER OF CASE** FBI Headquarters File 92-3171-1201 Top Hoodlum Program – Anti Racketeering. Daily Summary

CG 6486-C advised this date that information received by Doris Fanelli was that, "The man (Sam Giancana) said he was going to Paris and Rome." From earlier conversation held with Chuck English it was apparent that Fanelli in contact with Giancana, probably telephonically.

Source advised that Marshall (Caifano) tried to contact Giancana at Armory on 9/8/63, and told Sam not in.

FEDERAL BUREAU OF INVESTIGATION

REPORTING OFFICE	OFFICE OF ORIGIN	DATE	INVESTIGATIVE PERIOD	
CHICAGO	CHICAGO	1963	September 17, 1963	
TITLE OF CASE		REPORT MADE BY		TYPED BY
				dkc
SAMUEL M. GIANCANA, aka		**CHARACTER OF CASE** FBI Headquarters File Number 92-3171-1210 Top Hoodlum Program – Anti Racketeering. Daily Summary		

CG 6632-C advised that Sam Giancana is presently attempting to remain in seclusion as he feels that he is in line to be subpoenaed soon to appear before the Senate Racket Committee hearings that are scheduled to commence in the future in Washington. This information would give credence to that furnish 9/16/63, to effect that Giancana back in Chicago but has only made his whereabouts known to a few persons.

FEDERAL BUREAU OF INVESTIGATION

REPORTING OFFICE	OFFICE OF ORIGIN	DATE	INVESTIGATIVE PERIOD	
CHICAGO	CHICAGO	1963	September 19, 1963	
TITLE OF CASE		REPORT MADE BY		TYPED BY
				dkc
SAMUEL M. GIANCANA, aka		**CHARACTER OF CASE** FBI Headquarters File Number 92-3171 Top Hoodlum Program – Anti Racketeering. Daily Summary		

On September 19, 1963, Sam Giancana and two individuals identified only as Sol and Jimmy held a discussion at which time the topic concerned James Hoffa and the Union Pension Fund, in particular the Central States Union Pension Fund. During the conversation it was learned that Giancana had recently attempted to obtain a three million dollar loan from Hoffa's union and was turned down by Hoffa. Giancana was extremely bitter and in his comments concerning this, advised the others present that there were times recently when Giancana could obtain any sum of money he desired from this fund but now with all the heat on he cannot obtain any money nor any favors. Giancana continued that at one point several years ago, he obtained a one and three quarter million dollar loan from Hoffa in the period of two days. In regard to this conversation, it is believed that the request for the three million dollar loan was in connection with a request by Frank Sinatra for a similar amount for the purpose of renovating the Cal Neva Lodge supposedly owned by Sinatra but believed in actuality to be owned by Giancana.

FEDERAL BUREAU OF INVESTIGATION

REPORTING OFFICE	OFFICE OF ORIGIN	DATE	INVESTIGATIVE PERIOD
CHICAGO	CHICAGO	1963	September 27, 1963

TITLE OF CASE	REPORT MADE BY	TYPED BY
SAMUEL M. GIANCANA, aka		dkc
	CHARACTER OF CASE FBI Headquarters File Number 92-3171-1220 Top Hoodlum Program – Anti Racketeering. Daily Summary	

CG 6576-C advised that Pat Marcy had arranged a deal whereby Richard Cain agreed to set up a Sheriff's patrolman who had made an arrest of a client of Attorney Anthony V. Champagne. Source advised the patrolman, after being contacted by Champagne had advised Sheriff Richard Ogilvie that Champagne indicated a payoff could be made in this case. Ogilvie, after calling in Cain, arranged for patrolman to carry wire recorder to tape Champagne's payoff. However, through Cain's furnishing this information to Marcy, arrangement were made for Champagne to actually put patrolman in middle and make contact look as though Champagne was actually contacting patrolman to determine if his client's allegations that patrolman has shaken client down for $500 was true. Cain was then to arrest patrolmen instead of Champagne.

Through this maneuver, Cain also hoped to force Captain Noble, commanding officer of Homewood sub-station out as Noble has been tightening up on all Outfit joints located in south Cook County.

FEDERAL BUREAU OF INVESTIGATION

REPORTING OFFICE	OFFICE OF ORIGIN	DATE	INVESTIGATIVE PERIOD
CHICAGO	CHICAGO	1963	October 11, 1963

TITLE OF CASE	REPORT MADE BY	TYPED BY
SAMUEL M. GIANCANA, aka		dkc
	CHARACTER OF CASE FBI Headquarters File Number 92-3171-1230 Top Hoodlum Program – Anti Racketeering. Daily Summary	

CG 6486-C advised that Giancana held conversation with Charles English concerning Valachi testimony before Senate Committee. Both agreed that Valachi unable to hurt any of Chicago hoodlums but felt that he was doing a great deal of harm to New York mobsters. Biggest fear held by English was that government would be able to capitalize on this type of situation in the future in the obtaining of other informants, being able to show that they went along with Valachi and did not hold him accountable for his crimes.

In explaining significance of this type of hearing to Doris Fanelli (owner of Armory Lounge) it was explained that even though this informant did not put anyone in jail it caused irreparable harm to their reputations in their respective communities.

Source advised that Giancana playing golf on a daily basis with Chuck English as one of his playing partners.

FEDERAL BUREAU OF INVESTIGATION

REPORTING OFFICE	OFFICE OF ORIGIN	DATE	INVESTIGATIVE PERIOD	
CHICAGO	CHICAGO	1963	October 14, 1963	
TITLE OF CASE		REPORT MADE BY		TYPED BY
				dkc
SAMUEL M. GIANCANA, aka		CHARACTER OF CASE		
		FBI Headquarters File Number 92-3171-1232 Top Hoodlum Program – Anti Racketeering. Daily Summary		

CG 6576-C advised Anthony Tisci met with Anthony Girolami and Pat Marcy which time discussion held concerning conflict of interest case involving Tisci arising for involvement in Giancana's civil rights are against the government. Indication from source was that Tisci has just received information from Washington to affect that FBI conducting interviews regarding this matter in Washington. This undoubtedly reference to recently conducted interviews by WFO with Congressman Roland Libonati concerning Tisci's duties as Libonati's secretary. Tisci apparently pressing Girolami for information concerning Chicago investigation into this matter and was advised by Girolami that he had absolutely no information and had been unable to gain any regarding this matter.

Girolami questioned Tisci as to whether Tisci would want Girolami to advise SA William Roemer of the Chicago Division of the fact that a subpoena had been issued for Tisci to act as a witness for Giancana feeling that should the government posses this information, it would substantially weaken case and possibly cause them to discontinue their investigation into this matter. From general tenor of conversation, Tisci appeared apprehensive over entire situation.

FEDERAL BUREAU OF INVESTIGATION

REPORTING OFFICE	OFFICE OF ORIGIN	DATE	INVESTIGATIVE PERIOD	
CHICAGO	CHICAGO	1963	October 16, 1963	
TITLE OF CASE		REPORT MADE BY		TYPED BY
				dkc
SAMUEL M. GIANCANA, aka		CHARACTER OF CASE		
		FBI Headquarters File 92-3171-1233 Top Hoodlum Program – Anti Racketeering. Daily Summary		

CG 6576-C advised Pat Marcy apprehensive over numerous reversals suffered by Chicago syndicate. In conversation with Buddy Jacobson, he indicated he was worried concerning opinions of Chicago top hoodlums as to his capabilities in handing these matters. Jacobson advised that in recent conversations with Sam Giancana and Paul DeLucia "Ricca" they had indicated they were extremely satisfied with Marcy's handling of various matters and that Jacobson assured Marcy that they felt that there was nothing any person could do at this time. Jacobson stated that he had never seen conditions as bad as they are in Chicago at this time. Jacobson continued that Ricca had advised him that the organization must be patient and wait for the pressure to lift. Jacobson indicated to Marcy that he had never seen a time when they had so little going for them. He continued that it was a shame to "have all this equipment and no place to move it." Marcy ended the discussion by advising that his day has become a scudding of serious problem which he has to attempt to cope with.

FEDERAL BUREAU OF INVESTIGATION

REPORTING OFFICE	OFFICE OF ORIGIN	DATE	INVESTIGATIVE PERIOD	
CHICAGO	CHICAGO	1963	October 16, 1963	
TITLE OF CASE		REPORT MADE BY		TYPED BY
		SA Marshall Rutland		dkc
SAMUEL M. GIANCANA, aka		CHARACTER OF CASE		
		FBI Headquarters File Number 92-3171-1231 Top Hoodlum Program – Anti Racketeering		

Synopsis:

Justices Elmer Schackenberg and Roger J. Kelly held emergency hearing in 7th Circuit Court of Appeals on 7/26/63 at which time they rendered a decision stating District Court order issued by Judge Richard Austin, whereby District Court issued preliminary injunction of FBI surveillance. Giancana's attorney filed notice for application for stay of order granted by Appellate Court with Supreme Court of U.S. on 8/3/63. Honorable Justice Thomas Clarke refused to hear motion. Government briefs for full hearing before Appellate Court filed 9/17/63. Giancana publicly acclaimed as member of "commission" during McClellan Hearings in Washington. Giancana's trip to Cal-Neva Lodge, Nevada basis for action taken by Nevada Gambling Commission in revoking license of interests held by Frank Sinatra in Cal-Neva and Sands Hotel in Las Vegas. Giancana reported planning to depart U.S. for period of six months to a year for purpose of evading more publicity and claims he will not return until publicity dies down. Giancana has issued instructions to all policy associates that they are to discontinue practice associates that they are to discontinue practical of attending weddings and funerals of hoodlums. Anthony Tisci, son-in-law of Giancana, presently subject of conflict of interest case arising from involvement in Giancana court proceedings. Phyllis McGuire told by sister to rid herself of Giancana association.

Relatives

On October 7, 1963, Anthony J. Giancana, the son of Joseph "Pepe" Giancana, Sam Giancana's Brother, was arrested by Missouri State Police in that state. Police advised that young Giancana was observed speeding at speeds up to 130 miles an hour and following his apprehension learned that he was running away from home.

Criminal Activities

During August of 1963, during hearings presided over by Senator John McClellan looking into the picture of organized crime throughout the U.S., Sam Giancana was identified by one Joseph Valachi, a self admitted member of the "La Cosa Nostra", to be a member of the "La Cosa Nostra" and was to be one of the ruling body of twelve individuals referred to as one of a "Commission" who duties are to rule on disputes and arguments pertinent to the operations of organized crime throughout the U.S.

It has been reported that a move may be in progress to oust Giancana as "Boss" and Jack Cerone to take his place. In this regard, it is pointed out that on July 29, 1963, a meeting was held at Staley's Restaurant in which some of the top members of the Chicago Organization were present. This meeting was most notable in that Giancana was not present. Those individuals present at the meeting were Murray Humphreys, Anthony Accardo, Paul DeLucia, Frank Ferraro, Gus Alex, Ralph Pierce, Jackie Cerone, Hy Godfrey, Joey Glimco, Fred "Jukebox" Smith and Attorneys Eugene Bernstein and Mike Brodkin. The full purpose of this meeting had never been determined; however, there is some indication that the Giancana situation was one of the prime topics of discussion.

In substantiation of the information furnished by CG T-2, CG T-3 advised in August, 1963, that because of Giancana's constant traveling outside of Chicago within the past several months, many decisions which are required to be made by Giancana have been left unmade and as a result underlings are receiving no direction as to their activity, rendering to a somewhat chaotic state within the Chicago Organization.

CG T-4 had furnished information in this regard to the effect that because of the situation developing within the Outfit, Anthony Accardo and Paul DeLucia "Ricca" have recently assumed a more active roll in the operations of the Chicago Organization. This informant has advised that these two individuals are attempting to keep the organization from breaking into several factions which in their opinion would make the entire organization extremely vulnerable to investigations being conducted primarily by Government investigators.

CG T-5 furnished information during September, 1963, which reflected that Sam Giancana was in attendance at a wedding of the son of Ben Fillichio. The wedding was attended by many of the top hoodlums in Chicago. Reportable Giancana, Anthony Accardo, Paul DeLucia, Frank Ferraro, and Murray Humphreys met in a private room reserved for this purpose during a reception held after the wedding. This meeting was held for the purpose of discussing the present situation of organized crime in Chicago.

Eddie Fisher and Dean Martin

CG T-9 advised that in September of 1963 he observed Sam Giancana in Las Vegas in the company of singing personality Eddie Fisher. Fisher was treating Giancana with a great deal of respect and difference to his every desire. On occasion he noted Giancana, Fisher and Dean Martin hanging out together, Martin to give same kind of respect as Fisher.

Phyllis McGuire

CG T-10 advised that there was some indication a rift had occurred between the McGuire Sisters and supposedly Dorothy McGuire had issues an ultimatum to her sister Phyllis that if she did not discontinue her association with Giancana, that Dorothy would refuse to sing with the sisters any longer.

First Ward, Chicago

It has been confidentially reported that Sam Giancana had definitely decided upon having Mike FioRito run in the next election for the position of Alderman of the First

Ward.

It had been learned that John D'Arco continues to hold some hope of regaining this position and has on occasion requested Pat Marcy to make contact with Giancana for the purpose of determining if Giancana will reconsider D'Arco for this position. D'Arco has further attempted to enlist the services of Frank Ferraro to go to Giancana on his behalf.

It was learned that Pat Marcy currently uses the code name of Doc or Doctor when conversing with close friends in reference to Sam Giancana.

FEDERAL BUREAU OF INVESTIGATION

REPORTING OFFICE	OFFICE OF ORIGIN	DATE	INVESTIGATIVE PERIOD
CHICAGO	CHICAGO	1963	October 17, 1963

TITLE OF CASE	REPORT MADE BY	TYPED BY
		dkc
SAMUEL M. GIANCANA, aka	**CHARACTER OF CASE** FBI Headquarters File Number 92-3171-1234 Top Hoodlum Program – Anti Racketeering. Daily Summary	

CG 6486-C advised that Sam Giancana met with Anthony Accardo, Charles "Chuckie" English, and Butch Blasi at the Armory Lounge. During conversation Giancana offered to lend Blasi some money to make a land purchase but was turned down by Blasi as he said that it would cause too much heat as the "G" would be investigating to see where he got that much money and the deal would not be worth it. Giancana became extremely agitated at this and began to curse the Government saying that he can't do a thing any more. He continued, "I'm just gona hit and run, hit and run ..... take care of them ....sneak here, sneak there ....get nothing violent."

FEDERAL BUREAU OF INVESTIGATION

REPORTING OFFICE	OFFICE OF ORIGIN	DATE	INVESTIGATIVE PERIOD
CHICAGO	CHICAGO	1963	October 18, 1963

TITLE OF CASE	REPORT MADE BY	TYPED BY
		dkc
SAMUEL M. GIANCANA, aka	**CHARACTER OF CASE** FBI Headquarters File Number 92-3171-1235 Top Hoodlum Program – Anti Racketeering. Daily Summary	

CG 6576-C advised Giancana extremely upset over intended court action concerning son-in-law Anthony Tisci. Source not clear over whether reference is to libel suit instituted by Tisci against Chicago American Newspaper and its reporter Sam Blair for $15,000,000 or to conflict of interest case against Tisci. Source reported that Giancana so concerned when advised of case by Attorney George Leighton that Leighton became too upset to tell Giancana that he would in all probability be called on to testify in this matter. Source indicates Leighton very upset over outcome of interview with Giancana.

CG 6486-C advised Giancana met October 12 last with Chuck English and met "with that guy on Western Avenue" during evening hours. Giancana continues to golf with English during day time hours.

First source indicated that Giancana presently under impression that Chicago agent assigned to his investigation in daily contact with Senate Racket Committee personnel and advising them as to who should be subpoenaed before committee.

FEDERAL BUREAU OF INVESTIGATION

REPORTING OFFICE	OFFICE OF ORIGIN	DATE	INVESTIGATIVE PERIOD
CHICAGO	CHICAGO	1963	October 23, 1963

TITLE OF CASE	REPORT MADE BY	TYPED BY
SAMUEL M. GIANCANA, aka		dkc

	CHARACTER OF CASE
	FBI Headquarters File Number 92-3171-1237 Top Hoodlum Program – Anti Racketeering. Daily Summary

Informant advised that from recent conversations with Anthony Tisci and Pat Marcy, it is his feeling that John D'Arco has been unable to re-establish himself in the good graces of Giancana and will retain position as democratic ward committeeman of the First Ward.

FEDERAL BUREAU OF INVESTIGATION

REPORTING OFFICE	OFFICE OF ORIGIN	DATE	INVESTIGATIVE PERIOD
CHICAGO	CHICAGO	1963	October 30, 1963

TITLE OF CASE	REPORT MADE BY	TYPED BY
SAMUEL M. GIANCANA, aka		dkc

	CHARACTER OF CASE
	FBI Headquarters File Number 92-3171-1239 Top Hoodlum Program – Anti Racketeering. Daily Summary

CG 6576-C advised that Giancana has met on three occasions during past week with Anthony Tisci during which times they have discussed situation on which Tisci was to contact Pat Marcy for answers. On evening of October 28 last Marcy met personally with Giancana to iron out certain problems. One of the situations presently under discussion is a new building erected in the First Ward in which Giancana has a strong interest.

CG 6486-C had advised that during the past week Giancana has not met Anthony Tisci at the Amory Lounge nor did Giancana meet with Marcy at Armory on October 28. New meeting place of Giancana not known at this time.

FEDERAL BUREAU OF INVESTIGATION

REPORTING OFFICE	OFFICE OF ORIGIN	DATE	INVESTIGATIVE PERIOD	
CHICAGO	CHICAGO	1963	November 2, 1963	
TITLE OF CASE		REPORT MADE BY		TYPED BY
				dkc
SAMUEL M. GIANCANA, aka		CHARACTER OF CASE		
		FBI Headquarters File Number 92-3171 Top Hoodlum Program – Anti Racketeering. Daily Summary		

CG 6486-C advised that Charles English held conversation with several individuals at Armory Lounge concerning recent narcotics arrests made in Chicago by Federal Narcotics Bureau which included arrest of Americo DiPietto. English advised that papers, while indicating funds from narcotics were channeled to Giancana, actually were aware that this is not so but just print this for publicity. Stated that "The FBI knows that he has nothing to do with narcotics. They know just what he is doing and where he is." Martin Accardo, brother of Anthony Accardo, also present and stated that Anthony is definitely against narcotics.

FEDERAL BUREAU OF INVESTIGATION

REPORTING OFFICE	OFFICE OF ORIGIN	DATE	INVESTIGATIVE PERIOD	
CHICAGO	CHICAGO	1963	November 5, 1963	
TITLE OF CASE		REPORT MADE BY		TYPED BY
				dkc
SAMUEL M. GIANCANA, aka		CHARACTER OF CASE		
		FBI Headquarters File 92-3171-1242 Top Hoodlum Program – Anti Racketeering. Daily Summary		

CG 6576-C continues to advise in meetings between Pat Marcy and Anthony Tisci that they are currently involved in a series of real estate transactions in which they are overseeing Giancana's interests in these various projects. This source indicates that Giancana issues instructions to Marcy through Tisci concerning most of the details surrounding these various projects. It is quite apparent from the information available that Giancana's name does not appear on any paper in connection with any of these projects but is merely receiving his cut through Marcy. The only known project divulged by this source in which Giancana expects to receive some remuneration is a new building development going up in the First Ward. According to source Marcy has indicated that they will receive their gain form this project through the obtaining of insurance from individuals who have been awarded building contracts on the project. Chicago will remain alert to any possibility of disclosing the rigged bidding that is known to be going for these projects.

FEDERAL BUREAU OF INVESTIGATION

REPORTING OFFICE	OFFICE OF ORIGIN	DATE	INVESTIGATIVE PERIOD	
CHICAGO	CHICAGO	1963	November 15, 1963	
TITLE OF CASE		REPORT MADE BY		TYPED BY
				dkc
SAMUEL M. GIANCANA, aka		**CHARACTER OF CASE** FBI Headquarters File Number 92-3171-1250 Top Hoodlum Program – Anti Racketeering. Daily Summary		

CG 6486-C advised that Frank "Buster" Wortman met with Charles English and Butch Blasi at Armory Lounge on 11/11/63. Lengthy discussion held about recent arrests of bookmakers at Sportsman's Park Race Track. Discussion in detail of case of Willie Russo referred to by English as "our guy" and to his 6 month sentence. Wortman spoke briefly concerning 5 of his men recently arrested in connection with policy operations. From discussion it was apparent that government entry into fields heretofore considered strictly under local jurisdiction has caused considerable unrest among hoodlums everywhere. Wortman left lounge prior to arrival of Giancana Later in the day Butch Blasi indicated that Giancana was "flying east to see her" presumably Phyllis McGuire.

This source advised that Giancana was present in lounge during late evening of November 12 and early morning of November 13 last. Had party at lounge lasting until 4:30 a.m. Present with Giancana was former paramour and noted entertainer Keely Smith who is currently appearing at Palmer House Hotel in Chicago. Smith present with Giancana, Chuck English and entertainer Jane Darwin in Armory Lounge for several hours during afternoon November 13 last. English brought Smith up to date on Giancana's troubles with FBI.

During discussion of court litigation being conducted Giancana stated in resigned voice, "I just want to be left alone. I don't want to be bothered any more. The FBI has got me on the ropes. I can't do anything." Also during discussion English advised he was happy to see surveillance end as Giancana's health was becoming seriously affected and English also afraid the way Sam was driving he would kill himself in an auto accident trying to lose the FBI. Indications are Giancana to see Kelly Smith during her entire stay in Chicago.

352

FEDERAL BUREAU OF INVESTIGATION

REPORTING OFFICE	OFFICE OF ORIGIN	DATE	INVESTIGATIVE PERIOD	
CHICAGO	CHICAGO	1963	November 16, 1963	

TITLE OF CASE	REPORT MADE BY	TYPED BY
		dkc
SAMUEL M. GIANCANA, aka	**CHARACTER OF CASE** FBI Headquarters File 92-3171-1252 Top Hoodlum Program – Anti Racketeering. Daily Summary	

CG 6486-C continues to furnish excellent information concerning present activities of Giancana. Since remodeling interior of lounge there has been an apparent change in the seating arrangement which has resulted in the placement of seats in close proximity to above source. Since placement of these chairs they have been utilized almost exclusively by Butch Blasi and Queenie Simonelli. It is felt that re-entry with prior bureau authority will eventually have to be made to either relocate present source or perhaps ass additional source to obtain full benefit of information available from private booth made expressly for Giancana. It is noted at this time it is difficult to pick up Giancana himself in present conversations.

Source learned that Butch Blasi, prior to picking up Giancana on 11/11/63, inquired of all persons present at Armory Lounge if anyone had a loaded gun. Roy Taglia advised that he had one in his glove compartment of his car and obtained it and gave it to Blasi. Source further advised possibility that a camera has been placed in interior of Lounge during remodeling.

During conversation between Giancana, Keely Smith, and Charles English it was determined that Giancana was now planning trip to south, possibly Florida with English. Source also advised that from conversations held within past week, it appears that Giancana is no longer seeing Phyllis McGiure and is somewhat upset over situation. Bartender at Armory Lounge given instructions that juke box records of McGiure Sisters not to be played when Giancana is in the lounge.

FEDERAL BUREAU OF INVESTIGATION

REPORTING OFFICE	OFFICE OF ORIGIN	DATE	INVESTIGATIVE PERIOD	
CHICAGO	CHICAGO	1963	November 20, 1963	
TITLE OF CASE		REPORT MADE BY		TYPED BY
				dkc
SAMUEL M. GIANCANA, aka		**CHARACTER OF CASE**		
		FBI Headquarters File Number 92-3171-1254 Top Hoodlum Program – Anti Racketeering. Daily Summary		

CG 6576-C advised 12/18 last that information made available to John D'Arco and Pat Marcy that a move is under way to promote some individual other that Michael FioRito for the position of Alderman of Chicago's First Ward. D'Arco and Marcy were joined by Buddy Jacobson in heated discussion concerning situation. From information available, Marcy and D'Arco surmised that Mayor Richard J. Daley is behind this move primarily because FioRito is unacceptable to him. Daley feels there is too much "heat", attendant upon FioRito's running for this position. Marcy commented he feels that Daley is possibly being pushed in this regard by "Washington." Marcy indicated that he was told to put "Frankie", believed to be Frank Annunzio, in consideration by Daley. Both D'Arco and Jacobson extremely irate over this possibility and claim they will have nothing to do with Annunzio's candidacy.

It was pointed out that Sam Giancana is not aware as of this development. D'Arco in his remarks expressed a strong desire to keep this information from Giancana at this time. D'Arco then advised he was extremely upset with Vito Marzullo who apparently was aware of the Mayor's feelings in this regard several days before they were made known to the First Ward organization. Those present felt they should fight this situation and would hold discussions with Marzullo and Daley prior to making a final decision.

FEDERAL BUREAU OF INVESTIGATION

REPORTING OFFICE	OFFICE OF ORIGIN	DATE	INVESTIGATIVE PERIOD	
CHICAGO	CHICAGO	1963	December 6, 1963	
TITLE OF CASE		REPORT MADE BY		TYPED BY
				dkc
SAMUEL M. GIANCANA, aka		**CHARACTER OF CASE**		
		FBI Headquarters File Number 92-3171-1269 Top Hoodlum Program – Anti Racketeering. Daily Summary		

CG 6576-C advised conversation between Anthony Tisci and Pat Marcy held 12/4/63 at which time it was decided that Congressman Roland Libonati should be advised that he has officially been ousted and will not be re-slated for re-election next November. It was recommended that "full committee repot be shown to him." From conversation it was learned that committee consists of John D'Arco, Alderman Vito Marzullo, and Anthony Girolami. Apparently there are other members of the committee, however, in name only, and are not contacted as to their desires in this situation.

Source further advised that foremost candidate to be slated in Libonati's place is Frank Annunzio, (listed as D'Annunnzio in report) former Democratic ward committeeman. Annunzio not overly enthusiastic over taking position and is hoping rather for appointment over taking position and is hoping rather for appointment as county commissioner. Annunzio has obtained residence within district for registration purposes.

FEDERAL BUREAU OF INVESTIGATION

REPORTING OFFICE	OFFICE OF ORIGIN	DATE	INVESTIGATIVE PERIOD	
CHICAGO	CHICAGO	1963	December 7, 1963	
TITLE OF CASE		REPORT MADE BY		TYPED BY
				dkc
SAMUEL M. GIANCANA, aka		CHARACTER OF CASE		
		FBI Headquarters File Number 92-3171-1265 Top Hoodlum Program – Anti Racketeering. Daily Summary		

CG 6486-C advised that Charles English in recent conversation with unknown discussed local situation as to effect that President Kennedy would have on FBI investigations into hoodlum activities, "I tell you in another two months the FBI will be like it was five years ago. They won't be around no more. They're gonna investigate them fair play for Cuba's. They call that more detrimental than us guys. They'll say these local problems at home, let the local police handle it. The FBI won't be investigating completive business. They won't be calling in businessmen and saying did they put the muscle on you and things like that. Are you scared? Did they use fear?"

Unknown went into case of Phil Alderisio and discussion then centered on troubles of Alderisio case.

FEDERAL BUREAU OF INVESTIGATION

REPORTING OFFICE	OFFICE OF ORIGIN	DATE	INVESTIGATIVE PERIOD
CHICAGO	CHICAGO	1963	December 11, 1963

TITLE OF CASE	REPORT MADE BY	TYPED BY
		dkc

SAMUEL M. GIANCANA, aka	CHARACTER OF CASE
	FBI Headquarters File Number 92-3171-1268 Top Hoodlum Program – Anti Racketeering. Daily Summary

CG informant advised that Sam Giancana has instructed that moves be made to make Alderman Robert Massey, 36th Ward, a local judge. It was advised that Massey is not real name. He is Italian and has at least one brother who is a member of the hoodlum element in Chicago who is close to Giancana. Massey is the type of politician who can be counted on by Giancana and other hoodlums for practically anything.

Later that date John D'Arco has called a special luncheon of select leaders of Italian community here at Sherman House Hotel today. Informant understands that he, Massey, Vito Marzullo, and D'Arco will be most prominent persons there. Purpose of meeting is to receive suggestions from above and other Italian here for successor to Libonati. Apparently not aware that Giancana has instructed Frank Annunzio is to receive this spot. Apparently D'Arco and Pat Marcy strategy is to follow strategy used with Donald Parrillo where all leading Italians are consulted as to their choices and then when Giancana's selection is thereafter announced it makes it appear that this selection was arrived at by Democratic process of sorts.

FEDERAL BUREAU OF INVESTIGATION

REPORTING OFFICE	OFFICE OF ORIGIN	DATE	INVESTIGATIVE PERIOD
CHICAGO	CHICAGO	1963	December 13, 1963

TITLE OF CASE	REPORT MADE BY	TYPED BY
		dkc

SAMUEL M. GIANCANA, aka	CHARACTER OF CASE
	FBI Headquarters File Number 92-3171-1272 Top Hoodlum Program – Anti Racketeering. Daily Summary

CG 6576-C advised Giancana had advised John D'Arco that he (Giancana) has someone who can control Frank Annunzio. Giancana advised D'Arco that the person he referred to is Judge Daniel Covelli. For information of Bureau, Covelli has been long noted as a close friend of many Chicago top hoodlums.

On December 12, last, Gus Kringas, the owner of Gus Kringas Steak House, a former notorious gambling joint, met with Tarquin "Qweenie" Simonelli. Kringas attempting to meet with Giancana; however, Giancana did not appear.

FEDERAL BUREAU OF INVESTIGATION

REPORTING OFFICE	OFFICE OF ORIGIN	DATE	INVESTIGATIVE PERIOD	
CHICAGO	CHICAGO	1963	December 18, 1963	
TITLE OF CASE		REPORT MADE BY		TYPED BY
				dkc
SAMUEL M. GIANCANA, aka		CHARACTER OF CASE		
		FBI Headquarters File Number 92-3171-1275 Top Hoodlum Program – Anti Racketeering. Daily Summary		

CG 6576-C advised that a party was held at the Armory Lounge on 12/15/63 for singer Vic Damone and apparently hosted by Giancana. Party attended by noted singing group, the Vagabonds. Source advised Pat Marcy in conversation with associates through this to be a very poor place to hold such a party and felt that such a celebration would only caused poor publicity for Damone and more publicity for Giancana. Damone appeared as the opening night entertainer at the New Chez Paree in Chicago several weeks ago on orders from Giancana.

FEDERAL BUREAU OF INVESTIGATION

REPORTING OFFICE	OFFICE OF ORIGIN	DATE	INVESTIGATIVE PERIOD	
CHICAGO	CHICAGO	1963	December 19, 1963	
TITLE OF CASE		REPORT MADE BY		TYPED BY
				dkc
SAMUEL M. GIANCANA, aka		CHARACTER OF CASE		
		FBI Headquarters File 92-3171-1274 Top Hoodlum Program – Anti Racketeering. Daily Summary		

CG 6486-C advised party held on 12/16/63 at Armory Lounge for airlines personnel, most of whom employed by Untied Airlines. Source advised that Party is annual Christmas party given by Johnny Carr, apparently a United Airlines supervisory official of sorts. Sam Giancana present during entire festivities. The Armory Lounge usually closed on Monday's but was opened specifically for above party.

It has been learned that Giancana utilizes United Airlines. Strong possibility exists Carr contact for tickets. It is believed that Butch Blasi picked up Phyllis McGuire at O'Hare Airport on 12/17/63 and driven to meet Giancana at Armory Lounge.

FEDERAL BUREAU OF INVESTIGATION

REPORTING OFFICE	OFFICE OF ORIGIN	DATE	INVESTIGATIVE PERIOD	
CHICAGO	CHICAGO	1963	December 21, 1963	
TITLE OF CASE		REPORT MADE BY		TYPED BY
				dkc
SAMUEL M. GIANCANA, aka		**CHARACTER OF CASE** FBI Headquarters File Number 92-3171-1277 Top Hoodlum Program – Anti Racketeering Daily Summary		

CG 6576-C furnished information reflecting payoffs made this month ostensibly under the guise of Christmas gifts to members of the Chicago PD assigned to the Marquette District. Money was given to Irv Gordon by Pat Marcy. Marcy said payoffs are low because it has been a bad year for business.

FEDERAL BUREAU OF INVESTIGATION

REPORTING OFFICE	OFFICE OF ORIGIN	DATE	INVESTIGATIVE PERIOD	
CHICAGO	CHICAGO	1963	December, 1963	
TITLE OF CASE		REPORT MADE BY		TYPED BY
				dkc
SAMUEL M. GIANCANA, aka		**CHARACTER OF CASE** FBI Headquarters File Number 92-3171 Top Hoodlum Program – Anti Racketeering.		

Additional FBI Information

1)   On 1-16-1963, Frank Sinatra was at the offices of Essex Productions, 9229 Sunset Boulevard, Chicago, and advised that he had no knowledge of Sam Giancana having any interest in the Villa Venice and that Giancana had nothing to do with his appearance at this club. Concerning the asso-

ciation of Sinatra with persons such as Giancana, Sinatra stated that in his business he met all kinds of people.

2)   CG informant advised that he heard Giancana had ordered all burglars or armed robbers to move out of Cicero, Illinois, when a lot of stolen merchandise had been recovered by States Attorney's Police in Cicero. This merchandise was stolen by Guy Mendolia and Giancana was so angered by the "resulting heat" that only the fact that Mendolia was his godson prevented Giancana from having Mendolia killed, but he indicated that any further transgressions would bring immediate retaliation.

3)   CG informant furnished information on July 1 and 3, 1963 concerning interstate transportation of stolen funds from Nevada gambling casinos. Informant advised that Sam Giancana did not trust any of his subordinates in the affairs of organized crime. He had considerable financial interest in Las Vegas gambling casinos and due to his distrust of his subordinates, Giancana made frequent trips to Las Vegas where he personal collected the proceeds from the money which was skimmed off the top of these gambling casinos and carry it back to Chicago. Source said that on some occasions the amount of money picked up by Giancana totaled almost half a million dollars. His practice was to fly to Los Angeles and then drive a rented car to Las Vegas. Source also added that he had learned that Marshall Caifano could do no wrong in the eyes of Giancana and was one of three "hit men" considered by Giancana to be the best in the business. I should be noted that Caifano may have returned some of the rented cars to Los Angeles that Giancana used.

4)   On 8-2-1963 the premises known as Alco Steel Service, 525 Rowell Street, Joliet, Illinois, were searched as it was believed there were 300 slot machines concealed on premises. Among other things found was a packing case containing slot machine parts which disclosed a shipping label from World Wide Distributors in Chicago to Automatic Coin in Joliet. It was noted that World Wide was reported to be an enterprise of Sam Giancana and Automatic Coin was reported to be an interest of Frank LaPorte, boss of vice and gambling in southeastern Cool County, Illinois.

Chapter 8

FEDERAL BUREAU OF INVESTIGATION

REPORTING OFFICE	OFFICE OF ORIGIN	DATE	INVESTIGATIVE PERIOD
CHICAGO	CHICAGO	1964	January 1, 1964

TITLE OF CASE	REPORT MADE BY	TYPED BY
SAMUEL M. GIANCANA, aka		dkc

CHARACTER OF CASE

FBI Headquarters File 92-3171-1282
Top Hoodlum Program – Anti Racketeering.
Daily Summery

Los Angeles advised that information received that division indicating Giancana, together with Phil Alderisio and Sam "Teets" Battaglia to meet with unknown persons in Los Angeles to discuss possible purchase of land and automobiles. Los Angeles informant advised Giancana to proceed from California to meeting in Arizona thereafter. Giancana observed at Armory Lounge December.

FEDERAL BUREAU OF INVESTIGATION

REPORTING OFFICE	OFFICE OF ORIGIN	DATE	INVESTIGATIVE PERIOD
CHICAGO	CHICAGO	1964	January 6, 1964

TITLE OF CASE	REPORT MADE BY	TYPED BY
SAMUEL M. GIANCANA, aka		dkc

CHARACTER OF CASE

FBI Headquarters File 92-3171-1286
Top Hoodlum Program – Anti Racketeering.
Daily Summery

Investigation Chicago indicates address 1340 Washington Boulevard, Chicago, Illinois, is that of Plumbers Chicago Journeymen Local Union 130. For information Honolulu Division, Steve M. Bailey is head of local 130, Plumbers Union, and is believed probably identical to Steven E. Bailey set forth in your tel. Information Chicago files reflects Bailey acquainted with local top hoodlums, however, no indebted to them. Former CG 6343-C furnished information in 1960 to the effect that Bailey known by Murray Humphreys, but that Bailey not in Humphreys' favor.

Chicago Division has no photos of Flood, however, is attempting to obtain a photo of Mrs. Flood from local newspapers who took same at time of recent Giancana trial at which Flood appeared as witness for Giancana. Upon receipt of same will forward AM to Honolulu. Description furnished unknown female number 2, age approx. 60 years old, resembles description of Rose Flood.

FEDERAL BUREAU OF INVESTIGATION

REPORTING OFFICE	OFFICE OF ORIGIN	DATE	INVESTIGATIVE PERIOD	
CHICAGO	CHICAGO	1964	January 9, 1964	
TITLE OF CASE		REPORT MADE BY		TYPED BY
				dkc
SAMUEL M. GIANCANA, aka		CHARACTER OF CASE		
		FBI Headquarters File 92-3171-1302 Top Hoodlum Program – Anti Racketeering. Daily Summery		

CG 6576-C advised that conversation held between Pat Marcy and Attorney Mike Brodkin concerning assignment of judges to case involving Chicago hoodlums Willie Messino, Joe Gagliano, and Marshall Caifano. Detailed discussion held concerning relative merits of various judges presently available under the new circuit system inaugurated on first of year. From discussion it is apparent that certain of the judges formerly relied upon by the First Ward organization to handle any hoodlum matters as directed have become apprehensive and are not as reliable as previously.

Following discussion it was decided that a new judge, Charles Barrett, a Republican would probably be the best person to hear the Caifano case. It was generally conceded that Caifano case not as serious as Messino-Gagliano case.

During conversation Brodkin related that he had just had a luncheon with Paul Ricca, Tony Accardo, Frank Ferraro, and Murray Humphreys at Jacques Restaurant. Brodkin stated that it was "just like old times." Continued that hoodlums not meeting as in past.

FEDERAL BUREAU OF INVESTIGATION

REPORTING OFFICE	OFFICE OF ORIGIN	DATE	INVESTIGATIVE PERIOD	
CHICAGO	CHICAGO	1964	January 11, 1964	
TITLE OF CASE		REPORT MADE BY		TYPED BY
				dkc
SAMUEL M. GIANCANA, aka		CHARACTER OF CASE		
		FBI Headquarters File 92-3171-1306 Top Hoodlum Program – Anti Racketeering. Daily Summery		

CG 6576-C advised that Pat Marcy met with Anthony Tisci this afternoon and advised that he had received three calls to effect that FBI has instituted an investigation of Anco Insurance Company. Source advised Marcy highly upset regarding this investigation and does not understand purpose. Tisci recommends that Marcy immediately obtain attorney and file injunction against FBI "just like we did." "You send a notice of this to Marlin Johnson, just like George Leighton did. You can be sure that something will be done. They aren't going to ignore it like they did the other case." "At least demand to know from Marlin Johnson what these men are doing here. We have not been indicted. There are no warrants." "Your civil rights are being denied under the 14th amendment."

During conversation discussion turned to Giancana case at which time Tisci advised Leighton is going to file an amended complaint in district court to attempt to have Judge Richard Austin give a final order. Tisci states that according to Leighton, the Supreme Court would not hear this case as it stands at this time in that the order handed down in original case is only a temporary order. Tisci continued that Giancana had told Leighton to amend the complaint and make it stronger. Giancana wants his complaint to show that he feels the judge did not go far enough in the limits of his injunction.

CG 6486-C advised that Armory Lounge broken into again during morning hours January 10 last but that apparently nothing taken from premises. Complaint given to Forest Park PD who sent officers to investigate. Police requested to furnish better patrol service to lounge during hours of closing.

FEDERAL BUREAU OF INVESTIGATION

REPORTING OFFICE	OFFICE OF ORIGIN	DATE	INVESTIGATIVE PERIOD
CHICAGO	CHICAGO	1964	January 13, 1964

TITLE OF CASE	REPORT MADE BY	TYPED BY
		dkc

	CHARACTER OF CASE
SAMUEL M. GIANCANA, aka	FBI Headquarters File 92-3171-1520 Top Hoodlum Program – Anti Racketeering. Daily Summary

CG advised Giancana at Fresh Meadows Golf Course 11/12 last in company of Sam Rosa, Sam Parde, Nicky Visco and Queenie Simonelli. During stay at club house Vince Solano entered and spoke to Giancana who immediately departed from associates to join person parked in car outside club house who was not visible to informant. Giancana remained in back seat with individual for approximately twenty minutes during which time Solano is chauffeur and bodyguard of lending Chicago hoodlum Ross Prio giving strong indication unknown individual identical to Prio.

Informant stated this date Giancana gave no indication of plans at this time to depart Chicago in near future. For info Miami, Jack Cerone and John Campanalli reported planning return to Chicago soon.

FEDERAL BUREAU OF INVESTIGATION

REPORTING OFFICE	OFFICE OF ORIGIN	DATE	INVESTIGATIVE PERIOD	
CHICAGO	CHICAGO	1964	January 1964	
TITLE OF CASE		REPORT MADE BY		TYPED BY
				dkc
SAMUEL M. GIANCANA, aka		CHARACTER OF CASE FBI Headquarters File 92-3171-1313 Top Hoodlum Program – Anti Racketeering. Honolulu Feild Office File 92-68		

Enclosed for Bureau are the following information on the golfing group in which Sam Giancana golfed with in January 1964 while in Honolulu, Hawaii.

Photo 1, picture of all five principals on 18th putting green, Waialae Country Club. Identified left to right as follows: John Campanelli, S. Rosie, Chuck Jones (golf pro at Mid Pacific Country Club, Honolulu), Sam Giancana and James Grange, aka J. Gates, Sr.

Photo 2 is Richard D. Flood sitting in the club house. Flood was part of the group when they arrived. Flood being used as bodygaurd for Giancana.

Photo 3 and 4 are photos of P. or S. or Dick Rosie on Waislae County Club fairway. In seeking to identify Rosie, check Barrington, Illinois since Rosie made station to station collect call from the Breakers Hotel, Honolulu. Rosie described as:

Age:	40
Height:	5' 6" to 5' 8"
Weight:	170 lbs.
Build:	Stocky
Complexion:	Dark, clean shaven but heavy beard
Eyes:	Dark, heavy eyebrows
Hair:	Black, thick and wavy with prominent side waves
Characteristics:	Deep raspy voice, Brooklyn or Chicago accent, Italian appearance; prominent nose, cleft center Of chin.

Photo 5 - left to right on golf cart, Chuck Jones (golf pro), and John Campanelli. Campanelli description:

Age:	About 40
Height:	6' 1"
Weight:	165 lbs.
Build:	Medium slender
Complexion:	Olive
Hair:	Black, turning grey
Posture:	Slight slouch

James Grange, (no photo) is currently using the name J. Gates Sr. Grange sent telegram to Berget Clark in Elmhurst, Illinois on 1-4-1964 stating, "Happy New Year - Sorry I am late to my regret I didn't call you before leaving. Will see you soon. With all my love, Mr. J. Gates - Staying at the Breakers Hotel, Waikiki."

Description of James Grange

Age:	55 to 60
Height:	5' 7"
Weight:	165 lbs.
Hair:	Silver gray, heavy sides, bald on top and front.

Race:	Apparently Italian, but could be mistaken for Jewish.

Complexion: Medium
Characteristics: Prominent Beaked nose.

FEDERAL BUREAU OF INVESTIGATION

REPORTING OFFICE	OFFICE OF ORIGIN	DATE	INVESTIGATIVE PERIOD	
CHICAGO	CHICAGO	1964	January 14, 1964	
TITLE OF CASE		REPORT MADE BY		TYPED BY
				dkc
SAMUEL M. GIANCANA, aka		CHARACTER OF CASE		
		FBI Headquarters File Number 92-3171-1305 Top Hoodlum Program – Anti Racketeering. Daily Summery		

CG 6486-C advised that Giancana returned to Chicago January 10 last and proceeded to residence in Oak Park where he remained for rest of day. Source stated that an individual known only as Louie has been making repeated inquiry at Armory Lounge and demands that he allowed to see Giancana. Louie claims that he is $13,000 into unnamed hoodlums and that only Giancana can help him. No information given informant as to whether meeting arranged for this individual.

Source further advised that Giancana undoubtedly owner of Armory Lounge. Doris Fanelli, in discussion with Chuck English, stated Giancana should consider selling restaurant. She feels that he might make such a decision when he sees how unprofitable operations were for the year 1963. Fanelli feels restaurant should be operated by man and wife combination or that Giancana should leave someone in restaurant to watch over operations. Recommendation has been made that the restaurant portion of the Lounge be closed, leaving only the bar open. From conversation it appears that financial situation of lounge is of little import to Giancana, but is maintained merely for the privacy that it provides for meetings with hoodlums and other associates.

Further conversation held about Marshall Caifano and Lewis Barbe, insurance agent, meeting at lounge. Some discussion held about inadvisability of using lounge for meetings but English advised that it makes no difference as the "G" knows everyone meets there anyhow.

Giancana appeared at lounge on January 12 last and remained for about six hours. Numerous individuals noted arrived and departed during time Giancana there.

FEDERAL BUREAU OF INVESTIGATION

REPORTING OFFICE	OFFICE OF ORIGIN	DATE	INVESTIGATIVE PERIOD
CHICAGO	CHICAGO	1964	January 15, 1964

TITLE OF CASE	REPORT MADE BY	TYPED BY
		dkc
SAMUEL M. GIANCANA, aka	**CHARACTER OF CASE** FBI Headquarters File Number 92-3171-1310 Top Hoodlum Program – Anti Racketeering. Daily Summery	

CG 6486-C advised that Charles English, in discussing recent news article stating that English is slated to replace Giancana as gangland chief, feels that Giancana is himself responsible for this type of article. In this connection English advised that Giancana is the person who has been circulating the information that he and Phyllis McGuire are no longer seeing each other which, according to English "you know is malarkey."

Photos taken by Honolulu office of Giancana golfing companions during recent Honolulu stay identified by Chicago agents as Johnny "Johnny Haircuts" Campanale and Sam "Slicker Sam" Rosa.

Giancana observed departing Armory Lounge on January 14 last dressed in business suit and "expensive looking coat and hat." Giancana returned to lounge at midnight with female believed to be Phyllis McGuire. Both remained to about 2 a.m.

FEDERAL BUREAU OF INVESTIGATION

REPORTING OFFICE	OFFICE OF ORIGIN	DATE	INVESTIGATIVE PERIOD
CHICAGO	CHICAGO	1964	January 17, 1964

TITLE OF CASE	REPORT MADE BY	TYPED BY
		dkc
SAMUEL M. GIANCANA, aka	**CHARACTER OF CASE** FBI Headquarters File Number 92-3171-1312 Top Hoodlum Program – Anti Racketeering. Daily Summery	

CG 6486-C advised that Giancana has issued orders to Butch Blasi "to keep everyone not invited out of the Armory Lounge." Blasi is to remain at the lounge as "bouncer" and is to see that anyone coming in to eat does that and nothing more and is not going to be allowed to linger there. Queenie Simonelli has been ordered to stay at Maggio's Steak House and not go to Armory anymore.

From above it is apparent that Giancana not concerned over fact that restaurant losing financial proposition as this source noted it was recently and intends to utilize same as meeting place of his desire. Source further learned that Giancana took extremely circuitous route in recent Hawaiian trip and was needled by Butch Blasi and Charles English concerning this. No details given as to exact route taken by Giancana.

FEDERAL BUREAU OF INVESTIGATION

REPORTING OFFICE	OFFICE OF ORIGIN	DATE	INVESTIGATIVE PERIOD	
CHICAGO	CHICAGO	1964	January 23, 1964	

TITLE OF CASE	REPORT MADE BY	TYPED BY
		dkc
SAMUEL M. GIANCANA, aka	**CHARACTER OF CASE** FBI Headquarters File Number 92-3171-1320 Top Hoodlum Program – Anti Racketeering. Daily Summery	

CG 6576-C advised that Pat Marcy called Judge Joseph Wosik into the First Ward offices to discuss arrested of certain arcade operators still to be tried. Source advised Marcy apologized to Wosik for making it necessary for these cases to be heard by him and indicated that originally they were scheduled to be heard by Judge Sullivan. However, Sullivan, who according to source is heavy drinker, went on binge and became too ill to hear cases, asking for continuances. Marcy at that point felt it best to make a chance and in his words "came to his old friend."

Marcy discussed at length just how Wosik should rule on films presented. Wosik strongly cautioned against making any ruling as to obscenity. Marcy slightly concerned lest States Attorney make an issue of obscenity of film. Wosik indicated he would follow Marcy's instructions and that organization should have no fear of outcome. Verbatim transcript of conversation being submitted in daily summary airtel.

Outcome of First Ward aldermanic election returned as expected with only possible surprise being the approximate 3,500 votes by Scala. Parrillo polled about eight thousand. Parrillo, in television interview over local station, commenting on outcome of election made serious blunder in intimating "left wing communist forces sided with Scala." When presses as to identity of these groups Parrillo stated he was referring to Independent voters of Illinois. A non partisan group of individuals interested in better government. TV newscaster Frank Reynolds immediately drew Parrillo out on his statement so that there could be no misunderstanding of his remarks.

FEDERAL BUREAU OF INVESTIGATION

REPORTING OFFICE	OFFICE OF ORIGIN	DATE	INVESTIGATIVE PERIOD	
CHICAGO	CHICAGO	1964	January 25, 1964	
TITLE OF CASE		REPORT MADE BY		TYPED BY
				dkc
SAMUEL M. GIANCANA, aka		CHARACTER OF CASE		
		FBI Headquarters File Number 92-3171-1318 Top Hoodlum Program – Anti Racketeering. Daily Summery		

CG 6576-C recently furnished information received during conversation between Pat Marcy and Anthony Tisci leaving no doubt but that chief investigator Richard Cain of the Cook County Sheriff's Office is working hand in hand with Marcy and Giancana. Marcy furnished Tisci with the following quotes made by Cain during recent conversations between he and Marcy, "He'd do anything. He told me." Marcy stated that he told Cain, "You told me you were going with us and you may get a chance to prove it someday." Marcy advised that Cain told him that he intensely disliked working for Sheriff Richard Ogilvie.

Above remarks came about following statements by Marcy to effect he felt Cain may have been responsible for recent bombing of Sahara Hotel. Marcy stated that Sahara owner Gene Authy had hired Cain to keep hoods out of the Sahara, but took him off the payroll after one week, thereby highly irritating Cain.

Marcy advised Tisci that if Cain was responsible for the bombing that he, Cain, would tell Marcy. Marcy stated that Cain would be out of town for several more days, but would find out if his assumption was correct when Cain returned. Source being followed closely about this situation.

FEDERAL BUREAU OF INVESTIGATION

REPORTING OFFICE	OFFICE OF ORIGIN	DATE	INVESTIGATIVE PERIOD	
CHICAGO	CHICAGO	1964	January 28, 1964	
TITLE OF CASE		REPORT MADE BY		TYPED BY
				dkc
SAMUEL M. GIANCANA, aka		CHARACTER OF CASE		
		FBI Headquarters File Number 92-3171-1321 Top Hoodlum Program – Anti Racketeering. Daily Summery		

CG 6576-C advised that Pat Marcy, just prior to his departure for Florida for a short vacation, left instructions to be given to Frank "Skid" Caruso, well known Chicago gambling operator who has operated large scale games in the First Ward area for many years, that all gambling operations are, "To stay down at least until I return." Instructions continued that Caruso was to meet with Marcy upon Marcy's return and discuss this situation.

FEDERAL BUREAU OF INVESTIGATION

REPORTING OFFICE	OFFICE OF ORIGIN	DATE	INVESTIGATIVE PERIOD	
CHICAGO	CHICAGO	1964	January 28, 1964	
TITLE OF CASE		REPORT MADE BY		TYPED BY
SAMUEL M. GIANCANA, aka		SA Marshall Ruthland		dkc
		CHARACTER OF CASE		
		FBI Headquarters File 92-3171-1322 Top Hoodlum Program – Anti Racketeering		

Synopsis:

All briefs have been filed with USDC, 7th District and hearing date presently being awaited. Giancana continues to meet on daily basis with leading members of Chicago organized crime in various locations. Giancana feels he has been greatly hampered by investigation of his activities conducted by FBI and has stated, "I'm all through. The FBI has me on the ropes." U.S. Congressman Roland Libonati publicly resigned from position and his successor, as selected by Giancana, to be Frank Annunzio. Giancana has given okay to several incumbent politicians Chicago area to again run for positions held. Giancana has given his okay to the selection of Donald Parrillo to run for the vacant position of First Ward alderman. Information received that Giancana has limited his meetings during the past three months to those persons in whom he has absolute trust. Other persons seeking to meet with Giancana singularly unsuccessful in their attempts to arrange for such meetings. During period Giancana reportedly visited the home of Frank Sinatra in Palm Springs, California, and continuing relationship with Phyllis McGuire. Giancana resumed relationship with noted entertainer Keeley Smith during this period. Vic Damone advised he appeared at opening of Chicago night club at request of Giancana. During trip to Hawaii in 1/64, Giancana and two Chicago hoodlums, Sam Rosa and John Campanalli. While in Hawaii, Giancana observed in the company of noted sports figure Joe DiMaggio and Chicago union official Steven Bailey.

Residence

CG T-1 advised that in December of 1963, Sam Giancana has been utilizing the residence of his associate and chauffeur, Dominic "Butch" Blasi, at 138 Park in River Forest, for about two days.

Miscellaneous

It was learned that Sam Giancana had issued instructions to Butch Blasi to see that the numerous hoodlums who had been hanging out at the Armory Lounge were told to go elsewhere. Included in this group were such close friends of Giancana as Tarquin Simonelli. Blasi was instructed that those persons coming to eat at the lounge would be allowed to do so but were to be hurried out as soon as they had finished eating. It was learned that Giancana did not wish to have these persons at the lounge because that it was causing too much heat on the restaurant and making it more difficult for him to utilize the establishment for his meetings.

FEDERAL BUREAU OF INVESTIGATION

REPORTING OFFICE	OFFICE OF ORIGIN	DATE	INVESTIGATIVE PERIOD	
CHICAGO	CHICAGO	1964	February 6, 1964	
TITLE OF CASE		REPORT MADE BY		TYPED BY
				dkc
SAMUEL M. GIANCANA, aka		CHARACTER OF CASE		
		FBI Headquarters File Number 92-3171-1327 Top Hoodlum Program – Anti Racketeering. Daily Summary		

During course of investigation to locate Americo DiPietto, a check of vehicles was made at Armory Lounge. Persons at lounge apparently alerted as to arrest of top hoodlum Phil Alderisio, and extremely alert to Bureau cars in area. As Bureau car departed, a car observed leaving Armory Lounge which proceeded to follow Bureau car some distance. As car came abreast of bureau car, it was determined that driver of vehicle was Giancana, accompanied by female who kept identity secret by crouching down on front seat of car. When Giancana observed bureau agent, who is known to Giancana, he proceeded to depart at great speed. No attempt made to follow Giancana.

CG 6486-C advised that meeting held at Armory Lounge between Giancana, Dominic Blasi, and others concerning the arrest of Phil Alderisio. CG 6576-C advised that hoodlum gambler Frank "Skid's" Caruso met with Pat Marcy upon Marcy's return from Florida and discussed Chinese gambling situation in operation in south end of First Ward, generally considered to be Caruso's territory. Marcy has paid local police to keep all Chinese games down for a month's duration. It this manner, all Chinese gambling will then be under his control.

Sam Giancana around 1964

FEDERAL BUREAU OF INVESTIGATION

REPORTING OFFICE	OFFICE OF ORIGIN	DATE	INVESTIGATIVE PERIOD	
CHICAGO	CHICAGO	1964	February 8, 1964	
TITLE OF CASE		REPORT MADE BY		TYPED BY
				dkc
SAMUEL M. GIANCANA, aka		CHARACTER OF CASE		
		FBI Headquarters File Number 92-3171 Top Hoodlum Program – Anti Racketeering. Daily Summary		

Giancana, Butch Blasi, and John Matassa observed together at Armory Lounge during late evening on February 6 last during spot surveillance.

CG 6576-C advised that Louis Arger met with Pat Marcy 2/6/64 to complain of continued arrest by First District policemen of Arger's establishments. Arger stated Captain James Riordan made arrest on 2/5 last. Arger extremely upset and wants Marcy to crack down, as he told Marcy, "After all you are the one who runs the First Ward." Marcy told Arger that, "Everyone is scared now Louis and they won't move like they used to. Things aren't like they used to be."

During discussion it was learned that Paul Quinn, Administrative Assistant to Superintendent O.W. Wilson of the Chicago PD is "looking for a hangout" to help out the strip joint owners. Marcy has requested Arger to immediately get $27 from each strip joint operator and total of $250 will be given to Quinn. Collection also to be taken up for several judges who have recently ruled favorably on strip cases. Each to be given $75. Specifically mentioned in this regard was Judge Sidney Jones who rendered most recent verdict in favor of strip joints.

FEDERAL BUREAU OF INVESTIGATION

REPORTING OFFICE	OFFICE OF ORIGIN	DATE	INVESTIGATIVE PERIOD	
CHICAGO	CHICAGO	1964	February 14, 1964	
TITLE OF CASE		REPORT MADE BY		TYPED BY
				dkc
SAMUEL M. GIANCANA, aka		CHARACTER OF CASE		
		FBI Headquarters File Number 92-3171-1333 Top Hoodlum Program – Anti Racketeering. Daily Summary		

CG 6486-C advised Giancana met with Butch Blasi, John Matassa, and unknown on 2/12/64. Matassa is now organizer for Local 272, Auto Chauffeur's Union. During discussion concerning old neighborhood, subject of one particular restaurant was frequented by all the big-time politicians, judges and lawyers. Blasi commented you could sit right there with them. To this Giancana commented, "In them days you didn't have to worry. There wasn't no "G" then."

Later discussion digressed to pending Federal sentencing of Donald Angelini, who was arrested during on track bookmaking raid August last. Unknown stated, "The only way they can get him is to frame him." Discussed sentence given to Red Alterie, another local gambler and bookmaker, who recently received 60 days, $2,000 fine and two years probation. All agreed that thing that hurt most was the two year probation.

FEDERAL BUREAU OF INVESTIGATION

REPORTING OFFICE	OFFICE OF ORIGIN	DATE	INVESTIGATIVE PERIOD	
CHICAGO	CHICAGO	1964	February 19, 1964	
TITLE OF CASE		REPORT MADE BY		TYPED BY dkc
SAMUEL M. GIANCANA, aka		**CHARACTER OF CASE** FBI Headquarters File 92-3171-1339 Top Hoodlum Program – Anti Racketeering. Daily Summary		

CG 6576-C advised Pat Marcy met with Chicago Policeman known only as John at which time lengthy discussion held concerning conditions in First District, and his continued harassment of First District strip joints. It was pointed out that owners of these establishments are fed up with continued arrests being made by Mandel even though they are paying him for protection. As Marcy states it is apparent that Mandel is making phony pinches to make the District look good. According to Marcy it would stand to reason that these joints are aware of Mandel's identity and would not commit any lead acts in his presence, knowing his reputation. It was also pointed out that in addition to taking money; Mandel is accused of illicit acts with girls employed by local joints.

Marcy stated something has to be done at this time and reiterated his statements of some months ago that he is the only person keeping Mandel from being harmed physically by the owners of the syndicate joints. Marcy stated he has held off having Mandel transferred by higher ups because Captain James Riordan, commanding officer, First District brought Mandel into district and Marcy did not want embarrass Riordan. Marcy, however, stressed fact that owners cannot stand anymore arrests as they are not making enough to pay lawyers, bonds and fines resulting from same. Will contact Riordan and give him one more chance to control Mandel and if that fails will see to it that he is transferred out. It is felt that if transfer accomplished, this situation could be utilized to embarrass crooked officials through proper publicity of transfer and reasons therefore, without jeopardy to source.

Marcy also in contact with Anthony Tisci wondered who would be replacement for Andrew Euzzino, presently and known as member of "West Side Bloc." Discussed as primary candidate was "Massey," a reference to Alderman Robert Massey, presently Alderman of 36th Ward and known to be pushed by Giancana for further advancement. Massey is individual who source reported was being pushed by Giancana for judgeship. Of interest in conversation, however, were Tisci's remarks that he is considering his brother, Nunzio Tisci, for this position. There is little doubt but that Giancana would accede to the desires of Tisci in this regard if Tisci made recommendation. Probably only drawback to such a recommendation would be prospect of too much adverse publicity in the linking of Tisci with Giancana.

CG informant advised that Charles Giancana presently negotiating for new quarter million dollar shopping center to be erected in Rosemont, IL. Informant advised that Giancana's name not listed in papers about project but is using local contractor named Pettino to front project.

FEDERAL BUREAU OF INVESTIGATION

REPORTING OFFICE	OFFICE OF ORIGIN	DATE	INVESTIGATIVE PERIOD	
CHICAGO	CHICAGO	1964		
TITLE OF CASE		REPORT MADE BY		TYPED BY
				dkc
SAMUEL M. GIANCANA, aka		CHARACTER OF CASE		
		FBI Headquarters File 92-3171-1342 Top Hoodlum Program – Anti Racketeering. Daily Summary		

CG 6576-C advised that Pat Marcy, following conversion with Chicago Attorney Mike Brodkin, issued instructions to Buddy Jacobson, First Ward political fixer, to make contact with Judge Richard Napoli, presently assignment Judge of Circuit Court of Cook County, for purpose of having Napoli changed venue of Caifano case, insurance fraud case involving Marshall Caifano, from Judge Walter Dahl to Judge Emmeti Morrissey, as Bureau aware Morrissey notorious in disregarding evidence or any other factors in case concerning hoodlums and at beck and call of First Ward politicians.

Above source indicated Giancana out of town since 2/21, last, however, no indication given as to whereabouts during period. Marcy gave Anthony Tisci two tickets to TV showing of heavyweight championship fight "if he gets back in town in time." Giancana in Western suburbs this afternoon.

FEDERAL BUREAU OF INVESTIGATION

REPORTING OFFICE	OFFICE OF ORIGIN	DATE	INVESTIGATIVE PERIOD	
CHICAGO	CHICAGO	1964	March 5, 1964	
TITLE OF CASE		REPORT MADE BY		TYPED BY
				dkc
SAMUEL M. GIANCANA, aka		CHARACTER OF CASE		
		FBI Headquarters File Number 92-3171-1354 Top Hoodlum Program – Anti Racketeering. Daily Summary		

CG 6576-C advised that Pat Marcy met with attorney Sam Papenek who is representing Star and Garter Lounge in most recent arrest charges of allowing soliciting on premises. Marcy advised that because of heat generated by TV program involving commissioner O.W. Wilson and three Chicago newspaper reports in which situation concerning First Ward strip joints discussed at length, Mayor Richard J. Daley ordered Star and Garter closed pending hearings resulting from last arrest. Marcy stated that until all four raised he had been able to handle situation and keep place opened. Stated that he has been in touch with Whitey Cronin, license appeal commissioner for city of Chicago who instructed Marcy to have Papenek be presented at hearing in Mayor Daley's Office at which time Cronin would attempt to have club opened. It is pointed out that Cronin is also a state senator representing Illinois 15th District. This source has furnished numerable references reflecting association between Marcy and Cronin and of fact that Cronin has been doing the bidding of Marcy for some time in similar situations.

It was noted that Marcy did tell Papenek that Cronin somewhat apprehensive on this occasion because of current publicity attendant to strip joint operations, but apparently still intends to do what he can for Marcy.

Marcy also met with Chicago policeman Pat O'Brien who was identified by source as being in charge of license investigations for area encompassing Loop and South Side. O'Brien indicated he has four men working for him at this time, including FNU McCarthy who was referred to by source recently as cracking down on bar on South Side owned by strongy Frank Ferraro. O'Brien advised that deputy superintendent Morris has issued instructions that his group is to investigate all bars and strip joints in their area and furnished report to Morris who will take appropriate action. Local investigators have been instructed not to do anything on there own to these locations. Discussion continued concerning "Heat generated by Sandy Smith on that program and the paper."

FEDERAL BUREAU OF INVESTIGATION

REPORTING OFFICE	OFFICE OF ORIGIN	DATE	INVESTIGATIVE PERIOD	
CHICAGO	CHICAGO	1964	March 6, 1964	
TITLE OF CASE		REPORT MADE BY		TYPED BY
				dkc
SAMUEL M. GIANCANA, aka		CHARACTER OF CASE		
		FBI Headquarters File Number 92-3171-1348 Top Hoodlum Program – Anti Racketeering. Daily Summary		

Personal property tax case against Giancana held before Judge Robert Ransom at Oak Park, Illinois March 4 last. Giancana failed to appear and was again represented by Attorney Anthony V. Champagne. In view of Giancana's failure to appear to contest tax case, judge ordered that claim be paid. Champagne advised that he would appeal to higher court. Giancana owes $592.80 for taxes in 1957. In previous hearings Champagne depicted Giancana with little money, no car, few cloths and a houseful of second hand furniture.

CG 6576-C advised that Pat Marcy talked with Romey (LNU) on 3/4, and was advised that Romety was "going to get the names of the twenty coppers on the list." It is pointed out that local newspapers, in referring to much publicized Federal report concerning corrupt policemen utilize the number twenty as to that number appearing in said report. Marcy advised John D'Arco, former First Ward Alderman, that Romey told him that "Gentile" is on the list. This factual, being a reference to Frank Gentile, recently promoted to sergeant, who formerly was First District traffic office known to be associated with hoodlums. Marcy also stated that "Quinn's name is there," A reference to Paul Quinn, administrative assistant to Commissioner O.W. Wilson, Marcy advised that Romey told him that he would be able to obtain entire list of names in near future.

Chicago has been unable to identify Romey to date. Pointed out that CG 6576-C has previously furnished information reflecting Romey to be close associate of Marcy however, this source has not furnished sufficient details to positively identify, efforts being made to accomplish this identification.

FEDERAL BUREAU OF INVESTIGATION

REPORTING OFFICE	OFFICE OF ORIGIN	DATE	INVESTIGATIVE PERIOD	
CHICAGO	CHICAGO	1964	March 10, 1964	
TITLE OF CASE		REPORT MADE BY		TYPED BY
				dkc
SAMUEL M. GIANCANA, aka		CHARACTER OF CASE		
		FBI Headquarters File 92-3171-1352 Top Hoodlum Program – Anti Racketeering. Daily Summary		

CG 6576-C advised that Pat Marcy and Anthony Tisci met with Alderman Donald Parillo for purpose of giving Parillo instructions on how to vote on any new legislation that city council attempts to enact as aid to local police in closing down local strip joints. Marcy contended that Parillo is to take the stand that legislation against unescorted woman in these bars would prohibit persons such as the Alderman's wife, as well as other legitimate women, from meeting their husband and others persons in bars. Parillo is to take the position that the innocent should not be penalized to curtail the actions of a few people who are doing wrong.

It was learned additionally that one of the reasons that Marcy is working so strongly to help one Anthony Tenerelli, a Sanitary District employee who was recently arrested for running a bar in which gambling was located, is that the bar is a Ralph Massuci, bookmaker and close friend and associate of Sam Giancana. According to source, Massuci operates his business from this location and following the arrest was responsible for engaging the services of his brother Robert Massey, Alderman of the 36th Ward, and close associates of Giancana, to handle the case. It is pointed out that few persons are aware that Ralph Massuci and Robert Massey are brothers as Ralph continues to use family name of Massuci rather than Massey. Noted that Marcy, since first leaning of case, has seen to it that Massey was taken off case and another attorney is being unitized to defend Tenerelli.

FEDERAL BUREAU OF INVESTIGATION

REPORTING OFFICE	OFFICE OF ORIGIN	DATE	INVESTIGATIVE PERIOD
CHICAGO	CHICAGO	1964	March 12, 1964

TITLE OF CASE	REPORT MADE BY	TYPED BY
		dkc

SAMUEL M. GIANCANA, aka	CHARACTER OF CASE FBI Headquarters File Number 92-3171 Top Hoodlum Program – Anti Racketeering. Daily Summary

CG 6576 advised that Pat Marcy recently learned of additional inquiry made by FBI into affairs of Anco Insurance. In discussing matter with John D'Arco and Anthony Tisci, Marcy asserted he was certain FBI has First Ward phones tapped and has learned of Anco's clients through phone conversations. Marcy stated to others present that FBI is attempting to show use of pressure to obtain clients for insurance business. Marcy continued that there has been no pressure used in any instance regarding insurance business. Marcy stated however, that they would have to contact Giancana immediately because it would be necessary to remove "Porky" from the payroll, now that he is committeeman. This is reference to Joseph Porcaro, recently selected as Republican Committeeman of 28th Ward who is also a salesman for Anco. It is known that Porcaro hired by Anco at request of Giancana and apparently his assent is needed to drop him for payroll. It was readily apparent that Marcy feels to have Porcaro remain in the employ of insurance company would bring undue publicity to this and possibly show additional ties between Giancana and First Ward politicians. It is well publicized fact in Chicago area that Porcaro is Giancana henchman.

Marcy further stated that "The only kinky thing connected with the insurance company is that Villa Venice, where that big nut owns us that money and we are making no effort to collect it." This source has previously advised that Leo Olson, operator and front of Villa Venice owed Anco approximately $8,000 which he has been unable to pay. No details concerning this debt were learned at that time. Chicago looking into possibility of Federal violation involved.

FEDERAL BUREAU OF INVESTIGATION

REPORTING OFFICE	OFFICE OF ORIGIN	DATE	INVESTIGATIVE PERIOD
CHICAGO	CHICAGO	1964	March 13, 1964

TITLE OF CASE	REPORT MADE BY	TYPED BY
		dkc
SAMUEL M. GIANCANA, aka	**CHARACTER OF CASE** FBI Headquarters File Number 92-3171-1357 Top Hoodlum Program – Anti Racketeering. Daily Summary	

CG 6486-C advised that Frank Ferraro met with Sam Giancana at Armory Lounge during 3/11 last. From excerpts of conversation obtained, it appeared that Gincana was being consulted by Ferraro concerning Ferraro's health status. Ferraro was known to have advised Giancana that he was advised by his physician that he should have an immediate operation. Apparently Ferraro is somewhat hesitant as to whether he should go into hospital and was heard to remark to Giancana that "I will go if you will go up there with me."

A short while later Ferraro conversed with Doris Fanelli, individual who operated Armory Lounge for Giancana, and indicated that he had decided to go ahead with operation "in all probability." Fanelli cautioned him to be sure that it is necessary "As it is always serious when you go under the knife."

FEDERAL BUREAU OF INVESTIGATION

REPORTING OFFICE	OFFICE OF ORIGIN	DATE	INVESTIGATIVE PERIOD
CHICAGO	CHICAGO	1964	March 19, 1964

TITLE OF CASE	REPORT MADE BY	TYPED BY
		dkc
SAMUEL M. GIANCANA, aka	**CHARACTER OF CASE** FBI Headquarters File 92-3171-1360 Top Hoodlum Program – Anti Racketeering. Daily Summary	

CG 6486-C advised Giancana spending great portion of every day at Armory Lounge. Chuck English spent several hours with Giancana on March 18 last.

Chicago informant advised that Charles Giancana, brother of subject, presently negotiating for new quarter million dollar shopping center to be erected in Rosemont, Illinois. Informant advised Giancana's name not listed in papers about project but is using local contractors named Pettino to front project.

FEDERAL BUREAU OF INVESTIGATION

REPORTING OFFICE	OFFICE OF ORIGIN	DATE	INVESTIGATIVE PERIOD	
CHICAGO	CHICAGO	1964	March 21, 1964	
TITLE OF CASE		REPORT MADE BY		TYPED BY
				dkc
SAMUEL M. GIANCANA, aka		CHARACTER OF CASE		
		FBI Headquarters File Number 92-3171-1363 Top Hoodlum Program – Anti Racketeering. Daily Summery Report		

CG informant advised late on the night of 3/16, he was surreptiously contacted by Jack Cerone. Cerone several times informed informant that he did not want Giancana to know of contact and informant should inform no one of contact. He mentioned several things suggesting to informant "something is going on in the Outfit" and specifically mentioned bad health of Frank Ferraro. Informant feels that Cerone was feeling him out to determine extent of informant's loyalty to Giancana and hoodlums close to Giancana. Noted this informant was a fairly close boyhood friend of Cerone.

Informant speculated that there may be impending shakeups in organized crime here and that Cerone probably feels that he is contender for top spot should Giancana be replaced. Note that source has advised that info about health of Ferraro is closely held secret and that Murray Humphreys obviously in unaware that Cerone knows.

Informant feels that Cerone is certainly one of 23 hoodlums here who are logical successors to Giancana, if stories of Giancana's replacement have any accuracy. Informant advised that not only is Cerone an intelligent, articulate person who reads every best seller written, but he undoubtedly would have the backing of Anthony Accardo and Paul Ricca, former members of the commission here. Noted Cerone was top lieutenant of Accardo when Accardo was in Giancana's position here and is still constant companion and confidant of Accardo. Informant feels that Cerone is not as highly regarded by Giancana as he is by Accardo and Ricca, and that some contest may be going on here as to Giancana's successor.

In this regard it is felt by Chicago that Fiore "Fifi" Buccieri would be equally logical as successor to Giancana and that Giancana himself very well might favor Buccieri. If such contest is going on Cerone may well be attempting to determine the quality of his support and is attempting to determine where the loyalties of certain hoodlums and their contacts lie. It should be kept in mind that at no time did Cerone advise informant that Giancana is to be replaced or that he is under consideration. Most of the above is speculation of informant based on things Cerone said and his knowledge of Hoodlum Empire.

Informant also advised that health of Cerone is not without complications. Advised that within past 6 years or so Cerone has had at least 2 heart attacks and a very serious automobile accident which caused serious injury to his leg. However, Cerone has apparently fairly well recovered from heart attacks and has rehabilitated leg to extent that it is stronger than before and he can golf daily during golf season.

FEDERAL BUREAU OF INVESTIGATION

REPORTING OFFICE	OFFICE OF ORIGIN	DATE	INVESTIGATIVE PERIOD	
CHICAGO	CHICAGO	1964	March 24, 1964	

TITLE OF CASE	REPORT MADE BY	TYPED BY
		dkc
SAMUEL M. GIANCANA, aka	**CHARACTER OF CASE** FBI Headquarters File Number 92-3171-1369 Top Hoodlum Program – Anti Racketeering. Daily Summery Report	

CG 6486-C had advised on a daily basis since March 17, last that Giancana has met with close associates Charles English and Butch Blasi at the Armory Lounge. Giancana when advising of very important meeting indicated it would be of top level nature and instructed English to be sure he did not do any drinking prior to attending meeting.

CG 6502-C indicated a person believed to be Giancana met with Gus Alex by Alex's apartment on March 21, last.

FEDERAL BUREAU OF INVESTIGATION

REPORTING OFFICE	OFFICE OF ORIGIN	DATE	INVESTIGATIVE PERIOD	
CHICAGO	CHICAGO	1964	March 24, 1964	

TITLE OF CASE	REPORT MADE BY	TYPED BY
		dkc
SAMUEL M. GIANCANA, aka	**CHARACTER OF CASE** FBI Headquarters File Number 92-3171-1369 Top Hoodlum Program – Anti Racketeering. Daily Summery Report	

CG 6486-C had advised on a daily basis since March 17, last that Giancana has met with close associates Charles English and Butch Blasi at the Armory Lounge. Giancana when advising of very important meeting indicated it would be of top level nature and instructed English to be sure he did not do any drinking prior to attending meeting.

CG 6502-C indicated a person believed to be Giancana met with Gus Alex by Alex's apartment on March 21, last.

FEDERAL BUREAU OF INVESTIGATION

REPORTING OFFICE	OFFICE OF ORIGIN	DATE	INVESTIGATIVE PERIOD
CHICAGO	CHICAGO	1964	March 26, 1964

TITLE OF CASE	REPORT MADE BY	TYPED BY
SAMUEL M. GIANCANA, aka		dkc

CHARACTER OF CASE

FBI Headquarters File 92-3171-1366
Top Hoodlum Program – Anti Racketeering.
Daily Summery Report

CG 6486-C advised that Willie Daddono met Giancana at Armory Lounge at which time he brought Giancana up to date on Daddono's activities while in Florida. Noted that Daddono returned from Florida during past week. Source advised that Daddono stated he met in Florida with Frank Esposito and a Doctor Chance, not further identified. No pertinent information developed about Daddono's activities in Florida. Source advised that Daddono and Giancana removed themselves from vicinity of source while still in conversation and no information of value received about any possible instructions given Daddono his return.

Source again reflected no meeting held at lounge on Monday last, however large group present on Tuesday, It is pointed out that Chicago informant has indicated that in past, Tuesday main meeting day for west side hoodlums at Armory.

FEDERAL BUREAU OF INVESTIGATION

REPORTING OFFICE	OFFICE OF ORIGIN	DATE	INVESTIGATIVE PERIOD
CHICAGO	CHICAGO	1964	March 31, 1964

TITLE OF CASE	REPORT MADE BY	TYPED BY
SAMUEL M. GIANCANA, aka		dkc

CHARACTER OF CASE

FBI Headquarters File Number 92-3171-1370
Top Hoodlum Program – Anti Racketeering.
Daily Summery Report

CG 6486-C advised Giancana met with Charles English, Butch Blasi, and others at west side headquarters several days during week of March 23-27, last.

On one occasion discussion held at which time particular discussion held regarding health of several of Chicago top hoodlums at which time particular discussion held regarding Jimmy Allegretti. Conversation centered upon Allegretti's merely spends the days there are sneaks out at night time. Giancana and English held short conversation during which Giancana indicated he and English attempting to have some property condemned and were successful in accomplishing this. No indication of property in question given. Several conversations held concerning poor state of business at Armory Lounge and of desire to sell same.

CG 6576-C advised Buddy Jacobson as assistant to First Ward Alderman, conferred with attorney Mike Brodkin, concerning attempts to fix current court case pending against Holiday Lounge, one of Chicago's notorious strip joints. Jacobson advised he was meeting with Judge Sidney Jones regarding this case and that present plans are to have case postponed until after April 7. It was learned Pat Marcy is returning from his extended vacation on April 7 and Jacobson advised that all matters are being delayed until Marcy's return from him to handle.

FEDERAL BUREAU OF INVESTIGATION

REPORTING OFFICE	OFFICE OF ORIGIN	DATE	INVESTIGATIVE PERIOD	
CHICAGO	CHICAGO	1964	April 14, 1964	
TITLE OF CASE		REPORT MADE BY		TYPED BY
				dkc
SAMUEL M. GIANCANA, aka		CHARACTER OF CASE		
		FBI Headquarters File 92-3171-1376 Top Hoodlum Program – Anti Racketeering, Daily Summery		

Investigation at Chicago indicates no increased police activity at Armory Lounge since closing. Observation and source indicate Giancana not observed at lounge since April 11 last. Possibility exists Giancana visiting Keeley Smith in Las Vegas. Source indicates no associates of Giancana have frequented lounge during evening hours since April 6.

Authority requested to attempt re-entry of lounge under full security for purpose of relocating source. Chicago feels re-entry during period lounge closed provides greater degree of security as well as greater period in which to complete operation.

FEDERAL BUREAU OF INVESTIGATION

REPORTING OFFICE	OFFICE OF ORIGIN	DATE	INVESTIGATIVE PERIOD	
CHICAGO	CHICAGO	1964	April 16, 1964	
TITLE OF CASE		REPORT MADE BY		TYPED BY
				dkc
SAMUEL M. GIANCANA, aka		CHARACTER OF CASE		
		FBI Headquarters File Number 92-3171 Top Hoodlum Program – Anti Racketeering, Daily Summery		

Re-Entry into Armory Lounge accomplished without incident during early morning hours April 16 instant. One of the two units located on premises resituated adjacent to bar in front portion of lounge where it appears in excellent position to cover pertinent area of lounge. Re-Entry disclosed extent or re-modeling within lounge has in fact added extra security to second unit located adjacent to booth formerly utilized exclusively by Giancana. Also of interest was observation of newly constructed lattice-type partition further securing Giancana's booth. Chicago feels this location undoubtedly will be further utilized by Giancana in future. Chicago feels one more entry will be necessary to insure most complete coverage of lounge.

FEDERAL BUREAU OF INVESTIGATION

REPORTING OFFICE	OFFICE OF ORIGIN	DATE	INVESTIGATIVE PERIOD	
CHICAGO	CHICAGO	1964	April 22, 1964	
TITLE OF CASE		REPORT MADE BY		TYPED BY
				dkc
SAMUEL M. GIANCANA, aka		CHARACTER OF CASE		
		FBI Headquarters File 92-3171-1381		
		Top Hoodlum Program – Anti Racketeering		

Illegal Activities

CG T-4 advised in March that information has been received to the effect that Sam Giancana is considering retiring as a member of the "Commission" and that according to the information made available that the person in line to replace Giancana as the Chicago representative to the "Commission" is Frank Ferraro. Among other individuals recently stated as possible successors to Giancana's position as boss are Jackie Cerone and Phil Alderisio.

It was believed that Charles English is the man between Giancana and the Chicago organization and the New York origination. CG T-17 advised that English in this capacity, travels to New York on the average of once a week and takes great care on these occasions to see that his departures are unknown to anyone.

CG T-3 advised that also in late March, Giancana met with Frank Ferraro at Ferraro's request for advice as to how Ferraro should handle his health problem. It is pointed out that Ferraro recently learned that he has a rather serious illness and at the time of his learning of this illness, it was recommended that he should go to the Mayo Clinic for a full scale check up and possible surgery. It was learned that Ferraro was undecided as to whether he should do this or not and it was for this purpose as well as to advise Giancana as to this illness, that he met with him.

Associates of Giancana's

William Daddono

Cg T-3 advised that William Daddono has been meeting on the average of two or three times a week since January with Giancana. It is pointed out that Daddono, several years ago, was reputed to be Giancana's top lieutenant and at one time reportedly in line to take over for Giancana organization in the future years. Recent information had indicated Daddono to have fallen in favor with leading gang bosses. Apparently Daddono has again curried Giancana's favor and is now meeting regularly with them.

Vic Damone

Based on information received indicating Vic Damone, a notes singer and nightclub performer was seen in the company of Sam Giancana. During an interview it was also determined as to the extent of Damone's interest in the Vic Damone Pizza Company in which he has as partners Frank Buccieri and Joseph Grieco, two hoodlums.

Frank Esposito

Frank Esposito is the head of the County Municipal Workers and Street Laborers Union and head of the AFL-CIO Construction and General Laborers District Council of Chicago. The Chicago Office was in receipt of information in early 1962 indicating that Esposito was scheduled to be killed by members of the Chicago syndicate. At that time the local authorities in Miami were advised of this information by the FBI and through their interventions succeeded in preventing this murder. In the summer of 1963 a newspaper article told the story. During March, 1962, Esposito was encountered by an FBI agent in the Miami area while vacationing and was interviewed. Details of the interview are set forth hereafter. Frank Esposito advised s follows:

He recently read an article in the "Chicago Sun Times" by Sandy Smith, whereby it was stated that he, Esposito, was scheduled to be executed by the Chicago criminal organization during the winter of 1962. Esposito described the article as "pure hogwash" in that there would be no reason for "them" to harm him. He has never had any dealings with them except to "help some of them young fellows out" occasionally.

Esposito repeatedly denied that he was in anyway associated with the so called "Syndicate" in Chicago. He said that in his capacity as head of the Municipal Employees and General Laborers Union in Chicago, he would see to that "unfortunate young fellows" who had minor troubles would be put on the city pay roll if possible. Esposito said he has dedicated his life to assisting the needy and unfortunate. He said he is well respected in the Italian American Community of Chicago and deserves that respect.

Mr. Esposito denied being acquainted with Jack Cerone, Sam Giancana, or Anthony Accardo, except by name and possibly seeing them at wakes, weddings, and funerals.

John Lardino

John Lardino is the former business agent of Local 450, Hotel Clerks, Restaurant Employees and Bartenders Union. In March 1964, Lardino meet surreptitiously with several of Chicago's top hoodlum among whom was Sam Giancana.

Phyllis McGuire

CG T-11 advised that Miss McGuire continues to call Sam Giancana on numerous occasions.

Rocco Potenzo

CG T-2 and CG T-3 have advised that Rocco Potenzo has been meeting on average of two or three days a week with Giancana.

Frank Smith

CG T-2 and CG T-3 have recently advised that Frank "Turk" Smith has been meeting on a frequent basis with Giancana since the first portion of 1964. Frank Smith is active in the juke box field in the Chicago area being president of Garfield Amusement Company which deals primarily in juke boxes. He is the brother of Fred "Jukebox" Smith, old time Chicago hoodlum. He was observed playing golf with Giancana on the average of once a week.

<u>Politics</u>

It was learned in February, 1964, that Alderman Robert Massey, Democratic Alderman in Chicago's 36th Ward, was being considered as a replacement as State Representative from the 27th District where he would replace Andrew Euzzino. It was learned that this change was being considered by Sam Giancana. Another possibility to replace Euzzino if such a replacement was, in fact, made was Nunzio Tisci, the brother of Anthony Tisci, son-in-law of Giancana.

It was learned in March, 1964, that officials of the Anco Insurance Company were planning to meet with Sam Giancana for the purpose of discussing the employment by that firm of Joseph Porcaro. Porcaro is presently the Republican Ward Committeeman in the 28th Ward and is an individual who has had strong backing of Giancana in recent political movements. It was learned that the officers of the insurance company were apprehensive regarding Porcaro's employment because of a recent investigation conducted by the FBI into the affairs to the insurance company. It was felt that to keep Porcaro on the payroll would lend adverse publicity to the company and for this reason Giancana was to be contacted for the purpose of replacing Porcaro.

FEDERAL BUREAU OF INVESTIGATION

REPORTING OFFICE	OFFICE OF ORIGIN	DATE	INVESTIGATIVE PERIOD	
CHICAGO	CHICAGO	1964	April 25, 1964	
TITLE OF CASE		REPORT MADE BY		TYPED BY
				dkc
SAMUEL M. GIANCANA, aka		CHARACTER OF CASE FBI Headquarters File Number 92-3171-1383 Top Hoodlum Program – Anti Racketeering. Daily Summary		

CG 6576-C advised that group consisting of Sam Rosa, Mr. Flood, and Johnny Matassa observed dining at Imperial Inn, Chicago motel located in the Loop, Chicago. It may be that Dominic Blasi is in the hospital after having suffered a heart attack.

FEDERAL BUREAU OF INVESTIGATION

REPORTING OFFICE	OFFICE OF ORIGIN	DATE	INVESTIGATIVE PERIOD
CHICAGO	CHICAGO	1964	May 7, 1964

TITLE OF CASE	REPORT MADE BY	TYPED BY
SAMUEL M. GIANCANA, aka		dkc

CHARACTER OF CASE

FBI Headquarters File Number 92-3171-1394
Top Hoodlum Program – Anti Racketeering.
Daily Summary

CG 6576-C advised Pat Marcy met with Judge Daniel Covelli on evening of May 4, last at Covelli's request. Covelli, according to Marcy, had been drinking when he met Marcy and immediately launched into a tirade against "any lawyer coming into my court-room and thinking he can tell me what to do." Apparently Marcy had made a request of Covelli concerning certain case to be heard in his court and the lawyer was instructed that arrangements had been made with the judge. Covelli then became antagonized with lawyer's manner and handling of case.

During meeting Covelli asked Marcy who he was doing this for and was told for Giancana. Covelli then stated that he wanted to talk to Giancana himself regarding this matter. Marcy stated that he had contacted Anthony Tisci and advised him of the fore-going and requested that he tell Giancana that Covelli wants to meet with him. Marcy very heated over this and wants Giancana to tell Covelli who is boss and that orders from Marcy are to be obeyed.

FEDERAL BUREAU OF INVESTIGATION

REPORTING OFFICE	OFFICE OF ORIGIN	DATE	INVESTIGATIVE PERIOD
CHICAGO	CHICAGO	1964	May 15, 1964

TITLE OF CASE	REPORT MADE BY	TYPED BY
SAMUEL M. GIANCANA, aka		dkc

CHARACTER OF CASE

FBI Headquarters File 92-3171-1398
Top Hoodlum Program – Anti Racketeering.
Daily Summary

CG 6576-C advised Anthony "Puleo" DeRosa, minor Chicago hoodlum, met with Pat Marcy and John D'Arco to discus possibility of aid for DeRosa in pending case resulting out of arrest of DeRosa and six other Chicago ex-convict hoodlums recently on charges of voting without restoration of civil rights.

DeRosa advised his attorney apprehensive over this matter and advised DeRosa that he felt it would be hard to out the "fix" in this case. DeRosa advised that he un-derstands his case assigned to Judge Emmeti Morrissey. As Bureau is aware Morrissey close contact of First Ward organization and caters to desires of Marcy.

Anthony Tisci later joined the group and was questioned as to affect DeRosa's not ever having been confined would have on the situation. Although DeRosa was convicted he claims not to have been confined following this conviction. Tisci advised that there is no law on this and he does not know what effect this would have.

FEDERAL BUREAU OF INVESTIGATION

REPORTING OFFICE	OFFICE OF ORIGIN	DATE	INVESTIGATIVE PERIOD	
CHICAGO	CHICAGO	1964	May 21, 1964	
TITLE OF CASE		**REPORT MADE BY**		**TYPED BY** dkc
SAMUEL M. GIANCANA, aka		**CHARACTER OF CASE** FBI Headquarters File 92-3171-1402 Top Hoodlum Program – Anti Racketeering. Daily Summary		

CG 6576-C advised that Pat Marcy met with Anthony Tisci at 4:30 pm this date. Marcy advised Tisci that it was urgent that he meet with Giancana tonight regarding situation concerning Judge Covelli of which Bureau advised last week. As noted Covelli insists on seeing Giancana before complying with wishes of Marcy concerning pending court case presently being heard by Covelli and Marcy wants Giancana to advise Covelli that instructions from Marcy are the same as instructions from Giancana.

Tisci advised Marcy at this time that Giancana not in Chicago and will not return until Friday, May 22, next. No indication given as to whereabouts of Giancana.

FEDERAL BUREAU OF INVESTIGATION

REPORTING OFFICE	OFFICE OF ORIGIN	DATE	INVESTIGATIVE PERIOD	
CHICAGO	CHICAGO	1964	May 28, 1964	
TITLE OF CASE		**REPORT MADE BY**		**TYPED BY** dkc
SAMUEL M. GIANCANA, aka		**CHARACTER OF CASE** FBI Headquarters File Number 92-3171-1404 Top Hoodlum Program – Anti Racketeering. Daily Summary		

CG 6576-C advised that Pat Marcy during conversation with arcade and strip joint owner Louis Arger advised Arger that there is no hope in reopening any of the seven joints close to date. Marcy continued that they will attempt to keep the remaining two locations opened until November and hope for a "favorable election" and hope that they can open up again after that. To emphasize the situation, Marcy stated that "I went to the man and I offered him a (obscene) package a mile high, and it was the first time he's turned my money down. Pat, I can't take your money, I've got to (obscene) you." Forgoing sum apparently offered to liquor license commissioner in attempt to forestall revocation of license of Chez Dot stripe joint.

FEDERAL BUREAU OF INVESTIGATION

REPORTING OFFICE	OFFICE OF ORIGIN	DATE	INVESTIGATIVE PERIOD
CHICAGO	CHICAGO	1964	June 2, 1964

TITLE OF CASE	REPORT MADE BY	TYPED BY
		dkc
SAMUEL M. GIANCANA, aka	**CHARACTER OF CASE** FBI Headquarters File 92-3171-1408 Top Hoodlum Program – Anti Racketeering. Daily Summary	

Las Vegas informant advised that Sam Giancana observed in Indianapolis with Keeley Smith on May 31, 1964.

FEDERAL BUREAU OF INVESTIGATION

REPORTING OFFICE	OFFICE OF ORIGIN	DATE	INVESTIGATIVE PERIOD
CHICAGO	CHICAGO	1964	June 4, 1964

TITLE OF CASE	REPORT MADE BY	TYPED BY
		dkc
SAMUEL M. GIANCANA, aka	**CHARACTER OF CASE** FBI Headquarters File Number 92-3171-1410 Top Hoodlum Program – Anti Racketeering Daily Summary	

CG 6486-C advised Charles English appeared at Armory Lounge and is having serious marital difficulties at present time. He feels the FBI is trying to have his wife become an informant but states, "She doesn't know anything." Wife highly upset over serious illness of her father and according to English is making life miserable for him. Later in conversation with John Matassa, English stated he has over 50 people working for him at one time and that he has to keep them in line. He continued that "You have to watch them closely and if they get out of line you have to whack them good." English talking about on track bookmaking situation in Chicago stated, "We got a lot of problems." English advised that he will not be going to the wedding of Anthony Accardo's son at the Villa Venice but would send his contribution. He feels there will be too much publicity attendant upon the affair.

FEDERAL BUREAU OF INVESTIGATION

REPORTING OFFICE	OFFICE OF ORIGIN	DATE	INVESTIGATIVE PERIOD
CHICAGO	CHICAGO	1964	June 6, 1964

TITLE OF CASE	REPORT MADE BY	TYPED BY
		dkc

SAMUEL M. GIANCANA, aka	CHARACTER OF CASE FBI Headquarters File Number 92-3171-1411 Top Hoodlum Program – Anti Racketeering. Daily Summary

CG 6486-C advised that Joey Aiuppa appeared at Armory Lounge on June 4, last in a attempt to contact Giancana concerning his strip joints in Cicero which were closed several months ago by raiders of Cook County States Attorney for indecent shows and has remained closed. Aiuppa in contact with Butch Blasi and stated that he wants Giancana, "to make some contacts at the courts." Blasi advised Aiuppa that Giancana not in Chicago and will bring matter up upon his return and contact Aiuppa.

In general conversation Aiuppa advised that "things are down," presumably in Cicero, due to recent "heat" generated by newspapers, but expects the town will open up again after the elections in November.

FEDERAL BUREAU OF INVESTIGATION

REPORTING OFFICE	OFFICE OF ORIGIN	DATE	INVESTIGATIVE PERIOD
CHICAGO	CHICAGO	1964	June 9, 1964

TITLE OF CASE	REPORT MADE BY	TYPED BY
		dkc

SAMUEL M. GIANCANA, aka	CHARACTER OF CASE FBI Headquarters File 92-3171-1415 Top Hoodlum Program – Anti Racketeering. Daily Summary

CG 6486-C advised Butch Blasi advised while on the phone that several big people anxious to meet with Giancana on important matters. Giancana still out of town. Blasi mentioned that one of the matters to be discussed was that of whether politicians would be allowed to attend wedding of son of Anthony Accardo which is taking place on June 10, 1964. In view of this, and assuming he is aware that Accardo himself desires to talk over this matter, it is believed trip must be of business nature to deem it important enough to remain on trip instead of returning home to talk with someone of Accardo's stature.

FEDERAL BUREAU OF INVESTIGATION

REPORTING OFFICE	OFFICE OF ORIGIN	DATE	INVESTIGATIVE PERIOD	
CHICAGO	CHICAGO	1964	June 10, 1964	
TITLE OF CASE		REPORT MADE BY		TYPED BY
				dkc
SAMUEL M. GIANCANA, aka		**CHARACTER OF CASE** FBI Headquarters File Number 92-3171 Top Hoodlum Program – Anti Racketeering. Daily Summary		

CG 6486-C advised that Giancana returned to Chicago on 6/9 last and met Charles English, Butch Blasi and Rocco Potenzo at Armory Lounge. Potenzo, who was most insistent that he speak with Giancana in private tonight. When Giancana told Potenzo that he would not be able to take the time he was told, "I'll tell you why I got to tell you. While you was away these others tried to get you," Giancana cursed and advised Potenzo not to worry. He advised that he could take care of himself. He then instructed Potenzo that he would be at the lounge every night and Potenzo should contact him there.

Above would indicate Potenzo told Giancana of some of activities on parts of persons not identified to jeopardize the position of Giancana. It is felt that Potenzo will further relate details concerning same in near future.

During the evening Butch Blasi was heard advising Giancana "Here is the money Fifi (Buccieri) sent you, $4,000."

An FBI surveillance photo taken from the rear of the Armory Lounge. The Lounge is circled by Agents.

FEDERAL BUREAU OF INVESTIGATION

REPORTING OFFICE	OFFICE OF ORIGIN	DATE	INVESTIGATIVE PERIOD	
CHICAGO	CHICAGO	1964	June 16, 1964	
TITLE OF CASE		REPORT MADE BY		TYPED BY
				dkc
SAMUEL M. GIANCANA, aka		**CHARACTER OF CASE** FBI Headquarters File Number 92-3171-1416 Top Hoodlum Program – Anti Racketeering. Daily Summary		

CG 6486-C advised that Hy Godfrey appeared at the Armory Lounge requesting an urgent meeting with Giancana or Butch Blasi. Godfrey was informed Giancana was at the golf course. Blasi, when later advised of Godfrey visit, was highly agitated and indicated he did not want to be bothered with Godfrey. Source indicated that Blasi later advised Giancana of Godfrey matter and stated he left $3,000 for Giancana. Of particular note was information given to Godfrey that Giancana might be located at Pucci's Restaurant located about two blocks west of the Armory Lounge. Blasi also advised Giancana that "little Larry wants to get in touch with you urgently." This probably reference to Larry Rassano, Cicero hoodlum and manager of Joey Aiuppa's Turf Lounge in Cicero. It is pointed out that Aiuppa attempted to contact Giancana last week concerning another of his Cicero clubs which has been closed for purpose of having Giancana make some contacts to help Aiuppa re-open his clubs.

It is noted that source advised that Hy Godfrey advised Murray Humphreys that Giancana could not make meeting requested by Humphreys from June 15, as he would be leaving town on the evening of June 13. CG 6486-C advised Giancana still in town on the 14th. This would indicate Giancana merely putting off Humphreys with excuse when not interested in meet.

FEDERAL BUREAU OF INVESTIGATION

REPORTING OFFICE	OFFICE OF ORIGIN	DATE	INVESTIGATIVE PERIOD	
CHICAGO	CHICAGO	1964	June 17, 1964	
TITLE OF CASE		REPORT MADE BY		TYPED BY
				dkc
SAMUEL M. GIANCANA, aka		**CHARACTER OF CASE** FBI Headquarters File Number 92-3171-1417 Top Hoodlum Program – Anti Racketeering. Daily Summary		

Prior to Giancana's departing for a golf tournament, he met with Joey O'Brien (Aiuppa), James "Cowboy" Mirro, and Joe "Fifkie" Corngold. Discussion with O'Brien concerned about the reopening of closed Cicero strip and gambling joints. Giancana advised that he would have Butch Blasi check into this matter while Giancana away.

Source advised that Giancana will be gone for a week. During that period source stated that Blasi was given numerous matters to handle aside from above concerning O'Brien. Among contacts to be made were with "Curley" (Murray Humphreys), "That Federal man" and "Billy."

FEDERAL BUREAU OF INVESTIGATION

REPORTING OFFICE	OFFICE OF ORIGIN	DATE	INVESTIGATIVE PERIOD	
CHICAGO	CHICAGO	1964	June 18, 1964	
TITLE OF CASE		REPORT MADE BY		TYPED BY
				dkc
SAMUEL M. GIANCANA, aka		CHARACTER OF CASE		
		FBI Headquarters File 92-3171-1419 Top Hoodlum Program – Anti Racketeering. Daily Summary		

CG 6486 advised that just prior to leaving Chicago Giancana met with James "Cowboy" Mirro and Jimmy Capezio and discussed an unidentified gambling game presently being operated by them. Mirro indicated game was just recently started and doing well on weekends but has not as yet caught on during week. Statement made by Mirro, "we have a lot of lookers who will probably jump in latter." Giancana advised both that he wanted to see them both as soon as he gets back into town and to be advised of progress of game. Above three persons later joined by Joe Marks, a small time hoodlum who once held interest in the Amber Light Caf, where Joe Corngold operated gambling interest for Giancana, and was utilized by Giancana as a meeting place.

FEDERAL BUREAU OF INVESTIGATION

REPORTING OFFICE	OFFICE OF ORIGIN	DATE	INVESTIGATIVE PERIOD	
CHICAGO	CHICAGO	1964	June 20, 1964	
TITLE OF CASE		REPORT MADE BY		TYPED BY
				dkc
SAMUEL M. GIANCANA, aka		CHARACTER OF CASE		
		FBI Headquarters File Number 92-3171 Top Hoodlum Program – Anti Racketeering. Daily Summary		

Chicago recently in receipt of complaint alleging that Kenron Awning Co., Cicero, Illinois, suspected of bookmaking activities since complainant observed a large number of phones on premises. Noted Kenron is a large awning company in which top hoodlum Leonard Patrick is alleged to have an interest in. On 6/18, last CG6576-C advised that Pat Marcy, John D'Arco and Anthony Tisci had conversation which apparently refers to above situation. Tisci indicated that "the redhead" (Richard Cain) received info that an awning company which has about 50 phones, is believed to be a wire room and is attempting to notify Giancana prior to any contemplated investigation. Tisci and Marcy apparently contacted Butch Blasi and were advised that this awning company is a legitimate business and to instruct "the redhead" to leave it alone.

FEDERAL BUREAU OF INVESTIGATION

REPORTING OFFICE	OFFICE OF ORIGIN	DATE	INVESTIGATIVE PERIOD	
CHICAGO	CHICAGO	1964	June 22, 1964	
TITLE OF CASE		REPORT MADE BY		TYPED BY
				dkc
SAMUEL M. GIANCANA, aka		**CHARACTER OF CASE** FBI Headquarters File Number 92-3171-1421 Top Hoodlum Program – Anti Racketeering. Daily Summary		

CG 6486-C advised Giancana held conversation with several hoodlums at Armory Lounge shortly after returning to Chicago. Heard discussing the wedding of son of Anthony Accardo held June 10, 1964 and of numerous investigating agencies who had personnel covering the affair. Giancana spoke at length over FBI surveillance during summer of 1963 and indicated that he was unable to accomplish anything during period of surveillance. According to Giancana "they had me tied up. I couldn't go nowhere alone." Giancana continued that his court proceedings were a last ditch effort, which he did not feel that its inception would succeed. Giancana now feels that each and every case involving government or local police should be brought to court if for no other reason than the agency in question will defer further action until matter decided. Giancana believes these tactics should be also pursued against local press though libel actions to curtail wave of bad publicity afforded Chicago hoodlums which reduces their activities.

FEDERAL BUREAU OF INVESTIGATION

REPORTING OFFICE	OFFICE OF ORIGIN	DATE	INVESTIGATIVE PERIOD	
CHICAGO	CHICAGO	1964	June 25, 1964	
TITLE OF CASE		REPORT MADE BY		TYPED BY
				dkc
SAMUEL M. GIANCANA, aka		**CHARACTER OF CASE** FBI Headquarters File 92-3171-1425 Top Hoodlum Program – Anti Racketeering. Daily Summary		

Information has been received that the word has been passed to all hoodlum juice lenders that they are to discontinue use of muscle with juice operations at this time as too much heat generated on juice activities in area by federal and local law enforcement officials. Information did not indicate if permanent or just until publicity subsides.

Information also advised Sam DeStefano, reportedly Chicago's leading money lender, had "words" with Sam Giancana and reportedly told Giancana off. Chicago feels second information probably connected to that of juice operations and knowing background of DeStefano feels it highly plausible that he would tell Giancana off in this regard, Chicago following matter closely.

FEDERAL BUREAU OF INVESTIGATION

REPORTING OFFICE	OFFICE OF ORIGIN	DATE	INVESTIGATIVE PERIOD
CHICAGO	CHICAGO	1964	June 29, 1964

TITLE OF CASE	REPORT MADE BY	TYPED BY
SAMUEL M. GIANCANA, aka		dkc

CHARACTER OF CASE
FBI Headquarters File Number 92-3171-1426
Top Hoodlum Program – Anti Racketeering.
Daily Summary

CG 6486-C advised Giancana not known to be in Chicago area since June 25 last. It was learned Giancana met with that night Anthony Tisci and discussed certain matters of interest to Giancana and to Pat Marcy. Marcy known to have requested Tisci to press for an answer on certain matters o which "that guy went out on a limb for Moe."

FEDERAL BUREAU OF INVESTIGATION

REPORTING OFFICE	OFFICE OF ORIGIN	DATE	INVESTIGATIVE PERIOD
CHICAGO	CHICAGO	1964	July 1, 1964

TITLE OF CASE	REPORT MADE BY	TYPED BY
SAMUEL M. GIANCANA, aka		dkc

CHARACTER OF CASE
FBI Headquarters File Number 92-3171-1427
Top Hoodlum Program – Anti Racketeering.
Daily Summary

CG 6486-C advised Charles English advised Butch Blasi of decision of US Court of Appeals concerning Giancana matter and indicated extreme displeasure of that courts findings. English stated that he could not understand how the court could hold special agents in Chicago in contempt and yet not find that FBI within jurisdiction of court. English indicated that Blasi should immediately contact Giancana for purpose of alerting him to decision and suggest that he use devious means to return to Chicago as "those (obscene) "G" guys will be all over him when he gets back in town." Blasi felt that if such is the situation Giancana may spend considerably less time in Chicago area as he has often expressed irritation over his inability to "do anything" during surveillance.

FEDERAL BUREAU OF INVESTIGATION

REPORTING OFFICE	OFFICE OF ORIGIN	DATE	INVESTIGATIVE PERIOD
CHICAGO	CHICAGO	1964	July 6, 1964

TITLE OF CASE	REPORT MADE BY	TYPED BY
SAMUEL M. GIANCANA, aka		dkc
	CHARACTER OF CASE	
	FBI Headquarters File Number 92-3171-1428 Top Hoodlum Program – Anti Racketeering. Daily Summary	

CG 6576-C advised Pat Marcy left two envelopes in care of Buddy Jacobson instructing that $600 to paid to Lieutenant Mark Conlin of the Chicago PD and $1,600 to go to Captain O'Donnell.

Marcy, who departed Chicago on July 3, for his summer home advised Jacobson that he would call him on July 7, with instructions as to where he should meet with the above individuals. Marcy pointed out to Jacobson that instructions have been given Conlin's not to come to First Ward offices any longer. These instructions undoubtedly issued after Marcy made aware of Conlin's name being included in report concerning police corruption furnished to Commissioner O.W. Wilson.

FEDERAL BUREAU OF INVESTIGATION

REPORTING OFFICE	OFFICE OF ORIGIN	DATE	INVESTIGATIVE PERIOD
CHICAGO	CHICAGO	1964	July 14, 1964

TITLE OF CASE	REPORT MADE BY	TYPED BY
SAMUEL M. GIANCANA, aka		dkc
	CHARACTER OF CASE	
	FBI Headquarters File Number 92-3171-1440 Top Hoodlum Program – Anti Racketeering. Daily Summary	

Re-entry into Armory Lounge accomplished without incident during early hours this date. Investigation disclosed both sources shorted out. Attempt made to replace with new units, however, unsuccessful in this regard. Because of extremely heavy police patrol of area, including check of premises from outside, personnel required to depart while sufficient darkness remained to cover same. No indication given that police evidence any suspicion of entry to location. Chicago contemplates re-entry at earliest possible date provided full security assured. No activity noted Giancana residence from fixed plant locations.

FEDERAL BUREAU OF INVESTIGATION

REPORTING OFFICE	OFFICE OF ORIGIN	DATE	INVESTIGATIVE PERIOD
CHICAGO	CHICAGO	1964	July 21, 1964

TITLE OF CASE	REPORT MADE BY	TYPED BY
		dkc
SAMUEL M. GIANCANA, aka	CHARACTER OF CASE	
	FBI Headquarters File 92-3171-1441 Top Hoodlum Program – Anti Racketeering. Daily Summary	

Upon Giancana's return to Chicago area Pat Marcy immediately made contact with Anthony Tisci and Anthony Girolami concerning subpoenas issued in libel suit being pressed by William Fishman, owner of crossroads Restaurant, against Chicago Sun Times newspaper and its reporter Sandy Smith for statement made by Smith that Fishman is a gangster.

Marcy concerned over information indicating his brother Paul Marcy to be subpoenaed in this case and this would place Paul Marcy's job with country in jeopardy. Marcy obtained legal advice over manner in which persons being requested to give depositions in this matter must answer. Tisci advised each person should be in company of his respective attorney during questioning and allow attorneys to determine what is pertinent. Marcy indicated he is not concerned over subpoena for himself.

Marcy later had Frank "Boomby" Fiore, local bailiff, meet with him and discuss Fiore's subpoena. Fiore initially stated he would go and furnish deposition in matter alone but was subsequently convinces by Marcy that he would be better advised to have attorney present to prevent and embarrassing circumstances.

FEDERAL BUREAU OF INVESTIGATION

REPORTING OFFICE	OFFICE OF ORIGIN	DATE	INVESTIGATIVE PERIOD
CHICAGO	CHICAGO	1964	July 27, 1964

TITLE OF CASE	REPORT MADE BY	TYPED BY
	SA Marshall Rutland	dkc
SAMUEL M. GIANCANA, aka	CHARACTER OF CASE	
	FBI Headquarters File Number 92-3171-1447 Top Hoodlum Program – Anti Racketeering	

Synopsis:

In June 1964, U.S. Circuit Court of Appeals for the 7th Circuit returned decisions arising from Giancana's suit against government instituted on 1963. Judge Rodger J. Keley wrote opinion concerning preliminary injunction case against FBI surveillance and ruled that judgment of lower court be vacated and returned since the district court did not have jurisdiction. Keley based opinion on fact that complaint defective because it failed to show damages exceeded the value of $10,000. Judge Elmer J. Schnackenberg affirmed the opinion while Judge Luther M. Swygert dissented. Judge Schnackenberg wrote opinion in alleged criminal contempt situation against SAC Marlin Johnson and upheld USDC finding in this mater. Judge Swygert concurred with opinion of Judge Schnackenberg found that question put to Johnson were material and relevant to the issues and it did not appear from the records that these exhibits about which Johnson was questioned were ever in the file of the Department of Justice and as a result Johnson was in contempt in refusing to answer questions pertaining thereto. US Attorney's Office, Chicago, filed a motion on July 10, 1964, requesting extension of time in which to file petition for rehearing of contempt matter before Circuit Court. Executive Assistant to the Attorney General of the US desires to appeal contempt citation to Supreme Court. Giancana reportedly has issued instructions to all syndicate "juice" operators that they are to discontinue all violence in the collection of "juice" loans because of publicity generated on these activities. Additional rumors heard concerning replacement of Giancana as head of Chicago syndicate. Giancana continues meeting with local hoodlums although noted to have been absent from Chicago area approximately 6 weeks during period mid April to mid July. Giancana observed in Lake Worth, Florida together with Tarquin "Queenie" Simonelli and also believed present in Miami area in company of Phyllis McGuire. Giancana reported to have financed Chicago businessman to buy out partner and obtained full control of Reddi Whip Corporation of Chicago. While in Chicago area Giancana observed frequenting on almost daily basis the Drake Oakbrook Hotel.

Miscellaneous Information

CG T-1 furnished information in May, 1964, indicating that the property located at 1505 North 16th Avenue, Melrose Park, and the building located thereupon in owned in actuality by Sam Giancana. This source further indicated that Giancana owns additional buildings in that area, however, the particular buildings are unknown to the source. The source was also unable to identify the man in whose name the property is held but stated that the person merely fronts as owner on the behalf of Giancana.

Illegal Activities

CG T-2 advised in June, 1964, that Sam Giancana issued orders to Fifi Buccieri to see that all violence and beating cease in connection with the collection of "juice" loans. According to the informant, instructions have been given that the collectors are to obtain whatever money they can get from their victims without any threats of violence. The informant continued that this decision was brought about by the extreme "heat" placed on "juice" activities by federal, state and local authorities. Sam DeStefano is the cause of all the publicity attendant to this type of operation. This informant indicated there is some possibility that DeStefano might possibly be slated "for the trunk."

As a result of the foregoing orders many of the leading west side "juice" operators, including Fifi Buccieri and Sam Battaglia, have decided to get out of the "juice" business and are presently attempting to determine what plan of action to follow with the moneys received in this business and what to do with the business.

CG T-4 corroborated the information furnished by CG T-3 concerning instructions to juice operators to discontinue the use of muscle tactics in the collection of loans outstanding. According to CG T-4 Sam DeStefano reportedly Chicago's leading money lender, "had words with Giancana" concerning this edict and reportedly "told Giancana off."

CG T-4 advised that from his knowledge of DeStefano he feels it highly likely that he would dare to tell Giancana off in Chicago. This informant, when questioned as to the possibility of DeStefano ending up in a trunk, while admitting he had not heard anything specific concerning this, felt that it would not be an unlikely concerning this, felt that it would not be an unlikely end for DeStefano.

CG T-5 advised that while in Florida he talked to several persons familiar with Giancana who informed him that Giancana was getting ready to step down from his position. He informed that the 2 men mentioned were known to him as "Milwaukee Phil" and "The Bug." That would be similar to Felix "Milwaukee Phil" Alderisio and Johnny "The Bug" Varelli. It is pointed out that both of these individuals have attained fairly high status with in the Chicago organization in the past years and that information has been received to the effect that Alderisio might be in line to replace Giancana.

However, it is the consensus of opinion at this time after reviewing all information concerning the numerous rumors regarding Giancana's demise as head of the Chicago organization that there is limited basis of fact upon which to support any specific consideration at this time that Giancana is about to retire as the head of the Chicago mob.

Associates

Joe E. Lewis

A physical surveillance conducted by agents of the Chicago division on April 25, 1964, revealed that Sam Giancana to present in the company of three other persons one of whom was identified as Birgit Clark, a female with whom Giancana has maintained a acquaintance for several years. The other two were identified as Mr. and Mrs. Partepelio.

During the course of the evening, Giancana was observed to proceed to a small bar adjacent to the Camelia House and there to engage in conversation with nationally notes comedian Joe E. Lewis, Following a conversation for some 20 minutes, Lewis excused him self for the purpose of performing. Upon completion of his act, Lewis was noted to join Giancana at a ringside table.

CG T-11 informant advised that spoke with Lewis while he was in Chicago. This individual indicated that the topic of Giancana arose and that Lewis indicated that he has known Giancana for several years but failed to recall when or where or through whom he was first introduced to Giancana. According to this source, Giancana had requested Lewis to accompany him on several other occasions during Lewis's stay in Chicago which invitations were turned down by Lewis.

Sam Rosa

CG T-7 advised in April 1964, that Sam "Slicker Sam" Rosa was having financial troubles following a recent arrest in a gambling operation and as a result had been in contact with Sam Giancana to either borrow some money or to obtain some sort of job with Giancana's organization. According to this source, Giancana refused both request of Rosa thereby causing Rosa to be extremely unhappy with Giancana and other member of the Chicago syndicate.

It was pointed out that Rosa was one of the individuals who accompanied Giancana to Hawaii during the early portion of January 1964. Rosa's latest arrest was made during a gambling raid in Highwood, Illinois, which raid was one of several recently instituted by the Illinois State police based on warrants by the Chicago Division of FBI.

Keely Smith

The Las Vegas Division advised on June 1, 1964, that a Las Vegas informant, who had recently attended the Indianapolis 500 mile auto race, stated that while he was attending he had seen Keely Smith in the company of Sam Giancana.

Jack Sussman

CG T-7 advised in March 31, 1964, that Jack Sussman, the owner of the Roosevelt Coffee Shop located on Roosevelt Road just east of Halsted Street, is a close confident of Sam Giancana and Tony Accardo. The informant stated that Sussman used to accompany both Accardo and Giancana to New York City for the purpose of attending major prize fights held in that city.

John Campanale

Johnny "Haircuts" Campanale has been in almost daily companion with Sam Giancana. When Giancana in town, Campanale is a golf companion in Giancana's foursome and Campanale will also spend several evenings a week in Giancana's company. According to source, Campanale is, next to Butch Blasi, the person who is most aware of Giancana's whereabouts.

The informant further advised that Campanale himself operates a small bookmaking operation in the western suburbs out of one or two restaurants.

Activities in the Lake Worth Area

On June 17, 1964, CG T-12 advised that he observed on the course at the Palm Beach National Golf Club, rural Lake Worth, Florida, Giancana, Phyllis McGuire and James Fiore, the care taker at the residence of Leslie "Killer Kane" Kruse, 1902 Notre Dame Boulevard, Lake Worth. The informant said that this was the first time in almost five years since Giancana in that area.

FEDERAL BUREAU OF INVESTIGATION

REPORTING OFFICE	OFFICE OF ORIGIN	DATE	INVESTIGATIVE PERIOD	
CHICAGO	CHICAGO	1964	July 31, 1964	
TITLE OF CASE		**REPORT MADE BY**		**TYPED BY**
				dkc
SAMUEL M. GIANCANA, aka		**CHARACTER OF CASE** FBI Headquarters File Number 92-3171-1448 Top Hoodlum Program – Anti Racketeering. Daily Summary		

Charles English was interviewed and indicated that Giancana is out of town and would not divulge either location nor intended return. English feels FBI responsible for sending a photo of English with another woman to his wife which has caused serious rift in marriage.

English observed in company of Jack Cerone prior to interview. It was learned from independent source that Cerone met with English to iron out problem concerning Joseph Gagliano which Cerone was unable to handle himself. Nature of problem unknown. Chicago informant advised this date that Giancana observed at noon with Bergit Clark having lunch at Drake Oakbrook Hotel, Chicago.

FEDERAL BUREAU OF INVESTIGATION

REPORTING OFFICE	OFFICE OF ORIGIN	DATE	INVESTIGATIVE PERIOD	
CHICAGO	CHICAGO	1964	August 3, 1964	
TITLE OF CASE		**REPORT MADE BY**		**TYPED BY**
				dkc
SAMUEL M. GIANCANA, aka		**CHARACTER OF CASE** FBI Headquarters File 92-3171-1450 Top Hoodlum Program – Anti Racketeering. Daily Summary		

CG 6576-C advised of discussion with Pat Marcy, John D'Arco and James C. Renzino, Attorney. Renzino revealed position of First Ward Republican Committeeman had been urged on him by Peter C. Granata, Illinois State Representative, presently functioning as Republican Committeeman in the First Ward. Granata indicated this position had been lined up with approval of Tim Sheehan, Cook County chairman, Republican Party. Renzino in discussion pointed out his association of eight or nine years with Marcy and D'Arco in First Ward regular Democratic headquarters although he is generally known as a Republican.

Renzino explained he was registered to vote in Chicago's 18th Ward but if he takes the new position can register from 240 West 26th Street, Chicago. Renzino stated he and Granata would further discuss this proposal with D'Arco. Renzino indicated Granata might possibly discuss this matter with D'Arco over the weekend of August 1, last. During which time D'Arco should also give through to this matter. Renzino said in addition "You clear it with Gussie (Gus Alex) and if Gussie wants to talk to me and wants to know why I'm in this thing, I didn't ask for it." D'Arco assured Renzino that "we'll work together." Renzino made statement that "Whenever the orders are to be followed, I'll follow them." Renzino further assured D'Arco "You'll know in detail what moves are made, who I'm called in by, and what to do."

FEDERAL BUREAU OF INVESTIGATION

REPORTING OFFICE	OFFICE OF ORIGIN	DATE	INVESTIGATIVE PERIOD	
CHICAGO	CHICAGO	1964	August 6, 1964	
TITLE OF CASE		REPORT MADE BY		TYPED BY
				dkc
SAMUEL M. GIANCANA, aka		CHARACTER OF CASE FBI Headquarters File Number 92-3171-1451 Top Hoodlum Program – Anti Racketeering. Daily Summary		

During conversation between Hy Godfrey and Pat Marcy concerning a "fix" in gambling matters, Marcy suggested contact with Jack Cerone. Godfrey stated he was going "out west" and would probably see Cerone at the Armory Lounge. In later conversation between John D'Arco, Marcy, and Buddy Jacobson, D'Arco concerned about judgeship appointments. Marcy said Giancana instructed him to handle "it" that way. D'Arco was concerned since Giancana had been in town and apparently departed without leaving further instructions concerning judgeship. This refers to Giancana's selection of Robert Masset as nominee for Circuit Judge.

FEDERAL BUREAU OF INVESTIGATION

REPORTING OFFICE	OFFICE OF ORIGIN	DATE	INVESTIGATIVE PERIOD	
CHICAGO	CHICAGO	1964	August 19, 1964	
TITLE OF CASE		REPORT MADE BY		TYPED BY
				dkc
SAMUEL M. GIANCANA, aka		CHARACTER OF CASE FBI Headquarters File Number 92-3171-1459 Top Hoodlum Program – Anti Racketeering. Daily Summary		

CG 6547-C advised that this afternoon Mike Brodkin, Chicago Attorney, and Pat Marcy conversed concerning conference Brodkin had with Judge Austin during course of James Hoffa trial. In essence Brodkin rehashed information previously obtained from CG 6758-C.

However, during course of conversation, Brodkin made reference to previous conversation between him and Judge Austin when Brodkin "wanted a favor for Giancana that time." Brodkin indicated that on that occasion he has spoken to Austin after Austin had been approached on the same situation by D'Arco who is First Ward Democratic Committeeman. Brodkin remarked he told Austin "You help D'Arco. This is first opportunity he's had to redeem himself in the eyes of certain people. This means more to him than anything he ever did in his life."

Brodkin also commented Austin recently told him "You know the FBI has got you in a report with me, how close you are to me. They know you and Bieber made contact with Judge Austin through John D'Arco."

FEDERAL BUREAU OF INVESTIGATION

REPORTING OFFICE	OFFICE OF ORIGIN	DATE	INVESTIGATIVE PERIOD	
CHICAGO	CHICAGO	1964	August 26, 1964	
TITLE OF CASE		REPORT MADE BY		TYPED BY
				dkc
SAMUEL M. GIANCANA, aka		CHARACTER OF CASE		
		FBI Headquarters File Number 92-3171-1461 Top Hoodlum Program – Anti Racketeering. Daily Summary		

CG 6576-C advised that Pat Marcy and Buddy Jacobson attended the wake of Frank Ferraro Monday evening although realizing this to be against edict issued by Giancana concerning attendance by politically connected persons at hoodlum waked and weddings. Source advised Jacobson first to encounter Giancana who was also present and was greeted by Giancana with words "hello Jew (obscene)." Giancana then continues to berate Jacobson for appearing and requested explanation for presence. Jacobson stated that he attended because of lengthy friendship with Ferraro. Jacobson claims after discussion that Giancana culmed somewhat.

Marcy advised that Giancana did not berate him for attendance but left it understood that he was not pleased at same. Marcy stated that there was little doubt that edict to be enforced strictly in future. Marcy gave no indication as to whether he would go to funeral or not.

Jacobson also advised that he attempted to have private conference with Giancana but was rebuffed. Giancana apparently indicated that he would not meet with anyone during time spent at wake and further indicated reason was that he did not desire to get tied up as he had prior plans. Information received this date from Cleveland division indicates that "short bald man" entered rooms of Phyllis McGuire late Monday night and apparently spent rest of night with her. Giancana was observed at breakfast this AM with McGuire but sat in matter so that waitress unable to identify. Giancana plans to attend Ferraro funeral Wednesday.

CG 6576-C advised that Wilson Moy, chief operator of gambling operations in Chinatown section under control of Frank "Skid" Caruso, met with Pat Marcy this date and requested permission to open up operations again by 8/27 next. Moy's operation has been closed since raid on location at 209 Cermak on 8/21 last by Chicago PD based on warrant obtained by FBI. Moy indicated being hurt greatly financially by lengthy shutdown. Requested permission to re-open game at 214 west 22nd Place, which location directly behind former location.

Marcy advised that he would have to wait for several days while he "checked some things out." Marcy advised that he is not concerned over local police but rather extremely concerned over FBI. Marcy states that FBI seems to have complete knowledge of local gambling operations. Advised Moy to re-contact in day or so.

Marcy in conversation with Buddy Jacobson learned that Paul Ricca and Tony Accardo at wake of Frank Ferraro during evening of August 25, last in contradiction of Giancana made any remarks to either of these individuals.

Marcy indicated strict orders given by Giancana that no one to attend and feels that there might be strong repercussions over failure to adhere to instructions. Apparently Marcy acceded to orders of Giancana and did not attend funeral held this AM.

One exception was Gus Alex, an extremely close life long friend of Ferraro who did attend the wake.

FEDERAL BUREAU OF INVESTIGATION

REPORTING OFFICE	OFFICE OF ORIGIN	DATE	INVESTIGATIVE PERIOD	
CHICAGO	CHICAGO	1964	August 28, 1964	
TITLE OF CASE		REPORT MADE BY		TYPED BY
				dkc
SAMUEL M. GIANCANA, aka		CHARACTER OF CASE FBI Headquarters File Number 92-3171-1462 Top Hoodlum Program – Anti Racketeering. Daily Summary		

Giancana in attendance at burial of Frank Ferraro in company of Butch Blasi and Jackie Cerone. In view of orders given out by Giancana to other members of Chicago underworld to affect that they were not to attend, forgoing rather strange. It is noted that Murray Humphreys, among others, acceded to Giancana desires and did not attend burial, although not in agreement with Giancana over this issue.

Romey, who has previously been reported as close associate of Pat Marcy, identified as being Romie Nappi. Chicago indices negative about Nappi.

FEDERAL BUREAU OF INVESTIGATION

REPORTING OFFICE	OFFICE OF ORIGIN	DATE	INVESTIGATIVE PERIOD	
CHICAGO	CHICAGO	1964	September 5, 1964	
TITLE OF CASE		**REPORT MADE BY**		**TYPED BY** dkc
SAMUEL M. GIANCANA, aka		**CHARACTER OF CASE** FBI Headquarters File 92-3171-1470 Top Hoodlum Program – Anti Racketeering. Daily Summary		

Upon return from Democratic convention John D'Arco briefed by Pat Marcy on recent activities within Chicago area and was told that "everything is down. The "G" put down the Chinaman and they are out in Maxwell Street." Marcy explained that he has advised that Chinese gambling operations remain down as FBI aware of all the gambling locations and will, merely knock it over as soon as it goes up again."

Marcy also advised D'Arco that his information indicated strong like hood that Ralph Pierce would assume Frank Ferraro's position in syndicate operations at which D'Arco stated "he can't be a boss." It is assumed D'Arco making reference to fact Pierce not Italian. Marcy, in answer to this, stated, "But the number two man could be boss." Apparently Marcy feels that while Ralph Pierce would be in overall charge of Ferraro's enterprises, his lieutenant, if an Italian would be the boss insofar as "The Family" is concerned.

CG T-1 advised John Roselli was in Chicago for the purpose of meeting with Sam Giancana. Reason for visit unknown.

FEDERAL BUREAU OF INVESTIGATION

REPORTING OFFICE	OFFICE OF ORIGIN	DATE	INVESTIGATIVE PERIOD	
CHICAGO	CHICAGO	1964	September 18, 1964	
TITLE OF CASE		**REPORT MADE BY**		**TYPED BY** dkc
SAMUEL M. GIANCANA, aka		**CHARACTER OF CASE** FBI Headquarters File Number 92-3171-1479 Top Hoodlum Program – Anti Racketeering		

Highly confidential source advised that Pat Marcy advised Anthony Tisci that many leading hoodlums scheduled to be subpoenaed for depositions in William Fishman libel action against Chicago Sun Times have "ducked out of town." It is apparent Marcy has contact at Sun Times who is advising him of dates persons are scheduled to be served as he furnished Tisci with information that Gus Alex and Murray Humphreys to be served in October, and Ralph Pierce to be served next week. Marcy advised that Mousey Garambone has "ducked town." Strong possibility exists that Marcy receiving information through Judge Walter Kowalski who in turn receiving same from Karen Walsh, managing editor of times. It is pointed out that this source has previously advised that Marcy instructed Kowalski to contact Walsh in this matter.

FEDERAL BUREAU OF INVESTIGATION

REPORTING OFFICE	OFFICE OF ORIGIN	DATE	INVESTIGATIVE PERIOD	
CHICAGO	CHICAGO	1964	September 22, 1964	
TITLE OF CASE		REPORT MADE BY		TYPED BY
				dkc
SAMUEL M. GIANCANA, aka		CHARACTER OF CASE FBI Headquarters File Number 92-3171-1485 Top Hoodlum Program – Anti Racketeering. Daily Summary		

CG 6576-C advised that Frank Annunzio is trying to meet with Giancana to straighten out some undisclosed matters buy to date has been unable to make contact with Giancana, Giancana also avoiding contact with these persons is fact Giancana aware that subpoena presently outstanding from him in connection with two separate libel actions being pressed at this time against local papers. Giancana feels it would be poor time to be seen in company of local politicians thereby giving fuel for another situation which previously arose following the disclosure of his meeting with John D'Arco in suburban restaurant several years ago. As a result, Giancana presently limiting associations to meetings with hoodlum's associates and any messages he has for politicians being relayed be Anthony Tisci.

FEDERAL BUREAU OF INVESTIGATION

REPORTING OFFICE	OFFICE OF ORIGIN	DATE	INVESTIGATIVE PERIOD	
CHICAGO	CHICAGO	1964	October 1, 1964	
TITLE OF CASE		REPORT MADE BY		TYPED BY
				dkc
SAMUEL M. GIANCANA, aka		CHARACTER OF CASE FBI Headquarters File Number 92-3171-1490 Top Hoodlum Program – Anti Racketeering. Daily Summary		

CG informant advised that following recent gambling raid conducted in Rosemont, IL, based on FBI warrant, a raid on a wire room operating in an apartment building owned by the Mayor of Rosemont Donald Stevens, contact made with Charles Giancana, aka Charles Kane, Sam Giancana's brother by Mayor of Rosemont for purpose of having Kane contact brother with request to have Giancana order Rocco Potenzo to take his various operations out of Rosemont because of publicity being afforded town. Contact made with Kane because of large financial and real estate holdings in that town (2 million dollars) and was pointed out that these would lose value if publicity continued.

Informant advised that Potenzo contacted Rosemont Mayor 9/28, last and advised that "The Cigar" told him to get out of Rosemont. Potenzo claimed to Mayor that he had been out of Chicago for six months and was not aware of these operations but indicated that he would clear out immediately.

FEDERAL BUREAU OF INVESTIGATION

REPORTING OFFICE	OFFICE OF ORIGIN	DATE	INVESTIGATIVE PERIOD	
CHICAGO	CHICAGO	1964	October 1, 1964	
TITLE OF CASE		REPORT MADE BY		TYPED BY
				dkc
SAMUEL M. GIANCANA, aka		**CHARACTER OF CASE** FBI Headquarters File 92-3171-1502 Top Hoodlum Program – Anti Racketeering. Daily Summary		

During a contact held with AUSA's David Schippers and Robert Bailey concerning another matter, the topic of Federal grand jury hearings into narcotics whereby immunity could be granted to witnesses appearing before such a jury was discussed. The Bureau agents proposed the possibility of convening such a grand jury to probe the ties between narcotics traffic in Chicago and members of organized crime, basing this on the recent arrest and subsequent conviction of Chicago hoodlum Americo DiPietto, as ringleader of a large narcotics ring allegedly sponsored by Sam Giancana.

It was suggested that a starting point for a tie-in that would eventually lead to the subpoenaing of Sam Giancana would be calling of such persons as James "Cowboy" Mirro and Ernest "Rocky" Infelice, two extremely close associates of DiPietto's who can be closely associated with Giancana. It is felt that other persons such as Charles Nicoletti, a lieutenant of Giancana who has a conviction on a narcotics violation and is rumored at this time to be involved in narcotics traffic in this area, could be reasonably called into such a proceeding, together with other lesser hoodlums having narcotics convictions in their backgrounds. It is further contemplated by AUSA's that any persons who could be reasonably assumed to derive income from narcotics proceeds such as all of the leaders of organized crime in Chicago, i.e. Gus Alex, Ross Prio, Tony Accardo, Paul Ricca, Jack Cerone, etc., could be called before such a panel.

It is assumed that after showing the connection of these persons to narcotics dealings that the probe could then branch out into various other facets of organized crime in this area and throughout the country. It is the contention of the AUSA's with whom this matter was discussed that in such a grand jury hearing as proposed, that once a connection had been shown between the witness and the subject matter that they can proceed questioning on a broad front concerning corollary matters.

It is felt that questioning of Giancana would also touch on his association with Vito Genovese, "Commission" member, now serving time for narcotics traffic and from there the probe could attempt to develop the presence of "the Commission" and facts surrounding La Cosa Nostra.

In actuality, it is felt that, even though granted immunity, Giancana would not likely talk before any grand jury, at which time contempt proceedings could be instituted against him. The other alternative, of course, is the possibility of Giancana furnishing false information at which time perjury proceedings could be instituted. In this regard it is pointed out that in the event such a tack should be initiated, agents of the Chicago division familiar with Giancana and organized crime would have to work very closely with the AUSA's selected to conduct such hearings, in the preparation of subject matter on which witnesses were to be questioned so that in the event certain of the witnesses felt they could better serve their purpose by giving false information, we would be in a strong position to back up a perjury proceeding.

FEDERAL BUREAU OF INVESTIGATION

REPORTING OFFICE	OFFICE OF ORIGIN	DATE	INVESTIGATIVE PERIOD	
CHICAGO	CHICAGO	1964	October 8, 1964	
TITLE OF CASE		REPORT MADE BY		TYPED BY
				dkc
SAMUEL M. GIANCANA, aka		CHARACTER OF CASE		
		FBI Headquarters File 92-3171-1494 Top Hoodlum Program – Anti Racketeering. Daily Summary		

Highly confidential source advised Hy Godfrey appeared at residence of Sam Giancana early 10/8 to obtain permission from Giancana to leave Chicago area for vacation to Hot Springs. He also brought Giancana pastries for party Giancana intends to have at residence this date.

When later questioning Murray Humphreys as to why he needed Giancana's permission to leave Chicago when he had sanction of Humphreys and Gus Alex to do so. Humphreys replied "He's the boss, his ok is what you need, not me or Gussie." Humphreys also gave similar response when Godfrey informed him Giancana instructed Godfrey he must contact Giancana more often when Godfrey returns, Godfrey, like Humphreys and Alex, does not have high regard for Giancana. However, Humphreys cautioned him to follow orders of Giancana.

FEDERAL BUREAU OF INVESTIGATION

REPORTING OFFICE	OFFICE OF ORIGIN	DATE	INVESTIGATIVE PERIOD	
CHICAGO	CHICAGO	1964	October 13, 1964	
TITLE OF CASE		REPORT MADE BY		TYPED BY
				dkc
SAMUEL M. GIANCANA, aka		CHARACTER OF CASE		
		FBI Headquarters File 92-3171-1510 Top Hoodlum Program – Anti Racketeering. Daily Summary		

CG T-4 advised that on October 13, 1964, two individuals from Kansas City arrived in Chicago indicating that they had a pre-arranged meeting scheduled with Sam Giancana. Giancana not in Chicago but in New York. These individuals were directed to Butch Blasi to see what they should do concerning their meeting and when Giancana would return.

FEDERAL BUREAU OF INVESTIGATION

REPORTING OFFICE	OFFICE OF ORIGIN	DATE	INVESTIGATIVE PERIOD	
CHICAGO	CHICAGO	1964	October 14, 1964	
TITLE OF CASE		REPORT MADE BY		TYPED BY
				dkc
SAMUEL M. GIANCANA, aka		**CHARACTER OF CASE** FBI Headquarters File Number 92-3171-1503 Top Hoodlum Program – Anti Racketeering. Daily Summary		

Preliminary investigation into background of Romie Nappi shows he is associated with Phil Mesi in concern known as life time plastics located on northwest side of Chicago. Mesi has been reported by Chicago informant as one of the top men in Jackie Cerone organization and known to be a long time bookmaker handing particularly bets of prominent politicians, including Pat Marcy. As Bureau aware Nappi has influential connections within the Chicago Police Department whereby he is able to obtain copies of highly confidential material, especially within intelligence unit. Investigation indicates both Mesi and Nappi spend a great portion of the day at business location.

Bureau permission requested to institute survey of premises at lifetime plastics to obtain possible coverage of activities of Nappi and Mesi.

FEDERAL BUREAU OF INVESTIGATION

REPORTING OFFICE	OFFICE OF ORIGIN	DATE	INVESTIGATIVE PERIOD	
CHICAGO	CHICAGO	1964	October 16, 1964	
TITLE OF CASE		REPORT MADE BY		TYPED BY
				dkc
SAMUEL M. GIANCANA, aka		**CHARACTER OF CASE** FBI Headquarters File 92-3171-1500 Top Hoodlum Program – Anti Racketeering. Daily Summary		

CG advised 10/16 that on evening of 10/15 he received word that changes are imminent in hoodlum group here and that on that night a big meeting was held in Chicago relative to these changes. Informant advised Sam Battaglia has been tapped for additional power and responsibilities up to and perhaps including replacement of Giancana. However, informant's information not clear whether Giancana being replaced, or if Battaglia replacement for Frank Ferraro. Informant advised Jack Cerone might have received power now being assumed by Battaglia except that he has a "drinking problem" and is also blamed for heat brought on organized crime here by his underlings, Joseph Gagliano and William

Messino who recently tried for their involvement in juice operation of Cerone and now under prosecution for involvement gambling operations of Cerone.

CG recently advised that he learned from Helene Amato, wife of Joseph Amato, hoodlum, that Sam Battaglia promoted to number 2 spot in Chicago criminal group night before Frank Ferraro died.

CG advised that Sam Giancana returned to Chicago area on 10/15 last and held a large party at Armory Lounge.

FEDERAL BUREAU OF INVESTIGATION

REPORTING OFFICE	OFFICE OF ORIGIN	DATE	INVESTIGATIVE PERIOD
CHICAGO	CHICAGO	1964	October 20, 1964

TITLE OF CASE	REPORT MADE BY	TYPED BY
		dkc

TITLE OF CASE	CHARACTER OF CASE
SAMUEL M. GIANCANA, aka	FBI Headquarters File Number 92-3171 Top Hoodlum Program – Anti Racketeering. Daily Summary

Survey of Armory Lounge being reinstituted for purpose of determining patterns of police and hoodlum prior to making re-entry for purpose of re-establishment of microphone surveillance that location. CG informant alerted for information about Giancana department from city during which period Chicago intends re-entry.

Giancana observed October 20 instant meeting with Butch Blasi, at west side restaurant. Above informant advised Giancana planned golf date this P.M. with hoodlum associate John Campanalli. Informant advised Giancana won $3,000 on recent World Series which he used to throw party for close associates. One of the guest invited at the party was Nick Visco, a large scale bookmaker operating on the Northwest side of Chicago.

It was learned effective this date Lieutenant Joseph Mueller, Chicago PD had been named to head gambling unit of Vice Control Division switching his position as head of License Control Bureau with Lieutenant John Corless, former gambling head. Noted CG-6576-C furnished considerable information showing close relationship between Muller and Pat Marcy of the First Ward. Marcy utilized Mueller on numerous occasions in connections with arrests made in various establishments holding liquor licenses. Lieutenant Corless has been extremely cooperative with FBI in gambling matters and appeared to be very reliable and capable.

FEDERAL BUREAU OF INVESTIGATION

REPORTING OFFICE	OFFICE OF ORIGIN	DATE	INVESTIGATIVE PERIOD	
CHICAGO	CHICAGO	1964	October 26, 1964	
TITLE OF CASE		REPORT MADE BY		TYPED BY
				dkc
SAMUEL M. GIANCANA, aka		**CHARACTER OF CASE** FBI Headquarters File 92-3171-1504 Top Hoodlum Program – Anti Racketeering. Daily Summary		

CG informant advised that noted singer Johnny Desmond and comedian named Frank Ford flew into Chicago from Las Vegas and both were picked up at airport by Queenie Simonelli and brought to Fresh Meadow Golf Course where they played golf with Sam Giancana. Following completion of match both were returned to airport and ostensibly flew back to Las Vegas. Informant states Ford flew into Chicago previous week end and played golf with Giancana, however, remained at that time only long enough to play nine holes. Informant believes both individuals possibly appearing at Stardust Hotel, Las Vegas.

Las Vegas requested to determine if either of above known to be in Las Vegas and if any hoodlum connections heretofore known on part of either.

Giancana known to have placed approximately six calls to Las Vegas and Phoenix on Saturday, 10/24 last, as well as one to New York.

FEDERAL BUREAU OF INVESTIGATION

REPORTING OFFICE	OFFICE OF ORIGIN	DATE	INVESTIGATIVE PERIOD	
CHICAGO	CHICAGO	1964	October 27, 1964	
TITLE OF CASE		REPORT MADE BY		TYPED BY
				dkc
SAMUEL M. GIANCANA, aka		**CHARACTER OF CASE** FBI Headquarters File Number 92-3171-1505 Top Hoodlum Program – Anti Racketeering. Daily Summary		

CG 6576-C advised 10/27 that Pat Marcy had a meeting with Anthony Tisci for the purpose of sending message to Giancana concerning "Earloft" that Marcy had picked up. Marcy stated word he received is that plans are under way by authorities to do something about persons found voting in forthcoming elections who have convictions and did not have voting rights restored. Marcy requested Tisci to see that Giancana receives this information and suggested Giancana issue orders that persons having such a record be sure not to vote. Marcy stated because of this situation he himself will not vote. Marcy worried over persons such as his brother Paul Marcy being caught in this situation. Marcy having someone go to Springfield and correct that situation immediately following election so that no such event will occur in future.

Giancana now using Pucci's Restaurant located on Roosevelt Road in Forest Park, Illinois, to some extent to meet with friends and associates during the evening hours. Phyllis McGuire able to make contact with Giancana at this restaurant.

FEDERAL BUREAU OF INVESTIGATION

REPORTING OFFICE	OFFICE OF ORIGIN	DATE	INVESTIGATIVE PERIOD
CHICAGO	CHICAGO	1964	October 29, 1964

TITLE OF CASE	REPORT MADE BY		TYPED BY
			dkc
SAMUEL M. GIANCANA, aka	**CHARACTER OF CASE** FBI Headquarters File Number 92-3171-1507 Top Hoodlum Program – Anti Racketeering. Daily Summary		

CG 6576-C advised Pat Marcy, John D'Arco and Alderman Don Parrillo held lengthy discussion concerning income during which D'Arco complained that he "Is hurting, there ain't nothing going and more par nothing. There ain't no more money coming in. There just ain't no more rackets." Parrillo queried others as to whether they were presently receiving any income at all from two remaining strip joints operating in Loop area and was informed that they were not getting one penny. Marcy commented "Every one of the joints is dead."

To add a humorous note, D'Arco then commented in a tone that sounded as though to have to go through with this would be similar to begging and almost an unthinkable thing to do that, "We got to start with something legitimate." Marcy followed statement by saying they had never been in anything legitimate before which highly amused all three present.

FEDERAL BUREAU OF INVESTIGATION

REPORTING OFFICE	OFFICE OF ORIGIN	DATE	INVESTIGATIVE PERIOD
CHICAGO	CHICAGO	1964	November 3, 1964

TITLE OF CASE	REPORT MADE BY		TYPED BY
			dkc
SAMUEL M. GIANCANA, aka	**CHARACTER OF CASE** FBI Headquarters File Number 92-3171-1509 Top Hoodlum Program – Anti Racketeering. Daily Summary		

MI Informant advised Milwaukee top hoodlum Frank Balistrieri visited Chicago recently when Felix "Milwaukee Phil" Alderisio was elevated to the number 2 spot in Chicago, not Sam Battaglia.

CG informant recently advised Alderisio given position of number 2 man here following death of Frank Ferraro. Former CG informant advised on 11/2 that he was advised previous day Alderisio now controls gambling in Loop with Gus Alex, taking the spot of Ferraro in this regard. This information came to former informant from Loop bookmaker who therefore in position to know. On 11/2 Mike Brodkin instructed his secretary to contact Alderisio and have him contact Alex. Since these two hoodlums are not closely associated heretofore this tends to confirm information that Alderisio took Ferraro's spot with Alex. Investigation Chicago has established close relationship in past between Battaglia and Alderisio. Both have been observed together frequently and have been financially interested in legitimate enterprise together. All above info lends credence to information both have recently risen in power. However, no info obtained indicating Giancana has lost any power or that he does not remain top leader here.

FEDERAL BUREAU OF INVESTIGATION

REPORTING OFFICE	OFFICE OF ORIGIN	DATE	INVESTIGATIVE PERIOD
CHICAGO	CHICAGO	1964	November 5, 1964

TITLE OF CASE	REPORT MADE BY	TYPED BY
		dkc
SAMUEL M. GIANCANA, aka	CHARACTER OF CASE FBI Headquarters File Number 92-3171-1515 Top Hoodlum Program – Anti Racketeering. Daily Summary	

Ausa David Schippers advised that he has been instructed by USA Edward Hanrahan to immediately proceed with plan to call Sam Giancana as witness before Federal Grand Jury and offer him immunity under Federal statutes. Schippers advised plans to confer with Agents commencing Monday next for purpose of preparing necessary background material to be utilized in connection with Giancana's appearance.

Schippers advised USA Hanrahan enthusiastic about proposed plan and has instructed Schippers to pursue Sam vigorously. Hanrahan now of opinion direct action against Giancana more propitious rather than to proceed against Giancana underlings such as James Mirro and Rocky Infelice as previously contemplated.

At such time as proceedings become public knowledge Hanrahan states he will advise news media purpose of proceedings are to provide government with information concerning Giancana's activities in organized crime and detailed information concerning machinations of other persons connected with organized crime, Chicago area, which information has not previously been available because of witnesses use of fifth amendment and is not merely for purpose of citing Giancana for contempt or perjury.

TO: Special Investigative Division

FROM: ☐ Intelligence   ☐ General Investigative   ☐ Special Investigative

REQUEST FOR SEARCH OF SPECIAL INDICES

Date of request	Requesting Agent
3-23-78	Don Hartpson

Please complete following and return one copy to:

Hafner / Register

_____ , Division - ☐ Intelligence
  Section   ☐ General Investigative
                   ☐ Special Investigative

NAMES TO BE SEARCHED	KNOWN ALIASES	Results of Criminal and Security Special Indices Search (attach separate sheet, if necessary)
Sam Momo Giancana	GIANCANA, SAM	GIANCANA, SAM
GIANCANA, MOE	GIANCANA, SAM	3/8/62 D BOSTON
CG 6788-C*	CG 6186-C*	MM 799-C* 10/7/64
1/11/65	8/17/61	LV 72-C* CG 6788-C*
CG 6550-C*	NY 3986-C*	5/15/62 1/12/65
3/31/63	3/11/64	LV 48C* CG 6343-C*
CG 6546-C*	CG 6550-C*	7/7/61 12/4/61
9/28/62	4/24/63	NEWARK CG 6576-C*
GIANCANA, MOMO	CG 6568-C*	6/8/63 10/23/62
aka SAM, MOONEY	1/21/63	LV 88-C* CG 6343-C*
NEWARK 4/16/62	CG 6705-C*	9/14/62 7/30/59
GIANCANA, MOONEY	6/22/64	LV 64-C* NY 4099-S*
BOSTON 6/2/65	MM 857-C*	4/11/62 2/20/65
	2/22/63 D	DE 919-C* SAM M.
190-0	MM 920-C*	VOL. 3 7/8/63 Req./SA. J.E. DECKER
Bufile	4/24/64 D	9/16/63 9/17/68, ANSWER TO
	MM 845-C*	Searched by TAYLOR AG 10/14/68 POS.
	10/1/63 D	Date 3/29/78
	MM 794-C*	
	2/11/62 D	OVER ⇒

Here is a FBI report listing most of the FBI investigations and the cities in which Sam Giancana was a subject in.

FEDERAL BUREAU OF INVESTIGATION

REPORTING OFFICE	OFFICE OF ORIGIN	DATE	INVESTIGATIVE PERIOD
CHICAGO	CHICAGO	1964	November 7, 1964

TITLE OF CASE	REPORT MADE BY	TYPED BY
SAMUEL M. GIANCANA, aka		dkc

CHARACTER OF CASE
FBI Headquarters File Number 92-3171-1512
Top Hoodlum Program – Anti Racketeering.
Daily Summary

CG 6576-C advised Pat Marcy met 11/5 last with John D'Arco and Buddy Jacobson for discussion of present situation concerning income to these individuals. Marcy feels now that election is out of the way persons present should begin in earnest to attempt to augment their income. Marcy stated in very serious tone that they should get together in immediate future with "Moe" (Giancana) and tell him of situation as it exists. Marcy did not give any indication as to method in which he expected to receive help from Giancana but indicates that Giancana will allow more freedom to operate on part of First Ward politicians.

Jacobson and D'Arco in wholehearted agreement with Marcy's plans. D'Arco insistent that Marcy remember that all three present be included in any deals, indicating some concern over being left out of any arrangements.

FEDERAL BUREAU OF INVESTIGATION

REPORTING OFFICE	OFFICE OF ORIGIN	DATE	INVESTIGATIVE PERIOD
CHICAGO	CHICAGO	1964	November 12, 1964

TITLE OF CASE	REPORT MADE BY	TYPED BY
SAMUEL M. GIANCANA, aka		dkc

CHARACTER OF CASE
FBI Headquarters File 92-3171-1514
Top Hoodlum Program – Anti Racketeering.
Daily Summary

Jack Cerone, Lou Rosanova, and approximately ten others arrived in Miami 11/12 from Chicago and proceeded to Kings Bay Country Club, South Dade County, Florida. Giancana not observed. Limousine drive who took group to club advised that there are a total of 11 in group, said party named Lou was talking as though he, Lou, owned this club, said mentioned golf tournament.

FEDERAL BUREAU OF INVESTIGATION

REPORTING OFFICE	OFFICE OF ORIGIN	DATE	INVESTIGATIVE PERIOD	
CHICAGO	CHICAGO	1964	November 12, 1964	
TITLE OF CASE		REPORT MADE BY		TYPED BY
				dkc
SAMUEL M. GIANCANA, aka		CHARACTER OF CASE		
		FBI Headquarters File 92-3171-1514 Top Hoodlum Program – Anti Racketeering. Daily Summary		

Information about stag party at Kings Bay Club and fact that certain Chicago hoodlums would be in attendance. Observation by Agents indicated Monte Carlo type party with crap game. Only known hoodlums there were Jack Cerone, Lou Rosanova and Pete Sarnoff, who is owner of the Golden Nugget Motel and Lounge, MM, and an associate of Cerone. Sam Giancana and Anthony Accardo not observed.

Jack Cerone was arrested for vagrancy during event, before alleged girlie activity commenced. As result, crap table folded, and one female belly dancer performed an act described by so as lewd or lascivious.

FEDERAL BUREAU OF INVESTIGATION

REPORTING OFFICE	OFFICE OF ORIGIN	DATE	INVESTIGATIVE PERIOD	
CHICAGO	CHICAGO	1964	December 4, 1964	
TITLE OF CASE		REPORT MADE BY		TYPED BY
				dkc
SAMUEL M. GIANCANA, aka		CHARACTER OF CASE		
		FBI Headquarters File 92-3171-1524 Top Hoodlum Program – Anti Racketeering. Daily Summary		

Chicago highly confidential source advised Giancana recently held meetings with Chicago political associates to determine what individual is to be placed in position of alderman left vacant by recent elections of Robert Massey to position of Circuit Court Judge. As previously noted Giancana plans to utilize 36th Ward as base of political operations feeling that because of changes within makeup of First Ward that change now called for.

Source indicated that no one has been decided upon to fill above position but Giancana, through Sanitary District chairman Frank Chesrow, made his desires known to Mayor Richard J. Daley to leave 36th Ward alone and not interfere with designs of Giancana organization. Source advised that Massey also has been sent as emissary to Daley in this regard. Causing some concern to Giancana group is fact that USA Edward Hanrahan has met with Daley and injected his own candidate into proceedings.

Source advised First Ward politicians feel Giancana made grave error in having Massey resign aldermanic position for position of judge without building up some individual within ward to continue in Massey's place without controversy. Source advised that decision to run Massey for judge made because of request of Ralph Massuci upon Giancana. Noted Massuci, local gambler and brother of Massey and long time friend of Giancana.

FEDERAL BUREAU OF INVESTIGATION

REPORTING OFFICE	OFFICE OF ORIGIN	DATE	INVESTIGATIVE PERIOD	
CHICAGO	CHICAGO	1964	December 7, 1964	
TITLE OF CASE		REPORT MADE BY		TYPED BY
				dkc
SAMUEL M. GIANCANA, aka		CHARACTER OF CASE		
		FBI Headquarters File 92-3171-1525 Top Hoodlum Program – Anti Racketeering. Daily Summary		

CG 6576-C advised Captain Mark Thanasouras introduced Pat Marcy to one lieutenant Leo Sheehan who has been designated to act as "Bag Man" for First District Police officers, replacing recently transferred Lieutenant Mark Conlin. Marcy instructed Sheehan to contact him, Marcy, on third or forth of each month. Marcy explained that Sheehan is never to use his last name on Marcy's phone but if Marcy not in, merely to state that "Leo called" and leave a number for Marcy to call back. Source advised that unknown amount of money given to Sheehan on 12/4 last. Source stated that Sheehan has been assigned First District for past six years, previously serving for many years in Park District Police Force, now discontinued unit of Chicago Police Force. Source noted Thanasouras remained present during entire negotiations between Marcy and Sheehan. Marcy instructed Sheehan that "You are on call all day now, whenever I need your help." Source learned that Sheehan resides Chicago South side.

FEDERAL BUREAU OF INVESTIGATION

REPORTING OFFICE	OFFICE OF ORIGIN	DATE	INVESTIGATIVE PERIOD	
CHICAGO	CHICAGO	1964	December 8, 1964	
TITLE OF CASE		REPORT MADE BY		TYPED BY
				dkc
SAMUEL M. GIANCANA, aka		CHARACTER OF CASE		
		FBI Headquarters File 92-3171-1526 Top Hoodlum Program – Anti Racketeering. Daily Summary		

CG 6576-C advised that Pat Marcy recently made contact with Chicago policeman identified as Sam Papich who is vice coordinator for 21st District, which district abuts south end of 1st District. Primary purpose of contact learned concerns gambling operations in Chinatown, which area is split between 1st and 21st Districts. During conversation Marcy explained reason that Chinatown is "down" is because "The "G" is in there now. There is no use in having them open up now and have the "G" tell them (Police) to go in and pinch them again." Marcy explained that he feels that after first of year they will be able to allow Chinese to open up again.

Papich given code name with which to contact Marcy in future. It was explained to Papich that he was not to personally visit First Ward offices again and also not to talk about anything over phone as Marcy's phones are all "tapped."

Papich advised he would also keep Marcy apprised of conditions existing within the 21st District. Also meeting with Marcy was Louis Arger who discussed closed strip joints in First Ward. Marcy explained there is no possibility of opening up at this time as there is too much heat still focused on First Ward and stated "They" (apparently First Ward Police) are still afraid of Sandy Smith, "Sun Times" reporter whose stories on First Ward strip joints initiated action closing these establishments. Marcy explained they would take another look at situation after first of year to determine possibility of reopening some of clubs.

FEDERAL BUREAU OF INVESTIGATION

REPORTING OFFICE	OFFICE OF ORIGIN	DATE	INVESTIGATIVE PERIOD	
CHICAGO	CHICAGO	1964	December 9, 1964	
TITLE OF CASE		REPORT MADE BY		TYPED BY
				dkc
SAMUEL M. GIANCANA, aka		CHARACTER OF CASE		
		FBI Headquarters File Number 92-3171-1523 Top Hoodlum Program – Anti Racketeering. Daily Summary		

CG 6576-C advised First Ward politicians continue to discuss current activities concerning attempts to fill position of alderman in 36th Ward. Pat Marcy and John D'Arco showing concern over apparent lack of recognition being given to First Ward people and their ideas in this matter. D'Arco feels Giancana has made up his mind in this matter and therefore will not bend. D'Arco stated that in dealing with Giancana they have to remember that, "It is different than dealing with Joe Batters (Anthony Accardo) because Giancana has no brains." Marcy concerned over lack of ability to arrange meeting with Giancana personally to discuss this situation. Marcy claims Anthony Tisci will not make appointment for Marcy and is wondering if this is because of Giancana instructions or if Tisci doing this on own initiative. Marcy plans to let matter ride for short period before demanding meeting to straighten situation out.

FEDERAL BUREAU OF INVESTIGATION

REPORTING OFFICE	OFFICE OF ORIGIN	DATE	INVESTIGATIVE PERIOD	
CHICAGO	CHICAGO	1964	December 10, 1964	
TITLE OF CASE		REPORT MADE BY		TYPED BY
				dkc
SAMUEL M. GIANCANA, aka		CHARACTER OF CASE		
		FBI Headquarters File 92-3171-1527 Top Hoodlum Program – Anti Racketeering. Daily Summary		

CG 6576-C advised Giancana again holding meetings with individuals desiring to talk with him. According to Anthony Tisci Giancana busier than ever before. On two consecutive evenings on which Pat Marcy attempted to set up appointment with Giancana, Tisci stated Giancana had appointment set for five, seven, and 8:30 PM each night. Marcy also attempted to arrange for meeting between Giancana and Richard Cain, preferably "out of town."

Marcy advised that in response to contact with Butch Blasi on 12/7 last concerning appointment with Giancana that Blasi returned call morning of 12/9 last and advised that while Giancana in town, he would not be able to meet with Marcy because "he's got some people in town." Marcy advised that Gus Alex had confirmed this later in day. Chicago attempting to determine who persons referred to might be. Possibility exists this might be Don Ferraro, New York City, who arrived in Chicago.

FEDERAL BUREAU OF INVESTIGATION

REPORTING OFFICE	OFFICE OF ORIGIN	DATE	INVESTIGATIVE PERIOD	
CHICAGO	CHICAGO	1964	December 15, 1964	

TITLE OF CASE	REPORT MADE BY	TYPED BY
SAMUEL M. GIANCANA, aka		dkc

CHARACTER OF CASE

FBI Headquarters File Number 92-3171-1528
Top Hoodlum Program – Anti Racketeering.
Daily Summary

CG 6576-C advised that Pat Marcy held lengthy discussion with Romie Nappi 12/11 last and outlined changed in leadership of Chicago syndicate. Marcy stated that he had learned that "This guy, after the first of the year is going to be the boss, Teetz. He said Moe Giancana (has got to stay in the background) and this guy won't have any trouble." Discussion then continued on how hard an individual Battaglia is to deal with and of fact that he feels that he always has to be right. Point in discussion indicated that possibility exists that Giancana and Anthony Accardo had heated argument prior to discussion also tells as to how First Ward people stand with Battaglia, with general feeling that they are in good stead.

Members of the First Ward held separate meetings with Anthony Accardo and Phil Alderisio in attempt to determine if rumors that Giancana about to be displaced by Sam Battaglia as overall leader are true.

Most bothersome aspect of situation is fact that Giancana will not set appointment with Pat Marcy or John D'Arco at this time supposedly because he is too busy with out of town visitors. One particular item of importance which Marcy wishes to clear up is amount of money Giancana desires to invest in new banking venture being started in First Ward. From information furnished it appears funds are to be syndicate funds rather than personal funds of Giancana's and his word will be necessary before final action can be taken in matter.

Marcy, D'Arco and Buddy Jacobson all planned separate meeting evening 12/12 with individuals who they hope can enlighten them as to which group to fall in with. Marcy feels that without final word from Giancana that they would be foolish to think that someone else has taken over his position. Marcy also feels that Giancana would not gracefully step aside at this unless he had fully decided in his own mind that he would be better off without the burden of leadership upon his shoulders.

It is noted in conversations individuals had with Accardo he has apparently indicated some charges in mill but would not definitely state that Giancana out. However, it is also to be noted that bulk of information from Accardo given to Buddy Jacobson, who is Jewish, giving rise to possibility that full situation not being explained to him at this time.

FEDERAL BUREAU OF INVESTIGATION

REPORTING OFFICE	OFFICE OF ORIGIN	DATE	INVESTIGATIVE PERIOD
CHICAGO	CHICAGO	1964	December 18, 1964

TITLE OF CASE	REPORT MADE BY	TYPED BY
		dkc
SAMUEL M. GIANCANA, aka	CHARACTER OF CASE	
	FBI Headquarters File 92-3171-1531 Top Hoodlum Program – Anti Racketeering. Daily Summary	

CG informant advised Giancana planning trip to Peru 1/5 next in connection with opening gambling enterprise in that country. This informant highly pertinent in light of info received from CG 6576-C concerning report compiled by Richard Cain, who was recently convicted for perjury, during recent trip to Peru. Report given to Gus Alex who in turn passed same on to Giancana. Source advised during discussion of project between these two, Alex advised against going into deal on basis that they know little about Peru and that venture would be costly. Alex indicated project would involve construction of large building and operation would not be "A store front type venture." New York advised of above for consideration of subpoena of Giancana in connection with grand jury.

FEDERAL BUREAU OF INVESTIGATION

REPORTING OFFICE	OFFICE OF ORIGIN	DATE	INVESTIGATIVE PERIOD
CHICAGO	CHICAGO	1964	December 21, 1964

TITLE OF CASE	REPORT MADE BY	TYPED BY
		dkc
SAMUEL M. GIANCANA, aka	CHARACTER OF CASE	
	FBI Headquarters File Number 92-3171-1533 Top Hoodlum Program – Anti Racketeering. Daily Summary	

CG 6576-C advised Anthony Tisci met 12/17 last with Pat Marcy upon return from New York City. Advised meeting arranged from John D'Arco at 4 pm that date with Giancana at "regular place." Marcy immediately made contact with D'Arco to advise him of meet and to arrange for him to meet with Marcy prior to seeing Giancana. During this meeting Marcy and D'Arco discussed sums of money and from best indication Marcy ended up giving D'Arco total of $10,000 to be delivered to Giancana. No indication given as reason for this payment nor where funds came from. Previously noted D'Arco reportedly arranged meeting to determine how much money Giancana was to invest I banking deal being planned in First Ward.

FEDERAL BUREAU OF INVESTIGATION

REPORTING OFFICE	OFFICE OF ORIGIN	DATE	INVESTIGATIVE PERIOD	
CHICAGO	CHICAGO	1964	December 28, 1964	

TITLE OF CASE	REPORT MADE BY	TYPED BY
		dkc
SAMUEL M. GIANCANA, aka	**CHARACTER OF CASE** FBI Headquarters File 92-3171-1535 Top Hoodlum Program – Anti Racketeering. Daily Summary	

CG 6576-C advised that Chicago policeman identified as Tony (LNU) met with Pat Marcy to advise him that during recent week he learned that "The G is in your building." Tony continued that he learned some type of recording device being used but not aware of location of device. From description given individual not familiar with electronic equipment and appears to be attempting to impress Marcy with his knowledge. When unable to be specific as to location or type of device used, Marcy appeared to disregard import of information. Advised policeman that "G" has all types of equipment. From continued conversation both seemed to feel that any type of device in use in the building would be phone tap of some type and Marcy assured individual that he does not use phones for any business. From Marcy's manner it would appear that he is not concerned with this information. Chicago following source closely to determine if Marcy has First Ward offices "cleaned" again.

FBI list of names used by Sam Giancana as of 1964.

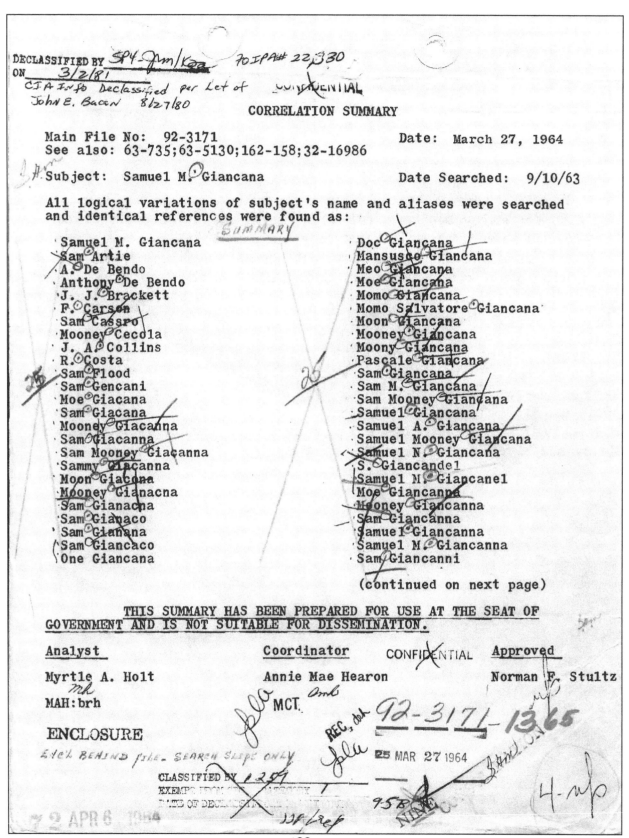

DECLASSIFIED BY SP4 *Jm/Kaa* 7O IPA# 22,330
ON 3/2/81
CIA Info Declassified per Let of *CONFIDENTIAL*
John E. Bacon 8/27/80

CORRELATION SUMMARY

Main File No: 92-3171
See also: 63-735;63-5130;162-158;32-16986

Date: March 27, 1964

Subject: Samuel M. Giancana

Date Searched: 9/10/63

All logical variations of subject's name and aliases were searched
and identical references were found as:

Summary

Samuel M. Giancana
Sam Artie
A. De Bendo
Anthony De Bendo
J. J. Brackett
F. Carson
Sam Cassro
Mooney Cecola
J. A. Collins
R. Costa
Sam Flood
Sam Gencani
Moe Giacana
Sam Giacana
Mooney Giacanna
Sam Giacanna
Sam Mooney Giacanna
Sammy Giacanna
Moon Giacona
Mooney Gianacna
Sam Gianacna
Sam Gianaco
Sam Gianana
Sam Giancaco
One Giancana

Doc Giancana
Mansusco Giancana
Meo Giancana
Moe Giancana
Momo Giancana
Momo Salvatore Giancana
Moon Giancana
Mooney Giancana
Moony Giancana
Pascale Giancana
Sam Giancana
Sam M. Giancana
Sam Mooney Giancana
Samuel Giancana
Samuel A. Giancana
Samuel Mooney Giancana
Samuel N. Giancana
S. Giancandel
Samuel M. Giancanel
Moe Giancanna
Mooney Giancanna
Sam Giancanna
Samuel Giancanna
Samuel M. Giancanna
Sam Giancanni

(continued on next page)

<u>THIS SUMMARY HAS BEEN PREPARED FOR USE AT THE SEAT OF
GOVERNMENT AND IS NOT SUITABLE FOR DISSEMINATION.</u>

<u>Analyst</u>

Myrtle A. Holt
mh
MAH:brh

<u>Coordinator</u>

Annie Mae Hearon

MCT.

CONFIDENTIAL

<u>Approved</u>

Norman F. Stultz

REC. *da* 92-3171-1365

ENCLOSURE

Ench BEHIND file. SEARCH SLIPS ONLY

25 MAR 27 1964

CLASSIFIED BY 1259
EXEMPT FROM GDS CATEGORY
DATE OF DECLASSIFICATION

958 NINE

2 APR 6 1964

422

(continued)   SUMMARY

Moma Giancano   R. J. Landolt
Mooney Giancano   Albert Mancuso
Sam Giancano   Michael Mancuso
Samuel Giancano   Michael J. Mancuso
Samuel M. Giancano   Michael Mancusso
Sam Giancarpa   One Mansusco
Sam Gianciana   Sam Mansusco
Mooney Gianciano   Albert Manusco
Sam Gianciano   Albert Masusco
Mooney Giancina   Sam Montana
Sam Giancina   One Mooney
Sam Giancinia   J. Mooney
Sam Giancino   Sam Mooney
Samuel N. Giancone   Tom Mooney
Sam Giancorra   Sam Moony
Gilormo Giangana   Sam Morris
Sam Gincana   Russell Paige
Sam Gincani   Sam Pearl
Mooney Gincanna   James Perno
Sam Gincanna   S. Perry
Sam Giacanni   Thomas Rosenberg
Sam Gincano   Sam Russo
Sam Gincina   Frank De Santo
Sam Ginncana   John De Santos
Sam Ginoina   Sam Schwartz
Sam Ginsberg   Morris Simon
Samuel M. Goldfield   Mooney Wanunah
T. Isci   Sam Wood
R. Landolt

Also searched as Cigars Giancana. See page 62 in summary.

        This is a summary of information obtained from a review
of all "see" references to the subject in Bureau files under the
names and aliases listed above. All references under the above
names containing data identical with the subject have been included
except those listed at the end of this summary as not having been
reviewed, or those determined to contain the same information as
the main file.

        This summary is designed to furnish a synopsis of the
information set out in each reference. In many cases the original
serial will contain the information in much more detail.

Chapter 9

FEDERAL BUREAU OF INVESTIGATION

REPORTING OFFICE	OFFICE OF ORIGIN	DATE	INVESTIGATIVE PERIOD
CHICAGO	CHICAGO	1965	January 4, 1965

TITLE OF CASE	REPORT MADE BY	TYPED BY
		dkc
SAMUEL M. GIANCANA, aka	**CHARACTER OF CASE** FBI Headquarters File 92-3171-1538 Top Hoodlum Program – Anti Racketeering. Daily Summary	

Chicago recently in receipt of information that subject planned visit to Peru as of January 5, next, possibly in connection with new gambling venture. Chicago source advised this date that subject accompanied by Sam Rosa, aka. Slicker Sam, may have left Chicago yesterday possibly en-route to Miami for flight to Peru.

FEDERAL BUREAU OF INVESTIGATION

REPORTING OFFICE	OFFICE OF ORIGIN	DATE	INVESTIGATIVE PERIOD
CHICAGO	CHICAGO	1965	January 12, 1965

TITLE OF CASE	REPORT MADE BY	TYPED BY
		dkc
SAMUEL M. GIANCANA, aka	**CHARACTER OF CASE** FBI Headquarters File Number 92-3171-1543 Top Hoodlum Program – Anti Racketeering. Daily Summary	

CG informant advised 1/11 he just returned from Washington D.C. where he attended swearing in of Congressman Frank Annunzio, who replaced Roland V. Libonati. Advised also there were Anthony Tisci, John D'Arco, and Pat Marcy who obviously will be very close to Annunzio. Tisci in fact will be in charge of Chicago office of Annunzio with offices in Federal building here. Informant believes Annunzio will be much more effective congressman than Libonati, both for Giancana and for constituents.

Informant has been asked by Mayor Richard J. Daley to resume role of Alderman. Informant has informed Tisci of proposition with request to see Giancana since he fears personal and family safety if he takes position without sanction of Giancana. However, Tisci has not effected appointment. Informant still feels Sam Battaglia is now more powerful here than Giancana but can give no specific reason for such opinion.

Informant attended New Years Eve party in company of other Italian public officials and legitimate businessmen at new Riverwoods Country Club being managed by Lou Rosanova, hoodlum associate. As coincidence next table was occupied by Anthony Accardo, Sam Battaglia, Felix Alderisio, Paul DeLucia and one other not known to informant. Informant feels there is significant in this grouping with Accardo and DeLucia being former bosses here; Battaglia being present boss opinion of informant and Alderisio obviously also top echelon hoodlum here at present. Noted Giancana known to be in Honolulu New Year's Eve so his absence not particularly significant.

FEDERAL BUREAU OF INVESTIGATION

REPORTING OFFICE	OFFICE OF ORIGIN	DATE	INVESTIGATIVE PERIOD	
CHICAGO	CHICAGO	1965	January 15, 1965	
TITLE OF CASE		REPORT MADE BY		TYPED BY
				dkc
SAMUEL M. GIANCANA, aka		CHARACTER OF CASE FBI Headquarters File 92-3171-1545 Top Hoodlum Program – Anti Racketeering. Daily Summary		

CG informant advised this date that meeting scheduled for noon this date at "The Spot" restaurant owned by Johnny "Haircuts" Campanalli which to be attended by approximately 15 of Giancana's closest associates. To be in attendance were Butch Blasi, Queenie Simonelli, Campanalli and Charles English. Informant stated Giancana also suppose to attend but was not sure what effect his appearance before Grand Jury in New York City would have.

Physical surveillance that location 1 pm reflected vehicles of Blasi, Simonelli, Sam Rosa, Joe Marks, and John Matassa. Informant believed he would be able to determine those persons in attendance and will advise 1/15 next. Nature of meeting unknown but informant believes he will be able to determine.

FEDERAL BUREAU OF INVESTIGATION

REPORTING OFFICE	OFFICE OF ORIGIN	DATE	INVESTIGATIVE PERIOD	
CHICAGO	CHICAGO	1965	January 27, 1965	
TITLE OF CASE		REPORT MADE BY		TYPED BY
				dkc
SAMUEL M. GIANCANA, aka		CHARACTER OF CASE FBI Headquarters File 92-3171-1555 Top Hoodlum Program – Anti Racketeering. Daily Summary		

Interview with Bergit Clark was conducted on January 13, 1965 at her residence at 844 Parkside Avenue, Elmhurst, Illinois, at which time she advised that she had known Sam Giancana for several years. Clark was rather antagonistic towards the agents interviewing her and refused to allow them to enter her home claiming fear for her person stating that she was alone at that time. In response to several questions concerning her being able to help the FBI, Clark responded that there was nothing she could do to help the agents nor did she have any information that could possibly assist them in their investigation.

It was positively determined that during this interview that Clark was the female companion of Giancana on several occasions specifically when Giancana and Clark attended show put on by Joe E. Lewis.

It should be noted that during a conversation with Agnes Coyne, a personal friend of Giancana's, she told agents that in regards to Bergit Clark, she has been a constant companion of Giancana's for approximately five years. Coyne advised that it is common knowledge to persons at the Armory Lounge that Clark managed to win Giancana's favor though her immoral activities which Coyne claims are rather well known to persons familiar with Clark.

Coyne advised that rumors persist that the home in which Clark lives which in had been purchased by Giancana in that the furnishings and her car are also gifts from Giancana.

Coyne continued that from her observations, Clark, while enjoying the presence of Giancana, is extremely concerned over her relationship with Giancana and becomes extremely terrified when persons questions her concerning this relationship.

Residence

CG T-1 Advised that in December, 1964, that information had come to the attention that Sam Giancana maintained a residence in Schaumberg, Illinois. Investigation disclosed that the house reportedly Giancana's is directly across the street from the one owned by Charles Giancana. Investigation in this neighborhood disclosed that the residence of the home purportedly Giancana's is a family named Littler. Background information conducted on this family gives no indication of any connection with Giancana and it is felt that the information given to the informant is erroneous and that the information actually pertained to Giancana's brother's home.

Miscellaneous

During the course of several surveillances conducted it has been noted that Giancana had made a habit of utilizing public phones for the purposes of making his phone calls.

CG T-3 advised that during December 1964, approximately $2,000 was spent by the owners of the Caravelle Motel in Rosemont, Illinois, for the purpose of renovating and refinishing one of the rooms located in this motel. According to informant, this room is used by Sam Giancana and Phyllis McGuire during her visits in Chicago.

CG T-5 advised that in early November, 1964, a meeting consisting of Sam Giancana, Tony Accardo, Joseph DiVarco, Ross Prio, and others met in a restaurant on Chicago's north side. This meeting was followed by another in December where Giancana, Accardo, Paul DeLucia, John Campanale, Butch Blasi, Tarquin Simonelli, Marshall Caifano, Chuck English and Sam Rosa met at the Armory Lounge.

Giancana and Phyllis McGuire reported to be in Hawaii during December, 1964 and January 1965 under the name of Mr. and Mrs. Bianco.

FEDERAL BUREAU OF INVESTIGATION

REPORTING OFFICE	OFFICE OF ORIGIN	DATE	INVESTIGATIVE PERIOD
CHICAGO	CHICAGO	1965	February 2, 1965

TITLE OF CASE	REPORT MADE BY	TYPED BY
		dkc

	CHARACTER OF CASE
SAMUEL M. GIANCANA, aka	FBI Headquarters File Number 92-3171-1561 Top Hoodlum Program – Anti Racketeering. Daily Summary

Andrew Snyder, presently serving concurrent state and federal charges for bank burglary at Pontiac, Illinois State Prison interviewed Chicago concerning possible information reflecting Giancana ownership of former North Avenue Steak House Restaurant. Noted Snyder operated this establishment from late 1958 to early 1960. Snyder advised while he knows in his own mind that Giancana was true owner of Restaurant, he never dealt directly with him, but rather through Joseph DeTolve. Snyder advised that during this period of management he paid $400 per month to DeTolve. Noted DeTolve maiden name of Giancana's late wife.

Of particular pertinence was information by Snyder which shows association between Giancana, Americo DiPietto, convicted narcotics hoodlum, Rocky Infelice and James Mirro.

FEDERAL BUREAU OF INVESTIGATION

REPORTING OFFICE	OFFICE OF ORIGIN	DATE	INVESTIGATIVE PERIOD
CHICAGO	CHICAGO	1965	February 4, 1965

TITLE OF CASE	REPORT MADE BY	TYPED BY
		dkc

	CHARACTER OF CASE
SAMUEL M. GIANCANA, aka	FBI Headquarters File 92-3171-1569 Top Hoodlum Program – Anti Racketeering. Daily Summary

CG 6576-C advised Anthony "Tony X" Esposito Sr., local labor leader in contact with Pat Marcy 23 last in connection with death of unnamed individual who, according to Esposito headed another large labor union in Chicago area. From conversation it appears that orders have been given to install individual of Italian extraction as next head of union. In this regard Esposito advised majority of union members in that union are of Irish descent and feels attempt to install Italian will lead to trouble within union. For that reason Esposito requested Marcy contact Sam Giancana and arrange appointment for Esposito so that Esposito can fully explain this situation to Giancana before proceeding with any attempts to install new leadership.

Another highly confidential source advised Murray Humphreys attempting to arrange meet with Giancana for either 24 or 25 instant. Nature of meet not divulged.

FEDERAL BUREAU OF INVESTIGATION

REPORTING OFFICE	OFFICE OF ORIGIN	DATE	INVESTIGATIVE PERIOD
CHICAGO	CHICAGO	1965	February 5, 1965

TITLE OF CASE	REPORT MADE BY	TYPED BY
		dkc
SAMUEL M. GIANCANA, aka	**CHARACTER OF CASE**	
	FBI Headquarters File Number 92-3171 Top Hoodlum Program – Anti Racketeering. Daily Summary	

CG 6476-C advised Pat Marcy telling unknown that Anthony "Tony X" Esposito Sr. spent 4 hours with Sam Giancana evening last. Meeting pertained to the replacement of Charles LoVerdi, recently deceased head of the Pipe Fitters Union in Chicago.

FEDERAL BUREAU OF INVESTIGATION

REPORTING OFFICE	OFFICE OF ORIGIN	DATE	INVESTIGATIVE PERIOD
CHICAGO	CHICAGO	1965	February 9, 1965

TITLE OF CASE	REPORT MADE BY	TYPED BY
		dkc
SAMUEL M. GIANCANA, aka	**CHARACTER OF CASE**	
	FBI Headquarters File Number 92-3171-1571 Top Hoodlum Program – Anti Racketeering. Daily Summary	

Highly confidential source advised Pat Marcy made reservations through Kenneth Leonard for eight persons at Playboy Club evening February 8 last. Noted, Leonard, Anthony "Tony X" Esposito Sr., Chicago labor union leader together with five other persons, not presently identified in attendance ay performance of Frank Ford, featured entertainer of show commencing Monday last. Ford identical to individual reported in contact with Sam Giancana fall of 1964 together with singer Johnny Desmond. Info received at that time indicated both flew into Chicago from Las Vegas for purpose of meeting with Giancana, purpose unknown.

Noted following performance Ford proceeded to Marcy's table where he remained until time of last performance. Also noted was fact female accompanying Ford remained at Marcy table during entire evening.

Original information indicated Anthony Tisci to accompany Marcy during evening, however, Tisci not in attendance with Marcy group. Chicago contemplates interview of Ford concerning Giancana connections, UACB.

FEDERAL BUREAU OF INVESTIGATION

REPORTING OFFICE	OFFICE OF ORIGIN	DATE	INVESTIGATIVE PERIOD
CHICAGO	CHICAGO	1965	February 11, 1965

TITLE OF CASE	REPORT MADE BY	TYPED BY
		dkc

	CHARACTER OF CASE
SAMUEL M. GIANCANA, aka	FBI Headquarters File Number 92-3171-1575 Top Hoodlum Program – Anti Racketeering. Daily Summary

Highly confidential source advised Murray Humphreys instructed Hy Godfrey 2/9 last to contact Giancana to line up meeting between Humphreys and Giancana in immediate future. Meet was to be at unknown west side Chicago location. Afternoon 2/10 off duty investigative clerk John E. Whalen, Chicago. Observed Giancana and Humphreys at booth in Oakside Restaurant, Oak Park. He immediately contacted Chicago office. Agents immediately proceeded to Oakside Restaurant where they were able to observe discreetly Humphreys and Giancana. Portions of conversation as over heard by agents concerned efforts Chicago group to influence members Illinois general assembly against anti-crime bills presently pending there. Waitress subsequently developed as witness to meeting.

Above orally furnished AUSA David Schippers, who advised this, is key piece of info which he believes will insure successful outcome of grand jury proceedings. AUSA Schippers feels agent's testimony about above will not only be key testimony vs. Giancana but now feels that Humphreys can be brought before grand jury and will consider offering Humphreys immunity as to this meeting so that resultant contempt or perjury can be developed against Humphreys as well as Giancana. Schippers desires utilizing three FBI agents as agents of FGJ to insure that all info developed during proceedings can be discussed and developed as situation warrants. This will be done unless advised to contrary by bureau.

FEDERAL BUREAU OF INVESTIGATION

REPORTING OFFICE	OFFICE OF ORIGIN	DATE	INVESTIGATIVE PERIOD
CHICAGO	CHICAGO	1965	February 19, 1965

TITLE OF CASE	REPORT MADE BY	TYPED BY
		dkc

	CHARACTER OF CASE
SAMUEL M. GIANCANA, aka	FBI Headquarters File 92-3171-1579 Top Hoodlum Program – Anti Racketeering. Daily Summary

Chicago informant advised Giancana observed at noon this date at Drake Oak Brook Hotel in company of Rose Flood, sister-in-law of Giancana.

CG 6576-C advised Giancana scheduled 2 PM meet this date with John D'Arco. Source further advised Pat Marcy met with Captain Louis Capparelli, Commanding Officer, Monroe Police District and Irving Gordon, Chicago market master and political fixer. Marcy explaining meeting to D'Arco, stated that, "You know we took care of your predecessor, and we'll take care of you." Capparelli acknowledged knowing of payments to previous commanding officer Captain John Hartnett who was promoted to assistant Deputy Superintendent in charge for field services. No amount given.

Capparelli indicated he had been disappointed when he took over this command that no one, apparently referring to politicians such as Marcy and D'Arco, had welcomed him to his new position and ostensibly advised him of how he is to be taken care of monetarily.

FEDERAL BUREAU OF INVESTIGATION

REPORTING OFFICE	OFFICE OF ORIGIN	DATE	INVESTIGATIVE PERIOD	
CHICAGO	CHICAGO	1965	March 2, 1965	
TITLE OF CASE		REPORT MADE BY		TYPED BY
				dkc
SAMUEL M. GIANCANA, aka		CHARACTER OF CASE		
		FBI Headquarters File Number 92-3171-1582 Top Hoodlum Program – Anti Racketeering. Daily Summary		

Entertainer Frank Ford interviewed March 1 last concerning Chicago associations and admitted knowing labor official Anthony "Tony X" Esposito Sr. and Pat Marcy. Claims association comes through friendship with Anthony "Sonny" Esposito Jr., son of Esposito Sr., whom he met in Boston, Massachusetts, area some years ago. Esposito had father contact Ford upon arrival in Chicago for present appearance at Playboy Club.

Ford advised that his closest Chicago association is with labor official Anthony "Tony X" Esposito Sr. and through Esposito has meet other individuals in Chicago among them being Frank Esposito and Pat Marcy, who Ford described as a Chicago Democratic politician.

Ford shown photo of Giancana and claimed not to know him. When memory refreshed, he recalled meeting John Desmond in Chicago on late September and playing round of golf with Desmond and two other individuals one of whom he claimed was the owner of the club, who he described as elderly, tall, and graying and forth individual whose description he could not recall. Remembered that club in far western suburbs. Stated Giancana definitely not forth member of group. Noted informant previously advised Giancana and Chuck English part of golfing group.

As interview continued, it became obvious Ford not being truthful and attempted to change subject matter continuously. Interview discontinued when it became obvious that Ford although courteous but evasive did not plan to cooperate. Giancana not observed to depart O'Hare airport for New York during evening of March 1 last.

CG 6576-C advised Pat Marcy, while explaining problems concerning the writing of insurance for Lormar Distributing Company, made the following statement, "Foreget that you are changing the structure of this partnership and are now adding Moe's name on there. If Chuckie English had left it with us there would be nothing to changing the trust, but now it will be rough." No further mention made of Giancana in this conversation as to whether his name appearing in trust agreement concerning Lormar, or whether his name to be set forth in open as part of business.

FEDERAL BUREAU OF INVESTIGATION

REPORTING OFFICE	OFFICE OF ORIGIN	DATE	INVESTIGATIVE PERIOD	
CHICAGO	CHICAGO	1965	March 19, 1965	
TITLE OF CASE		REPORT MADE BY		TYPED BY
				dkc
SAMUEL M. GIANCANA, aka		CHARACTER OF CASE		
		FBI Headquarters File Number 92-3171-1592 Top Hoodlum Program – Anti Racketeering. Daily Summary		

Chicago informant advised in conversation with Frank Buccieri, brother of Fifi Buccieri, Giancana lieutenant who has been reported to be gaining stature in Chicago syndicate, that Fifi no longer making decisions or settling disputes in Giancana's absence. Informant states this now is being handled by a three man board comprised of Sam Battaglia, Phil Alderisio, and Jackie Cerone, in addition all must agree on decision rendered otherwise judgment left for Giancana upon return. Informant gave no indication reason for change.

Information received from second informant indicates hoodlum Rocco Pranno, in conversation with friend, indicated Giancana no longer top man in Chicago and that position now held by Sam Battaglia. Pranno concerned over future. Stated Giancana in trouble because of troubles with FBI and current publicity.

FEDERAL BUREAU OF INVESTIGATION

REPORTING OFFICE	OFFICE OF ORIGIN	DATE	INVESTIGATIVE PERIOD	
CHICAGO	CHICAGO	1965	April 2, 1965	
TITLE OF CASE		REPORT MADE BY		TYPED BY
				dkc
SAMUEL M. GIANCANA, aka		CHARACTER OF CASE		
		FBI Headquarters File Number 92-3171-1605 Top Hoodlum Program – Anti Racketeering. Daily Summary		

CG 65766-C advised further concerning reported change of Chicago syndicate leadership from Giancana to Sam "Teets" Battaglia that reason behind same is Giancana's desire to remove some of pressure now being exerted on him as leader of this group. Source advised Giancana feels assured that FBI has an informant within syndicate circles on high level who is furnishing them with specific details concerning hoodlum activities. This thought second by John D'Arco who retold situation concerning meeting between himself and Giancana held at Czech Lodge in 1961 which was uncovered by FBI. D'Arco advised that FBI tried to contact him before this meeting and tell him of its purpose, which according to D'Arco was known to them some time prior to actual meeting.

Noted Pat Marcy stated to all that as far as he is concerned Giancana still boss and person to contact for approval on all matters.

CG informant advised Giancana in Chicago all week. Observed to be holding meetings at Armory Lounge Tuesday and Wednesday afternoons this week with Butch Blasi.

FEDERAL BUREAU OF INVESTIGATION

REPORTING OFFICE	OFFICE OF ORIGIN	DATE	INVESTIGATIVE PERIOD	
CHICAGO	CHICAGO	1965	April 23, 1965	
TITLE OF CASE		REPORT MADE BY		TYPED BY
				dkc
SAMUEL M. GIANCANA, aka		**CHARACTER OF CASE** FBI Headquarters File 92-3171-1613 Top Hoodlum Program – Anti Racketeering. Daily Summary		

CG 6576-C advised Sam Rosa recently met with Pat Marcy for purpose of having Marcy obtain permit to change "Fag" bar that Rosa operates into strip joint. Marcy, after learning Rosa had not previously cleared this with Giancana, instructed him to do so before going further in matter. When given these instructions Rosa questioned whether he should see Giancana or "Teete" Battaglia. This indicates some substantiation of recent information reflecting Battaglia assuming more power, it being noted Rosa now daily golfing companion of Giancana and seemingly would know who has power to ok such transactions. Marcy instructed Rosa to see Giancana about this stating that is why Marcy has instructions.

Informant also added that Felix Alderisio asked informant to order two refrigerated beer coolers to be given as a present to Sam Giancana. He instructed Tony Panzica to deliver the coolers to Dominic "Butch" Blasi who would deliver them to Giancana at the Armory Lounge.

Giancana golfed on April 22 at Cog Hill Club with Chuck English, Johnny Campanelli, Sam Parde, and CG informant.

FEDERAL BUREAU OF INVESTIGATION

REPORTING OFFICE	OFFICE OF ORIGIN	DATE	INVESTIGATIVE PERIOD	
CHICAGO	CHICAGO	1965	April 30, 1965	
TITLE OF CASE		REPORT MADE BY		TYPED BY
				dkc
SAMUEL M. GIANCANA, aka		**CHARACTER OF CASE**		
		FBI Headquarters File 92-3171-1622 Top Hoodlum Program – Anti Racketeering. Daily Summary		

CG 6486-C advised Giancana made phone call to "Mr. Korshak" from the Armory Lounge. Identified him self as "Dr. Moe" and stated "I'm on my way." Korshak believed to be identical with Attorney Sidney Korshak. Source advised earlier in evening Giancana in contact with one Mike (LNU) concerning situation in Stone Park and Northlake, two western suburbs generally known to be under domination of hoodlum Rocco Pranno.

From discussion appears Giancana placed Steve Anselmo in position of power in Stone Park having replaced former henchman of Pranno. Anselmo known associate of Giancana and constant patron at Armory Lounge past four years. Source further disclosed Giancana replacing Pranno personnel and Pranno no longer receiving financial lickback from operations in Stone Park and Northlake. Chicago office revealed that Stephen Anselmo was an attorney and political figure in the western suburb of Chicago. Stephen Anselmo is connected with political group which was just voted into office in Stone Park on a reform ticket in the April, 1965 elections. Anselmo is known to have been a frequent visitor at the Armory Lounge during the past several years and has been reported to be friendly with Giancana, Blasi and other habitues of the Armory Lounge.

Mike (LNU) possibly identical to Mike Marino, partner of Pranno in Key Club and close associate of Giancana.

Giancana, Chuck English, Butch Blasi, and Marshall Caifano met at Armory Lounge 4/29 last and discussed Giancana appearance before FGJ New York. General fear among all present that Giancana about to be trapped in hearings. Feel government plans to utilize immunity statues when Giancana next called. English initially states Supreme Court has reversed previous cases where immunity granted but is corrected by Giancana who stated "They already have a gambler on it in New York." Upon learning above all became apprehends over forthcoming proceedings. General consensus is Giancana would not be able to answer any questions, and to do so would open him to perjury. Feels government probably approaching these hearings with this end in mind. As English stated "If he talks they'll play 20 questions with him and before he knows it they will convict him on own answers, he can't win that way."

FEDERAL BUREAU OF INVESTIGATION

REPORTING OFFICE	OFFICE OF ORIGIN	DATE	INVESTIGATIVE PERIOD	
CHICAGO	CHICAGO	1965	May 3, 1965	

TITLE OF CASE	REPORT MADE BY	TYPED BY
SAMUEL M. GIANCANA, aka		dkc
	CHARACTER OF CASE FBI Headquarters File 92-3171-1641 Top Hoodlum Program – Anti Racketeering. Daily Summary	

Highly confidential source advised John D'Arco, Pat Marcy, and Romie Nappi conferred April 28 last. Nappi advised he learned Sam Battaglia assumed position as number 2 man of the Chicago group following the death of Frank Ferraro. Advised Giancana remains boss of the Chicago group but indications are sometime in future Battaglia will assume this role. Did not give source his info. D'Arco and Marcy indicated this info made more sense than info previously given them that Battaglia replaced Giancana. Also appears to be logical to Chicago office, since all other sources indicate other Chicago top hoodlums continue to seek meeting with Giancana for approval their interests. No such meetings know to be requested with Battaglia to date.

FEDERAL BUREAU OF INVESTIGATION

REPORTING OFFICE	OFFICE OF ORIGIN	DATE	INVESTIGATIVE PERIOD	
CHICAGO	CHICAGO	1965	May 4, 1965	

TITLE OF CASE	REPORT MADE BY	TYPED BY
SAMUEL M. GIANCANA, aka		dkc
	CHARACTER OF CASE FBI Headquarters File 92-3171-1568 Top Hoodlum Program – Anti Racketeering. Daily Summary	

CG 6576-C advised Anthony Tisci recently contacted Anthony Girolami concerning situation whereby Mayor Richard J. Daley had requested Girolami to again take position of alderman within 28th Ward, which position now vacant. As Bureau aware Girolami presently clerk of probate court, unable to give mayor answer to request until situation explained to Giancana and his desired known. Tisci advised source Giancana had issued instructions to Girolami that he is not to take alderman position regardless of pressures exerted by Daley. Girolami has so advised Daley of his stand.

Daley explained his reasons for desiring Girolami's return to alderman position are that city council now top heavy with Negro alderman and with 28th Ward now 65 percent Negro, mayor foresees another Negro being elected to council. Girolami has advised that he will guarantee white alderman will assume this position.

Source further advised Giancana apprehensive over recent Supreme Court decision not to hear his case feeling FBI will again intensify its surveillance of his activities. Giancana feels that he will again be forced into period where he is unable to make any contacts if such action is resumed. Giancana feels last period of surveillance was cause of present state of unrest within Chicago organization and does not desire situation to worsen. Apparently others within organization tightly controlled he must remain in constant contact with underlings. Chicago news media recently quoted Federal Judge Richard Austin as stating he believes Giancana's Attorney will file amended complaint showing $10,000 damage incurred by Giancana resulting from FBI surveillance.

FEDERAL BUREAU OF INVESTIGATION

REPORTING OFFICE	OFFICE OF ORIGIN	DATE	INVESTIGATIVE PERIOD	
CHICAGO	CHICAGO	1965	May 7, 1965	
TITLE OF CASE		REPORT MADE BY		TYPED BY
				dkc
SAMUEL M. GIANCANA, aka		CHARACTER OF CASE		
		FBI Headquarters File Number 92-3171-1633 Top Hoodlum Program – Anti Racketeering. Daily Summary		

CG 6486-C advised Attorney Mike Brodkin met with Giancana, Butch Blasi, Frank Smith, brother of Fred "Jukebox" Smith and Eddie Vogel at Armory Lounge late May 5. Discussed fact Nick Montos in touch with hoodlum Ralph Pierce within past several months and advised he has made "connections in Georgia" whereby he feels he can obtain new trial for $5,500. Brodkin stated Montos talked about warden of prison about a possible escape situation and added, "If Nick can make things easy for himself, he will." Discussed recent trip to Las Vegas by Vogel and Gus Alex, with indications that Albert Frabotta also there. Giancana present Armory May 6 last and instructed Blasi to make contact with Illinois State Senator Bernard Neistein. Nature of contact not discussed. Source advised Giancana plans to be in Chicago May 7, but has given indication plans to leave city "Day or so after Friday."

FEDERAL BUREAU OF INVESTIGATION

REPORTING OFFICE	OFFICE OF ORIGIN	DATE	INVESTIGATIVE PERIOD	
CHICAGO	CHICAGO	1965	May 10, 1965	

TITLE OF CASE	REPORT MADE BY		TYPED BY
			dkc
SAMUEL M. GIANCANA, aka	**CHARACTER OF CASE**		
	FBI Headquarters File Number 92-3171-1637 Top Hoodlum Program – Anti Racketeering. Daily Summary		

CG 6486-C advised Giancana returned to Armory Lounge following subpoena service by Bu-agents May 9 last. Concerning purpose behind grand jury. Giancana's feels greatest possibility concerns testimony given by Paul DeLucia during recent deportation hearings. Blasi advised, "You brought it all on your self." Apparently for be-rating agents in the past. Giancana stated he should have cursed agents as strongly as he did "at airport." Of note was feelings of Giancana that he can call agents any type of vile invectives and get away with it. Boasted that "If anyone ever called me those names I'd kill them."

CG 6576-C advised Pat Marcy in contact with Chicago Policeman John Auriemma early AM instant about service of Giancana. Marcy advised he has heard 25 subpoenas to be issued. Requested Auriemma attempt to learn identity of persons to be served and purpose. Marcy extremely concerned over purpose of federal investigation.

During conversation between Blasi and Giancana about general crime situation is a follows:

Blasi: You know you look at these things and it seems like we're in worse shape now them we ever were. Look at this Attorney General.

Giancana: What do you expect. Bobby put him in, I don't know that things are any worse, but I tell you they got their fingers in there.

Blasi: ..Johnson...was he the attorney general? The senator? Was he the prosecutor? He was either the Attorney General or the prosecutor for the state of Texas.

Giancana: He cleaned the (obscene) state of slot machines ..that was where he got his name. The top man...all the gambling.

FEDERAL BUREAU OF INVESTIGATION

REPORTING OFFICE	OFFICE OF ORIGIN	DATE	INVESTIGATIVE PERIOD
CHICAGO	CHICAGO	1965	May 21, 1965

TITLE OF CASE	REPORT MADE BY	TYPED BY
		dkc
SAMUEL M. GIANCANA, aka	**CHARACTER OF CASE** FBI Headquarters File 92-3171-1661 Top Hoodlum Program – Anti Racketeering. Daily Summary	

Richard Cain served with subpoenas by bureau agents May 20 instant without incident, for appearance tomorrow. Highly confidential source advised today that John D'Arco concerned over not having received government subpoena to date. Considering one of two possibilities. First to go to Mayor Richard J. Daley and have him find out if subpoena outstanding for D'Arco and if so why not served. Secondly, to appear without subpoena before FGJ on May 21, next.

Anthony V. Champagne telephonically contacted Chicago Division inquiring if subpoena outstanding for Patricia Clark, former girl friend of Giancana.

FEDERAL BUREAU OF INVESTIGATION

REPORTING OFFICE	OFFICE OF ORIGIN	DATE	INVESTIGATIVE PERIOD
CHICAGO	CHICAGO	1965	May 25, 1965

TITLE OF CASE	REPORT MADE BY	TYPED BY
		dkc
SAMUEL M. GIANCANA, aka	**CHARACTER OF CASE** FBI Headquarters File 92-3171-1664 Top Hoodlum Program – Anti Racketeering. Daily Summary	

CG 6576-C advised Don Parrillo, First Ward Alderman, complained to Pat Marcy that his, Parillo's brother, forced him out of ABNK (Republic National) and Insurance Company owned by brothers because of adverse publicity heaped on Parrillo in connection with his position as alderman. Parrillo will continue ownership of Loan Company. Parillo very upset because, "They think because I'm alderman of this ward I get a million dollars." Also complained no one associated with Democratic organization, especially Anthony Tisci, has done any favors for him.

CG 6486-C advised Giancana upset over present FGJ proceedings. Butch Blasi states Giancana feels this investigation tied into New York appearance which were merely for purpose of giving Chicago time to prepare present case. Also this served purpose of keeping Giancana's whereabouts known. Source states Giancana became concerned after second Chicago appearance because questioning much more direct and apparently aimed at specific situations. Actual goal of government still not known but feeling is they might be trying new "Anti Racketeering" laws. Source states "All they need are phone calls and travel." Giancana also concerned over learning Phyllis McGuire did not take Fifth Amendment to all questions.

FEDERAL BUREAU OF INVESTIGATION

REPORTING OFFICE	OFFICE OF ORIGIN	DATE	INVESTIGATIVE PERIOD	
CHICAGO	CHICAGO	1965	May 28, 1965	
TITLE OF CASE		REPORT MADE BY		TYPED BY
				dkc
SAMUEL M. GIANCANA, aka		CHARACTER OF CASE		
		FBI Headquarters File Number 92-3171-1672 Top Hoodlum Program – Anti Racketeering. Daily Summary		

Giancana appeared in Judge Campbell's court May 28 instant with Attorney Richard Gorman and instructed to return June 1. Highly confidential source advised Murray Humphreys and Gus Alex with Giancana 9:00 A.M. this date "way out west." Purpose of meeting unknown.

CG 6486-C advised Giancana met with Chuckie English May 27 last at Armory Lounge and explained grave situation facing him in his next appearance. English suggested Giancana return to Grand Jury and answer questions by stating, "I can't remember." Giancana answered, "They (presumably his attorney) sat that's no good." Later source advised Butch Blasi told by English that immunity came as great shock to Giancana. Blasi feels Giancana, "In trouble, what can he do?"

CG 6758-C advised Mike Brodkin and Attorney Richard Gorman conferred today concerning Giancana matter and conducted extensive review of possible cases to be cited to forgo utilization of immunity provision. Gorman stated Giancana departing from Washington, D.C., this PM apparently to confer with attorney Williams. Gorman claims Williams to appear before Judge Campbell Tuesday next and "No matter what Williams says Judge Campbell is going to order Giancana to jail. If it was some other judge we'd have a chance, but not with Judge Campbell."

FEDERAL BUREAU OF INVESTIGATION

REPORTING OFFICE	OFFICE OF ORIGIN	DATE	INVESTIGATIVE PERIOD	
CHICAGO	CHICAGO	1965	June 3, 1965	
TITLE OF CASE		REPORT MADE BY		TYPED BY
				dkc
SAMUEL M. GIANCANA, aka		CHARACTER OF CASE		
		FBI Headquarters File 92-3171-1681 Top Hoodlum Program – Anti Racketeering. Daily Summary		

Attorney Richard Gorman appeared before 7th Circuit Court of Appeals at which time he filed an emergency motion for stay of Judge Campbell's order Giancana to jail, pending appeal.

CG T-7 indicated that several top-ranking hoodlums and their associates felt that the grant of immunity was the strongest blow that the government ever wielded against organized crime and that the general contention of these individuals was that the attorneys who have been receiving substantially high incomes through these many years from the hoodlums had best think up some defense for this government tactic.

CG T-3 advised that Butch Blasi had indicated that as a result of the Grand Jury proceedings, the Armory Lounge would be closed down for a while as all of the persons frequenting the lounge will be following Giancana. Blasi indicated to this individual that all of those subsequently called before the Grand Jury would have to follow Giancana's precedent in refusing to accept the grant of immunity.

CG T-14 advised that E. Bennett Williams indicated that he had indicated to Giancana that he desired to drop Giancana as a client based on Giancana's refusal to follow his advice which was to accept the grant immunity and answer the questions placed to him by the Grand Jury.

FEDERAL BUREAU OF INVESTIGATION

REPORTING OFFICE	OFFICE OF ORIGIN	DATE	INVESTIGATIVE PERIOD	
CHICAGO	CHICAGO	1965	June 7, 1965	
TITLE OF CASE		REPORT MADE BY		TYPED BY
				dkc
SAMUEL M. GIANCANA, aka		CHARACTER OF CASE		
		FBI Headquarters File Number 92-3171-1687 Top Hoodlum Program – Anti Racketeering. Daily Summary		

Giancana in need of medical care Sunday night. Examined by Dr. Edward Malters, County jail physician, who advised Giancana suffering from peptic condition of upper stomach. Malters states condition gives evidence of ulcer or fact that Giancana suffering from acute nervous condition.

USA Edward Hanrahan advised that his wife received a phone call from unidentified male who stated, "If Giancana is not out of jail by next Friday we will wash your husband's face in acid."

FEDERAL BUREAU OF INVESTIGATION

REPORTING OFFICE	OFFICE OF ORIGIN	DATE	INVESTIGATIVE PERIOD	
CHICAGO	CHICAGO	1965	June 9, 1965	
TITLE OF CASE		REPORT MADE BY		TYPED BY
				dkc
SAMUEL M. GIANCANA, aka		CHARACTER OF CASE		
		FBI Headquarters File Number 92-3171-1686 Top Hoodlum Program – Anti Racketeering. Daily Summary		

Government attorneys, Chicago, completed work on brief to be filed late afternoon June 9. Court documents of appeals in response to petition filed by Giancana's attorney. Matter now will be reviewed by appeals court to determine if Giancana should be released on bond pending appeal from contempt ruling.

Following Giancana's first appearance before Federal Grand Jury in New York City during early part of year, meeting held in Chicago to decide who would handle Chicago hoodlum affairs should Giancana go to jail. Most logical hoodlums mentioned are Sam Battaglia and Fiore "Fifi" Buccieri. However, due to reported rift between Buccieri and Battaglia, Chicago hoodlums felt factional dispute might arise.

According to source, Charles English reportedly was decided upon since English supposedly acceptable to both parties.

FEDERAL BUREAU OF INVESTIGATION

REPORTING OFFICE	OFFICE OF ORIGIN	DATE	INVESTIGATIVE PERIOD	
CHICAGO	CHICAGO	1965	June 15, 1965	
TITLE OF CASE		REPORT MADE BY		TYPED BY
				dkc
SAMUEL M. GIANCANA, aka		CHARACTER OF CASE		
		FBI Headquarters File Number 92-3171-1700 Top Hoodlum Program – Anti Racketeering. Daily Summary		

CG 6576-C advised Anthony Tisci recently in Washington, DC where he met with Congressman Frank Annunzio to discuss Tisci's situation and employment following involvement in Giancana Grand Jury proceedings. Source advised Annunzio told Tisci that reason Tisci brought into matter is that FBI feels Tisci responsible for Giancana going into court two years ago and therefore had a responsibility to "Get Tisci." Annunzio continued "Government knows you are the direct link" but this could not be proved. (Apparently link between Giancana and political pawns.) Annunzio states to keep Tisci on as assistant would be "Another slap in the face" to government which would merely serve to keep their investigation going. Therefore, according to source, Tisci to be innocent victim" of whole situation.

Tisci advised Pat Marcy, concerning appeal now before Supreme Court Justice Tom Clark, that no one, (Giancana's Attorneys) feels that Clark will release Giancana. Feeling is he will advise that they have not used all legal means available in lower courts and will advise them to return to appellate court. Tisci feels when government has Giancana in jail through summer, and his attorneys then proceed before Supreme Court, government will drop suit, according to Tisci, because they have no case.

FEDERAL BUREAU OF INVESTIGATION

REPORTING OFFICE	OFFICE OF ORIGIN	DATE	INVESTIGATIVE PERIOD
CHICAGO	CHICAGO	1965	June 29, 1965

TITLE OF CASE	REPORT MADE BY	TYPED BY
		dkc
SAMUEL M. GIANCANA, aka	**CHARACTER OF CASE**	
	FBI Headquarters File 92-3171-1712 Top Hoodlum Program – Anti Racketeering. Daily Summary	

CG informant advised that Sam Battaglia currently handing affairs of Giancana during latter's confinement and has assumed role of top leader here.

Informant advised this delegation of authority to Battaglia has angered Jackie Cerone who feels he should be top man in Giancana's absence. Informant advised Cerone feels he has backing of former top leaders Anthony Accardo and Paul DeLucia and may try power play.

This info may explain purpose of meeting between Gus Alex, Paul DeLucia, Ralph Pierce and Jackie Cerone at Rookery Restaurant June 28 last. Cerone and DeLucia may be attempting to line up support of members of Humphreys group in this regard.

FEDERAL BUREAU OF INVESTIGATION

REPORTING OFFICE	OFFICE OF ORIGIN	DATE	INVESTIGATIVE PERIOD
CHICAGO	CHICAGO	1965	July 2, 1965

TITLE OF CASE	REPORT MADE BY	TYPED BY
		dkc
SAMUEL M. GIANCANA, aka	**CHARACTER OF CASE**	
	FBI Headquarters File Number 92-3171-1713 Top Hoodlum Program – Anti Racketeering. Daily Summary	

U.S. Congressman Frank Annunzio issued a statement to Chicago newspapers indicating complete confidence in his assistant Anthony Tisci and indicated no intention of requesting his resignation from position as Congressional assistant because of adverse publicity resulting from recent Grand Jury appearances. Above apparently maneuver to set stage for letter furnished local papers by Tisci to Annunzio thanking him for this confidence but indicated that for reasons of health and upon advice from his personal physician, he was tending his resignation.

FEDERAL BUREAU OF INVESTIGATION

REPORTING OFFICE	OFFICE OF ORIGIN	DATE	INVESTIGATIVE PERIOD	
CHICAGO	CHICAGO	1965	August 16, 1965	
TITLE OF CASE		REPORT MADE BY		TYPED BY
				dkc
SAMUEL M. GIANCANA, aka		CHARACTER OF CASE		
		FBI Headquarters File Number 92-3171-1734 Top Hoodlum Program – Anti Racketeering. Daily Summary		

Associates

Charles Giancana

CG T-16 advised that Charles Giancana, aka Charles Kane, continues to engage in the construction business on a large scale in the Rosemont, Illinois, area with his partner Sam Pisetti. Giancana meets practically on a daily basis with Donald Stephens, Rosemont's Mayor, concerning financing and zoning regulations in the Rosemont area.

Chuck Giancana has recently expressed extreme bitterness over the imprisonment of his brother, Sam, and has repeatedly stated that "Moe will have his day yet."

Sam Lewis

Sam Lewis, a former operator of Parr Loan Company, was reported by CG T-14 to be one of the five persons among who was Sam Giancana, whom control organized crime in the Chicago area. Lewis, whose true name is Salvatore Carmen Lusi, was reported to meet on a weekly basis with Giancana to discuss matters concerning organized crime in the Chicago area.

Melvin "Potsy" Pearl

CG T-17 advised that he received information that Melvin "Potsy" Pearl is a "front" for Sam Giancana in several ventures one of which is the owner ship of an apartment building located at 22 East Pearson. Melvin's brother is Sam Pearl, an attorney whose office is at 100 North La Salle Street in Chicago. In addition, Peral reportedly recently took two circuit court magistrates, Wallace Cargman and Harry Schrier, to the Armory Lounge where both were introduced to Sam Giancana.

Phyllis McGuire

During the investigation to locate Phyllis McGuire for the purpose of serving her with a subpoena to appear before Grand Jury it was learned that she recently rented an apartment in Ft. Lauderdale, Florida. The apartment building, named the Villa Frasca, is located at 3220 Bay View Drive. It is reportedly owned by Liberty Frasca of Chicago and the Manager, Charles Alesi, is also from Chicago and associated with Sam Giancana. It was noted that during attempts by the Miami Division to locate McGuire, both Alesi and his wife were uncooperative and told conflicting stories about McGuire and her whereabouts.

Business Enterprises

Oasis Vending Company
3259 West Chicago Avenue
Chicago, Illinois

CG T-19 advised in May, 1965, that an associate, one Pat Petrone, had advised that Oasis Vending Company was owned by Petrone and that Giancana had originally loaned Petrone the money to start this company. Petrone never advised the informant of the amount of money received from Giancana. Petrone died on April 29, 1965.

During late April, 1965, a meeting was held between Sam Giancana, "Milwaukee Phil" Alderisio and Sam Battaglia for the purpose of discussing and deciding upon an individual who could front for these individuals in certain legitimate enterprises operated by the Chicago syndicate.

FEDERAL BUREAU OF INVESTIGATION

REPORTING OFFICE	OFFICE OF ORIGIN	DATE	INVESTIGATIVE PERIOD	
CHICAGO	CHICAGO	1965	August 22, 1965	
TITLE OF CASE		REPORT MADE BY		TYPED BY
				dkc
SAMUEL M. GIANCANA, aka		**CHARACTER OF CASE** FBI Headquarters File 92-3171-1737 Top Hoodlum Program – Anti Racketeering. Daily Summary		

Sandy Smith, crime reporter advised today that Anthony "Tony X" Esposito, Charles Nicosia, Pat Marcy and Anthony Tisci arrested on August 20, last by St. Louis PD at alleged hoodlum meeting at Chase Hotel, St. Louis. Group reportedly in contact with one Stephen P. Gorman, brick layer contractor, and associate of hoodlum Buster Wortman.

For St. Louis, Anthony "Tony X" Esposito is the brother of Frank Esposito, powerful Chicago labor official who was slated for gangland slaying in February 1962 on orders from Sam Giancana, however contact resended due to FBI intervention. Nicosia is employee of hoodlum dominated Democratic First Ward, Chicago. Also on payroll of Chicago Judge Thaddeus Adesko as security evaluator for inheritance tax cases and works with Illinois state attorney's general's office. Marcy is secretary of Chicago's First Ward and political contact man for Giancana. Tisci is son-in-law of Giancana who recently resigned as administrative assistant to U.S. congressman.

Smith stated purpose of St. Louis meeting not known, however is writing articles for Sun Times under Ray Brennan by-line indicating Marcy and Tisci carrying messages to Wortman and St. Louis hoodlum Nick Civella from Giancana who still confined county jail Chicago since June one last. St. Louis obtained details of arrest and advice.

FEDERAL BUREAU OF INVESTIGATION

REPORTING OFFICE	OFFICE OF ORIGIN	DATE	INVESTIGATIVE PERIOD	
CHICAGO	CHICAGO	1965	August 23, 1965	
TITLE OF CASE		REPORT MADE BY		TYPED BY
				dkc
SAMUEL M. GIANCANA, aka		CHARACTER OF CASE		
		FBI Headquarters File Number 92-3171-1738 Top Hoodlum Program – Anti Racketeering. Daily Summary		

About Chicago tel August 22, last concerning reported arrest of Anthony "Tony X" Esposito, Charles Nicosia, Pat Marcy, and Anthony Tisci by St. Louis PD, 8/20/65.

St. Louis Division advised intelligence unit, St. Louis PD, received info that Esposito using a one hundred dollar a day presidential Suite, Chase Hotel, St. Louis, which suite billed to Stephen Gorman Brick Company. Due to expenses incurred and suspicious circumstances, St. Louis PD attempted to interview Esposito in hotel suite and found him to be in company of Nicosia, Marcy and Tisci. Group called in for questioning and no arrest made. During interview all claimed to have attended state fair, Springfield, previous night and traveled to St. Louis for dinner.

CG informant advised today that purpose of travel of above group was to attend Governor's day at state fair in Springfield. As is annual custom group then traveled to St. Louis to cabaret inasmuch as more pleasures available St. Louis than Springfield. Informant certain travel was for pleasure only.

Chapter 10

FEDERAL BUREAU OF INVESTIGATION

REPORTING OFFICE	OFFICE OF ORIGIN	DATE	INVESTIGATIVE PERIOD	
CHICAGO	CHICAGO	1966	February 7, 1966	
TITLE OF CASE		REPORT MADE BY		TYPED BY
				dkc
SAMUEL M. GIANCANA, aka		**CHARACTER OF CASE** FBI Headquarters File Number 92-3171 Top Hoodlum Program – Anti Racketeering. Daily Summary		

In connection with the 2/6/66 bombing of Mario's Barber Shop, 6745 West North Avenue, Oak Park, the investigation conducted by the Oak Park PD revealed that Mario Cervi, owner of the shop, was previously employed at the Galewood Barber Shop, 6964 West North Avenue, Oak Park. It was believed that Galewood catered to hoodlum element inasmuch as its owner, Joseph Serucusa, was believed to be Sam Giancana's personal barber, and his automobile had been observed on numerous occasions at Giancana's residence in Oak Park. It was felt that Cervi kept a list of his clientele while employed at Galewood and it was possible that he brought his former clientele to his new place of business. The Oak Park PD had no suspects or motives for the bombing.

FEDERAL BUREAU OF INVESTIGATION

REPORTING OFFICE	OFFICE OF ORIGIN	DATE	INVESTIGATIVE PERIOD	
CHICAGO	CHICAGO	1966	May 17, 1966	
TITLE OF CASE		REPORT MADE BY		TYPED BY
				dkc
SAMUEL M. GIANCANA, aka		**CHARACTER OF CASE** FBI Headquarters File Number 92-3171 Top Hoodlum Program – Anti Racketeering. Daily Summary		

On May 17, 1966, a meeting was held between Colonel Sheffield Edwards, former Director of Security, CIA, and John "Johnny" Roselli concerning the FBI wanting to talk to "Johnny" alone. Edwards thought that Johnny believed that if he talked to the FBI alone, Sam Giancana, who was in jail in Chicago, or Sam's friends would believe he was "talking" which would be fatal for Johnny as he knew a lot about Sam. As the result of the Bureau's contact with Roselli, he went to the CIA for protection. CIA in the past compromised them selves by dealing with Roselli when they had him contact Giancana, head of the Chicago LCN family, to get someone to assassinate Fidel Castro in Cuba.

FEDERAL BUREAU OF INVESTIGATION

REPORTING OFFICE	OFFICE OF ORIGIN	DATE	INVESTIGATIVE PERIOD
CHICAGO	CHICAGO	1966	July 20, 1966

TITLE OF CASE	REPORT MADE BY	TYPED BY
SAMUEL M. GIANCANA, aka		dkc

CHARACTER OF CASE

FBI Headquarters File Number 92-3171-1871
Top Hoodlum Program – Anti Racketeering.
Daily Summary

Fiore "Fifi" Buccieri advised informant that Sam Giancana left Chicago immediately upon being released "Because he was afraid of being subpoenaed." Informant feels Giancana, not knowing whether he was to be subject of additional government proceedings or not, made himself scarce to avoid any possibility of additional confrontations.

Informant feels direct result of absence of Giancana and reluctance of Sam Battaglia to assume aggressive leadership in absence of Giancana is that Chicago underworld continues to suffer from lack of leadership and that Buccieri-Battaglia dispute is direct result and appears to be worsening.

FEDERAL BUREAU OF INVESTIGATION

REPORTING OFFICE	OFFICE OF ORIGIN	DATE	INVESTIGATIVE PERIOD
CHICAGO	CHICAGO	1966	August 11, 1966

TITLE OF CASE	REPORT MADE BY	TYPED BY
SAMUEL M. GIANCANA, aka		dkc

CHARACTER OF CASE

FBI Headquarters File Number 92-3171-1874
Top Hoodlum Program – Anti Racketeering.
Daily Summary

CG informant advised he was visited at his home by Sam Giancana who was accompanied by a man introduced as Fiore Buccieri. After a few moments of general conversation Giancana asked informant if he would take a job. Conversation indicated that job would be in New York City within two weeks. Informant background and general tenor of conversation led informant to believe that job might be a contract to hit some unknown. Giancana and Buccieri left to let informant think it over and said they would return in about an hour after visiting a friend in the area. After their departure informant left home to place call to Chicago office. Upon his return his wife advised that Giancana and Buccieri has returned to his home during his absence and left message that informant should come to grill at Harlem and Addison the next day.

Informant advised previously that he learned from Paul "Peanuts" Panczko, Chicago top jewel thief that Giancana had been in London and would return to Chicago during mid week.

Informant's background unverified as yet but he states he served time with Panzcko in Tennessee where he killed an inmate at Panzcko's request. Also allegedly killed one more inmate and a prison guard. Informant was in federal tier at Cook County jail during portion of time Giancana was there and allegedly acted as messenger boy and bodyguard for Giancana while in jail having been introduced and recommended by Panzcko in effort to get some type of job with Giancana who had allegedly promised him a favor while in jail. Panzcko stated that this man was an "excellent hit man" and a "stand up guy" and would vouch for him.

<table>
<tr><td colspan="4" align="center">**FEDERAL BUREAU OF INVESTIGATION**</td></tr>
<tr><td>REPORTING OFFICE

CHICAGO</td><td>OFFICE OF ORIGIN

CHICAGO</td><td>DATE

1966</td><td>INVESTIGATIVE PERIOD

August 15, 1966</td></tr>
<tr><td>TITLE OF CASE

SAMUEL M. GIANCANA, aka</td><td colspan="2">REPORT MADE BY</td><td>TYPED BY

dkc</td></tr>
<tr><td></td><td colspan="3">CHARACTER OF CASE
FBI Headquarters File Number 92-3171
Top Hoodlum Program – Anti Racketeering.
Daily Summary</td></tr>
</table>

Further information advising of Giancana and Fiori Buccieri contact with CG informant about possible, "Contract to hit unknown in New York City."

Informant given phone message August 11, last to be at grill at Harlem and Addison, Chicago. Informant was picked up at that spot by two unknown white males who drove him to Chicago downtown. After waiting about one hour a white male entered the car and introduced himself as "Tony the Bull." One of the original passengers left at this point and informant, Tony and the driver proceeded to drive in restaurant in Maywood where they stated about three hours, apparently killing time. At about seven PM they drove to western suburb believed to be Lyons, Illinois, where they all entered an apartment house basement. This spot was used as a telephone bookmaking location. At this location they were met by Fiore Buccieri.

Buccieri, the informant and Tony the Bull then drove short way to Baldi's Restaurant in Lyons. On arrival Buccieri began discussing the job for informant. He made it clear that job was a "Contract" to kill someone in NYC who was a person of some prominence in Chicago criminal group. Killing will occur sometime within next two weeks and informant is to keep himself in readiness. Tony the Bull will be his "back up man" Buccieri told informant that victim would drive to site selected for killing by a man who was not to be harmed and who would "walk away after the job." Informant shown photograph of driver at which time Tony said, "I know him, there won't be any accident." Informant and Buccieri settled on a fee of $2,600 for the job. Half will be given to informant, together with the plane tickets, by Tony as they leave for New York. Remainder will be paid by Tony after completion of hit. Tony will remain in NYC while informant returns to Chicago.

Buccieri asked what type of weapon he liked, rifle or revolver? Informant requested a 357 Magnum for which Buccieri will supply a shoulder holster. Buccieri advised a person in Chicago who would supply the type of point sight informant prefers. Buccieri stated that sound of gunfire at the site of killing will not be a problem. Buccieri told informant that victim should be killed in car or just as he gets out of car. Tony asked if they should "Take him to the scrap pile" after killing, to which Buccieri replied in affirmative.

Buccieri indicated that victim was to be killed for stealing money from the Outfit but was not an informant. Victim will be leaving for NYC in near future. Informant identified photos of Buccieri and Giancana, as persons making initial contact. Tony possibly former boxer as he has cauliflower left ear and scar tissue over eyes. Informant desires to go through with scheme up to but not including murder. Suggests possibility that he might take some medicine at last moment to make him ill and preclude his participation.

Informant feels his acceptance of contract and knowledge of Tony's scheduled participation make it impossible to back out of job at this time without attracting suspicion and jeopardizing his life.

CG informant advised that "Tony the Bull" contacted him late night on 8/14 last at informants home. Tony showed informant photo of Butch Blasi and specifically designated Blasi as man they were to kill. Plans have been changed according to Tony and hit will take place in Chicago on 8/15 or 8/16. Informant advised to remain in home in readiness for contact by Tony. In order to delay above plans about slaying of Blasi, arrangements have been made through SAC contact to have informant enter emergency room and have his right leg placed in cast thus immobilizing him.

Conference held with Captain William Duffy, Director, Intelligence Unit, CPD, who was advised of above situation. Duffy will have informant probation revoked at appropriate time to further remove informant from involvement. Thereafter serious consideration will be given to interview with Blasi to acquaint him with murder plot with possibility existing of developing Blasi as an informant.

Coverage by Bureau agents being afforded in vicinity of informant's home to identify Tony the Bull and to further verify informants story. Informant believes Tony is from the Detroit area but this alias is unknown to Detroit office.

After further investigation, Agents confronted him with overwhelming evidence developed in this matter as well as the many discrepancies uncovered. For more than one hour he continued to remain steadfast in his story when finally he admitted that the entire story was false. He stated that he fabricated this tale because of his dislike for local law enforcement which stemmed from his difficulties during his extensive incarceration in various state institutions in Tennessee.

FEDERAL BUREAU OF INVESTIGATION

REPORTING OFFICE	OFFICE OF ORIGIN	DATE	INVESTIGATIVE PERIOD	
CHICAGO	CHICAGO	1966	August 31, 1966	
TITLE OF CASE		REPORT MADE BY		TYPED BY
				dkc
SAMUEL M. GIANCANA, aka		CHARACTER OF CASE		
		FBI Headquarters File Number 92-3171 Top Hoodlum Program – Anti Racketeering. Daily Summary		

Present whereabouts of Giancana unknown, however, Chicago source advised he observed Giancana at Giancana's residence on Sunday, 8/7 last and at service station two blocks from Giancana's residence.

In view of frequent travel of Giancana and since he is known to be in telephonic contact with key subordinates and associates to keep arrest activities of organize crime here while elsewhere, bureau requested to approve check of toll calls from following persons and locations: Dominic Blasi, Anthony V. Champagne, Tarquin "Queenie" Simonelli, Anthony Tisci, John Matassa, Phyllis McGuire, Armory Lounge and Giancana's residence.

FEDERAL BUREAU OF INVESTIGATION

REPORTING OFFICE	OFFICE OF ORIGIN	DATE	INVESTIGATIVE PERIOD	
CHICAGO	CHICAGO	1966	September 16, 1966	
TITLE OF CASE		REPORT MADE BY		TYPED BY
				dkc
SAMUEL M. GIANCANA, aka		CHARACTER OF CASE		
		FBI Headquarters File Number 92-3171-1895 Top Hoodlum Program – Anti Racketeering. Daily Summary		

CG informant advised that he recently overheard conversation indicating Giancana was in Chicago during past two weeks playing cards with William "Willie Potatoes" Daddono and two others. Informant is closely associated with Daddono and knows Daddono frequently plays cards at Melrose Park residence of Pasquale "Buck" Clementi, a gambler and juice collector for Daddono group.

Dominic Blasi was contacted and interviewed at length; however, declined to indicate Giancana's present whereabouts. Stated FBI must be aware from investigation of Blasi that Blasi has not been with Giancana since release from jail. Blasi advised Anthony Tisci has had increasing heart problems since his appearance before FGJ and has been advised by physician to leave Chicago area for Arizona and then go to Mayo Clinic in January for surgery.

Blasi advised James Perno is moving out of Giancana's residence and is purchasing Tisci's residence. Blasi advised FGJ appearances of Tisci affected him more than any other Giancana associate. At present time Tisci in bad financial position and at loss to know how he will make a living in Arizona and pay for doctor bills. When it was suggested Giancana would undoubtedly assist Tisci since Tisci married to Giancana's daughter and Tisci's troubles were brought on due to his association with Giancana. Blasi scoffed that although Giancana lavishly cared for "any skirt." He is frugal with members of his family. Blasi cited as example Giancana's brother, Joseph, who must "hustle hot watches" for a living.

Blasi advised he received a phone call from Phyllis McGuire three weeks ago from Colorado Springs. Although Blasi declined to discuss nature of call, point he made was that Giancana not seeing McGuire at this time. Stated Giancana frequently kept McGuire at Blasi's residence when they were intimate but "as you guys know" McGuire has not been at Blasi's since Giancana went to jail.

Blasi advised he felt certain when agents contacted him Sept. 15, he was to be served with subpoena to reappear before FGJ since all members of Chicago group "are waiting for the other shoe to drop."

FEDERAL BUREAU OF INVESTIGATION

REPORTING OFFICE	OFFICE OF ORIGIN	DATE	INVESTIGATIVE PERIOD	
CHICAGO	CHICAGO	1966	September 19, 1966	
TITLE OF CASE		REPORT MADE BY		TYPED BY
				dkc
SAMUEL M. GIANCANA, aka		CHARACTER OF CASE		
		FBI Headquarters File 92-3171-1893 Top Hoodlum Program – Anti Racketeering. Daily Summary		

Based on info several members of the Chicago group are now frequenting Giannotti's Restaurant (formerly Armory Lounge). Immediately after Agents entered front door of Giannotti's, Sam Giancana fled out rear door. This info was verified by George Colucci who was present. In addition to above, following members were observed at Giannotti's, Dominic Blasi, Sam English, Fiore Buccieri and James "Turk" Torello. Also present were Frank "Lefty" Rosenthal, Miami gambler and handicapper, Joseph Rossetti, currency exchange front for group, and Joe Scaramuzzo, a local gunsmith associated with group. Earlier in evening Rosenthal was observed with Dave Yaras, Frank Buccieri, and Joseph Ferriola at Duncan YMCA on west side of Chicago.

FEDERAL BUREAU OF INVESTIGATION

REPORTING OFFICE	OFFICE OF ORIGIN	DATE	INVESTIGATIVE PERIOD
CHICAGO	CHICAGO	1966	September 27, 1966

TITLE OF CASE	REPORT MADE BY	TYPED BY
	Special Agent William F. Roemer, Jr.	dkc
SAMUEL M. GIANCANA, aka	**CHARACTER OF CASE**	
	FBI Headquarters File number 92-3171-1899, Top Hoodlum Program – Anti Racketeering	

Synopsis:

Sam Giancana has been observed at his residence at 1147 South Wenonah, Oak Park, on only one or two occasions during past three months. He has not been observed in the company of Phyllis McGuire. Dominic "Butch" Blasi refused to furnish any information current whereabouts of Giancana, but claimed he has not been in recent company with Giancana. Information developed indicating that Giancana has absented himself from Chicago area and has not made himself available for frequent contacts with other leader's organized crime Chicago area.

Determine whereabouts of Sam Giancana Summer 1966

Chicago T-1 advised that he has observed the residence of Sam Giancana at 1147 S. Wenonah, Oak Park, on an almost daily basis during summer of 1966. This informant had advised that he has not seen Giancana at all or in the vicinity of his residence. This informant advised that the James Perno family has resided in the Giancana house during the summer of 1966, and that the gardener, Joseph DiPersio, arrives at the residence early each morning in order to care for the lawn and outside condition of the home. Frequently a woman believed to be Bonnie Lou Tisci, arrives with her small children for visits of several hours.

CG T-3 advised that a wedding anniversary party was held on the evening of August 5, 1966, for James and Marie Perno at the Villa Venice Restaurant. Giancana did not attend however a telegram was received for the Perno's from Giancana wishing them congratulations.

CG T-4 advised that he observed Giancana at his home on August 7, 1966.

CG T-7 advised that the Armory Lounge, 7421 W. Roosevelt Road, Forest Park, Illinois, became known as Nick Giannotti's Restaurant and Lounge, when it was purchased by Nick Giannotti in June of 1966. On September 14, 1966, Nick Giannotti was interviewed by SA's John Bassett and William Roemer Jr. that he is not personal acquainted with Sam Giancana. He agreed that he would feel certain, however, that he would learn if Giancana should ever visit his restaurant and lounge.

Travel of Sam Giancana

Milwaukee, Wisconsin

CG T-8 advised that he learned that on the night of June 15, 1966, Sam Giancana was in Milwaukee, Wisconsin, in the company of Frank Balistrieri, the boss of organized crime in Milwaukee. The informant stated he learned that Giancana and Balistrieri were at the "Scene," a downtown Milwaukee night club operated by Balistrieri. The informant advised that he was unable to learn of the nature or purpose of the meeting of these two individuals.

Miscellaneous

CG T-2 advised that he has learned that Washington D.C. attorney Edward Williams claims that it was through his personal efforts that Sam Giancana was not brought back before the Federal Grand Jury in Chicago following his release from Cook County Jail on May 31, 1966, and cited for contempt again. The informant advised that Williams sent a message to the Chicago underworld and particularly to Giancana that it should be kept in mind that he, Williams was the only man in the world who could pull a deal like he did to keep Giancana out of Jail. Informant advised, however, that in his understanding that Giancana does not accept Williams at his word and instead blames Williams for giving him bad advice about how he should conduct himself before a Federal Grand Jury in Chicago.

CG T-5 advised that Phyllis McGuire and her sisters came to Colorado Springs, Colorado, to entertain at the 17th annual convention of the National District Attorneys Association Foundation, which was held at the Hilton Hotel in Denver. Informant advised that it is his understanding that the affair which previously existed between Phyllis McGiure and Sam Giancana had been terminated. This informant advised that Giancana is aware of the present romantic relationship between Phyllis McGuire and Mike Davis and that Giancana has no interest in there activities.

FEDERAL BUREAU OF INVESTIGATION

REPORTING OFFICE	OFFICE OF ORIGIN	DATE	INVESTIGATIVE PERIOD	
CHICAGO	CHICAGO	1966	October 5, 1966	
TITLE OF CASE		REPORT MADE BY		TYPED BY
				dkc
SAMUEL M. GIANCANA, aka		CHARACTER OF CASE		
		FBI Headquarters File Number 92-3171 Top Hoodlum Program – Anti Racketeering. Daily Summary		

As Bureau aware, Giancana has failed to take an active role in leadership of organized crime here since time he commenced his one year incarceration, June, 1965. At present time, Chicago source generally report that Giancana apparently has now returned to Chicago area. However, Giancana has not been observed at any of his known hangouts and apparently is making no effort this time to resume strong leadership role.

Because of Giancana's incarceration and his subsequent absence there has been no strong leadership of the Chicago criminal group. This had caused factional disputes and dissatisfaction among various hoodlum groups most notable of which is obvious widening rift between Fiore Buccieri group and Frank LaPorte group. Chicago had received information during the past two years that members of the Buccieri organization were moving in on territory of Frank LaPorte in South Cook County. It was reported that Fifi Buccieri has been feuding with LaPorte for last 18 months.

CG informant advised James Torello, bodyguard for Buccieri, had interest in Eagles-a-go-go Club owned by LaPorte but operated by Bob and Joe Davis, both of whom are closely associated with Torello and Buccieri.

On March 1, last, Clarence Forrest, bartender at above club, was forcibly removed from club and shot and killed. Forrest was reportedly killed for spying on LaPorte and his associates for Buccieri group. CG informant advised that Forrest was killed by Louis Pratico, former Chicago Heights policeman and bodyguard of Frank LaPorte, and Marvin O'Lena, Sgt. Blue Island Police Dept. August Pratico's body was found dead in ditch in Chicago Heights. Informant also advised that close associate of James Catuara told him that he has been given job of obtaining two stolen cars for Catuara, which are to be utilized for two additional murders. Informant advised that Catuara had "contract" for Pratico murder and Catuara is known to be close associate with Buccieri group.

During last evening of 10/4 last Bu-Agents observed vehicles belonging to Dominic Blasi, Joseph Aiuppa, and James Torello parked at Towne Hotel in Cicero owned by Aiuppa. James Torello and Fiore Buccieri were observed leaving from back door of hotel and departed in Torello's car. At same time Blasi left via front door of hotel.

Above hoodlums not usually known to meet at this hotel and possibility exists that meeting was for purpose of discussing feud between Buccieri and LaPorte groups.

FEDERAL BUREAU OF INVESTIGATION

REPORTING OFFICE	OFFICE OF ORIGIN	DATE	INVESTIGATIVE PERIOD	
CHICAGO	CHICAGO	1966	November 3, 1966	
TITLE OF CASE		REPORT MADE BY		TYPED BY
				dkc
SAMUEL M. GIANCANA, aka		CHARACTER OF CASE		
		FBI Headquarters File Number 92-3171-1903 Top Hoodlum Program – Anti Racketeering. Daily Summary		

CG informant advised that he understands Sam Giancana is no longer occupying top command position in organized crime here at present. Both Sam Battaglia and Jack Cerone were offered opportunity to succeed Giancana but both have declined such offer. On the other hand, Fiore "Fifi" Buccieri and Felix Alderisio have openly sought top position, however, neither acceptable to other top leaders.

During recent chance meeting with Fifi Buccieri by agents of this office, Buccieri claimed he has not seen Giancana since release of Giancana from jail last June and that Giancana "Has only been seen there twice" since then.

FEDERAL BUREAU OF INVESTIGATION

REPORTING OFFICE	OFFICE OF ORIGIN	DATE	INVESTIGATIVE PERIOD	
CHICAGO	CHICAGO	1966	November 21, 1966	
TITLE OF CASE		REPORT MADE BY		TYPED BY
		Special Agent William F. Roemer, Jr.		dkc
SAMUEL M. GIANCANA, aka		CHARACTER OF CASE		
		FBI Headquarters File 92-3171-1907 Top Hoodlum Program – Anti Racketeering		

Recent Position of Giancana in Outfit

CG T-4 who is in a position to know, advised that in Chicago "The Mafia" and "The Outfit" are two different organizations which have an influence on organized crime in the Chicago area. This informant stated that whereas the Mafia and the "La Cosa Nostra" is the controlling hoodlum organization in all parts of the country, this is not true in Chicago. This informant stated that in Chicago, the controlling hoodlum organization is known as the "Outfit" or "The Syndicate" or "The Life". Informant stated that whereas some individuals are members of either one organization or the other, others are members of either one organization or the other, others are members of both organizations. This informant stated that Giancana was a member of "the Mafia" when he took over as "boss" of the "Outfit." The informant stated that this was necessary so that Giancana could represent Chicago at the "Board" meeting which consisted of representatives of the "Mafia" families from all over the country. Informant stated that the "Outfit" was built by Al Capone and today is considered to be the strongest criminal family in the US.

CG T-5 advised that he is acquainted with the organization which controls organized crime in the Chicago area. He stated that there is no doubt in his mind that the Chicago criminal organization which controls organized crime in the Chicago area has for some time been controlled by Anthony Accardo and Paul Ricca. It is the contention of this informant that Sam Giancana and Sam Battaglia have been powerful leaders of organized crime in the Chicago area, but that when it comes to final matters of policy it is Ricca and Accardo who make the final decisions.

Financial Interest of Giancana in Las Vegas, Casinos

CG T-6 advised in October, 1966, that the owners of records in the Stardust Hotel in Las Vegas, Nevada such as Morris Kleinman, Morris Dalitz and Sam Tucker would like to divest themselves of their financial holdings in the Stardust Hotel but are having a difficult time in this regard with the leaders of organized crime in the Chicago area headed by Sam Giancana who have financial interest in the Stardust Hotel. Informant stated that Kleinman, Dalitz and Tucker in October, 1966 were conducting negotiations for the sale of their holdings in the Desert Inn Casino and hotel in Las Vegas due to the "current heat being generated by the FBI and future heat the FBI will generate" in the Las Vegas area in regard to investigations of "skimming." The informant was unable to furnish any other information concerning whatever interest Giancana and his associates in Chicago may have in the Stardust Hotel.

CG T-7 advised that he understands that Sam Giancana and Carlos Marcello of New Orleans have hidden interests in the Tropicana Hotel and Casino in Las Vegas. However, he was unable to furnish any information concerning details of whatever holdings Giancana and Marcello might have in the Tropicana.

CG T-8 advised that he was informed by an individual who is in a position to know, that Sam Giancana and Gus Alex have acquired points in the Dunes Hotel and Gambling Casino in Las Vegas, and that they are the only leaders of organized crime in Chicago who have a financial interest in the Dunes. However, this informant was unable to furnish any further information concerning the interest of Alex and Giancana in the Dunes Hotel.

Investigation to Determine the Present Whereabouts of Giancana

SA's William Roemer and John Bassett on approximately 50 or 60 occasions have observed the residence of Giancana in Oak Park, and the known hangouts and meeting places of Giancana in the Chicago area. On none of these occasions has SA's Roemer or Bassett observed Giancana.

Andrew J. DeTolve, the brother of Rose Flood, the nice of Sam Giancana, who is extremely close to Giancana, died on November 5, 1966, and was buried in the Chicago area on November 7, 1966. Officers under the direction of Lieutenant Frank Nash, Chicago PD, observed the wake and his burial. On no occasion was Giancana observed.

Captain William Duffy, Chicago PD advised on October 24, 1966, that he had received information from the intelligence Unit of the Los Angeles PD, indicating that Sam Giancana and Anthony Accardo were scheduled to attend an "Appalachian type meeting" in the Los Angeles area in the near future. This meeting is to be attended by leaders of organized crime in the US.

FEDERAL BUREAU OF INVESTIGATION

REPORTING OFFICE	OFFICE OF ORIGIN	DATE	INVESTIGATIVE PERIOD
CHICAGO	CHICAGO	1966	December 16, 1966

TITLE OF CASE	REPORT MADE BY	TYPED BY
		dkc
SAMUEL M. GIANCANA, aka	**CHARACTER OF CASE** FBI Headquarters File 92-3171-1922 Top Hoodlum Program – Anti Racketeering. Daily Summary	

CG informant advised he attended wake and funeral of Joseph Imburgio Bulger; Chicago hoodlum attorney very closely associated all leaders in Chicago hoodlum group for past three decades. Stated that although all other leaders of organized crime here attended wake and or funeral, Giancana did not attend. It appears Gincana continues to be in Mexico or South America and undoughtedly continues to meet with Phyllis McGuire there.

Chapter 11

FEDERAL BUREAU OF INVESTIGATION

REPORTING OFFICE	OFFICE OF ORIGIN	DATE	INVESTIGATIVE PERIOD
CHICAGO	CHICAGO	1967	January 12, 1967

TITLE OF CASE	REPORT MADE BY	TYPED BY
		dkc

SAMUEL M. GIANCANA, aka

CHARACTER OF CASE

FBI Headquarters File 92-3171-1938
Top Hoodlum Program – Anti Racketeering. Daily Summary

Info developed that Charles Giancana, aka, "Chuck Kane," brother of Sam Giancana, within past year has become involved as principle in building projects and in a construction company in general area of Rosemont, Illinois. Charles Giancana is completing a shopping plaza in Rosemont called Rosemont Plaza which includes some business establishments. It has also been learned that Rocco Potenzo has been given choice location in Rosemont Plaza for his liquor store, Plaza Liquors which is reportedly fronted for Potenzo by one Al Doty. Charles Giancana is also building an apartment building in Rosemont called River Rose Apartments and has or had an interest in a construction company, name of which not known at this time. Charles Giancana owns and is selling seven houses on Astelle Street in Rosemont for $23,000 each.

No info developed indicating Charles Giancana is a member of Chicago hoodlum group or that Charles Giancana ever independently acquired wealth which obviously would be necessary to finance above projects. It appears logical that source of Charles Giancana's new financial status is his brother, Sam Giancana. Appears Sam Giancana, who is indefinitely out of the country, is using his brother to invest in legitimate companies as front for him. Chicago opening an investigation of Charles Giancana to ascertain complete background of his transactions, source of his financing, scope of his operations, profits obtained and identity of associates.

FEDERAL BUREAU OF INVESTIGATION

REPORTING OFFICE	OFFICE OF ORIGIN	DATE	INVESTIGATIVE PERIOD
CHICAGO	CHICAGO	1967	January 13, 1967

TITLE OF CASE	REPORT MADE BY	TYPED BY
		dkc

SAMUEL M. GIANCANA, aka

CHARACTER OF CASE

FBI Headquarters File 92-3171-1939
Top Hoodlum Program – Anti Racketeering. Daily Summary

CG informant advised he has learned Richard Cain, former chief investigator, Cook County Sheriff's office, telephonically contacted Richard B. Ogilvie, his former employer now president, Cook County Board of Commissioners, and advised he had just returned to Chicago from lengthy stay in San Francisco and stated he wanted to meet with him on very important matter. When Ogilvie refused to meet with Cain, Cain told him it was important for Republican Party that John Waner, Republican candidate for mayor, Chicago, be put in touch with Cain since Cain has important info which Warner can use to defeat Mayor Richard J. Daley. Cain wanted to trade the info for a "favor."

Since it is known Cain has just returned from stay with Sam Giancana in Mexico, it is possible he is carrying message about bride to be used by Warner for campaign purposes or does in fact have info given him by Giancana which can be used against Daley. In any event, it would definitely appear Cain is performing task for Chicago hoodlum group.

Attention in this regard directed to info provided by confidential source that Chicago group through intermediary offered campaign funds to Benjamin Adamowski when he ran for mayor against Daley. Also noted that since it is known Cain recently associating with Peter Granata, tool of Chicago group in Illinois legislature, he may be used in political area by Chicago group.

Anthony G. Girolami finds him self in poor position in that his protege, Angelo Provenzan, present Alderman of 28th Ward, has refused to run for re-election. Chicago hoodlum group instrumental in having Joseph Jambrone file not that aldermanic office. Jambrone's connections with Chicago group so well known in 28th Ward no candidate could be found to run against him except three Negroes. As result, Jambrone definite favorite to win. Girolami feels this will be blow against law enforcement in view of Jambrone's obvious close association with such highly placed Chicago hoodlums as Jack Cerone, Joseph Gagliano and William Messino. On other hand, Girolami will lose face with Mayor Daley and lose power in ward if Negro candidate should beat Jambrone. Girolami recourse is to "drag feet" while pretending to assist Jambrone's campaign.

FEDERAL BUREAU OF INVESTIGATION

REPORTING OFFICE	OFFICE OF ORIGIN	DATE	INVESTIGATIVE PERIOD	
CHICAGO	CHICAGO	1967	January 19, 1967	
TITLE OF CASE		REPORT MADE BY		TYPED BY
				dkc
SAMUEL M. GIANCANA, aka		CHARACTER OF CASE		
		FBI Headquarters File Number 92-3171-1946 Top Hoodlum Program – Anti Racketeering. Daily Summary		

CG informant advised he recently returned from visit to Rocco Pranno who is presently confined at Federal Penitentiary, Terre Haute, Indiana. Pranno, who was confined with Giancana in Cook County jail when Gincana released told informant Giancana completely disgusted with his circumstances at time of release. Pranno related Giancana's morale completely shattered, and Giancana told him he intended to completely disassociate himself from organized crime and "Go to an island and relax for the rest of his life." Pranno stated Giancana convinced government would call him back before FGJ and continue intensive efforts to reconfine him. Pranno told informant Giancana felt government would always focused primary investigation efforts on leader organized crime and Giancana did not desire to spend any more time in confinement. Giancana made obscene comments about his associates and stated he intended to "Leave everything behind. They can have everything I got."

Pranno informed informant that felling is Giancana may have "flipped" over to side of FBI upon his release since Giancana has not been subpoenaed back before FGJ or in any other way subjected to any type of prospective action. Pranno feels Giancana must have made some type of "deal" with government in return for this consideration.

Pranno told the informant that when Giancana left the County Jail, he gave Pranno his watch and ring.

FEDERAL BUREAU OF INVESTIGATION

REPORTING OFFICE	OFFICE OF ORIGIN	DATE	INVESTIGATIVE PERIOD	
CHICAGO	CHICAGO	1967	January 26, 1967	
TITLE OF CASE		REPORT MADE BY		TYPED BY
		SA William F. Roemer, Jr.		dkc
SAMUEL M. GIANCANA, aka		CHARACTER OF CASE		
		FBI Headquarters File number 92-3171-1954, Top Hoodlum Program – Anti Racketeering		

Synopsis:

Giancana not observed at his residence or elsewhere in Chicago area during past three months. Giancana allegedly has disassociated himself from leadership position in organized crime, Chicago area. Giancana observed in Mexico City, Mexico on 12/66 and in San Juan, Puerto Rico, during January, 1967. Also believed to have been in other Mexican cities and possibly in Buenos Aires, Argentina during 12/66 and 1/67, Giancana in contact with Phyllis McGuire in Mexico City and San Juan.

Disassociation of Sam Giancana from Leadership in Chicago

In late December, 1966, CG T-3 advised that it was Sam Battaglia who has assumed the leadership position given up by Giancana. This informant advised that several of the top leaders of organized crime as of late December, 1966 had become disgusted with the operation of organized crime under the leadership of Battaglia and were openly expressing their deep dissatisfaction with the leadership provided by Battaglia. These leaders included John "Jackie" Cerone and Charles English.

CG T-3 advised that as of late December, 1966 Giancana had not been in the Chicago area for many months and that it is well known to the members of the Outfit that Giancana had intended to give up his US citizenship and become a permanent citizen of Mexico.

CG T-2 advised that he had a conversation with one of the closes associates of Giancana during the middle of December, 1966. During this conversation the informant was told that Giancana was then in Mexico where he had taken over a farm and where he was spending all of his time. This informant also stated that he was told that Giancana and Phyllis McGuire might be married during the Christmas season of 1966.

CG T-8 advised that Gincana arrived in San Juan on 1/13/67 and was staying at the Sheraton Hotel with Phyllis McGuire who is appearing at the Sheraton Hotel in San Juan for an engagement.

458

FEDERAL BUREAU OF INVESTIGATION

REPORTING OFFICE	OFFICE OF ORIGIN	DATE	INVESTIGATIVE PERIOD
CHICAGO	CHICAGO	1967	February 9, 1967

TITLE OF CASE	REPORT MADE BY	TYPED BY
		dkc
SAMUEL M. GIANCANA, aka	**CHARACTER OF CASE** FBI Headquarters File Number 92-3171 Top Hoodlum Program – Anti Racketeering. Daily Summary	

Extensive financial interest if Charles Giancana in Rosemont, Illinois. Chicago Tribune carries front page article by Robert Wiedrich entitled, "Gangsters build own community in vicinity of O'Hare." Article states "Crime syndicate gangsters have established a three million dollar complex of thirty seven apartment buildings and shopping center near O'Hare Airport." Article disclosed that general manager this development is Charles Giancana, deposed operating boss of the crime syndicate who is now hiding in Mexico City.

Wiedrich reported that when he commenced an interview of Charles Giancana, Giancana accused him, "You got to be with the G, you know more about this place that any newspaper guy would." Giancana denied any of the money for the development came from his brother but instead from saving and loans company. He stated his corporation, Four G's Construction Company, Inc., put up fourteen thousand dollars for each unit which sold for seventy three thousand dollars in apartment buildings alone. Giancana refused to identify what his interest is in the three hundred thousand dollar Rosemont shopping plaza where Rocco Potenza has prime location for his "Plaza Liquor" store.

Wiedrich also interviewed Mayor Donald Stephens of Rosemont, who, while claiming he, "wished Giancana would get out of town" admitted he owned two of the seventy three thousand dollar units in Giancana's development.

FEDERAL BUREAU OF INVESTIGATION

REPORTING OFFICE	OFFICE OF ORIGIN	DATE	INVESTIGATIVE PERIOD
CHICAGO	CHICAGO	1967	February 15, 1967

TITLE OF CASE	REPORT MADE BY	TYPED BY
		dkc
SAMUEL M. GIANCANA, aka	**CHARACTER OF CASE** FBI Headquarters File 92-3171-1959 Top Hoodlum Program – Anti Racketeering. Daily Summary	

Information received from CG informant that Sam Giancana currently resides in a 15 room penthouse at Club Nacionale, Acapulco, Mexico, in which he reportedly has an interest. Suite described as including a secret elevator, $15,000 worth of paintings, staffed by a cook imported from Italy, a butler, two maids and several bodyguards.

Informant advised Giancana has been visited in Mexico by hoodlums Sam Battaglia, Sam English, his brother Chuck English, Gus Alex, Joe DiVarco, Lennie Patrick, Dave Yaras, Frank Sinatra and Dean Martin.

Informant also stated Giancana allegedly has many government officials in Acapulco paid off and operates almost as a dictator there.

FEDERAL BUREAU OF INVESTIGATION

REPORTING OFFICE	OFFICE OF ORIGIN	DATE	INVESTIGATIVE PERIOD
CHICAGO	CHICAGO	1967	February 20, 1967

TITLE OF CASE	REPORT MADE BY	TYPED BY
		dkc
SAMUEL M. GIANCANA, aka	**CHARACTER OF CASE** FBI Headquarters File Number 92-3171-1966 Top Hoodlum Program – Anti Racketeering. Daily Summary	

CG informant advised last week that Sam Giancana definitely in the Grand Bahamas, possibly Freeport, playing golf with John "Haircuts" Campanalli and Sam "Slicker Sam" Rosa. Informant also advised "Chi Chi" Rodriquez, prominent golf pro, also golfed with Campanali in Grand Bahamas.

Miami reported William Messino spotted in Miami with Jack Cerone and believed to meet with Giancana soon at Kings Bay Club.

FEDERAL BUREAU OF INVESTIGATION

REPORTING OFFICE	OFFICE OF ORIGIN	DATE	INVESTIGATIVE PERIOD
CHICAGO	CHICAGO	1967	March 4, 1967

TITLE OF CASE	REPORT MADE BY	TYPED BY
		dkc
SAMUEL M. GIANCANA, aka	**CHARACTER OF CASE** FBI Headquarters File Number 92-3171 Top Hoodlum Program – Anti Racketeering. Daily Summary	

For info to Bureau an oven exploded in the kitchen of the Villa Venice in Northfield which caused extensive fire damage to the super club. One employee injured and dining room was a total lost. No indication of arson at this time. The Villa Venice has long been called a fire trap by local fire marshal. Fire insurance for Villa Venice handled by Anco Insurance Company which is controlled by John D'Arco. It is believed that Giancana will be amply reimbursed by Anco Insurance Company for fire loss and will take advantage of settlement to dispose of his holdings in Villa Venice.

FEDERAL BUREAU OF INVESTIGATION

REPORTING OFFICE	OFFICE OF ORIGIN	DATE	INVESTIGATIVE PERIOD	
CHICAGO	CHICAGO	1967	March 9, 1967	
TITLE OF CASE		REPORT MADE BY		TYPED BY
				dkc
SAMUEL M. GIANCANA, aka		CHARACTER OF CASE		
		FBI Headquarters File Number 92-3171 Top Hoodlum Program – Anti Racketeering. Daily Summary		

Captain William Duffy, Director, Intelligence unit, Chicago PD, advised he suspects LT. Peter Henry Hutley is close associate and possibly related to John D'Arco by marriage. As bureau aware D'Arco was completely controlled by Sam Giancana and his associates. Duffy advised LT. Nutley presently on furlough and has requested extension of furlough to travel to Padova, Italy, "to settle an estate." Duffy suspects travel is for purpose of organized crime. Passport agency states reason given by Nutley for passport was to "Purchase brooms from a factory in Padova, Italy." In view of discrepancy story given to Chicago PD with that passport agency, Captain Duff's suspicions may be justified.

Chicago files contain info on one Peter Nutley who attended the wedding of Mike Briatta in 1962. Mike Briatta is an associate of Gus Alex and is related to D'Arco by marriage.

FEDERAL BUREAU OF INVESTIGATION

REPORTING OFFICE	OFFICE OF ORIGIN	DATE	INVESTIGATIVE PERIOD	
CHICAGO	CHICAGO	1967	April 4, 1967	
TITLE OF CASE		REPORT MADE BY		TYPED BY
				dkc
SAMUEL M. GIANCANA, aka		CHARACTER OF CASE		
		FBI Headquarters File Number 92-3171 Top Hoodlum Program – Anti Racketeering. Daily Summary		

Possible visit of Sam Giancana to new residence of Anthony Tisci in Tucson area. Records of postal authorities Chicago reflect that when Tisci moved from Chicago he gave forwarding address of 2300 North 74th Court, Elmwood Park, Illinois. Investigation determined this is the residence of the Tisci family. Postal carrier advised mail for the Tisci family is being delivered there.

As bureau and Phoenix aware, following Chicago hoodlums known to have residences in Tucson, area: Sam English, Joseph Corngold, Nick Palermo, Joseph Amato, and Charles English.

FEDERAL BUREAU OF INVESTIGATION

REPORTING OFFICE	OFFICE OF ORIGIN	DATE	INVESTIGATIVE PERIOD
CHICAGO	CHICAGO	1967	April 25, 1967

TITLE OF CASE	REPORT MADE BY		TYPED BY
			dkc
SAMUEL M. GIANCANA, aka	**CHARACTER OF CASE** FBI Headquarters File 92-3171-1973 Top Hoodlum Program – Anti Racketeering. Daily Summary		

Informant advised Sam Giancana and Frank Sinatra reportedly scheduled to be in NYC on the 27th. Insofar as Chicago able to ascertain, Giancana has not been observed in Chicago and has been in Mexico and Caribbean countries since then.

Los Angeles and Las Vegas request to attempt to determine where abouts of Sinatra, as Giancana may be traveling with him. New York will attempt to subpoena Giancana for appearance before FGJ there when he arrives in NYC.

FEDERAL BUREAU OF INVESTIGATION

REPORTING OFFICE	OFFICE OF ORIGIN	DATE	INVESTIGATIVE PERIOD
CHICAGO	CHICAGO	1967	May 4, 1967

TITLE OF CASE	REPORT MADE BY		TYPED BY
			dkc
SAMUEL M. GIANCANA, aka	**CHARACTER OF CASE** FBI Headquarters File Number 92-3171-2006 Top Hoodlum Program – Anti Racketeering. Daily Summary		

Informant advised that he recently returned from European tour with his wife and wife of Felix Alderisio. He mentioned to Alderisio upon return that he and Alderisio's wife had enjoyed their visit, especially to Majorca, on island of Palma, off coast of Spain. At this point Alderisio expressed great interest and told informant he should have advised Alderisio of his intention to go with Alderisio's wife to Majorca because "That's where Sam is," reference to Giancana. Alderisio told informant that has he known he would have had Giancana entertain informant and Alderisio's wife.

FEDERAL BUREAU OF INVESTIGATION

REPORTING OFFICE	OFFICE OF ORIGIN	DATE	INVESTIGATIVE PERIOD	
CHICAGO	CHICAGO	1967	May 18, 1967	
TITLE OF CASE		**REPORT MADE BY**		**TYPED BY**
		William F. Roemer, Jr.		dkc
SAMUEL M. GIANCANA, aka		**CHARACTER OF CASE**		
		FBI Headquarters File number 92-3171-2011 Top Hoodlum Program – Anti Racketeering		

Associates of Sam Giancana

Anthony Tisci

CG T-2 advised that Anthony Tisci sold his home at 1834 South Austin, Chicago, and has moved to Arizona where he is located in the Tucson area near the Rimrock Ranch, owned by Charles and Sam English, associates of Giancana. This informant has learned that Giancana intends to visit with the Tisci family in near future.

On May 4, 1967, the above information was verified in that it was determined that Tisci and his wife Bonnie Lou, and their two sons and a family butler are presently residing at 4545 North Camino Escuela, Tucson, Arizona foothills.

Richard Cain

On March 6, 1967, CG T-3 and T-4 advised that Richard Cain was observed at the Mexico City Airport, where he was questioned by Mexican Immigration Agents. Cain informed Agents he was waiting for his wife whom he identified as Harriette Blake Cain. She arrived by air from Chicago and was reportedly to appear as a singer on the local television program of one Raul Astor.

Travel of Sam Giancana

CG T-5 advised in the middle of April, 1967 that recently he heard the statement from either Fiore "Fifi" Buccieri or from Joseph Ferriola, that Sam Giancana was then "having a big time in Mexico."

Miscellaneous

On April 18, 1967, CG T-8 advised that the only engagements of which he is presently aware for the McGuire Sisters, are an appearance on the Ed Sullivan Show, on April 23, 1967, in New York City and an appearance at fair in Calgary, Alberta, Canada, July 6 through 15, 1967. Source stated that Calgary appearance is presently scheduled to be the last engagement for the McGuire Sisters as a group. Source states that present plans are for the McGuire Sisters to break-up as a team in September, 1967. Phyllis McGuire, will at that time, continue her career as a single.

Chicago PD advised on April 25, 1967, that Geraldine Sonne, sister of Jack Cerone, died in Chicago. Captain William Duffy advised that the wake and funeral was converted by the Chicago PD, who advised numerous leaders and prominent members of organized crime in the Chicago area in attendance including many of Giancana's close associates. Giancana was not observed at wake or funeral.

CG T-9 advised in late April, 1967, that he learned that Sam Giancana and his associate, entertainer Frank Sinatra, would be in New York City for the purpose of meeting with one Herbert Schwartzman to discuss an invention of Schwartzman which he desired to put on the market. It was the information of this informant that Schwartzman desired financing from Giancana and Sinatra.

CG T-3 advised on July 20, 1967, that at that time Frank Sinatra was entertaining in Miami and was living at the Fontainebleau Hotel in Miami. This informant, who knows Giancana on sight, advised that he observed Sinatra during the nightly show at the Fontainebleau and while a guest at the hotel and while engaged in the filming of a movie to be known as "Tony Rome" and that at no time did he observe Giancana in the presence of Sinatra or elsewhere.

On April 27, 1967, Herbert Schartzman was contacted by agents of the New York Office. He claimed to own 65 per cent of an electric stimulation process which would be announced to the public on April 28, 1967 at the Hotel Plaza in New York City. During discussion he volunteered that three days prior to April 27, 1967 he was with Frank Sinatra in Miami and that Sinatra was interested in acquiring Mexican rights to this machine. Schwartzman denied any knowledge of any hoodlum interest in his product. Investigation by Agents of the New York Office on April 28, 1967, at the Hotel Plaza in New York City during the public release of the above product did not determine that either Frank Sinatra or Sam Giancana appeared.

(Chicago Tribune Article attached here, May 7, 1967.)

FEDERAL BUREAU OF INVESTIGATION

REPORTING OFFICE	OFFICE OF ORIGIN	DATE	INVESTIGATIVE PERIOD	
CHICAGO	CHICAGO	1967	May 23, 1967	
TITLE OF CASE		REPORT MADE BY		TYPED BY
				dkc
SAMUEL M. GIANCANA, aka		CHARACTER OF CASE		
		FBI Headquarters File 92-3171-2013 Top Hoodlum Program – Anti Racketeering. Daily Summary		

Former close associate of Giancana's advised he was contacted by one of the daughters of Sam Giancana two weeks ago. During contact daughter told informant she has not see Giancana since his release from jail and that Giancana had not been home since that time. Stated she is unaware of his whereabouts and that she has received only one phone call from him since his release, that being a long distance call.

Daughter also advised that Francine, another daughter, is engaged and scheduled to be married in August and assumes Giancana will be present for his daughter's wedding.

Informant, who is close to other associates of Giancana, such as Anthony Accardo, Charles English and Paul DeLucia, stated to his knowledge Giancana has not returned to Chicago area since his release and remains in Latin America. Informant stated he would be surprised, knowing that Bonnie Lou, Giancana's daughter married to Anthony Tisci, is closest member of family to Giancana, if she and Tisci were not in contact with Giancana. Informant, who is aware that Tisci's now live in Arizona, feels that it is likely Giancana will visit there.

FEDERAL BUREAU OF INVESTIGATION

REPORTING OFFICE	OFFICE OF ORIGIN	DATE	INVESTIGATIVE PERIOD	
CHICAGO	CHICAGO	1967	June 15, 1967	
TITLE OF CASE		REPORT MADE BY		TYPED BY
				dkc
SAMUEL M. GIANCANA, aka		CHARACTER OF CASE		
		FBI Headquarters File Number 92-3171 Top Hoodlum Program – Anti Racketeering. Daily Summary		

Coverage activities Phyllis McGuire while in Chicago continues through source William Goldbaum, hairdresser for Giancana family, and physical observations. At no time has it been determined she has met with Giancana.

Source advised he went to Giancana residence early evening of June 14, last. Giancana's daughter, Francine, and relatives Rose Flood and Marie Perno had prepared Italian dinner for McGuire with source then delivered to McGuire SP Palmer house. Source stated no sign of Giancana at residence and no indication received through family he is in area. Stated McGuire stayed in hotel throughout day rehearsing and preparing cosmetically.

At first performance on June 14, last, approximately eight members of Giancana family, including above, observed in audience. Mike Davis, according to source is current romantic interest of McGuire, and Murray Kane, personal manager of McGuire, also present. No Chicago hoodlums observed except Charles Lucania, associate of Chicago hoodlums. Although Phoenix has advised Anthony Tisci in Chicago, he and wife, Giancana's daughter Bonnie Lou were not present with Giancana family at McGuire performance.

Contact with source following performance determined that McGuire intended to spend time with Davis following performance and she was not observed leaving hotel. Source feels strongly that Davis would not be in Chicago with her if she intended to meet Giancana here and repeated his previous opinion Chicago is last place in the world Giancana will appear.

Although discreet coverage of McGuire will continue, it does not appear likely she will meet Giancana during her stay here.

FEDERAL BUREAU OF INVESTIGATION

REPORTING OFFICE	OFFICE OF ORIGIN	DATE	INVESTIGATIVE PERIOD	
CHICAGO	CHICAGO	1967	June 19, 1967	
TITLE OF CASE		REPORT MADE BY		TYPED BY
				dkc
SAMUEL M. GIANCANA, aka		CHARACTER OF CASE		
		FBI Headquarters File Number 92-3171 Top Hoodlum Program – Anti Racketeering. Daily Summary		

Efforts made to contact Phyllis McGuire in line with objectives. McGuire would not accept house calls, so contact made with her manager, Murray Kane. He agreed to contact her with request for interview by agents and he agreed to re-contact agents. When Kane had not re-contacted Chicago office, re-contact was made with him. He stated he had not been able to contact Miss McGuire yet and promised to re-contact Chicago within hour. When re-contacted not made, Chicago attempted on several occasions to re-contact Kane without result. For these reasons, McGuire left Chicago June 17, without being interviewed.

FEDERAL BUREAU OF INVESTIGATION

REPORTING OFFICE	OFFICE OF ORIGIN	DATE	INVESTIGATIVE PERIOD	
CHICAGO	CHICAGO	1967	June 22, 1967	
TITLE OF CASE		REPORT MADE BY		TYPED BY
				dkc
SAMUEL M. GIANCANA, aka		CHARACTER OF CASE		
		FBI Headquarters File Number 92-3171-2047 Top Hoodlum Program – Anti Racketeering. Daily Summary		

Wake and funeral held for the mother of Anthony Accardo, leader of the Chicago group. Chicago source and officers, Chicago PD, who attended wake advised wake with two noteworthy exceptions. These were Sam Giancana, who has not been known to be in Chicago area since just after his release from jail, and Paul Ricca, whose trial for perjury scheduled to commence in fall and who is attempting to be most circumspect with open association of Chicago hoodlums.

FEDERAL BUREAU OF INVESTIGATION

REPORTING OFFICE	OFFICE OF ORIGIN	DATE	INVESTIGATIVE PERIOD	
CHICAGO	CHICAGO	1967	July, 1967	
TITLE OF CASE		REPORT MADE BY		TYPED BY
		William F. Roemer, Jr.		dkc
SAMUEL M. GIANCANA, aka		CHARACTER OF CASE		
		FBI Headquarters File number 92-3171, Top Hoodlum Program – Anti Racketeering		

CG T-1 advised that as of early June, 1967, Giancana continued to travel in and out of Mexico. He stated that Joe Esposito, also known as Joe Esty, a resident of San Diego, California, and a former Chicagoan who is the son of "Diamond Joe" Esposito, a hoodlum leader in the 1920's and a Chicago labor racketeer, is the contact man for Giancana in that he reportedly makes connections for Giancana in Mexico where Esposito has numerous highly placed contracts. It is noted that Esposito, age 50, resides in San Diego at the present time, moving there during 1955 after he was caught stealing as an employee of the Public Administrator of the State of Illinois and discharged. Esposito is known to be any associate of Giancana and of Frank LaPorte, another leader of organized crime in Chicago, who spends considerable time in California.

CG T-14 advised that Richard Cain stated that the FBI has "destroyed Giancana and the Outfit," a reference by Cain to organized crime in Chicago. Cain told CG T-14 that the FBI in Chicago has "wiped out" gambling and vice to the point where it is no longer lucrative or sufficient to support "The Outfit." And that "The Outfit" presently is nonexistent. Cain stated that since there is now so much "aggravation" attached to being a leader of organized crime, all top leaders have given up their position and since they are all "millionaires" anyway, have decided to relax and enjoy their wealth without becoming involved with the FBI.

CG T-15 advised as approximately the same period of time that Gus Alex, a leader of organized crime has the responsibility for maintaining contact with public officials and obtaining favorable treatment for members of organized crime, in mid-May, 1967, expressed great interest in insuring that Richard Scalzetti Cain was given the best legal representation which could be obtained in Chicago when he is retried for perjury before the Cook County Grand Jury. It is noted that Cain was convicted of this perjury but that his conviction was reversed by the Illinois Supreme Court. It is expected that he will be retried by the Cook County States Attorneys Office in the fall of 1967.

CG T-5 advised that Tony Accardo and Paul De Lucia "Ricca" are currently in command of the organized criminal element in the Chicago area.

CG T-6 advised that he has been informed by a top leader of organized crime in Miami who is in a position to know, that Tony Accardo has been made boss of the Chicago "Family" of the La Costra Nostra, replacing Sam Giancana.

Interview of Roma Paige

It is noted that Sam Giancana had an intimate relationship with Roma Paige prior to the romantic interest which Giancana developed with entertainer Phyllis McGuire. During the interview of Paige she explained the nature of her relationship with Giancana. She is employed as a model in New York City and was introduced to Giancana during the time she was in Chicago, engaged in theatrical work. She advised this was about ten years ago and she associated with Giancana for a year. Paige stated she left Giancana of her own volition and maintained that she did so because she had nothing to gain by maintaining such a relationship.

It should be noted in the interview she referred to one Tony Dale. CG T-13 has identified Dale as being Anthony Agenellino, a leader of organized crime in New Jersey who is allied with Anthony "Little Pussy" Russo, the leader of organized crime in the New Jersey shore area.

FEDERAL BUREAU OF INVESTIGATION

REPORTING OFFICE	OFFICE OF ORIGIN	DATE	INVESTIGATIVE PERIOD
CHICAGO	CHICAGO	1967	August 18, 1967

TITLE OF CASE	REPORT MADE BY	TYPED BY
		dkc

	CHARACTER OF CASE
SAMUEL M. GIANCANA, aka	FBI Headquarters File Number 92-3171 Top Hoodlum Program – Anti Racketeering. Daily Summary

CG informant advised according to Joseph Leonardi, first cousin of Giancana, that Sam Giancana still in Mexico where he has been ordered by other leaders of the Chicago group to remain for at least a year or two. Although informant unable to advise of reasons for this order, it appears reason would be in line with info provided by Richard Cain that leadership here fells group better off with Giancana away from Chicago due to what they feel is personal animosity he has caused toward him on part of FBI.

Information recently disclosed that Anthony Accardo and Jack Cerone have been almost daily companions of Paul DeLucia, aka Paul "The Waiter" Ricca. Observations of these meetings by Chicago agents indicates that Accardo and Cerone give Ricca considerable respect and deference and indicate he has greater authority at this time than Accardo and Cerone.

As Bureau aware, Ricca was top leader of the Chicago group prior to his incarceration for conviction in Hollywood extortion case in the mid 1940's and was succeeded as boss by Accardo and then Giancana. Also noted Miami informant has advised Ricca again Chicago representative on "The Commission." It would appear from above that Ricca has resumed top position in leadership of the Chicago group with Accardo assisting Ricca.

FEDERAL BUREAU OF INVESTIGATION

REPORTING OFFICE	OFFICE OF ORIGIN	DATE	INVESTIGATIVE PERIOD	
CHICAGO	CHICAGO	1967	September 6, 1967	
TITLE OF CASE		REPORT MADE BY		TYPED BY
				dkc
SAMUEL M. GIANCANA, aka		CHARACTER OF CASE		
		FBI Headquarters File Number 92-3171-2095 Top Hoodlum Program – Anti Racketeering. Daily Summary		

MM Informant advised that recent wave of bombings in Miami and Miami Beach were a result of "orders from Mooney of Chicago." The most recent of these bombings involved Miami TJT John Clarence Cook. On 8/22/67, a bomb exploded in the front of Cook's Miami residence which destroyed his 1967 Eldorado, his 18 foot runabout boat and the front of his residence. On 8/23/67 another bomb was successfully planted in the back of Cook's residence on his 26 foot cruiser, which bomb totally destroyed this craft.

MM advised that "Mooney" ordered these last two bombings against Cook and that Frank "Lefty" Rosenthal received the contract. Informant advised that the cause of dissatisfaction against Cook involved Cook's holding out on some $300,000 in rare coins which Cook had taken in a series of burglaries over the past several months.

Regarding other bombings, "Mooney" has ordered that all bookmakers in the Miami area be brought under the jurisdiction and control of Chicago and emphasized this authority with the bombing of recalcitrance. Among these were "Chappy" Rand, Irving "Mickey" Zion and Alphie Mart, all Miami Beach and Miami bookmakers and all victims of bombing attacks.

Informant said that these orders specifically excludes the Italian bookmakers and gamblers. Informant was asked if these orders emanated from Mooney personally and states he has no knowledge of Mooney's presence in Miami, either now or in recent past. Informant was asked if this information was contrary to the fact that Mooney has been replaced as boss of Chicago and replied that it was not, but merely indicates that the gambling action which is successfully operated in Miami as a result of these bombings will go to Mooney and or the Chicago family.

Informant advised that with regard to Cook, the contract is now to kill him. An unsuccessful attempt was made on 8/25/67 to shoot Cook and two shots were fired at him, both of which missed.

FEDERAL BUREAU OF INVESTIGATION

REPORTING OFFICE	OFFICE OF ORIGIN	DATE	INVESTIGATIVE PERIOD
CHICAGO	CHICAGO	1967	September 27, 1967

TITLE OF CASE	REPORT MADE BY	TYPED BY
		dkc
SAMUEL M. GIANCANA, aka	**CHARACTER OF CASE**	
	FBI Headquarters File 92-3171-2107 Top Hoodlum Program – Anti Racketeering. Daily Summary	

CG T-7, who has been a close associate of Giancana, advised that as of the middle of August, 1967, Giancana has completely divorced him self from the leadership of organized crime in the Chicago area. This informant advised that Giancana "has a piggy bank full," and needs no more money to live lavishly the rest of his life. He, therefore, wants no more part of the aggravation which attaches to leadership. This informant advised that Giancana now realizes that the biggest mistake of his life was attempting to enjoin the FBI from surveillances of him in 1963. The informant stated that Giancana fully realized he cannot win in the long run and that other top leaders in the Chicago area are convinced that the Chicago group is better off with him out of the picture due to their general belief that the FBI had developed a personal animosity against Giancana. Giancana fully believes that there is a subpoena outstanding against him as the first step towards reinstituting immunity proceedings and for this reason has not and will not return to the Chicago area.

The informant advised that the FBI has been primarily responsible for "destroying Chicago" as a money producer for the organized criminals in Chicago. He claims that the biggest producer of income in Chicago was casino-type gambling which catered to the "high rollers." Informant credited the FBI raids on such establishments as completely abolishing this income and stated that very little money is now coming in from bookmaking since most bettors are "two dollar punks and how much are you going to make from them?" This informant advised that the "Jet Age" is completely revolutionizing organized crime in Chicago. He said the "Jet Age" had now made it possible for "high rollers" who make huge profits possible for organized crime to fly to London, Las Vegas, South America and the Caribbean in short periods of time and do their gambling there with the added nicely that they are not subject to arrest there. This informant claims that the Chicago hoodlum group had realized the potential of progress in air travel and had "gotten in on the ground floor" with financial investments in those areas. In regards to London, this informant describes that country as "being where Chicago was in 1929," in so far as ability to cope with law and enforcement problems there.

FEDERAL BUREAU OF INVESTIGATION

REPORTING OFFICE	OFFICE OF ORIGIN	DATE	INVESTIGATIVE PERIOD	
CHICAGO	CHICAGO	1967	November 7, 1967	
TITLE OF CASE		REPORT MADE BY		TYPED BY
				dkc
SAMUEL M. GIANCANA, aka		CHARACTER OF CASE		
		FBI Headquarters File Number 92-3171		
		Top Hoodlum Program – Anti Racketeering.		
		Daily Summary		

As Bureau aware, Chicago division has been in continuous contact with Joseph D'Argento, major Chicago thief, who is confined in secluded jail in Chicago area after having requested removal from Leavenworth in fear of his life.

D'Argento was confined in Cook County Jail at same time as Giancana in 1965-66. He advised Warden Jack Johnson tries to run a good jail but allows himself to be dominated by influential inmates. Stated when Giancana there he has "everything" he wanted. Stated when Giancana paid to have as inmate under his influence, one (FNU) Ross, placed in bundle room so that whenever any associate of Giancana outside jail desired to bring packages they would be delivered to Giancana. In this matter Giancana enjoyed his favorite foods, liquor, money, etc.

D'Argento was told by Paul "Peanuts" Panczko, another major thief who was also confined in Cook County Jail at the same time, that Panczko and others were able to make arrangements to have sexual relations with female prisoners on Saturdays for about $25.

D'Argento was told by Chicago hoodlum leader Marshall Caifano, who was in jail part of time D'Argento was there, that he was able to perfect arrangements to have relations with his girl friend in Warden Johnson's private office.

D'Argento claims that Walter Makowski, deputy warden, is Warden Johnson's "bag man" in that he is intermediary between Johnson and inmates who pay for preferential treatment. He recalls that when he was "barn boss," the unofficial representative of inmates in his jail tier, he was shaken down by Johnson and Makowski for $50.

Above info furnished to Joseph Woods, Cook County Sheriff on highly confidential basis. Woods is presently taking steps to solidify his ultimate action of Johnson's removal.

FEDERAL BUREAU OF INVESTIGATION

REPORTING OFFICE	OFFICE OF ORIGIN	DATE	INVESTIGATIVE PERIOD	
CHICAGO	CHICAGO	1967	November 22, 1967	
TITLE OF CASE		**REPORT MADE BY**		**TYPED BY**
SAMUEL M. GIANCANA, aka		William F. Roemer, Jr.		dkc
		CHARACTER OF CASE		
		FBI Headquarters File number 92-3171-2120, Top Hoodlum Program – Anti Racketeering		

Marriage of Giancana's youngest daughter, Francine, August 16, 1967

Monsignor Wagener and Reverand LeVoy, pastor and assistant, St. Bernardine Church, Oak Park, Illinois, the parish to which the Giancana family belonged, advised SA William Roemer, Jr., October 20, 1967, that several months before, Francine Giancana, the youngest daughter of Sam Giancana, made arrangements at the parish to be married on November 18, 1967. Monsignor Wagener and Father LeVoy advised that the wedding was to be highly elaborate, attended by hundreds, with a lavish reception thereafter. However, in mid-summer, 1967, Francine Giancana informed the priests that her father would be unable to attend the wedding and she, therefore, requested that since her circumstances dictated, that she be married as secretly as possible, that she be dispensed with hav- ing the bans published and that the marriage be performed as quietly as possible on a week day morning with only a handful of the members of her immediate family present. The priests advised that her wishes were granted and she was married August 16, 1967, a Wednesday, at 10:30 a.m. with just two witnesses and several members of the immediate family present. Father LeVoy performed the ceremony which was attended by Monsignor Wagener. Although Father LeVoy advised that he was not acquainted with Sam Giancana, Monsignor Wagener, who sat in the rear of the church during the ceremony, advised that he is well acquainted with Giancana, and he advised that Giancana definitely did not at- tend the ceremony. Francine Giancana was married to Jerome DePalma.

Associates of Giancana

Jerome DePalma

Francine Giancana married Jerome DePalma in St. Bernadine Church in Oak Park. Records on Depalma state that he was baptized in Our Lady of Lourdes Church in Chicago on August 3, 1944, the son of Anthony and Elizabeth DePalma. He has a brother named Arthur DePalma who was his witness at his marriage.

Contact was made by SA William Roemer, at 2439 South Millard on November 1, 1967. Mrs. Arthur DePalma, the sister-in-law of Jerome, advised that Jerome DePalma no longer resided at that address. She advised that he was employed by the U.S. Gymsum Company, in Chicago.

Contact was made with DePalma on November 1, 1967. It was requested that he make himself available for an interview. However, DePalma immediately refused to submit to an interview and referred SA Roemer to his attorney, whom he identified as Anthony V. Champagne, Sam Giancana's associate.

On November 2, 1967, Harry Judd, Personnel Director, U.S. Gypsum Company, Chicago, advised that DePalma commenced employment as an accountant at the U. S. Gypsum Company, on April 11, 1967, following his graduation from the University of Illinois, located at Navy Pier, Chicago, in 1967. He currently is assigned to the Cost Reporting Department of U.S. Gypsum. His salary is $615.00 a month. Depalma was born on July 26, 1944, and is 6' tall, 237 pounds, with black hair.

Bergit Clark

On September 27, 1967, the Los Angeles Office of the FBI telephonically advised that an armed robbery occurred at the Lakin Et Cie Company, Los Angeles in March 1965 which $467,107.25 was taken in jewelry. In September 1967, one of the rings from the robbery valued at $10,000 was turned in to be fixed by Bergit Clark. Bergit Clark was interviewed by SA Robert Baker in September 1967 about the stolen ring. She advised she is the office manager of the Central Envelope and Lithograph Company in Forest Park. She confirmed that she had recently ordered repairs for the ring. She advised that she had received the ring as a gift, but refused to name the donor. During the conversation, she indicated that she had had "bad friends" and this ring incident will place her and her son in extreme danger. She stated she does not want the ring returned to her, now that she knows that it was stolen, and adamantly stated no actual knowledge of the original source of this ring.

Refusal of Mexican Government to Grant Immigrant Status to Giancana

Sam Giancana has made inquiry through Mexican attorney as to the possibility of obtaining permanent immigrant status in Mexico. In September, 1967, CG T-9 advised that he had been in contact with a high official of the Mexican Government concerning the matter. During this contact, the Mexican official advised that Giancana was almost given immigrant status in Mexico by the Mexican Government without knowing the full circumstances of Giancana's background. CG T-9 advised that this official was vehement that Giancana and his type of person would not be granted any status in Mexico and would be expelled from Mexico if found in national territory. It is noted that as of the time of the interview, Giancana had just left his residence in Cuernavaca, Mexico, and had not as of that time returned to Cuernavaca.

Current Position of Sam Giancana in Organized Crime

CG T-4 who is a leader of organized crime in a city other than Chicago advised that organized crime in Chicago is being run by Tony Accardo through John "Jackie" Cerone. This informant advised that Cerone is in daily contact with Accardo and that policy is made by these two leaders of organized crime. Giancana does not have a current voice in the affairs of organized crime in the Chicago area.

FEDERAL BUREAU OF INVESTIGATION

REPORTING OFFICE	OFFICE OF ORIGIN	DATE	INVESTIGATIVE PERIOD	
CHICAGO	CHICAGO	1967	1967	
TITLE OF CASE		REPORT MADE BY		TYPED BY
				dkc
SAMUEL M. GIANCANA, aka		**CHARACTER OF CASE**		
		FBI Headquarters File Number 92-10034-2 Phyllis McGuire, Top Hoodlum Program – Anti Racketeering. Tampa reporting		

The Chicago office has developed a source closely associated with Phyllis McGuire who has informed the Chicago Office that she has broken off her relationship with Giancana and intends to marry Mike Davis when the wife of Davis passes on. It is noted that Davis is married to a very wealthy owner of the Denver Post, Helen Bonfield, who is very elderly and ill. However, in view of the fact that as recently as 8 months ago McGuire was known to travel out of the country, obviously to meet with Giancana, it is believed that there is still an association which exists between them.

Mike Davis reported that Phyllis McGuire has often complained to him that she has been "harassed" by the FBI due to her former relationship with Giancana and that she thoroughly resents the fact that she has attracted the attention of the FBI. He states that in his opinion she would be very antagonistic if interviewed by FBI agents. Although he has told her that by coming involved with Giancana she was "inviting trouble" and that the FBI was merely doing its job by looking into the activities of Giancana and his associates.

Davis further related on a confidential basis that his wife, Helen Bonfils, is a very wealthy woman and is now over 80 years of age and in poor health and that she realizes that he needs the companionship of a younger woman. He stated that she knows all about his relationship with Phyllis McGuire and appears to have a personal affection for McGuire and has never raised any objection to Davis traveling all over the country with Phyllis McGuire.

Photographs of Phyllis McGuire and Edward Michael Davis from March 1967.

FBI surveillance photos of Sam Giancana's hill top mansion at Nubes 2, Cuernavaca, Morelos, Mexico from August 1967.

478

Chapter 12

FEDERAL BUREAU OF INVESTIGATION

REPORTING OFFICE	OFFICE OF ORIGIN	DATE	INVESTIGATIVE PERIOD
CHICAGO	CHICAGO	1968	January 26, 1968

TITLE OF CASE	REPORT MADE BY	TYPED BY
	William F. Roemer, Jr.	dkc
SAMUEL M. GIANCANA, aka	**CHARACTER OF CASE** FBI Headquarters File 92-3171-2127 Top Hoodlum Program – Anti Racketeering	

Synopsis:

Giancana has not resumed his residence in Chicago area. Investigation in vicinity of luxurious residence at Nubes Number 2, Cuernavaca, Mexico, indicates this residence currently unoccupied. Realtor who handles sale of this property advised that it currently belongs to the company Las Nubes, SA, which Jorge Castillo is Giancana's Attorney in Mexico. Inquiry has determined that Giancana has a bank account at the Banco de Mexico. However, no further information concerning this account yet available. Influential member organized crime, Chicago, advised informant that although Giancana continued to direct affairs of organized crime in Chicago, from Mexico, when he initially went to Mexico, in 1966, Giancana has disconnected himself from affairs of organized crime and leader of organized crime activity in residence of Phyllis McGuire, former girl-friend of Giancana, advised that Giancana has not been observed in McGuire home.

Current Whereabouts of Sam Giancana

CG T-2 advised that he understands that Giancana and Phyllis McGuire were living together in a house in Cuernavaca, Mexico, as of late November, 1967. Giancana using alias.

CG T-7, who visits frequently in Cuernavaca, advised on several occasions through December 13, 1967, that the house at Nubes Number 2, does not give appearance of being occupied. She noted that the house has an upstairs sun deck with shutters and porch furniture and that as of December, 1967, the shutters were down and the porch furniture has been taken in.

CG T-6 advised that he has heard from leaders of organized crime in Chicago that Richard Cain has purchased a large home in Columbia or Peru, and intended to move there shortly. This informant stated that he knows that Cain is very close to Sam Giancana and he therefore suspects that if Cain purchased a large home, that home is probably Giancana's. This informant stated Cain is a very vicious man who allegedly has killed four or five people.

FEDERAL BUREAU OF INVESTIGATION

REPORTING OFFICE	OFFICE OF ORIGIN	DATE	INVESTIGATIVE PERIOD
CHICAGO	CHICAGO	1968	February 17, 1968

TITLE OF CASE	REPORT MADE BY	TYPED BY
		dkc

SAMUEL M. GIANCANA, aka	**CHARACTER OF CASE**
	FBI Headquarters File Number 92-3171
	Top Hoodlum Program – Anti Racketeering.
	Daily Summary

Pat Marcy discussed the possibility that Victor Arrigo might be considered as new First Ward Alderman. Arrigo has clean image and is well respected in the Italian-American communities in Chicago.

Miami Division advised February 16, last that John D'Arco was observed in the Thunderbird Motel in Miami Beach meeting with Anthony Accardo. As Bureau aware, Accardo has shared active leadership in affairs of organized crime in Chicago with Jack Cerone and Paul Ricca, since departure of Sam Giancana from Chicago area. Circumstances of D'Arco meeting with Accardo reminiscent with D'Arco meeting with Giancana at Chez Lounge in December 1962, just prior to aldermanic election involving D'Arco. At that time it was Giancana's decision to depose D'Arco as candidate for alderman. This meeting indicates that Accardo at this time is possibly directing First Ward situation.

FEDERAL BUREAU OF INVESTIGATION

REPORTING OFFICE	OFFICE OF ORIGIN	DATE	INVESTIGATIVE PERIOD
CHICAGO	CHICAGO	1968	February 20, 1968

TITLE OF CASE	REPORT MADE BY	TYPED BY
		dkc

SAMUEL M. GIANCANA, aka	**CHARACTER OF CASE**
	FBI Headquarters File Number 92-3171
	Top Hoodlum Program – Anti Racketeering.
	Daily Summary

Resignation of Donald Parrillo Alderman, First Ward, Chicago. After Mayor Richard J. Daley advised press on 2/19 last that he had not received any notice from Parrillo indicating he might resign, Parrillo held press conference 2/20 announcing his resignation. Parrillo advised he intends to move from First Ward residence to Barrington, Illinois. Again announced he resigned since his duties as alderman interfered with his banking business.

Art Petacque, crime reporter for the Chicago Sun Times, confidently advised that John D'Arco was recently overheard asking Judge Daniel Covelli whether Covelli's son would desire to be alderman. Judge Covelli was mentioned prominently as potential USDC Judge here who indicated he was aware his background would not enable him to pass investigation and Judge Alexander Napoli received appointment instead.

At conference Parrillo indicated that Victor Arrigo, Chicago Attorney and state representative was possible replacement. No info available indicating Arrigo association with organized crime here.

FEDERAL BUREAU OF INVESTIGATION

REPORTING OFFICE	OFFICE OF ORIGIN	DATE	INVESTIGATIVE PERIOD	
CHICAGO	CHICAGO	1968	March 19, 1968	
TITLE OF CASE		REPORT MADE BY		TYPED BY
		William F. Roemer, Jr		dkc
SAMUEL M. GIANCANA, aka		CHARACTER OF CASE		
		FBI Headquarters File number 92-3171-2135 Top Hoodlum Program – Anti Racketeering		

Current Whereabouts of Sam Giancana

CG T-2 advised that information was received from the manager of a golf course in Cuernavaca, Mexico, where Giancana has been in the habit of playing golf prior to the fall of 1967, that as of January 7, 1968, Giancana has returned to the golf club.

On January 23, 1968, CG T-3 advised that inquiry in Cuernavaca tended to confirm that Giancana was back in his residence at Nuves 2, Rancho Telela, Cuernavaca, Mexico.

CG T-3 advised that working in this vicinity advised that the house is presently being occupied by a person other than the servant, presumably by the owner who answers Giancana's description. CG T-3 advised that the person resembling Giancana rarely leaves the premises but is frequently visited by his attorney, Castillo, who is also the administrator of the property. Aside from trips to town, the person resembling Giancana occasionally goes to the Club de Cuernavaca, usually on Wednesdays or Thursdays.

FEDERAL BUREAU OF INVESTIGATION

REPORTING OFFICE	OFFICE OF ORIGIN	DATE	INVESTIGATIVE PERIOD	
CHICAGO	CHICAGO	1968	May 3, 1968	
TITLE OF CASE		REPORT MADE BY		TYPED BY
				dkc
SAMUEL M. GIANCANA, aka		CHARACTER OF CASE		
		FBI Headquarters File Number 92-3171 Top Hoodlum Program – Anti Racketeering. Daily Summary		

Giannotti's Restaurant and Cocktail Lounge, formerly the Armory Lounge is now owned by Joseph Aiuppa and not Sam Giancana. Interview of Giannotti by Chicago Division concerning association with Aiuppa reveled Giannotti has no lease or other interest in premises. Giannotti advised Aiuppa would not give lease and about six months after going into business there, Aiuppa raised rent from $250 a month to $350 a month, which is mailed to his residence. Failure to have lease is violation of beneficial interest provision of Liquor Control Act.

Hearings will be held and plans to have subpoenas issued to Giannotti, Joseph Aiuppa, his brothers Sam Aiuppa and James Aiuppa who operate Country Investments Company, prior landlord of Giannotti's and possibly hoodlums Ralph Pierce and William Aloisio who have been known to frequent lounge.

FEDERAL BUREAU OF INVESTIGATION

REPORTING OFFICE	OFFICE OF ORIGIN	DATE	INVESTIGATIVE PERIOD	
CHICAGO	CHICAGO	1968	June 12, 1968	
TITLE OF CASE		REPORT MADE BY		TYPED BY
				dkc
SAMUEL M. GIANCANA, aka		CHARACTER OF CASE		
		FBI Headquarters File Number 92-3171 Top Hoodlum Program – Anti Racketeering. Daily Summary		

Miami advised Giancana identified using aliases Mickey Mancuso and John Williams at gambling casinos in Freeport, Bahamas. Giancana first known to use the alias of Marcuso in 1957 when he, Anthony Accardo, and Paul DeLucia flew to Los Angeles where they were met by Anthony Pinelli and Frank Ferraro.

FEDERAL BUREAU OF INVESTIGATION

REPORTING OFFICE	OFFICE OF ORIGIN	DATE	INVESTIGATIVE PERIOD
CHICAGO	CHICAGO	1968	September 23, 1968

TITLE OF CASE	REPORT MADE BY	TYPED BY
SAMUEL M. GIANCANA, aka	William F. Roemer, Jr.	dkc

CHARACTER OF CASE

FBI Headquarters File number 92-3171-2152
Top Hoodlum Program – Anti Racketeering

Synopsis:

Giancana has returned to residence he has been utilizing during past two years in Mexico. Further information developed indicating that when Giancana originally established this residence, he was accompanied by Richard Cain, using the name Richard Scaizetti. Giancana also using name Scaizetti and introduced Cain as his nephew. Permanent residence of Giancana in Oak Park, Illinois, now being utilized by Anthony Tisci and Tisci wife, Giancana's daughter Bonnie Lou. In July, residence of Tisci in Tucson, Arizona, was hit by two blasts from shotgun. However, it appears act was prank on part of two juveniles.

Miscellaneous

As reported above, the son-in-law of Sam Giancana, Anthony Phillip Tisci and Giancana's daughter are presently spending the summer at the residence of Giancana ay 1147 South Wenonah, Oak Park. It is noted that Tisci, a former resident of Chicago, left the Chicago area due to heart condition approximately a year and a half ago, and are now residing in Tucson, Arizona.

On July 4, 1968, two blasts for a shot gun were fired at the residence of Tisci in Tucson. One of the blasts went through the front window while the other one hit the rear window of a car owned by the care taker of Tisci's residence. Investigation by the Police Department determined that it was possible that these shotgun blasts were fired by two boys who were annoyed with the caretaker over a verbal alteration which occurred between them in the past and that the boys were reportedly intoxicated and celebrating the 4th of July. The investigation conducted by the Pima Country, Arizona, Sheriff's Office indicated that there was no evidence of any hoodlum activity and/or warfare involved.

FEDERAL BUREAU OF INVESTIGATION

REPORTING OFFICE	OFFICE OF ORIGIN	DATE	INVESTIGATIVE PERIOD	
CHICAGO	CHICAGO	1968	November 18, 1968	

TITLE OF CASE	REPORT MADE BY	TYPED BY
SAMUEL M. GIANCANA, aka		dkc

CHARACTER OF CASE

FBI Headquarters File 92-3171-2234
Top Hoodlum Program – Anti Racketeering.
Daily Summary

Synopsis:

Sam Giancana continues to reside in luxurious mansion at Nu Bes Number 2, Rancho Tetela, Cuernavaca, Morelos, Mexico. Giancana not observed in Chicago for the last two years. Investigation vicinity of residence of Phyllis McGuire, former mistress of Giancana, in Las Vegas, Nevada, indicates Giancana has not visited McGuire there and that she is living there with her current paramour, Mike Davis.

Giancana observed at in his residence in Mexico by CG T-2. Informant advised Giancana was wearing a black turtle neck sweater and smoking his usual large cigar. He advised, however, that he looked thinner than he was when last seen by CG T-2.

Chapter 13

<table>
<tr>
<td colspan="4" align="center"><h2>FEDERAL BUREAU OF INVESTIGATION</h2></td>
</tr>
<tr>
<td>REPORTING OFFICE

CHICAGO</td>
<td>OFFICE OF ORIGIN

CHICAGO</td>
<td>DATE

1969</td>
<td>INVESTIGATIVE PERIOD

January 7, 1969</td>
</tr>
<tr>
<td rowspan="2">TITLE OF CASE

SAMUEL M. GIANCANA, aka</td>
<td colspan="2">REPORT MADE BY</td>
<td>TYPED BY
dkc</td>
</tr>
<tr>
<td colspan="3">CHARACTER OF CASE
FBI Headquarters File 92-3171-2238
Top Hoodlum Program – Anti Racketeer-
ing. Daily Summary</td>
</tr>
</table>

As Bureau aware, current status of investigation of Giancana through Legat, Mexico City, indicates that whereas Giancana apparently continues to maintain residence in Cuernavaca, Mexico, and to reside there on a semi-permanent basis, it would appear he is absent from this residence occasionally. However, he has not been known to return to US.

Former PC advised that he has been advised by Richard Cain, Giancana's traveling companion and confidant, has been traveling abroad for purpose of setting up gambling locations. Cain did not definitely so state but former PC advised he feels Cain was sent abroad for this purpose by Giancana. Noted that previous investigation has indicated this to be true.

Former PC advised that in very recent conversations with William "Willie Potatoes" Daddono, he was informed by Daddono that at present time, Giancana is in Barcelona, Spain, where he is establishing gambling operation and also investing in parking lots.

Daddano informed former PC that Giancana is now closely associated with New York families and has very little or no association with his former associates in Chicago. Noted that Daddono indicated his source for this info was Frank Carbo with whom Daddono was, until recently, confined in Federal Penitentiary in Atlanta. Noted Carbo former prominent member organized crime in New York. However, former PC also speculated Daddono would know of Giancana's lack of close association with Chicago group of his own direct knowledge since Daddono continued as a leader Chicago group long after Giancana left the Chicago area.

Former PC also advised that Giancana and Phyllis McGuire, his former paramour, have completely severed their relationship because Giancana strenuously objected to her alleged excessive drinking. Noted McGuire now residing luxurious mansion in Las Vegas area with current paramour, Mike Davis.

Bureau request to advise appropriate legal to conduct investigation vicinity Barcelona, Spain, in attempt to verify current absence of Giancana from his residence in Cuernavaca.

For the purpose of evaluation of above info, noted that all three participants in conversations from which info obtained, former PC, Daddono and Cain,
are know to each other as having been close to Giancana and their appears to be
no reason why they would attempt to deceive each other with false info. Close
contact being maintained with former PC and Bureau will be kept advised of developments.

FEDERAL BUREAU OF INVESTIGATION

REPORTING OFFICE	OFFICE OF ORIGIN	DATE	INVESTIGATIVE PERIOD	
CHICAGO	CHICAGO	1969	January 20, 1969	
TITLE OF CASE		REPORT MADE BY		TYPED BY
				dkc
SAMUEL M. GIANCANA, aka		**CHARACTER OF CASE**		
		FBI Headquarters File 92-3171-2240 Top Hoodlum Program – Anti Racketeering. Daily Summary		

Synopsis:

Information has been obtained that Sam Giancana at present time is interested in
a fishing business in Mexico and that he has had an unknown individual believed to be
named "Luigi" who is operating in the Las Vegas area as a Lieutenant for Giancana has
been soliciting orders for fish to be shipped into Las Vegas hotels from his business in
Mexico.

FEDERAL BUREAU OF INVESTIGATION

REPORTING OFFICE	OFFICE OF ORIGIN	DATE	INVESTIGATIVE PERIOD	
CHICAGO	CHICAGO	1969	January 21, 1969	
TITLE OF CASE		REPORT MADE BY		TYPED BY
				dkc
SAMUEL M. GIANCANA, aka		**CHARACTER OF CASE**		
		FBI Headquarters File 92-3171-2239 Top Hoodlum Program – Anti Racketeering. Daily Summary		

CG investigation advised 1/20, last that new account has been open at Central
National Bank. Chicago, in name of Davis S. Chesrow and Thomas Keane DBA Rush Walton
property with deposit of four hundred thousand dollars.
As Bureau aware, Davis S. Chesrow (true name Cesario) is Chicago attorney who is
close associate of Pat Marcy and John D'Arco of First Ward regular Democratic Organization and of Giancana. He is a member of the Chesrow family active in Chicago poli-

tics, all of whom are associates of leaders of organized crime here. On January 11, last as Gov. Samuel Shapiro was going out of office, he appointed Chesrow and ten others to fill vacancies as superior court judges in Cook County. However, a suit against this action has been filed by new Illinois State AG challenging these appointments so that at present Chesrow is a Cook County judge but Supreme Court has ordered that no cases be assigned him and others until case is decided.

Thomas Keane, Democratic Ward Committeeman and Alderman of the 31st Ward in Chicago. Alderman Keane is generally considered second most powerful politician in Chicago, second only to Mayor Richard J. Daley, his close political ally. Keane is chairman of Finance Committee of City Council, the most strategic and important committee.

This info appears significant in view of info previously received about manipulations of Giancana in Cheswick Corp. In spring of 1965, at that time Sam Giancana, who apparently owned twenty five percent of Cheswick Corp, with David Chesrow and a man named Chadwick, ordered Pat Marcy and Anthony Tisci to direct that new corporation be formed in order that his interests could be increased and Chadwick's diminished.

It would appear possible that new corp. now formed as result of Giancana's directives in this regard and that power influence of Keane is now associated with it. Cheswick Corp. was formed as holding company of several parking lots, Chicago area. Noted that parking lots appear to be special interest of Giancana. Noted info recently received Giancana allegedly presently in Barcelona, Spain investing in parking lots.

CG informant recently advised that in return for bribe Keane allegedly was man to see in order to obtain liquor licenses for night clubs, restaurants and taverns in Rush Street night club area of Chicago. Noted Rush and Walton in Chicago is in that area.

Springfield requested to check records of corporation division of secretary of state to determine background of Rush Waldon Corporation, one 134 South LaSalle Street, Chicago and identify all officers.

FEDERAL BUREAU OF INVESTIGATION

REPORTING OFFICE	OFFICE OF ORIGIN	DATE	INVESTIGATIVE PERIOD	
CHICAGO	CHICAGO	1969	February 13, 1969	
TITLE OF CASE		REPORT MADE BY		TYPED BY
				dkc
SAMUEL M. GIANCANA, aka		CHARACTER OF CASE		
		FBI Headquarters File Number 92-3171 Top Hoodlum Program – Anti Racketeering. Daily Summary		

As bureau aware, John Matassa has instituted suit against Chicago Crime Commission (CCC) and several newspapers here following his inclusion by the CCC in their "spotlight" brochure on organized crime figures.

Elliott Anderson, Chief Investigator, CCC, advised that the CCC has decided to combat Matassa's suit by subpoenaing hoodlum associates of Matassa and compelling them to give depositions about their association with Matassa. Noted CCC aware this is procedure which has influenced other individuals to drop libel suit in Chicago in recent past.

Anderson advised he served subpoenas on February 11 and 12, last on Charles and Sam English for purpose of bringing them into CCC attorneys to give depositions. Anderson also advised subpoena is outstanding for Giancana to be served when and if Giancana returns to this area in future.

FEDERAL BUREAU OF INVESTIGATION

REPORTING OFFICE	OFFICE OF ORIGIN	DATE	INVESTIGATIVE PERIOD	
CHICAGO	CHICAGO	1969	March 3, 1969	

TITLE OF CASE	REPORT MADE BY	TYPED BY
		dkc
SAMUEL M. GIANCANA, aka	CHARACTER OF CASE	
	FBI Headquarters File 92-3171-2214 Top Hoodlum Program – Anti Racketeering. Daily Summary	

Charles and Sam English had been subpoenaed to give depositions in libel suit brought by John Matassa, former chauffeur and bodyguard from Sam Giancana when Giancana was top leader of organized crime in Chicago, against Chicago Crime Commission (CCC).

Elliott Anderson, Chief Investigator, CCC, advised English brothers appeared as scheduled on February 27, last and took the Fifth Amendment to all questions. Immediately following their appearance, Donald Ruben, prominent Chicago libel attorney retained to represent CCC, advised Matassa's attorney that subpoena for Giancana had been obtained and that efforts were being made to locate him for service and that subpoenas were about to be issued for following upper echelon leaders of organized crime in Chicago; Anthony Accardo, Gus Alex, John "Jackie" Cerone, Fiore Buccieri and Paul DeLucia, aka, Paul "The Waiter" Ricca. Anderson pointed out this threat received mention in press accounts of appearances of English brothers. Anderson advised that threat was merely bluff to influence leaders of organized crime here to order Matassa to drop suit to preclude their being subpoenaed.

Anderson advised March 3, that on this date attorney for Matassa appeared before Judge Nicholas Bua and requested suit be dropped. Judge Bua then ordered dismissal of suit with prejudice.

Noted this method has proved successful now on several occasions and appears to be answer for libel suit brought by hoodlums and their associates.

FEDERAL BUREAU OF INVESTIGATION

REPORTING OFFICE	OFFICE OF ORIGIN	DATE	INVESTIGATIVE PERIOD
CHICAGO	CHICAGO	1969	March 19, 1969

TITLE OF CASE	REPORT MADE BY	TYPED BY
	William F. Roemer, Jr.	dkc

TITLE OF CASE

SAMUEL M. GIANCANA, aka

CHARACTER OF CASE

FBI Headquarters File number 92-3171-2146
Top Hoodlum Program – Anti Racketeering

Synopsis:

  Investigation in Cuernavaca, Mexico has established that house Giancana living in has been for sale but has either been sold or has been removed from the market. Subpoena for Giancana issued by Chicago Crime Commission. Subpoena was for purpose of obtaining testimony of Giancana regarding suit brought vs. Commission by former chauffeur for Giancana, John Matassa. However, prior to location of Giancana, suit was dropped by Matassa.

FEDERAL BUREAU OF INVESTIGATION

REPORTING OFFICE	OFFICE OF ORIGIN	DATE	INVESTIGATIVE PERIOD
CHICAGO	CHICAGO	1969	May 18, 1969

TITLE OF CASE	REPORT MADE BY	TYPED BY
	William F. Roemer, Jr.	dkc

TITLE OF CASE

SAMUEL M. GIANCANA, aka

CHARACTER OF CASE

FBI Headquarters File 92-3171-2148
Top Hoodlum Program – Anti Racketeering

Synopsis:

  Residence in Cuernavaca, Mexico where Giancana known to be residing in past two years continues to be occupied. Investigation continuing to determine weather Giancana continues residence there. Information developed indicating possibility Giancana intends to return to US in June following his receipt of legal advice that he will be safe from legal process at that time. Movie actor Dale Robertson advised that he has known Giancana for some 20 years but has not been closely associated with him and understands he is now living in Mexico.

Interview with Dale Robertson

  On 2/27/69, Dale Robertson, movie entertainer, was interviewed at his residence in the Los Angeles area. He advised that approximately twenty years ago he met Sam Giancana at a golf course in Banff, Canada, and since that time has been friendly with him. Robertson stated that at this initial meeting with Giancana he had no idea of who Giancana was and Giancana told him that he was a car salesman in Chicago. Robertson stated that it was not until sometime later that he learned the true background concerning Giancana. Robertson stated that he is not proud of his association with Giancana as he was disappointed to learn about him and he truly wishes that Giancana had a different background as he was always pleasant to him and always acted like a gentlemen in his presence. Robertson stated that he has not seen Giancana recently and understands he is now living out of the country in Mexico. Robertson also advised that he is acquainted with other individuals through Giancana such as Milwaukee Phil Alderisio and Sam Battaglia. Robertson also recalled that several years ago Giancana had given him two Doberman dogs and that these dogs were brought to him on behalf of Giancana by Rocco Potenzo. He also advised that in the latter part of 1968, he ate at a restaurant called the Steak Joint in the Old Town section of Chicago with Potenzo.

Robertson denied that he has any business dealings with Giancana or any of the people whom he has meet through Giancana.

FEDERAL BUREAU OF INVESTIGATION

REPORTING OFFICE	OFFICE OF ORIGIN	DATE	INVESTIGATIVE PERIOD	
CHICAGO	CHICAGO	1969	July 18, 1969	
TITLE OF CASE		REPORT MADE BY		TYPED BY
		William F. Roemer, Jr.		dkc
SAMUEL M. GIANCANA, aka		CHARACTER OF CASE		
		FBI Headquarters File number 92-3171 Top Hoodlum Program – Anti Racketeering		

Synopsis:

Exact whereabouts of Giancana at present time unknown. Information has been received that his former residence in Cuernavaca, Mexico, is now for sale and apparently subject not presently residing there. Subject's Mexican attorney, Jorge Castillo has advised source that subject definitely not in Mexico at present time and indicated that subject had been in U.S. for 7 days in recent past, but is no longer in U.S. Information also received Giancana presently residing Rio de Janeiro, Brazil. This source indicated that subject living with "Contessa." This source also indicated subject has been in Chicago and that he had put on a considerable amount of weight, wears a mustache and toupee. Informant advised that he understands Giancana now almost entirely unrecognizable to people who have known him for years.

Current Whereabouts of Giancana

CG T-2 advised that he understands that Giancana is currently spending a considerable amount of time in Rio de Janeiro, Brazil where he may be involved in some type of gambling operation. The informant understands that Giancana is extremely well off financially. He stated further that his information is that there is a "Contessa" in Rio de Janeiro with whom Giancana is living. However, he was unable to furnish any further details concerning this relationship or the exact location of Giancana's present where about.

FEDERAL BUREAU OF INVESTIGATION

REPORTING OFFICE	OFFICE OF ORIGIN	DATE	INVESTIGATIVE PERIOD	
CHICAGO	CHICAGO	1969	September 19, 1969	
TITLE OF CASE		REPORT MADE BY		TYPED BY
		William F. Roemer, Jr.		dkc
SAMUEL M. GIANCANA, aka		CHARACTER OF CASE		
		FBI Headquarters File number 92-3171-2257 Top Hoodlum Program – Anti Racketeering		

Synopsis:

Giancana believed to be using alias Sam DePalma and residing in Penthouse #1, Amsterdam #82, Mexico City. Informant advised that "DePalma" is also maintaining a residence in Cuernavaca, Mexico.

FEDERAL BUREAU OF INVESTIGATION

REPORTING OFFICE	OFFICE OF ORIGIN	DATE	INVESTIGATIVE PERIOD	
CHICAGO	CHICAGO	1969	November 20, 1969	
TITLE OF CASE		REPORT MADE BY		TYPED BY
				dkc
SAMUEL M. GIANCANA, aka		CHARACTER OF CASE		
		FBI Headquarters File Number 92-3171-2266 Top Hoodlum Program – Anti Racketeering		

The current status of hierarchy of organized crime in Chicago is one of disorganization and confusion. Former CTE advised that currently Giancana has no plans to return to Chicago and certainly no plans to ever resume leadership of organized crime here.

Information advised Giancana's successor, Sam Battaglia, proved for short time he was in power, to be able successor to Giancana and his leadership was effective. However, following his conviction and incarceration leadership passed to John Cerone, who although capable was not effective leader and needed constant guidance and support of Anthony Accardo and Paul Ricca to rule.

Following the arrest of Jack Cerone by Chicago, Cerone was allowed to withdraw from leadership and position as "boss" temporarily passed to Felix Alderisio, who ruled for short period of time until recently incarcerated on extortion charge which he had been appealing for years.

Organized crime leadership then again prevailed upon Cerone to return as acting boss, at least for indefinite period until Battaglia is released from jail or until another capable leader established.

CTE advised such is situation as of current time. Cerone is acting boss who is advised on practically every decision by Accardo and Ricca, CTE, who for years has been close to Cerone, advised that older leaders are well off financially from investments made with income received when organized crime in Chicago was highly profitable, but younger members who depend on current income are "starving" and therefore restless.

CTE advised that Frank Annunzio, US Congressman, is currently being used by Cerone to relay orders from organized crime to Italian-American political leaders and other public officials. CTE identified following as top Italian-American politicians in Chicago at present who are under influence of organized crime and who look to Congressman Annunzio for orders; Vito Marzullo, John D'Arco, Louis Garripo Sr., Anthony Laurino, all Democratic Committeemen in Chicago and Joseph Jambrone, Democratic Alderman, 28th Ward. Jambrone is very close to Cerone and one of his closest friends for twenty some years had been Cerone's top Lieutenant, Joseph "Gags" Gagliano.

CTE advised that Annunzio had indicated to members of his Italian-American bloc that Cerone at present had ordered that "Thing be held together" through present "tough times" until organized crime in Chicago is able to reestablish it's self possibly when Battaglia returns to take command again. Group has been instructed that Italian-Americans under influence of organized crime should continue to band closely together and to bring along such people as themselves so that when "things get better" a nucleolus will be available from which to build.

Noted contact with former CTE at present is on very limited basis inasmuch as he feels that his status in Italian American community is as law and order office holder and although other public officials from this bloc must deal with him for their own good in view of his position, they deal with him at arms length. As result former CTE must be most circumspect and information he provides must be handled with utmost discretion.

FEDERAL BUREAU OF INVESTIGATION

REPORTING OFFICE	OFFICE OF ORIGIN	DATE	INVESTIGATIVE PERIOD	
CHICAGO	CHICAGO	1969	November 25, 1969	
TITLE OF CASE		REPORT MADE BY		TYPED BY
		William F. Roemer, Jr.		dkc
SAMUEL M. GIANCANA, aka		CHARACTER OF CASE		
		FBI Headquarters File 92-3171-2268 Top Hoodlum Program – Anti Racketeering		

Synopsis:

Giancana continuing to reside in Mexico using apartment in Mexico City and residence in Cuernavaca, Mexico. Giancana allegedly visited in Acapulco, Mexico, during Christmas season, 1968, by Sidney Korshak, Chicago, Los Angeles and Las Vegas Attorney. Giancana has visited US on at least two occasions during past year and has often been visited by his two daughters. However, no indication that Giancana has been in Chicago area, or in mid-west states. On two occasions when Giancana known to be in US. He was in personal contact with Phyllis McGuire, the entertainer who has been girl friend of his for several years. These meetings took place in Las Vegas, Nevada, where McGuire presently residing. Interviews with McGuire indicates that Giancana came to her aid at her request from Mexico, when she was threatened with an extortion threat by unknown individuals who used Giancana's name.

Chapter 14

FEDERAL BUREAU OF INVESTIGATION

REPORTING OFFICE	OFFICE OF ORIGIN	DATE	INVESTIGATIVE PERIOD	
CHICAGO	CHICAGO	1970	March 24, 1970	
TITLE OF CASE		REPORT MADE BY		TYPED BY
		William F. Roemer, Jr.		dkc
SAMUEL M. GIANCANA, aka		**CHARACTER OF CASE**		
		FBI Headquarters File number 92-3171-2293		
		Top Hoodlum Program – Anti Racketeering		

Synopsis:

Giancana continues to maintain residences in Mexico. One is a penthouse in Mexico City, and the other is a luxurious mansion in Cuernavaca. Although information previously reported indicated that Giancana visited the US in order to visit with his family over Christmas vacation, his son-in-law Anthony Tisci, when interviewed advised such not factual and instead Giancana's daughter, Bonnie Lou, Tisci's wife, along with Tisci and their children visited with Giancana in Mexico City, Mexico, during the 1969 Christmas holidays. Tisci verified Giancana has not visited the US recently. In regard to information previously reported that the purpose of Giancana's visit in particular was to visit his youngest daughter, Francine, who supposedly was to have a baby during the Christmas season. Tisci advised that Francine did not have a baby at that time and instead did not have her baby until first part of March, 1970. Tisci advised further to his knowledge Giancana has not visited Francine recently. Tisci did admit that Giancana is in frequent telephone contact with Bonnie Lou Tisci from Mexico City.

FEDERAL BUREAU OF INVESTIGATION

REPORTING OFFICE	OFFICE OF ORIGIN	DATE	INVESTIGATIVE PERIOD	
CHICAGO	CHICAGO	1970	May 20, 1970	
TITLE OF CASE		REPORT MADE BY		TYPED BY
		William F. Roemer, Jr.		dkc
SAMUEL M. GIANCANA, aka		**CHARACTER OF CASE**		
		FBI Headquarters File 92-3171-2299		
		Top Hoodlum Program – Anti Racketeering		

Synopsis:

Information set out herein indicates that Giancana has spent considerable time in Acapulco and Jamaica. Information indicating possibly that leaders of organized crime in

494

the United States, such as Anthony Accardo and Meyer Lansky have visited Giancana in Mexico, in recent weeks.

Miscellaneous

CG T-1 advised that Giancana is subject to a wide variety of moods and that, at the present time he varies from contentment to widespread dissatisfaction with his status in life as the present time. This information advised that Giancana has been known to become enraged over trifles, apparently because of his rather confined existence. When he is in a particularly black mood, his condition resembles temporary insanity.

CG T-1 and CG T-2 both advised that one of Giancana's constant companions in Mexico, as of this time is his attorney, Jorge Castillo.

Investigation of Anthony Accardo has recently determined that Accardo, former leader of organized crime in Chicago, who preceded Giancana in this capacity, has recently traveled to Acapulco, Mexico, and was possibly in contact there with Giancana.

CG T-2 advised that since a newspaper article appearing in Mexico, concerning the presence there or an Italian Gangster who utilizes the alias of "Sam DiPlama", an obvious reference to Giancana, Giancana has been very circumspect concerning his activity and associates.

This informant advised that Giancana has recently been in Jamaica, and speculated that since Meyer Lansky has recently been in Acapulco, and in Jamaica, that Giancana has been in contact with Lansky at either or both locations.

FEDERAL BUREAU OF INVESTIGATION

REPORTING OFFICE	OFFICE OF ORIGIN	DATE	INVESTIGATIVE PERIOD	
CHICAGO	CHICAGO	1970	July 20, 1970	
TITLE OF CASE		REPORT MADE BY		TYPED BY
		William F. Roemer, Jr.		dkc
SAMUEL M. GIANCANA, aka		CHARACTER OF CASE		
		FBI Headquarters File number 92-3171-2310 Top Hoodlum Program – Anti Racketeering		

Synopsis:

Giancana continues residences in Mexico; however, he has been known to have visited New York City on two occasions within past year. Giancana apparently contemplating marriage with manicurist from Los Angeles, California, area who has been visiting him in Mexico in recent months.

Miscellaneous

CG T-1 advised further that Giancana has been romantically involved in the past year or so with two females in Mexico. One of these is possibly identical with a manicurist from Los Angeles area and the other is a young entertainer by the name of Janice Harper. She is a former New York showgirl who lived with Giancana when he was in

Acapulco.

The subject has been known to be associated with George B. Unger, a jeweler with employment at 30 West 47th Street, in New York City. Contact was made with Unger by SA Edmund J. Pistey on May 26, 1970, and Unger furnished the following information:

"Unger advised he operates a jewelry manufacturing and retailing business at the above address and has a wide range of customers, many of whom are well known entertainment and political figures. He has known Sam and Joseph Giancana for approximately ten years. During the late 1950's and early 1960's he sold a great deal of jewelry to all members of the cast of the Arthur Godfrey Show. The McGuire Sisters were regular features of this show. On one occasion about ten years ago he delivered a piece of jewelry to Phyllis McGuire at her dressing room in a New York City television studio. Sam Giancana was with McGuire at the time and was introduced to him by McGuire.

Thereafter, Giancana himself stopped by his jewelry store on a number of occasions to purchase jewelry and gradually his relationship with Giancana developed into a social as well as business one. He has golfed with Giancana an frequently has dined with him.

Over the years, Giancana purchased a great deal of jewelry from him, much of it was for Phyllis McGuire. He always gave Giancana a fair price and in return for this Giancana "steered" customers to him. Among these customers who to this day continued to purchase jewelry from him are Frank Sinatra, Sinatra's mother, singer Eddie Fisher and Sammy Davis Jr. He never paid Giancana any commissions on any sales to these customers.

He last saw Giancana approximately one year ago when Giancana was in New York City for a few days. On this occasion they went to dinner at an unrecalled restaurant.

Since this time he has been called by Giancana on occasion and has himself called Giancana. Since he last saw Giancana, Giancana has been living in Cuernavaca, Mexico. This is the same location already known to the Chicago Office.

He was last called by Giancana about one month ago at which time Giancana asked to order a wrist watch for himself. The calls he has received from Giancana have all involved talk regarding jewelry purchases or just light social talk.

Approximately six or seven months ago Giancana called to advise that his sister Antoinette was coming to New York City to have a delicate eye operation by a New York City specialist. He offered his New York City apartment to Giancana's sister during her recuperation. This offer was accepted and Antoinette resided at this apartment for approximately two weeks.

His relationship with Giancana is wholly legitimate. He has never engaged in any illegal activity with Giancana nor has Giancana ever discussed any illegal activity with him.

Shortly after meeting Giancana, Giancana introduced him to his brother Joseph. While he has always enjoyed the company of Sam, he finds Joseph to be a most unpleasant person. He has seen or been in contact with Joseph on very infrequent occasions. He knows Joseph to be very heavy gambler.

As a favor to Sam, he agreed to pay commissions to Joseph on any jewelry sales Joseph would make for him. From approximately 1965-1968, Joseph made numerous sales in Chicago area. Over this period, he paid Joseph "several thousand dollars" in commissions. All these payments were by check and were documented in his books. He has agreed to make available these records through his accountant. He had no contact with Joseph for one and a half years."

FEDERAL BUREAU OF INVESTIGATION

REPORTING OFFICE	OFFICE OF ORIGIN	DATE	INVESTIGATIVE PERIOD	
CHICAGO	CHICAGO	1970	September 17, 1970	

TITLE OF CASE	REPORT MADE BY	TYPED BY
SAMUEL M. GIANCANA, aka	William F. Roemer, Jr.	dkc

CHARACTER OF CASE

FBI Headquarters File number 92-3171-2318

Top Hoodlum Program – Anti Racketeering

Synopsis:

Giancana continues to maintain his 3 residences in Mexico. Janice Harper, entertainer, admitted long association with Giancana. Admits visiting him in Acapulco 1/1970. George Unger, New York City jeweler and close associate of Giancana, advised he is unaware of Giancana's reported presence in New York City in May and June, 1970.

Associates

Janice Harper

It is noted that information has previously been reported that one Janice Harper, am entertainer who recently was signed by Roulette Records, has been seen with Giancana in Acapulco in January, 1970.

Moe Morton

Richard Gliebe, Chief, Organized Crime Unit, Illinois Bureau of Investigation, testified before the Illinois Racing Board on July 15, 1970, that he and three of his agents conducted an undercover investigation in Acapulco, Mexico. Gliebe testified that he was informed by a confidant of one Moe Morton that Sam Giancana is a close associate of Morton, former owner of the Acapulco Towers in Acapulco and that Giancana was observed on the yacht of Morton in Acapulco in 1969 engaged in a serious and lengthy conversation with Morton. It is noted that information has previously been reported that Giancana spent time in December and January of the past year at the Acapulco Towers and that the Acapulco Towers has been owned by Sidney R. Korshak and associates of Korshak's. It is noted that Korshak is a Chicago, Las Vegas and Los Angeles attorney known to be closely associated with Giancana.

Louis Joseph Lederer

CG T-2 advised that recently Giancana perfected arrangements whereby the Shah of Iran has allowed the construction and operation of a gambling casino to be opened in Teheran, Iran. This informant advised that Louis Lederer, a former Chicago gambling figure who has represented the Chicago group in Las Vegas for the past two decades, is to be in charge of the casino in Teheran, Iran. Informant stated Lederer purchased one hundred slot machines in London, England, for use in casino. Informant also stated Giancana used contacts to influence sister of the Shah of Iran to persuade her brother to allow gambling. The Shaw will not allow any foreigners outside of Lederer and perhaps one or two key employees therefore Lederer at present is conducting school for dealers and other casino employees with Iranians as students who will man gambling posts when casino opens.

On August 26, 1970, SA William F. Roemer, Jr., made contact at the residence of Lederer in Chicago, 860 Lake Shore Drive, and determined from the housekeeper there that at the present time Lederer and his wife are out of the U.S. and will not return for "at least a couple of months".

Lederer was born on August 22, 1906, at Farmer City, Illinois. He is married to Loretta Cunningham, who was born in Chicago on June 28, 1906, and who is believed to be traveling with him. In the 1950's Lederer owned ten percent of the Sands Hotel in Las Vegas and when Frank Costello was wounded in an assassination attempt in May, 1957, Lederer's handwriting appeared on memo notes of the Tropicana Hotel's profits found on person of Costello. In 1963 Lederer traveled with Leslie Kruse to Santo Domingo where they attempted to open gambling casino in the Paz Hotel. In 1969 Lederer traveled to Europe with Chicago mobster Frank LaPorte. Lederer is obviously an acknowledged expert on casino gambling.

In view of background of Lederer, his association with Lederer organized crime throughout the country, his expertise in casino gambling and his apparent knowledge of current hoodlum activities he is being considered as target under tecip and attempts will be made to contact him.

FEDERAL BUREAU OF INVESTIGATION

REPORTING OFFICE	OFFICE OF ORIGIN	DATE	INVESTIGATIVE PERIOD	
CHICAGO	CHICAGO	1970	November 20, 1970	
TITLE OF CASE		REPORT MADE BY		TYPED BY
SAMUEL M. GIANCANA, aka		William F. Roemer, Jr.		dkc
		CHARACTER OF CASE		
		FBI Headquarters File number 92-3171-2321 Top Hoodlum Program – Anti Racketeering		

Synopsis:

Giancana is suffering from a kidney ailment and possibly visited medical facility in Houston, Texas, in the mid 1970's for treatment. Information obtained there was possibly Giancana visited relatives in the US, however, knowledgeable source in the vicinity of Giancana's residence in Oak Park, was able to furnish no information indicating that Giancana was observed in his former neighborhood there.

Miscellaneous

CG T-5 advised that Giancana has sold the Mercedes Benz which he has been driving and is now driving a new Ford Galaxy. It is noted that this car has been observed at his Amsterdam 82 apartment in Mexico City. He also advised he heard reports that the subject may have been in Canada in August, and may also have spent some considerable time in Acapulco during the early fall.

In the middle of September, CG T-5 advised that he learned that Giancana had left Mexico City and had traveled to Houston, Texas, on September 13, 1970, supposedly to go to a medical center for treatment of his kidney problem; However, the source was aware that Giancana was in Mexico on September 12, 1970, and mentioned no such plans. He indicated that he had played golf on the morning. According to this source, Giancana is looking well, sporting a full beard as of that time.

Chapter 15

FEDERAL BUREAU OF INVESTIGATION

REPORTING OFFICE	OFFICE OF ORIGIN	DATE	INVESTIGATIVE PERIOD	
CHICAGO	CHICAGO	1971	January 1971	
TITLE OF CASE		REPORT MADE BY		TYPED BY
SAMUEL M. GIANCANA, aka		William F. Roemer, Jr.		dkc
		CHARACTER OF CASE FBI Headquarters File 92-3171 Top Hoodlum Program – Anti Racketeering		

It was reported in 1963 Mafia don Sam Giancana met with and offered to ex-Cuban revolutionary Edward I. Arthur a large sum of money to arrange the assassination of Fidel Castro inasmuch as Castro, after receiving a Mafia bribe to allow them to continue business in Cuba, arrested and booted them out of the country.

FEDERAL BUREAU OF INVESTIGATION

REPORTING OFFICE	OFFICE OF ORIGIN	DATE	INVESTIGATIVE PERIOD	
CHICAGO	CHICAGO	1971	March 18, 1971	
TITLE OF CASE		REPORT MADE BY		TYPED BY
SAMUEL M. GIANCANA, aka		William F. Roemer, Jr.		dkc
		CHARACTER OF CASE FBI Headquarters File 92-3171-2328 Top Hoodlum Program – Anti Racketeering		

Synopsis:

Giancana continues to maintain residences in Cuernavaca, Mexico, and one in Mexico City. He spent New Years Eve in Acapulco but except for that occasion has apparently spent the rest of his time at his residences in Mexico. Informant advised he understands Giancana intends to remain in Mexico, until 1973 when he feels that Statute of Limitations will have run against all charges which may be pending against him in the United States. Another informant advised that Giancana's function of setting up casinos in foreign countries has been successful but not nearly as lucrative as expected inasmuch as profits from these casinos has not met expectations.

CG T-1 advised that Giancana continues to maintain the three residences in Mexico. One of these is a luxurious home located in Nubes #2, Rancho Tetala, Cuernavaca, Mexico. The other is another luxurious home located at Quanta San Cristobal, Colonia Las Quindas, also located in Cuernavaca.

CG T-3 advised that he has learned that Giancana has busied himself while out of the United States with the function of setting up gambling casinos for organized crime in Chicago, to be located in foreign countries such as the one fronted by Lou Lederer, in Teheran, Iran. The informant advised, however, that form information coming to his attention he does not believe that these casinos have been nearly as lucrative and profitable as were expected and that return there from in not sufficient to make any of the hoodlums who are participating in the profits rich.

FEDERAL BUREAU OF INVESTIGATION

REPORTING OFFICE	OFFICE OF ORIGIN	DATE	INVESTIGATIVE PERIOD	
CHICAGO	CHICAGO	1971	May 18, 1971	
TITLE OF CASE		REPORT MADE BY		TYPED BY
				dkc
SAMUEL M. GIANCANA, aka		CHARACTER OF CASE		
		FBI Headquarters File 92-3171-2331		
		Top Hoodlum Program – Anti Racketeering		

Recap reported information from an informant that Antonio Caponigro was believed to be visiting Sam Giancana in Mexico and he believed that Meyer Lansky might also be in Mexico.

On 4/2/71 informant advised that he had not had any personal contact with Sam Giancana for several weeks but heard from mutual friends that subject departed Mexico City about 3/27/71, possibly for Central or South America.

FEDERAL BUREAU OF INVESTIGATION

REPORTING OFFICE	OFFICE OF ORIGIN	DATE	INVESTIGATIVE PERIOD	
CHICAGO	CHICAGO	1971	December 14, 1971	
TITLE OF CASE		REPORT MADE BY		TYPED BY
				dkc
SAMUEL M. GIANCANA, aka		CHARACTER OF CASE		
		FBI Headquarters File Number 92-3171-2349		
		Top Hoodlum Program – Anti Racketeering		

For information Honolulu Giancana is former top leader of organized crime in Chicago. Intelligence Unit, Chicago PD advised 12/13 from Honolulu PD that sometime this month Giancana met in Hawaii with person using name of Aaron "Obie" Oberlander and Frank Rosenthal. Oberlander and Rosenthal are Chicago and Las Vegas gambling figures and underlings of Chicago organized crime boss Fiore "Fifi" Buccieri and Ross Prio. Honolulu PD indicated Oberlander and Rosenthal came to Hawaii from Las Vegas and meeting allegedly concerned gambling operations to be organized in Hawaii.

Honolulu contact Honolulu PD and ascertain full details above and conduct whatever investigation deemed warranted there.

As Bureau and Honolulu aware, Honolulu recently confirmed travel of Ken Eto to Hawaii and contacts of Eto there. Noted Eto is also gambling operator in Buccieri group. Possibility therefore exists visit of Eto may have had some connection with visit of Giancana ET AL. Noted that Eto and Oberlander traveled to Puerto Rico on several occasions in early 1960's to investigate gambling possibilities there.

FEDERAL BUREAU OF INVESTIGATION

REPORTING OFFICE	OFFICE OF ORIGIN	DATE	INVESTIGATIVE PERIOD	
CHICAGO	CHICAGO	1971	December 15, 1971	

TITLE OF CASE	REPORT MADE BY	TYPED BY
SAMUEL M. GIANCANA, aka		dkc

	CHARACTER OF CASE
SAMUEL M. GIANCANA, aka	FBI Headquarters File 92-3171-2350 Top Hoodlum Program – Anti Racketeering. Daily Summary

Las Vegas informant advised that the informant has been in personal daily contact with Aaron Leon Oberlander, casino manager of the Silver Nugget Casino. North Las Vegas,, Nevada, and knows positively Oberlander has not left state of Nevada since February or March, last when Oberlander and wife went to Hawaii for a short vacation. In addition, CI advised he has personally seen Frank Rosenthal at least once a week on Tuesday of each week when Rosenthal usually in the company of Elliot Paul Price, Charles Turner, Theodore Lipson, Wilbur Stromberg and others know to the interested offices. In addition, Rosenthal has been observed on almost a daily basis by agents of the Las Vegas office usually at or near Churchill Downs Sports Book. It is, however, possible that Rosenthal may have taken a trip to Hawaii recently; also possible that individual using the name of Oberlander traveled to Hawaii. Las Vegas contacting knowledgeable informants and will advised.

Officer Tony Granito, Intelligent Unit, Honolulu Police Department, (HPD) advised December 14, last that Giancana, Frank Rosenthal and Albert Frabotta not know to have been in Honolulu and no meeting occurred about alleged gambling operations to be organized in Hawaii. Granito stated Nevada Game and Control Board requested investigation to determine if Aaron Oberlander resided and worked in Honolulu in 1968. HPD could not initially verify this information, believing that Frabotta had used the name of Oberlander in the past and reportedly worked for Giancana. Officer Granito contacted Chicago PD for back ground on Frabotta, Giancana and whether they had any connections with Frank Rosenthal. HPD since learned true identity of Aaron Oberlander and verified Oberlander in Honolulu in 1968. HPD believed Oberlander, Frabotta and Rosenthal all originally from Chicago.

Inquiry made Chicago PD about Rosenthal since some of Honolulu leading gambling figures recently moved to Las Vegas and have been seen with Rosenthal. Officer Granito and Sgt. Lyle Dupont, HPD, advised that Granito's call had apparently been completely misunderstood by Chicago PD as there had been no recent meetings in Honolulu and one of the above known to have been in Honolulu since Oberlander in Hawaii in 1968.

As Chicago is aware, Ken Eto traveled to Hawaii in July 1967. Eto has not been known to have visited Hawaii since that time.

Chapter 16

Synopsis:

Giancana currently believed to be traveling Europe, although he continues to maintain his residence in Cuernavaca, Mexico, and uses this residence as the base of his current operations. Giancana not currently active in the affairs of organized crime and, as matter of fact, has not been in Chicago since 6/66. However Giancana continues to exercise some influence on certain aspects of organized crime in Chicago, and currently uses three individuals as "care takers" of his affairs in Chicago.

These are Pat Marcy, Administrative Assistant to the regular Democratic Organization of the First Ward in Chicago; Anthony V. Champagne, long time attorney for Giancana and Dominic "Butch" Blasi, who functioned as body guard, chauffer, and appointment secretary when Giancana was the top boss of organized crime in Chicago. Giancana, with millions of dollars in wealth, is investing his money in various international enterprises, most of them legitimate.

FEDERAL BUREAU OF INVESTIGATION

REPORTING OFFICE	OFFICE OF ORIGIN	DATE	INVESTIGATIVE PERIOD
CHICAGO	CHICAGO	1972	September 19, 1972

TITLE OF CASE	REPORT MADE BY		TYPED BY
	William F. Roemer, Jr.		dkc
SAMUEL M. GIANCANA, aka	**CHARACTER OF CASE**		
	FBI Headquarters File 92-3171-2371 Top Hoodlum Program – Anti Racketeering		

Synopsis:

Information developed indicating that Giancana is currently utilizing services of Richard Scalzetti Cain as messenger and courier and possibly in narcotics traffic.

Richard Cain

CG T-2 advised that he has learned that Richard Cain, who for years been a close confident of Giancana, continues to be in Madrid, Spain, as of mid-August, 1972. Informant advised that he understands that Cain manages a small casino and house of prostitution in Madrid. He also learned that Cain continually works in close contact with Giancana who, according to this source, continues to reside in Mexico, but who travels extensively.

CG T-2 advised it is his information that Cain's primary role in Madrid is to established contacts with narcotics dealers there and in other parts of Europe and to arrange for narcotic shipments from Madrid to the United States.

Chapter 17

FEDERAL BUREAU OF INVESTIGATION

REPORTING OFFICE	OFFICE OF ORIGIN	DATE	INVESTIGATIVE PERIOD
CHICAGO	CHICAGO	1973	January 19, 1973

TITLE OF CASE	REPORT MADE BY	TYPED BY
SAMUEL M. GIANCANA, aka	William F. Roemer, Jr.	dkc

CHARACTER OF CASE

FBI Headquarters File number 92-3171-2379
Top Hoodlum Program – Anti Racketeering

Synopsis:

Giancana believed to have recently been in Spain and also reportedly visited the Chicago area during the Christmas holidays of 1972. Giancana has apparently given up his penthouse in Mexico City. Interest of Giancana in the United States being cared for by Dominic "Butch" Blasi, long time underling of Giancana.

FEDERAL BUREAU OF INVESTIGATION

REPORTING OFFICE	OFFICE OF ORIGIN	DATE	INVESTIGATIVE PERIOD
CHICAGO	CHICAGO	1973	March 20, 1973

TITLE OF CASE	REPORT MADE BY	TYPED BY
SAMUEL M. GIANCANA, aka	William F. Roemer, Jr.	dkc

CHARACTER OF CASE

FBI Headquarters File number 92-3171-2388
Top Hoodlum Program – Anti Racketeering

Synopsis:

Giancana reportedly is operating extensively slot machines in Guatemala through a front. Giancana reportedly maintaining residences in Mexico and an apartment in Beirut, Lebanon. Giancana also reportedly in monthly contact with leadership of organized crime in Chicago. Giancana reportedly in Hawaii during Christmas season 1972. Giancana continues to maintain P.O. Box 1066, in Cuernavaca, Mexico under the name Scalzetti.

Details Chicago

CG T-1 advised that within the past year of two, Sam Giancana, former top leader of organized crime in Chicago, has established numerous slot machines in Guatemala where slot machines at are legal. Informant advised that these slot machines are out in the open in the airport and in other public places. According to CG T-1, subject Giancana has control of these machines through a front man from Miami. Identity unknown to the informant.

In this regard, it is noted that Giancana traveled to Guatemala shortly after he left the United States in 1966, and in fact, obtained a passport at the Untied States Embassy in Guatemala. Investigation has determined indication that Giancana may be utilizing Guatemala as a staging area for his travels in and out of Mexico.

CG-T6 advised that subject has an apartment in Beirut. It is noted that this information has previously been received from another informant and previously reported. CG T-1 advised that Giancana has a very good contact in the Government in Beirut who meets him when he arrives in order to ease Giancana's entry into Beirut. Cg T-2 has advised that Giancana's Mexican Attorney, Jorge Castillo, recently exhibited a postcard from Giancana from Beirut to a high Mexican Immigration official in order to demonstrate to the immigration Official in order to demonstrate to the immigration Official that Giancana was not then in Mexico.

CG T-1 advised that Giancana was in Hawaii over Christmas, 1972, and speculated that his presence there might relate to a new gambling law being proposed in Hawaii.

CG T-1 advised that as of early January, 1973, Giancana was in San Francisco. CG T-1 advised on that occasion that Giancana has several homes in Mexico and apartments in Paris and Beirut. He also added that Giancana meets every month with the current head of organized crime in Chicago and has a foolproof way of getting in and out of Mexico. However, he could provide no further details concerning this contact.

FEDERAL BUREAU OF INVESTIGATION

REPORTING OFFICE	OFFICE OF ORIGIN	DATE	INVESTIGATIVE PERIOD		
CHICAGO	CHICAGO	1973	October 15, 1973		
TITLE OF CASE		REPORT MADE BY			TYPED BY
					dkc
SAMUEL M. GIANCANA, aka		CHARACTER OF CASE			
		FBI Headquarters File Number 92-3171-2404 Top Hoodlum Program – Anti Racketeering			

Allard Roen, General Manager, Rancho La Costa, San Diego, California, advised that Sam Giancana is not registered at La Costa and he has no information concerning his current whereabouts.

The Frank Fitzsimmons Teamster annual golf invitational tournament ended at La Costa on 10-14-73. Informants have no knowledge regarding Giancana being there. However, coverage of persons staying at La Costa is extremely difficult.

Lou Rosanova, Chicago hoodlum, is well acquainted with Giancana. He attended the gold tournament and left 10-14-73. It is assumed he returned to the Savannah Inn and Country Club which he operates in Savannah, Georgia.

Another close acquaintance of subject who has been residing in the San Diego area is Moe Morton. It is suggested Los Angeles locate Morton and John Roselli to determine if Giancana is in contact with them.

FEDERAL BUREAU OF INVESTIGATION

REPORTING OFFICE	OFFICE OF ORIGIN	DATE	INVESTIGATIVE PERIOD		
CHICAGO	CHICAGO	1973	October 25, 1973		
TITLE OF CASE		REPORT MADE BY			TYPED BY
					dkc
SAMUEL M. GIANCANA, aka		CHARACTER OF CASE			
		FBI Headquarters File Number 92-3171-2406 Top Hoodlum Program – Anti Racketeering. Daily Summary			

Former Chicago PC attempted to interest Giancana in financing a gambling ship in Maltese waters after his contact with the government established legality, but after Giancana made personal survey of situation, he declined investment.

Giancana reportable was playing golf with a group including Bob Lerner, the brother of Alan Jay Lerner, who has written Broadway shows such as "My Fair Lady" and "Camelot."

Chapter 18

FEDERAL BUREAU OF INVESTIGATION

REPORTING OFFICE	OFFICE OF ORIGIN	DATE	INVESTIGATIVE PERIOD
CHICAGO	CHICAGO	1974	January 23, 1974

TITLE OF CASE	REPORT MADE BY	TYPED BY
SAMUEL M. GIANCANA, aka	William F. Roemer, Jr.	dkc

	CHARACTER OF CASE
	FBI Headquarters File number 92-3171-2413 Top Hoodlum Program – Anti Racketeering

Synopsis:

Giancana has traveled extensively in Rome, Greece, Mid-East and London, during the past year. Giancana entered U.S. at New Orleans on 10/6/73 and again on 12/10/73. In 12/73 Giancana was in Washington D.C. where he contacted Passport Agency to renew passport. On both occasions when in the U.S. he apparently traveled to California to visit his girl friend, whom he reportedly intends to marry in the near future. Giancana reportedly has been in Chicago area on two occasions in the past year under surreptitious circumstances. On one occasion he was in town for purposes of visiting family at time of death of Rose Flood, his aunt, who was extremely close to him. On another occasion he met surreptitiously in area remote from Chicago with leaders of organized crime in Chicago. Informant advised he understands that these meetings were set up upon directions of Giancana to his former general functionary Dominic "Butch" Blasi. Giancana apparently visited Hawaii with "Carolyn" sometime around turn of year, 1974. Giancana currently bald, only occasionally wears toupee, almost always wears hat when traveling, now has short white beard.

Details

CG T-1 advised that as of the end of October, 1973, Giancana was in Mexico. He stated that that is the usual procedure of Giancana to sneak across the border, by the usual method of having two women, who reside in Texas drive across the border to Mexico, pick up Giancana and then drive him back across into Texas. This procedure causes a minimum of interrogation at the crossing point by the customs service since the woman advised custom service that all there including Giancana have just come into Mexico from Texas for the purpose of having dinner and are now returning.

CG T-1 advised that he understands that the daughters of Giancana, three in number, have visited with Giancana on special occasions such as birthdays and holidays in Mexico and in various cities in Europe where Giancana frequently travels.

FEDERAL BUREAU OF INVESTIGATION

REPORTING OFFICE	OFFICE OF ORIGIN	DATE	INVESTIGATIVE PERIOD	
CHICAGO	CHICAGO	1974	March 18, 1974	
TITLE OF CASE		REPORT MADE BY		TYPED BY
		William F. Roemer, Jr.		dkc
SAMUEL M. GIANCANA, aka		CHARACTER OF CASE		
		FBI Headquarters File number 92-3171-2426 Top Hoodlum Program – Anti Racketeering		

Synopsis:

Fianc' of Giancana identified as Mrs. Carolyn Morris, divorced wife of Edwin "Buzz" Morris, President, Edwin Morris Publishing Company, New York City, the leading music publisher in the world. Mrs. Morris resides in Santa Monica, California, age 52, and has two sons. Maiden name Crumly and originally from Kansas City, Missouri. She is closest friend of actress Lauren Bacall. Has traveled extensively with Giancana for past 2 ½ years.

Carolyn Morris

Alan Jay Lerner, Music Composer, New York, advised after having telephonically contacted his sister-in-law, Teresa Lerner in Mexico City, Mexico, that the current girl friend of Sam Giancana is Carolyn Morris, the ex-wife of Edwin "Buzz" Morris. Lerner advised that he had known, through his brother, Robert Lerner, who is a next door neighbor of Giancana in Mexico that Giancana is an American gangster.

Following the above contact of Alan Jay Lerner, contact was made with CG T-1. Informant advised Edwin and Carolyn Morris separated three years ago after Edwin Morris fell in love with a girl named "Fudge," who was associated with the rock group known as "Fudge and the Yum Yums." Edwin and Carolyn Morris had been married for approximately 30 years and "Fudge" is a 22 year old girl. Upon the divorce of Edwin and Carolyn Morris, Edwin Morris gave Carolyn 15% of one of his publishing corporations, which was worth to Carolyn Morris some $18 million. He has also given her a monthly income of some $5,000 and is also providing for the care of his two sons who are in their 20's.

CG T-1 advised that Carolyn Morris resides at 1025 Ocean Avenue, Santa Monica, California. Carolyn Morris is age 52, 5'5" tall, 110 pounds, blonde hair, very well groomed and cultured. She has two sons, Steven, age 27, and Chris, age 28. CG T-1 advised that Carolyn Morris, Lauren Bacall, and another girl were roommates at the age of 17 when the three of them intended a career on the stage and in movies. However, the other two girls married well, while Lauren Bacall went on to stardom in theatrical circles.

CG T-1 advised that in November, 1973, Carolyn received a $50,000 diamond ring from Giancana and they currently consider themselves engaged to be married. They have been going together for the past few years. CG T-1 described Carolyn as a very cultured person who is very romantically involved with Giancana.

United States Government records show that Carolyn Crumly Morris was born on August 31, 1922, at Colby, Kansas. She was married on September 10, 1945, to Edwin Morris who was born on December 18, 1906, at Pittsburgh, Pennsylvania, and was divorced from Morris on April 15, 1970.

Chicago Details

CG T-2 advised that he has obtained information which leads him to suspect that Giancana is in contact on infrequent occasions with Gus Alex at the residence of Alex in Florida and with Tony Accardo in Palm Springs, California. Informant stated that he believes that Giancana continues to exert some influence over the affairs of organized crime in Chicago and that although he does not physically come into the Chicago area except under very infrequent occasions and under most surreptitious circumstances, he makes contact with Alex when Alex travels to his residence in Fort Lauderdale and with Accardo in Palm Springs, California, as they both were during the entire winter season of 1973-1974. However, CG T-2 was unable to furnish and specific information concerning any dates of travel of Giancana to visit Alex or Accardo or the nature of any business which may have discussed or of any interest in common between these individuals.

Discussion among Giancana's associates that he had been traveling throughout the world and that he was on a Safari in Africa earlier in 1972. Former chauffeur of subject, Camilo Rodriguez, as having told another individual that subject, known to Rodriguez as Sam DePalma, had left Mexico for Italy around the end of 1972.

CAROLYN CRUMLY MORRIS
April 1971

SAM M. GIANCANA
July 1971

FEDERAL BUREAU OF INVESTIGATION

REPORTING OFFICE	OFFICE OF ORIGIN	DATE	INVESTIGATIVE PERIOD	
CHICAGO	CHICAGO	1974	July 19, 1974	

TITLE OF CASE	REPORT MADE BY	TYPED BY
		dkc

	CHARACTER OF CASE
SAMUEL M. GIANCANA, aka	FBI Headquarters File Number 92-3171 Top Hoodlum Program – Anti Racketeering. Daily Summary

Chicago placed call to San Antonio, July 19, 1974. As Bureau and San Antonio aware, subject, former top leader of organized crime Chicago who voluntarily fled country after release from jail in Chicago in June, 1966, is being expelled from Mexico where he has been residing since.

Giancana scheduled to arrive in Sam Antonio at 10:55 am today. U.S. Customs has nationwide stop outstanding for Giancana and is being alerted to Giancana's arrival for search of person and belongings.

Contact with strike force, Chicago, has determined that justice dept. has authorized subpoena calling for appearance Giancana before FGJ Chicago on July 23, 1974. San Antonio advised that arrangements have been made through USM to have subpoena ticket prepared immediately for service by FBI there upon arrival of Giancana in San Antonio. In event Giancana claims to be pauper, funds authorized by strike force for his travel to Chicago.

San Antonio following service of subpoena attempt to ascertain itinerary of Giancana upon his departure of San Antonio so that Giancana's U.S. residency can be established.

FEDERAL BUREAU OF INVESTIGATION

REPORTING OFFICE	OFFICE OF ORIGIN	DATE	INVESTIGATIVE PERIOD	
CHICAGO	CHICAGO	1974	July 19, 1974	

TITLE OF CASE	REPORT MADE BY	TYPED BY
		dkc

	CHARACTER OF CASE
SAMUEL M. GIANCANA, aka	FBI Headquarters File Number 92-3171-2442 Top Hoodlum Program – Anti Racketeering. Daily Summary

Following receipt of information from San Antonio that Giancana had been placed aboard American Airlines. Giancana was observed debarking from that fight at 2:23 pm today, at Chicago O'Hare airport.

Chicago advises that Sam Giancana was interviewed upon his arrival in Chicago on 7/19/74. Giancana very docile during interview and described himself as an "old broken-down man." He was extremely disturbed at the situation he found himself in, that is returning to Chicago to face another Federal Grand Jury inquiry. Giancana denied having anything to do with the murder of Richard Cain and stated that he was hit for "pushing too many people."

Following interview by BuAgents, Chicago PD officers took Giancana to their headquarters for continuing interviews regarding the Cain murder. They subsequently advised Giancana furnished no further information concerning that murder and merely stated he was "thousands of miles away." Giancana indicated he would remain in Chicago to complete his appearance before the Federal Grand Jury on 7/23/74, and would then in all likelihood depart the city.

FEDERAL BUREAU OF INVESTIGATION

REPORTING OFFICE	OFFICE OF ORIGIN	DATE	INVESTIGATIVE PERIOD	
CHICAGO	CHICAGO	1974	July 23, 1974	
TITLE OF CASE		REPORT MADE BY		TYPED BY
				dkc
SAMUEL M. GIANCANA, aka		CHARACTER OF CASE		
		FBI Headquarters File Number 92-3171-2448 Top Hoodlum Program – Anti Racketeering. Daily Summary		

Giancana appeared before FGJ, Chicago July 23, 1974, accompanied by veteran Chicago attorney George Callahan. Giancana took Fifth Amendment to all questions asked.

When waiting FGJ appearance, Giancana ruffled by situation which he referred to as "farce" when 35 reporters surrounded his residence in Oak Park. This morning awaiting him to appear to travel to Federal building.

It is present plan of action to request permission of department to immunize Giancana. Preliminary discussions in this regard with William Lynch, Organized Crime Section, Department of Justice, have indicated that department would look favorably on such a request. Toward this end, Giancana was continued under subpoena until September 17, 1974. This upset Giancana considerably and he advised he desired to "Get all this over with so I can get out of town again."

FEDERAL BUREAU OF INVESTIGATION

REPORTING OFFICE	OFFICE OF ORIGIN	DATE	INVESTIGATIVE PERIOD	
CHICAGO	CHICAGO	1974	December 17, 1974	
TITLE OF CASE		REPORT MADE BY		TYPED BY
				dkc
SAMUEL M. GIANCANA, aka		CHARACTER OF CASE		
		FBI Headquarters File Number 92-3171-2448 Top Hoodlum Program – Anti Racketeering		

On 12/17/1974, Giancana appeared on subpoena before Federal Grand Jury (FGJ), Chicago where he invoked the Fifth Amendment Privilege to all questions prior to his being brought before the United States District Court Judge (USDCJ) Edwin Robson, who granted Giancana immunity and ordered him to return before FGJ and answer questions. Giancana there upon returned to Grand Jury where he answered a few general questions before being ordered to return to present further Grand Jury testimony on January 14, 1975.

FEDERAL BUREAU OF INVESTIGATION

REPORTING OFFICE	OFFICE OF ORIGIN	DATE	INVESTIGATIVE PERIOD	
CHICAGO	CHICAGO	1974	December, 1974	
TITLE OF CASE		REPORT MADE BY		TYPED BY
		William F. Roemer, Jr.		dkc
SAMUEL M. GIANCANA, aka		CHARACTER OF CASE		
		FBI Headquarters File number 92-3171-2539 Top Hoodlum Program – Anti Racketeering		

CG T-5 advised that during mid December, 1974, Sam Giancana engaged in a number of meetings with Jack Cerone. It is noted that Cerone was one of the successors to Giancana as a top leader of organized crime and directed the affairs of organized crime in Chicago for a period of time while Giancana was in Mexico, during the late 1960's. Another participant in the meeting between Cerone and Giancana on at least one occasion was Tony Spilotro, a prominent member of organized crime in Chicago.

Chapter 19

FEDERAL BUREAU OF INVESTIGATION

REPORTING OFFICE	OFFICE OF ORIGIN	DATE	INVESTIGATIVE PERIOD	
CHICAGO	CHICAGO	1975	January 16, 1975	
TITLE OF CASE		REPORT MADE BY		TYPED BY
				dkc
SAMUEL M. GIANCANA, aka		CHARACTER OF CASE		
		FBI Headquarters File 92-3171 Top Hoodlum Program – Anti Racketeering		

1/15/1975, and butel to Chicago same date. Giancana appeared in chambers of USDC Judge Edwin Robson, wherein it was agreed that electronic surveillance hearing would be waived until such time as questioning of Giancana by FGJ relates to matters which may have been tainted by unlawful Elsur logs.

Judge Robson therefore ordered Giancana to answer all questions under grant of use immunity which may be put to him by the FGJ which relate to events which occurred subsequent to May, 1966, or during period he was in self imposed exile from US. Giancana was ordered to return to give further testimony before FGJ on February 11, 1975.

FEDERAL BUREAU OF INVESTIGATION

REPORTING OFFICE	OFFICE OF ORIGIN	DATE	INVESTIGATIVE PERIOD	
CHICAGO	CHICAGO	1975		
TITLE OF CASE		REPORT MADE BY		TYPED BY
		William F, Roemer Jr.		dkc
SAMUEL M. GIANCANA, aka		CHARACTER OF CASE		
		FBI Headquarters File 92-3171-2640 Top Hoodlum Program – Anti Racketeering		

Synopsis:

Giancana taken into custody at his residence in Cuernavaca, Mexico, by Mexican authorities on 7/18/74. Upon his arrival in the US at San Antonio, Texas, Giancana was served a subpoena calling for his appearance on 7/23/74 before the FGJ in Chicago. Upon arrival in Chicago he submitted to interview of Chicago office of FBI and denied that he had any knowledge of facts of murder of his close associate, Richard Cain, in Chicago, December, 1973. He was then pointed out to officers of Intelligence Unit Chicago PD who took him to Police Headquarters in Chicago and interviewed him in concerning his knowledge of murder of Cain.

Giancana appeared before FGJ on morning of 7/23/74. Upon leaving his residence some 35 representatives of the Chicago news media attempted interview and large number waited for him at the Federal Building. Shortly after his appearance, Giancana left the Chicago area and was not observed back in Chicago area until second week of September, 1974. Information previously reported that Giancana maintained residence in Lebanon. Investigation in Beirut indicates that he had temporary membership in Golf Club of Lebanon. However, residence not located. Giancana continued under subpoena by FGJ. Shortly after Giancana returned to Chicago he conferred with top leaders of organized crime in Chicago including Gus Alex, Joseph Aiuppa, and possibly Anthony J. Accardo. Also possibly with Les Kruse, upper echelon leader of organized crime who had traveled for Giancana in foreign countries in the past surveying gambling opportunities.

FEDERAL BUREAU OF INVESTIGATION

REPORTING OFFICE	OFFICE OF ORIGIN	DATE	INVESTIGATIVE PERIOD	
CHICAGO	CHICAGO	1975	June 20, 1975	
TITLE OF CASE		REPORT MADE BY		TYPED BY
				dkc
SAMUEL M. GIANCANA, aka		CHARACTER OF CASE FBI Headquarters File Number 92-3171 Top Hoodlum Program – Anti Racketeering. Daily Summary		

Chicago advised further details received on Giancana's slaying indicate body found face up on floor of kitchen in basement apartment utilized by Giancana. Six 22. Caliber bullet holes were found in Giancana's neck. Body found by Joseph DiPersio, Giancana's housekeeper and Oak Park Fire Department telephonically contacted at 11:53pm, 6/19/75, concerning slaying. Giancana found with both arms above his shoulders, wallet in his hand devoid of money, and $1,400 in U.S. currency on his person. Body clothed in sport shirt, slacks, and slippers. Chicago Police Department Intelligence Unit advised Giancana released from Methodist Hospital, Houston, Texas, on 6/19/75. Intelligence Unit there fore instituted surveillance during late evening hours that date and noted family gathering took place consisting of Giancana's daughter Francine, her husband Jerry DePalma, and their daughter. Giancana associate Chuck English present earlier in evening and vehicle possibly belonging to "Butch" Blasi, Giancana's long-time chauffeur and confidant observed in area of subject's residence. Chicago following and will furnish pertinent details as received.

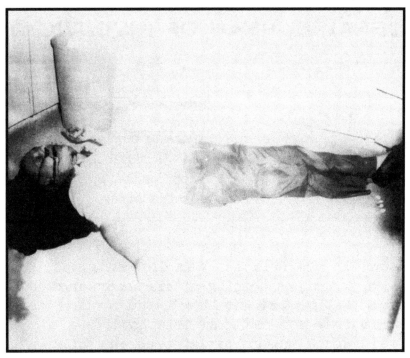

Oak Park Police photo of Sam Giancana shot to death.

FEDERAL BUREAU OF INVESTIGATION

REPORTING OFFICE	OFFICE OF ORIGIN	DATE	INVESTIGATIVE PERIOD	
CHICAGO	CHICAGO	1975	June 23, 1975	
TITLE OF CASE		REPORT MADE BY		TYPED BY
				dkc
SAMUEL M. GIANCANA, aka		CHARACTER OF CASE		
		FBI Headquarters File Number 92-3171-2597 Top Hoodlum Program – Anti Racketeering. Daily Summary		

CG informant advised that the day Giancana was murdered, June 19, 1975; Dominic Blasi had spent a considerable portion of the day with Giancana. Source advised that Blasi noted Giancana to be in good spirits and in apparent relaxed mood, indicating he was not aware he was to be killed later that evening.

On June 21, 1975, Chicago PD, working with customs, O'Hare International Airport, Chicago, advised that Phyllis McGuire, former paramour of Giancana, had just checked through customs with ten pieces of luggage. Chicago PD informed that McGuire was just returning from France. McGuire was met at airport by Charles English who escorted her to Chicago to attend subject's wake and funeral.

As Bureau aware, subject was waked at Moniclair Funeral Home, Chicago. Wake was covered by Chicago PD who noted that wake was restricted to family and close personal friends of subject. Subject buried at Mt. Carmel Cemetery and placed in the mausoleum housing his wife Angelina. Chicago PD advised instant date funeral procession was limited to a small group of hoodlums and family members.

FEDERAL BUREAU OF INVESTIGATION

REPORTING OFFICE	OFFICE OF ORIGIN	DATE	INVESTIGATIVE PERIOD	
CHICAGO	CHICAGO	1975	June 23, 1975	
TITLE OF CASE		REPORT MADE BY		TYPED BY
				dkc
SAMUEL M. GIANCANA, aka		CHARACTER OF CASE		
		FBI Headquarters File 92-3171-2601 Top Hoodlum Program – Anti Racketeering. Daily Summary		

Carolyn Morris, girl friend of Sam Giancana, stated that she loved subject very much, but knows nothing of his underworld activity as he shielded her form that part of his life to the point of not permitting her to talk to him from her residence telephone.

She claimed subject was not having problems with anyone to her knowledge and had been contacted by no one since entering the hospital in Houston except his daughters Bonnie and Franci, and their husbands.

She said she had no information to indicate subject had been contacted by any investigative committee or agency, however, when subject called her either June 17, or 18, he remarked that he had already had visitors and they had been very nice. This was a term, according to Morris, subject used when referring to FBI in particular, but law enforcement in general. She took this to mean that FBI or some law enforcement agency had contacted him at the Warwick Hotel, Houston following his release from the hospital.

She also recalled that while she was sitting in subject's hospital room about the first week in June, a man identifying him self as a Houston newspaper reporter wanted to interview subject stating that he was the only reporter in Houston who knew about subject was in that hospital. She told him subject too ill and not permitted visitors. Next day a small article in a Houston paper related above incident, but no follow up and reporter did not return to hospital.

The plan when she left Houston was for Bonnie and Anthony Tisci to take subject to the plane in Houston and for Franci and Jerry De Palma to pick him up at the airport in Chicago and drive him home.

Morris advised that subject often cooked in the basement kitchen late at night and invariably prepared more food than those present would consume.

He never carried cash in his wallet, only credit cards, photographs and phone numbers, the latter in a scrambled code known only to him. Cash carried in large money clip in shape of regular paperclip, a gift from his deceased wife. Morris unable to identify suspects or motive for subjects murder.

FEDERAL BUREAU OF INVESTIGATION

REPORTING OFFICE	OFFICE OF ORIGIN	DATE	INVESTIGATIVE PERIOD	
CHICAGO	CHICAGO	1975	June 25, 1975	
TITLE OF CASE		REPORT MADE BY		TYPED BY
				dkc
SAMUEL M. GIANCANA, aka		CHARACTER OF CASE		
		FBI Headquarters File Number 92-3171 Top Hoodlum Program – Anti Racketeering. Daily Summary		

CG informant advised that Sam Giancana had left the Chicago area during early, May 1975, and traveled to California where he was to meet with his current paramour Carolyn Morris. Following short visit to California, he went to Houston, Texas, to meet with an Arab with whom he had become acquainted when he was residing in Beirut, Lebanon. Shortly after arriving in Houston, he was met there by Mexican attorney Jorge Castillo.

Source advised that when Giancana suffered from a gall bladder attack, Castillo, being well acquainted with Houston physician Dr. De Bakey, prevailed upon Dr. De Bakey to be attending physician for Giancana. Source advised that when hospitalized, Giancana called for Dominic "Butch" Blasi and his son-in-law Jerome DePalma to be with him in Houston. Following his second visit to the hospital, with complications suffered as a result of the gall bladder operation, Carolyn Morris was asked to come and visit with Giancana.

Carolyn Morris interviewed by Los Angeles FBI on June 23, 1975, and advised she had checked out of the Warwick Hotel on June 16, 1975, and returned to her Santa Monica, California residence same date.

Morris stated Giancana released from Methodist Hospital June 17, 1975, and contact her telephonically, presumably from Houston, that date. She was contacted the following date by Giancana and learned from him he would be returning to his Oak Park, residence on June 19, 1975. She received another telephone call from Bonnie Tisci, Tucson, Arizona, advising her that subject had wanted her to call him. She stated that it was too late to call to Chicago, and did not call, deciding to call next day. She received a telephone call early June 20, 1975, from Bonnie Tisci, and learned that subject was dead, Bonnie telling her he had died of a heart attack. Morris subsequently called Giancana residence and learned from house keeper Giancana had been shot.

Chicago advised that information received from columnist Jack Mabley that following murder of Giancana, Mabley received anonymous telephone call indicating murder had been committed by a group referred to as the "young turks." The caller referred to a previous phone call made following the murder of Richard Cain in December, 1973, at which time the caller stated that the murder of Cain was carried out by "old timers" from River Forest intimating it was sanctioned by La Cosa Nostra leaders Tony Accardo and Sam Giancana. At the time of the earlier call, the caller told Mabley that the "young turks" would soon kill one of the "old timers." The most recent call received by Mabley stated that they had now carried out their threat to "hit" one of the leaders of organized crime and that within the next six months Tony Accardo will also be killed.

According to this source, two men were on the "hit team," both from out of town and were paid $250,000 for the hit. Source claimed both left within an hour of killing. The "young turks" group is a loose knit band of fringe and dissident members of younger years who feel that they are not receiving enough money from organized crime rackets in Chicago and have attempted to obtain greater piece of action from older leaders of Chicago "family."

It is noted that Giancana was not telling any mob secrets, nor, as best can be determined, was he attempting to take over operation of the Chicago organized criminal element. Giancana, since returning to the U.S., was maintaining a low profile and was contacted by only very few of the organized criminal element to include Charles English and Dominic "Butch" Blasi, who was pall bearer at Giancana's funeral. Those in attendance at Giancana's funeral did not include Anthony Accardo and members of the "River Forest" group who normally would have been present out of respect for Giancana as former boss of the Chicago group.

It is also noted that Oak Park Police Chief Reichert advised he was one of first on scene at the Giancana residence following call to their department on June 19, 1975, and moments later was followed by Jerome DePalma, son-in-law to Giancana. Reichert noted of particular interest the reaction of DePalma upon entering the basement were Giancana lay on the floor in a pool of blood. Reichert stated that DePalma appeared calm and in possession of his emotions showing no reaction to the deceased. He was followed into the basement by his wife Francine DePalma, who was not permitted to view her father lying on the floor, but was rather ushered out of the room and to an upstairs room. Reichert advised upon the return of DePalma to the basement, DePalma feigned an emotional display and began hitting his fist into the wall until he was asked to leave the room by the Oak Park Police Department.

COP Reichert also noted the reaction of Carmen Manno, son-in-law to Giancana, when he viewed Giancana's body on the basement floor. He advised that Manno displayed no show of emotion, viewed the body and said nothing. He appeared to show no remorse and remained out of the way while Oak Park conducted their crime scene search.

FEDERAL BUREAU OF INVESTIGATION

REPORTING OFFICE	OFFICE OF ORIGIN	DATE	INVESTIGATIVE PERIOD	
CHICAGO	CHICAGO	1975	June 27, 1975	
TITLE OF CASE		REPORT MADE BY		TYPED BY
				dkc
SAMUEL M. GIANCANA, aka		CHARACTER OF CASE		
		FBI Headquarters File Number 92-3171-2600 Top Hoodlum Program – Anti Racketeering. Daily Summary		

CG informant, a Chicago LCN member, who was a close associate of Giancana in past, advised on June 25, 1975, that after Giancana's death he tried to find out about funeral arrangements in an effort to attend both wake and funeral. He first called William Marzullo, Chicago undertaker located near Giancana's residence, and was told Montclair Funeral Home, was where majority of hoodlums are waked, was handing this matter. Marzulo told CTE at this time that "This is a private family affair and it will do you no good- you won't get in." CTE then made further inquiry and was told by a relative close to hoodlum leader Joseph Aiuppa, "Don't go or they'll call you in."

Informant stated rather than explain to mob bosses why he attended, he gave up the idea. Since the funeral CTE learned that none of the "big people" such as Anthony Accardo, Joseph Aiuppa or James "Turk" Torello or others attended Giancana's funeral. He stated it was clear Giancana's family did not want "these people" to attend.

Above info is consistent with that set forth in retell in which another Chicago source advised that only close personal friends of Giancana were permitted to attend wake and had to be admitted personally by Giancana family members at funeral home.

In view of above, it appears that mob leaders had agreed to a request of Giancana family to make services a family affair with as little hoodlum notoriety as possible and had issued instructions to outfit members to stay away which apparently was reason for noticeable lack of hoodlums in attendance except for Charles English and Dominic Blasi who are close personal friends of Giancana family.

In later contacts with "Outfit people" informant noted that the matter of Giancana's death was not to be discussed with anyone. He interpreted this as fact that LCN leaders were not obviously concerned or disturbed over death of Giancana which would logically rule out theory that Giancana could have been ailed by "young turks" causing mob unrest.

Also CG informant, whose identity as upper echelon leader in organized crime is known to Bureau, was encountered during brief change meeting on June 26, 1975, and he commented that recent newspaper article (Jack Mabley) which linked Giancana's death to power play by young turks was incorrect. He also stated without embellishment that "if you knew the truth you wouldn't believe it" which implies unusual circumstances surrounding Giancana's death.

It therefore appears at this time, based in available info and circumstances that Giancana's death either had the approval of current leadership, the reason for which have not yet become apparent or it was possibly a crime of passion involving a member of Giancana family or household. This situation being closely followed and Bureau will be advised of developments.

FEDERAL BUREAU OF INVESTIGATION

REPORTING OFFICE	OFFICE OF ORIGIN	DATE	INVESTIGATIVE PERIOD	
CHICAGO	CHICAGO	1975	June 30, 1975	
TITLE OF CASE		REPORT MADE BY		TYPED BY
				dkc
SAMUEL M. GIANCANA, aka		**CHARACTER OF CASE** FBI Headquarters File Number 92-3171-2611 Top Hoodlum Program – Anti Racketeering. Daily Summary		

For info of Bureau, Bernard Carey, Cook County States Attorney, Chicago, caused to be issued subpoenas for appearance hoodlums Charles English and Dominic "Butch" Blasi before Cook County Grand Jury to be conversed in the near future.

Cook County States Attorney has inventoried all items contained in desk and file cabinet and has made copies of the items. They have also listened to Giancana tapes seized with negative results pertaining to possible solution of Giancana murder. PSI,

Chicago is assisting Cook County States Attorney in analysis papers and items found in desk and file cabinet.

Hoodlum leader confided to source that Chicago Outfit was glad to be rid of Giancana and that the killing of Giancana was a sanctioned contract hit. Source was told that Giancana, upon his return to the U.S., has been short of funds, has not been able to get his money out of Mexico, and has attempted to muscle his way into certain hoodlum financial interests much to the chagrin of leaders of organized crime, Chicago. LCN leadership, Chicago, would not condone this by Giancana and ordered his execution.

For further info, Bureau, Peter Vaira, AIC, Chicago strike force, and William Lynch, Chief Organized Crime, Department of Justice, Washington, D.C., have been requested to appear before the Jackson Committee in the near future to testify about their knowledge of activities of Sam Giancana.

FEDERAL BUREAU OF INVESTIGATION

REPORTING OFFICE	OFFICE OF ORIGIN	DATE	INVESTIGATIVE PERIOD	
CHICAGO	CHICAGO	1975	July 1, 1975	
TITLE OF CASE		REPORT MADE BY		TYPED BY
				dkc
SAMUEL M. GIANCANA, aka		CHARACTER OF CASE		
		FBI Headquarters File Number 92-3171-2604 Top Hoodlum Program – Anti Racketeering. Daily Summary		

Kenneth Gillis, Cook County States Attorney's Office, who is in charge of the Giancana murder investigation, advised June 30, 1975, their office made copies of items contained in desk and file cabinet seized under search warrant from the residence of Sam Giancana, Oak Park, Illinois. Gillis said he would make copies of all items seized available to FBI as soon as litigation regarding search warrant is resolved. Gillis advised of note among items seized was a guest list containing dollar amounts next to names of apparent contributors to the wedding of one of Giancana's daughters. This list is at least 10 years old since it contained name of Murray Humphreys, former upper echelon leader in Chicago, who died November 23, 1965. Humphreys donation to wedding couple was listed as $2500. Others on wedding list were Alderman Vito Marzullo, 25th Ward; John D'Arco, First Ward Democratic Committeeman; and Circuit Court Judges Sorrentino, Syracuse and Covelli. Gillis said that there were eight judges on list who apparently donated cash gifts to bride and groom with the notation $500 next to Judge Covelli's name. Noted that Judge Daniel Covelli is one who issued a temporary restraining order to prevent the States Attorney's Office from inspecting Giancana's property, which order came at the request of Giancana's daughters.

Total amount of money received by couple was approximately 120,000. Gillis advised that among those items in the desk seized was a box containing .22 caliber bullets, however, no rifle or .22 caliber hand gun was found in desk. It was opinion of Gillis that someone has gone through the desk prior to it's being seized by his office. His reason for saying this was that photographs belonging to Giancana found in desk went only to 1970, and thereafter nothing after 1970 could be found.

Gillis stated of particular note, the top drawer of the file cabinet was a safe into which they were not able to penetrate. His office is awaiting decision by Circuit

Court Judge Hechinger as to how to proceed in opening this safe. He advised that the file cabinet, desk and tape recorder seized is now located in a sealed room in his office and will not be reopened until such time as motions filed in Judge Covelli's court and Judge Hechinger's court and ruled upon.

Gillis advised that he expected Charles English and Dominic "Butch" Blasi to be served with Cook County Jury subpoenas on June 30, 1975, requesting their appearance before the Grand Jury to testify about murder of Giancana. Also that he expected English and Blasi to plead their Fifth Amendment privilege and decline to testify.

FEDERAL BUREAU OF INVESTIGATION

REPORTING OFFICE	OFFICE OF ORIGIN	DATE	INVESTIGATIVE PERIOD
CHICAGO	CHICAGO	1975	July 2, 1975

TITLE OF CASE	REPORT MADE BY	TYPED BY
		dkc

SAMUEL M. GIANCANA, aka	**CHARACTER OF CASE** FBI Headquarters File Number 92-3171-2602 Top Hoodlum Program – Anti Racketeering. Daily Summary

As Bureau aware, Cook County States Attorney's Office, Chicago, has in its possession some papers and documents seized under search warrant from Giancana residence. Appearing in July 1, 1975, issue of "Chicago Daily News", column of Mike Royko in article captioned "The Giancana Wedding Gifts", was a list of names of some of several hundred guest who made monetary contributions at wedding of Giancana's daughter, Bonnie Lou, to Anthony Tisci. In previous tel. some of these guest were made known to bureau to include Circuit Court Judge Daniel Covelli.

In addition to those individuals previously noted to Bureau. Article reflected that wedding list also contained following individuals:

Pat Petrone "deceased", 25th Ward Alderman, $200 gift; Fred Roti, Alderman from First Ward, Chicago, $200 gift, Frank Chesrow, former President of Metropolitan Sanitary District of Chicago, present member of Cook County Board of Commissioners, $200 gift; Anthony DeTolve, former Illinois State Senator, nephew to Giancana by marriage, $200 gift; John Kringas, member of Chicago zoning board of appeals, partner with Vito Marzullo, Alderman in a lucrative funeral home, $50 gift; James J. Adduci, former Illinois State Reprehensive, $20 gift; James Rinella, former Illinois State Representative, $20 gift, Louis Briatta, father-in-law to Chicago Mayor Daley's son, John Daley, who recently married Briatta's daughter, $100 gift.

Further info bureau, Charles English and Dominic "Butch" Blasi have been subpoenaed and are expected to appear before Cook County Grand Jury during week of July 7-11, 1975.

FEDERAL BUREAU OF INVESTIGATION

REPORTING OFFICE	OFFICE OF ORIGIN	DATE	INVESTIGATIVE PERIOD
CHICAGO	CHICAGO	1975	July 3, 1975

TITLE OF CASE	REPORT MADE BY	TYPED BY
		dkc
SAMUEL M. GIANCANA, aka	**CHARACTER OF CASE** FBI Headquarters File 92-3171-2603 Top Hoodlum Program – Anti Racketeering. Daily Summary	

Chicago, in previous teletype, reported that Phyllis McGuire had come to Chicago from France on June 21, 1975. McGuire was met at airport by Charles English and subsequently brought her to a Chicago hotel. Source advised that wile McGuire in Chicago she was chauffeured around Chicago by Chicago Police Lieutenant August Locallo and Chicago Patrolman Vincent Santore, who possibly were working as security personnel with Marriott Hotel, Chicago. Noted Lt. Locallo known to be closely associated with many Chicago hoodlums and his brother, Victor Locallo, was convicted in 1969 for anti-gambling.

Source advised that prior to departing Chicago, Phyllis McGuire was brought to the upper avenue National Bank were she is reported to have removed contents from a safe deposit box.

Las Vegas is requested to interview Phyllis McGuire and determine if she, in fact, did have a safe deposit box in Chicago, and if so, by whom chauffeured, and what was removed from this box in addition to details surrounding her attendance at the wake and funeral of Giancana.

FEDERAL BUREAU OF INVESTIGATION

REPORTING OFFICE	OFFICE OF ORIGIN	DATE	INVESTIGATIVE PERIOD
CHICAGO	CHICAGO	1975	July 7, 1975

TITLE OF CASE	REPORT MADE BY	TYPED BY
		dkc
SAMUEL M. GIANCANA, aka	**CHARACTER OF CASE** FBI Headquarters File Number 92-3171 Top Hoodlum Program – Anti Racketeering. Daily Summary	

For info bureau, Houston furnished copy of synopsis of surveillance of Sam Giancana while Giancana in Houston, Texas. Surveillance of Giancana instituted by Houston PD, Criminal Intelligence Division (CID). On June 4, 1975, when CID made aware Giancana in Houston by Harris County Assistant District Attorney. CID surveillance placed Jerome DePalma, Anthony Tisci, Carolyn Morris, Albert N. Jamail and Edward Mike Davis at Warwick Hotel, Houston, during surveillance. Surveillance by CID continued until 18, 1975, after which Houston informed Giancana had been killed in his Oak Park, Illinois, residence, evening of June 19, 1975.

For info Bureau, Albert Jamail, owner-operator of Jim Jamail and Sons Grocery Store, 3114 Kirby Drive, Houston, was observed in several occasions visiting Giancana while Giancana in Methodist Hospital undergoing treatment for removal of gall bladder. Jamail interviewed by CID on June 20, 1975, at Jamail's place of business where he told officers he has first met Giancana was shopping in a store with Anthony Tisci. Jamail was asked to identify individuals visiting Giancana while he was in hospital and stayed only persons he knew to visit Giancana were himself, his wife, Giancana's daughters Francine and Bonnie, Jerome DePalma, Anthony Tisci and Carolyn Morris. Jamail stated he operated a personal service store and had taken food to the hospital for Giancana and his family members. Jamail stated he had reserved a room for Tisci at Warwick Hotel under name of Tony Thomas upon request of one of Giancana's daughters. Jamail stated that on the day of Giancana's dismissal from the hospital, June 17, 1975, several vehicles belonging to Jamail were sent to the hospital in an effort to get Giancana out of the hospital without being confronted by reporters. Jamail stated the last day he talked to Giancana was June 18, 1975.

Info received by CID that when Giancana released from hospital, he walked down stairs to third floor, went to a recovery room, placed a hospital gown over his street cloths, got on a stretcher, was covered with a sheet and then taken by hospital attendants down an elevator to the basement and wheeled him through a tunnel to the main hospital building to a loading dock where he then got off the stretcher, entered a hospital vehicle which drove him to Warwick Hotel.

On June 23, 1975, CID obtained Warwick Hotel registration folio for room 239, room occupied by Anthony Tisci under the name of Tony Thomas. Folio revealed credit for room was okayed by Mr. Durr in room 539. Registration folio for room 539 was obtained and revealed that B. Dunn occupied room 539 from June 9, 1975, to June 11, 1975, representing Tiger Oil Company, 1920 Colorado Street Bank Building, Denver, Colorado. It was further determined that Mike Davis, president of Tiger Oil was registered in Warwick at this time. CID determined that Giancana was taken from Warwick Hotel on June 17, 1975, by Limousine Service International. To host International Hotel at Intercontinental Airport, Houston. Trip ticket from limousine service indicated Tiger Oil Company may have made arrangements for limousine.

Jamail again contacted June 23, 1975, by CID at which time he stated he had contacted a girl friend of his to get three rooms in Host Hotel in her name. Jamail went to the hotel at approximately 7:00 pm on June 17, 1975, to Giancana's room 1022 where he conversed with Giancana for several minutes and left. Jamail advised Tisci was staying in one of the other rooms and did not know who stayed in remaining room. Jamail received telephone call from Giancana on June 18, 1975, at approximately 3:00 pm and told him he was leaving within the hour.

CID went to Host Hotel on June 23, 1975, and determined from hotel records that Jonie Hartman had made reservations for three rooms on June 17, 1975, reserved room were assigned as follows: 1012 under name James Thief; 1022 under name Bernard Corrigan and 1020 under name Leo Stacy. Hotel records indicate six long distance phone calls made from room 1022 to phone numbers subscribed to following individuals:

Anthony Tisci, 7940 North Portofino Circle, Tucson, Arizona;
Jorge Castillo Zepeda, Lava 135 Jardin Del Pedregal, Villa Pbergon, Mexico City;
Carolyn Morris, 1025 Ocean Avenue, Santa Monica, California;
Jorge Castillo Zereda, Plaza De La Republica, 321 Piso, Mexico City;
Jane A. Kennedy, 214 Balboa, El Paso, Texas;
Jerome DePalma, 3771 Ivanhoe Court, Schiller Park, Illinois;

FEDERAL BUREAU OF INVESTIGATION

REPORTING OFFICE	OFFICE OF ORIGIN	DATE	INVESTIGATIVE PERIOD	
CHICAGO	CHICAGO	1975	July 11, 1975	

TITLE OF CASE	REPORT MADE BY	TYPED BY
		dkc
SAMUEL M. GIANCANA, aka	**CHARACTER OF CASE** FBI Headquarters File Number 92-3171 Top Hoodlum Program – Anti Racketeering. Daily Summary	

For info Baltimore, Giancana former LCN boss, Chicago, was murdered in his Oak Park, Illinois, residence late evening, June 19, 1975, with 22. caliber automatic pistol. Weapon has not been recovered; however, local police have recovered seven spent cartridge casings during crime scene search. This matter under investigation.

Marconi De Tunno, an informant of James Nilan, Sergeant, Delaware State Police, Dover, Delaware, told Nilan he knew who has shot and killed Giancana. Informant advised contract to kill Giancana issued approximately six months ago but for unknown reason was not fulfilled until June 19, 1975. Informant advised hit man paid initial $4,000 and not aware if other promised to hit man upon completion of job. Informant advises he was shown money by hit man. Informant advised hit man travels frequently between Chicago and east coast, and when in Delaware, resides with female prostitute. Informant advised hit man is former Hells Angeles motorcycle gang member from California.

Informant states there were four persons who knew he had contract for Giancana. Informant advises at present only he and hit man remain, as other two individuals are no longer around. Informant extremely fearful for his life and afraid he, as well as hit man will be killed by Chicago Outfit.

Informant subsequently contacted on July 8, 1975, and advised hit man uses name Billy Frank, Billy Watson, Billy F. and Billy A.

FEDERAL BUREAU OF INVESTIGATION

REPORTING OFFICE	OFFICE OF ORIGIN	DATE	INVESTIGATIVE PERIOD	
CHICAGO	CHICAGO	1975	July 14, 1975	

TITLE OF CASE	REPORT MADE BY	TYPED BY
		dkc
SAMUEL M. GIANCANA, aka	**CHARACTER OF CASE** FBI Headquarters File Number 92-3171 Top Hoodlum Program – Anti Racketeering. Daily Summary	

Edward Mike Davis, owner, Tiger Oil Company, was interviewed July 12, 1975, and advised as follows:

Davis, as well as numerous employees of Tiger Oil Company frequently stays at Warwick Hotel in Houston, Texas. Davis normally at Warwick at least one day a week in connection with Tiger Oil Company business in Houston, area. National and international general office of Tiger Oil being moved to Denver, Colorado, from Houston, effective August 12, 1975.

Davis furnished identities of Jerome DePalma and Anthony Tisci as son-in-law of Giancana. Identified Albert Jamail as owner of grocery store, declined to identify Carolyn Morris. Davis stated he was, of course, aware when Giancana entered the hospital, and did not recall the number of times he visited Giancana in the hospital, but stated it was several.

Davis stated that he did not arrange for limousine service for Giancana from the hospital to the airport, and has no knowledge of anyone else connected with Tiger Oil Company furnishing this service. Davis stated that Tiger Oil Company has issued limousine service for various figures in connection with business with Tiger Oil Company.

Davis stated he was in Chicago following the death of Sam Giancana, and stayed at the Hyatt Regency Hotel. Davis did not attend funeral, but did visit funeral home on one occasion during time body was being viewed.

Davis stated he does not now nor has never had a safety deposit box either under his name of Tiger Oil Company, anywhere in Chicago. Davis stated that he and Phyllis McGuire have never been legally married.

Davis stated that he has never received any messages, which he considered a threat to his personal safety from any source subsequent to the death of Giancana.

FEDERAL BUREAU OF INVESTIGATION

REPORTING OFFICE	OFFICE OF ORIGIN	DATE	INVESTIGATIVE PERIOD	
CHICAGO	CHICAGO	1975	July 23, 1975	
TITLE OF CASE		REPORT MADE BY		TYPED BY
				dkc
SAMUEL M. GIANCANA, aka		CHARACTER OF CASE		
		FBI Headquarters File Number 92-3171-2623 Top Hoodlum Program – Anti Racketeering. Daily Summary		

Assistant States Attorney James Meltreger advised that Dominic "Butch" Blasi and Charles English, scheduled to appear before Cook County Grand Jury on July 22, 1975, did not appear as scheduled because SAQ continued their subpoenas until sometime in August, 1975. Meltreger stated reason for continuance was that current Cook County Grand Jury term expires end July, 1975, and it was felt case should be presented to Grand Jury whose term would be longer in order to hear evidence of investigation about the Giancana murder. Meltreger advised further decision to grant immunity to Blasi and or English held in abeyance pending further investigation about murder.

FEDERAL BUREAU OF INVESTIGATION

REPORTING OFFICE	OFFICE OF ORIGIN	DATE	INVESTIGATIVE PERIOD	
CHICAGO	CHICAGO	1975	October 16, 1975	
TITLE OF CASE		REPORT MADE BY		TYPED BY
				dkc
SAMUEL M. GIANCANA, aka		CHARACTER OF CASE		
		FBI Headquarters File Number 92-3171-2639 Top Hoodlum Program – Anti Racketeering. Daily Summary		

As Bureau aware Chicago documents and items contained in safe, file cabinet and desk seized pursuant to search warrant for Giancana residence. On September 16, 1975, Bu Agents returned to Dominic Gentile, Giancana family attorney, photographs of Giancana family members, photos taken while Giancana in Mexico depicting Phyllis McGuire and Carolyn Morris, and other photos deemed not necessary in furtherance of investigation. Other items among those seized were returned to Dominic Gentile consisting of keys and stock certificated for which receipts among the Giancana possessions documented their purchase.

Among those stock certificates returned were 6000 shares Baltimore Transit Company Stock, 2550 shares DiGiorgio Corporation, 500 shares advance-Ross Corp. and 4000 shares of Utah Shale Land Corp.

During conversation with Dominic Gentile it was learned that heir to the Giancana estate have not found a massive cash horde as had been expected. Giancana died without telling family members where he kept cash other than that documented in savings pass book accounts. Gentile indicated the single most valuable asset of the Giancana estate would be land holdings in Mexico, however with his limited working knowledge of the Spanish language it would appear that Jorge Castillo would stand to gain all Mexican assets of Giancana's inasmuch as all of this property and assets are listed in the name of Castillo, Castillo's wife, and the Castillo law firm representing Giancana. Gentile is of the property and assets acquired by Sam Giancana in Mexico.

Gentile also indicated that the heirs to the Giancana estate, the three daughters, are fighting among themselves as to how to divide the estate, and do not want to spend more money on attorney's fees to find more wealth in the estate.

For info Bureau, Chicago presently correlating trust documents as they may lead to possible federal violations as they pertain to Chicago LCN figures Charles English and Dominic Blasi. Remaining thrust of this investigation is being directed toward this end.

FEDERAL BUREAU OF INVESTIGATION

REPORTING OFFICE	OFFICE OF ORIGIN	DATE	INVESTIGATIVE PERIOD	
CHICAGO	CHICAGO	1975	November 5, 1975	
TITLE OF CASE		**REPORT MADE BY**		**TYPED BY**
		William W. Thurman		dkc
SAMUEL M. GIANCANA, aka		**CHARACTER OF CASE** FBI Headquarters File number 92-3171-2640, Top Hoodlum Program – Anti Racketeering		

Synopsis:

Information relative to Jorge Castillo Zepeda and interviews of Zepeda set forth. Interview of Guy Marks set forth. Investigation relative to Carolyn Crumly Morris, Giancana's latest girlfriend, set forth. Investigation relative to gal bladder operation and Giancana's hospital visit, Methodist Hospital, Houston, Texas, during May, 1975, and early June, 1975, set forth. Interview of Marie Perno, former housekeeper at Giancana residence, 6/16/75, set forth. Interview of Marie Perno following murder of Giancana set forth. Interviews of Phyllis McGuire and Mike Davis as Las Vegas, Nevada, set forth. Interview of Albert Jamail, Houston, Texas, set forth. Interviews of Sharon Messer and her sister, Jane Kennedy, El Paso, Texas, set forth. Interviews of Morris Pearl and Sam Pearl, Chicago real estate investors set forth. Interview of Nicholas J. Falagrady, Garland, Texas, set forth.

Details

On April 15, 1975, CG T-1 advised that as of mid April, 1975, Giancana has been in the Chicago area for the past two weeks. Source advised that following the appearance of Carolyn Morris before the Federal Grand Jury (FGJ) in Chicago, in March, 1975, Giancana and Carolyn Morris left the Chicago area where they intended to spend a considerable period of time together. Carolyn Morris has a serious illness in her family and stayed in California alone while Giancana returned to Chicago. Source indicated that Morris and Giancana had not seen one another since this time, however, are in telephonic contact.

Relative to Giancana's health, source indicated that Giancana has a very nervous stomach and was having difficulty with his stomach.

Source advised that Charles English had returned to Chicago after spending the winter in Florida, and is again in contact with Giancana. Source stated that the two individuals who are regularly in contact with Giancana are English and Dominic Blasi.

During April, 1975, source indicated that Charles English and Giancana have resumed their golfing habits in Chicago and were using the Cog Hill Golf Course.

Jorge Castillo Zepeda

Various sources have indicated that Castillo is a Mexican City attorney with offices at Plaza de la Republica 32. He resides with his wife, Maria Luisa Carranza Iraza De Castillo.

"The next 3 sections blacked out by the Government"

During this period Giancana's addresses in Mexico were unknown. However, among documents furnished for Harriette Blake Cain was Post Office box 1066, Cuernavaca, Morelos, Mexico, and it was determined that this box was listed to Richard Scalzitti, address Calle de Nubes #2, Rancho Tetela, Cuernavaca. It was determined that this house was held in the name of a corporation known as "Las Nubes, S.A." (Translation the Clouds, Inc.) of which the only significant share holder and executive was listed as Jorge Castillo Z. , Attorney, age 44 (in 1965), born Shreveport, Louisiana, address Luna 135, Pedregal, Mexico City. The corporation was formed in January of 1965 with a capitalization of 52,000 pesos, established in Cuernavaca, Morelos, to deal in real estate with 500 shares of which 646 were in the name of Castillo. The remaining four hares at one share each were in the names Raul Riquelme, Sara Perex, Maria Luisa Gonzalez and Porfirio Locano, conjectured to be personnel in Castillo's office.

A Mercedes seen parked at the Nubes address was determined also to be registered in the name Las Nubes.

Various sources including a former house servant have confirmed that the actual occupant and owner of Nubes #2 was Giancana.

Information was received in April of 1968 that Castillo identified as Giancana's attorney had petitioned the Mexican Government to review their decision not to grant Giancana immigrant status in Mexico. He denied that Giancana had any relationship with the underworld although acknowledging that he was a former part owner of gambling casinos. He claimed Giancana had been retired since 1950 and that since that time had been persecuted by the FBI. He contended that Giancana could not be a criminal because he has been residing in the United States and had not been arrested for any crimes. He said Giancana had not returned to Mexico since he was requested to leave in October of 1966. There have been various indications of continuing contact between Giancana and Castillo over the years. For example, Giancana was reported to have attended a New Year's party given by Castillo in Acapulco New Year's 1970.

At some point the house at Nubes #2 was reportedly sold to a Mexican politician and about November, 1969, Giancana, calling him self Sam DePalma, through his attorney Castillo purchased a luxury house known as Quinta San Cristobal in the Las Quintas area in Cuernavaca. This house reportedly was purchased in cash with the money being paid by a check sighed by Castillo against a Mexican bank. Reportedly the house was purchased in the name of a company called "San Cristobal" formed for this purpose.

In addition, it was established through various sources that Giancana maintained a penthouse at Amsterdam 82 in Mexico City and the arrangements for this apartment were also made through Castillo. Reportedly Giancana as Sam DePalma played golf as a guest of Castillo.

Reportedly Giancana attended a wedding at Mexico City November 10, 1973, in the company of Castillo and was at the wedding on one of the Castillo children in the spring of 1974.

It is known that a number of telephone calls were made to Castillo's office and home telephones from San Cristobal house at about the time of Giancana's deportation and Castillo is reported to have gone to the offices of Mexican Immigration at this concerning this matter.

The following investigation was conducted at Sherman Oaks, California, Los Angeles Division of the FBI:

Guy Marks, 4249 Woodcliff Road, California, was interviewed at his residence in the present of his wife. Marks advised that he is a night club and television entertainer. He advised of the continuing investigation interest by the FBI in Samuel Giancana.

Marks said that he first met Giancana in the early 1950's when he, Marks, was appearing at an unrecalled night club in Miami, Florida. He did not recall having been introduced by a third party. At that time he did not know anything about Giancana's business or social activity.

He said that he did a few things for Giancana that made him laugh and they have been on friendly terms ever since. He said that he had no further significant contact with Giancana until the mid to late 1960's.

Marks advised that, during that period, he had career and health problems and, while living alone in the above residence, "I flipped completely out." At that time Giancana maintained occasional personal contact with him and encouraged him to get back on his feet, according to Marks.

Marks advised that he never asked for, or accepted money, as either a gift or a loan, form Giancana. He said that to his knowledge, Giancana has had no influence on his career in the entertainment field. When asked when the last time he had seem Giancana was, he replied, "Three or four weeks ago." He said that it had been in his, Marks', house and that Giancana was accompanied by Carolyn Morris. He said that this was the only time Giancana had ever been in his house.

Subsequently, during the interview, he remarked that when Giancana comes to his house the two of them go out to the golf course together. He then agreed that Giancana had been in his house on several occasions.

When asked how the arrangements are made for Giancana to visit him, he replied that Giancana phones him from an unknown location in the Los Angeles area, not from long distance, and then is driven to the Marks' residence, usually by Carolyn. He said he cannot identify anyone else who may have driven Giancana to his house.

Marks advised that he does not, and has never known, where Giancana stays when he is in the Los Angeles area.

At Chicago, Illinois

CG T-1 advised that when Frank Sinatra came to Chicago during the week of May 4, 1975, he sent word that while he was in town he was going to throw a party for his Chicago Italian friends. This party was subsequently held at Giannotti's Restaurant on Roosevelt Road in Forest Park. Source advised that Giannotti is the individual who took over the Armory Lounge after Giancana used it for several years as his headquarters. Source advised that people like Dominic "Butch" Blasi were contacted and especially invited to be present. However, when Sam Giancana, the former top boss of organized crime Chicago, indicated that he did not care to attend and was not receptive to Sinatra's invitation, the rest of Giancana's entourage also refrained from attending. Source advised that for this reason he does not believe that any of the leaders and prominent members of organized crime who received invitations to Sinatra's party attended in view of the attitude of Giancana.

In reviewing the relationship between Giancana and Sinatra, source advised that through the election campaign of John Kennedy in the early 1960's and for several years prior to this time, Giancana was very close to Sinatra. However, during the campaign of John Kennedy in the early 1960's, Giancana apparently made certain representations to the commission that Sinatra would be able to have influence behind the scenes in the Kennedy administration. When Kennedy was successfully elected and when Giancana did not materialize when Kennedy administration, especially the department of Justice under Robert Kennedy which intensified the investigation of organized crime, Giancana lost considerable face because of the reliance of the leadership of organized crime on Sinatra's representations and Giancana never forgave Sinatra for this situation. Source advised that as of May of 1975, Giancana considers Sinatra to be a "phony" and as of this time whereas Giancana and Sinatra had been close friends, they are now completely on the outs with each other.

Source advised that as of this time Giancana is not close to any of the well known entertainers with whom he associated in the past such as Dean Martin, Leo Durocher, Joey Bishop, and Shecky Green. Source advised that the only entertainer with whom Giancana has any particular association now is his old mistress, Phyllis McGuire, of the McGuire Sisters, which at one time enjoyed some fame.

Concerning Phyllis McGuire, source advised that she is now living in a man and wife relationship with Mike Davis in Las Vegas, Nevada. Davis is the owner of Tiger Oil Company in Denver, Colorado, and is a multimillionaire. Source commented that it is remarkable that he resembles very closely the physical characteristics of Giancana.

Source also advised that another individual currently having severe financial hardships, who was a very prominent money maker for organized crime in years past is Rocco Potenza. Source advised that Potenza was a top gambling chieftain for Giancana during the 1960's and made considerable money for Giancana. However, after Giancana left the leadership of organized crime in 1966, Potenza went "straight down hill" with the result that in resent years a collection has been taken up for him by his associates in organized crime, who are sympathetic to his plight. Source advised that Potenza's situation is further complicated by the fact that his sons of his current wife, about his eighth, are narcotics addicts.

On June 10, 1975, CG T-2 furnished the following information:

Source advised that Sam Giancana left the Chicago area during May, 1975, and traveled to California where he was to be in contact with his girlfriend, Carolyn Morris. Following a short visit to California he left there for Houston, Texas, where he was to meet an Arab with whom he had become acquainted when he had resided in Beirut, Lebanon. Shortly after arriving in Houston, he was joined there by Jorge Castello, The attorney from Mexico who represented Giancana when Giancana resided in Mexico during the late 1960's and early 1970's.

In Mid-May of 1975, Giancana suffered a gall bladder attack. Castillo, being well acquainted with the famous Houston Physician, Doctor De Bakey, prevailed upon Doctor De Bakey to be the attending physician for Giancana and Giancana was admitted to a Houston hospital where he was operated on by Doctor De Bakey himself who removed his gall blatter.

Source advised at this point Giancana called for his closest associates, which were Butch Blasi and Jerry DePalma. Blasi and DePalma immediately went to Houston on or about May 12, 1975, where they visited with Giancana in the hospital and after his release from the hospital at the Warwick Hotel in Houston, where Giancana resided in an attempt to recuperate from his operation.

However, late on Saturday night in mid-May, Giancana became very ill and attempted to contact Doctor De Bakey. However, Doctor De Bakey was out of the city of Houston, and Giancana was referred to an associate of De Bakey, a female doctor, who immediately instructed that Giancana be retaken to the hospital in Houston where he subsequently was operated on again for a blood clot which was a post-operative condition which resulted as a result of the gall bladder operation.

Source advised that Giancana instructed that no one other than his immediate family be advised of his physical problems. This specifically excluded Chuckie English, a long time close associate of Giancana. The only person who were advised and who as of June 10, 1975, are aware of the physical problems of Giancana are Tony Tisci, and his wife Bonnie, Giancana's daughter; Jerry DePalma; Butch Blasi and his wife, Connie; Francine, a daughter of Giancana and Antoinette (Toni) another daughter. However, in view of the fact that Toni is divorced from her husband and is outranged as a result there of from Giancana she was specifically excluded from being invited to visit Giancana in Houston. The other traveled to Houston during the illness of Giancana to visit him, but Antoinette was specifically advised not to come in view of the fact that following her divorce from her husband during which she gave up custody of her five children Giancana has excluded her from the family.

Source advised that no one else including the top leadership of organized crime in Chicago, and including English, another of the closest associates of Giancana, are aware of Giancana's physical problems at the present time, this being at the specific instructions of Giancana.

Source advised that one other person who visited Giancana at his request in Houston, was Carolyn Morris and apparently their relationship has been resumed, it is being noted that following her appearance before a FGJ in Chicago, she became somewhat disenchanted with the emotional relationship with Giancana.

Source advised that another person who was advised of the problems of Giancana but who was not invited to visit him in Houston was Phyllis McGuire, the entertainer who formerly was a mistress of Giancana and with whom he still enjoys a compatible but not physical relationship.

Marie Perno

Marie Perno, 1126 South Hannah Avenue, Forest Park, was interviewed at her residence and furnished the following information:

Marie Perno advised that up until approximately three years ago she had resided at the residence of Sam Giancana, 1147 South Wenonah, Oak Park. She had resided at this residence since death of Sam Giancana's wife, Angie, in 1954. She stated that circumstances surrounding her taking residence at Giancana's house were such that prior to 1954 she had become very close to Angeline Giancana. She explained that her mother, Ann Tumminello and Angeline Giancana were sisters, she being a niece of Sam Giancana and his wife. She related that Angeline Giancana had had a heart condition since she had been 17 years old, had been very athletic and competed in swimming meets and other athletic events. She stated that Angeline was preparing to enter a swim meet at age 17, and during the course of the physical it was determined that she had a heart condition.

Marie Perno stated that Angeline went to a private physician and was told that strenuous activity for the remainder of her life would have to be curtailed, otherwise this activity would kill her. She stated that Angeline took the doctor's advice and refrained from any other strenuous activities. She advised that because of Angeline's condition, Marie was asked to assist Angeline by her grandmother at whatever she could do to help her around the house with her three children. Marie Perno stated that for many years, even after she had married James Perno and had a daughter, Andrea Perno, she continued to assist her aunt with the upkeep of the house and the raising of the three daughters, Annette, Bonnie, and Francine.

Marie Perno stated that in 1954 she was taking care of the Giancana children while Sam Giancana and Angeline Giancana were on a vacation trip to Florida. While in Florida, Angeline, at this time, age 42 (approximate), had a heart attack, and within two weeks died in Florida. She stated that prior to Angeline's death, she personally had been asked by Angeline to take care of her family and the house in the event she died. She advised that after the death of Angeline, the family met and discussed who was going to raise Francine, the youngest of the Giancana children, and who was going to take care of the other two daughters who were in their late teens. She advised that there was very little to discuss as she had already been asked to take care of the family by Angeline, and had spent considerable time at the Giancana household taking care of the children. It was decided that she and her husband, along with their daughter, would move into the house and take care of the house and children.

She stated at this time in her life she and her husband had purchased a home in Melrose Park, Illinois, and were residing in this residence. She stated that she and her husband were experiencing financial difficulty at this time and it looked as if they would eventually lose their Melrose Park residence. Reluctantly, she and her husband disposed of their real property pertaining to the Melrose Park residence and moved into the Giancana residence to take care of Francine and the remainder of the family. She stated that she lived in the Giancana residence for approximately 21 years, raised Francine and her own daughter, Andrea, both of whom are now married.

While residing in the residence, she was permitted to move in with not only her family, but also her mother, Ann Tumminello, now 83 years old, and with whom she now resides. She explained that while working at the Giancana residence, she had to prepare meals for them each evening after twenty-one years as is if she has spent her life taking care of a hotel and cooking gourmet meals for a banquet, in addition to running the household of Giancana.

Marie Perno stated that frequent individuals as the Giancana residence were Rose Flood and her husband, who would remain at the household for extended periods of time. She explained that Rose Flood was Sam Giancana's sister and she legally would have been the one to take care of Giancana's children after Angeline died, however, the undertaking was trust upon her.

Marie Perno stated that during the years she took care of the residence, she never did know what Sam Giancana was up to or when to expect him at the residence. She stated that he would come and go as he pleased, however, on those occasions when he was at the residence; he never once was heard to swear to raise his voice. She stated that he treated his children and family members very well and made sure they were excellently cared for. She advised that Sam Giancana, as she knew him, was a good man and, in fact, has donated money to have churches built and donated to other charitable causes.

Marie Perno stated that while residing at the Giancana residence, her husband, James Perno, was employed at the Central Envelope Company, Chicago. She stated that this company was owned in part by Mr. DeTolve, a relative to Giancana. She stated that approximately two years ago, DeTolve retired from the business, sold his interest in the business and her husband was no longer employed at the Central Envelope Company.

Marie Perno stated approximately three years ago, her husband received a telephone call from Sam Giancana to the effect that the Perno's were asked to leave the Giancana residence. She stated that James Perno told Giancana it would not be an inconvenience for his wife to move and hung up the telephone.

She advised that she now resides in Forest Park with her mother and her divorce from James Perno will be final in July, 1975. She stated the reason that she was asked to leave the Giancana residence was that Rose Flood's husband was retired in 1972, and could not afford to maintain his residence on his retirement income. Rose Flood (now deceased) appealed to Sam Giancana who told her she could live at his house and that the Perno's could leave inasmuch as the children were all married and had left the Oak Park residence.

She stated that presently there is no one residing in the Oak Park residence and the home is being cared for by DiPersio, the grounds keeper. She stated to the best of her knowledge DiPersio is not residing in the house.

Regarding her husband, she stated that he is now employed as a projectionist at the Harlem-Cermak Cinema.

Marie Perno advised she is not bitter towards Sam Giancana, who provided a roof over her head and food for her and her family for approximately 21 years. She stated that the individual with whom she is disappointed with is her husband, on whom she was going to rely for support following the move from the Giancana residence. She advised that the reason for relying on her husband for support was that for all the years she worked at the Giancana's residence, she received no wages, and as such, nothing was paid in by her to Social Security.

She advised that the attorney for her husband in the divorce agreement was Jerry DePalma, husband of Francine Giancana. She stated that during the years she raised Francine, she regarded Francine as her own daughter and noted that Andrea, her own daughter, and Francine were very close.

Marie Perno added that she is aware that Sam Giancana had financially backed individuals whom he has put through law school and through medical school. She also stated that Sam Giancana knows many influential people and people in high places as a result of his contacts.

Marie Perno was question concerning her possible knowledge about who had shot and killed Sam Giancana on June 19, 1975. She advised she did not hear that Giancana had been shot until approximately 8:30 AM the next day following Giancana's murder. She recalled she had received a telephone call from a friend of hers early in the morning (8:00 AM), who had asked her to come over to her house as soon as possible. She advised that she put on her house coat, got into her car and began the drive to her friend's house.

She stated on her way to her friend's house, she was listening to a news broadcast in her car and heard that Sam Giancana had been killed the night before. She stated she did not get to her friend's house, but rather drove over to the Giancana residence to see if she could lend assistance to Francine DePalma, nee Giancana, as she knew this would seriously affect her.

Marie Perno advised that when she arrived at the DePalma residence, she was let into the house by Francine's mother-in-law who was looking after Francine's daughter. She attempted to talk to Francine, but found it very difficult as Francine had been given a sedative and she was incoherent. She recalled Francine kept answering her questions with the reply "I don't know." Marie Perno stated following her visit she returned to her own residence.

Marie Perno stated that latter the same day she met with Sam Giancana's other daughters and during the discussion of what kind of wake and funeral to have for Giancana, suggested that a wake not be held. She suggested that the family just have a burial so as to avoid a big spectacle. She stated the family members did want a wake, and she could not defer them from this decision. She suggested that the wake be restricted to family members only and have the wake as a family affair and limit the wake to family members only. She recalled that she asked that Sam Giancana be permitted to die with dignity.

She stated that the family must have done as she suggested as the wake and funeral were restricted to family members only. She stated that none of Mooney's "friends" appeared at the wake or funeral, and obviously the word got out about who was wanted at the wake and funeral. She stated that she herself attended the wake and funeral and did not note anyone other than family members present.

She advised relative to the time she resided at 1147, South Wehonah, Oak Park, that the back door to the residence was always open when she was in the kitchen on the street level of the house. She explained that she spent much of her time preparing meals for the Giancana family, and when the kitchen kept the back door open, as she could see anyone coming or going through this door. She added that newspaper accounts of the murder to Giancana indicated that the murder had used the back door to the residence. She stated this door was frequently left unlocked.

Marie Perno advised relative to the time she resided at the Giancana residence, she never knew Sam Giancana to raise his voice. Relative to the murder, she stated she did not know who would have killed Giancana, as to her he was always a good person. She stated that prior to the time Giancana had gone to Mexico, he had purchased a riding mower with an attachment for clearing snow from walks and drives. She stated that often Mooney would start his riding mower, mow his own lawn and be done so fast he would continue cutting lawns until all the neighbors' lawns were also cut. She stated that during the winter months Mooney would get up early, start his riding mower, and drive around the block clearing everyone's walks and driveways, after first doing his own. She added at Christmas time Mooney would tell Marie Perno to order a basket of fruit and meat to be delivered Christmas day to every neighbor on the block. She stated none of the food baskets were ever returned.

Marie Perno stated that Mooney has paid for the windows, the marble, and the railings in the St. Bernadine Church, Forest Park, and had donated these items in the name of his wife whereon her name had been placed on a small plaque and mounted on the items donated. Following the murder to Giancana, the Giancana family asked a priest from St. Bernadine's Church to officiate at the wake or funeral, and the family was informed the priest would not officiate.

Marie Perno advised that following the death of Giancana, she was talking to Antoinette Manno, daughter of Giancana's, who related to her what problems they had while attending school. She advised that although she had been taking care of the Giancana children Antoinette had never told her what they had to put up with while in school. Marie Perno advised that the Giancana children attended parochial school. She learned from Antoinette that both Antoinette and Bonnie Lou were frequently dragged in the rest room, stripped of their outer garments, and beaten with sticks and kicked by their classmates because they were the daughters of Sam Giancana. Marie Perno advised the younger Giancana daughter, Francine, attended school with her own daughter who protected her from the other children, and thugs she did not have to put up with or sustain the beatings the other children were given. Marie Perno advised that from the death of Giancana, some good will come in that the family can now have peace of mind.

Marie Perno stated she is still very close to Francine DePalma, nee Giancana, and that Francine calls her on the telephone on almost a daily basis. Regarding the death of Sam Giancana, she stated the whole set of circumstances seems strange, and she hopes, through Francine, to learn some of the details.

Marie Perno added that at the time of Sam Giancana's death, his present housekeeper, Joseph DiPersio, was very hard of hearing and has emphysema.

It should be noted during the interview that Marie Perno appeared to be in good spirits and could exercise control over her emotions. During an earlier interview, she was very distraught and interrupted the interview five to six times to cry, at which point interviewing agents would wait for her to gain her composure until the interview could be continued.

Details of Crime Scene

On June 19, 1975, officers from Oak Park, PD in response to an assistance call from the Oak Park Fire Department ambulance at the residence of Sam Giancana were met at the rear entrance by several firemen who had responded to the call. The police were informed that a shooting victim was lying inside, dead, on the floor in the basement. The police were led into the basement where Giancana was observed lying in a pool of blood on his back. Giancana was observed by investigating officers to have his left keg crossed over his right, his arms outstretched, his slacks unbuttoned at the waist, and his wallet to the left of his head between his left hand and his head.

Reporting officers upon entering the basement observed the outer screen door of the basement closed, but was unlocked. The kitchen area of the basement was brightly lit and a frying pan was observed on the right rear burner of the store which was to the right of Giancana. Six .22 caliber casings were found in the kitchen.

Investigating officers interviewed Joseph DiPersio, Giancana's housekeeper, who was home at the time of the murder. DiPersio stated to the Oak Park Police that he had awakened from a nap at approximately 7:00pm, June 19, 1975, and observed Giancana walking down the stairs to the basement with his daughter and son-in-law Mr. and Mrs. Jerome DePalma. DiPersio stated he went back into the house and went to the basement to repair a pipe in the basement ceiling which was dripping. At this time, DiPersio stated that Giancana was alone and assisted him in repairing the pipe. When finished, DiPersio ask if Giancana needed anything and Giancana told him he would call DiPersio if he needed anything. DiPersio stated he then went up to the first floor of the residence and watched the news and the beginning of the Johnny Carson Show. At approximately 11:00 pm, DiPersio related to the police that he went to the basement stairway and called to Giancana. When he did not get a reply, he went down to the basement and observed Giancana lying on the floor. DiPersio stated that he called to his wife to call for an ambulance. In response to questioning by the police, DiPersio indicated that no one else was in the house other than himself, his wife, and Giancana. He also stated the basement door to the residence was never locked.

Investigation officers also interviewed Ann DiPersio, wife of Joseph DiPersio, who stated that she had prepared dinner for Giancana, Giancana's daughter, and son-in-law and their daughter at approximately 5:30 pm. At approximately 7:00 pm, Giancana and his daughter, grand daughter, and son-in-law went down to the basement and remained there until approximately 9:30 pm when Jerome DePalma came up to the first floor to get his wife's purse. The remainder of information furnished by Mrs. DiPersio corroborated with that of her husband.

Investigating officers also interviewed the ambulance drivers who stated they were met at the ambulance by Joseph DiPersio who made the comment, "He's down in the basement, you might already be too late." The fireman stated they followed DiPersio into the basement where Giancana was found in a pool of blood. The fireman felt the radial artery and the carotid artery and found no pulse. They also noted that upon feeling the extremities that the extremities were cold. The fireman stated that a this point called the police.

Of note in the police report, it was reflecting the Oak Park PD was not called to the scene of the murder until 11:53 pm.

Investigating officers attempted to interview Jerome DePalma, who declined to submit to interview, investigating officers also conducted a neighborhood investigation with negative results.

A re-interview with Giancana's housekeeper Joseph DiPersio

Joe DiPersio entered the United States from North Central Italy (Abruzzi) with his parents in 1900 at the age of six years. He and his father were friendly with Sam Giancana's father as both resided in the same neighborhood in Chicago. Approximately thirty years ago Joe DiPersio was out of a job and as such, Sam Giancana's father asked him if he would like to take care of Sam Giancana's house, i.e., maintain the lawns, landscaping and perform odd jobs around Sam Giancana house and make repairs as necessary. Joe DiPersio consented to this and as such has been working for Giancana since this time in the capacity described above.

Joe DiPersio began residing in the Sam Giancana residence in Oak Park approximately two years ago following the death of Rose Flood, who was taking care of the house for Giancana. Joe DiPersio and his wife moved into the residence as Rose Flood's husband, Richard Flood, and alcoholic Irishman, could not take care of him self, let alone the Giancana residence. Joe DiPersio and his wife moved into the residence at the request of Giancana, who subsequently asked Richard Flood to leave. Richard Flood now resides in a nursing home on the north side of Chicago.

Prior to the time that Rose Flood and her husband resided in the Giancana residence, the house was occupied by James and Marie Perno who had resided in the house for 17 years following the death of Giancana's wife, Angeline. At the time Angeline Giancana died the family decided that the Perno's were best suited to take care of the Giancana children as the Perno's had one child of their own, were young, and could manage the three Giancana daughters. Marie Perno was the niece to Sam "Mooney" Giancana by marriage.

James and Marie Perno resided in the Giancana residence until such time as the Giancana daughters had all married and left the house. After leaving the house several of the daughters were asked not to bother coming back to the house by Marie Perno as she was tired of taking care of them and finally had the house clean, didn't want to clean up after them and more as she had done it for 17 years. The daughters complained to their father who asked Marie and James Perno to move out of the house. It was at this time that Rose Flood and Richard Flood moved into the house.

Joe DiPersio and his wife were present in the Giancana house the evening Giancana was murdered. Giancana had returned to Oak Park the day before he was murdered (June 19, 1975), to recuperate following removal of his gall bladder in Texas. The evening Giancana was murdered Joe DiPersio's wife had fixed Giancana some chicken for his dinner and he was in the process of eating the chicken in the upstairs family-TV room when his daughter, Francine DePalma, her husband Jerry DePalma, and their young daughter came to the Giancana residence to visit with Sam Giancana. While Sam Giancana finished his dinner Jerry DePalma asked if there was any corned beef in the house and was instructed there was and proceeded to make himself a corn beef sandwich. He returned to the table where Sam Giancana was finishing his dinner.

The dinner completed, sometime after 7:00 pm. Sam Giancana, Francine DePalma, Jerry DePalma, and Sam Giancana's granddaughter went to the basement area of the Giancana's residence where they all remained until approximately 10:30 pm. At this time one of the DePalma's came upstairs to retrieve some of their belongings preparatory to going home. DiPersio recalled the Johnny Carson Show was just coming on the television in the family room. DiPersio walked out onto the back porch area located at the rear of the residence and noted the DePalma's were departing. He recalled the evening was warm and was enjoying the cool night air when Sam "Mooney" Giancana called to him form the garage area of the property to come and take a walk with him.

Joe DiPersio went over to Mooney and accompanied Giancana on a walk. Giancana had asked DiPersio to accompany him as Giancana was afraid he might fall down, as he was still weak from the recent surgery. Giancana took DiPersio's arm and the two proceeded to the corner of Filmore and the next block west of the Giancana residence.

During the course of their walk DiPersio noted a lot of automobile traffic on Filmore Street along which they were walking close to the Giancana residence and mentioned this to Giancana who gesticulated in reply that he did not give a damn. DiPersio could not tell if the automobile traffic and individuals he noted in the area at this time of night were police officers or not as these individuals frequently spent many hours observing the Giancana residence from across the church yard and church yard alley way caddy corner from Giancana's residence.

He and Giancana returned to the Giancana residence following their walk and

DiPersio accompanied Giancana into the basement area of the residence by entering the house through the rear cellar door entrance, which door was open. This door led down a flight of stairs to a steel door which was also open behind a screen / storm door combination. Giancana entered the basement and DiPersio returned to the upstairs portion of the house. DiPersio estimated that he and Giancana took approximately fifteen minutes to take their walk.

After being upstairs for approximately fifteen minutes Mooney called to him from downstairs and he went downstairs to see what Mooney wanted. When he got downstairs to the basement Mooney pointed out to DiPersio that water was dripping from the ceiling of the dining room area to the floor. He and Mooney discussed what the problem could be.

Shortly after noting the dripping water Dominic "Butch" Blasi entered the basement dining area from the basement kitchen, sat down at the basement dining table and asked if there was any scotch in the house. DiPersio got him some ice and Blasi proceeded to drink scotch while he and Giancana attempted to determine what was causing the water to drip onto the basement dining room floor. DiPersio removed several acoustic tiles from the ceiling of the dining room in the area of the water drip and noted that the water was coming from a drain pipe taking water from the bathroom located directly above the area of the leak. DiPersio got some buckets and put them under the slow leak. It was decided the pipe could be fixed in the morning.

DiPersio cleaned up the mess on the dining room floor and stacked the wet acoustical tiles out of the traffic areas in the basement. He asked Sam Giancana if he needed anything else and Giancana told him if he did need anything he would call him. DiPersio then went upstairs and joined his wife in the family room located on the first level of the house. He left Mooney and Blasi alone in the basement dining room. On the way into the family room DiPersio closed a sliding door between the stairs and the upstairs kitchen. He joined his wife at approximately 11:20 pm and watched part of the Johnny Carson show with her. He also noted his wife had the air conditioner on in the television area and as such the television was turned on rather loudly.

DiPersio and his wife watched television for approximately one-half hour at which time Joe DiPersio stood up and looked through the rear window area and noted that Blasi's car was not in the driveway. DiPersio then went to the door way, which door he had earlier closed, as he and his wife wished to retire, he opened the door and called downstairs to Mooney. Giancana did not answer and he then proceeded downstairs to see if Giancana was alright. Once downstairs DiPersio noted that Giancana was not in the basement dining area and that the sliding door between the basement kitchen and the basement dining room was partially closed permitting him to see that Giancana was lying on the basement kitchen floor.

DiPersio slid open the door and noted that Giancana was lying on the basement kitchen floor face up, with blood underneath his head. He also noted that on the stove in the kitchen area, with the gas burner turned on full blast, was a small frying pan containing Italian sausage, spinach, and beans. DiPersio immediately turned the gas off under the frying pan, took the pan off the burner and in the process burned his hand. He then called upstairs to his wife, told her not to come downstairs and to immediately call an ambulance since Mooney had been hurt. He felt for Mooney's pulse and could not find one.

A few minutes later an ambulance driver arrived and DiPersio was instructed by the driver that Mooney was dead and he had been shot in the head. DiPersio stated he did not see very well and in the excitement did not note that Giancana had been shot in the head.

DiPersio advised that Sam Giancana was a very meticulous man and as such at the end of the evening he would close and lock the basement door leading to the outside when he was ready to retire. He stated that on the evening Giancana was killed the back door was not locked while he and Mooney took their walk and anyone could enter the house from this entrance and hide in the basement as there were two possible places to hide in the basement that night; one being the utility room and the other being a storage closet. When things were quiet it is possible someone could easily sneak up behind Mooney and shoot him in the head.

DiPersio noted the last person, to best of his knowledge, to see Giancana alive was Blasi and that Blasi was the most trusted of Giancana's associates. It was very rare for Giancana to be visited by anyone at night, especially Blasi, who rarely was at the house in the evening. Blasi generally visited Giancana during the daylight hours. In the evening hours if Giancana wanted to get in touch with someone he would slip out the back door and make a phone call.

DiPersio also noted that on the evening Giancana was murdered he did not see Chuck English at the residence and has not see Chuck English for approximately four months. Chuck English generally visited the house during the day time.

DiPersio explained that he and his wife stayed at the Giancana residence for $10.00 per day and that he had not been paid by Giancana since January, 1975. The evening Giancana was murdered and prior to the time Blasi came to the residence DiPersio mentioned to Giancana he had not been paid for a considerable period of time. Giancana also owed a considerable amount of money on bills which had accrued at the house in his absence and Giancana replied that they would take care of the whole matter in the morning and pay all the bills, including DiPersio's salary. DiPersio indicated that Mooney did not mention he had any money on his person but when he was searching following the murder $1,400 was found in his pocket. Giancana never carried money in his wallet and reserved the wallet for carrying credit cards.

After Giancana had been murdered Blasi stopped by the Giancana residence many days later and asked DiPersio how things were going. DiPersio explained to Blasi that many bills were mounting at the house and he could not pay them. Blasi asked that all bills at the house be forwarded to him and that he would take care of them.

Approximately two weeks ago, late in the evening, DiPersio's wife answered a telephone call at the Giancana residence and was immediately set upon by a male caller who used very abusive language to her regarding her husband. DiPersio took the telephone himself and the caller used profanity to explain that the caller was coming to the Giancana residence to kill DiPersio and his "bitch" wife if he did not keep his mouth shut. DiPersio then proceeded to call the unidentified male caller every name he could think of in Italian and hung up the telephone in anger. DiPersio recalled he heard background music as if the caller was calling from a tavern.

DiPersio recognized the voice of the caller as being an individual he thought he knew, however, he decline to further identify him. As a result of the telephone call he and his wife have been apprehensive about remaining in the Giancana residence. DiPersio has had the telephone number at the Giancana residence changed and has experienced no further problem with receiving telephonic threats.

DiPersio and his wife, although residing in the Giancana residence, have maintained a flat in Cicero, Illinois and both will be more relaxed when they move back to their flat. DiPersio advised that appraisers have examined the contents of the residence and is of the opinion the Giancana family members will soon place the residence on the open market for sale.

During the period of time that DiPersio has known Giancana, Giancana at no time confided in him what it was he did to earn a living; however, DiPersio was of the opinion that whether Giancana controlled many "books" or was prominent in the rackets, Giancana was the boss. On those occasions when DiPersio was present and Charles English or "Butchie" Blasi came to see Mooney, DiPersio was asked to leave and he, therefore, was not privy to discussions of "business" between Giancana and his associates. Giancana was afraid of no one and as such left the basement door open and unlocked until such time he was ready to go to bed in the evening.

During this period of time that DiPersio has resided in the Giancana residence, he and his wife have noted in particular two vehicles apparently watching the Giancana residence. He described one vehicle as being a red, late model car and the other being a camper with blue curtains. They have noted these vehicles on several occasions during the evening hours and on one occasion early in the morning the camper was observed in the alley next to the garage with two men and a woman parked at this location. DiPersio watched these individuals for several minutes and the vehicle left.

Relative to the leak in the basement, DiPersio noted that the day following Giancana's murder his wife recalled that Mooney had taken a shower the day before. He checked the shower stall and noted that the water was running slowly from the shower stall and noted that the water was on and turned the water off. After turning the water off the leak in the basement ceased. DiPersio ultimately caulked the drain in the shower and replaced the acoustical tile in the basement ceiling.

DiPersio recalled the evening Giancana was murdered Blasi was wearing a short sleeve shirt and pants. He could not recall if Blasi was wearing the shirt outside of his pants or tucked into his trousers.

Relative to Judith Campbell Exner, DiPersio advised that he had seen her several times at the Giancana residence as he had seen many of the women Giancana brought to the house.

In conclusion, DiPersio was of the opinion that whoever killed Giancana was an individual who was very close to Giancana and was fully aware of the layout of the house and, in addition, knew Giancana spent the majority of his time in the basement. As an example of the killer's knowledge of the residence, DiPersio noted when he found the body of Giancana, the door separating the downstairs dining room and the kitchen area was almost fully closed. This door was never closed by Giancana and was recessed in the wall.

On June 20, 1975, Member of the Oak Park PD and the Cook County State's Attorney's Office, Chicago, went to the Giancana residence to re-examine the crime scene. These persons were ultimately admitted to the residence.

On June 20, 1975, CG T-3 advised that a vehicle matching the description of that belonging to Charles English was observed at the Giancana residence the evening of June 19, 1975. CG T-3 also advised that a vehicle matching the description of a vehicle known to be driven by Dominic "Butch" Blasi was observed at the residence the evening of June 19, 1975.

On June 20, 1975, Attorney in Chief, Chicago Strike Force, Peter Vaira, advised that murder of Sam Giancana did not constitute violation of Obstruction of Justice and therefore the FBI would not be called to investigate the murder.

Autopsy examination of Sam Giancana revealed that Giancana was shot once in the rear of the head, behind his right ear and lower than right ear, with the six remaining shots entering the head and neck regions anteriorly. The cause of death was attributed to gun shot wounds of the head. The projectiles were recovered and turned over to the Oak Park PD. The murder weapon was determined to be .22 caliber.

On June 23, 1975, the Los Angeles Division, FBI, advised that their agent had interviewed Carolyn Morris. Morris advised she had been staying in Houston, Texas, while Giancana was also in Houston. She was residing at the Warwick Hotel until June 18, 1975, at which time she returned to her Santa Monica, California residence. She stated that Giancana was released from Methodist Hospital on June 17, 1975, and she was in telephonic communication with Giancana on that date. Giancana, she presumes, called her from the Warwick Hotel.

Morris advised that Giancana called her again on June 18, 1975, and he told her he would be at his Oak Park home on June 19, 1975. The following evening she received a telephone call from Giancana's daughter, Bonnie Tisci, Tucson, Arizona, advising her that Giancana was home, and wanted her to call him. She opted not to call him because of the late hour, 11:30 pm (Chicago time) and to call him the next morning. At approximately 1:15 am the next morning, she received a telephone call from Tisci, telling her that Giancana was dead, and died from an apparent heart attack.

Morris advised that several hours later she called the Giancana residence, and spoke with Ann DiPersio, housekeeper. DiPersio told her that Giancana had been shot to death and the house was full of reporters and television people.

Carolyn Morris was not able to identify any suspects or a motive for the murder of Giancana. She stated that she was in love with Giancana; however, during their association Giancana told her nothing of his underworld activity and shielded her from this part of his life.

On June 23, 1075, Giancana was buried at Mt. Carmel Cemetery, Hillside, Illinois, and placed in the mausoleum housing his wife Angelina. Wake a funeral of Giancana was limited to family members and a small group of hoodlum mourners.

On June 24, 1975, a search warrant was obtained by the Cook County State's Attorney's office, Chicago, for a desk, file cabinet, and tape recorder previously observed in the residence of Sam Giancana during the search of the crime scene basement area on June 20, 1975. The above items were seized by Illinois Bureau of Investigation (IBI) agents and brought to the offices of the Cook County State's Attorney, Chicago.

On June 25, 1975, Jerome DePalma, Attorney and son-in-law to Giancana, filed a motion for injection to restrict opening of the desk and file cabinet and to restrict the Cook County State's Attorney's Office from processing the tapes on the tape recorder.

This motion was filed before Circuit Court Judge Daniel Covelli, who ruled in favor of the motion. To counter the injunction of Judge Covelli, Judge Hechinger demanded the Cook County State's Attorney's Office and IBI to immediately open the desk and file cabinet, process the tape on the tape recorder in addition to other tapes seized, and submit an inventory to him on June 25, 1975. Following the preparation of the inventory, the items seized were placed under seal in the offices of the State's Attorney's office.

On June 27, 1975, the Cook County State's Attorney's Office issued Cook County Grand Jury subpoenas for the appearance of Charles English and Dominic Blasi to appear in the near future the Grand Jury convened to investigate the murder of Sam Giancana.

On August 18, 1975, Dominic Gentile, Attorney for Giancana family members, appeared before Chief Judge James Parsons, NDI, USDC, and withdrew the motion to quash the FGJ subpoena. Judge Parsons granted the withdrawal of the motion. Reason for withdrawal of the motion was that after opening a safe contained in the file cabinet seized by Cook County State's Attorney's Office three handguns were discovered. Giancana family members did not want to accept ownership of these weapons due to the fact of the possible implications of these weapons.

On August 13, 1975, River Forest, maintenance personal, while in the process of cutting grass in the forest preserve adjacent to Thacker Street, River Forest, discovered a .22 caliber automatic pistol with a silencer, lying in the grass. This weapon was turned over to the River Forest Police Department.

The revolver was described as a Hi Standard Dura Matic, .22 long rifle, ten shot automatic with a seven and on forth by one and one fourth inch aluminum silencer. The revolver had serial number 1450968. This weapon was not listed as stolen in the National Crime Information Center (NCIC)

On August 21, 1975, items seized by the Cook County State's Attorney's Office from Giancana residence were obtained by Bureau Agents.

Relative to the .22 caliber automatic discovered in the grass adjacent to the Forest Preserve, ballistics tests conducted by the State of Illinois, determined that the above described weapon was the weapon used to kill Sam Giancana. Subsequent investigation reveals this weapon was sold to Moore-Handley, Incorporated, Miami Florida, on June 20, 1965.

Birmingham Division at Pelham, Alabama

On August 28, 1975, B.H. Wells, Vice President, Moore-Handley, Inc, Pelham, Alabama, advised their records revealed a Hi Standard .22 caliber six and one half inch barrel, blue, Dura Matic automatic pistol, model number 91-25, serial number 1450898 (instead of 1450968) was received by Moore-Handley from Hi Standard Company April 25, 1965. This weapon sold on August 9, 1965, to Tamaimi Gun Shop, Miami, Florida. Records at Moore-Handley indicated the above described weapon and one other were shipped to Tamiami Gun Shop by registry number Y-7002.

On August 29, 1975, Julio Fares, Manager Tamaimi Gun Shop, advised that no record exists for the acquisition of weapons in 1965. Fares advised he is part of new owners of gun shop purchased in 1973. Fares stated that previous owner, Roy Katon, Cotal Gables, Florida, had maintained incomplete records. Katon was in Spain at this time and due not to return until January, 1976.

In a similar development, Alcohol Tobacco and Firearms advised they had attempted to trace this same weapon on August 27, 1975, with negative results. Noted, no latent fingerprints were found on the weapon, magazine, or silencer.

Suspect

The chief suspect in this murder remains as Dominic Blasi; however, circumstantial evidence is not sufficient enough to indict Blasi for the murder. Several theories have been set forth regarding the reason Giancana was murdered. One theory set forth has been that upon Giancana's return to the U.S., Giancana wanted to re-establish himself as the operating head of the Chicago LCN and as such would be asking an individual in the Chicago LCN, after nine years absence, to move over and let him run the family as he has in the past. In this regard, he would have obviously been cutting someone out of a position they had earned based on their ability to handle the job, and as such he was murdered.

A second theory regarding the murder of Giancana was that there is an element of the Chicago family, in a secondary role within the family who feel they are ready to run the family and as such must move the elder statesmen from their positions of influence through murder as the elder statesmen refused to relinquished their positions of leadership based on their many years.

It has also come to the attention of the Chicago Division through a reliable source that Sam Giancana had been having an affair with Nancy Spilotro, wife of Anthony Spilotro. On those instances when Nancy Spilotro was in the Chicago area, Giancana and Nancy Spilotro would get together. This source indicated that Anthony Spilotro had learned of his wife's indiscretions and Giancana was murdered because of his "carrying on" with Nancy Spilotro.

It is believed that the motive for the murder of Giancana was not robbery, as Giancana had approximately $1,400 cash on his person at the time of the murder, and it did not appear any of his credit cards were missing from his person.

Interview with Phyllis McGuire

Phyllis McGuire advised that she completed an engagement at a local hotel in Las Vegas in the middle of June, 1975, and decided to take a vacation in Europe. Accordingly, she traveled to Paris, France, where she arrived on June 19, 1975. She had only been in her hotel room for a very short time when she received a call from Edward Mike Davis, with whom she resides in Las Vegas, advising her that Sam Giancana had been killed in Chicago.

McGuire stated that, of course, it is public knowledge that she and Giancana had been extremely close during the period 1959 through approximately 1964 or 1965. She stated that at one time she was very much in love with Giancana but had finally come to realize that in view of the age difference and Giancana's background, the relationship should cease. Accordingly, in 1964 or 1965, the romantic involvement between she and

Giancana was slowly terminated. She stated, however, that she had been in touch with Giancana from time to time primarily by telephone over the years.

She stated based on the above events she was uncertain as to what action she should take but felt that she should travel to Chicago to pay her respects to the daughters of Giancana.

She departed Paris by Air France, flying to Montreal, Canada, then to Chicago, where she arrived on the afternoon of June 21, 1975. McGuire declined to identify the individual who met her at the airport but stated it was definitely not Charles English of Dominic "Butch" Blasi.

McGuire was driven to the Hyatt House Regency Hotel where he had been pre-registered. She stated she does not know who pre-registered her or what name was used for her at the hotel.

McGuire stayed in view of the wide spread news media interest in both her and Giancana; she took appropriate action to avoid the news media as much as possible.

She stated that on the day Giancana's body was first available for viewing, she went to the funeral home on that night after the funeral home was ostensibly closed. She stated she entered the room in the funeral home where Giancana's body was located and spent five to seven minutes in the room alone with the body. She left the funeral home and returned to her hotel. She again visited the funeral home, date not recalled, but believes it was the night prior to the funeral. McGuire stated she did not attend either the rosary or the funeral.

McGuire declined to identify the individual who drove her to and from the funeral home but stated it was an individual she has known for several years and that it was not Charles English or Dominic "Butch" Blasi.

McGuire stated that a short time after the funeral, one of Giancana's daughters came to the hotel and visited with her for a short time. Following this she left Chicago and returned to Las Vegas later on the same day of the funeral.

McGuire stated that she has never had a safe deposit box in Chicago area under her name or any other name and that she did not visit any bank in the Chicago area while she was there on this particular trip. She stated that to the best of her recollection she has never been in any bank in the Chicago area in her life.

She stated that she and Edward Mike Davis are not legally married although they did secure a marriage license some time ago but a civil marriage ceremony has never been performed. At the beginning of the interview, McGuire stated that she was extremely apprehensive for her own safety in view of her relationship with Giancana. She said, however, that she has received no type of communication at this point which she considers a threat to her in any manner.

McGuire stated that she contemplates frequent travel during the next few months and requested that if further interviews are necessary by the FBI, that the same be handled by the contacting Agents and stated she would keep these Agents informed of her exact whereabouts at all times.

Informants

Past information, on 6/2/75, CG informant advised SA F. Ford that "Potsy" Peral is operating his bookmaking operation on his own on the north side of Chicago. Source stated there is an excellent chance that in the very near future his entire operation will be placed under Lenny Patrick. From what he can gather, source stated Sam Giancana no longer gets any income from Pearl's operations.

Source stated that Giancana is very much on his own and prefers it that way. Source advised that like a number of old time Mafia leaders, Giancana has accumulated great wealth and is not interested in acquiring a source of income from Chicago area Mafia operations. Source stated there had been no conversation concerning Giancana and apparently Giancana is not presenting any problems to the present Mafia bosses.

On 7/8/75, CG informant advised that nothing had changed since Giancana had been killed. The word is still out that "he had it coming" and Accardo, Aiuppa, and the rest of the people are satisfied the job was "well done".

Source indicated it was his guess that someone very close to Sam was contacted and ordered to do the job. When orders come from the top, you cannot get off. This guy could well have been Charles English or Dominic Blasi. Source indicated that both had complete confidence of Giancana and would have no trouble getting into Giancana's house.

On 7/9/75, CG informant advised there is no question Giancana was "knocked off" with the approval of the top Mafia members. During the past week, informant stated he has been at several hoodlum hangouts, including the Hollywood Lounge in Cicero, Illinois. No one discusses Giancana and there is no talk about "revenge" as there would be if the murder was not authorized.

On 7/15/75, CG informant advised that Giancana's death still is not discussed by any mob members. It is now well known that "Sam got someone high up pretty mad." Source indicated that Giancana brought it on himself by whatever he said or did since returning from Mexico.

Source indicated that two LCN members were very close to Giancana. He stated that one or the other probably got a phone call from one of the committee. Whoever received the call would have no choice.

On August 20, 1975, CG T-1 furnished the following information:

Source advised that the family of Sam Giancana has conducted a diligent search for any will which was executed by Giancana prior to his death. No such will has been located. The family assumed a will was contained in the safe which was confiscated under a search warrant by the Cook County States Attorney's Office and which was impounded by order of Judge Daniel Covelli. No will was found in the safe and is therefore the conclusion of the family of Giancana as of the middle of August, 1975, that Giancana did not execute a will. Therefore all of his possessions will be divided equally between his three daughters, his only heirs.

Source advised that although veteran associates of Giancana such as James Perno, Joe DiPersio, Dominic Blasi and Charles English felt they were beneficiaries of monies left to them by Giancana inasmuch as he had indicated by statements throughout his life time to them that they would be taken care of by Giancana when he died, known of them had received a penny from Giancana.

Source advised that he understands that Charles English and Dominic Blasi, who have been the subjects of subpoena ever since the killing of Giancana in June have now been again continued until 9/24/75.

Source advised that Charles English had been so upset due to his involvement in the investigation of the killing of Giancana that he recently suffered his third heart attack and was confined in the hospital for a short period of time. However, he has now been released and is again at home in River Forest.

Autopsy

Autopsy examination of Sam Giancana revealed that Giancana was shot once in the rear of the head, behind his right ear and lower than the right ear, with the six remaining shots entering the head and neck regions anterior. The cause of death was attributed to gun shot wounds of the head. The projectiles were recovered and turned over to the Oak Park PD. The murder weapon was determined to be a .22 caliber.

Sam Giancana's house at 1147 South Wenonah Avenue, Oak Park, Illinois.

FEDERAL BUREAU OF INVESTIGATION

REPORTING OFFICE	OFFICE OF ORIGIN	DATE	INVESTIGATIVE PERIOD	
CHICAGO	CHICAGO	1975	December 2, 1975	

TITLE OF CASE	REPORT MADE BY	TYPED BY
		dkc
SAMUEL M. GIANCANA, aka	**CHARACTER OF CASE** FBI Headquarters File number 92-3171-2642 Samuel M. Giancana, Top Hoodlum Program – Anti Racketeering	

On instant date, safe deposit box at Berwyn National Bank, in name of Sam DeTolve, opened. It was determined this safe deposit box was being used by Sam Giancana as the box was rented in the name of DeTolve after the death of DeTolve. Present when safe deposit box was open was Francine DePalma, Richard Fredo, Giancana family attorney, and Robert Door, representing the State of Illinois. Safe deposit box was empty at time of being opened. Richard Fredo advised that last record of entry to this safe deposit box was on January 17, 1975, in the name of Sam DeTolve.

In conversation with Richard Fredo, only liquid assets to Giancana heirs at present time are the Giancana residence, 1147 S. Wenohan, Oak Park, Illinois, and $55,000 in savings account. Giancana's assets in Mexico consisting of several supermarkets, the Quinta San Cuernavaca residence, and several loans outstanding.

Chapter 20

FEDERAL BUREAU OF INVESTIGATION

REPORTING OFFICE	OFFICE OF ORIGIN	DATE	INVESTIGATIVE PERIOD
CHICAGO	CHICAGO	1976	January 30, 1976

TITLE OF CASE	REPORT MADE BY	TYPED BY
SAMUEL M. GIANCANA, aka	William W. Thurman, Jr.	dkc

	CHARACTER OF CASE
	FBI Headquarters File number 92-3171
	Top Hoodlum Program – Anti Racketeering

Relative to the investigation of the murder of Sam Giancana being conducted by the Cook County State's Attorney's Office, Chicago, Jerome DePalma, Giancana's son-in-law and Francine DePalma, subject's daughter, appeared before the Cook County Grand Jury and both invoked the Fifth Amendment privilege and declined to testify. Both were asked to return to the Grand Jury on November 14, 1975.

On November 14, 1975, Jerome DePalma again invoked his Fifth Amendment privilege and declined to testify. On the same date Francine DePalma also appeared before the Grand Jury and testified subsequent to being granted immunity by Chief Judge, Cook County Circuit Court. Jerome DePalma was instructed to reappear on November 21, 1975.

On November 18, 1975, Dominic Joseph Blasi, chief murder suspect in this investigation, appeared before the Cook County Grand Jury and invoked his Fifth Amendment privilege. He was directed to return on December 12, 1975.

On December 12, 1975, Joseph DiPersio and his wife Ann appeared before the Grand Jury. Both were subsequently granted immunity and testified.

During November, 1975, Giancana's family heirs hired Richard Fredo, Probate Attorney, to administrate the estate of Sam Giancana. On December 2, 1975, safe deposit box number 502, Berwyn National Bank, in the name of Sam DeTolve was opened. This safe deposit box was being used by

Sam Giancana as the key for this box was found among those items seized from the Giancana residence. The safe deposit box was found empty at the time it was open. Last entry to this box was on January 17, 1975, in the name of Sam DeTolve.

The Giancana assets in Mexico, consisting of Quinta San Cristobal, several loans, and Mexican bonds, are all in the name of Giancana's Mexican attorney, Jorge Castillo. It was learned that Jerome DePalma attempted to contact Castillo relative to the Giancana Mexican assets and Castillo appeared **very vague** pertaining to the Giancana interests.

FEDERAL BUREAU OF INVESTIGATION

REPORTING OFFICE	OFFICE OF ORIGIN	DATE	INVESTIGATIVE PERIOD
CHICAGO	CHICAGO	1976	September 17, 1976

TITLE OF CASE	REPORT MADE BY	TYPED BY
SAMUEL M. GIANCANA, aka	William W. Thurman, Jr.	dkc

CHARACTER OF CASE

FBI File number 92-3171-2652
Top Hoodlum Program – Anti Racketeering

Administrative

Investigative period is somewhat lengthy, however, this matter has been kept current through inter and intra office communications. It was determined that this investigation be kept open after being reopened 2/13/76, in order to satisfactorily resolve the Sam Giancana estate which was placed in probate in absence of a will. At this time all matters of Bureau interest concerning the Sam Giancana estate have been resolved and Chicago is closing this matter.

Synopsis:

Attempts to locate records pertaining to the Sam Giancana murder weapon from the Tamiami Gun Shop, Miami, Florida, negative. Records indicating a value of the personal estate of Sam Giancana estimated at $132,583.16 as filed in Circuit Court of Cook County, Illinois, County Department-Probate Division, 2/4/76. Heirs to the Giancana estate received

$63,867.40 from the sale of personal effects consisting of a collection of porcelain figurines, jewelry, French antique furniture, prints and paintings, during June, 1976. The Giancana residence, 1147 South Wenonah, Oak Park, was sold for 69,500 and this amount will be added to the estate of Giancana. Noted a commission of $4,170 was paid to the realtor of the house, the realtor was Dominic Blasi.

Giancana's residence

The home itself is a two story brick residence with a completely finished basement. The residence has six large bedrooms, three full baths, two half baths, a formal dining room and a large living room with a vaulted ceiling, a small kitchen and a family room on the ground level and second story of the residence. The basement, fully finished, has a fully furnished kitchen complete with refrigerator-freezer combination built into the wall, a large dining room with 2 $\frac{1}{2}$ thick solid brick walls, a wine cellar and combination utility room/work room complete with work bench.

Details

Investigation in this matter was reopened on 2/13/1976, upon receipt of information to the effect that a tape recording had been made of the murder of Sam Giancana and that this recording could possibly lead to the identity of the murderer or murderers of Giancana in the basement of his Oak Park, residence on June 19, 1975. Subsequent investigation relative to this tape disclosed that the tape recording was in fact one which had been among the possessions seized pursuant to the issuance of a search warrant following the murder of Giancana at the Giancana residence. A review of this tape did not reveal that it was recorded the evening of the murder and in fact gunshots heard on the tape were from background noise from the television show "Kojak."

On September 15, 1976, Richard P. Fredo advised that the auction of the personal effects of Giancana's residence (consisting of a collection of quality porcelain figurines, jewelry, French antique furniture and prints and paintings) grossed the heirs $79,464 with a net figure of $63,867.40. The difference between the net and gross figures went for commission on the sale of the items and for repair of some of the porcelain and furniture. The Giancana residence was sold for $69,500 and a commission of $4,170 was paid to the realtor Dominic "Butch" Blasi.

On June 17, 1977, Joseph DiPersio was re-interviewed concerning murder of his former employer. DiPersio was specifically queried regarding the .22 caliber High Standard Dura-Matic murder weapon and the .22 caliber long rifle ammunition found in the Giancana residence during the execution of a search warrant. DiPersio related to his knowledge Giancana kept no weapons in the residence. On a number of occasions DiPersio searched the residence specifically looking for a weapon, however, he found none. DiPersio expressed some anxiety about residing in the Giancana home, particularly when Giancana was not present. A number of prowler incidents in the vicinity of the residence made DiPersio and his spouse fearful which prompted DiPersio to request Giancana for a gun. Giancana refused DiPersio's request advising him a gun was unnecessary since no one would ever harm he or his spouse.

Photographs of the .22 caliber High Standard Dura-Matic pistol were displayed to DiPersio. He was unable to make an identification of this pistol and he never recalled observing it in the Giancana residence. Regarding the .22 caliber ammunition found in Giancana's desk located in the residence basement, DiPersio claimed he never had access to this desk and he was unaware of its contents. It was DiPersio's belief that Giancana had the only key to the desk.

The main FBI investigation on Sam Giancana is being placed in a closed status.

The FBI file was closed and the murder of Sam Giancana was never solved. In June 1978, a Thomas Hampson, who was the senior investigator for the Illinois legislative investigation commission, made a report about his findings on the Giancana murder. His theory was that the death of Giancana involved the fact that Giancana and Joseph Bannano, New York City mob boss, were at odds with each other. Bonnano attempted to take over the New York families of organized crime and failed. According to Hampson, Giancana voted to kill Bannano while the remainder of the Commission decided to kidnap him instead. After the kidnapping, the Commission gave Bonnano Arizona as his own area. As a result of Giancana's incarceration from his refusal to testify, Giancana lost his power in Chicago and took isolation in Mexico. Before this time either if any cooperation existed between the Chicago organization and the Arizona organization because of the animosity between Giancana and Bannano. Once Giancana was out of power, a profitable exchange began developing between Chicago and Arizona. Chicago organized crime figures were frequently traveling to Arizona.

After a period of exile Giancana wanted to regain possession of the Chicago mob. Several opposing factors existed. First, those in power in Chicago did not want to relinquish to Giancana; second, even though a profitable exchange existed between Chicago and Arizona, the old animosity between Giancana and Bonnano still existed and Bannano refused to do business with Giancana; third, the Organized Crime Commission did not favor the publicity that Giancana always drew.

As a result of their action, particularly Bonnano's influence, the Commission decided to kill Giancana. Hampson stated that Chuck English and Harry Altman are the two primary suspects as the trigger men in the shooting. Hampson discounted that Giancana was killed because of his testimony before the Senate, his possible testimony before and grand jury or anything connected with the CIA or CIA plots.

The Giancana Family

In years to follow many stories and theories as to why Giancana was killed were hatched. Mobster Aladena "Jimmy the Weasel" Fratianno told the feds that Giancana was killed because he agreed to cooperate if federal authorities would give him a cover and make it look like he was being forced back to Chicago to testify. When the Chicago mob found out it was all planed, Giancana was killed. However, government officials stick to the story that Giancana never gave up any information and was never cooperating with anyone.

The theory that Giancana was demanding his old job back was reported, but, if so, no one ever talked and confirmed that story, at least, not that the public knows. The story of Sam Giancana has become an interest to almost anyone who hears it. His daughters and grandchildren will continue to make sure his story stays alive in any form that is possible.

In 1977 an FBI informant came forward to the FBI with information about Giancana and his love life at the time of his murder. The report reads, *"Source advised relative to Sam Giancana, that near the time of Giancana's killing (June 19, 1975), Giancana was having an affair with Nancy Spilotro, wife of Tony Spilotro. Source indicated Giancana always had a propensity to 'entertain' several women at the same time, independent of each other, regardless of his feelings for individual women. Regarding Nancy Spilotro, source indicated Nancy Spilotro would stay at the Spilotro residence located several blocks away from the Giancana Oak Park, Illinois, residence, and on these occasions, Giancana had 'access' to Nancy Spilotro."* The information was an allegation and the FBI had no proof this actually occurred.

Years ago an old time Chicago police officer who was on duty the night of the Giancana murder told the story that Chicago police had been watching the house the night of the murder and moments before the killing the police officers assigned to watch the house were ordered away from the house. When this officer questioned why the officers were pulled at the moment of the murder he found no answers.

Sam's brother Joseph Giancana was the subject of his own FBI investigation in the 1970's.

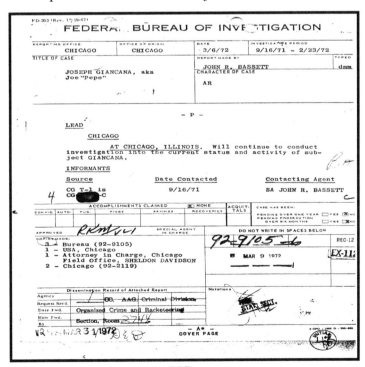

Joseph "Pepe" Giancana was born on May 9, 1920, and was 12 years younger than his big brother Sam. One report stated that Joseph was a half brother to Sam. He would go on to marry his wife Maria "Mary" and have three children, Anthony, James and Donna. His known address was 1938 Wenonah Avenue in Berwyn, Illinois and later in life lived in Bloomingdale, Illinois.

Earliest reports attached were from April 1945 when a Corp. Joseph Giancana, living at 2816 Lexington Street in Chicago, received an honorable discharge from the military at the A.A.F. regional and convalescent hospital in Miami Beach, Florida. He had served 16 months in the Central Pacific zone. It was not know if this was the brother of Sam Giancana.

By 1961, Joe Giancana was listed as being involved in gambling and "juice" operations in Cicero, Illinois. He was connected to Gus' Steak House at 4817 Roosevelt Road and a handbook in the rear of a bar at 11th Street and Cicero Avenue. He was listed as being partners with Frank "Sharkey" Eulo and Gus Kringas. He was also linked to Sam "Mad Sam" DeStefano's "juice" racket in Cicero.

In April 1963 government authorities raided Tony and Carry's Tavern at 1442 S. Cicero Avenue in Cicero and arrested Michael Baker, James Leo, Charles Hruby, Michael LoSurdo, Paul Abraham and Hyman Fogelbaum. Abraham and Fogelbaum refused to testify before a county grand jury. Taken in the raid were dice tables, betting cards and $350. The tavern was reported to be operated by Joe Giancana and was known as "Pepe's dice game."

In 1967 the FBI concluded that Joseph Giancana was a "made" member of the Chicago Outfit of the La Cosa Nostra.

In July 1969, Joseph was involved in a collision involving property damage from speeding. The car he had been driving was registered to Celozzi-Ettleston Chevrolet car dealer ship at 15W600 Roosevelt Road, owned buy Joe Giancana's brother-in-law. A month later Joe Giancana was called to testify before a federal grand jury investigating organized crime. Also called were Fiore "Fifi" Buccieri, Joseph "Gags" Gagliano, James "Turk" Torello, Angelo Kokas, John Manzella, Louis Manzella and Salvatore Molose.

A 1970 report stated that Joseph Giancana had not been seen in Rosemont Illinois for almost 2 years. Giancana use to frequent Rosemont where he sold various types of jewelry and trinkets.

In December 1971, federal authorities discovered that Joseph Giancana and his son were paid employees working behind mutual windows at Chicago race tracks. From there they could take bets for the mob. During the investigation he was learned that Giancana was observed dispensing tickets at the $5 window at the Aurora Downs Race Track in 1970. Also discovered on payrolls of area racetracks were Michael Bates, a known gambler from Cicero, Carmen Buccieri, the nephew of Fifi Buccieri and the Esposito brothers, Anthony "Sonny" Esposito Jr. and his brother Frank "Butch" Esposito had jobs working the windows at Sportsman Park race track for the mob. Another was William McGuire, a former Chicago police officer who was alleged to be a "front man" for the syndicate to muscle into legitimate businesses. McGuire was associated with Frank DeStefano, brother of mobster Rocco DeStefano, in an illegal garbage dump operation. The investigation disclosed that mob bookies were making up to $100,000-a-day in profits at the race tracks. The investigation also revealed that Robert "Big Bob" McCullough, a one time Capone gangster, had many of the concessions at Chicago race tracks in his pockets. One example was he controlled all the parking lots at Sportsman's Park in Cicero. When McCullough wanted to put mobsters on the payroll working the windows he would call one time Illinois Secretary of State Paul Powell, who in return would call track officials and get the gangsters their jobs.

In February 1973 an FBI informant said that Joseph Giancana, Sam Giancana and Nick Nitti were holding a meeting at the Blue Max Night Club inside the Regency Hyatt House in Rosemont,

Illinois. The informant also added that alleged mob associate Ben Stein was also present in the Blue Max but gave orders to the head waiter that he was not to be seated in the same area and the Giancana brothers.

Joseph "Pepe" Giancana died on May 2, 1996 in Bloomingdale, Illinois. Sam's other brother, Charles Giancana, aka Charles Kane, died on January 7, 2001 and both are buried at Queen of Heaven Cemetery in Hillside, Illinois.

Joseph Giancana's Grave

Charles Giancana's Grave

It was not reported if Joseph's two son's James and Anthony ever followed in there fathers foot steps but reports did appear from time to time concerning them. In 1999 a report that James S. Giancana was arrested and charged with assault. According to the report James approached a woman and while shaking his hands told the woman *"I will get a gun and blow your head off."* However, James Giancana was found not guilty. The report did not confirm that this was the son of Joseph.

As for his other son Anthony, he had repeated problems with the law. In October 1963 Anthony J. Giancana was arrested by Missouri police after a 38-mile auto chase on U.S. Highway 66. When police tried to pull him over for speeding a chase ensued with speeds up to 130 miles-an-hour. When police would try and pull up next to the speeding car Giancana would try and run them off the road. He was finally stopped when police set up a road block near Waynesville, Missouri. When the young Giancana was asked what his name was, he answered, *"none of your business."* Then he gave a fictitious name, they looked on his drivers license and saw the name Anthony Giancana. However, when the policeman read that his birthdates was March 17, 1946, he thought the young Anthony was much younger and suspected a fake birth date. His license said he was 17-years-old, when his father arrived he told them that he was 16-years-old and Chicago Police records said he was 15-years-old with a birth date of June 17, 1948. When asked why he was speeding and what he was doing in Missouri, he told the police that he took the car with out his parents knowing and, *"I just wanted to get as far away as I could."*

He was charged with careless and imprudent driving and speeding. He was sentenced to 60 days in jail. The story did not end there, the next day while in jail the young Anthony set his mattress and two blankets on fire. Police also discovered that he almost had the glass removed completely from his window in his cell. And the story did not end there, the next day he complained he was feeling ill, so he was taken to the local hospital where he escaped from police custody. Police recaptured him as he was trying to hitch hike on U.S. Highway 66. One of the retired trooper named Joe Kearse remembered the day and said that when Giancana's parents were called, his mother Mary showed-up in her luxury vehicle and was accompanied by two very large bodyguards.

Anthony J. Giancana was married on July 11, 1965, to a bohemian girl from Berwyn, Illinois. The FBI reported that arrangements were made for them to live in one of the apartments in Rosemont, Illinois, which was owned by Charles Giancana. There is a listing of an Anthony J. Giancana divorcing a Nancy L. Giancana in divorce court from 1982. Anthony Giancana had six children, Carmen, Angela, Timothy, Danine, Michael, and Nicholas.

In December 1995, Anthony Giancana was pulled over by police while driving a black 1987 Chrysler Sedan with a head light out on the vehicle. Police discovered that his license had been revoked and he was placed into double locked handcuffs and arrested. At the time of his arrest police information had him living at 1-B Dale Place in Bloomingdale, Illinois. He was listed as 5'11" in height, 195 pounds, brown hair, brown eyes and a tattoo of a dagger on his left arm and a rose on his left shoulder.

One of the last reports on Anthony Giancana was when he was arrested in June 2000 once again for driving on a revoked license; he spent three days in the custody of the Sheriff's department in jail. Anthony J. Giancana was listed as a veteran of the Vietnam War when he died in December 2003.

File Card

Anthony J. Giancana
Born: June 17, 1948
Death: December 4, 2003 (Obituary date)

Known Arrest Record and Court Hearings

Date	Description	Agency
10-1963	Careless driving and speeding	Missouri PD
10-1963	Prison break	Missouri Jail
1979	Unknown	DuPage
1980	Unknown	DuPage
1981	Unknown	DuPage
6-30-1982	Driving while licensed revoked	Glen Ellyn PD
3-23-1983	Driving while licensed revoked	Elmhurst PD
12-7-1995	Driving while licensed revoked	DuPage
6-2000	Driving while licensed revoked	DuPage Sheriff

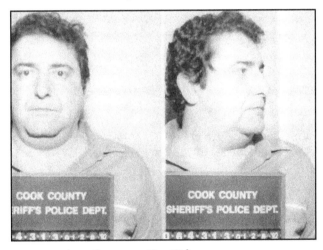

Anthony J. Giancana

Timothy Giancana

Some reports alleged that Joseph Giancana's grand children have had some scrapes with law enforcement. According to court documents under the Giancana name that match the names of Joseph's grand children, Timothy Giancana has been arrested for and spent time in prison on burglary, theft, criminal damage to property, possession of Cannabis, auto theft, obstructing justice, DUI, reckless driving, illegal transport of alcohol, possession of stolen property, disorderly conduct, unlawful use of credit card, criminal trespass to land, resisting a police officer, aggravated battery and driving under a suspended license. As of 2008 he was serving time in an Illinois State prison for burglary. A Michael Giancana has been arrested for possession of drug paraphernalia, obstruction of justice and driving while license suspended. None of the reports mentioned if Michael and Timothy were the sons of Anthony J. Giancana or related to Joseph and Sam Giancana. It is alleged that from Joseph Giancana on down to his grand children there have been over 55 issued traffic violations.

Sam Giancana's Official FBI Bio Card

Name	Samuel M. Giancana
Aliases	Sam Mooney, Momo Salvatore Giancana, Gilormo Giancana, Samuel Giancanna, Sam Gianaco, Sam Gincani, Sam Giancano, Sam Gencani, Sam Gincana, Sam - Gincanni, Sam Gincanna, Sam Gincina, Sam Ginoina, Sam Giacana, Sam Gianana, Sam Ginncana, Sam Giancanel, Sam Flood, Albert Manusco, Albert Masusco, R. J. Landolt, Mr. Goldfield, Mooney Cecola, Sam Russo, J.J. Brackett, Sam Bianco, Dr. Moe, Sam DeTolve, Mickey Mancuso, John Williams, Sam DePalma,
Race	White
Sex	Male
Dates of Birth	June 15, 1908, *(as contained on birth certificate maintained at Holy Guardian Angel Church, Chicago, and delayed birth certificate filed by subject and his attorney at the Bureau of Vital Statistics at Chicago in 1955.)* May 24, 1908, *(as contained on birth certificate No. 5915 files with the Bureau of Vital Statistics, Chicago, on June 30, 1908, by midwife of Giancana, Chicago, Illinois.)*
Place of Birth	Chicago, Illinois
Height	5'9"
Weight	170 pounds
Build	Medium
Hair	Black, slightly wavy, receding in front and at temples
Eyes	Brown
Complexion	Dark
Occupation	No known legitimate employment
FBI Number	58437
Social Security #	326-18-6902
Residence	1147 Wenonah Avenue, Oak Park, Illinois (1945 to present) 2822 West Lexington (1945) 914 South Hermitage (1944) 1148 South Monitor, 2022 West Lexington (1939)
Marital Status	Widower
Relatives	Angeline Giancana, nee Angeline DeTolve (deceased April 23, 1954, Florida)
Daughter Giancana	Annette, also known as "Toni", date of birth June 23, 1935, Chicago, Illinois; resides with
Daughter	Bonnie Lou, date of birth April 29, 1938, Chicago, Illinois; resides with Giancana
Daughter	Francine, date of birth July 15, 1945, Chicago, Illinois; resides with Giancana.
Father	Antonio Giancana (deceased)
Mother	Mrs. Antonia Giancana (deceased)
Brothers	Joseph Giancana Charles Giancana
Sisters	Mrs. Josephine Benedetto
	Mrs. Mary Faraggia
	Mrs. Victoria Citro

Sisers	Miss Antonietta Giancana
	Mrs. Lena Campo
	Mrs. Celozzi
Son-in-law	Carmen Manno (Husband of daughter Annette)
Son-in-law	Anthony Tisci (Husband of daughter Bonnie Lou)
Son-in-law	Jerry DePalma (Husband of daughter Francine)

Some of Giancana's Assosiates Listed in the Files

Anthony Joseph Accardo
1906-1992

Tony Accardo, also known as "Joe Batters", "The Big Tuna", "The Old Man", and smiply "Joe." Top mob boss and Consiglieri from the 1940's to 1990's.

The FBI's 1964 offical listing of Accardo, "Anthony Accardo currently resides at 1407 North Ashland, River Forest, Illinois. He is not known to be gainfully employes in any Legitimate enterprise which necssitates his physical appearance.

Accardo is a member of La Cosa Nostra and was for approximately ten years the Chicago representative to "the Commission" of the La Cosa Nostra. During this tenure Accardo was the head of the organized criminal element in Chicago and surrounding areas. He was replaced as the representative on the "Commission" by Sam Giancana. Since his relacment Accardo, like Paul Ricca (De Lucia), has been considered as an "elder statesman." Accardo is respected by the organization and continues to wield influence. He is sought after for counsel and his opinions are listened to and carefully considered.

Accardo is not known to be active in any particular phase of orgainzed crime. He reportedly has entered into legitimate financial investments in the United States; however, none of the reported investments have been verified. He and Ricca are reported to be interested in racing and gambling in Mexico City, Mexico. Accardo continues in a close capacity with those persons recignized as the hierchy of the Chicago criminal element.

Joseph John Aiuppa
1907-1997

Joey Aiuppa was mostly know as Joey O'Brien. Top mob boss and underboss from 1970's to 1990's.

The FBI's offical listing of him in 1964 is as follows, "Joseph John Aiuppa, a white male, born on December 1, 1907, Melrose Park, Illinois, continues to reside at 4 Yorkshire Woods, Oak Brook, Illinois.

This address was formerly Elmhurst, Illinois, but was changed due to the reallocation of the Oak Brook Villiage. According to Oak Brook Police Department, Aiuppa lives a quit, sedated life as a country gentleman in their area. Aiuppa has had a notorious beackgroud since the early 1930's. One alleged report regarding Aiuppa's activities in the early 1930's was that Aiuppa was a "trigger man" for Claude Maddox, deceased, a notoriouos Cicero hoddlum. He was alleged to have been an expert bank robber and had killed many a men when Maddox, whose true name is John E. Moore, wanted individuals killed or done away with. Aiuppa allegedly furnished hiding places for members of the John Dillinger gang during the early 1930's. Aiuppa Aiuppa was reportedly a charter member of Local 450, Hotel, Resturant Employees and Bartenders Union, and had appeared before the Senate committee investigating crime in the early 1950's, however, refused to testify by citing the Fith Amendment of the Constitution. Aiuppa also obtained notoriety during the Mc-Clellan Committee hearings investigation labor racketeers and hoodlums on which Robert F. Kennedy was Chief Council.

Aiuppa's domain is generally considered to be the notorious "vice strip" in the 4800 block of West Cermak Road, Cicero, Illinois. Aiuppa can usually be found in or about the Towne Hotel and the Towne Snack Shop in that area. The 4800 block of West Cermak Road had in the past been the location for Frolics Club and the Magic Lounge, two notorious places of amusement where strip shows and "B Girls" hustling tricks operated with immunity for protection. Both of these businesses are now closed as a result of raids conducted by the Cook County Sheriff's Office.

Aiuppa is still considered to be the man in charge of Cicero gambling and "strip joints" and his authority for the direction of these activities is shared with aonther well known hoodlum, William Daddono, also known as "Potatoes." Aiuppa's underling is considered to be Joseph Corngold, who has for a long time been considered the gambling boss in Cicero, Illinois, operating the El Patio gambling spot in Cicero for the past 20 years. Sam Giancana reportedly the leader of Chicago's organized crime element can be considered as assosciate of Aiuppa. During August, 1964, Aiuppa has been observed with James "Cowboy" Mirro.

Aiuppa untilizes the Towne Hotel and the Towne Hotel Snack Shop as a meeting place where he can discuss his various activities with his friends and associates. FBI agents conducting a surveillance in the vacinity of the Towne Hotel have noted that Vincent Inserro, also known as "The Saint", who is considered to be a professional killer for the Outfit, has been observed on numerous occashions entering and leaving the Towne Hotel.

Aiuppa's appeal for his conviction for the illegal possession and transportaion of mouring doves at the United States District Court, Kansas City, Kansas, is still pending and the case is scheduled to be argued before the Circuit Court of Appeals in Denver, Colorado, on September 21, 1964.

Aiuppa is described as a white male, 5'5 ½", 180 pounds, brown hair, brown eyes, and should be considered armed and dangerous inasmuch as he is a reported "trigger man" for hoodlums."

Felix Anthony Alderisio
1912-1971

Felix Alderisio was know in the mob circles as "Philly" and "Milwaukee Phil". Mob underboss and capo in the 1960's and 70's.

The FBI's 1964 listing is as follows, "Felix Alderisio resides at 505 Berkeley Drive, Riverside, Illinois. Alderisio has been characterized as a "hit" man and is said to be an independent operator answerable only to Sam "Mooney" Giancana. Approximately four or five years ago Alderisio was considered only a muscleman and was noted for his rough, uncouth appearance. He once appeared at a hoodlums wedding wearing a sports shirt and no tie. At present, Alderisio's rise in stature in the hoodlum element has been meteoric and he has emerged as a daper fresser who posses as a successful businessman. He invariable dresses immaculately and on occasion when picked up by the Chicago Police has had from $800 to $2,5000 in his pocket. It has been alleged that he is considered in some areas as scond in command to Sam Giancana, and would be considered to replace Giancana when he steps out of the top spot."

Gus Alex
1916-1998

Gus Alex, also know as Gussie, Slim, and Shotgun. Mob boss of the old First Ward in Chicago 1940's to 2000. Highest ranking non-Italian boss in the Chicago outfit.

The FBI's listing in 1964 is as follows, "Gus Alex is forty-eight years old, although his birth date had varied according to different documents prepared by Alex. He is 5'10" in height, 190 pounds, black graying hair, brown eyes, and dark complexioned. He is very neat and impeccably dressed at all times. He currently resides in Apartment 10C, 1150 North Lake Shore Drive, Chicago, Illinois. Alex prides himself in his personal appearance and good physique and is known by his hoodlum associates by names such as "Slim", "Shoulders", "The Greek", and "Gussie".

Alex in the past has been in poor health and suffered from depressive neurosis, having been hospitalized several times in a mental hospital in New Canaan, Connecticut. Inquiry at this hospital recently indicated he has not received any treatment there since 1961. He is known to be a worrier and to take a quantity of pills each day. He is very much aware of FBI and police interest in him and his activities making him extremely surveillance conscious and difficult to follow.

Alex is considered one of the leaders of organized crime in Chicago having responsibility for the First Ward of Chicago which includes the Loop area and near South Side as well as near West Side. He receives income from gambling, prostitutes, strip joints, arcades and loan shark activities. He was closely associated in these activities with the late Frank Ferraro, top hoodlum and reputed "Treasure" for the underworld in Chicago. Alex has been associated with organized crime all his life having been born and raised in the near South Side where he became associated with Ferraro and others. He rose to his present position after the death of Jake Guzik for whom he was chuffer and bodyguard, prior to Guzik's death in 1956. Alex interests in prostitution, strip joint operations and arcades are directed by Louis Arger, who is responsible to Alex."

Samuel Battaglia
1908-1973

Sam Battaglia was known to many as "Teets." Top mob boss and capo in the 1950's and 1960's. His 1964 FBI bio page reads as follows, "Salvatore Battaglia is a high ranking member of the Chicago "Outfit" who is considered by many to be second only to Giancana in importance. He resides at 1114 North Ridgeland, Oak Park, Illinois, and also has a large farm, known as Free Meadows Stock Farm Pingree Grove Illinois. Battaglia is in general control of the Western suburbs of Chicago in "juice", prostitution and gambling. Lieutenants of Battaglia are Felix Alderisio and Marshall Caifano."

Dominic Joseph Blasi
1911-1993

Dom Blasi went by the name of "Butch." Butch Blasi acted as Sam Giancana's right hand man in the capacity that of an under boss, chauffeur and bodyguard.

His 1963 FBI bio card reads as follows, "Dominic Joseph Blasi, born September 9, 1911, Chicago, Illinois, and currently resides at 1138 Park Avenue, River Forest, Illinois. Blasi is generally considered as the closest confidant of Samuel Giancana, reputed leader of organized crime element in Chi-

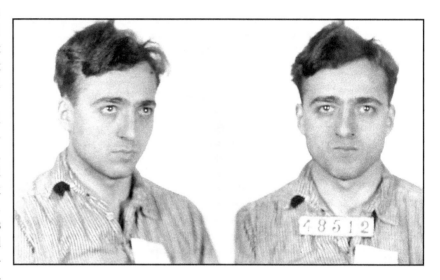

cago area. Blasi has extensive criminal background dating back to 1932, includes arrest for larceny, robbery and conviction of counterfeiting in 1936. Present legitimate occupation is that of building contractor and real estate investor. He continues as Giancana's contact man and personal messenger for Giancana in the Chicago area."

Joseph Borsellino
1927-1995

Joseph Borsellino was born on August 10, 1927 in Chicago, Illinois, and was listed as living at 1620 S. Central Park Avenue in 1945. Police record indicates Borsellino was arrested on charges of ranging from battery to murder. In December 1945 Borsellino was arrested for allegedly attempting to rape a 17-year-old girl at Addison Street and Central Avenue in Chicago. Also arrested with Borsellino were Leonard Dicker, Julius Gilman and George La Flame, the three had been charged with being accessories to the crime and disorderly conduct. Joseph Borsellino died on October 11, 1995 in Cicero, Illinois.

Louis Briatta
1908-1996

Louie Briatta, sometimes known as "Louie the Barber" was an under boss and collector for Gus Alex in the old First Ward. His official FBI listing in 1964 is as follows, "Louis Briatta lists his date of birth as November 20, 1908, at Chicago, Illinois. He resides with his wife and family in the second floor apartment at 1074 West Polk Street, Chicago, Illinois. He also maintains a summer residence at Grand Beach, Michigan. He is a white male, 5'6" tall, 165 pounds, brown hair and brown eyes. He is related by marriage to former First Ward Alderman John D'Arco and still maintains clout through the First Ward organization now headed by a nominal alderman, Donald Parrillo, although actually controlled by Sam Giancana, according to reliable sources.

Briatta is reportedly still involved in syndicate bookmaking and juice operations in the Chicago First Ward and he is under the control of First Ward gambling and vice overseer, Gus Alex.

Fiore Buccieri
1904-1973

Fiore Buccieri, known as "Fifi" and "The Noise" was a long time capo, hit man, and later under boss in the 1960's and 70's. He started out as a labor slugger for the Chicago Embalmers Union. His police record contains arrest for bribery, murder, burglary, larceny, receiving stolen property and arson. He was known to have a large estate in Lake Geneva, Wisconsin where he would train other mobsters to kill.

John Michael Caifano
1911-2003

Known mostly as Marshall Caifano he was one of Sam Giancana's main guys in the 1960's.

His FBI bio listing in 1964 is as follows, "Marshall Caifano is considered to be an enforcer and killer for the "Outfit", both in Chicago and, when directed by Sam Giancana, nationally. Caifano is considered to be a ranking member of the "Outfit" in Chicago.

Caifano recently sued the State of Nevada and others in a case involving the "Black Book" restrictions. On September 25, 1964, a U.S. Court Judge at Las Vegas ruled against Caifano and upheld the right of Nevada to bar certain individuals from gambling casinos.

Richard Cain
1924-1973

Real name Richard Scalezetti. A former Chicago Police vice Detective and Chief Investigator for the Cook County Sheriff's office from 1962 to1964. Know to be a close associate and confidant of Sam Giancana. He was convicted of perjury before a Cook County Grand Jury and discharged from the Sheriff's Office. In the early 1970's Cain traveled to Mexico and other Latin American countries as a courier for Giancana. He was murdered in 1973.

John Phillip Cerone Sr.
1914-1996

Know as Jackie Cerone or "Jackie the Lackey". Top mob boss, under boss, capo, hit man, and consiglieri. Jackie Cerone was mostly known as a bodyguard and chauffer for Tony Accardo.

His official FBI 1965 bio listing is as follows, "Jack Cerone, an Anthony Accardo protégé, is highly respected and influentially placed in the organized criminal element in Chicago. Cerone reportedly has been considered as a possible successor to Sam Giancana if and when he resigns.

Cerone exercises influence and control over vice, gambling, and illegal activities on the west side of Chicago. These operations are handled for him by Joseph "Joe Gags" Gagliano and William Messino. Cerone continues to exercise control in the Melrose Park, Schiller Park areas through Frank "Skippy" Cerone, a cousin.

Cerone has influence in political areas resulting from numerous political contacts. Because of his "clout" he has been able to effect smooth operations in several wards in the Chicago area. Jack Cerone is considered to be a logical successor to Giancana because of his backing by Accardo and Paul Ricca; because of his influence, power and prestige, because of his political contacts and because of his intelligent manner and excellent personal appearance. Cerone is ambitious and continually active in the operation of his own affairs and the organized criminal element.

William Daddono Sr.
1912-1975

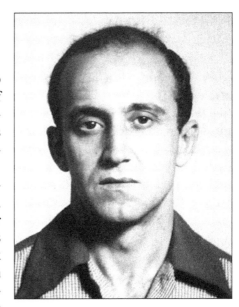

Willie Daddono, always spelled Daddano, was a tough mob capo, at times acted as under boss. He went under the nick name of "Willie Potatoes." He was known as a top leader in the Outfit assigned the responsibility of settling disputes between major thieves and burglars and disciplining those who cause problems which affect the crime syndicate.

His 1965 FBI bio reads, "William Daddano, who is commonly known as Willie "Potatoes", was born on December 28, 1912, at Chicago, Illinois. He resides with his wife and six minor children at 8109 West 26th Street, North Riverside, Illinois. He has a police record dating back to March, 1938 and is a convicted bank burglar. He has been questioned by law enforcement authorities in Chicago in connection with several gangland slayings. He is a former gambler who developed into a "muscle man" for the Chicago syndicate and at one time was recognized as the chief executioner for the Chicago organization.

His name was formerly linked with coin machine operations in Kane, Mc Henry, and Will Counties in the Chicago area and also with the garbage disposal industry. He is a close associate of most of the well known major hoodlums in the Chicago area and has been closely connected with Joseph Aiuppa in the control of vice and gambling in Cicero. He also apparently controls such individuals as Vincent Inserro, Anthony "Puleo" DeRosa, and James "Mugsy" Tortoriello.

Paul DeLucia
1897-1972

Real name Paul Maglio in Italy but changed his name to Felice DeLucia. Mostly know as Paul "The Waiter" Ricca. Took over as top boss of the old Capone gang after the death of Frank Nitti. He was then made top Consiglieri in the mob and Chicago reprehensive to the world.

His 1965 FBI bio card reads as followed, "Paul DeLucia is well known, long-time Chicago area hoodlum whose background dates back to the Capone era. Prior to 1920, DeLucia fled Italy to avoid prosecution for two murders and arrived in the United States on false papers issued to one Paul Maglio. After 1920, DeLucia rose from bookkeeper to bodyguard and "killer" for Al Capone to head man of the Capone gang when Capone was in prison and Frank Nitti had killed him self. In 1943, DeLucia began a 10 year sentence for violation of the Anti-Racketeering Act and while in prison, his leadership of the Capone gang was taken over by Anthony Accardo. In 1947, DeLucia was paroled and after a minor battle for control with Accardo, DeLucia once again became the power controlling the Chicago criminal organization but shared this power with Accardo. Thereafter, Accardo was tried for income tax evasion and DeLucia lost his citizenship and was ordered deported. In addition in 1958, thereafter, Sam Giancana was given titular control of the Chicago criminal organization but Accardo and DeLucia reportedly continued to exercise actual control of same. In 1961, DeLucia was released from prison and since that time, both he and Accardo had declared themselves to be "retired" but in reality they continued to actively direct the operations of the Chicago Criminal Organization.

Americo DiPietto
1914-1990

Americo "Pete" DiPietto, spelled sometimes DePietto, was a New York native who came to Chicago to become a trusted hoodlum under the Giancana organization. DePietto had been arrested over 20 times from charges of armed robbery to possession of stolen property. He was found guilty and sentenced to 20 years in prison for being the main boss in a 10 million-dollar-a-year narcotics ring.

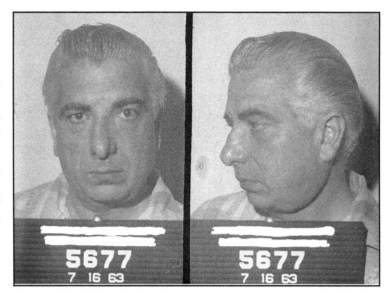

Samuel DeStefano
1909-1973

Sam DeStefano, known as "Mad Sam" was an independent organized crime boss outside the Chicago outfit. He was known as the "king" of "juice" and loan sharking operations in Chicago. He was killed in 1973 by 2 shotgun blast.

John D'Arco
1912-1994

John D'Arco, the mob's man in Chicago politics held the old First Ward Alderman seat until Sam Giancana made him quit by faking a heart-attack. He remained the mob's man in city politics under the title of Democratic Committeeman.

566

Charles Carmen English
1914-1985

Chuckie English was one of the mob's top operators in gambling and a kingpin in the jukebox industry. Chuckie was a top capo under Sam Giancana and became one of Giancana's most trusted men.

His 1965 FBI bio card reads as follows, "Charles English is a lieutenant for top hoodlum Sam Giancana. Whenever Giancana is in Chicago area, English can usually be seen in his company.

Charles English is in charge of all track bookmaking for Giancana in the Chicago area. The English organization is stationed in the 29th Ward, Chicago. Due to the arrest of 15 bookies operating at Sportsman's Park Race Track in August, 1965, the English organization has been hurt financially due to the lose of lucrative amount of income. However, information received that the English's are in charge of most of the other track bookmaking that is still going on." He was killed in 1985.

Frank Anthony Esposito
1900-1969

"Frankie X" as he was known to his friends was the mobs man in labor. Being a close friend to Sam Giancana, he controlled over 35,000 union men as he held the position of President of the Chicago Joint Council of Labor and President of Chicago Local 1001, which controlled the city of Chicago union workers. Esposito was the hand picked successor of Mike "Dago Mike" Carrozzo, Al Capone's and Frank Nitti's hand picked man to control most Chicago labor union in the 1920's and 30's

Anthony Frank Esposito Sr.
1910-1969

Known as "Tony X", brother of "Frankie X" who took over as president of the Chicago labor unions. He was one of Giancana's guys in union affairs while being involved in mob gambling and old First Ward matters.

Frank Ferraro
1911-1964

Born Frank Sortino with the nick name of "Strongy," Ferraro was the mob's Italian boss of the old First Ward in the 1950's and 1960's. He was used mostly in political matters and labor. He was used by Giancana as an adviser to solve mob problems.

Robert Kennedy said in 1959, "Gus Alex and Frank Ferraro ate two of the most ruthless and vicious hoodlums in Chicago, and that they have complete control of Chicago's First Ward."

Joseph Paul Glimco Sr.
1909-1991

Joey Glimco was a short, tough, and mean union boss of the Taxi Cab Drivers Union Local 777 who was trained by the old time union sluggers. Joey Glimco had a "cut" of the action from Sam Giancana.

During the year when Giancana was boss it was reported Glimco received and accepted money and other things of value from employers with intent to influence him with respect to his actions, decisions, and duties as an official of a labor organization. Items received by Glimco included a 1961 XXE Jaguar automobile, tailor-made suits, and other items given to Glimco and his family. The Glimco family is still active in Chicago Local 777 as of 2009.

Murray Humphreys
1899-1965

Known as "The Camel" in the newspapers and "Hump" or "Curly" to his mob cronies. Humphreys was one of the highest ranking non-Italian mob members in Chicago. Hump's field of expertise was that of labor unions and law matters.

His official FBI bio in 1965 read, "Murray Humphreys is the only leader of the old Capone gang in Chicago who continues to be active in the affairs of organized crime in Chicago today. He is 65 years of age, having been born on April 1, 1899, in Chicago, Illinois. He resides in Apartment 5131, 300 North State Street, Chicago. This is the location of the apartment complex generally known as Marina City. Humphreys is of Welch descent.

Although having only a formal education though the fourth grade, Humphreys is a most articulate individual. Due to the fact that he makes a very presentable appearance it is his function to be the contact man used by organized hoodlums in the Chicago area with legitimate labor leaders, public officials, politicians, businessmen and attorneys, not only in Chicago but throughout the Unites States.

Humphreys has no specific area or sphere of activity in the affairs of organized crime for which he is responsible as is generally the case with his hoodlum associates. It is his function to direct strategy utilized by his hoodlum associates when these individuals come under prosecution by Federal, local or state authorities. He works very close with defense attorneys used by these hoodlums and prepares witnesses and directs other strategy in their cases. The counsel of Humphreys is also solicited by his hoodlum associates when they plan new endeavors such as the investment of gambling in other areas as in Las Vegas and the Grand Bahamas Island and in legitimate businesses. Generally speaking it is Humphreys function to serve as a counselor and advisor to his associates in organized crime in Chicago.

In view of the fact that Humphreys has no specific area or sphere of activity except that set out above, he has very little use for a group of underlings such as other Chicago criminal leaders. Humphreys does, however, utilize the services of one Hy Godfrey as a messenger, chauffeur, bodyguard and errand boy. He also used one Edward Ryan in this regard. Ryan is a former underling of Frank "Buster" Wortman in the East St. Louis, Illinois area and formerly managed hotels in Chicago.

Humphreys closest hoodlum associates are Gus Alex, Ralph Pierce and Leslie Kruse. He was extremely close to Frank Ferraro, who died of chest cancer in August, 1964."

Pat Marcy
1914-1993

Pat Marcy, real last name Marciano, controlled the old First Ward Democratic offices and politicians. Marcy was also Sam Giancana's voice to all the judges, police officials, and politicians under the control of Giancana and the mob. He remained the mob's fixer until his death in 1993.

John Matassa
1922-1976

One time Chicago Policeman who became Sam Giancana's chauffeur and bodyguard. Later was involved in the Teamsters and other labor unions in Chicago.

Phyllis McGuire
1931-

Member of the McGuire Sisters sing group in the 1960's. Born in Middletown, Ohio, Phyllis McGuire and he sisters Christine and Dorothy became a staple on Las Vegas entertainment scene. She became Sam Giancana's girl friend in the 1960's. In 1968 the McGuire Sisters retired and Phyllis began a solo act. She resides in her Las Vegas mansion as of 2009 with the McGuire Sisters occasional performing together on special engagements.

Charles Nicoletti
1916-1977

Known as "Chuckie" was an outfit Capo and syndicate enforcer in the 1950's, 60's and 70's. Was inline to be under boss before he was killed.

His 1965 FBI bio card read, "Charles "Chuckie" Nicoletti, a white male individual, born December 3, 1916, currently resides at 1638 North Broadway, Melrose Park, Illinois.

This individual reportedly is responsible for most of the gangland executions for the organized crime group in Chicago, allegedly he is usually present at the scene on the occasion of each slaying. In 1962, he was arrested along with Felix "Milwaukee Phil" Alderisio in a specially rigged automobile which automobile has been described as being a "hit" car utilized by organized crime circles in connection with their murders. This automobile contained secret compartments for storage of weapons and other items used in connection with an execution.

Nicoletti has previously been convicted on a narcotics charge and he is close associate of Alderiso, Sam DeStefano, Sam Giancana, Sam "Teets" Battaglia and Fiore "Fifi" Buccieri." He was killed in 1977.

Rocco Potenza
1912-

Known as "The Parrot", Rocco was born on September 24, 1912. He was one of Sam Giancana's top men running many of his operations in the Northern section of Cook County cover the area just south of Evanston, Illinois near Lake Michigan. His arrest record contained arrest for gambling and a suspect in bombings.

One of the last reports on Rocco Potenza came in 1947 when he, fellow mobsters Rocky Infelice, Americo DiPietto, Charles "Specs" DiCaro, Wayne Brock and Mario Garelli filed a law suit after they lost their jobs at Chicago McCormick Place convention center when a federal investigation was launched into alleged union shake downs and payroll padding.

Rocco Pranno
1918-1979

Rocco Salvatore Pranno was one of Sam Giancana's main guys in controlling operations west of Chicago in the 1960's. Being born on December 18, 1916, 1917 or 1918, in Chicago, all dates given to police, the six foot vicious hood enjoyed throwing treats and enforcing them with a baseball bat. He used the alias of Joe Martin, James Martell, Joe Martell, Judge Conway, Rocky Bretell, Jim Pionno and Robert Parno.

His 1965 FBI card reads as follows, "Rocco Salvatore Pranno lives at 1608 North 39th Street, Stone Park, Illinois. He is the owner of D'Ors Supper Club at 1741 North Mannheim Road, Stone Park, and allegedly had complete control of the Village of Stone Park for legal and illegal activities. Pranno's control was bolstered by the fact that his cousin, Andrew Signorelli, was Chief of Police of the Stone Park PD. Pranno is considered to be a "muscle man" inasmuch as he is quick tempered and untilies threats of physical harm in the event his orders are not carried out. Pranno was involved in an infiltration of Chicago hoodlums into Kane County area   o f Illinois and was subsequently subpoenaed to testify before the McClellan Committee investigating racketeering. The committee revealed testimony that Pranno, a convicted robber and burglar, untilized "terror tactics" against gamblers and juke box operators in an effort to gain control of the "rackets" in Kane County.

Recently the Chief of Police at Stone Park has been changed and Pranno's activities have been diminished. Pranno's business at the Supper Club has been failing. Pranno in the past has received notorious publicity when he beat up a school teacher after an argument at his super club."

Pranno also had control in Northlake, Illinois where his other cousin Daniel Provenzano was Chief of Police in that city. In the 1960's areas listed under his control were Stone Park, Northlake, Franklin Park, Shiller Park, portions of Melrose Park, and Lisle Illinois.

Sam Rosa
1919-1998

A well known friend and associate of Sam Giancana's nick named "Slicker Sam." He controlled many of Giancana's operations based out of Melrose Park, Illinois.

Frank Sinatra
1915-1998

Frank Sinatra was a singer, movie star, and self proclaimed "tuff guy" who was known as a member of the "Rat Pack" comedy group. He was born in Hoboken, New Jersey and had an arrest record with the charge of "seduction" from 1938. Sinatra had had sexual intercourse with a married woman with the promises that he would marry her at a later date. The charge of "seduction" was also listed as the crime of adultery.

Anthony Phillip Tisci
1929-2002

Lawyer and son-in-law to Sam Giancana who was used in Giancana's political structure of the old First Ward in Chicago.

James Vincent Torello
1930-1979

Known as "Turk" in the underworld, Torello served as hit man, Capo, and late in his carrier was considered one of the top Outfit bosses.

Chicago Criminal Organization Under Giancana 1960's

Governing Board

Sam Giancana
Murray Humphreys
Gus Alex
Frank Ferraro
Ross Prio

Ex-Officio

Tony Accardo
Paul DeLucia

Enforcement

Sam Alex
Fiore Buccieri
Jack Cerone
Phil Alderisio
William Daddono
Dave Yaras
Charles Nicoletti

Loop - First Ward

Gus Alex-Frank Ferraro
Louis Briatta
Tom Briatta
Mike Briatta
Maish Baer
Frank Caruso
Joe Caruso
James Catuara
Ralph Ciangi
Louis Arger
Nick Garambone
John Cumitilli
Tony DeRosa
Sid Frazin
Hy Godfrey
Nathan Ladon
Joe Laino
Angelo LaPietra
James LaPierta
Tony Maenza
Charles Nicosia
James Pulano
Louis Tornabene
John D'Arco Sr.
Frank Roti
Frank Tornabene
Tony Tornabene
Leo Manfredi
Frank Micelli
Lee Lanio

Political Contacts
Legal Advice

Murray Humphreys
Pat Marcy
Paul Marcy
John D'Arco Sr.
Frank Annunzio
Fred Roti
Rocco Armando
Mattias Bauler
Eugene Bernstein
Mike Brodkin
Joseph Bulger
Frank Chesrow
Elmer Conti
Anthony DeTolve
Peter Granata
Buddy Jacobson
Marshall Korshak
Roland Libonati
Vito Marzullo
Thomas O'Brien
Joseph Porcaro
Joe "Pep" Briatta
Steve Anselmo
Tony Tisci
Anthony Champagne
Anthony Giroliami

Labor

Joesph Glimco Sr.
Anthony Esposito Sr.
Frank Esposito
Vince Solano Sr.
Joseph Spingola Sr.
Thomas Crivellone
Louis Celano
John Lardino
Eco James Coli
Gus Zapas
Leonard Gianola
Michael Kennedy
Sandy O'Brien
Dom Senese
William Hogan Sr.
Joseph Aiello
Al Pilotto
James Caporale
Tony Gianfrancesco
Peter Fosco
Nick Cantone
Mike Schivarelli
John Matassa
Ernest Gibbs

Juice Loans

Sam DeStefano
Tony Spilotro
Mario DeStefano
William Jackson
Charles Crimaldi
Sam Gallo
Sam Lewis
Carmen Bastone
Angelo Bastone
Sal Bastone
Rocky Joyce
Joseph Lombardi
Joe LaMantia
Steve Annoreno
Sam Bills
John Monteleone
Wayne Brock
Frank Rinelli
Vito Spillone
Frank Teutonico
Joe Spadavecchio
Thomas Immerso
Joe Amari
Morris Goldstein
Joe Grieco
Ju Ju Grieco
Donald Grieco
Al Saigh
Mike Castaldo
Peter Ori

Chicago Criminal Organization under Giancana 1960's

Westside

Fifi Buccieri
Sam Battaglia
Joseph Aiuppa
Jack Cerone
Charles Nicoletti
Charles English
Joseph Corngold
Rocco Pranno
Joseph Gagliano
William Messino
Marshall Caifano
Joseph Ferriola
Frank Buccieri
Rocco Salvatore
Ralph Capone
Dom Blasi
Frank Eulo
Bob Ansoni
Sam English
John Matassa
James Torello
Salvatore De Rose
Rocco Infelice
Don Angelini
Dom Cortino
Tony Eldorado
Rocco DeStefano
Mike Spranze
Joe Giancana
John Varles
Vincent Inserro
Frank Cerone
Buck Ortenzi
Larry Rassano
Sam Cesario
Lou Rosanova
Rocco DeGrazio
James Mirro
Tony Pitello
John DeBiase
Frank Torraco
Charles Tourino Jr.
Dominic Volpe
Sam Ariola
Ned Bakes
Joe Colucci
Americo DiPietto
John Manzella
Rocco Paternoster
Joe Siciliano
Tarquin Simonelli
Joe Accardo
Frank Eldorado
Nick Visco
Frank Teutonico

Westside Continued

Frank Manno
Nick Manno
Tony Esposito Jr.
Rocco Potenza
Leo Rugendorf
Frank Zimmerman
William Block
Gus Liebe
John DiFranzo
Pasty DiConstanzo
Al Sarno
Chris Cardi
Joseph Lombardo
Anthony Battaglia
Joseph Battaglia
Joe Rocco
Angelo Jannotta
Joe Ambile
Rich Derrico
Gerald Nargie
Guy Cervone
John Zitto
Nick DeGrazio
John Tarrara
Bill Del Percio
Elmer Del Percio
Joe Scaccia
Mike Biancofior
Jay Campise
John Carr
Sander Caravello
John Cimitile
Pasquale Clementi
Marco D'Amico
Frank Covello
Louis DiRiggi
Peter DeStito
John Fecarotta
William Petrocelli
Tony Renallo
George Vertucci
Mike Briatta Jr.
Jimmy Torraco

Lake County

Joe Amato
Les Kruse
Tom Griffin
George Rauff

Northside

Ross Prio
Jimmy Allegretti
Phil Alderisio
Joseph DiVarco
Lenny Patrick
Dave Yaras
Marshall Caifano
Albert Frabotta
Len Gianola
Bob Furey
Andy Louchious
William Aloisio
Anthony DeMonte
Dom DiBello
Dom Nuccio
Dom Brancato
Joe Arnold
Ken Eto
Anthony Overlander
Sam Lisciandrello
Joe Lisciandrello
Frank Lisciandrello
Sam Mesi
Sam Faruggia
Frank Fratto
Mike Glitta
Frank Orlando
Larry Buonaguidi
Joe LaBarbara
Cosmo Orlando
Ben Policheri
Bill Gold
Bob Furey
Phil Katz
Irving Dworetzky
Tony Monaco
John Varelli
Frank Calabrese
Louis Eboli
Sam Castonzo
Joe Siciliano
Joe Volpe
Phil Mesi

Coin Machines

Edward Vogel
Thomas Smith

NorthWest

Rocco Pranno
Jasper Pellicane
Nick Bravos
Sam Rosa
George Bravos
Ben Fillichio

South Suburban

Frank LaPorte
Al Pilotto
Francis Curry
Babe Tuffanelli
J. Guzzino
D. Palerno
Frank Luzi
Joseph Costello
R. Bacino
James Roti
James Catuara
James Cordovano
Tony DeLordo
Charles DiCaro
Joe DiCaro
Tony Panzica
Joe Caruso
Arthur Markovitz
Mike Markovitz
Guido Fidanzi
Billy Dauber

McHenery County

Joe Amato
Lou Czarnocki

DuPage-Kane County

William Daddono
Mike Caldarulo

The Resting Place of Sam Giancana
Mount Carmel Cemetery

A map of the locations where some of Chicago's mobsters are buried at Mount Carmel Cemetery in Hillside, Illinois.

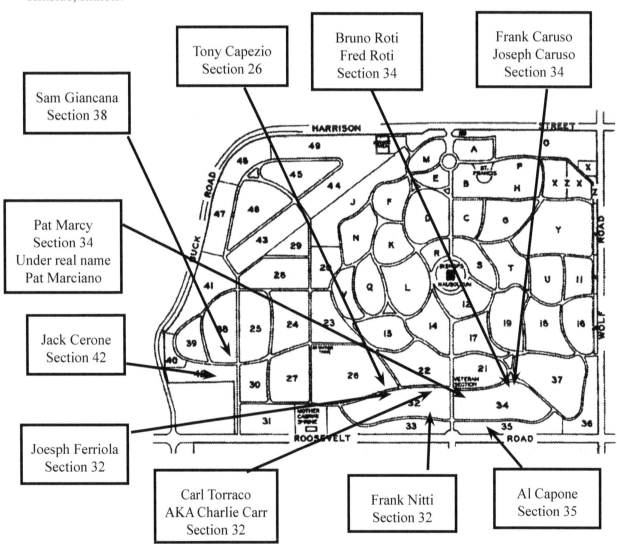

Across the street from Mount Carmel Cemetery is Queen of Heaven Cemetery where some of the Giancana's friends were laid to rest. They are:

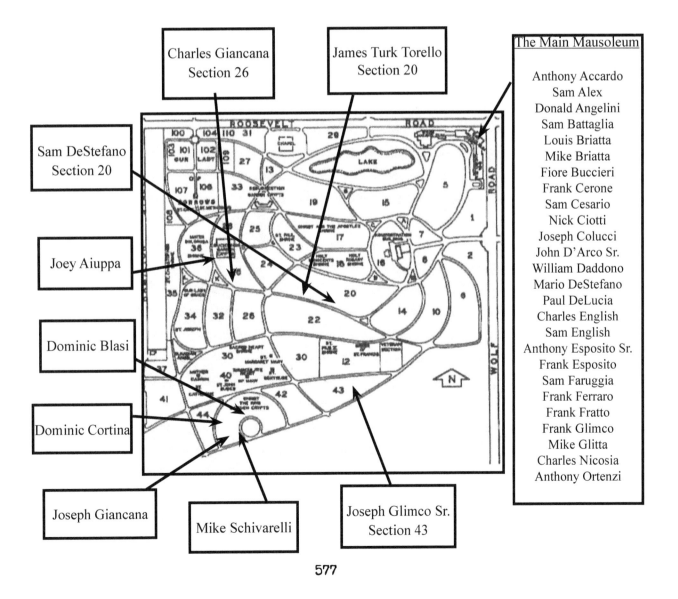

Charles Giancana
Section 26

James Turk Torello
Section 20

The Main Mausoleum

Anthony Accardo
Sam Alex
Donald Angelini
Sam Battaglia
Louis Briatta
Mike Briatta
Fiore Buccieri
Frank Cerone
Sam Cesario
Nick Ciotti
Joseph Colucci
John D'Arco Sr.
William Daddono
Mario DeStefano
Paul DeLucia
Charles English
Sam English
Anthony Esposito Sr.
Frank Esposito
Sam Faruggia
Frank Ferraro
Frank Fratto
Frank Glimco
Mike Glitta
Charles Nicosia
Anthony Ortenzi

Sam DeStefano
Section 20

Joey Aiuppa

Dominic Blasi

Dominic Cortina

Joseph Giancana

Mike Schivarelli

Joseph Glimco Sr.
Section 43

Other source documents used

Books

Dark, Tony. A Mob of His Own: Samuel Mad Sam DeStefano and the Chicago Mobs's Juice Rackets, Hosehead Productions, 2008

Demaris, Ovid. Captive City: Chicago in Chains, New York: Lyle Stuart, 1969

FBI Files

General File 62-9-9-1616
Giancana, Sam 92-3171

Senate Committee Hearings on Labor 1958

To Kimmy sunshine
&
Grand-mal-mar

Without your help, this book would not be possible!

Cover art by Frank Menaloscino

Contact author at tonydark35@yahoo.com

ALSO AVAILABLE

A Mob of his Own

The story of Sammuel "Mad Sam" DeStefano and the Chicago "Juice" Racket

By

Tony Dark

ISBN 978-0-615-17496-9

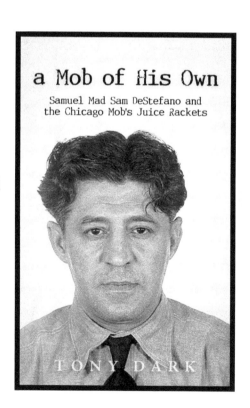

a Mob of His Own

Samuel Mad Sam DeStefano and
the Chicago Mob's Juice Rackets

TONY DARK

INDEX

Baer, Maishie "Morris Saletko" 252, 573,
Baer, Sam 51,
Bailey, Robert 406,
Bailey, Steve 360, 370,
Bailey, Thomas 55,
Baker, Barney 157, 158,
Baker, Michael 554,
Baker, Robert (FBI Agent) 160, 473,
Bakes, Mike 182,
Bakes, Ned 574,
Balistreri, Frank 235, 411, 452,
Balletti, Arthur James 141, 196,
Bannano, Joseph 552,
Baragiano Italy 75,
Barbe, Lewis 366,
Barclay, Toya 87,
Barnes, Stuart 111, 114, 115,
Baron, Charles "Babe" 158, 214, 232,
Barradio, Frank 60,
Barrett, Charles 361,
Barrett, Eddie 123,
Bartell, Bart 215,
Bartoli, Fred 169, 192, 220,
Bartoli, Sam 171,
Bassett, John (FBI Agent) 203, 206, 212, 219, 255, 451, 455,
Bastone, Angelo 573,
Bastone, Carmen 573,
Bastone, Salvatore, "Sal" 573,
Bates, Michael 554,
Batista Regime 200, 232,
Battaglia, Angela 68,
Battaglia, Anthony 574,
Battaglia, Joseph 215, 574,
Battaglia, Sam "Teetz" 13, 26, 30, 67, 68, 82, 104, 110, 117, 125, 127, 154, 170, 174, 195, 208, 215, 240, 271, 285, 360, 397, 408, 409, 411, 412, 419, 424, 425, 431, 432, 434, 440, 441, 443, 446, 453, 458, 460, 490, 492, 562, 570, 574, 577,
Batters, Joe *See Anthony Accardo"*
Bauler, Mattias 573,
Baylay, Warren 221,
Becker, Ralph 116,
Becker, Norman "Minnie" 183,
Beckman, Mel 257, 301,
Belacastro, James "King of Bombers" 180,
Belgrad, Lester 141,
Bell, Lloyd 128,
Bellison, George 161,
Bellows, Charles 192,
Bellwood Illinois 193,
Benanty, Jack 323,
Beneduce, Daniel 62, 75,
Bennett, James 35,
Bennett, Tony 224, 242,
Bernas, Richard "Dick" 68, 83, 125, 178, 191, 219, 308,
Bernstein, Eugene (Lawyer) 178, 348, 573,
Berwyn Illinois 17, 27, 49, 78, 80, 183, 188,
Bianco 426,
Biancofiori, Mike 574,
Bieber, George 110, 402,
Biele, John 249,

Billett, Marvin 232,
Bills, Sam 573,
Bioff, Alan 107,
Bioff, Hyman 107,
Bioff, Willie 24, 30, 107,
Biondo, Joseph 249,
Bishop, Joey 190, 532,
Black Book (Nevada Gambling) 231,
Black Hand 6,
Blackhawk's, Chicago Hockey Team 277,
Black Onyx Night Club 142,
Blackie's Restaurant 180, 181,
Blair, Sam 349,
Blakely, James 82, 128,
Blasi, Constance "Connie" 255, 533,
Blasi, Dominic, "Butch" 80, 85, 177, 186, 194, 197, 201, 202, 207, 211, 212, 215, 216, 217, 224, 228, 229, 240, 244, 248, 250, 255, 256, 257, 267, 268, 269, 270, 282, 285, 287, 288, 290, 305, 311, 313, 314, 315, 318, 321, 325, 336, 340, 349, 352, 353, 357, 367, 370, 371, 372, 380, 381, 385, 389, 390, 391, 392, 394, 403, 407, 409, 418, 425, 426, 432, 433, 435, 436, 437, 438, 448, 449, 450, 451, 453, 504, 506, 509, 516, 517, 519, 520, 521, 523, 528, 529, 530, 531, 532, 533, 539, 540, 541, 542, 543, 544, 545, 549, 551, 562, 574, 577,
Blick, Walter 155,
Bloomingdale Illinois 554, 555, 556,
Block, William "Willie" 24, 574,
Blubock, Norman 272,
Bond, George 80, 85, 202,
Bonfield Helen 474,
Bonnano, Joseph 120, 122,
Boogie Woogie Night Club 27, 60,
Borsellino, Joseph 153, 164, 308, 562,
Bosics, Carlo 224,
Bouch, Albert 77,
Bouche, Albert "Pape" 82, 83,
Bougadis, George 156,
Boyle, John 25,
Brackett, J.J. 337
Bradi, Lawrence *See Lawrence Buonaguidi"*
Brady, Louis "Lou" 113, 217, 218, 254,
Bradhill, Lucille 73,
Brancamp, Leo 64,
Brancato, Dominick 57, 574,
Brancato, Dom "Nags" 23, 66,
Bravos, George "George the Greek" 229, 258, 278, 574,
Bravos, Nicholas "Nick the Greek" 258, 574,
Brazil 490, 491,
Brennan, Ray 444,
Briatta, Joseph "Pep" 573,
Briatta, Louis "Lou the Barber" 104, 130, 131, 202, 250, 253, 297, 298, 299, 523, 563, 573, 577,
Briatta, Mike 461, 573, 577,
Briatta, Mike Jr. 574,
Briatta, Tom 573,
Brickhouse, Jack 331,
Bridewell Prison 26,
Britt, Mae 189,
Brock, Wayne 571, 573,
Brodkin, Michael (Lawyer) 70, 104, 110, 348, 361, 374, 381,

D

H

J

I

LeVoy, Reverand 472,
Levy, Morris 249,
Lewis, Eddie 184,
Lewis, Jackie 185,
Lewis, Joe E. 205, 398, 426,
Lewis, Robert "Bobby" 184,
Lewis, Sam "Lusi" 184, 185, 209, 210, 442, 573,
Lewis, Sam Jr. 184
Leydon, Butch 110,
Liberatore, Ercole 56,
Libonati, Roland (Congressman) 113, 227, 296, 319, 322, 323,
346, 354, 356, 370, 424, 573,
Libton, Sonny 228,
Lido Motel 172, 272,
Liebe, August "Gust" 183, 574,
Lifton, Robert 203,
Lincoln, Abe 105,
Lincoln Park Chicago 57,
Lipson, Theodore 503,
Lisciandrello, Frank 574,
Lisciandrello, Joe 574,
Lisciandrello, Sam 574,
Liston, Sonny 230, 286,
Litberg, Morris 307,
Littler Family 426,
Local 5, of the Chicago Heights Hod Carriers Union Chicago
Heights 254,
Local 46, Laundry Workers Union of Chicago 144, 160,
Local 110, Movie Operators Projectors Union of Chicago 104,
105, 106, 107, 108,
Local 130, Plumbers Chicago Journeymen Union 360,
Local 134, International Brotherhood of Electrical Workers
Union of Chicago 11, 271, 273,
Local 272, Auto Chauffeur's Union Chicago 372,
Local 450, Hotel Clerks, Restaurant Employees and Bartenders
Union Chicago 384, 560,
Local 593 of the Hotel and Apartment Hotel Service Workers
and Miscellaneous Restaurant Employees Union 136,
Local 777, Taxi Cab Union Chicago 23, 65, 136, 568,
Local 1001 of the County Municipal Employees and Foremen's
Union Chicago 273, 384, 567,
Locallo, August (Police Lieutenant) 524,
Locallo, Victor 524,
Locano, Profirio 530,
Locke, Andrea 98,
Locke, Arlene 99,
Locke, Nelson 53, 54,
Lohman, Joseph 123,
Lombardi, Joseph "Pretty Boy" 573,
Lombardo, Antonio "Scourge" 577,
Lombardo, Joey "The Clown" 574,
Lombardozzi, Carmine 148, 249,
London England 498,
Lormar, Chuck 97,
Lormar Distributing Company 73, 97, 110, 151, 181, 330, 430,
Los Angeles, California 15, 28, 51, 119, 125, 473, 482, 490,
495,
Losasso, Guido 76,
LoSurdo, Michael 554,
Louchious, Andy 574,
Louisville Kentucky 18,

LoVerde, Frank 251,
Loverdi, Butch 192, 308,
LoVerdi, Charles 428,
Lownes, Vic 150,
Lubino, Joe 134,
Lucania, Charles 465,
Luchese, Thomas 120, 122, 126,
Luciano, Charles "Lucky" 55, 147,
Luciaus, Andy 174,
Luke, Kan Jung 119,
Lulinski, George 332,
Lulinski, John 332, 333,
Lupo, Mario 195,
Lusi, Salvatore Carmen "See Sam Lewis"
Luzi, Frank 574,
Lynch, John 333,
Lynch, William 513, 522,

M

Mabley, Jack 519, 521,
Mack, Tony 24, 290,
Maddox, Claude "Screwy" 82, 104, 105, 106, 107, 560,
Maenza, Tony "Poppy" 573,
Mafia 6, 11, 27, 80, 158, 206, 221, 272, 454, 544, 545,
Magaddino, Peter 122,
Magaddino, Steve 121, 122,
Maggio's Steak House 367,
Maglio, Paul "See Paul DeLucia"
Magill, John 285,
Maheu, Robert (FBI Agent) 196, 198, 232,
Mahoney, John 158,
Madigan, John 332,
Makowski, Walter 471,
Malters, Edward Dr. 439,
Mancuso, Michael 51,
Mandl, Richard 108,
Manfredi, Leo 573,
Mangano, Lawrence "Dago" 57,
Manning, Pat 49, 66,
Manno, Carmen 86, 87, 91, 103, 104, 520, 559,
Manno, Frank 574,
Manno, Jeff 103, 278, 280,
Manno, Nick 574,
Mano, Patrick 66, 67,
Manzella, John 554, 574,
Manzella, Louis 554,
Marcello, Carlos 454, 455,
Marcello, Sam 29,
Marciano, Pat "See Pat Marcy"
Marcus, H.L. 146,
Marcus, Leon 15, 54, 60, 71, 92, 145, 146, 192,
Marcy, Pat 105, 189, 287, 290, 291, 292, 297, 299, 300, 302,
303, 311, 313, 315, 317, 318, 319, 320, 322, 324, 331, 340,
343, 345, 346, 347, 349, 350, 351, 352, 354, 356, 357, 358,
361, 368, 371, 372, 373, 374, 375, 376, 377, 382, 386, 387,
392, 395, 396, 400, 401, 402, 403, 404, 408, 409, 410, 411,
414, 416, 417, 418, 419, 420, 421, 424, 427, 429, 430, 430,
432, 434, 436, 437, 440, 443, 444, 480, 486, 487, 504, 569,
573, 576,
Marcy, Paul 396, 410, 573,

Marino, Mike "The Brew" 148, 236, 433,
Maritote, John 107,
Markovitz, Arthur 574,
Markovitz, Mike 574,
Marks, Guy 529, 531,
Marks, Joe 145, 187, 392, 425,
Marola, Johnnie 308,
Marshall Fields 199,
Mart, Alphie 469,
Martello, Willy 206,
Martin, Dean 5, 113, 176, 177, 194, 240, 242, 289, 304, 305, 308, 348, 460, 532,
Martin, Joe 571,
Martin, Tony 107,
Martorano, Mike 202,
Marzullo, Vito (Alderman) 244, 292, 319, 323, 354, 355, 356, 492, 520, 522, 523, 573,
Massa, Andrew 191,
Massau, Moses 113,
Masset, Robert (Judge) 401,
Massey, Robert (Alderman) 356, 373, 376, 385, 415, 416,
Massuci, Ralph 376, 416,
Matarrese, Joseph 253,
Matassa, John Sr. 85, 101, 163, 165, 166, 167, 177, 208, 217, 224, 228, 229, 240, 244, 250, 252, 253, 268, 285, 286, 287, 290, 307, 308, 309, 310, 319, 372, 385, 388, 425, 428, 449, 487, 488, 489, 570, 573, 574,
Matthews, John (FBI Agent) 141,
Matthys, Francis (FBI Agent) 27, 183,
Maxwell Street Chicago 404,
May, Sam 37,
Mayo Clinic Minnesota 383, 450,
Maywood Park Harness Association 175, 277,
Maywood Park Illinois 75, 167, 277, 278, 447,
Maywood Race Track 280,
McCall, John 28,
McClellan Committee 74, 83, 347, 560, 571,
McClellan, John 100, 129, 347,
McClintock, Harold 162,
McCormick Place 571,
McCullough, Robert "Big Bob" 554,
McCulloch, Harry (Police Sergeant) 152,
McCullough, H.R. (FBI Agent) 51,
McDonagh, Captain 118,
McDonald, Frank 332, 333,
McDonald, John 178,
McDonald, Tommy "MacDonald" 192, 195, 232,
McGloon, Thomas (Senator) 105,
McGuire, Christine 133, 134, 137, 147, 261, 276, 570,
McGuire, Dorthy 133, 134, 348, 570,
McGuire, Peter 227,
McGuire, Phyllis 5, 125, 126, 131, 133, 134, 135, 137, 141, 148, 149, 164, 187, 195, 196, 198, 199, 200, 201, 203, 204, 205, 206, 224, 226, 234, 247, 255, 261, 262, 265, 273, 284, 288, 305, 308, 309, 310, 312, 318, 323, 324, 336, 337, 339, 347, 348, 352, 353, 357, 367, 370, 384, 397, 399, 402, 410, 426, 437, 442, 449, 450, 451, 452, 455, 458, 463, 465, 466, 467, 474, 475, 479, 484, 485, 493, 496, 517, 524, 527, 528, 529, 532, 533, 543, 544, 570,
McGuire, William 554,

McKeigue, James (U.S. Marshal) 77,
McKenna, Flicka 135,
McLaughlin, Eugene "Red"
McRoberts, Earl Dr. 135,
Meccia, John 3,
Medlevine, Don 150, 167,
Mellott, Frank (FBI Agent) 53, 55, 59, 64, 65, 70, 72, 74, 75, 79, 82, 88,
Melrose Park Illinois 54, 69, 71, 75, 80, 88, 116, 140, 154, 155, 156, 160, 165, 183, 185, 187, 191, 214, 215, 249, 272, 274, 276, 397, 449, 534, 560, 564, 570, 571, 572,
Meltreger, James 528,
Memerovski, 118,
Menalocino, Frank 666
Mendino, Joseph "Crackers" 170, 174, 184,
Mendolia, Guy 359,
Meo, Alfred-Albert "Chuck" 82, 83, 85, 96, 209, 219, 304, 308,
Meo, James 77, 82, 83, 85, 89, 209, 219, 304,
Meo, Stella 77, 83, 89,
Meo, Tripolina "Trip" 82, 83,
Mercurio, Salvatore 170,
Mertes, Herb 157,
Mesi, Phil 408, 574,
Mesi, Sam 574, 577,
Messer, Sharon 529,
Messino, Mike 202,
Messino, William "Wee Willie" 152, 182, 229, 258, 338, 361, 409, 457, 460, 467, 564, 574,
Mexico 79, 87, 106, 107, 112, 114, 173, 312, 457, 458, 459, 460, 462, 463, 464, 473, 476, 479, 481, 483, 484, 485, 486, 489, 490, 491, 493, 494, 495, 496, 499, 500, 501, 502, 504, 505, 506, 507, 509, 510, 512, 514, 515, 522, 525, 529, 530, 531, 536, 550, 552, 559, 564,
Meyer, Emil 154,
MGM Lounge Chicago 127, 152, 221, 257, 271,
Miami, Florida 12, 101, 103, 104, 105, 113, 120, 149, 153, 162, 190, 248, 255, 260, 261, 262, 263, 264, 272, 306, 316, 318, 424, 464, 468, 469,
Miceli, James 37,
Michell, Allen 274,
Micelli, Frank "Chi Chi" 573,
Michelle, Helen 212,
Michigan Avenue 11, 69,
Midway Airport Chicago 108, 121, 173, 192,
Mike's Fish Restaurant Chicago 50, 103, 124, 138,
Milano, Carl 254,
Milano, Pete 218,
Miller, Edward H. 30,
Miller, G.S. 103,
Miller, Herbert 61,
Miller, Marilyn 125, 147, 148, 149,
Miller, Ross 240,
Milwaukee, Wisconsin 58, 63,
Miraglia, John 23,
Mirro, James "Cowboy" 30, 152, 172, 175, 207, 265, 278, 280, 316, 391, 392, 406, 412, 427, 560, 574,
Mist Club 193, 224,
Mitchell, Tuffy 113,
Moffat, William (Police Lieutenant) 87,
Molliter, Robert 114,

Molose, Salvator 554,
Monaco, Tony 574,
Moniclair Funeral Home 517, 520,
Montana, Joe 107, 279,
Monteleone, John 573,
Montello, Margaret 103,
Montgomery Wards 181,
Montos, Nick George 27, 192, 435,
Moore, John *"See Claude Maddox"*
Morelli, Freddy 296,
Morrelli, Blackie 279,
Morrelli, Carlo 279,
Morretti, Salvatore "Sal" 24, 117,
Morris, Carolyn 510, 511, 518, 519, 524, 525, 527, 528, 529, 530, 531, 532, 533, 541, 542,
Morris, Chris 510,
Morris, Eddie 111, 112, 113, 280,
Morris, Edwin "Buzz" 510, 511,
Morris, Joseph (Police Lieutenant) 23, 27, 28, 30, 66, 88, 167, 275,
Morris, Steven 510,
Morrissey, Emmeti 374, 386,
Morrison, Richard 131,
Morton, Arnold 150,
Morton, Moe 497, 508,
Moss, Harry 109,
Mount Carmel Cemetery 517, 542, 575, 576, 577,
Moy, Wilson 402, 403,
Mueller, Joseph 409,
Mundo, R. 23,
Munizzo, Tom 126, 127,
Murray, Gerard 174, 175,
Musolino, Josephine 52,
Napoli, Alexander (Judge) 481,

N

Napoli, James 249,
Napoli, Richard (Judge) 374,
Napolean, Jack *"See Sam DeStefano"*
Napolitano, James 122,
Nap, Jimmy 122,
Nappi, Romei "Romey" 375, 376, 403, 408, 419, 434,
Nardi, Edward 23, 49, 65,
Nardico, John 82,
Nardulli, Frank 177, 193,
Nargie, Gerald 574,
Nash, Frank (Sergeant) 151, 152, 293, 296, 455,
Navy Pier Chicago 473,
Neistien, Bernard (Senator) 105, 435,
Nestor, Fremont (Captain) 17, 18, 23, 24, 25, 59, 62, 65, 66, 69,
Nestor, Tiny (Lieutenant) 30,
Nestos, William Dr. 174,
New Jersey 468, 572,
New York 13, 28, 79, 80, 101, 105, 122, 133, 291, 323, 418, 446, 447, 448, 464, 467, 485, 495, 496, 497, 510, 552, 566,
Newey, Paul 126,
New Frontier Hotel and Casino 221,
Nicastro, Rose *"See Rose Eulo"*
Nicoletti, Charles "Chuckie" 29, 79, 80, 88, 89, 102, 104, 148,

181, 215, 221, 249, 259, 272, 281, 406, 570, 573, 574, 577,
Nicosia, Charles 443, 444, 573, 577,
Nilan, James (Police Sergeant) 526,
Niles Illinois 72, 115, 118, 155, 162, 165, 222, 259, 266
Nitti, Frank "The Enforcer" 107, 565, 567, 576,
Nitti, Nick 554,
Noble, (Police Captain) 345,
Nordi, Gus 81,
North Avenue Steak House 75, 138, 158, 167, 172, 173, 187, 188, 207, 274, 276, 278, 427,
Northlake Illinois 433, 571,
Norwood Park Illinois 175,
Nuccio, Dominic 53, 56, 57, 58, 66, 67, 574,
Nuzzio, Inez 56, 57, 58,

O

Oak Brook Illinois 560,
Oak Park Illinois 5, 15, 17, 23, 27, 30, 46, 55, 59, 62, 65, 68, 70, 79, 80, 92, 100, 101, 114, 120, 125, 134, 145, 147, 154, 155, 185, 202, 209, 210, 219, 253, 284, 322, 332, 366, 375, 445, 451, 455, 472, 483, 513, 516, 519, 520, 522, 524, 526, 535, 536, 538, 541, 545, 546, 548, 551, 553, 558, 562,
O'Banion, Dion 5,
Oberlander, Aaron "Obbie" 502, 503,
Odierno, Mary 55,
O'Brien, Joey *"See Joey Aiuppa"*
O'Brien, Pat 3,
O'Brien, Sandy 573,
O'Brien, Thomas 573,
O'Connell, Partick 375,
O'Connor, Edward (FBI Agent) 46,
O'Dierno, Anthony Jr. 64,
O'Dierno, Angelo 63, 64
O'Dierno, Frank 64,
O'Dierno, James 64,
O'Dierno, Jennie 64,
O'Dierno, Tony Sr.63, 64,
O'Donnell, (Police Captain) 395,
O'Donnell, Miles 239,
Ogilvie, Richard 238, 290, 311, 345, 369, 456, 457,
O'Hare Airport 157, 198, 203, 307, 325, 357, 430, 459, 512, 517,
O'Keefe, Denis 174,
O'Leary, John (FBI Agent) 156,
O'Leary, Martin (Police Sergeant) 453,
Olson, Leonard "Leo" 163, 219, 304, 377,
Olivette, Dominic 122,
Ori, Peter 573,
Orlando, Cosmo 574,
Orlando, Frank 574,
Orlando, Tony 61, 62,
Ortenzi, Anthony "Buck" 215, 258, 574, 577,
Otto, Julius 183,
Overlander, Anthony 574,
Owl Club 67, 203,

P

Pucci, 410,
Puerto Rico 458, 502,
Pulano, James 573,
Pyle, Palmer 313, 314,

Q

Queen of Heaven Cemetery 281, 555, 577,
Quinn, Paul 372, 375,

R

Ragen, William 274,
Rand, Chappy 469,
Ranelli, James (Judge) 375,
Ransom, Robert (Judge) 375,
Rantis, Peter 183,
Rassano, Larry "Little Larry" 391, 574,
Rauff, George 574,
Ray, Raymond 55,
Recorded Music Service Association 151, 152,
Red Hawk Gang 30,
Reed, Frank 148,
Reed, Robert C. (FBI Agent) 63,
Reichert, (Police Chief) 520,
Reilly, Edward 307,
Renallo, Anthony "Radio" 574,
Renzino, James C. 400, 401,
Reynolds, Frank 368,
Ricca, Paul "The Waiter" *"See Paul DeLucia"*
Ricci, Anthony "Tony" 28, 104, 105, 108,
Ricco, Diego 32, 61,
Ridi, 119,
Rinaldi, Eugene 193,
Rinella, Frank 573,
Rinella, James 523,
Riordan, James (Police Captain) 372, 373,
Riquelme, Raul 530,
River Forest Illinois 49, 74, 80, 105, 145, 158, 176, 183, 252, 370, 519, 520, 542, 559, 562,
River Forest State Bank 176,
River Grove Illinois 83, 155,
Riverside Illinois, 292, 561, 565,
Riverview Amusement Park 174,
Riverwoods Country Club 425,
Riviera Hotel and Casino 158, 213, 218, 232, 240,
Roberts, John (FBI Agent) 115, 120, 167, 248,
Robertson, Dale 489, 490,
Robson, Edwin (Judge) 514, 515,
Rocco, Joe 574,
Rodriguez, Camilo 511,
Rodriquez, Chi Chi 460,
Roe, Theodore 26, 70,
Roemer, William Jr. (FBI Agent) 6, 102, 107, 111, 115, 120, 133, 180, 195, 199, 246, 297, 330, 333, 335, 336, 346, 451, 455, 458, 463, 467, 472, 479, 481, 483, 489, 490, 491, 493, 494, 495, 497, 498, 500, 504, 505, 506, 509, 510, 514, 515,
Roen, Allard 508,
Rodgers Park Illinois 174, 225,

Roger, James 68,
Rogers, John 32,
Rollins, Frank 61,
Romanelli, Michael 175,
Romano, Anthony 87,
Rosa, Sam "Slicker Sam" 305, 362, 367, 370, 385, 398, 424, 425, 426, 432, 460, 572, 574,
Rosanova, Lou "The Tailor" 274, 414, 415, 425, 508, 574,
Roselli, Johnny 158, 206, 213, 214, 232, 233, 240, 257, 404, 445, 508,
Rosemont Illinois 48, 87, 160, 173, 307, 314, 316, 373, 378, 405, 426, 442, 456, 459, 554, 556,
Rosenberg, Thomas (Alderman) 165, 167, 168,
Rosenthal, Frank "Lefty" 450, 469, 502, 503,
Rosi, Peter Dr. 77,
Rosie, Dick 364,
Rosie, S. 363,
Ross, 471,
Ross, Paul 81,
Rossetti, Anthony 78,
Rossetti, Joseph 450,
Rossi, Paul 81,
Rosthal, Robert 187,
Rothchild, Maurice 182,
Roti, Bruno Sr. 576,
Roti, Frank 573,
Roti, Fred B. 293, 295, 313, 318, 523, 573, 576,
Roti, F. S. 49,
Roti, James 574,
Roti, R.S. 23,
Rowan, Dan 141, 196, 198, 204,
Royko, Mike 523,
Ruben, Donald 488,
Rubirosa, Porfirio 337,
Rugendorf, Leo 574,
Runyon, Damon 133,
Rush Street Chicago 121, 149, 251, 272, 308, 487,
Russell, David 335,
Russell, Harry 29,
Russell, John Jr. 166,
Russell, Tony 62,
Russo, Anthony "Little Pussy" 306, 468,
Russo, Thomas 61, 62, 175,
Russo, Sam 335,
Russo, Willie 352,
Rutland, Marshall (FBI Agent) 330, 334, 335, 347, 370, 396,
Ryan, Daniel 133,
Ryan, Edward 569,

S

Sabatino, Betty 79, 101,
Sabatino, Mike 79, 101,
Sahara North Motel 272, 273, 287, 289, 307, 308, 321, 369,
Saigh, Alfred 573,
Sain, Frank 256,
Salvatore, M. 68,
Salvatore, Rocco 574, 577,
Salerno Brothers Funeral Home 103,
Saletko, Morris *"See Mashie Bear"*

CPSIA information can be obtained
at www.ICGtesting.com
Printed in the USA
LVHW060321120419
613943LV00002B/37/P